The behavior and decision-making processes of the U.S. Supreme Court have often been examined using the legal model, which holds that Supreme Court decisions are based on the "plain meaning" of the Constitution, the intent of the framers, and precedent. In this book, Professors Segal and Spaeth investigate the decisions and the decision-making processes of the Supreme Court using an alternative framework: the attitudinal model, which holds that Supreme Court decisions are based on the attitudes and values of the justices.

Using the highly reliable U.S. Supreme Court Judicial Database, compiled by Professor Spaeth, the authors examine all stages of the Court's decision-making processes, from staffing and access to case selection, votes on the merits, opinion assignments and opinion coalitions, and judicial restraint and activism, and succeed in explaining and predicting behavior with a great degree of accuracy. They also include a framework for understanding the impact of judicial decisions and the place of the Court in the American political system. By using an attitudinal model to explain the justices' decision making and that of other policy makers, this book demythologizes the Court and its decisions while greatly extending our knowledge and understanding.

THE SUPREME COURT AND
THE ATTITUDINAL MODEL

THE SUPREME COURT AND THE ATTITUDINAL MODEL

JEFFREY A. SEGAL
State University of New York, Stony Brook

HAROLD J. SPAETH
Michigan State University

CAMBRIDGE
UNIVERSITY PRESS

Published by the Press Syndicate of the University of Cambridge
The Pitt Building, Trumpington Street, Cambridge CB2 1RP
40 West 20th Street, New York, NY 10011-4211, USA
10 Stamford Road, Oakleigh, Victoria 3166, Australia

First published 1993

Printed in the United States of America

Library of Congress Cataloging-in-Publication Data
Segal, Jeffrey Allan.
The Supreme Court and the attitudinal model / Jeffrey A. Segal and
Harold J. Spaeth.
p.   cm.
Includes index.
ISBN 0-521-41130-0. – ISBN 0-521-42293-0 (pbk.)
1. United States. Supreme Court.   2. United States –
Constitutional law – Interpretation and construction.   3. Judicial
process–United States.   I. Spaeth, Harold J.   II. Title.
KF8742.S43   1992
347.73'26 – dc20
[347.30735]   92-2387
                                                                 CIP

A catalog record for this book is available from the British Library

ISBN 0-521-41130-0 hardback
ISBN 0-521-42293-0 paperback

In memory of my parents, Eli and Billie Segal
Jeffrey A. Segal

For Jean
Harold J. Spaeth

Contents

Tables and figures

TABLES

FIGURES

Preface

The purpose of this book is to scientifically analyze and explain the Supreme Court, its processes, and its decisions, from an attitudinal perspective. To the extent that we are successful in doing so, we hope that it will encourage others to use the scientific method to extend, develop, and refine the work contained in the book, and apply it not only to the Supreme Court but to other judicial bodies as well. Although political scientists have written much about the Court, most of it has been historical, anecdotal, legalistic, tendentious, or doctrinal – the stuff for which historians, journalists, legal scholars, and philosophers are trained. Sad to say, political scientists tend to discard science when the Court is their subject.

We grind no ideological axes. Though we have our individual policy preferences, we march to markedly different beats. To the extent possible, we have attempted to allow the facts to speak for themselves. And to the extent that in marshaling the facts our work results in the demolition of many cherished beliefs, of laypersons as well as scholars, to that extent does conventional wisdom about the Court and the judicial system lack scientific validity and rest on myth instead of data.

Although attitude research has contributed much to our knowledge and understanding of the Court, it has tended to focus only on the final vote on the merits – the votes of the justices as specified in the Court's Reports. Here, however, we apply attitude theory and the model based on it to all stages of the Court's decisional process.

Our subject is the U.S. Supreme Court. We hold no brief either for the lower federal courts or for the state courts. The extent to which the attitudinal model applies to their decisions awaits future research. In presenting the attitudinal model toward the end of Chapter 2, we note the unique environment in which the justices operate. That that environment facilitates the operation of the attitudinal model cannot be gainsaid. That is to say, the features of the Court's environment that we identify provide conditions sufficient for the operation of the attitudinal model. Whether they are necessary to its operation requires scientific analysis of other courts. It is our judgment that the attitudinal model will explain the decision making of other courts to the extent that the environment of these courts approximates that of the Supreme Court. The least correlation will obtain among closely supervised trial courts that lack power to control their dockets.

We build on the work of Glendon Schubert, as it has been developed and expanded by other scholars as well as ourselves. The result is the presentation of an attitudinal model, in contradistinction to the legal model that typically characterizes other books that examine the Court. Unlike the legal model, our attitudinal model enables us to systematically explain – validly and reliably – how the Court operates and why the justices behave as they do. In the course of validating our model, we critique the assumptions on which the legal model rests and demonstrate that it lacks operational relevance.

Chapter 1 explains what courts do and why their activity results in policy making. In presenting the legal model in Chapter 2, we emphasize its current garb, interpretivism, along with its antithesis, the non-interpretivist position. We then contrast the legal model with the attitudinal one, and show why it has particular relevance for Supreme Court decision making.

In keeping with the Court's policy-making role, we present in Chapter 3 a political history of the Court, one that outlines the ideological considerations that have motivated the thrust of the Court's decisions since its inception,

Chapter 4 deals with the nomination and confirmation of the justices. We identify the factors affecting their nomination and present a brief case study of the five failed nominations between the effort to elevate Abe Fortas to the chief justiceship and the withdrawal of Douglas Ginsburg from consideration. We also pay special attention to the barely successful Thomas nomination. An aggregate analysis of all nominations is provided, followed by an individual-level focus on the votes of senators on the two dozen nominations between Earl Warren and Clarence Thomas. The resulting model accurately predicts 95 percent of the senators' confirmation votes.

Chapter 5 describes the legal requirements litigants must meet to gain access to the Court, and the procedures and criteria the justices employ to select the cases they choose to decide. We demonstrate that at this level of activity, as at the final vote on the merits, the individual justices' personal policy preferences explain their behavior.

In Chapter 6 we demonstrate that the components of the attitudinal model – the facts of the case and the ideology of the justices (measured either directly through previous votes or indirectly through content analysis) – successfully explain and predict the votes of Supreme Court justices. Notwithstanding allegations of voting fluidity between the original (conference) vote on the merits and the final (or Report) vote, analysis demonstrates the overall validity of the attitudinal model. Because of the possibility that various non-attitudinal factors may affect the justices' decisions – roles, the Solicitor General, Congress, public opinion, and interest groups – we also test for their presence. Except for the influence of the Solicitor General, little systematic evidence supports appreciable effect by any of the others.

Chapter 7 systematically considers majority-opinion assignments, the resulting patterns, and the reasons they were made. We demonstrate that attitudinal considerations govern majority-opinion assignments by both the Chief Justice and the senior associate justice in the majority. We then consider opinion coalitions. Unfortunately, a majority-opinion coalition does not always form. When this happens, only a non-authoritative judgment of the Court results. We investigate the reasons for these judgments by determining which justices are responsible for the resulting breakdown in collegiality. We also investigate opinion coalitions generally: Who joins with whom and why.

In Chapter 8 we consider the relationship of the Court's policy making and the operation of constitutional democracy. We begin with an examination of judicial review and the debate it has engendered. The extent to which the Warren, Burger, and Rehnquist Court justices have exercised judicial restraint is empirically documented and evaluated, with particular attention paid the votes and opinions of Justice Frankfurter, the apotheosis of judicial restraint. We find virtually no evidence of restraint. The chapter closes with an assessment of the record of the Warren, Burger, and Rehnquist courts insofar as declarations of unconstitutionality and alterations of precedent are concerned.

Chapter 9 provides a framework for understanding the "impact" of the Court's decisions, focusing on the parties to litigation, compliance by the interpreting and implementing populations, and the impact of the Court's decisions insofar as the exclusionary rule of the Fourth Amendment, reapportionment, school desegregation, and abortion are concerned.

We conclude in Chapter 10 with consideration of criticisms of the attitudinal model.

Assessment of the operation of any theoretically grounded model requires highly reliable data. Although we have utilized data from a variety of sources, we have overwhelmingly depended on those contained in the U.S. Supreme Court Judicial Database, a multiphase project conceived and designed for multi-investigator use by Harold Spaeth, who compiled the data in it with the financial assistance of the National Science Foundation. The data, of known reliability, are updated at the end of each term of the Court, and encompass a wide range of variables that bear on the behavior of the Court and the individual justices. These cover background, chronological, substantive, outcome, and voting and opinion variables.[1]

Except for our treatment of the Court's political history, we concentrate on the activity, decisions, and policies of the last half of the twentieth century. We do so for two reasons. First, though antiquarianism has its place, it ought not to upstage the here and now, at least not in an arena as dynamic as that of the Court. Second, the database on which we primarily rely dates from the beginning of the Warren Court in 1953; hence, the focus on activity since then. But we

---

[1] The database is freely available for use by faculty and students at institutions that are members of the Interuniversity Consortium for Political and Social Research in Ann Arbor, Michigan, as Study #9422.

do not totally ignore the nineteenth century in testing our theory. Thus, we explain the Taney Court's policy making from an empirically replicable attitudinal perspective.

Note also that although we test the operation of the attitudinal model more heavily in certain areas than in others because of the availability of data – for example, search and seizure – we also apply it across the board, though with different degrees of success, as the appendix to Chapter 6 indicates. It may well be that some areas of the law lack salience in the minds of the justices, with the result that decisions in those areas are driven by non-attitudinal factors. If so, we have not discovered them.

Because of our emphasis on the present day, many of the cases that we cite postdate the availability of the bound volumes of the *United States Reports*, which contain the official record of the Court's decisions. In its place, we use the privately printed *Lawyers' Edition* of the *United States Reports*.[2]

We wish to acknowledge the assistance of scholars without whose help this book could never have been written: Michael F. Altfeld, Saul Brenner, Charles M. Cameron, Albert D. Cover, Lee Epstein, Timothy M. Hagle, Thomas H. Hammond, Donald R. Songer, and Thomas G. Walker. For better or for worse, the day of the solitary scholar buried behind the stacks of a library or the equipment of a laboratory who successfully advances human knowledge without personal interaction and collaboration with others is history. We gratefully thank these individuals whose wisdom, understanding, and knowledge have so appreciably enhanced ours – deficient though ours remains. We also thank Megan Perillo, who provided invaluable research assistance, and Christine Segal, who first suggested the need for what became Chapter 3.

We are fortunate to have had Emily Loose as our editor at Cambridge University Press and Ronald Cohen as our manuscript editor. Both display a light and unobtrusive touch, which in our judgment is the hallmark of editorial excellence.

Much of the research that appears in the book was undertaken with the financial support of the National Science Foundation through grants SES-8313733, SES-8812935, SES-8842925, and SES-9112755. We thank the NSF very much. Without its support, our knowledge and understanding of the Court would be primitive indeed.

---

[2] Rochester, NY: Lawyers Cooperative Publishing Co.

1

Introduction: Supreme Court
policy making

We live in a democracy, but within that democracy we give the nine unelected, virtually unremovable members of the Supreme Court broad discretion to determine, for instance, whether abortions should be allowed, death penalties inflicted, and homosexuality criminally punished. Although the justices might claim for public consumption that they do not make public policy, that they merely interpret the law, the truth is closer to Chief Justice (then Governor) Charles Evans Hughes's declaration: "We are under a Constitution, but the Constitution is what the judges say it is."[1]

This chapter focuses on why the Supreme Court, along with other American courts, makes policy. We initially present a set of reasons for judicial policy making. Though these reasons are crucial to our understanding of the institution's importance, they do not tell us anything about the considerations that cause the justices to make the choices that produce the Court's policies. In Chapter 2, we describe and critique the legal model of decision making, which purportedly identifies the criteria that cause the justices to decide their cases the way they do, and the school of interpretivist thought that takes its cue from one of the variants of the legal model. As we demonstrate, the legal model serves only to cloak – to conceal – the motivations that cause the justices to decide as they do. As an alternative, we present an attitudinal model, based on the political attitudes and values of the justices, that does explain why the justices vote as they do.

WHAT COURTS DO

In order to explain why justices vote as they do, we begin with a specification of what courts themselves do. From the most general and non-technical standpoint, they resolve disputes. Not all disputes, of course. Only those that possess certain characteristics. The party initiating legal action must be a "proper plaintiff," and the court in which the dispute is brought must be a "proper forum." That is, it must have the authority – the jurisdiction – to resolve the dispute. For example, courts generally, and the federal courts in particular, may only

---

[1] Quoted in Craig Ducat and Harold Chase, *Constitutional Interpretation*, 4th ed. (New York: West, 1988), p. 3.

resolve a "case" or "controversy."[2] In Chapter 5 we detail the specific characteristics that enable a litigant to be a proper plaintiff and those pertaining to
the proper forum.

The Supreme Court has described the judiciary's function as follows:

> Perhaps no characteristic of an organized and cohesive society is more fundamental than
> its creation and enforcement of a system of rules defining the various rights and duties
> of its members, enabling them to govern their affairs and definitively settle their differences
> in an orderly, predictable manner. Without such a "legal system," social organization
> and cohesion are virtually impossible; with the ability to seek regularized resolution of
> conflict individuals are capable of interdependent action that enables them to strive for
> achievements without the anxieties that would beset them in a disorganized society. Put
> more succinctly, it is this injection of the rule of law that allows society to reap the
> benefits of what political theorists call the "state of nature."[3]

The Court also noted that courts are not the only available means for resolving
disputes. Indeed, "private structuring of individual relationships and repair of
their breach is largely encouraged in American life, subject only to the caveat
that the formal judicial process, if resorted to, is paramount."[4]

The process whereby courts resolve disputes produces a decision. This decision, unless overruled by a higher court, is binding on the parties to the dispute.
If a higher court does overrule the trial or a lower appellate court, then its
decision replaces the earlier one. A court's decision, binding the litigants, is
authoritative in the sense that non-judicial decision makers, such as legislators
or executive officials, cannot alter or nullify it.[5] Judicial authority is not subverted
by the possibility that the legislature may at some point in the future alter the
law that the court applied to the case it decided,[6] or that a constitutional amend-

---

[2] For all practical purposes, the two terms are synonymous. A "case" includes all judicial proceedings, whereas a "controversy" is a civil matter. As Justice Iredell pointed out in the lead
opinion in *Chishom v. Georgia*, 2 Dallas 419 (1792), at 432: "It cannot be presumed that the
general word, 'controversies[,]' was intended to include any proceedings that relate to criminal
cases . . . " Although the Eleventh Amendment nullified the Court's decision in *Chishom v.
Georgia*, Iredell's distinction survives.

[3] *Boddie v. Connecticut*, 401 U.S. 371 (1971), at 374.

[4] Id. at 375. Also see Christine Harrington, *Shadow Justice* (Westport, CT: Greenwood Press,
1985).

[5] This assumes, of course, that the court in question had authority to resolve the dispute in the
first place. If, for example, a court were to decide a matter for which a legislative or executive
agency has ultimate responsibility, its decision lacks authority.

[6] A recent example of Congressional override involves the Court's decision in *Ohio v. Betts*, 106
L Ed 2d 134 (1989), which held that the Age Discrimination in Employment Act did not require
an employer to justify differential benefits for older workers on the basis of cost. Lower benefits
are valid unless imposed for a discriminatory purpose. A county's speech pathologist was di-
agnosed as having Alzheimer's disease at age fifty-eight. She continued working until sixty-one.
The state retirement system prohibits workers over sixty from receiving disability benefits. She
lost her case.
   If concurred in by the House of Representatives and approved by the President, Senate action
protecting workers' insurance, severance, and disability benefits will overturn the Court's deci-

ment may undo the Court's decision, as the Eleventh Amendment undid *Chisholm v. Georgia*, which permitted a nonresident to sue a state in federal court.[7]

Not only does a constitutional amendment not subvert judicial authority, courts themselves – ultimately the Supreme Court – authoritatively determine the sanctioning amendment's meaning. Although the Court's interpretation of an amendment that overturns one of its decision may give the amendment the effect its words or purpose conveys, this need not be the case. Thus, the Twenty-Sixth Amendment, ratified in 1971, did indeed enable eighteen-year-olds to vote in state and federal elections, which was indisputably its purpose.[8] But the Fourteenth and Sixteenth Amendments are a different matter. The former clearly overturned the Court's decision in *Scott v. Sandford*[9] and was meant to give blacks legal equality with whites. Scholars disagree about what other objectives the Amendment had, but it does appear that the prohibition of sex discrimination was not among them.[10] Nonetheless, in 1971 the Court held that the equal protection clause of the Fourteenth Amendment encompassed women.[11] As for the Sixteenth Amendment, it substantially, but not completely, reversed the Court's decisions in *Pollock v. Farmers' Loan and Trust Co.*, which declared unconstitutional the income tax that Congress had enacted in 1894.[12] In 1913, the requisite number of states ratified an amendment that authorized Congress to levy a tax on income "from whatever source derived." The language is unequivocal. Yet for the next twenty-six years the Supreme Court ruled that this language *excluded* the salaries of federal judges. Why the exclusion? Because Article III, Section 1, of the original Constitution orders that judges' salaries "not be diminished during their continuance in office." Though it is an elementary legal principle that later language erases incompatible earlier language, the justices ruled that any taxation of their salaries, and those of their lower court colleagues, would obviously diminish them.[13] Finally, in 1939, the justices overruled their predecessors and unselfishly allowed themselves to be taxed.[14]

---

sion. See Richard L. Berke, "Senate, 94-1, Votes to Protect Benefits of Older Workers," *New York Times*, September 25, 1990, p. C16.

[7] 2 Dallas 419 (1793). Although it has virtually never happened, Congress can grant relief to a losing litigant by way of a private bill, assuming no constitutional violation occurs in doing so.

[8] Thereby overruling *Oregon v. Mitchell*, 400 U.S. 112 (1970), which voided an act of Congress that authorized eighteen-year-olds to vote in state elections.

[9] 19 Howard 393 (1857).

[10] See *Bradwell v. Illinois*, 16 Wallace 130 (1873).

[11] *Reed v. Reed*, 404 U.S. 71 (1971).

[12] 157 U.S. 429 (1895) and 158 U.S. 601 (1895).

[13] See *Evans v. Gore*, 253 U.S. 245 (1920), and *Miles v. Graham*, 268 U.S. 501 (1925).

[14] *O'Malley v. Woodrough*, 307 U.S. 277 (1939). The subjection of federal judges "to a general tax . . . merely [recognizes] . . . that judges are also citizens, and that their particular function in government does not generate an immunity from sharing with their fellow citizens the material burden of the government whose Constitution and laws they are charged with administering." Id. at 282.

Judges as policy makers

The authoritative character of judicial decisions results because judges make policy. Policy making involves choosing among alternative courses of action, where the choice binds the behavior of those subject to the policy-maker's action. Phrased more succinctly, a policy maker authoritatively allocates resources.

Although the typical judicial decision will only authoritatively allocate the limited resources at issue between the parties to a lawsuit, the resources allocated at appellate court levels commonly affect persons other than the litigants. Appellate courts support their decisions with opinions precisely because of their broader impact, so that persons who find themselves in similar situations may be apprised of the fate that may befall them if they engage in actions akin to those of the relevant litigant.

Note, however, that trial court decisions may also have wide-ranging policy effects. Few cases are appealed; as a result, unappealed decisions become as authoritative as those of a supreme court. Multi-party litigation is becoming increasingly common. A class of thousands of human or legal persons may institute a single lawsuit, the decision in which binds all participants – for example, all taxpayers in the State of California, or all stockholders of General Motors. Organizations frequently sue or are sued as surrogates for their members – for example, the Sierra Club or the Teamsters Union. A lawsuit brought by or against the United States or a state or local government may have very broad and pervasive effects.

Courts make policy only on matters that they have authority to decide – that is, within their jurisdiction. The subjects of the jurisdiction of American courts range from the purely trivial to matters of utmost societal importance. As an eminent Canadian jurist phrases it:

Reading through an American constitutional law text is like walking through modern human existence in an afternoon. From a woman's control of her own body to the Vietnam war and from desegregation of schools to drunken drivers, it is hard to imagine a facet of American existence that has not been subjected to constitutional scrutiny.[15]

American courts derive their jurisdiction from the constitution that established them and/or from legislative enactments. Because judges' decisions adjudicate the legality of contested matters, judges of necessity make law. Only those who believe in fairy tales deny this statement. Even so, Americans find it unsettling to admit to judicial policy making because we have surrounded judicial decisions with a panoply of myth, the essence of which avers that judges and their decisions are objective, impartial, and dispassionate. In the language of Chief Justice John Marshall:

Judicial power, as contradistinguished from the power of the laws, has no existence. Courts are the mere instruments of the law and can will nothing. When they are said to

[15]   Bertha Wilson, "The making of a constitution," 71 *Judicature* 334 (1988).

exercise a discretion, it is a mere legal discretion, a discretion to be exercised in discerning the course prescribed by law; and, when that is discerned, it is the duty of the court to follow it. Judicial power is never exercised for the purpose of giving effect to the will of the judge; always for the purpose of giving effect to the will of the legislature . . .[16]

More than Marshall's words, myth makers favor the language of Justice Owen Roberts in *United States v. Butler*, to which five of his colleagues subscribed:

It is sometimes said that the court assumes a power to overrule or control the action of the people's representatives. This is a misconception. The Constitution is the supreme law of the land ordained and established by the people. All legislation must conform to the principles it lays down. When an act of Congress is appropriately challenged in the courts as not conforming to the constitutional mandate, the judicial branch of the Government has only one duty – to lay the article of the Constitution which is invoked beside the statute which is challenged and to decide whether the latter squares with the former.[17]

One might wish that such statements only harked back to an earlier time and that today everyone admits that "judges make law."[18] Unfortunately, this is not the case. The assertion that judges merely "find" or "discover" the law, and do not ever make it, continues to be propounded with the same vigor as of yore, even though, as one authority documents, "Seventeenth-century Americans viewed lawmaking and judging as synonymous activities."[19] Three cases illustrate this.

The very framing of the issue that we purport to decide today – whether our decision . . . shall "apply" retroactively – presupposes a view of our decisions as *creating* the law, as opposed to *declaring* what the law already is. Such a view is contrary to that understanding of "the judicial Power," US Const, Art III, Sec. 1, cl 1, which is not only the common and traditional one, but which is the only one that can justify courts in denying force and effect to the unconstitutional enactments of duly elected legislatures . . . To hold a governmental act to be unconstitutional is not to announce that we forbid it, but that the *Constitution* forbids it . . .[20]

These words were written by Justice Scalia, a justice whom many view as the Court's brightest member. Apparently, intelligence does not preclude self-deception. Alternatively, perhaps he believes it appropriate to apply a bit of "spin" to his opinions. At least Scalia spoke only for himself here, unlike Justice Roberts in the quotation from *United States v. Butler*, the first illustrative case. Even so, Scalia's remarks are puzzling. If it is he and his colleagues through whom the Constitution speaks, and not vice-versa, how can he consistently assert a few paragraphs later that he might not adhere to what "the *Constitution* forbids"? Thus:

---

[16] *Osborn v. Bank of the United States*, 9 Wheaton 738 (1824), at 866.

[17] 297 U.S. 1 (1936), at 62.

[18] Wilson, op.cit. fn. 15 supra, p. 334.

[19] Kermit L. Hall, *The Magic Mirror: Law in American History* (New York: Oxford University Press, 1989), p. 17.

[20] *American Trucking Assns. v. Smith*, 110 L Ed 2d 148 (1990), at 174. The emphasis is in the original.

Stare decisis — that is to say, a respect for the needs of stability in our legal system — would normally cause me to adhere to a decision of this Court [sic] already rendered as to the unconstitutionality of a particular type of state law.[21]

Note the use of the phrase, "a decision of this Court." Scalia presumably distinguishes between "what the Constitution forbids" or commands, and the Court's decisions. Some of the latter must only contain matters that a majority of lawmaking justices forbid or command. Scalia has provided no objective criteria for determining in which decisions the Constitution speaks and which merely voice the willful utterances of a biased majority. Perhaps those from which he dissents?

Notwithstanding the justices' denials, Congress commonly authorizes the Court to make law. Consider, for example, federal subsidization of allegedly obscene arts projects. A heated 1989 controversy over support for the exhibition of the work of a deceased gay photographer, Robert Mapplethorpe, ended with the repeal of explicit anti-obscenity curbs that Congress had imposed on the National Endowment for the Arts. In October 1990, by a vote of 382–42, the House of Representatives authorized the federal courts, rather than Congress, to make such determinations.[22]

The second of the three illustrative cases required the Court to directly answer the question whether judges make policy. The Age Discrimination in Employment Act exempts appointed state court judges from its ban on mandatory retirement, and the Court construed the relevant language – "appointees . . . 'on a policymaking level' " – to encompass judges. But not without considerable waffling. The majority noted that exemption only requires judges to function on a policymaking level, not that they "actually make policy." And though "It is at least ambiguous whether a state judge is an 'appointee' on the policymaking level," nonetheless "we conclude that the petition[ing judges] fall presumptively under the policymaking exception."[23] Justices White and Stevens, concurring in the result, had no hesitation in calling a spade a spade. Using Webster's definition of policy, they concluded by quoting the lower court whose decision the Supreme Court reviewed: "Each judge, as a separate and independent judicial officer, is at the very top of his particular 'policymaking' chain, responding . . . only to a higher appellate court."[24]

---

[21] Id. at 176.

[22] Robert M. Andrews, "House says let courts decide what's obscene," Associated Press wire story, October 12, 1990.

[23] *Gregory v. Ashcroft*, 115 L Ed 2d 410 (1991), at 427, 428.

[24] Id. at 440. Justice Blackmun, whom Marshall joined, dissented, refusing to accept Webster's definition as authoritative: "I hesitate to classify judges as policymakers . . . Although some part of a judge's task may be to fill in the interstices of legislative enactments, the *primary* task of a judicial officer is to apply rules reflecting the policy choices made by, or on behalf of, those elected to legislative and executive positions." At 441, note 1. The dissent relied on the opinion of Judge Amalya Kearse of the Second Circuit who flatly asserted that "the performance of traditional judicial functions is not policy making." Linda Greenhouse, "Justices to Hear Retirement Age Case," *New York Times*, November 27, 1990, p. A12. Judge Kearse's opinion,

Unfortunately, the justices further muddied matters in the last of three illustrative cases, one that was decided on the same day as *Gregory v. Ashcroft*. The issue was the retroactive application of a decision that declared unconstitutional a state statute that discriminatorily taxed liquor produced out of state.[25] The six-member majority required four opinions to state their varied positions, none of which commanded more than three votes.[26] Justice White continued the realistic thrust of his *Ashcroft* opinion by acerbically criticizing the opinion of Justice Scalia, who, it will be recalled, wrote the opinion quoted in the first illustrative case. This time, Blackmun and Marshall, the two *Ashcroft* dissenters, joined Scalia's opinion, which read:

I am not so naive (nor do I think our forebears were) as to be unaware that judges in a real sense "make" law. But they make it *as judges make it*, which is to say *as though* they were "finding" it – discerning what the law *is*, rather than decreeing what it is today *changed to*, or what it will *tomorrow* be. Of course, this mode of action poses "difficulties of a . . . practical sort . . . when courts decide to overrule prior precedent. (Italics in original.)[27]

White replied:

. . . even though the Justice is not naive enough (nor does he think the Framers were naive enough) to be unaware that judges in a real sense "make" law, he suggests that judges (in an unreal sense, I suppose) should never concede that they do and must claim that they do no more than discover it, hence suggesting that there are citizens who are naive enough to believe them.[28]

The foregoing evidence, such as it is, suggests that the fairy tale of a discretionless judiciary survives, even though its mouthpieces carry their tongues in their cheeks.

REASONS FOR JUDICIAL POLICY MAKING

No other nation empowers its courts to resolve so broad a range of disputes as does the United States. Neither does any other nation concede to its courts such authoritative decision making. Furthermore, in making their decisions, the courts do so with a minimum of interference from other governmental bodies or officials.

Why do American judges have such virtually untrammeled policy-making authority? Five interrelated factors provide an answer: fundamental law, distrust of governmental power, federalism, separation of powers, and judicial review. Because they are so closely interconnected, we cannot empirically judge their relative importance.

and one from the Eastern District of Virginia, are the only ones that held judges not to be policymakers. The majority of judges, holding to the contrary, are listed at 438, note 2.

[25] *Bacchus Imports, Ltd v. Dias*, 468 U.S. 263 (1984).

[26] *James B. Beam Distilling Co. v. Georgia*, 115 L Ed 2d 481 (1991).

[27] Id. at 497.

[28] Id. at 495.

Fundamental law

The original English colonizers of New England brought with them the concept of a fundamental law: the idea that all human and governmental action should accord with the word of God or the strictures of nature as the leadership of the particular settlement decreed.[29] These individuals had left Europe because they were unwilling or unable to conform to the teachings of England's established church. Their arrival in America did not produce religious harmony. Much of the settlement of Rhode Island and Connecticut, for example, resulted from the expulsion of dissenters from Plymouth and Massachusetts Bay.

The overtly religious motivations that inspired the founding of new settlements was reflected in the charters and constitutions that their inhabitants devised. Although the theocratic parochialism of the early colonies, if not of specific towns and villages within each of them, had largely vanished by the beginning of the Revolutionary War, the notion of a fundamental law retained its vitality.[30]

The environment in which the colonists found themselves did not lend itself to the stabilizing influences of the Old World. Religious diversity flourished. Dissenters – with or without a theomanic preacher – merely had to move a few miles west to establish their own kindred community. The process of westward settlement produced marked social and economic turbulence, which continued throughout the nineteenth century and into the twentieth century, and persists still. The industrial and technological revolutions transformed a society of yeoman farmers and artisans into one of urban employees. Culturally, well before the Revolution, the original English settlers had been supplemented by substantial numbers from the Netherlands, Germany, Scotland, and Ireland, to say nothing of the forcible importation of African slaves. The cultural diversity that resulted became vastly more eclectic with the mass immigration of the latter half of the nineteenth century and the early years of the twentieth century.

The changes in lifestyle and status that these and associated forces have wrought preclude the establishment of a fixed and stable religious, social, economic, or cultural system. Indeed, Americans generally view change in these areas of human activity to be desirable, considering them synonymous with progress and freedom. Only in the political realm do we view drastic change as undesirable.

This schizoid orientation reflects the reality of American life. No one can function well in an unduly dynamic environment. To a substantial extent, human beings are creatures of habit. Economic misfortune, the unexpected breakup of personal relationships, and the demolition of cherished beliefs produces trauma. Life becomes frightening to those who find events in the saddle riding herd on them. But the political sphere appears to be an arena amenable to stability. This

---

[29]   Hall, op. cit. fn. 19 supra, pp. 12–17, 24–27.
[30]   See Edward S. Corwin, *The "Higher Law" Background of American Constitutional Law* (Ithaca: Cornell University Press, 1955).

was the goal the Framers set for themselves when they gathered in Philadelphia in the summer of 1787: to transpose the religious notion of a fundamental law into a secular context, to enshrine the Constitution that they intended to create as a secular substitute for Holy Writ.

The fact that the Constitution has lasted longer than that of any other nation is evidence of the Framers' success. Its long life has added political stability to the distinguishing features of American life. Although a resurrected Framer might be appalled at the size of the governmental system he helped create, he most assuredly would recognize the workings of what he had wrought. Other societies may achieve stability through an established church, to which the citizenry pays at least pro forma obeisance, or through the hierarchical social control that a hereditary caste or group exercises. Alternatively, the economic system may prove unchanging, as in a non-industrialized society where subsistence farming occupies all but a privileged elite. Or national boundaries may coincide with ethnic or tribal lines, insuring cultural homogeneity. In these environments, the political sphere provides the vehicle for change. Radical regime changes, bloody or otherwise, become commonplace. Not so in the United States. The Constitution and its system of government furnish us with our link to the unchanging.

Distrust of governmental power

Judicial policy making also inheres in our historic distrust of governmental power, especially that exercised from a central level. Like the concept of fundamental law, this factor also dates from the colonial era. Americans viewed British insistence that they defray the costs of the French and Indian War, which ended in 1763, as inimical to their rights and liberties. Opposition to these policies led to the onset of the Revolution, which coincided with an internal struggle for control of the newly formed governments that the patriots (i.e., the non-Loyalists) established in each of the colonies. This internal struggle roughly pitted the socioeconomic elite, such as it was, against the rural yeomanry and urban artisans. It was continuing apace when the Framers convened in Philadelphia in 1787.

Unsettled economic conditions that persisted beyond the end of the Revolution severely strained the governmental capabilities of both the Continental Congress and the individual states. The Articles of Confederation, which took effect in 1781, made no provision for a chief executive or a federal judiciary; the Continental Congress had no power to levy taxes; nor could it exercise any of its limited powers over individuals; amendment of the Articles required unanimous approval of the thirteen state legislatures. A number of states yielded to debtor demands and printed large quantities of paper money that they issued as legal tender, while others enacted stay laws that lengthened the period of time during which debtors could legally pay their creditors. To protect their own interests, some states imposed tariffs and other trade barriers that inhibited the free flow of interstate commerce. Of the money that Congress requested to defray the costs of the Confederation and the Revolutionary War, the states paid so little that Congress could not meet the interest payments on the national debt.

Support for strengthening the governmental system came from a number of sources: leaders who believed that the power of a single state to prevent change endangered them all; merchants and shipowners concerned about commercial restrictions; frontiersmen threatened by Indian attacks; and veterans and members of the Continental Congress who had developed national loyalties. Of the fifty-five delegates to the Constitutional Convention, thirty-nine had served in Congress, at least thirty were veterans, eight had signed the Declaration of Independence, and all were experienced in the politics of their respective states.

They clearly recognized that any effort to replace the Articles of Confederation with a more capable government required the creation of a system that no single interest or ''faction'' (to use the word then in vogue) could control or dominate; one that – from the broadest standpoint – neither the ''haves'' nor the ''have nots'' could dominate. The governmental capability of the federal level had to be strengthened while that of the states required diminution. The hoped for result was a system in which neither level would do much governing. The federal government would be empowered to defend the Union, coin money, operate a postal system, regulate interstate commerce, and – needless to say — levy taxes. The states would be saddled with restrictions to prevent them from interfering with the responsibilities given to the federal level, as Article I, Section 10, illustrates:

1. No State shall enter into any treaty, alliance, or confederation; . . . coin money; emit bills of credit; make anything but gold and silver coin a tender in payment of debts; pass any bill of attainder, *ex post facto* law, or law impairing the obligation of contracts . . .

2. No State shall, without the consent of the Congress, lay any imposts or duties on imports or exports; . . . the net produce of all duties and imposts . . . shall be for the use of the treasury of the United States; and all such laws shall be subject to the revision and control of the Congress.

3. No State shall, without the consent of the Congress, lay any duty of tonnage, keep troops, or ships of war in time of peace, enter into any agreement or compact with another State, or with a foreign power, or engage in war, unless actually invaded, or in such imminent danger as will not admit of delay.

The federal government did not escape similar strictures. Section 9 of Article I, for example, contains eight clauses of ''thou shalt nots'' that specify things that Congress may not do.

In short, the Framers limited the powers of government in two different ways. First, they severely limited what government could do. Second, they specified in considerable detail the *way* in which government could exercise the powers that it did possess. Thus, Article III stipulates that persons accused of committing a federal crime, other than impeachment, be tried by a jury, and Article I, Section 7, details the procedure whereby a bill becomes a law. The sum total of these substantive and procedural limitations on the exercise of power is clear evidence of the "constitutionalism" of the Constitution.[31]

The resulting system gained the support of the major elements of American society, though not without a sharp and hard fought struggle. The lower socio-economic echelons stood to benefit from limited government because they lacked experience in the affairs of state. Some had been deprived of the right to vote or hold public office because of property qualifications. Others, though entitled to vote and hold office, lacked the political seasoning of their more experienced neighbors. Their preference for states' rights and local self-government made them suspicious of what might become a strong and efficient centralized government. If not in their own experience, then in that of their ancestors, government had been a vehicle of oppression and tyranny. For the many who lived along the frontier, the utility of a federal government was limited to an occasional band of cavalry to pacify unruly natives.

Nor were the landed gentry and mercantile interests necessarily opposed to a government invulnerable to any group's effective control. They chiefly feared loss of position on the socioeconomic ladder. As long as governmental power was not used against them, they sensibly assumed that they could perpetuate their position in society, given their education and wealth and the status that accompanied it.

Consequently, for self-interested reasons that varied from one group and segment to another, the Jeffersonian ideal that that government is best that governs least quickly became an article of faith for Americans generally. Subsequent developments insured its retention: The lure of the frontier and the opportunities it provided individuals to begin again, the immigrating refugees of the nineteenth and twentieth centuries for whom government was synonymous with tyranny and oppression, the Darwinian thesis of the survival of the fittest, the gospel of wealth, and rugged individualism all paid homage to the concept of limited government.

Federalism

In addition to rigorously circumscribing the powers of government, the Framers divided those that were provided between the national government and the states. For the most part, certain powers are delegated to the federal government, whereas others are reserved to the states. Some, however, are shared, such as the power to tax.

The constitutional language that pertains to this geographical division of power lacks precision. As a result, the Supreme Court has confronted a constant stream of litigation that has required the justices to determine the relative power of the federal government vis-à-vis the states. The Court's first major case, *Chisholm*

---

[31] For a classic treatment of constitutionalism, see Charles H. McIlwain, *Constitutionalism: Ancient and Modern*, rev. ed. (Ithaca: Cornell University Press, 1947).

v. Georgia,[32] concerned federal-state relations. Resolution of these conflicts tilts in favor of the federal government in part because of the language of the supremacy clause (Article VI, Section 2):

> This Constitution, and the laws of the United States which shall be made in pursuance thereof; and all treaties made, or which shall be made, under the authority of the United States, shall be the supreme law of the land; and the Judges in every State shall be bound thereby, anything in the Constitution or laws of any State to the contrary notwithstanding.

The resolution of federal-state conflicts also tilts in favor of the federal government because the Supreme Court has arrogated to itself the authority to ultimately decide these disputes. It did so early in the nineteenth century, in a pair of landmark decisions, *Martin v, Hunter's Lessee* and *Cohens v. Virginia*.[33]

But even though the constitutional language favors federal supremacy, and the ultimate decision maker is an arm of the federal government, centralization of power has not characterized American politics, as Chapter 3 on the political history of the Court shows. The Court's decisions have caused the degree of centralization/decentralization to vary from one period to another. Indeed, during the late nineteenth and early twentieth centuries when the Court was writing the doctrines of laissez-faire economics into the Constitution, the justices even-handedly struck down anti-business regulations regardless of the governmental level from which they emanated.

Apart from the operation of the justices' personal policy preferences, the limited jurisdiction of the federal courts and the separate constitutional existence of the state judicial systems have enabled the states to resist a variety of centralizing tendencies rather successfully. We address these matters in the next major section of this chapter, The Federal and State Judicial Systems.

Separation of powers

Separation of powers compartmentalizes government into three separate branches, in the sense that each exercises powers distinct from the others and does so with its own personnel. The effect of this arrangement precludes any branch from compelling action by the other two. Instead, separation of powers institutionalizes conflict, particularly between the Congress and the President. To prevent one branch from overpowering another, each is provided with certain powers that functionally belong to one of the other branches. These are the so-called checks and balances. Thus, the President constitutionally possesses the legislative power to veto Congress' actions, while the Senate participates in the selection of executive officials through the constitutional requirement of advice and consent. Both check the courts – the President by nominating judges, and Congress by consenting to their selection (Senate only)

---

[32]   2 Dallas 419 (1793).
[33]   1 Wheaton 304 (1816) and 6 Wheaton 264 (1821).

and determining their number and jurisdiction. The courts in turn check the President and Congress through the power of judicial review, which we discuss next.

The Framers were most concerned about the exercise of legislative power. To lessen their fears, they divided Congress into two separate chambers, the Senate and the House of Representatives, with the membership chosen from distinct constituencies (except for those states that have only a single representative) and with a different term of office. They required that a bill pass both houses with identical provisions, down to the last comma, before it could be sent to the President for signature or veto. The judiciary, by contrast, escaped relatively unscathed. The Framers did not view the courts as a threat to the constitutionalism they so carefully crafted. They were more concerned lest the judges become subservient to either of the other branches. To insure the judiciary's independence, the Framers provided them with lifetime tenure, no reduction in salary, and created a selection process that neither the President nor Congress could control.

Separation of powers enables the Supreme Court to resolve authoritatively justiciable disputes that pit Congress and the President against one another.[34] A politically charged example concerned the Gramm-Rudman Balanced Budget and Deficit Reduction Act of 1985. Congress assigned one of its own employees, the Comptroller General, responsibility for determining the cuts needed to reduce the budget deficit. By a 7-to-2 vote, the Supreme Court declared the provision unconstitutional because a person removable by Congress was given the executive power to estimate, allocate, and order the spending cuts required to satisfy the deficit targeted by the law. The Court ruled that because Congress could remove the Comptroller General from office, he was "subservient" to it.[35] The fact that Congress had never done so during the sixty-five years of the office's existence did not sway the majority.

Notwithstanding the publicity that attended this decision, the dispute turned on a trivial technicality. The Court did not void the fallback provision that allows the regular legislative process to effectuate the cuts; neither does the decision preclude Congress from merely repealing the provision that allows it to remove the Comptroller, or from bestowing the Comptroller's power on an official whom Congress can remove only through impeachment. Either of these options would make the official "executive" rather than "legislative." This arguably is a distinction without a difference.

The creation of the judiciary as an independent coordinate branch of the government has appreciably promoted the policy-making capabilities of federal judges in general, and that of the Supreme Court in particular. Absent functional

---

[34] Many such disputes are "political questions." The plaintiff lacks standing to sue because the Court believes the matter – though within the courts' subject matter jurisdiction – should be resolved by the "political" branches of government themselves. We discuss this matter in the section on standing to sue in Chapter 5.

[35] *Bowsher v. Synar*, 478 U.S. 714 (1986), at 727. The dissenters were White and Blackmun.

independence, the judges would likely be viewed – along with other government officials – as mere politicians and bureaucrats. Their efforts to distinguish themselves and their activities as principled, even-handed, and nonpartisan would likely be unsuccessful, with the result that the public would view them as on a level with the persons of minimal competence and dubious ethics who engage in the dirty business of politics.

Judicial review

The most striking evidence of judicial independence is a court's exercise of the power of judicial review. Although the power to declare an action of the other branches of government incompatible with the content of the fundamental law is nowhere specified in the Constitution, its exercise comports with the motivations and concerns that led to the drafting and ratification of the document.

First, if the Constitution is to be the fundamental law of the land, some body must be able to decide whether the actions of government conform to it. Such decisions may theoretically be made by Congress and/or the President. After all, they do take the same oath as federal judges to preserve, protect, and defᵣ d the Constitution of the United States. But the competition between the Congᵣess and the President that separation of powers engenders may cause either of them to take a less than objective view of the constitutionality of their own conduct as opposed to that of the other branch. Unseemly squabbles would likely result. How much better to leave such decisions to the judges. Not only are they independent of the other branches, but their lifetime appointment also insulates them from factious electoral pressures.

Second, inasmuch as separation of powers insures conflict between the executive and legislative branches, does it not make sense to position the judiciary, which, as we have seen, is beholden to neither of them, as the balance of power?

Third, given the federal system, a decision maker is also needed to authoritatively resolve disputes between the federal government and the states. The opacity of the constitutional provisions governing their relationship magnifies the need for such an ''umpire.'' To allow the ''political'' branches of the federal government or the states themselves to resolve such disputes would unduly centralize or decentralize governmental authority depending on which level makes the decisions.

Enunciation of the doctrine of judicial review. John Marshall, newly ensconced as Chief Justice, unhesitatingly seized the opportunity that the case of *Marbury v. Madison*[36] presented and formally enunciated the doctrine of judicial review. In the closing days of John Adams' administration, the Federalist-controlled Congress passed an act that provided for forty-two new judges. Adams quickly

---

[36]　1 Cranch 137 (1803).

nominated ardent Federalists to these positions, and on March 3, 1801, the last day of the Adams administration and the last day of the lame-duck holdover Congress, the Senate approved the nominations. The appointments would have legal effect when each nominee received a sealed commission of office from Secretary of State John Marshall, who was then serving in that position as well as Chief Justice.

Not all the commissions were delivered by the appointed hour of midnight. Jefferson's Secretary of State, James Madison, refused to deliver the remainder. William Marbury, one of the nonrecipients, went directly to the Supreme Court and requested a writ of mandamus that would order Madison to deliver him his commission. Marbury argued that the Judiciary Act of 1789 gave the Supreme Court original jurisdiction to issue such writs.

Marshall, speaking for a unanimous Court, ruled that Marbury had a right to the commission, but the Court had no power to order its delivery. Section 13 of the Judiciary Act, which purportedly expanded the Court's original jurisdiction, was unconstitutional because the Constitution specifies the Court's original jurisdiction, with all other matters being heard only on appeal. The issuance of writs of mandamus does not appear among the listed subjects of original jurisdiction. By expanding the Court's original jurisdiction, the Judiciary Act violated the Constitution.

According to the elementary canons of judicial ethics, Marshall, as the individual responsible for the controversy that gave rise to the lawsuit, should have recused himself.[37] Marshall, however, realized that no better opportunity to formulate judicial review would occur.[38] The case, aptly described as a "trivial squabble over a few petty political plums,"[39] should never have been decided by the Supreme Court in the first place. As Marshall's opinion makes clear, in bringing his case to the Supreme Court, Marbury entered the wrong forum and should merely have been directed to the appropriate federal district court. Marshall, however, did not allow either legal or ethical niceties to deprive him of his opportunity.

Marshall held that any action by Congress to expand the Court's original jurisdiction to include subjects not specified in the Constitution was unconstitutional.[40] The fact that the First Congress enacted the law – the Judiciary

---

[37] Special Committee on Standards of Judicial Conduct, "Code of Judicial Conduct," in *Code of Professional Responsibility and Code of Judicial Conduct* (Chicago: American Bar Assn., 1978), pp. 62, 63.

[38] Subsequent events proved Marshall correct. Not until fifty-four years later, in *Scott v. Sandford*, 19 Howard 393 (1857), did the Court declare another act of Congress unconstitutional. Unlike *Marbury v. Madison*, the decision in that case, which led directly to the Civil War, was hardly conducive to the continued vitality of judicial review.

[39] John A. Garraty, "The Case of the Missing Commissions," in John A. Garraty, ed., *Quarrels That Have Shaped the Constitution* (New York: Harper & Row, 1964), p. 13.

[40] Significantly, Marshall's decision did not require executive action for its enforcement. Furthermore, he ruled against a member of his own political party. Madison and the Jeffersonians won

Act of 1789 – and that a disproportionate number of its members had been delegates to the Constitutional Convention – Marshall, significantly, was not among them – did not give Marshall pause. If any group of persons knew the meaning and intention of the Constitution's provisions, it was the members of the First Congress. Furthermore, the provision of the Judiciary Act declared unconstitutional was authored by Oliver Ellsworth, Marshall's predecessor as Chief Justice. The irony of a Chief Justice of the United States, a member of the First Congress, and a delegate to the Constitutional Convention, violating his oath of office by writing a statute that contravened the fundamental law of which he was also an author apparently did not strike Marshall as at all peculiar.

Even more mind-boggling is the fact that nothing in the language of the statute – Section 13 of the Judiciary Act of 1789 – even remotely suggests an expansion of the Supreme Court's original jurisdiction! After listing the cases in which the Supreme Court might exercise original jurisdiction, the statute catalogs the matters over which the Court has appellate jurisdiction:

The supreme court shall also have appellate jurisdiction from the circuit courts and the courts of the several states, in the cases herein after specially provided for. And shall have power to issue writs of prohibition to the district courts when proceeding as courts of admiralty and maritime jurisdiction; and writs of MANDAMUS, in cases warranted by the principles and usages of law, to any courts appointed, or persons holding office, under the authority of the United States.

This is the only language that concerns Marbury's case. Marshall clearly had absolutely nothing to declare unconstitutional![41] He simply formulated the doctrine of judicial review without applying it to any specific statutory language. As further evidence of this fact, nowhere in *Marbury v. Madison* does Marshall quote the foregoing language. This may well be the only case in the Court's Reports in which the prevailing opinion does not cite the language declared unconstitutional. The only reference to the provision antedates Marshall's opinion of the Court where the Reporter, William Cranch, in recording the testimony of the witnesses and the arguments of the attorneys, notes that Marbury's attorney, Charles Lee, made mention of it.[42]

In the course of his opinion, Marshall tenders a view of judicial competence and integrity in which he presents arguments and makes assertions that humiliate and debase the other branches. These assertions, mind you, are ones that Americans have unquestioningly come to accept. Thus,

It is a proposition too plain to be contested, that the constitution controls any legislative act repugnant to it; or, that the legislature may alter the constitution by an ordinary act.[43]

---

the battle (although not the war, as history has shown). From the perspective of the average citizen, what better evidence of the objectivity and impartiality of judicial decision making!

[41] In support of our assertion, see Charles Warren, *The Supreme Court in United States History* (Boston: Little, Brown, 1922), I, 242, and William W. Van Alstyne, ''A Critical Guide to Marbury v. Madison,'' 1969 *Duke Law Journal* 1, at 15.

[42] 1 Cranch 137, at 148. Marshall's opinion begins at the end of page 153.

[43] Id. at 177.

Of course. The statement is logically impeccable. But consider the implications: that Congress, aided if not necessarily abetted by the President, is fully capable of acting unconstitutionally. Query: Why do we not make the same presumption about the justices themselves?

Marshall returns to the foregoing argument when he writes that those who controvert the principle that the Constitution is the fundamental law

> must close their eyes on the constitution, and see only the law.
> This doctrine would subvert the very foundation of all written constitutions. . . . It would declare that if the legislature shall do that which is expressly forbidden, such act, notwithstanding the express prohibition, is effectual.[44]

Again, this is an indisputable proposition. But again consider the implication: Marshall assumes that Congress would consciously and deliberately behave unconstitutionally – even though, as we have seen, Congress did nothing of the sort here. If we couple this fact with Marshall's deviousness and his dubious ethics, can we say the same of the Court? Might it not be as appropriate, if not more so, to consider the possibility that the justices might void a constitutional law or uphold an unconstitutional one?

In a final argument, Marshall lays logic aside and, with an indignant flourish, rhetorically poses the ethical question:

> Why otherwise does it [the Constitution] direct the judges to take an oath to support it? This oath certainly applies in an especial manner, to their conduct in their official character. How immoral to impose it on them, if they were to be used as the instruments, and the knowing instruments, for violating what they swear to support! . . .
> Why does a judge swear to discharge his duties agreeably to the constitution of the United States, if that constitution forms no rule for his government?[45]

The fact that all federal officials take the same oath gave Marshall no more pause than it gives us today. What is sauce for the goose is *not* sauce for the gander. Only politicians betray their oaths of office, not judges. If the doctrine of judicial review did not congruently fit the Framers' concept of fundamental law and their – and our – distrust of elected officials, would we not direct the logic and implications of Marshall's reasoning – to say nothing of his behavior here – against the Court itself?

The mythology of judging

Given our acceptance of judicial supremacy as evidenced by the doctrine of judicial review and the other reasons supporting authoritative judicial and Supreme Court policy making, why do we find it necessary to surround courts and judges with myth? Assertions that judicial decisions are objective, dispassionate, and impartial are obviously belied by the fact that different courts and different

---

[44]   Id. at 178.
[45]   Id. at 179.

judges do not decide the same question or issue the same way, to say nothing of the fact that appellate court decisions – particularly those of the United States Supreme Court – typically contain dissenting votes. So, too, a single personnel change may fundamentally alter the course of constitutional law.[46]

Insofar as judicial and Supreme Court policy making are concerned, mythology basically exists because judges play God with regard to the life, liberty, and property of those who appear before them. No matter the issue – trivial or earthshaking – the final decision rests with a court. But playing God is not a proper task for mere mortals. And so mythology is born. Judges are said to have no discretion; they do not announce their decisions. It is rather the law or the Constitution speaking though them that dictates the outcome. If any policy results, fundamental law and governmental actions compatible therewith have mandated it, not the judge. Judges, therefore, are objective, dispassionate, and impartial. To insure that facts do not becloud the myth we adopt an ostrich posture.

To support the mythology, devices have been created to inculcate respect and reverence for judges. Secrecy and mystery shroud the decision-making process. Thus, we garb judges in distinctive dress. And although society attires some governmental personnel other than judges in uniforms – the military, the police, and some postal workers – none wears a black robe, the most solemn and mysterious of outfits. Courthouses and courtrooms replicate churches and temples. Instead of altars, they contain elevated benches to which all who enter must look *up*. The proceedings are ritualized, accompanied by pomp and ceremony, and conducted (at least before the demise of legalistic jargon) in a language largely unintelligible to laypersons. The religious imagery evoked in Chief Justice Taft's statements about the utility of the judicial robe typify the matter:

It is well that judges should be clothed in robes, not only, that those who witness the administration of justice should be properly advised that the function performed is one different from, and higher than, that which a man discharges as a citizen in the ordinary walks of life; but also, in order to impress the judge himself with the constant consciousness that he is a high priest of the temple of justice and is surrounded with obligations of a sacred character that he cannot escape. . . .[47]

Hence the dominance of the judiciary. Governmental affairs become judicial affairs in the sense that their outcome often depends on a court's decision, most authoritatively those of the United States Supreme Court. Aided and abetted by a mythology that blunts criticism and insulates them from the hue and cry, judges blithely go about their business, obligated to none but themselves. As enigmatic

---

[46]   See Jeffrey A. Segal and Harold J. Spaeth, "Decisional trends on the Warren and Burger Courts: results from the Supreme Court Data Base Project," 73 *Judicature* 103 (1989), 104–105.

[47]   William Howard Taft, *Present Day Problems* (New York: Dodd, Mead, 1908), pp. 63–64. Judge Jerome Frank candidly and incisively critiqued the symbolism surrounding judicial decision making as "the cult of the robe" in his classic *Courts on Trial* (New York: Atheneum, 1963), pp. 254–261.

technicians, as so many Delphic oracles, they objectively dispense revealed truth
and wisdom. As one astute commentator irreverently observed:

Like oysters in our cloisters we avoid the storm and strife.
Some President appoints us, and we're put away for life.
When Congress passes laws that lack historical foundation,
We hasten from a huddle and reverse the legislation.
The sainted Constitution, that great document for students,
Provides an airtight alibi for all our jurisprudence.
So don't blame us if now and then we seem to act like bounders;
Blame Hamilton and Franklin and the patriotic founders.[48]

THE FEDERAL AND STATE JUDICIAL SYSTEMS

As a result of federalism, the United States has two separate and autonomous
court systems: those of the states and that of the federal government. The subject-
matter jurisdiction of the federal courts is limited to "federal questions" – those
whose resolution depends on a provision of the Constitution, an act of Congress,
or a treaty of the United States[49] – and cases that arise under "diversity of
citizenship" – those that do not contain a federal question, but that may yet be
heard in a federal court if the parties are residents of different states. By contrast,
the jurisdiction of the state courts covers a much wider range of subjects. This
results in concurrent state court jurisdiction over many matters that are also
appropriate for resolution by the federal courts. The opposite situation, however,
does not hold: The federal courts do not have concurrent jurisdiction with the
state courts over matters that do not contain a federal question or involve diversity
of citizenship.[50] In other words, the federal courts lack exclusive jurisdiction,
except over such peculiarly federal matters as admiralty and maritime cases and

---

[48] Arthur Lippmann, "Song of the Supreme Court," *Life Magazine*, August 1935, p. 7.

[49] The Constitution also gives the Supreme Court jurisdiction "to controversies between two or
more States" and "to all cases affecting ambassadors, other public ministers and consuls."
Such disputes need not concern any constitutional provision or federal statute or treaty. They
rarely occur, however, and when they do they take on the character of a local or purely private
dispute. They are not of broad public policy significance.

[50] Minor exceptions exist. The federal courts may constitutionally exercise "supplementary jurisdiction" – that is, ancillary and pendent jurisdiction. See the Judicial Improvements Act of 1990,
28 *U.S. Code* 1367. If a jurisdictionally sufficient claim exists, either party, as well as third
parties, may join with that jurisdictionally sufficient claim other jurisdictionally *in*sufficient claims
that any of them may have if these additional claims "derive from a common nucleus of operative
fact." *United Mine Workers v. Gibbs*, 383 U.S. 715 (1966), at 725. If the federal trial court
finds that this condition exists, the multiple claims will be joined with the others and the entire
dispute decided. This policy lessens piecemeal litigation and promotes judicial economy.
    Pendent jurisdiction involves joining state-law claims to a jurisdictionally sufficient federal
question, whereas ancillary jurisdiction involves joining claims of persons other than the original
plaintiff to the lawsuit – for example, the respondent's counterclaim, or those of a third party
who alleges an interest in the property that the lawsuit concerns.
    Chapter 5 contains a more detailed description of ancillary and pendant jurisdiction as part
of our discussion of the jurisdiction of the federal courts.

federal crimes, with the result that plaintiffs commonly have a choice of forums in which to bring their cases.[51]

To apportion jurisdictional responsibility between itself and the lower federal courts on the one hand, and the state courts on the other, the Supreme Court utilizes three constitutional provisions – the supremacy clause, the Eleventh Amendment's doctrine of sovereign immunity, and the full faith and credit clause – plus three policies of its own design – comity, an adequate and independent state ground for decision, and the rules governing choice of law. A discussion of each follows.

National supremacy

The existence of concurrent jurisdiction produces conflict. This conflict typically pits the Supreme Court against the courts of the various states. To resolve these conflicts, the Framers provided in the supremacy clause – Article VI, Section 2, of the Constitution – that

This Constitution, and the laws of the United States which shall be made in pursuance thereof; and all treaties made, or which shall be made, under the authority of the United States, shall be the supreme law of the land; and the Judges in every State shall be bound thereby, anything in the Constitution or laws of any State to the contrary notwithstanding.

Although this language clearly establishes the supremacy of federal law, it does not say who shall decide such cases. The First Congress eliminated this omission, and in the famous Section 25 of the Judiciary Act of 1789, authorized the Supreme Court to review state court decisions that involved a federal question:

That a final judgment or decree in any suit, in the highest court of law or equity of a State in which a decision in the suit could be had, where is drawn in question the validity of a treaty or statute of or an authority exercised under the United States, and the decision is against their validity; or where is drawn in question the validity of a statute of, or an authority exercised under any State, on the ground of their being repugnant to the constitution, treaties or laws of the United States, and the decision is in favor of their validity, or where is drawn in question the construction of any clause of the constitution, or of a treaty, or statute of, or commission held under the United States, and the decision is against the title, right, privilege or exemption specifically set up or claimed by either party, under such clause of the said constitution, treaty, statute or commission, may be re-examined and reversed or affirmed in the Supreme Court of the United States.[52]

Except for the Supreme Court and its original jurisdiction,[53] Congress creates the lower federal courts and determines – within the subject matter specified in

---

[51] This does not mean that when the federal or state or local governments initiate litigation they cross jurisdictional lines to do so. Neither federal nor local prosecutors, for example, have authority to file charges in any court other than those of which they are officers.

[52] 1 *U.S. Statutes at Large* 85–86.

[53] "In all cases affecting ambassadors, other public ministers and consuls, and those in which a State shall be party, the Supreme Court shall have original jurisdiction." Article III, Section 2, Clause 2.

Article III, Section 2, Clause 1 – which courts may decide what sorts of cases. In authorizing the Supreme Court to review state court decisions that contained a federal question, Congress withheld Supreme Court review until the losing litigant had exhausted all remedies under state law – typically a final judgment[54] by the state supreme court.

This jurisdictional grant, however, did not settle matters. Congress had not seen fit to provide the federal trial courts with jurisdiction to hear federal questions, preferring to leave such matters to the state courts. Not until after the Civil War did Congress invest the federal courts with first instance federal question jurisdiction. As a result, such cases were heard in the state courts. State court judges did not take kindly to Supreme Court review of their decisions, alleging that though they were bound by the supremacy clause, they were not obliged to adhere to the Supreme Court's interpretation of the Constitution, acts of Congress, or treaties of the United States. They asserted that to be so bound would materially impair state sovereignty and the independence of state courts.

In what is arguably the most important decision it has ever made, *Martin v. Hunter's Lessee*, the Supreme Court unequivocally rejected the states' contentions:

> Judges of equal learning and integrity, in different states, might differently interpret a statute, or a treaty of the United States, or even the constitution itself. If there were no revising authority to control these jarring and discordant judgments, and harmonize them into uniformity, the laws, the treaties, the constitution of the United States would be different in different states, and might, perhaps, never have . . . the same construction, obligation, or efficacy, in any two states. The public mischiefs that would attend such a state of things would be truly deplorable . . . the appellate jurisdiction must continue to be the only adequate remedy for such evils.[55]

Precisely. Without such power, each provision of the Constitution, every act of Congress, and every treaty would have a different meaning in each of the fifty states. The United States would be no more united than the United Nations is or Yugoslavia was. Each state would be as sovereign as any petty principality or third world polity. What constitutes taxable income, the status of women and minors, the meaning of due process and equal protection, the scope and applicability of the First Amendment, the reasonableness of searches and seizures, whether the Constitution recognizes any kind of right to privacy, would vary from state to state as each of fifty autonomous state supreme courts decreed.

Note further that this link, this bit of glue, that binds the fifty states into a single entity couples together only the courts at the top of each hierarchy – the state and federal supreme courts. And that the 176 operative words in Section 25 of the Judiciary Act of 1789 emanate from Congress – and what Congress grants, Congress may revoke. Indeed, until well after the Civil War, bills were regularly introduced to do just that.

---

[54] A "final judgment" typically means any decree or order from which an appeal lies. See, for example, Rule 54(a) of the Federal Rules of Civil Procedure.

[55] 1 Wheaton 304 (1816), at 348.

To be completely accurate, we should also note the existence of an alternative link between the federal and state court systems, which dates from 1867: the use of the writ of habeas corpus.[56] Persons convicted of crime under state law who allege that their convictions violate the federal Constitution may petition the federal district court where they are incarcerated to review their state court convictions. In order to do so, convicts must have complied with the state's contemporaneous objection rule, which requires them to raise their federal question – typically the admission of evidence from an allegedly illegal search or seizure – at the time the evidence is introduced. If the state court fails to give full and fair consideration to their federal question, they may petition the federal district court in the locale where the state court sits for a writ of habeas corpus once they have exhausted their appeals under state law.

The federal courts use the writ of habeas corpus sparingly. Although the Warren Court had opened this door rather widely in the mid-1960s in decisions such as *Dombrowski v. Pfister*,[57] in which a civil rights organization enjoined state officials from prosecuting it under the state's subversive activities statutes, the Burger Court substantially closed it by the early 1980s.[58]

The system of comity[59]

The decision in *Martin v. Hunter's Lessee* did not make the state courts superfluous to the resolution of federal questions for two reasons. First, the Supreme Court accepts review of an exceptionally small proportion of state court decisions, whether or not they arise on a writ of habeas corpus. Rejected cases, as well as those that the Supreme Court affirms, become the law of the land – at least that of the state involved. Second, mindful of the tender sensibilities of the states and their judges (which sensibilities are markedly less pronounced than they were prior to the Civil War), the Supreme Court has devised a system of comity for the purpose of minimizing conflict between the two judicial systems. Speaking though Hugo Black, the justices described it in the following maudlin language:

---

[56]   28 *U.S. Code*, sections 2241–2255.

[57]   380 U.S. 479 (1965).

[58]   See, for example, *Stone v. Powell*, 428 U.S. 465 (1976); *Engle v. Isaac*, 456 U.S. 107 (1982); *United States v. Frady*, 456 U.S. 152 (1982). The Rehnquist Court barred it further in *McCleskey v. Zant*, 113 L Ed 2d 517 (1991), a ruling that essentially limited state prisoners to a single habeas petition, and in *Coleman v. Thompson*, 115 L Ed 2d 640 (1991), which held that state prisoners' failure to comply with the state's procedural requirements forfeits their right to bring a habeas petition in federal court. This decision over-ruled *Fay v. Noia*, 372 U.S. 391 (1963), a liberal landmark ruling that allowed prisoners access to the federal court as long as they had not "deliberately by-passed" the state's appeals process. 372 U.S. at 438. *Fay v. Noia* itself overruled a precedent, *Darr v. Burford*, 339 U.S. 200 (1950), further evidencing the Court's tergiversation in this area of federal-state relations.

[59]   As explained later, comity refers to the effect the federal government accords the laws and judicial actions of the state and local governments, not as a matter of obligation but out of deference and respect.

... a proper respect for state functions, a recognition of the fact that the entire country is made up of a Union of separate state governments, and a continuance of the belief that the National Government will fare best if the States and their institutions are left free to perform their separate functions in their separate ways. This, perhaps for lack of a better and clearer way to describe it, is referred to by many as "Our Federalism," and one familiar with the profound debates that ushered our Federal Constitution into existence is bound to respect those who remain loyal to the ideals and dreams of "Our Federalism." The concept does not mean blind deference to "States' Rights" any more than it means centralization of control over every important issue in our National Government and its courts. The Framers rejected both these courses. What the concept does represent is a system in which there is sensitivity to the legitimate interests of both State and National Governments, and in which the National Government, anxious though it may be to vindicate and protect federal rights and federal interests, always endeavors to do so in ways that will not unduly interfere with the legitimate activities of the States. It should never be forgotten that this slogan, "Our Federalism," born in the early struggling days of our Union of States, occupies a highly important place in our Nation's history and its future.[60]

The vehicle by which the Court implements comity is the abstention doctrine, "whereby the federal courts 'exercising a wise discretion,' restrain their authority because of 'scrupulous regard for the rightful independence of the state governments' and for the smooth working of the federal judiciary."[61] Thus, the abstention doctrine requires the federal courts to avoid intruding themselves into ongoing state judicial proceedings or otherwise duplicating litigation already begun in a state court. Exceptions are narrowly confined. State proceedings may be enjoined on a showing of "irreparable injury" that is "both great and immediate."[62] A plaintiff is not likely to meet this standard in other than extreme cases of bad faith prosecution or official harassment. Efforts to remove a state initiated case from a state court to a federal court are governed by equally stringent criteria.[63]

One notable exception to comity's disapproval of removal involved the case of Pete Rose, then manager of the Cincinnati Reds baseball team, who sued Major League Baseball Commissioner, A. Bartlett Giamatti. Rose, a Cincinnati native and local hero, had been investigated by the Commissioner's office for alleged gambling activities both as an an active player and as a manager. Despite explicit language in Rose's contract with the Reds that gave the Commissioner the authority to

investigate ... any act, transaction or practice charged, alleged or suspected to be not in the best interests of the national game of baseball ... to determine, after investigation, what preventative, remedial or punitive action is appropriate in the circumstances and to take such action ... as the case may be ...[64]

---

[60]　*Younger v. Harris*, 401 U.S. 37 (1971), at 44–45.

[61]　*Railroad Commission of Texas v. Pullman Co.*, 312 U.S. 496 (1941), at 501.

[62]　*Younger v. Harris*, 401 U.S. 37 (1971), at 46.

[63]　For example, *Johnson v. Mississippi*, 421 U.S. 213 (1975); *Arizona v. Manypenny*, 451 U.S. 232 (1981).

[64]　Murray Chass, "Judge Blocks Giamatti's Hearing On Betting Charges Against Rose," *New York Times*, June 26, 1989, p. A1.

Rose sought an injunction against further action by Giamatti. He also named the Reds and Major League Baseball as defendants. As both do business in Ohio, he was able to file his claim in an Ohio court.

The judge, an elected official who was obviously mindful of Rose's great popularity, ignored the express language of the contract, as well as sixty years of unbroken precedents giving the Commissioner broad disciplinary powers over baseball, and temporarily enjoined Giamatti from further action. It is not irrelevant to note that the local judge presided over a televised hearing.

Giamatti, concerned about the fairness of the proceedings, sought access to a federal court in Columbus. For technical reasons, the federal court could take jurisdiction only if Major League Baseball and the Reds were deleted as defendants. Such efforts are almost always denied, but not in this case. One month after the Cincinnati judge issued his injunction, the federal judge in "an extraordinary technical ruling" removed Baseball and the Reds from Rose's suit and took jurisdiction of the case.[65] Without the protection provided him by the local Cincinnati judge, Rose accepted a plea bargain that banished him from baseball for life, subject to possible reinstatement at the Commissioner's discretion. In August 1990, Rose began serving a five-month sentence for income tax evasion.

Normally, once state proceedings have commenced, litigants must almost always avail themselves of and exhaust the state's administrative and judicial remedies before they take their federal questions into a federal court. Accordingly, determination of the constitutionality of state laws and regulations rests initially with the state courts themselves. If the state courts resolve the federal questions their cases contain compatibly with federal law, the need for Supreme Court review disappears.

Apart from the deference that comity pays to the state courts, abstention also impedes prompt federal court protection of federal rights. According to Justice Douglas, who opposed abstention more than any of his colleagues, "We do a great disservice when we send . . . tired and exhausted litigants into the desert in search of this Holy Grail that is already in the keeping of the federal court."[66]

Sovereign immunity[67]

Although the doctrine of sovereign immunity has had far less effect on the relationships between the state and federal courts than the system of comity and the abstention doctrine, it has the potential to appreciably expand the scope of state court policy making.

Sovereign immunity had its genesis in *Chisholm v. Georgia*, discussed earlier.

---

[65] Murray Chass, "Judge Rules That Rose Case Should Go to a Federal Court," *New York Times*, August 1, 1989, p. B7.

[66] *Harris County Commissioners Court v. Moore*, 420 U.S. 77 (1975), at 91.

[67] The immunity from suit that government has from liability for its actions.

In reaction to the Court's decision allowing nonresidents to sue a state in the federal courts, Congress proposed and the states ratified the Eleventh Amendment in 1798, which decreed that "The judicial power of the United States shall not be construed to extend to any suit in law or equity, commenced or prosecuted against one of the United States by citizens of another State, or by citizens or subjects of any foreign State."

The Supreme Court has construed this language narrowly. Immunity applies only to the states as states, not to local governments or to officials of either state or local governments. The Court has rationalized this distinction on the theory that illegally acting officials do so in a private capacity rather than in their governmental capacity.[68] In general, only suits for money damages are barred. Furthermore, Section 5 of the Fourteenth Amendment, which gives Congress the power to enact legislation to enforce the other provisions of the Fourteenth Amendment – particularly the right of persons not to be deprived of due process or denied the equal protection of the law – overrides the bar to nonresident suits. The federal courts may therefore try damage suits brought by persons whose civil rights a state has abridged.

The primary advocate for an expansion of sovereign immunity has been Chief Justice Rehnquist. He has argued that the Eleventh Amendment, along with Article III, rests "on important concepts of sovereignty that do not find expression in the literal terms of those provisions, but which are of constitutional dimension because their derogation would undermine the logic of the constitutional scheme."[69] Rehnquist, accordingly, reads the Eleventh Amendment to bar an unconsenting state from suit in the courts of a sister state.

The full faith and credit clause

Another constitutional provision that has had relatively little impact on federal-state relationships is the full faith and credit clause of Article IV, Section 1: "Full faith and credit shall be given in each State to the public acts, records, and judicial proceedings of every other State." A long line of decisions has construed the clause to apply only to final state court judgments in civil, not criminal, cases. These judgments have the same force and effect in the courts of other states as they do in the rendering state, provided that the original court had not exercised jurisdiction over a non-resident defendant in a way that violates due process of law.[70] A federal statute requires the same of federal courts.

---

[68] *Ex parte Young*, 209 U.S. 123 (1908).

[69] *Nevada v. Hall*, 440 U.S. 410 (1979), at 439.

[70] A state court's decision over a non-resident defendant does not violate due process if it meets the "minimum contacts" test of *International Shoe Co. v. Washington*, 326 U.S. 310 (1945). If defendants are not present in the forum state, the court has personal jurisdiction over them if they have had "certain minimum contacts with it such that the maintenance of the suit does not offend 'traditional notions of fair play and substantial justice.' " 326 U.S. at 316. The jurisdictional problems that out-of-state defendants pose are described in the first section of Chapter 5.

Most such cases concern commercial transactions, insurance, and various forms of compensation. These are automatically enforced. Not so those that pertain to child custody, support, and spousal alimony. These lack the necessary finality to trigger full faith and credit because they are subject to ongoing modification as the best interests of the benefitted party require – for example, a minor child.[71] As the Supreme Court recently observed: ''Because courts entering custody orders generally retain the power to modify them, courts in other States were no less entitled to change the terms of custody according to their own views of the child's best interest.''[72] The Supreme Court, of course, is free to alter its stance and subject domestic relations to the operation of the clause. Its failure to do so enables litigants to avoid or alter their responsibilities by the simple expedient of crossing a state line.

Adequate and independent state grounds for decision

From a policy-making standpoint, this aspect of the relationship between the federal and state courts differs markedly from the Court's use of comity and the abstention doctrine. Whereas comity views the state courts as conscientious and competent construers of federal questions, the Court's use of adequate and independent state grounds for decision cuts both ways: On the one hand, it allows the Court to view state judges as devious decision makers who employ their own laws and constitutional provisions to concoct policies at variance with those mandated by the Supreme Court. On the other, it permits state court decisions to escape review by the Supreme or other federal courts when a majority of the justices so prefer.

Historically, the Supreme Court had supplemented the abstention doctrine with the self-imposed assumption that if a state court decision contained a federal question that was intermixed with questions of solely state concern, the state court's decision rested ''on an adequate and independent state ground.'' In other words, if the state court did not clearly indicate that its decision was based on state law as opposed to federal law, the Supreme Court simply assumed that the state court decided the case on the basis of its own law. This traditional orientation comported fully with the fact that the subject-matter jurisdiction that the Constitution authorizes the federal courts to exercise makes them courts of limited jurisdiction and that in the federal scheme of things, the autonomy of the state courts is limited only by the supremacy clause.

Accordingly, the crucial inquiry for the justices in every state court case that contains both state and federal questions was twofold: Does the state court decision rest on non-federal grounds? If so, is that nonfederal ground adequate

---

[71]   In *Ford v. Ford*, 371 U.S. 187 (1962), for example, the Supreme Court unanimously ruled that a Virginia decree that gave custody to the parents of three minor children for only a specific part of the year did not prevent the mother from filing suit in a South Carolina court for full custody.

[72]   *Thompson v. Thompson*, 98 L Ed 2d 512 (1988), at 521.

to support the state court's decision? If the answer to both questions is "yes," the justices would refuse to review the case. Unless the party petitioning the Supreme Court for review could persuade the justices to the contrary, the Court assumed that the state court based its decision on its own law, and that that law was sufficient to support the state court's decision.

In 1983, in a run-of-the-mill vehicular search and seizure case, the Burger Court reversed its historic policy and ruled that when

... a state court decision fairly appears to rest primarily on federal law, or to be interwoven with the federal law, and when the adequacy and independence of any possible state law ground is not clear from the face of the opinion, we will accept ... that the state court decided the case the way it did because it believed that federal law required it to do so.[73]

To overcome this new – and contradictory – presumption, the state court bore the burden of demonstrating that the federal cases and authorities that it cited in its opinion did "not themselves compel the result that the [state] court has reached," but were used only for "guidance." How might the state court meet this burden? "If the state court decision indicates clearly and expressly that it is alternatively based on *bona fide separate*, adequate, and independent grounds, we, of course, will not undertake to review the decision." (Italics added.)[74] Not only must state courts apparently issue a plain statement denying reliance on federal law, but they must also persuade the justices that this reliance is genuine. The addition of the word, "separate," to "bona fide," "adequate," and "independent" should enable the justices to review any state court decision they wish so long as it makes reference to some federal authority.

Why did the moderately conservative Burger Court, with a reputation of deference to the states, suddenly change its tune?

Analysis of decisions in which the majority used *Michigan v. Long* to review state court decisions shows it to be a means to overturn liberal state decisions upholding the rights of persons accused or convicted of crime, particularly those involving unreasonable searches and seizures.[75]

[73] *Michigan v. Long*, 463 U.S. 1032 (1983), at 1040–1041. The Court upheld a protective search of those portions of the passenger compartment of an automobile in which a weapon could be placed or hidden. The police had stopped to investigate after Long's car had swerved into a ditch. The search yielded a pouch containing marijuana.

[74] Id. at 1041.

[75] In its three remaining terms after *Long*, the Burger Court used the ruling as authority to review state court decisions in ten cases. Eight of them overturned liberal state court decisions, five of which concerned searches and seizures, and one each jury instructions, double jeopardy, and the due process rights of prisoners. The Burger Court used *Long* twice to produce a liberal outcome: in a death penalty case and in one that concerned a state court's jurisdiction over an Indian tribe. See Harold J. Spaeth, "Justice Sandra Day O'Connor: An Assessment," in D. Grier Stephenson, Jr. (ed.), *An Essential Safeguard* (Westport, CT: Greenwood Press, 1991), pp. 81–98.

The use of *Long* in the Indian case indicates that its scope is not limited to cases that adjudicate the rights of persons accused or convicted of crime.

The Rehnquist Court, during its early years, has continued to use *Long* as the Burger Court did.

The *Long* presumption, however, could not produce a conservative outcome when applied to cases seeking entree to the federal courts by way of a writ of habeas corpus. Petitioners in such cases are persons convicted of crime in state courts who allege that they are in custody in violation of the Constitution or federal law. From a conservative standpoint, reviewing decisions of convicted persons wastes scarce judicial resources. Although the Court initially applied the *Long* presumption to petitions for habeas corpus,[76] it quickly qualified this decision by establishing as a predicate "that the decision of the last state court to which the petitioner presented his federal claims must fairly appear to rest primarily on federal law or to be interwoven with federal law."[77] Consequently, considerations of comity rather than the *Long* presumption actually control access by state convicted felons. The conservative Rehnquist Court majority has thereby managed to have its cake and eat it also. If a state court renders a liberal decision, the justices assume the presence of a federal question; but when the state's decision is conservative, any ambiguity redounds to the state's benefit.

Choice of law

As we have noted, in cases where federal and state law conflict, the Constitution mandates the supremacy of federal law. But what of those cases in which no controlling federal law exists? These rarely concern federal questions, but they do regularly pertain to cases arising under "diversity of citizenship."[78] This results because Article III, Section 2, extends federal court jurisdiction to cases "between citizens of different States." The Framers apparently thought that the parties in these cases should have a choice of forum because of the possibility of prejudice against the out-of-state litigant.[79] The substantive issues in these cases are those that, absent diversity jurisdiction, are grist for state judicial mills: commercial transactions, contracts, torts, and property. Since 1789, Congress has required the federal courts to apply the "law of the several states" to the resolution of these disputes.

The Supreme Court initially defined the "law of the several states" to mean only their statutes and constitutions, not their judge-made, or common, law.[80] Given that legislatures enacted little law before the twentieth century, and that constitutions paid more attention to limitations on the scope of governmental power than they did to its exercise, the range of common law was extensive.

---

[76] *Harris v. Reed*, 489 U.S. 255 (1989).

[77] *Coleman v. Thompson*, 115 L Ed 2d 640 (1991), at 660. Also see *Ylst v. Nunnemaker*, 115 L Ed 2d 706 (1991).

[78] We discuss diversity jurisdiction in Chapter 5.

[79] Nowhere in the pages cited diversity jurisdiction in the "Index by Clauses of the Constitution," in James H. Hutson, ed., *Supplement to Max Farrand's The Records of the Federal Convention of 1787* (New Haven: Yale University Press, 1987), pp. 350–351, does a statement of the reasons for diversity jurisdiction appear.

[80] *Swift v. Tyson*, 16 Peters 1 (1842).

Consequently, the federal courts were individually free to make their own law to resolve diversity cases. Litigants engaged in forum shopping in order to evade the state or federal court whose law did not support the shopper's contentions and/or to find the court whose law best presaged a favorable outcome.

In 1938, the Court overruled *Swift v. Tyson* and held that the federal courts' creation of common law derogated states' rights.[81] The refusal of federal courts, sitting in diversity, to follow the common law of the state in which they are located is an unconstitutional assumption of power:

> ... whether the law of the State ... be declared by its Legislature in a statute or by its highest court in a decision is not a matter of federal concern. There is no federal general common law. Congress has no power to declare substantive rules of common law applicable in a State whether they be local in their nature or "general," be they commercial law or a part of the law of torts. And no clause in the Constitution purports to confer such a power upon the federal courts.[82]

Thus ended the preference that *Swift v. Tyson* and its progeny had effectively accorded the out-of-state litigant.

The *Erie* decision left certain areas gray. *Erie* did not apply to matters governed by the Constitution or acts of Congress. One such matter is the rules of procedure that the federal courts use. Thus, federal courts need only apply the "substantive" law of the state in which they sit because in the same year that *Erie* was decided, Congress enacted the Federal Rules of Civil Procedure. But apart from the Federal Rules, the distinction between substance and procedure lacked clarity. The Court therefore devised an "outcome determinative" rule.[83] A rule is "substantive" if it controls the outcome of the case, even though it solely concerns matters of procedure – for example, a statute of limitations briefer than that provided by federal law, or a law that bars suits by out-of-state corporations if they failed to comply with the state's corporation filing law.

To surmount the argument that rules of procedure are never neutral, but necessarily affect the outcome of the case, the Court declared all subjects covered by the Federal Rules to be procedural regardless of whether or not they determine the outcome of the case.[84] Furthermore, if a matter not covered by the Federal Rules nonetheless affects "a strong federal policy,"[85] that matter also is to be treated as procedural. Thus, the federal interest in disposing of complex mul-

---

[81]   *Erie Railroad v. Tompkins*, 304 U.S. 64 (1938). The facts of the case provide a classical illustration of forum shopping. Tompkins, a Pennsylvania resident, brought a tort action for injuries suffered by something projecting from a passing train while he walked along the Erie's tracks. The railroad was a New York corporation. Tompkins chose to file in the New York federal district court because Pennsylvania common law viewed persons walking along a railroad right of way as trespassers. The New York federal court favored the rule of *Swift v. Tyson*. It therefore exercised its own independent judgment and held the railroad liable.

[82]   Id. at 78.

[83]   *Guaranty Trust v. York*, 326 U.S. 99 (1945).

[84]   *Hanna v. Plumer*, 380 U.S. 460 (1965).

[85]   *Byrd v. Blue Ridge Rural Electric Cooperative, Inc.*, 356 U.S. 525 (1958), at 538.

tiparty litigation in a single trial overrides a state law that prohibits nonresidents from suing out-of-state corporations, and the federal preference for jury determination of factual issues subordinates a state law that requires a judge to decide unemployment compensation cases.

Summary

Use of these six considerations governing the relationship between the state and federal court systems not only affects their relative autonomy, it also enables the Court to adapt its policy making to the substantive personal policy preferences of its members. Thus, for example, the willingness of the Burger and Rehnquist Courts' conservative majority to subordinate considerations of federalism to its substantive policy preferences insofar as adequate state grounds for decision are concerned should occasion no surprise. Matters of procedure, whether they be a court-created rule or a constitutional provision are regularly invoked when the majority supports the merits of the lower court's decision. The justices, of course, do defer, but they do not do so blindly. Justices who are conservative on criminal procedure (Rehnquist, Burger, O'Connor, Powell, White, Blackmun, Scalia, and Kennedy) apparently thought the Court's traditional standard of review unduly hindered them from reversing liberal state court decisions. They therefore changed the rules of the game so that their substantively conservative policy preferences could continue to be accommodated.[86]

CONCLUSIONS

This chapter has specified the five interrelated features of the Constitution that enable the federal courts in general, and the Supreme Court in particular, to function as authoritative policy makers. The view of Americans that the Constitution is the fundamental law establishes it as the benchmark from which the legitimacy of all governmental action is to be judged. The popular belief that that government is best that governs least has produced an abiding distrust of government, politicians, and bureaucrats. That distrust, however, does not extend to judges and their decisions. The constitutional division of governmental power between the states and Washington, as well as that among the three branches of the federal government, requires some entity to resolve the conflicts that this division and separation produces. By its enunciation of the doctrine of judicial review in *Marbury v. Madison*, the Supreme Court arrogated to itself the authority to guard against subversion of the fundamental law and to concomitantly resolve the conflicts that federalism and separation of powers produce.

---

[86] The constitutional provisions and Court-made policies governing the relationship between the state and federal courts are not the only instruments that the Court utilizes to justify and rationalize its policy preferences. As we discuss in Chapter 8, at least as important is the deference, or lack of it, that judicial restraint and judicial activism provide.

Because the Constitution limits the subject-matter jurisdiction of the federal courts on the one hand, and provides for the existence of autonomous state courts on the other, the Supreme Court has had to share policy making with the courts of the individual states. Apportionment of this jurisdictional responsibility rests on three constitutional provisions – the supremacy clause, sovereign immunity, and full faith and credit – and three criteria of the Supreme Court's own creation: the system of comity, adequate and independent state grounds for decision, and the rules governing whether state or federal law should be used to resolve a given dispute. By subjecting their initial formulation to redefinition, the Supreme Court has been able to increase or decrease its policy-making capacity vis-à-vis the state courts to conform to the justices' fluctuating preferences toward centralization/decentralization and their substantive support of liberal or conservative policies.

2

Models of decision making

In this chapter we present two distinct models of Supreme Court decision making: legal and attitudinal. The justices and their apologists claim that the former explains their decisions while denying that the latter has any effect at all. We analyze the accuracy of the justices' assertions.

Before discussing the legal and attitudinal models, it may be useful to discuss what a model is and why it is used. A model represents reality; it does not constitute reality itself. A model purposefully ignores certain aspects of reality and focuses instead on a selected set of crucial factors. A successful model achieves two often contradictory goals: It explains the behavior in question, and it does so simply and parsimoniously. A model that does not validly and reliably explain the behavior in question – be it the votes of Supreme Court justices, the decisions of dictators to invade neighboring countries, or the collapse of Soviet power in Eastern Europe – is obviously of little value. But an unduly complex model that explains behavior may be almost as worthless, for it is axiomatic mathematically that one can always perfectly "explain" behavior when the number of variables equals the number of cases. Thus the goals of explanation and parsimony are often contradictory, for the more variables one uses the more behavior one can "explain." For instance, a justice's vote in a particular equal protection case may be based on an encounter the justice had with a member of the group in question earlier in the day. A vote in another case might depend on a different random event. Nevertheless, a good model would ignore such idiosyncratic factors and highlight instead variables that explain a high percentage of the behavior in question.

We start with the legal model, which postulates that the decisions of the Court are based on the facts of the case in light of the plain meaning of statutes and the Constitution, the intent of the framers, precedent, and a balancing of societal interests. We further assess the legal model in light of the assertions of "interpretivism," which currently appears to be the most popular mode of legalistic analysis. We then consider the attitudinal model, which antithetically to the legal model claims that the decisions of the Court are based on the facts of the case in light of the ideological attitudes and values of the justices.

THE LEGAL MODEL

The legal model that we describe and critique has four variants that the justices themselves employ: plain meaning, intent of the framers (or legislators), precedent, and balancing. Although the justices, except for Scalia and Stevens, express no preference for one rather than another,[1] legal philosophers and apodictical and tendentious analysts do, as we will show in our discussion of interpretivism, which follows our specification of the legal model.

The legal model differs from the attitudinal model in several respects. First, though one may empirically distinguish the variants of the former, the justices will frequently use more than one of them to explain why they ruled as they did in a particular case. Occasionally they will interweave two of the variants, but most often they appear seriatim. The attitudinal model, by contrast, rests on a common set of assumptions. Variations result because some researchers prefer to use a microanalytical focus, whereas others proceed macroanalytically. Thus, some delineate differences in the operation of the psychological determinant of behavior that is identified as the factor that motivates, and thus explains, the justice's and, by extension, the Court's decisions in a specific area of the Court's decision making (e.g., death penalty or affirmative action), whereas others attempt to identify the commonality of the justices' attitudes toward civil liberties generally.

Second, the attitudinal model also differs from the legal model in that the justices, as mentioned, do not admit the validity of the former as an explanation of their decisions. To do so would give the lie to the mythology that the justices, their lower court colleagues, and off-the-bench apologists have so insistently and persistently verbalized: that judges exercise little or no discretion; that they do not speak; rather, the Constitution and the laws speak through them. Accordingly, judicial decisions merely apply the law objectively, dispassionately, and impartially.

Third, the two types of models also differ in that the legal has not, and perhaps cannot, be subject to systematic empirical falsification. This is because the various modes of legal decision making cannot be operationalized evenhandedly. For example, both parties to a lawsuit typically find no dearth of precedents to support their contrary assertions. This is especially true in appellate tribunals, which, through docket control, can weed out frivolous cases. If one or more of the participating judges writes a dissent, he will likely cite as many precedents in support of his decision as the majority does. So also with regard to the other variants of the legal model. The majority opinion, along with the dissent(s), will commonly use equally effectively and plausibly the same variant to arrive at diametrically opposite conclusions. The attitudinal

---

[1]   As we shall see, Scalia and Stevens have expressed opposition to the intent of the Framers or legislators, as the case may be. Strictly speaking, then, they disapprove of one of the variants of the legal model rather than expressing support for any of the others.

model, by contrast, operationalizes its constructs in an intersubjectively transmissible fashion and provides empirical support for its conclusions. In short,
the attitudinal model can and has been empirically tested; the legal model has
not, and in all probability cannot.

Because the legal model serves only to rationalize the Court's decisions and
to cloak the reality of the Court's decision-making process, we make no attempt
to discuss the variants of that model in any architectonic order. No such system
exists. Furthermore, as mentioned, the justices' opinions frequently intermingle
elements of one model with another. The justices most frequently assert that
they reach their decisions through plain meaning and intent, with intent the
subject of most scholarly commentary. To avoid premature specification of an
undue number of variations on a single model, we begin with an analysis of
plain meaning.

Plain meaning

This version applies not only to the language of statutes and constitutions, but
also to the words of judicially formulated rules. It simply holds that judges rest
their decisions on the plain meaning of the pertinent language. So if Article 1,
Section 10, of the Constitution declares that no state shall pass any law impairing
the obligation of contract, then the Court will strike down any law that does so.
Alternatively, courts should not judicially create rights that the Constitution does
not explicitly contain.

For several reasons, construction through plain meaning possesses a chame-
leonic quality that spans the color spectrum. First, English as a language lacks
precision. Virtually all words have a multiplicity of meanings, as the most
nodding acquaintance with a dictionary will attest. Meanings, moreover, may
directly conflict. For example, the common legal word, "sanction," means to
reward as well as to punish. The penumbral quality of a given word, especially
in combination with others, insures wide ranging discretion by those charged
with construing the overall meaning of the pertinent set of words. Second,
legislators and framers of constitutional language typically fail to define their
terms – legislators because of the need to effect a compromise, framers because
of their inability to anticipate the future. Third, one statutory or constitutional
provision or court rule may conflict with another. And although some language
may be clearer than other, the meaning of words under construction in the types
of cases heard by the Supreme Court, as we shall see next, is likely to be
particularly opaque.

A commonly used example of plain meaning pertains to the operative language
of the Mann Act, a classic bit of Congressional morals legislation.[2]

---

[2] We trust that the irony of Congress's concern with morals legislation is not lost on the reader.
   The Court, of course, also legislates morality. For example, *Barnes v. Glen Theater*, 115 L Ed
   2d 504 (1991), which permits state and local governments to outlaw nude dancing.

... any person who shall knowingly transport or cause to be transported, or aid or assist in obtaining transportation for, or in transporting, in interstate or foreign commerce ... any woman or girl for the purpose of prostitution or debauchery, or for any other immoral purpose, or with the intent and purpose to induce, entice, or compel such woman or girl to become a prostitute or to give herself up to debauchery, or to engage in any other immoral purpose ... shall be deemed guilty of a felony.[3]

The first case concerned three men who transported their mistresses across a state line. By a vote of 5 to 3, the Court affirmed their convictions on the basis that the phrase, "immoral purpose," included persuading a woman to become a "concubine and mistress," even though the venture was nonremunerative.[4] The second case involved a madam and her husband who took two of their employees with them on a vacation to Yellowstone National Park, crossing state lines on the way. The employees did not work until after they returned from vacation. By a 5-to-4 vote, the Court reversed the employers' convictions, ruling that there was no immoral purpose inasmuch as the purpose of the trip "was to provide innocent recreation and a holiday" for their employees.[5] The third case pertained to a group of polygamous Mormons who had transported their several wives across state lines. Justice Douglas, speaking for himself and four of his colleagues, ruled that "the establishment or maintenance of polygamous house-holds is a notorious example of promiscuity." Justice Murphy demurred: "Etym-ologically, the words 'polygyny' and 'polygamy' are quite distinct from 'prostitution,' 'debauchery' and words of that ilk."[6] Presumably the crucial consideration for Douglas, who was married four times, is that multiple wives are permissible so long as a man has them consecutively, rather than concurrently.

At the constitutional level, an oft-cited example of plain meaning concerns the creative use that the Marshall and Taney Courts made of the word "citizens," as it is used with reference to the diversity jurisdiction of the federal courts. To avoid subjecting fledgling American business enterprise to the potentially harsh mercies of out-of-state courts, Marshall ruled that a corporation was a "citizen" notwithstanding that no dictionary defined it as such. Marshall reasoned that inasmuch as corporations are artificial entities created by law, one should look to the human reality behind the legal facade, the stockholders.[7] And if they were all domiciled in a state different from that of the other party to the litigation, diversity existed.[8]

Marshall's creative solution worked well as long as American business re-mained localistic. But once a corporation's stockholders no longer resided in a

---

[3] 18 *U.S. Code Annotated* 398, section 2. The Court held the statute constitutional as an appropriate exercise of Congress's power to regulate interstate commerce in *Hoke v. United States*, 227 U.S. 308 (1913).

[4] *Caminetti v. United States*, 242 U.S. 470 (1917), at 483.

[5] *Mortensen v. United States*, 322 U.S. 369 (1944), at 375.

[6] *Cleveland v. United States*, 329 U.S. 14 (1946), at 19, 26.

[7] *Bank of the United States v. Deveaux*, 5 Cranch 84 (1810). For the details of diversity jurisdiction, see Chapter 5.

[8] *Strawbridge v. Curtis*, 3 Cranch 267 (1806).

single state, the corporation lost its access to the federal courts unless – this time compatibly with lexicographic plain meaning – diversity was complete – that is, no party on one side of the dispute held citizenship in the same state as a party on the other side of the dispute. In 1845, the Taney Court, not noted either for its support of business or federal power, rescued business from the specter of localistic tyranny. Observing that *Deveaux* and *Strawbridge* had "never been satisfactory to the bar," and that Marshall himself had "repeatedly expressed regret that those decisions had been made," the Court ruled that the words of the Constitution did not prohibit Congress from giving "the courts jurisdiction between citizens in many other forms than that in which it has been conferred."[9] Hence, for purposes of federal jurisdiction, a corporation was a citizen of the state of its incorporation. The result:

The most remarkable fiction in American law. A conclusive and irrebuttable presumption . . . that all stockholders of a corporation were citizens of the state in which the corporation was chartered. By operation of this fiction, every one of the shareholders of General Motors Corporation is a citizen of Delaware despite the fact that there are more share-holders than there are Delawareans.[10]

One need not retreat to cases of ancient vintage to document the deficiencies of plain meaning as an explanation of the Court's decisions. Three cases from a four-month period of 1990 nicely suffice. The question in the first case was the meaning of the words "adjustment" and "recovery" with regard to the Social Security Act's old-age benefits. The majority defined the terms to the recipient's detriment; the dissenters conversely. The majority supported its construction by defining the words as they are defined in another section of the statute. The majority said this approach is "reasonable, if not necessary," while confessing that its definition is not "an inevitable interpretation of the statute, but it is assuredly a permissible one."[11]

The dissenters, in an opinion of equal length, asserted that the majority's construction is "inconsistent with both common sense and the plain terms of the statute," and supplemented their linguistic analysis by concluding that the majority's interpretation "defeat[s] clear congressional intent." The dissent does admit, albeit grudgingly, "that students of language could justify" the majority's result if intent were ignored.[12]

The second case, decided by the same voting alignment as the first (Rehnquist, White, O'Connor, Scalia, and Kennedy versus Brennan, Marshall, Blackmun,

[9] *Louisville, Cincinnati and Charleston Railroad. Co. v. Letson*, 2 Howard 497 (1845), at 555, 554. To shore up its creative use of "citizens," the Court peremptorily asserted that its decision "will be admitted by all to be coincident with the policy of the Constitution." Id. at 556. Note also that the Court's reliance on plain meaning enabled it to severely constrict the applicability of Marshall's decisions in *Deveaux* and *Strawbridge*, thereby illustrating the ability of one application of the plain meaning model to undo another.

[10] John P. Frank, *Justice Daniel Dissenting* (Cambridge: Harvard University Press, 1964), p. 219.

[11] *Sullivan v. Everhart*, 108 L Ed 2d 72 (1990), at 82, 83.

[12] Id. at 85, 89, 92.

and Stevens, presented the question of whether a "child's insurance benefits" under one provision of the Social Security Act constituted "child support" under another provision of the same Act. The majority turned not to Webster but to Black's Law Dictionary to determine the "common usage" of child support. The dissenters did the opposite. The majority, however, ruled the common usage of child support "to have become a term of art," and "any attempt to break down the term into its constituent words is not apt to illuminate its meaning."[13]

Whether the supplementation of plain meaning with "term of art" warrants segmenting this version of the legal model into two distinct subtypes will apparently need to await future legalistic developments and usage. Notwithstanding, the dissenters again supplemented their focus on "ordinary English usage" with reference to its purpose.[14]

The third case not only illustrates an additional shortcoming of plain meaning, it also demonstrates the inutility of the major alternative model to plain meaning: legislative intent.[15] The case turned on the meaning of the phrase, "non-curriculum related student group," as used in a federal statute that requires public schools to give student religious groups equal access to school facilities that other extracurricular groups have. The majority held that the statute did not violate the establishment clause of the First Amendment, but that a high school's refusal to allow students to form a Christian club did violate the law.

The prevailing opinion observed that not only did the law fail to define "non-curriculum related student group," even the law's sponsors did not know what it meant.[16] Given the inadequacy of both plain meaning and intent to resolve the problem, the majority simply rested its judgment on the "logic" of a 1981 decision. In dissent, Justice Stevens targeted yet another deficiency of plain meaning:

The Court relies heavily on the dictionary's definition of "curriculum." . . . That word, of course, is not the Act's; moreover the word "noncurriculum" is not in the dictionary. Neither Webster nor Congress has authorized us to assume that "noncurriculum" is a precise antonym of the word "curriculum." "Nonplus," for example, does not mean "minus" and it would be incorrect to assume that a "nonentity" is not an "entity" at all.[17]

As a final example, we cite the Court's own words in an important First Amendment freedom case to further falsify plain meaning as a reliable guide to why the Court decides a case the way it does. The Court begins by quoting itself to the effect that "above all else, the First Amendment means that government has no power to restrict expression because of its message, its ideas, its subject matter, or its content." This unequivocal language is followed by citations to

---

[13] *Sullivan v. Stroop*, 110 L Ed 2d 438 (1990), at 445.
[14] Id. at 453, 447.
[15] *Westside Community Schools v. Mergens*, 110 L Ed 2d 191 (1990).
[16] Id. at 207, 211. The dissenting opinion also agreed with this assertion. At 236.
[17] Id. at 242.

seven cases that arose in seven different contexts, in addition to the one that the Court was quoting. Immediately thereafter, the following language appears:

This statement . . . read literally . . . would absolutely preclude any regulation of expressive activity predicated in whole or in part on the content of the communication. But we learned long ago that broad statements of principle, no matter how correct in the context in which they are made, are sometimes qualified by contrary decisions before the absolute limit of the stated principle is reached.[18]

In short, plain meaning does not explain the Court's decisions because the justices plainly do not necessarily mean what they say. Nor do they provide criteria that inform analysts when they intend to act as snollygosters or pseudologists.

Akin to equivocation about the First Amendment is the longstanding rule that the Constitution's absolute prohibition on laws impairing the obligation of contract is not to be read literally. Rather, the Court will uphold such laws, so long as they are reasonable. "Laws which restrict a party to those gains reasonably to be expected from the contract are not subject to attack under the Contract Clause, notwithstanding that they technically alter an obligation of contract."[19]

Rights not explicitly found in the Constitution, such as travel and privacy, are currently upheld with the strictest scrutiny.[20] This is not to say that the justices decided these cases incorrectly; we only note that if the Court can read rights out of the Constitution that it *explicitly* contains while simultaneously reading into the Constitution rights that it does *not explicitly* embrace, the plain meaning rule obviously fails as an explanation of what the Court has done.[21]

Legislative and Framers' intent

Legislative and framers' intent refers to construing statutes and the Constitution according to the preferences of those who originally drafted and supported them. The sole substantive difference between these two types of intent is that the former pertains to the interpretation of statutes, whereas the latter construes constitutional provisions. As guides to the justices' decisions, neither improves upon plain meaning. Indeed, as we saw earlier, and as we shall further observe, these two versions not infrequently support an opposite result in cases before the Court. Inasmuch as the Court provides no empirically supportable basis for choosing meaning over intent, or vice-versa, a justice's choice of one in preference to the other necessarily rests on considerations other than the model itself.[22]

[18] *Young v. American Mini Theatres*, 427 U.S. 50 (1976), at 65.
[19] *City of El Paso v. Simmons*, 379 U.S. 497 (1965), at 515.
[20] *Shapiro v. Thompson*, 394 U.S. 618 (1969); *Griswold v. Connecticut*, 381 U.S. 479 (1965).
[21] For a more limiting view on the role of plain meaning, see John Brigham, *Constitutional Language* (Westport, CT: Greenwood Press, 1978).
[22] The Court, however, does typically "begin with the text." *Gollust v. Mendell*, 115 L Ed 2d 109 (1991), at 118. Also see *Demarest v. Manspeaker*, 112 L Ed 2d 608 (1991): "In deciding a question of statutory construction, we begin of course with the language of the statute." At

Nonetheless, because many of those who ought to know better – morosophic legal scholars and students of the judiciary – believe that intent really explains the justices' behavior, it behooves us to demonstrate the falsity of such belief, as well as its fatuousness, not only by reference to the justices' words, but to the writings of commentators as well. And indeed, as we will show in the section of this chapter on the meaninglessness of the legal model, the choice based on intent may also be inconsistent and illogical.

Any assessment of intent must obviously depend on the record that the authors of the language left. This record varies as between constitutional and statutory language, as well as from one constitutional provision or statute to another. In the case of the original Constitution, we have only a "carelessly kept" Journal; Madison's notes, which he edited in 1819, thirty-two years after the events he reports; and a smattering of scattered notes from eight of the delegates to the Constitutional Convention.[23] None of these documents identifies the Framers' intentions in even the most rudimentary fashion. But even if these documents did contain assertions of purpose, a threshold question would still remain: who were the Framers? All fifty-five of the delegates who showed up at one time or another in Philadelphia during the summer of 1787? Some came and went.[24] Only thirty-nine signed the final document. Some probably had not read it. Assuredly, they were not all of a single mind. Apart from the delegates who refused to sign, should not the delegates to the various state conventions that were called to ratify the Constitution also be counted as Framers? Unfortunately, all commentators exclude these persons from consideration.

Apart from their fragmentary character, even the official records used to assess intent may be false and misleading. The *Congressional Record* is a prime case in point. Until 1978, members of Congress were free to add to, subtract from, edit, and insert remarks they never uttered on the floor of the House or the Senate, notwithstanding the law that requires the *Record* to be "substantially a verbatim report of the proceedings of Congress."[25]

---

614. And if, in the majority's "view, the plain language . . . disposes of the question before us," intent will not be assessed (*Toibb v. Radloff*, 115 L Ed 2d 145 (1991), at 151); with some exceptions, of course: "When we find the terms of a statute unambiguous, judicial inquiry should be complete except in rare and exceptional circumstances." *Freytag v. Commissioner*, 115 L Ed 2d 764 (1991), at 776. This language also appears in *Demarest v. Manspeaker*, 112 L Ed 2d at 616.

[23] Max Farrand, ed., *The Records of the Federal Convention of 1789*, rev. ed. (New Haven: Yale University Press, 1966), I, xiii. The eight delegates, in addition to Madison, were Robert Yates, Rufus King, James McHenry, William Pierce, William Paterson, Alexander Hamilton, Charles Pinckney, and George Mason.

[24] Yates, for example, whose notes "are next in importance" to Madison's. His notes cease with July 5, thereby omitting the crucial last two-and-a-half months of the Convention. Id. I, xv, xiv.

[25] Marjorie Hunter, "Case of the Missing Bullets," *New York Times*, May 15, 1985, p. 24. This change presumably decreased the likelihood that 112 pages of events could appear on a day when the Senate had met for only eight seconds, and the House not at all. Id. For other examples

But even if we assume complete and accurate records, the intent model cannot withstand scrutiny. Intentions are subjective and personal. As the demand for the services of psychiatrists and therapists attests, even optimate individuals do not necessarily know why they do what they do. At the group level, fathoming purpose or motivation becomes an exercise in futility. Moreover, the groups responsible for legal action – constitutional conventions and legislators – are usually sorely divided. The records of the original Constitution do document one pervasive activity: that the participants continually engaged in compromise. The upshot? Partisans on both sides of most every major constitutional issue have been able to support their contentions by equally plausible references to the Framers' intent. And given that the records pertaining to congressional legislation are much more voluminous than those of constitutional provisions, our observation applies to acts of Congress a fortiori. Grist for this mill includes the debates that preceded passage of the legislation; majority and minority committee reports; the statements and views of sponsors of the legislation; testimony and comments of individual legislators, government officials, and interested private entities given at committee and subcommittee hearings; and previous court decisions interpreting the statute.

Justice Scalia wrote precisely in a leading case that considered the constitutionality of a state statute:

The number of possible motivations, to begin with, is not binary, or indeed even finite. In the present case, for example, a particular legislator need not have voted for the Act either because he wanted to foster religion or because he wanted to improve education. He may have thought the bill would provide jobs for his district, or may have wanted to make amends with a faction of his party he had alienated on another vote, or he may have been a close friend of the bill's sponsor, or he may have been repaying a favor he owed the Majority Leader, or he may have hoped the Governor would appreciate his vote and make a fundraising appearance for him, or he may have been pressured to vote for a bill he disliked by a wealthy contributor or a flood of constituent mail, or he may have been seeking favorable publicity, or he may have been reluctant to hurt the feelings of a loyal staff member who worked on the bill, or he may have been mad at his wife who opposed the bill, or he may have been intoxicated and entirely *un*motivated when the vote was called, or he may have accidentally voted "yes" instead of "no," or, of course, he may have had (and very likely did have) a combination of some of the above and many other motivations. To look for *the sole purpose* of even a single legislator is probably to look for something that does not exist.

Putting that problem aside, however, where ought we to look for the individual legislator's purpose? We cannot ... assume that every member present ... agreed with the motivation expressed in a particular legislator's pre-enactment floor or committee statement.... Can we assume ... that they all agree with the motivation expressed in the staff-prepared committee reports ... [or] post-enactment floor statements? Or post-enactment testimony from legislators, obtained expressly for the lawsuit? ... media reports on ... legislative bargaining? All these sources, of course, are eminently manipulable.

... If a state senate approves a bill by a vote of 26 to 25, and only one intended solely

of how Congress doctors its official records, see Harold J. Spaeth, *Supreme Court Policy Making* (San Francisco: W.H. Freeman, 1979), p. 72, and the references cited therein.

to advance religion, is the law unconstitutional? What if 13 of 26 had that intent? What if 3 of the 26 had the impermissible intent, but 3 of the 25 voting against the bill were motivated by religious hostility or were simply attempting to "balance" the votes of their impermissibly motivated colleagues? Or is it possible that the intent of the bill's sponsor is alone enough to invalidate it – on a theory, perhaps, that even though everyone else's intent was pure, what they produced was the fruit of a forbidden tree.[26]

Others concur with Scalia and Stevens. Senator John C. Danforth, R-MO, for example: "Any judge who tries to make legislative history out of the free-for-all that takes place on the floor of the Senate is on very dangerous ground."[27] Lower federal court judges do not disagree. According to Alex Kozinski of the Ninth Circuit Court of Appeals: "Legislative history can be cited to support almost any proposition, and frequently is."[28]

The use to which intent may be put is perhaps best illustrated by cases in which it conflicts with plain meaning. We begin with the first major affirmative action case, *Regents of the University of California v. Bakke*. Four justices ruled that the quota system established by the medical school of the University of California at Davis violated the plain words of Title VI of the Civil Rights Act of 1964, which says that "No person in the United States shall, on the ground of race, color, or national origin, be excluded from participation in, be denied benefits of, or be subjected to discrimination under any program or activity receiving federal financial assistance." They cited the rule that a constitutional issue should be avoided if a case can fairly be decided on statutory grounds[29] and concluded that the "ban on exclusion is crystal clear. Race cannot be the basis for excluding anyone from participation in a federally funded program." Four other justices held these words not to mean what they said because Title VI was enacted "to induce voluntary compliance with the requirement of non-discriminatory treatment." That being so, "It is inconceivable that Congress intended to encourage voluntary efforts to eliminate the evil of racial discrimination while at the same time forbidding the voluntary use of race-conscious remedies." Justice Powell split the difference, ruling that race could be one of a number of factors governing admission to the medical school, but it could not be the only factor.[30]

---

[26]   *Edwards v. Aguillard*, 482 U.S. 578 (1987), at 636–638. Also see parallel language by Justice Stevens in *Rogers v. Lodge*, 458 U.S. 613 (1982), at 642–643.

     The other justices essentially disagree with Scalia's anti-intent position because "common sense suggests that inquiry benefits from reviewing additional information rather than ignoring it." *Wisconsin Public Intervenor v. Mortier*, 115 L Ed 2d 532 (1991), at 547, n. 4.

[27]   Robert Pear, "With Rights Act Comes Fight to Clarify Congress's Intent," *New York Times*, November 18, 1991, p.A1.

[28]   Id. An additional quotation from this same article explains why legislative history covers the waterfront of intent: "I would like to add some legislative history at the end of my remarks," Representative Henry J. Hyde, Republican of Illinois, said as he casually dropped a 9,000-word interpretive memorandum into the Congressional Record.

[29]   The rule cited here is, of course, the direct antithesis of Marshall's decision in *Marbury v. Madison*, discussed in Chapter 1.

[30]   438 U.S. 265 (1978), at 412, 418, 336, 319–320.

The next affirmative action case that the Court addressed also positioned meaning and intent adversely to one another, *Steelworkers v. Weber*. At issue was the meaning of Title VII of the same 1964 Civil Rights Act involved in *Bakke*, which makes it unlawful for an employer "to discriminate . . . because of . . . race." Over the objections of the two dissenters – Rehnquist and Burger – who said that the employers' quota system was plainly illegal, the five-member majority ruled the system legal because, citing an 1892 decision,

It is a "familiar rule that a thing may be within the letter of the statute and yet not within the statute, because not within its spirit, nor within the intention of its makers."[31]

To fail to so rule, said the majority, "would be ironic indeed if a law triggered by . . . concern over centuries of racial injustice . . . constituted the first legislative prohibition of all voluntary, private, race-conscious efforts to abolish . . . racial segregation."[32]

The message is clear: If all else fails, simply dust off this language and apply it to destroy plain meaning.[33] Though its use has been sporadic, by no means does this maxim have applicability only to affirmative action cases. Four years prior to *Steelworkers v. Weber*, the Court used it to deny a union's request for a jury when it was tried for criminal contempt even though the pertinent statute said that the accused shall enjoy a jury trial in "all cases of contempt."[34]

By no means does the Court always find it necessary to use the maxim when it wishes to rationalize policy on the basis of intent rather than plain meaning. It is able to do so very nicely without even passing reference to it. As an example, consider *Maryland v. Craig*, in which the majority said that the confrontation clause of the Sixth Amendment does not mean what it says because the purpose of the clause is to insure that evidence admitted against the accused is reliable and subject to "rigorous adversarial testing."[35] The four dissenters focused on the obvious:

Whatever else it may mean in addition, the defendant's constitutional right "to be confronted with witnesses against him" means, always and everywhere, at least what it explicitly says: the " 'right to meet face to face all those who appear and give evidence at trial.' "[36]

Note should also be made that the Court has at its disposal rules of its own creation that allow it to simultaneously disregard both plain meaning and intent, without replacing either of them with another variant of the legal model –

---

[31]   443 U.S. 193 (1979), at 199–200, 201.

[32]   Id. at 204.

[33]   The majority's view of intent contradicts not only the plain meaning of the Act, but the dissenters' view of intent as well. Rehnquist makes a compelling case, butressed by innumerable quotes from floor leader Hubert Humphrey (D-MN), that the intent of the framers of Title VII was to abolish *all* race-preferential treatment.

[34]   *Muniz v. Hoffman*, 422 U.S. 454 (1975), at 457.

[35]   111 L Ed 2d 666 (1990), at 678, 679.

[36]   Id. at 689.

precedent or balancing. Chief among such devices are the Ashwander Rules that Justice Brandeis formulated in a case of the same name. One such rule reads as follows:

> When the validity of an act of the Congress is drawn in question, and even if a serious doubt of constitutionality is raised, it is a cardinal principle that this Court will first ascertain whether a construction of the statute is fairly possible by which the question may be avoided.[37]

It conveniently enables the Court to concurrently disregard plain meaning and intent in order to concoct an alternative interpretation of statutory language of which the majority approves. Two examples will suffice. In *Webster v. Reproductive Services*[38] the Supreme Court construed a Missouri statute limiting abortion rights. Section 188.029 required doctors to perform such tests "as are necessary to make a finding" of viability on fetuses over twenty weeks of gestational age. As fetuses at twenty weeks have no lung capacity and thus are not viable, the statute, according to the lower court, required superfluous tests and thus imposed "unnecessary and significant health risks for both the mother and the fetus."[39] In order to interpret the statute in a way that would avoid constitutional difficulties, the plurality simply said that the statute did not absolutely require the mandated tests.

A second example involves a key provision of the Bankruptcy Reform Act of 1978, which makes certain household goods and personal possessions automatically exempt from the blanket liens that finance companies standardly obtain as security for consumer loans. On the basis of such liens, finance companies would seize the property of debtors who filed for bankruptcy. To avoid deciding whether the retroactive application of the provision would take creditors' property without due process of law, the Court unanimously rewrote the language, notwithstanding congressional intent, to deny protection to consumers who incurred their debts prior to the statute's enactment.[40]

Before considering intent in the context of the current debate over "interpretivism," note may be made of two recently contrived variations of intent: "subsequent legislative history" and the "principle intended" by the framers.

Although the opinion of the Court in which "subsequent legislative history"

---

[37] *Ashwander v. Tennessee Valley Authority*, 297 U.S. 288 (1936), at 348. Though the Ashwander Rules were formulated in a dissenting opinion, that has not precluded their use by judges at all levels of the judicial hierarchy to rationalize their decisions.

[38] 106 L Ed 2d 410 (1989).

[39] 851 F2d 1071, at 1075.

[40] *United States v. Security Industrial Bank*, 459 U.S. 70 (1982). A variation of the quoted Ashwander Rule was used to sustain the constitutionality of a statute conditioning minors' access to abortion: "Where fairly possible courts should construe a statute to avoid a danger of unconstitutionality." *Ohio v. Akron Reproductive Health Center*, 111 L Ed 2d 405 (1990), at 420. Unlike the Ashwander Rules, which were formulated in an opinion to which only the author – Brandeis – subscribed, this one had the support of a second justice, Burger, in addition to its author, Powell. *Planned Parenthood Assn. v. Ashcroft*, 462 U.S. 476 (1983), at 493.

made its initial appearance did not define it, Justice Scalia not only did so, but he also critiqued it, hopefully with enough sarcasm to insure an early demise.

> The legislative history of a statute is the history of its consideration and enactment. "Subsequent legislative history" – which presumably means the post-enactment history of a statute's consideration and enactment – is a contradiction in terms. The phrase is used to smuggle into judicial consideration legislators' expressions *not* of what a bill currently under consideration means (which, the theory goes, reflects what their colleagues understood they were voting for), but of what a law *previously enacted* means. . . .
>
> In my opinion, the views of a legislator concerning a statute already enacted are entitled to no more weight than the views of a judge concerning a statute not yet passed. . . .
>
> Arguments based on subsequent legislative history, like arguments based on antecedent futurity, should not be taken seriously, not even in a footnote.[41]

The creation of the other variation, "principle intended," occurred during the Senate Judiciary Committee hearings on the nomination of David H. Souter to the Supreme Court. In the course of his testimony, Souter reportedly said that the key to constitutional interpretation is the "principle intended" by its authors, not their "original intent."[42] Whether this variation will become a full-fledged competitor of plain old unvarnished "intent" remains to be seen. We assume that any such development will be found in Justice Souter's opinions rather than in any fugitive off-the-bench epistles, given his ability to avoid leaving any record of the latter sort to date.

Precedent

Precedent, or *stare decisis*, quite simply means adherence to what has been decided. Today's decisions are linked with those handed down yesterday. The law thereby develops a quality of connectedness, an appearance of stability. But no more than plain meaning and intent does precedent restrict the justices' discretion in the types of cases that come before the Court; nor does its use explain any better why the justices decide a particular case in favor of one party rather than the other.

Unlike plain meaning and the variations on intent, judges use precedent as an ostensible explanation for virtually every decision they make. Though it may appear in isolation from other aspects of the legal model, it much more often buttresses the meaning or the intent that the Court ascribes to the statute or the constitutional provision at issue. That is, the justices will support their judgment that a legal or constitutional provision means this rather than that by citing a number of previous decisions. As a result, the frequency accorded precedent far surpasses that accorded any other aspect of the legal model. Precedent also differs from plain meaning and intent inasmuch as no one disputes that the justices actually do base their decisions on previously decided cases in the sense

---

[41]   *Sullivan v. Finkelstein*, 110 L Ed 2d 563 (1990), at 577–578.

[42]   Aaron Epstein, "Souter's silence on abortion leads to criticism by groups," *Detroit News*, September 15, 1990, p. 1A.

that they almost always cite previously decided cases as authority for the disposition they make of the case at bar.

Precedent parallels meaning and intent in its application to both statutory construction and constitutional interpretation. As the justices unanimously explained:

Adherence to precedent is, in the usual case, a cardinal and guiding principal of adjudication, and "[c]onsiderations of stare decisis have special force in the area of statutory interpretation, for here, unlike in the context of constitutional interpretation, the legislative power is implicated, and Congress remains free to alter what we have done."[43]

But in cases concerning constitutional interpretation, the Court is more willing to reexamine its precedents because the Constitution is rarely amended and also – according to Chief Justice Taney – to insure that the reasoning on which such decisions depend remains cogent.[44] Justice Scalia recently restated the justification for the individual justice to discount constitutional precedents:

With some reservation concerning decisions that have become so embedded in our system of government that return is no longer possible ... I agree with Justice Douglas: "A judge looking at a constitutional decision may have compulsions to revere past history and accept what was once written. But he remembers above all else that it is the Constitution which he swore to support and defend, not the gloss which his predecessors have put on it." Douglas, Stare Decisis, 49 Colum L Rev 735, 736 (1949).[45]

Though precedent, like plain meaning and intent, looks backward, it does not appreciably restrict judicial discretion for a number of reasons. First, and most basic, precedents lie on both sides of most every controversy, at least at the appellate level. If losing litigants at trial did not have authority to support their contentions, no basis for appeal would exist. Even judges themselves recognize this fact. Judge Frank M. Coffin of the U.S. Court of Appeals for the First Circuit said:

"Precedent is certainly real and we learn to live with it. But if precedent clearly governed, a case would never get as far as the Court of Appeals: the parties would settle."[46]

That view was echoed by Judge Frank H. Easterbrook of the U.S. Court of Appeals for the Seventh Circuit, in Chicago.

"Given that litigation is so expensive, why are parties willing to take their cases up?" he asked. "It's because precedent doesn't govern. Precedent covers the major premise. But the mind-set of the judge governs the minor premise."[47]

---

[43] *California v. Federal Energy Regulatory Commission*, 109 L Ed 2d 474 (1990), at 486.

[44] *Mitchell v. W.T. Grant Co.*, 416 U.S. 600 (1974), at 628; *Passenger Cases*, 7 Howard 283 (1849), at 470. The Burger Court did not adhere to this stricture. Instead, it divided its forty-two instances of overruling equally, as Table 2.1 shows. By contrast, the Warren Court, as well as the Rehnquist Court during its first five terms, overturned constitutional decisions on more than twice as many occasions as they did nonconstitutional ones.

[45] *South Carolina v. Gathers*, 104 L Ed 2d 876 (1989), at 892.

[46] Linda Greenhouse, "Precedent for Lower Courts: Tyrant or Teacher," *New York Times*, January 29, 1988, p. 12.

[47] Ibid.

As further evidence that precedents exist to support the contentions of both parties, merely consult any appellate court case containing a dissenting opinion. This, as well as the majority opinion, will likely contain a substantial number of references to previously decided cases. Reference to these cases will undoubtedly show that those cited by the majority support its decision, whereas those specified by the dissent bolster its contrary judgment.

As an example, consider the first two campaign spending cases that the Rehnquist Court decided. In the first case, by a 5-to-4 vote, the justices declared unconstitutional a provision of the Federal Election Campaign Act as applied to a nonprofit corporation formed for "pro-life" purposes.[48] Not only did the corporation not need to set up a political action committee through which its funds must be filtered, it also has a First Amendment right to spend its own money directly. The majority as well as the dissenters located an abundance of precedents to support their respective contentions. The second case held that government could not only prohibit nonprofit corporations from contributing money directly to political candidates, but it could also forbid them from spending their own money on behalf of candidates. Because the three conservatives who held that the restrictions violated the First Amendment – Kennedy, O'Connor, and Scalia – were able simply to cite the precedents used in the preceding case, plus that decision itself, as authority for their position, it might superficially appear that the majority would not fare as well precedent-wise. Not so. The Court has taken a very dim view of censorship, which is what the statute at issue decreed, authorizing it only with respect to the military, prisoners, and minor children. Moreover, the Court has consistently stated that political speech is entitled to special protection. Indeed, Justice Thurgood Marshall in his opinion of the Court, admitted as much:

Certainly, the use of funds to support a political candidate is "speech"; independent campaign expenditures constitute "political expression 'at the core of our electoral process and of the First Amendment freedoms.' "[49]

Nevertheless, Marshall had no difficulty finding seven cases to support the law's constitutionality, including several citations to the majority opinion in *Massachusetts Citizens for Life* itself![50]

A second issue may be briefly adumbrated to further illustrate precedent's ability to serve contradictory masters simultaneously: the conditioning of government action in such a way that it inhibits the free exercise of religion. On the one hand, government may not deny individuals benefits (e.g., unemployment compensation for refusing to work on the Sabbath). But on the other, government may deny welfare benefits to an individual who refuses, for religious reasons,

---

[48]   *Federal Election Commission v. Massachusetts Citizens for Life*, 479 U.S. 238 (1986).

[49]   *Austin v. Michigan Chamber of Commerce*, 108 L Ed 2d 652 (1990), at 662–663.

[50]   Id. at 664–668.

to show a social security number; or construct a road that defiles government land that had traditionally been used by an Indian tribe for religious purposes.[51]

Not uncommonly, the majority itself will note the existence of alternative lines of precedent. The Court's landmark decision in *Griswold v. Connecticut* provides a most instructive example.[52] Not only did the majority identify alternative sets of precedents, it did so in a decision that shattered legal precedent by establishing a new right to privacy based substantially on a heretofore unused provision of the Constitution – the Ninth Amendment.[53] In ruling unconstitutional a law that criminalized a married couple's use of birth control, the Court rejected a discredited line of largely overruled cases.[54] Instead, the majority candidly recognized the lack of textual authority for its holding:

> The association of people is not mentioned in the Constitution nor in the Bill of Rights. The right to educate a child in a school of the parents' choice – whether public or private or parochial – is also not mentioned. Nor is the right to study any particular subject or any foreign language. Yet the First Amendment has been construed to include certain of those rights.[55]

The Court then proceeded to cite twelve cases to document the quoted language, which cases also became the authority for the right that its decision created.

As a more recent, but equally innovative, example of precedent's ability to use past decisions to create new and innovative law, consider *Cruzan v. Director, Missouri Department of Health*, in which the Court created a constitutional right to die.[56] To document the principle underlying the decision – "that a competent person has a constitutionally protected liberty interest in refusing unwanted medical treatment" – and thereby sustain the Court's ruling, Chief Justice Rehnquist cited five cases as precedent – one pertaining to compulsory vaccination, one to search and seizure, a third to forcible medication of prisoners, and the final pair to mandatory behavior modification, and the confinement of children.[57]

A second reason why precedent does not restrict judicial discretion is because it consists of two components: the court's decision and the material facts that the court took into account in arriving at its decision. Because the facts in two appellate cases invariably differ, and the degree of factual similarity and dissimilarity between any two given cases involves an intensely personal and subjective

---

[51] *Sherbert v. Verner*, 374 U.S. 398 (1963), and *Hobbie v. Florida Unemployment Appeals Commission*, 480 U.S. 136 (1987), versus *Bowen v. Roy*, 476 U.S. 693 (1986), and *Lyng v. Northwest Indian Cemetery Protective Assn.*, 485 U.S. 439 (1988). Also see *Employment Division, Oregon Dept. of Human Resources v. Smith*, 108 L Ed 2d 876 (1990), upholding the denial of unemployment benefits to persons who used peyote for religious purposes.

[52] 381 U.S. 479 (1965).

[53] It is especially instructive to note that the Court's precedent-shattering decision did *not* require it to formally overrule any precedent. It shattered precedent by creation, not destruction.

[54] That is, "Overtones of some arguments suggest that Lochner v. New York, 198 U.S. 45, should be our guide." 381 U.S. at 481–482.

[55] Id, at 482.

[56] 111 L Ed 2d 224 (1990).

[57] Id. at 241–242.

judgment, judges may pick and choose among precedents to find those that accord with their policy preferences, while simultaneously asserting that these are also the ones that best accord with the facts of the case at hand.

Third, jurists disagree over what constitutes a precedent. One school accepts the previously mentioned considerations: decision, plus material facts. The other ascertains the *ratio decidendi*, the underlying principle on which the case was decided. Defining the *ratio decidendi* in an intersubjectively transmissible fashion seems all but impossible; it does appear, however, to turn on a fairly basic principle, one typically more global than the rule of law that the court cites as authority for its decision.

Two cases involving the inheritance rights of illegitimate children provide an instructive example of this approach to precedent. The cases not only came from the same state, Louisiana. Each was decided incompatibly with the other, thereby providing courts and judges with authority to rule in favor of or against the children depending on the decision maker's subjective preferences. The first case held that the five illegitimate children of a woman could sue for damages because of her wrongful death due to negligent medical treatment. Starting "from the premise that illegitimate children are not 'nonpersons,' " (an obvious statement if there ever was one!) the Court ruled the statute prohibiting such actions unconstitutional because "the rights asserted here involve the intimate, familial relationship between a child and his own mother."[58] The second case, decided three years later, saw the three dissenters from the first case join with Nixon's first two appointees, Burger and Blackmun, to rule that Louisiana could constitutionally prohibit acknowledged illegitimate offspring from sharing their father's estate equally with his legitimate children. "*Levy* did not say . . . that a State can never treat an illegitimate child differently from legitimate offspring." The law has a rational basis: "promoting family life and of directing the disposition of property left within the State."[59] As a consequence, the Court has a perfectly good precedent on both sides of the matter: if it wishes to rule in favor of illegitimates, *Levy* and its progeny nicely suffice;[60] if it does not, *Labine* is preferable.[61]

Clearly, then, precedent as a legal model provides no guide to the justices' decisions. Instead, as Justice Marshall candidly observed, "the continued vitality of literally scores of decisions must be understood to depend on nothing more than the proclivities of the individuals who *now* comprise a majority of this Court."[62] All that one can say is that precedent is matter of good form, rather

---

[58] *Levy v. Louisiana*, 391 U.S. 68 (1968), at 70, 71.
[59] *Labine v. Vincent*, 401 U.S. 532 (1971), at 536.
[60] See *Weber v. Aetna Casualty & Surety Co.*, 406 U.S. 164 (1972); *Gomez v. Perez*, 409 U.S. 535 (1973); *New Jersey Welfare Rights Organization v. Cahill*, 411 U.S. 619 (1973); *Jimenez v. Weinberger*, 417 U.S. 628 (1974); and *Trimble v. Gordon*, 430 U.S. 762 (1977).
[61] See *Mathews v. Lucas*, 427 U.S. 495 (1976); *Norton v. Mathews*, 427 U.S. 524 (1976); *Fiallo v. Bell*, 430 U.S. 787 (1976); and *Lalli v. Lalli*, 439 U.S. 259 (1978).
[62] *Payne v. Tennessee* 115 L Ed 2d 720 (1991) at 753.

than a limit on the operation of judicial policy preferences. A court should lard its opinions with precedents, but doing so will not inhibit the exercise of discretion. And even if the court should confront a situation with but a single line of precedents – perhaps because it has only decided one case in point – it has devices that enable it to deviate from what has been decided, and to do so, moreover, compatibly with good legal form.

There are four such devices – obiter dicta, distinguishing a precedent, limiting (or extending) a precedent in principle, and overruling a precedent. The first two technically do not alter the scope of the precedent involved; the latter two do.

Obiter dicta. Obiter dicta, or simply dicta, indicate that specified portions of the opinion in a previously decided case consist of surplus language. As such, the reasoning contained in those portions do not control decision in the case at bar. An oft-cited example concerns the power of the President to remove federal officials from office. Congress had authorized the President to remove postmasters short of their four-year term of office only with the advice and consent of the Senate. In 1920, Woodrow Wilson removed the Portland, Oregon postmaster without Senate approval. In a lengthy opinion, William Howard Taft, the only person to occupy the White House and a seat on the Supreme Court, ruled that the President could remove any and all executive officials at will.[63] With the establishment of executive agencies during the early New Deal whose officials exercised quasi-legislative and quasi-judicial power, the question of presidential removal arose again. The Court thereupon declared *Myers* applicable only to those executive officials who exercised purely executive power. Congress could restrict the President's removal power of all other federal officials.[64]

Distinguishing a precedent. The other method of avoiding adherence to precedent without formally altering the precedent in question distinguishes the precedent. Its use merely requires the court to assert that the facts of the case before it sufficiently differ from the situational aspects of the precedent. The cases concerning the inheritance rights of illegitimates illustrate the matter well, particularly *Lalli v. Lalli*, where the plurality took especial pains to distinguish the situation therein from *Trimble v. Gordon*, which had been decided eighteen months earlier.[65] Lalli concerned a New York law that bars illegitimates from inheriting their fathers' estates unless the intestate father had gone to court and received judicial recognition of his paternity within two years of the child's birth. The *Trimble* majority had declared unconstitutional an Illinois law that allowed illegitimates to inherit only from intestate mothers, not fathers. The *Lalli* plurality stated that the New York law "is different in important respects" from the

---

[63] *Myers v. United States*, 272 U.S. 52 (1926).
[64] *Humphrey's Executor v. United States*, 295 U.S. 602 (1935).
[65] 439 U.S. 259 (1978), and 430 U.S. 762 (1977).

Illinois statute because "even a judicial determination of paternity was insufficient to permit inheritance" in Illinois, whereas "the marital status of the parents
is irrelevant" to New York. "A related difference" pertains to their respective
purposes. The Illinois law was "a means of encouraging legitimate family relationships," whereas "no such justification" supports the New York law. Its
purpose, instead, "is to provide for the just and orderly disposition of property
at death."[66]

Limiting a precedent in principle. The first and less drastic of the two methods
of formally altering precedent limits them in principle. A classic example concerns the matter of taxpayer's suits. Initially, the Court flatly prohibited them
as a means of challenging the purpose for which federal funds were spent. Given
that there are millions of federal taxpayers, their individual interests are minute
and indeterminable. Any individual taxpayer therefore suffers only an indirect
injury at best. Access to the federal courts, however, requires direct and substantial injury.[67] Forty-five years later, the Court qualified this policy by carving
out an exception to the flat ban. If the taxpayer challenged Congress's expenditure
on the basis that it exceeded some specific constitutional limitation on Congress's
power to tax and spend money (in this case, the establishment clause of the First
Amendment), then the taxpayer has standing to sue.[68]

A woman's right to an abortion provides a second example. In *Roe v. Wade*,[69]
the Court held that during the first trimester of pregnancy a woman had an
untrammeled right to an abortion. Subsequent decisions have qualified the holding in *Roe*, however, to read that women have a right to an abortion without
undue governmental interference.[70]

Overruling precedent. The other way in which a court may formally alter precedent is to overrule it. Because of the other means available to manipulate
precedent, none of which shatters the appearance of consistency and predictability
of judicial decision making to the extent that overruling does, it rarely occurs.
On the other hand, when the Court does overrule precedent, it tends to say so
in a rather straightforward fashion. Thus, we may determine the frequency of
overruling. As Table 2.1 shows, the Supreme Court has overruled its own
precedents only 105 times during the past 38 years. By comparison, it has
declared more than four times as many laws unconstitutional during this same
period.

Even so, when the Court decides to overrule itself, it not uncommonly will
do so – *mirabile dictu* – on the basis of precedent itself. In 1961, for example,

---

[66] 439 U.S. at 266, 267, 268.
[67] *Frothingham v. Mellon*, 262 U.S. 447 (1923).
[68] *Flast v. Cohen*, 392 U.S. 83 (1968).
[69] 410 U.S. 113 (1973).
[70] *Maher v. Roe*, 432 U.S. 464 (1977); *Webster v. Reproductive Health Services*, 106 L Ed 2d
      410 (1989).

Table 2.1. *Precedents overruled, 1953–1990 terms*

Court	Frequency	Ruling		% Const	N/Term
		Const	Non-Const		
Warren	42	29	13	69.0	2.6
Burger	44	30	14	68.2	2.6
Rehnquist	19	13	6	68.4	3.8
totals	105	72	33	68.6	2.8

the Court ruled that no person could be convicted on the basis of evidence secured from an unreasonable search or seizure, thereby overruling a 1949 decision that allowed state officials to use such evidence.[71] The Court noted that it had just prohibited the states from using the fruits of a coerced confession and cited that decision[72] as its authority to overrule *Wolf*: ''Why should not the same rule apply to what is tantamount to coerced testimony by way of unconstitutional seizure of goods, papers, effects, documents, etc.''[73]

A more recent example concerns a choice of law question: the extent to which state law rather than federal law governs a state's title to riverbeds within its boundaries. In 1973 the Court ruled that such controversies must be resolved on the basis of federal law.[74] Four years later, the Court overruled itself: ''Since one system of resolution of property disputes has been adhered to from 1845 until 1973, and the other only for the past three years, a return to the former would more closely conform to the expectations of property owners than would adherence to the latter.''[75]

Finally, one should not assume that when a court does adhere to precedent, no policy change can occur. Not uncommonly, adherence to precedent will not only alter the Court's policy, but will also *expand* the scope of the precedent to which the Court is adhering. A recent example concerns the direct purchaser rule, which limits those who may bring an action for the violation of the antitrust laws. The Court had held that only direct purchasers suffer a redressible injury, not their customers, who are indirect purchasers.[76] The rationale for the rule was problems of proof and apportionment of damages. But the Court applied the rule even where state law required the direct purchaser – here a public utility that had purchased gas from a producer and the pipeline that transported it – to pass

[71] *Wolf v. Colorado*, 338 U.S. 25 (1949).
[72] *Rogers v. Richmond*, 365 U.S. 534 (1961).
[73] *Mapp v. Ohio*, 367 U.S. 643 (1961), at 656.
[74] *Bonelli Cattle Co. v. Arizona*, 414 U.S. 313 (1973).
[75] *Oregon ex rel. State Land Board v. Corvallis Sand & Gravel Co.*, 429 U.S. 363 (1977), at 382.
[76] *Hanover Shoe, Inc. v. United Shoe Machinery Corp.*, 392 U.S. 481 (1968), and *Illinois Brick Co. v. Illinois*, 431 U.S. 720 (1977).

its costs on to its ratepayers, and to which the rule's rationale accordingly did not apply. As the dissent observed:

> . . . I cannot agree with the rigid and expansive holding that in no case, even in the utility context, would it be possible to determine in a reliable way a pass-through to consumers of an illegal overcharge that would measure the extent of their damage.[77]

Balancing

The final aspect of the legal model is balancing. It manifests itself most often when individual claims are set off against the interests of society, as reflected in a law that allegedly violates peoples' rights. More specific manifestations of balancing occur because neither constitutional nor legal rights form a seamless web. Conflict often occurs between them. Freedom of communication, as guaranteed by the First Amendment, may inhibit or preclude an accused's Sixth Amendment right to an impartial jury because of excessive publicity. Or the guarantee of free exercise of religion may conflict with the establishment clause, as when a public school on establishment grounds refuses to allow its students to form a religious organization.

In weighing the competing considerations that enter the balance, the Court will take one of two approaches: definitional or ad hoc balancing.[78] The former employs one or more hard-and-fast rules to rationalize a decision, such as the clear and present danger test, or others that similarly focus on a totality of the circumstances that surround the contested event. The ad hoc variety focuses exclusively on the individual case without reference to any previously formulated rule or test by which the case may be resolved. A classic example concerned efforts by the State of Alabama to force the NAACP to disclose its membership list. The NAACP refused to comply, alleging that disclosure would cause harm and harassment to its members. A unanimous Court weighed the effect of the law on the Association's membership against Alabama's interest in disclosure and concluded that the latter did not outweigh the deterrent effect disclosure would have on freedom of association.[79]

The Court has no reluctance to identify balancing by name, even though it provides no systematic guidance to what specific considerations are to be balanced nor an intersubjectively transmissible formula by which they are to be weighed. In an opinion upholding the constitutionality of sobriety check lanes, for example, the Court covered the nuances of balancing with its references to

---

[77] *Kansas and Missouri v. Utilicorp United Inc.*, 111 L Ed 2d 169 (1990), at 192.

[78] Recent decisions show a third type of balancing, cost-benefit analysis. Its use, however, appears to be associated with the other two types. See, for example, *United States v. Leon*, 468 U.S. 897 (1984). The case concerned the exclusionary rule of the Fourth Amendment, which precludes the admission of evidence obtained through an unreasonable search or seizure. Noting the social costs of the rule, the Court carved out a ''good-faith'' exception that allows the admission of evidence seized by the police under an invalid search warrant.

[79] *National Association for the Advancement of Colored People v. Alabama*, 357 U.S. 449 (1958).

"balancing factor," "balancing factors," "balancing test," and "balancing analysis."[80]

In one sense, balancing performs the function for the Supreme Court that the concept of reasonableness performs at the trial court level: a handy criterion by which to rationalize and justify a decision.[81] This, of course, is not necessarily bad. Both balancing and reasonableness provide courts with a degree of decisional flexibility that enables them to decide individual cases on their individual merits – however merits be defined – and thereby able to adapt their decisions to changing and variant circumstances and conditions.[82] Balancing and/or reasonableness are certainly superior to either the rigid-rule test, which straitjackets decision making into a framework where the literal application of the rule – no matter how foolish – controls the outcome,[83] or the subjective utility test, which commands that the personal quirks of the plaintiff should dictate the result.[84]

Like the other variations of the legal model, balancing frequently finds itself conflicting with one or the other of them. In *Maryland v. Craig*, which we discussed in connection with plain meaning, the dissent correctly identified the majority as using balancing to read out of the Constitution the plain meaning of the confrontation clause of the Sixth Amendment.[85]

INTERPRETIVISM

The belief that the text of the Constitution or the intent of the framers should bind Supreme Court justices is known as interpretivism. According to John Hart Ely, interpretivism is the "insistence that the work of the political branches is to be invalidated only in accordance with an inference whose starting point,

---

[80] *Michigan State Police v. Sitz*, 110 L Ed 412 (1990), at 422, 419, 420.

[81] We do not suggest that reasonableness is a criterion alien to the Supreme Court. It is not as the next footnote indicates.

[82] Notwithstanding the inherent subjectivity of the concept of reasonableness, the justices commonly label it an objective criterion – for example, "Reasonableness, in this as in many other contexts, is an objective standard, and the ultimate decision whether . . . [the lower court's decision] was dictated by precedent is based on an objective reading of the relevant cases." *Stringer v. Black*, 117 L Ed 2d 367 (1992), at 383.

[83] For example, this test as applied to the "law of nuisance . . . might prohibit radio playing above a specified decibel level after 10.00 p.m. – clearly a silly rule for a person residing on a 160-acre farm or in a college dormitory, where everyone likes the music, and peace and quite are as welcome as cockroaches or acne." Spaeth, op. cit. fn. 25 supra, p. 77.

[84] For example, that persons who intensely dislike rock music should recover more in damages than those who don't because their subjective loss of utility is greater.

[85] 111 L Ed 2d 666 (1990), at 692–694. Also see the opinions of Justice Scalia in *Employment Division, Oregon Human Resources Dept. v. Smith*, 108 L Ed 2d 876 (1990), at 882, and *Barnes v. Glen Theatre, Inc.*, 115 L Ed 2d 504 (1991), at 515. Scalia's hostility to balancing, at least as far as the First Amendment is concerned, is discussed in Paul M. Barrett, "Despite Expectations, Scalia Fails to Unify Conservatives on Court," *Wall Street Journal*, April 28, 1992, pp. A1, A6.

whose underlying premise, is fairly discoverable in the Constitution.''[86] Thus, an interpretivist would support the constitutionality of the death penalty, despite the Eighth Amendment's ban on cruel and unusual punishment, because the Fifth Amendment explicitly permits such capital punishment.[87] Similarly, interpretivists might argue that the Sixth Amendment's trial by jury means a unanimous jury of twelve citizens, because that's what the word ''jury'' meant in 1791.[88]

Although Supreme Court justices are generally loath to admit that their opinions go beyond a fair-minded interpretation of the text of the Constitution or the intent of the framers, candor requires admission that they sometimes do. In 1905 the Supreme Court declared that the State of New York did not have the right to limit the hours that bakers could work. The case, *Lochner v. New York*,[89] rested on a right to contract that the Court found implicit in the Fourteenth Amendment's due process clause. Of course, the Amendment says nothing about the right to contract. Moreover, the liberty guaranteed by the Amendment is not absolute. For these reasons, among others, *Lochner* received heavy criticism, and twenty-two years later the Court retreated from its protection of the right to contract.[90]

In 1965 the Court overturned a Connecticut law that prohibited anyone in the state, married or otherwise, from purchasing birth control devices.[91] The Court's majority opinion, written by Justice Douglas, created a general right to privacy. The decision did not rest on any specific Constitutional clause, but instead on the ''penumbras and emanations'' of the First, Third, Fourth, Fifth, Ninth, and Fourteenth Amendments. Like the right to contract, the right to privacy can nowhere be found in the Constitution.

The interpretivist position

The arguments for and against interpretation of the Constitution bound to the intent of the framers have dominated legalistic critiques of the Supreme Court in recent years. This is partially because the Court struck down anti-abortion laws in forty-six of the fifty states in *Roe v. Wade*[92] and because of its near

---

[86]   *Democracy and Distrust* (Cambridge: Harvard University Press, 1980), p. 2.

[87]   The Fifth Amendment explicitly or implicitly condones the death penalty in three separate phrases. 1) ''No person shall be held to answer for a capital or otherwise infamous crime, unless on a presentment or indictment of a grand jury . . . '' 2) ''nor shall any person be subject for the same offence to be twice put in jeopardy of life or limb . . . '' 3) ''nor be deprived of life, liberty or property without due process of law . . . '' The second clause above presumably suggests to interpretivists that not only is capital punishment acceptable, but dismemberment as well.

[88]   Raoul Berger, *Death Penalties* (Cambridge: Harvard University Press, 1982). But see *Williams v. Florida*, 399 U.S. 78 (1970), and *Apodaca v. Oregon*, 406 U.S. 404 (1972), for alternative views.

[89]   198 U.S. 45.

[90]   *West Coast Hotel v. Parrish*, 300 U.S. 379 (1937).

[91]   *Griswold v. Connecticut*, 381 U.S. 479.

[92]   410 U.S. 113 (1973).

overruling of this decision in *Webster v. Reproductive Services*.[93] The *Roe* opinion, like those in *Lochner* and *Griswold*, has only faint ties to the text of the Constitution or the intent of the framers.[94]

Additionally, interpretivism was seized upon as an issue by Reagan's Attorney General, Edwin Meese. According to Meese, the Court must follow a "Jurisprudence of Original Intention. . . . Those who framed the Constitution chose their words carefully; they debated at great length the most minute points. The language they chose meant something. It is incumbent upon the Court to determine what that meaning was."[95] Meese, though, was less concerned about original intent than he was the creation of a conservative jurisprudence. The Attorney General attacked the application of the Bill of Rights to the states, noting that those rights were originally intended to apply only to the national government. His tale of wrongful incorporation jumps from *Barron v. Baltimore*,[96] in which Chief Justice Marshall accurately asserted that the Framers did not intend the Bill of Rights to apply to the states, to *Gitlow v. New York*,[97] which first incorporated a non-economic provision of the Bill of Rights, without mentioning the intervening ratification of the Fourteenth Amendment, whose first section was thought by at least some of its proponents to overrule *Barron*.[98] One might also wonder why Meese opposed federal and state affirmative action programs. He contested the former on constitutional grounds even though no constitutional provision explicitly requires the national government to provide equal protection, and opposed state affirmative action although no proponent of the Fourteenth Amendment ever stated that the Amendment could be used to protect white Americans.[99]

An interpretivist almost as harsh as Meese, but with more scholarly credentials, is Raoul Berger. Berger's best known book, *Government by Judiciary*,[100] argues that the framers of the Fourteenth Amendment did not intend to incorporate the Bill of Rights, protect voting rights, or desegregate public schools. He quotes Representative James Wilson (R-IA) that "civil rights . . . do not mean that all

---

[93] 106 L Ed 2d 410 (1989).

[94] This is not to say that the *Roe* decision could not have been tied more firmly to the Constitution than it was in Justice Blackmun's majority opinion. One analyst forcefully argues the unconstitutionality of abortion laws based on the "involuntary servitude" clause of the Thirteenth Amendment. See Andrew Koppleman, "Forced Labor: A Thirteenth Amendment Defense of Abortion," unpublished manuscript, Yale University, 1990.

[95] Edwin Meese, Speech before American Bar Association, reprinted in *The Great Debate* (Washington D.C.: The Federalist Society, 1986) p. 9.

[96] 7 Peters 243 (1833).

[97] 268 U.S. 652 (1925).

[98] *Adamson v. California*, 332 U.S. 46 (1947), at 71–72. Justice Black attached a lengthy appendix to his dissenting opinion that supports his argument of full incorporation. At 92–123.

The first case to incorporate a provision of the Bill of Rights into the Constitution was *Chicago, Burlington and Quincy R. Co. v. Chicago*, 166 U.S. 266 (1897), which requires government to pay owners just compensation for taking their property.

[99] Meese, op. cit. fn. 95 supra, pp. 7–8.

[100] Cambridge: Harvard University Press, 1977.

citizens shall sit on juries, or that their children shall attend the same schools.'' Berger then declares that ''Wilson's statement is proof positive that segregation was excluded from the scope of the'' Fourteenth Amendment, as if a single statement by a single congressman could be proof positive of anything.[101]

The best defense of interpretivism is provided by former Supreme Court nominee Robert Bork. According to Bork, interpretivism solves the Madisonian problem of protecting minority rights without interfering with democratic rule.

One essential premise of the Madisonian model is majoritarianism. The model has also a counter-majoritarian premise, however, for it assumes there are some areas of life a majority should not control. There are some things a majority should not do to us no matter how democratically it decides to do them. These are areas properly left to individual freedom, and coercion by the majority in these aspects of life is tyranny.

Some see the model as containing an inherent, perhaps an insoluble, dilemma. Majority tyranny occurs if legislation invades the areas properly left to individual freedom. Minority tyranny occurs if the majority is prevented from ruling where its power is legitimate. Yet, quite obviously, neither the majority nor the minority can be trusted to define the freedom of the other. This dilemma is resolved in constitutional theory, and in popular understanding, by the Supreme Court's power to define both majority and minority freedom through the interpretation of the Constitution. Society consents to be ruled undemocratically within defined areas by certain enduring principles believed to be stated in, and placed beyond the reach of majorities, by the Constitution.

But this resolution of the dilemma imposes severe requirements upon the Court. For it follows that the Court's power is legitimate only if it has, and can demonstrate in reasoned opinions that it has, a valid theory, derived from the Constitution, of the respective spheres of majority and minority freedom. If it does not have such a theory but merely imposes its own values, or worse if it pretends to have a theory but actually follows its own predilections, the Court violates the postulates of the Madisonian model that alone justifies its power. It then necessarily abets the tyranny either of the majority or of the minority.[102]

From these premises Bork argues that the Court must ''stick close to the text and history (of the Constitution), and their fair implications and not construct new rights.''[103] His reading of the text and history of the Constitution leads him to conclude that the *Griswold* decision is unprincipled, that state courts can enforce racially discriminatory contracts despite the equal protection clause,[104] and that the First Amendment provides no protection whatsoever for scientific, literary, or artistic expression. All it protects is explicitly political communication, but even here, he excludes speech advocating the forceful overthrow of government.[105] These views had much to do with the Senate's refusal to confirm Bork for the Supreme Court in 1987.

---

[101]   Id. pp. 119–120, 120.
[102]   Robert Bork, ''Neutral Principles and Some First Amendment Problems,'' 47 *Indiana Law Journal* 1 (1971), 3.
[103]   Id. at 8.
[104]   See *Shelley v. Kraemer*, 334 U.S. 1 (1948).
[105]   Bork, op. cit. fn. 102 supra, pp. 27–30.

A somewhat kinder and gentler Bork appears as a federal circuit court of appeals judge in *Ollman v. Evans*, a libel suit by Marxist political scientist Bertell Ollman against syndicated columnists Evans and Novak. The offending passage declared that Ollman's "pamphleteering is hooted at by one political scientist in a major eastern university, whose scholarship and reputation as a liberal are well known. 'Ollman has no status within the profession, but is a pure and simple activist,' he said."[106] Ollman's suit included a survey of 317 "leading and representative" political scientists that "ranked him 10th (sic) in the entire field of all political scientists in terms of occupational prestige."[107]

Concurring with the majority opinion, Bork wrote an opinion that moved away from the narrow interpretivism he advocated in the *Indiana Law Journal*. Not only did he claim that questions of opinion should not be actionable, he went on to declare that the specific intent of the Framers of the First Amendment was not directly relevant to matters of libel. "Perhaps the framers did not envision libel actions as a major threat to that freedom. . . . But if over time, the libel action becomes a threat to the central meaning of the first amendment, why should not judges adapt their doctrines."[108] To the more modern Bork, the narrow question of what the Framers specifically had in mind is not as important as the value they sought to protect.

Despite the use of interpretivism by right-wing politicians and legal scholars, it is not necessarily a conservative doctrine. The Supreme Court justice who most consistently argued for interpretation bound to the text and history of the Constitution was Hugo Black, a most forceful advocate for freedom of speech and the incorporation of the Bill of Rights as binding on the states. He defended the former through the plain meaning of the First Amendment and the latter through his reading of the intent of the framers of the Fourteenth Amendment.[109] To Black, reading rights out of the Constitution posed a far greater danger to American freedoms than reading rights into it.

Additional arguments for the interpretivist position – as noted by Raoul Berger – are found in the writings of James Madison and Thomas Jefferson. According to Madison, "if the sense in which the Constitution was accepted and ratified by the Nation . . . be not the guide in expounding it, there can be no security for a consistent and stable government."[110] According to Jefferson, "our peculiar

---

[106] 750 F.2d 970 (1984), at 973.

[107] William B. Lockhart, Yale Kamisar, Jesse H. Choper, and Steven Shiffrin, *Constitutional Law*, 6th ed., 1989 Supplement (St. Paul: MN, West, 1989), p. 176.

[108] Id. at 996. This was still too expansive a view of constitutional interpretation for dissenting judge Antonin Scalia, who labeled the Evans and Novak opinion a "cooly crafted libel." Scalia went on to tie liberals and Marxists together, noting that the use of the expert opinion of the quoted but unnamed liberal was not the attack of an ideological enemy of Ollman, but the allegedly unbiased opinion of one who would be "sympathetic" to Ollman's beliefs.

[109] On freedom of speech, see *Barenblatt v. United States*, 360 U.S. 109 (1959). On the incorporation of the Bill of Rights, see *Adamson v. California*, 332 U.S. 46 (1947).

[110] Op. cit. fn. 100 supra, p. 364.

security is in the possession of a written constitution. Let us not make it a blank paper by construction."[111]

Finally, interpretivists question the alternatives to interpretivism. They argue that if the Constitution does not authoritatively guide the Court's decisions, the policy preferences of the majority of the justices will control. On what basis is it legitimate for us to be ruled by nine unelected people who do nothing more than make decisions based on their own values?

The non-interpretivist position

The deficiencies of interpretivism have led one critic to go so far as to claim that "the case for constitutional interpretation bound strictly to text and history is only slightly stronger than the case for the proposition that we inhabit a flat earth."[112]

The first deficiency is the lack of clarity about what constitutes intent. Interpretivists speak of decision making based on text and history, but often they do not coincide. The First Amendment states that Congress shall pass *no* law abridging the freedom of speech (emphasis added), but the history of the day suggests a narrower interpretation. Similarly, the Fourteenth Amendment says that states may not deny *any* person equal protection of the laws, not just blacks. Thus the language and intent differ. When this happens, interpretivists generally prefer history over text, but as Felix Frankfurter noted: "Remarks of a particular proponent of the Amendment, no matter how influential, are not to be deemed part of the Amendment. What was submitted for ratification was his proposal, not his speech."[113]

Assume that we base judicial interpretation on the speeches of and reports by proponents. The next question is whether it is possible to speak of "intent" when one refers to a group of people. On the one hand, one can probably assume that the Framers of the Constitution specifically intended that no one under the age of thirty-five could serve as President. But because of the clarity of the Constitutional command, no such case is likely to come to the Court. Alternatively, it is not clear that we can conceive of group intent about the Fourteenth Amendment. Radical Republican Senator Charles Sumner insisted that "separate education deprived blacks of their Fourteenth Amendment rights,"[114] whereas

---

[111]   Id.

[112]   Lief Carter, *Contemporary Constitutional Lawmaking* (New York: Pergamon Press, 1985), p. 41.

[113]   *Adamson v. California*, 332 U.S. 46 (1947), at 64. Yet just four years later Frankfurter wrote in dissent, "It has never been questioned in this Court that Committee reports, as well as statements by those in charge of a bill or of a report, are authoritative elucidations of the scope of a measure." *Schwegmann Bros. v. Calvert Distillers Corp.*, 341 U.S. 384 (1951), at 399–400. Apparently the choice between history and text is made on the basis of which better supports the writer's preferred position.

[114]   Judith Baer, *Equality Under the Constitution* (Ithaca: Cornell University Press, 1983), p. 96.

Lyman Trumbull (R-IL) viewed equal protection as only covering civil rights: "The right to go and come; the right to enforce contracts; the right to convey his property; the right to buy property – those general rights that belong to mankind everywhere."[115] "So, two of the leading figures of the Thirty-ninth Congress had a fundamental difference of opinion about what the amendment they had enacted meant."[116] Thus it may be impossible to refer to the "intent of the framers" as if such a singular intent actually existed.

If a singular intent does not exist, then by whose intent do we abide? According to Berger, the most important source is the draftsman, the person who wrote the bill, amendment, or clause.[117] Yet Berger himself frequently disregards or disparages the latitudinal interpretations of the Fourteenth Amendment by Section 1 co-author John Bingham (R-OH) in favor of more limited constructions by less consequential Republican proponents of the bill. Alternatively, we might opt for majority rule when the opinions of the Framers differ, but the multidimensional nature of most amendments makes the discovery of a single majority position improbable.[118]

If we are willing to accept the empirical existence of group intent – or if not, the ability to decide whose intent matters most – we must then determine what that intent is. For the Constitution, that task is Herculean. Madison's notes of the Constitutional Convention are notoriously incomplete as we pointed out earlier, and *The Federalist Papers*, however brilliant, are political propaganda. As Madison himself observed: "It is fair to keep in mind that the authors might sometimes be influenced by the zeal of advocates."[119] Determining intent as to the Bill of Rights is even more difficult, because the Amendments sailed through Congress with virtually no debate, and what little debate did occur was not transcribed verbatim. Although the congressional record of the Civil War amendments is far more complete, even here, it alone cannot tell us precisely what Congress intended:

Those torrents of words create as well as remove doubts. Not only did supporters and opponents dispute, but like the authors of *The Federalist*, supporters sometimes disagreed with each other. Even the modern *Congressional Record* is misnamed. Some speeches printed there were never made; some actually made may have been edited to include arguments, evidence, and witticisms absent from the originals. What the situation was for the Congresses that proposed the Fourteenth and Fifteenth Amendments is difficult to say, but the grammatical purity of the *Congressional Globe* indicates some redaction.[120]

---

[115] Id.
[116] Id. at 97.
[117] Op. cit. fn. 100 supra, p. 365.
[118] See Kenneth Arrow, *Social Choice and Individual Values* (New York: Wiley, 1951).
[119] James Madison, *Letters and Other Writings of James Madison* (Philadelphia: Lippincott, 1865) III, 436.
[120] Walter Murphy, James Fleming, and William Harris II, *American Constitutional Interpretation* (New York: Foundation Press, 1986) p. 305.

Former Supreme Court Justice William Brennan summarized these problems well:

There are those who find legitimacy in fidelity to what they call "the intentions of the Framers." In its most doctrinaire incarnation, this view demands that Justices discern exactly what the Framers thought about the question under consideration and simply follow that intention in resolving the case before them. It is a view that feigns self-effacing deference to the specific judgments of those who forged our original social compact. But in truth it is little more than arrogance cloaked as humility. It is arrogant to pretend that from our vantage we can gauge accurately the intent of the Framers on application of principle to specific, contemporary problems. All too often, sources of potential enlightenment such as the records of the ratification debates provide sparse or ambiguous evidence of the original intention. Typically, all that can be gleaned is that the Framers themselves did not agree about the application or meaning of particular constitutional provisions, and hid their differences in cloaks of generality. Indeed, it is far from clear whose intention is relevant – that of the drafters, the congressional disputants, or the ratifiers in the state? – or even whether the idea of an original intention is a coherent way of thinking about a jointly drafted document drawing its authority from a general assent of the states. And apart from the problematic nature of our sources, our distance of two centuries cannot but work as a prism refracting all we perceive. One cannot help but speculate that the chorus of lamentations calling for interpretation faithful to "original intention" — and proposing nullification of interpretations that fail this quick litmus test – must inevitably come from persons who have no familiarity with the historical record.[121]

Assume, notwithstanding, that an intent of the framers did exist, and that the historical record contains fairly clear evidence about it. For instance, let us state for argument's sake that *none* of the framers of the Eighth Amendment believed that the "cruel and unusual punishments" clause made death penalties unconstitutional, and that we are virtually certain that this is in fact true. Or we could assume that the framers of the Fourteenth Amendment did not intend the equal protection clause to protect women's rights. Should Supreme Court justices be bound by such intent? Justice Brennan believes not.

A position that upholds constitutional claims only if they were within the specific contemplation of the Framers in effect establishes a presumption of resolving textual ambiguities against the claim of constitutional right. It is far from clear what justifies such a presumption against claims of right. Nothing intrinsic in the nature of interpretation – if there is such a thing as the nature of interpretation – commands such a passive approach to ambiguity. This is a choice no less political than any other; it expresses antipathy to claims of minority rights against the majority. Those who would restrict claims of right to the values of 1789 specifically articulated in the Constitution turn a blind eye to social progress and eschew adaptation of overarching principles to changes of social circumstance.[122]

An obvious case to criticize on these grounds is *Olmstead v. United States*, in which Chief Justice Taft declared that the Fourth Amendment's protection

---

[121] William Brennan, "Speech at Georgetown University," reprinted in *The Great Debate* (Washington, D.C.: The Federalist Society, 1986), pp. 14–15.

[122] Id. at 15.

against unreasonable searches and seizures did not protect against wiretaps on telephone wires because such activity was not within "the meaning of the 4th Amendment."[123] Similarly, Justice Black argued in a later wiretapping case that the Court's duty is "to carry out as nearly as possible the original intent of the Framers."[124] Did the Framers intend to prohibit wiretapping? Obviously not, so to Black and other interpretivists, the Constitution leaves such activity totally unregulated.

Though in an entirely different case, Brennan responded that such questions ought not be decided by searching for the intent of the framers. "A more fruitful inquiry, it seems to me, is whether the practices here challenged threaten those consequences which the Framers deeply feared."[125] If wiretapping of one's home in search of evidence without probable cause and a warrant threatens the type of personal privacy protected by the Fourth Amendment, then the Amendment should also prohibit wiretapping.

Finally, even if one believes it possible to speak of the intent of the framers, to know what that intent is, and that such intent should be followed, one might still be able to reject the interpretivism of Raoul Berger and Robert Bork. For the intent of the original Framers may have been that future generations should not be narrowly bound by the intent of the Framers.

Many constitutional clauses are broadly written. The Eighth Amendment prohibits cruel and unusual punishments without defining them. The Fourteenth Amendment refers to an indeterminate due process and equal protection. No doubt many of the framers of these amendments had certain "conceptions" of what the language meant. But according to one constitutional theorist, Ronald Dworkin, it is the "concepts" of due process, equal protection, and cruel and unusual punishments that are written into the Constitution, not their conception.

Suppose I tell my children simply that I expect them not to treat others unfairly. I no doubt have in mind examples of the conduct I mean to discourage, but I would not accept that my "meaning" was limited to these examples, for two reasons. First I would expect my children to apply my instructions to situations I had not and could not have thought about. Second, I stand ready to admit that some particular act I had thought was fair was in fact unfair, or vice versa, if one of my children is able to convince me of that later; in that case I should want to say that my instructions covered the case he cited, not that I had changed my instructions. I might say that I meant the family to be guided by the *concept* of fairness, not by any *conception* of fairness I might have had in mind.[126]

---

[123]   277 U.S. 438 (1928), at 466.
[124]   *Berger v. New York*, 388 U.S. 41 (1967), at 87.
[125]   *Abington Township v. Schempp*, 374 U.S. 203 (1963), at 236.
[126]   *Taking Rights Seriously* (Cambridge: Harvard University Press, 1977), p. 134.

   Webster's dictionary makes no distinction between concept and conception. It defines both as an idea, although conception also refers to the act of becoming pregnant. Lawyers and judges, however, are highly skilled in the art of making distinctions without a difference. Once it becomes apparent logic or reason fails to sustain such artful word play, the maker becomes an ipsedixitist.

During the debate over the failed Equal Rights Amendment various, though not all, proponents declared that it would not require equal military duty for men and women (largely because such interpretations would make passage by three-quarters of the states more likely). Should the Supreme Court have been bound by such statements if the Amendment had passed? The interpretivist argument against interpretivism suggests that the framers would not necessarily want future Courts bound by such statements. Imagine war becoming so high-tech that soldiers no longer fight on battlefields; instead, computer scientists contend in laboratories. No conceivable reason warrants exempting female technicians from such activities.

Readers might ask themselves, if they were the framers of the cruel and unusual punishments clause, whether their specific conception of the clause should bind future generations, or whether posterity should define them for itself. Whatever the answer, we need no rely on hypotheticals. According to Madison, "as a guide to expounding and applying the provisions of the Constitution, the debates and incidental decisions of the Convention can have no authoritative character."[127] "Thus the dilemma: If one believes that 'intent' of the framers is binding, one must not consider that form of intent as binding."[128]

THE MEANINGLESSNESS OF THE LEGAL MODEL[129]

It is well established, via mathematical proofs, that every method of social or collective choice – every arrangement whereby individual choices are pooled to arrive at a collective decision — violates at least one principle required for reasonable and fair democratic decision making.[130] Although this observation applies with especial force to intent and to interpretivism, we elaborate on it here because it governs all variants of the legal model. It especially applies to intent and interpretivism because these variants explicitly rest on a method of social choice that we show to be without objective meaning. The application of

[127]   Op. cit. fn. 119 supra, III, 228. See also H. Jefferson Powell, "The Original Understanding of Original Intent," 98 *Harvard Law Review* 885 (1985).

[128]   Murphy, Fleming, and Harris, op. cit. fn. 120 supra, p. 305.

[129]   We wish to thank Thomas H. Hammond of Michigan State University for his help with this section of the book.

[130]   Kenneth Arrow, *Social Choice and Individual Values*, 2d ed. (New Haven: Yale University Press, 1963); William H. Riker, *Liberalism Against Populism* (San Francisco: W.H.Freeman, 1982), ch. 5; Frank H. Easterbrook, "Ways of Criticizing the Court," 95 *Harvard Law Review* 802 (1982).

   These desirable principles can be summarized in six seemingly innocuous rules: 1) Individuals are free to order their preferences as they see fit. 2) A winning choice may not be a loser, and vice versa – that is, if the voters prefer A to B and B to C, A must defeat C. 3) An outcome may not be imposed regardless of whether the citizenry approves of it or not. 4) If unanimity prevails for one option over another, the less preferred option cannot win. 5) Identical preference patterns may not produce different results. 6) No individual may function as a dictator. For a fuller statement of these conditions, see Riker, *Liberalism Against Populism*, pp. 116–119, and Easterbrook, "Ways of Criticizing the Court," pp. 823–831.

Table 2.2. *Hypothetical choices of three judges*

Choices	Judge 1	2	3
First Choice	A	C	B
Second Choice	B	A	C
Third Choice	C	B	A

social choice theory to intent and interpretivism does not amount to beating a dead horse, however. It rather shows that even if one can objectively fathom intent, it is likely to produce an arbitrary social choice.

To achieve a meaningful choice, the preferences of the decision makers must conform to decision rules that reflect the actors' sense of reasonableness. In American society, this tends to mean majority rule (or at least plurality rule, with the winner being the choice that garners more votes than any other option). Equal weight is accorded the vote of each participant – that is, one person, one vote. Further, among a range of choices – for example, A, B, C – each decision maker must be free to order them preferentially as he or she sees fit. Any system that precludes a person from choosing a particular preference order is dictatorial, and hence is morally unacceptable, unfair, and undemocratic. In exercising such choice, an option that no one chooses may not be imposed. Conversely, if everybody prefers A to B, then B may not become the social choice.

However, majority rule can produce cyclical legal judgments. It is obvious that the justices do indeed have a very wide range of purposes that they ascribe to the framers of a given constitutional or statutory provision, or to the language thereof. Consider, for example, a panel of three judges with the preferences shown in Table 2.2. Judge 1 prefers alternative A to alternative B, and also prefers alternative B to alternative C. Judge 2 prefers alternative C to A, and A to B. Judge C prefers alternative B to C, and C to A.

Assume that the panel of judges makes its decisions by majority rule. Alternative A will be defeated because judges 2 and 3 together prefer B. Alternative B will be defeated because judges 1 and 2 together prefer A. And to make matters complete, alternative C will be defeated because judges 1 and 3 together prefer B. The result is a social preference cycle among the three alternatives: Alternative A defeats alternative B, alternative B defeats alternative C, but alternative C defeats alternative A.

This cycling need not necessarily occur. If judge 3 prefers B to A, and C least of all, alternative A will win because it defeats *both* B and C. In this case, judges 1 and 2 prefer A to B, and judges 1 and 3 prefer A to C. C now becomes the least preferred option because 1 and 3 prefer B to C. But nothing *prevents* cycling from occurring. Cycling is always a potential problem.[131]

Given the likelihood that the preferences of legislators and framers lead to such intransitive collective choices as the quotation from Justice Scalia so graphically illustrates (see pp. 40–41), perhaps we ought to discard completely judicial efforts to fathom intent. If legislative and constitutional preferences are meaningless as social choices, interpretivism as a guide to judicial decision becomes unintelligible. So also strictures that courts and judges should exercise judicial restraint, a subject that we discuss in Chapter 8.

THE ATTITUDINAL MODEL

The legal model, as we have seen, holds that the Supreme Court decides disputes before it in light of the facts of the case vis-à-vis precedent, the plain meaning of the Constitution and statutes, the intent of the framers, and a balancing of societal versus constitutional interests. Statements of the Court and many legal scholars notwithstanding, we have shown that both litigants generally have precedents supporting them; both capably formulate arguments that the balance of societal interests rests in their respective favor; and both sides typically allege

---

[131] Professor, now Judge, Easterbrook provides a realistic example: "Suppose the Justices have studied the establishment clause, and different Justices reach different conclusions about the meaning of that provision. I assume . . . that each Justice comes to his own position after a process of reasoning deemed adequate and legitimate by traditional standards – that is, the positions are based on a study of the language and history of the clause and a careful analysis of the Court's earlier decisions, and each is internally consistent. I also assume that, in deciding a case, each Justice operates independently; each listens to, but is not bound by, the arguments of any other, and each votes according to his own conclusions. Three Justices conclude that all public acts that directly or indirectly aid religion violate the clause; call this position A for absolutism. Three more conclude that any public act is constitutional if it is neutral between religious and nonreligious institutions (N for neutrality). The remaining three conclude that the clause requires balancing, in which the purpose of the act, its effect on religion, and the extent of entanglement between between state and religion all play a role (B for balancing). . . .

"Each group of Justices, moreover, has a preferences between the two positions taken by the others. The Justices who take position N (neutrality) may believe that position B (balancing) more accurately reflects the design of the framers and the Court's cases than does position A (absolute ban on aid). The Justices who take position B may conclude that A is more nearly correct than N. And the Justices who take position A may conclude that N is more nearly correct than B. . . .

" . . . the Justices always vote according to their conclusions. But this voting will not lead them to agree on a rule, no matter how they go about the task. They cannot settle on rule A, because the Justices in groups 2 and 3 (a majority) believe that rule B is a more accurate construction of the clause than rule A. Yet rule B cannot be chosen either, because a majority (those in groups 1 and 3) would select rule N over rule B. And, to complete the cycle, a majority (in groups 1 and 2) would select rule A over rule N. No matter what the Court does, a majority would always vote to change the rule." Id., at 815–816. The foregoing hypothetical nicely describes the situation that prevails when a majority of the justices fails to agree on an opinion of the Court, and renders instead only a judgment of the Court.

that either the plain meaning of the Constitution and/or the intent of the framers supports its position.

If various aspects of the legal model can support either side of any given dispute that comes before the Court, then the legal model hardly satisfies as an explanation of Supreme Court decisions. By being able to explain everything, in the end it explains nothing.

We move now to an alternative explanation of the Court's decisions, the *attitudinal model*. This model holds that the Supreme Court decides disputes in light of the facts of the case vis-à-vis the ideological attitudes and values of the justices. Simply put, Rehnquist votes the way he does because he is extremely conservative; Marshall voted the way he did because he is extremely liberal. This framework will guide our work throughout the book, though we will not have an explicit test of the model until Chapter 6, "The Decision on the Merits." We turn now to the development of the attitudinal model and various formulations of it.

The legal realists

The attitudinal model has its genesis in the legal realist movement of the 1920s. The movement, led by Karl Llewellyn and Jerome Frank, among others, reacted to the conservative and formalistic jurisprudence then in vogue. According to the classical legal scholars of the time, law was

a complete and autonomous system of logically consistent principles, concepts and rules. The judge's techniques were socially neutral, his private views irrelevant; judging was more like finding than making, a matter of necessity rather than choice.[132]

Legal jurisprudence had hardly advanced since the great British jurist Sir William Blackstone wrote in the Eighteenth Century that judges "are the depositories of the laws; the living oracles, who must decide in all cases of doubt." They are sworn

to determine, not according to [their] own private judgment, but according to the known laws and customs of the land; not delegated to pronounce a new law, but to maintain and expound the old one. Yet this rule admits of exception, where the former determination is most evidently contrary to reason; much more if it be clearly contrary to the divine law. But even in such cases the subsequent judges do not pretend to make a new law, but to vindicate the old one from misrepresentation. For if it be found that the former decision is manifesly absurd or unjust, it is declared, not that such a sentence was *bad law*, but that it was *not law*.[133]

Against this nescient theory of a static law that judges merely find rather than make, the legal realists argued that lawmaking inhered in judging. According

[132] Yosal Rogat, "Legal Realism," in Paul Edwards, ed., *The Encyclopedia of Philosophy* (New York: Macmillan, 1972), p. 420.
[133] Quoted in Walter F. Murphy and C. Hermann Pritchett, eds., *Courts, Judges and Politics*, 4th ed. (New York: Random House, 1986), pp. 14, 15.

to Karl Llewellyn, the first principle of legal realism is the "conception of law in flux, of moving law, and of judicial creation of law."[134]

Judicial creation of law did not result because bad jurists sought power for themselves, but as inevitable fallout from an ever-changing society. According to Jerome Frank:

> The layman thinks that it would be possible so to revise the law books that they would be something like logarithm tables, that the lawyers could, if only they would, contrive some kind of legal sliderule for finding exact legal answers. . . .
>
> But the law as we have it is uncertain, indefinite, subject to incalculable changes. This condition the public ascribes to the men of law; the average person considers either that lawyers are grossly negligent or that they are guilty of malpractice, venally obscuring simple legal truths in order to foment needless litigation, engaging in a guild conspiracy of distortion and obfuscation in the interest of larger fees. . . .
>
> Yet the layman errs in his belief that this lack of precision and finality is to be ascribed to lawyers. The truth of the matter is that the popular notion of the possibilities of legal exactness is based upon a misconception. The law always has been, is now, and will ever continue to be, largely vague and variable. And how could this be otherwise? The law deals with human relations in their most complicated aspects. The whole confused, shifting helter-skelter of life parades before it – more confused than ever, in our kaleidoscope age.
>
> Even in a relatively static society, men have never been able to construct a comprehensive, eternalized set of rules anticipating all possible legal disputes and settling them in advance. Even in such a social order no one can foresee all the future permutations and combinations of events; situations are bound to occur which were never contemplated when the original rules were made. How much less is such a frozen legal system possible in modern times. . . . Our society would be straight-jacketed were not the courts, with the able assistance of lawyers, constantly overhauling the law and adapting it to the realities of ever-changing social, industrial and political conditions.[135]

If judges necessarily create law, how do they come to their decisions? To the legal realists, the answer clearly is not to be found in "legal rules and concepts insofar as they purport to *describe* what either courts or people are actually doing."[136] Judicial opinions containing such rules merely rationalize decisions; they are not the causes of them.

Without clear answers to how judges actually made decisions, the legal realists called for an empirical, scientific study of law,[137] taking as dictum the statement of Oliver Wendell Holmes, Jr., that "the prophecies of what courts will do in fact, and nothing more pretentious, are what I mean by law." "The object of our study, then, is prediction."[138]

---

[134] Karl Llewellyn, "Some Realism About Realism – Responding to Dean Pound," 44 *Harvard Law Review* 1237 (1931).

[135] Jerome Frank, *Law and the Modern Mind* (New York: Coward-McCann, 1949) pp. 5–7.

[136] Llewellyn, op. cit. fn. 134 supra, p. 1237.

[137] Hessel Yntema, "Legal Science and Reform," 34 *Columbia Law Review* 209 (1934).

[138] Oliver Wendell Holmes, "The Path of the Law," 10 *Harvard Law Review* 460–461, 457 (1897).

The behavioralists

Scholars only slowly responded to the call for scientific study of law. Jerome Frank attempted to use the theories of Sigmund Freud and Jean Piaget to explain judicial decisions, but little has come of this line of work.

Meanwhile, the heretofore misnomered discipline of political science began to test its theories scientifically. This movement, known as behavioralism, argued that

1. Political science can ultimately become a science capable of prediction and explanation. . . .
2. Political science should concern itself primarily, if not exclusively, with phenomena which can actually be observed. . . .
3. Data should be quantified and "findings" based upon quantifiable data. . . .
4. Research should be theory oriented and theory directed.[139]

Among early behavioral works was a 1948 book by C. Herman Pritchett entitled *The Roosevelt Court*. It systematically examined dissents, concurrences, voting blocs, and ideological configurations from the Court's nonunanimous decisions between 1937 and 1947. Pritchett did not provide a theory of Supreme Court decision making; yet he made the assumptions behind his work quite explicit. "This book, then, undertakes to study the politics and values of the Roosevelt Court through the nonunanimous opinions handed down by the justices" and acknowledged that the justices are "motivated by their own preferences."[140]

It was Glendon Schubert, drawing on the work of psychologist Clyde Coombs, who first provided a detailed attitudinal model of Supreme Court decision making.[141] Schubert assumed that case stimuli and the justices' values could be ideologically scaled. To illustrate: Imagine a search and seizure whose constitutionality the Court must determine. Assume the police searched a person's house with a valid warrant supported by probable cause. There were no extenuating circumstances. The search uncovers an incriminating diary. Now imagine a second search, similar to the first in that probable cause existed, but in which the police failed to obtain a warrant. Again, there were no extenuating circumstances.

According to Schubert, one can place these searches in ideological space. Because the search without a warrant can be considered less libertarian than the search with the warrant, we place the first search to the left of the second search. This is illustrated in Figure 2.1, where A represents the first search and B the second. Presumably, any search and seizure will be located on the line; depending

[139] Albert Somit and Joseph Tanenhaus, *The Development of Political Science* (Boston: Allyn and Bacon, 1967), pp. 177–78.
[140] (New York: Macmillan, 1948), pp. xii, xiii.
[141] Clyde Coombs, *A Theory of Data* (New York: Wiley, 1964); Glendon Schubert, *The Judicial Mind* (Evanston: Northwestern University Press, 1965). See also, Glendon Schubert, *The Judicial Mind Revisited* (New York: Oxford, 1974).

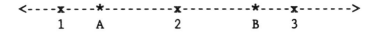

<--- x ---- * --------- x --------- * --- x ------->
1   A   2   B   3

Figure 2.1   Hypothetical justices and cases in attitudinal space

on case characteristics, the search will be to the left of A, between A and B (inclusive), or to the right of B. The less prior justification (probable cause or warrant) and the more severe the intrusion (home versus car, or full search versus frisk), the further to the right the search will fall. The more prior justification and the less intrusive the search, the further to the left it will be. The points on the line where the searches lie are referred to as j-points.

Next, we place the justices in ideological space. Consider three justices, 1, 2, and 3, who are respectively liberal, moderate, and conservative. They could easily be rank ordered on an ideological scale, with 1 on the left, 2 in the middle, and 3 on the right.

With some additional information we might be able to go a bit further and say that Justice 1 is so liberal that he would not even uphold the search in the first case, perhaps because he believes that police may not search and seize "mere evidence," such as papers and diaries.[142] Thus we could place Justice 1 to the left of Case A. Justice 2 might not be quite so strict as Justice 1; he would uphold the search of the home with a warrant, but would not uphold the warrantless search. Thus we could place Justice 2 to the right of Case A but to the left of Case B. Finally, Justice 3 might find the warrant requirement fairly unimportant and would uphold any search he considered reasonable. Because probable cause supported both searches, both are reasonable. Thus we could place Justice 3 to the right of Case B. The justices are placed in ideological space with the cases in Figure 2.1.

Schubert refers to the positions of the justices as their "ideal points" (i-points) though, as we shall see, the term is somewhat a misnomer. According to Schubert, a justice would vote to uphold all searches that are dominated by (i.e., are to the left of) the justice's ideal point and would vote to strike all searches that dominate (i.e., are to the right of) the justice's ideal point. If this is the situation, though, the *i*-points represent not the ideal points of each justice, but the indifference point. Justice 1 upholds all searches to the left of 1, rejects all searches to the right of 1, and is indifferent whether searches at 1 are upheld or overturned.

David Rohde and Harold Spaeth provided an alternative approach to Schubert's attitudinal model. According to them,

the primary goals of Supreme Court justices in the decision-making process are *policy goals*. Each member of the Court has preferences concerning the policy questions faced

---

[142]   See, for example, Justice Douglas's concurrence in *Berger v. New York*, 388 U.S. 41 (1967), at 64.

by the Court, and when the justices make decisions they want the outcomes to approximate as nearly as possible those policy preferences.[143]

Central to the Rohde and Spaeth model is the construct of attitudes. Quoting psychologist Milton Rokeach, they define an attitude as

a (1) relatively enduring, (2) organization of interrelated beliefs that describe, evaluate and advocate action with respect to an object or situation, (3) with each belief having cognitive, affective, and behavioral components. (4) Each one of these beliefs is a predisposition that, when suitably activated, results in some preferential response for the attitude object or situation, or toward the maintenance or preservation of the attitude itself. (5) Since an attitude object must always be encountered within some situation about which we also have an attitude, a minimum condition for social behavior is the activation of at least two interacting attitudes, one concerning the attitude object and the other concerning the situation.[144]

In their own words, "an attitude is nothing more than a set of interrelated beliefs about at least one object and the situation in which it is encountered."[145] The objects are the direct and indirect parties to the suit; the situations are the dominant legal issue in the case.

In focusing on attitudes, the Rohde-Spaeth model begins at a microanalytical level. They gather the Court's decisions into discrete sets of cases, each of which is organized on the basis of the "attitude situation" within which the "attitude object" is encountered. These are categorized as specifically in content as the decisions of the Court permit. The theory on which the model is based assumes that sets of these cases that form around similar objects and situations will correlate with one another to form issue areas (e.g., criminal procedure, First Amendment freedoms, judicial power, federalism) in which an interrelated set of attitudes – that is, a value – will explain the justices' behavior (e.g., freedom, equality, national supremacy, libertarianism).

Though attitudes may be said to have cognitive, affective, and behavioral components, our concern is with the votes of the justices, and thus the behavioral component of attitudes. These attitudes, and the values with which they associate, should cause a behaviorally predisposed justice to support certain legal claims and to oppose others, while other justices behave in an opposite fashion.

THE SUPREME COURT AND THE ATTITUDINAL MODEL

Members of the Supreme Court further their policy goals because they lack electoral or political accountability, ambition for higher office, and comprise a court of last resort that controls its own jurisdiction. Although the absence of these factors may hinder the personal policy-making capabilities of lower court judges, their presence enables the justices to vote as they individually see fit.

[143]   David W. Rohde and Harold J. Spaeth, *Supreme Court Decision Making* (San Francisco: W. H. Freeman, 1976) p. 72.
[144]   Id. at 75.
[145]   Id. at 76.

We start with the fact that unlike most other appellate courts, the Supreme Court controls its own docket. Although this does not guarantee that the justices will vote their policy preferences, it is a prerequisite for their doing so. Many meritless cases that no self-respecting judge would decide solely on the basis of his or her policy preferences undoubtedly exist. If Michael Dukakis filed a suit arguing that he should be declared winner of the 1988 presidential election, and if the Supreme Court had to decide the case, we would not expect the votes in the case to depend on whom the justices voted for in the election. Similarly, a soldier seeking to have the Persian Gulf war declared unconstitutional would hardly succeed, once Congress affirmed the President's action, regardless of the justices' preferences. But because the Supreme Court does have control over its docket, the justices would refuse to decide such meritless cases. Those that the Court does decide tender plausible legal arguments on both sides. For instances, if a case on the outcome of a presidential election should reach the Supreme Court, that would evidence legitimate arguments on both sides as a result of which the Court's decision might well turn on the personal preferences of the justices.

This is hardly idle speculation. In 1876, Democrat Samuel Tilden won the presidential election in the minds of all but the most partisan commentators, then and now. Voting irregularities in the (Republican) Reconstruction-controlled South produced twenty-one disputed electoral votes in three states. The Republican candidate, Rutherford B. Hayes, needed every one to be elected. Congress set up a fifteen-member commission to determine for which candidate the dispute electoral votes should be cast. The commission included ten Representatives and Senators (five Republicans, five Democrats) and five Supreme Court justices (three Republicans, two Democrats). On each of the twenty-one votes the three Republican justices joined the five Republicans to furnish Hayes with an 8-to-7 margin. Thus did the justices of the Supreme Court legitimize the most fraudulent presidential election in United States history.

With regard to electoral accountability – the first of the three factors mentioned – many state court judges are subject to electoral sanctions. Such judges do react to public opinion.[146] The evidence on life-tenured federal court judges suggests no such influence, however,[147] including those who sit on the Supreme Court. Relatedly, justices are virtually immune from political accountability. Congress can impeach Supreme Court justices, but this has only happened once, and the vote to remove failed.[148] The Court's appellate jurisdiction totally depends on

---

[146]   James Kuklinski and John Stanga, "Political Participation and Governmental Responsiveness," 73 *American Political Science Review* 1090 (1979); James Gibson, "Environmental Constraints on the Behavior of Judges, 14 *Law and Society Review* 343 (1980); Paul Brace and Melinda Gann Hall, "Neo-Institutionalism and Dissent in State Supreme Courts," 52 *Journal of Politics* 54 (1990).

[147]   Micheal Giles and Thomas G. Walker, "Judicial Policy-Making and Southern School Segregation," 37 *Journal of Politics* 917 (1975). See Chapter 6 for further discussion.

[148]   The Justice was Samuel Chase, a Federalist, whom the Jeffersonians impeached in 1804.

Congress, and Congress may alter it as it sees fit. Rarely has Congre͏͏
power to check the justices, however.[149] There is some evidence that
Roberts in 1937 and Harlan in 1959, reversed previously unpop͏͏͏
in the face of threats by Congress, but such examples are rare indeed.[150] Al͏͏͏
the President appoints the justices, he has no authority over them once they are
confirmed. *United States v. Nixon*[151] forcefully illustrates this point, where three
Nixon appointees joined a unanimous Court requiring the President to relinquish
the Watergate tapes, and thus delivered the coup de grace that forced Nixon to
resign.

With regard to the second factor, lower court judges may desire higher office
and thus be influenced by significant political others. Lobbying for a Supreme
Court seat from the lower courts, through speeches or through written opinions,
is not uncommon. One interested in reaching the high Court could hardly vote
his or her personal policy preferences on abortion during the Reagan or Bush
Administrations if those preferences were pro-choice. Lower court judges might
also be interested in other political positions besides the Supreme Court. Howell
Heflin (D-AL) went from the Supreme Court of Alabama to the United States
Senate. Thus we cannot assume that those interested in higher office will necessarily vote their personal policy preferences.

Efforts to seek higher office – assuming that such exists – is most improbable
for today's justices. During the first decade of the Court's existence, members
used the office as a stepping stone to run for positions such as governor,[152] but
today few – if any – positions have more power, prestige, and security than that
of Supreme Court justice. Three times this century members have resigned for
alternative (or at least the potential of alternative) political positions, but in only
one case was the move for a potentially higher office. That occurred in 1916,
when Charles Evans Hughes resigned in order to seek the presidency. The other
two cases occurred in 1942, when the exigencies of World War II led President
Roosevelt to ask James Byrnes to become Director of Economic Stabilization,
and in 1965, when President Johnson convinced Arthur Goldberg to become
United Nations Ambassador in order, Goldberg believed, to negotiate an end to
the Vietnam War.

Finally, other judges are subject to courts superior to their own. Unless they
wish to be reversed, they must follow the legal and policy pronouncements of
higher courts. Though the evidence is mixed, examination of appellate court

---

[149] One such instance occurred after the Civil War when Congress denied the Court authority to
hear appeals of persons detained by the military authorities. The Supreme Court complied with
Congress's decision in *Ex parte McCardle*, 7 Wallace 506 (1869).
[150] See Jeffrey A. Segal, "Courts, Executives and Legislatures," in John B. Gates and Charles
A. Johnson, eds., *The American Courts: A Critical Assessment* (Washington, DC: Congressional
Quarterly, 1990).
[151] 418 U.S. 683 (1974).
[152] The first Chief Justice, John Jay, twice ran for governor of New York while on the Supreme
Court, and left the bench when he finally won.

decisions in several different issue areas shows little overtly noncompliant behavior.[153] The Supreme Court, of course, sits at the pinnacle of both the federal and state judicial systems. No court overrules it.

This is not to say that finality characterizes all Supreme Court decisions. Congress can overturn judicial interpretations of statutory language and amendments can undo constitutional interpretation. Nevertheless, legislative inertia and the majorities needed to pass legislation make statutory overruling rather rare,[154] and the super-majorities needed to propose and ratify an amendment make constitutional overruling even rarer. Constitutional amendments have overturned only four Supreme Court decisions: The Eleventh Amendment (1798) overturned *Chisholm v. Georgia*,[155] which had allowed individuals to sue states in federal courts; the Fourteenth Amendment (1868) overturned *Scott v. Sandford*,[156] which had declared blacks ineligible for United States citizenship; the Sixteenth Amendment (1913) overturned *Pollock v. Farmer's Loan and Trust Company*,[157] which had struck down a federal income tax; and the Twenty-sixth Amendment (1971) overturned *Oregon v. Mitchell*,[158] which had struck down a federal law permitting 18-year-olds to vote in state elections.

SUMMARY AND CONCLUSIONS

In Chapter 1 we examined why the Supreme Court necessarily makes authoritative policy. In this chapter we examined the two different models that attempt to explain how justices make policy.

We initially considered the legal model abstractly and then as it is exemplified in the writings of the currently fashionable interpretivist school of jurisprudence. According to the legal model, justices make decisions based on the facts of the case in light of plain meaning, the intent of the framers, precedent, and a balancing of societal interests. Although the Court uses these factors to justify its decisions, they do not actually explain their outcome. Supporters certainly do not allow the well-documented theory of social choice to shake their belief in the cult of the robe.

Plain meaning assumes a mathematical exactness in the use of English that simply does not exist. Yet even when the constitutional language is fairly clear, the Court may behave with arrogation, reading into the Constitution rights that are not explicitly there, and reading out of the Constitution rights that it explicitly contains. Supporters of legislative or framers' intent must recognize the sparse-

---

[153]   See Donald R. Songer, "An Overview of Judicial Policymaking in the United States Courts of Appeals," in Gates and Johnson, op. cit. fn. 150 supra.

[154]   See Beth Henschen, "Statutory Interpretations of the Supreme Court," 11 *American Politics Quarterly* 441 (1983).

[155]   2 Dallas 419 (1793).

[156]   19 Howard 393 (1857).

[157]   U.S. 429, 158 U.S. 601 (1895).

[158]   400 U.S. 112 (1970).

ness of the historical record; that however "framer" is defined, different framers had different intentions; that intent often conflicts with plain meaning; and most notably, that the framers did not claim such prescience that only their motivations could rightfully bind future generations. Precedent clearly fails as an explanation of judicial decisions because in appellate cases precedents exist on both sides of controversies. And even when the weight of authority leans heavily toward one side, several legalistic methods enable courts and judges to avoid literal adherence to precedent. Justices can even cite precedents to avoid adhering to precedent. Finally, balancing fails as an explanation of Supreme Court decision making because it provides no objective criteria whatsoever for choosing one policy over another.

Against the legal model we present the attitudinal model, which holds that justices make decisions by considering the facts of the case in light of their ideological attitudes and values. The attitudinal model emanated from the criticisms of the classical legal model made by the legal realists in the 1920s. The behavioral school of political science that began to flower in the 1950s and continues to bloom today brought it to fruition. We presented two variants of the attitudinal model – one by Glendon Schubert, who based his work on the spatial theories of Clyde Coombs, and the other by David Rohde and Harold Spaeth, who based their work on the psychological theories of Milton Rokeach.

Because legal rules governing decision making (e.g., precedent, plain meaning) in the type of cases that come to Court do not limit discretion; because the justices need not respond to public opinion, Congress, or the President; and because the Supreme Court is the court of last resort, the justices, unlike their lower court colleagues, may freely implement their personal policy preferences as the attitudinal model specifies.

3

A political history of the Supreme Court

This chapter presents an overview of the role the Court has played as an authoritative policy maker during the course of American history. The mythology described in Chapter 1 that surrounds the Court and its decisions has decreed that the only proper perspective from which to view the Court is a legalistic one – namely, the legal model that we critiqued in Chapter 2. In order that we may place the model that we employ – the attitudinal one – in a proper perspective, we present this historical summary. In doing so, we differ from our legal and jurisprudential colleagues because we focus on the political effects of the Court's activity and not on how its decisions affected the course of the law and the doctrinal conflicts that resulted from it.

THE FIRST SUPREME COURT

The eleven years before John Marshall became Chief Justice are typically viewed as the first Supreme Court. If we adhere to the modern practice of identifying Courts by their Chief Justice, two Courts preceded Marshall: the Jay Court from 1790 to 1795, and the Ellsworth Court from 1796 to 1800. Neither of them left a legacy akin to that of their successor Courts. By our count, these two Courts decided a grand total of only sixty-one cases, an average of but five and a half per year. The number shrinks still further when one considers that the Court then held two terms per calendar year, unlike the current arrangement in which the Court normally convenes for a single term per year.

These Courts, however, did not want for eminent members. Jay himself was the third author of *The Federalist* Papers. Three of the five other original members served in the Constitutional Convention, as did Chief Justice Ellsworth and William Paterson, the author of the New Jersey Plan, whom Washington nominated in 1793. The others all supported ratification of the Constitution. Indeed, all of Washington's and Adams' nominees staunchly supported the Constitution and the federal government in its conflicts with the states.

The fact that six of the twelve justices who antedated Marshall resigned to take positions that by today's standards are of much lower status than service on the Court has certainly affected our judgment of the first two Courts. Jay left to accept the governorship of New York, while Ellsworth resigned to continue his career as a foreign diplomat. Indeed, when President Adams nominated Jay for a second term as Chief Justice after Ellsworth's resignation, Jay supplemented his declination for health reasons with the statement that the Court lacked "the energy, weight, and dignity which are essential to its affording due support to the national government."[1]

Nonetheless, the pre-Marshall Court was not a political nullity even though it did not decide a single case in five of its first twenty-two terms in addition to the August 1794 term – to which the Reports make no reference whatsoever[2] – and even though its first major decision produced such a storm of protest that a constitutional amendment was quickly proposed and ratified to overturn it. This case, *Chisholm v. Georgia,*[3] held that persons not resident in a state could nonetheless sue that state in federal court. Though the appropriately labeled Federalist Party controlled all three branches of the federal government, states' rights sentiments were sufficiently strong to occasion the adoption in 1798 of the Eleventh Amendment, which simply reads:

The judicial power of the United States shall not be construed to extend to any suit in law or equity, commenced or prosecuted against one of the United States by citizens of another State, or by citizens or subjects of any foreign State.

Perhaps the best way to comprehend the import of this rebuke is to note that on only three other occasions have the Court's decisions been similarly reversed: *Scott v. Sandford* by the Fourteenth Amendment, the income tax cases by the Sixteenth Amendment, and the 18-year-old vote by the Twenty-sixth Amendment.[4]

Notwithstanding, the early Court did decide one indisputably landmark case – *Calder v. Bull*[5] – which authoritatively defined the scope of ex post facto laws. The Court also rendered a second definitive judgment which, though important, was rather self-evident, given the language of the supremacy clause of the Constitution: that U.S. treaties overrode the provisions of conflicting state laws.[6] From a political perspective, however, the Court's initiation of the modern doctrine of standing to sue and the case or controversy requirement of Article III on which it largely rests were of greater importance than either of these

---

[1] Elder Witt, ed., *The Supreme Court and Its Work* (Washington: Congressional Quarterly, 1981), p. 114.

[2] The Court's reporter, A. J. Dallas, at 2 Dallas 479, explained the lack of cases during the August 1793 term as follows: "The malignant fever, which during this year, raged in the city of Philadelphia [where the Court was sitting], dispersed the great body of its inhabitants, and proved fatal to thousands, interrupted, likewise, the business of the courts; and I cannot trace, that any important cause was agitated in the present term." Similar conditions may explain the absence of any entries for the August 1794 term.

[3] 2 Dallas 419 (1793).

[4] 19 Howard 393 (1857); *Pollock v. Farmers' Loan and Trust Co.*, 157 U.S. 429, 158 U.S. 601 (1895); *Oregon v. Mitchell*, 400 U.S. 112 (1970).

[5] 3 Dallas 386 (1798).

[6] *Ware v. Hylton*, 3 Dallas 199 (1796).

decisions. The Court initially refused to decide a matter if its decision were susceptible of review by either Congress or the President because "Such revision and control . . . [is] radically inconsistent with the independence of that judicial power which is vested in the courts."[7] One year later, it extended this principle by refusing to render an advisory opinion at President Washington's request concerning United States' policies toward certain European nations.[8] The Court coupled its concern for judicial independence with fastidious attention to proper procedure by requiring, among other things, that the residence of the parties in cases arising under diversity jurisdiction be clearly spelled out, and that all matters must be brought to trial compatibly with the regular process of law.[9]

THE MARSHALL COURT

Unquestionably, John Marshall dominated his Court as no other justice has. Indeed, given the influence he exerted, one may plausibly argue that no person has had a greater effect on the course of American life – political or otherwise – than he. Under his aegis, the Marshall Court established three enduring legacies: the doctrine, if not the practice, of judicial supremacy; national supremacy; and an expansive view of federal power vis-à-vis that of the states.

Judicial supremacy

Judicial supremacy is rooted in the doctrine of judicial review that Marshall formulated and applied in *Marbury v. Madison*, which we discussed in Chapter 1. Although Marshall had no other opportunity to declare an act of Congress unconstitutional, and the second instance of its use, *Scott v. Sandford*, proved to be counterproductive, precipitating the Civil War, the doctrine survived full-blown and intact.

As we observed in Chapter 1, Marshall's tactics in deciding *Marbury* raise serious questions of propriety and decorum, and his arguments in the opinion of the Court demean the integrity of the other branches of government. Nonetheless, the decision gained sufficient acceptance among the American public to become the warp and woof of the constitutional fabric. In great part, this may have resulted from the political aspect of the decision. Marshall, after all, did rule against his political party and its well-known strategy, following its defeat in the election of 1800, to retreat into the judicial branch from whence it could lick its wounds preparatory to fighting another day. Second, the decision did not require enforcement. It automatically had force and effect without the need for executive action. Though Jefferson, Madison, and company were well aware

---

[7]   *Hayburn's Case*, 2 Dallas 409 (1792), at 410.

[8]   Charles Warren, *The Supreme Court in United States History* (Boston: Little Brown, 1922), I, 108–111.

[9]   *Bingham v. Cabot*, 3 Dallas 382 (1797); *Dewhurst v. Coulthard*, 3 Dallas 409 (1799).

of the constitutionally subordinate position in which *Marbury v. Madison* placed the legislative and executive branches, the average person, legally unsophisticated, likely saw the decision as a victory for principle over political expediency.

National supremacy

The second and third bequests of Marshall's legacy are closely interrelated: national supremacy and an expansive interpretation of the scope of federal power. Although they may superficially appear to be inseparable, this is not true in fact. Beginning with the Taney Court and continuing – largely without interruption – until the famous "switch in time" in 1937, the instruments of national supremacy were used to curb and confine the exercise of federal power and, during the heyday of laissez-faire, that of the states as well.

From a political standpoint, Marshall's effort to establish national supremacy met with the heaviest opposition. Although Article IV reads unequivocally, it nonetheless ran counter to deeply held states' rights sentiments. Marshall faced markedly less opposition to judicial review or the broad definition of federal power, even though the relevant constitutional language in these regards is either nonexistent or opaque. Furthermore, neither of these values contradicted others of equal force.

National supremacy required three major decisions to provide it with a firm foundation. In *Fairfax's Devisee v. Hunter's Lessee*,[10] the Court reversed a ruling of Virginia's supreme court concerning title to lands possessed by British subjects under provisions of the Jay Treaty of 1794. Virginia refused to accede to the Court's decision, arguing that though it was bound by the supremacy clause of the Constitution, it need not adhere to the Supreme Court's interpretation thereof. As a result of Virginia's noncompliance, the case returned to the Supreme Court three years later.[11] Construing the language in the Judiciary Act of 1789 that authorized Supreme Court review of state court decisions containing a federal question, the Court ruled that if a state were free to determine the compatibility of its own actions with those of the federal government, any given provision of the Constitution, act of Congress, or U.S. treaty would likely mean something different in each state. The uniformity of federal law would be chimerical along with the unity of the United States.

But not until the decision in *Cohens v. Virginia*[12] did the states' rights forces yield. Congress had authorized the District of Columbia to conduct a lottery for the purpose of financing public improvements. Virginia forbade lotteries. Its authorities arrested two District residents and convicted them of selling lottery tickets. Virginia protested the sellers' appeal of their case to the Supreme Court,

---

[10] 7 Cranch 603 (1813).

[11] *Martin v. Hunter's Lessee*, 1 Wheaton 305 (1816). Marshall did not participate in this case or its predecessor because he and his brother had a financial interest in the land in dispute.

[12] 6 Wheaton 264 (1821).

arguing that when a state is party to a lawsuit the Supreme Court has only original, not appellate, jurisdiction. Marshall, participating in this case, ruled that when a state took action against individuals who defended themselves on the basis of federal law, the Supreme Court did indeed have appellate jurisdiction. Addressing the merits, Marshall again displayed the political astuteness that served him in such good stead in *Marbury v. Madison,* and ruled that Congress did not intend the sale of lottery tickets outside the District of Columbia. Those who did so acted at their peril. Again, as in *Marbury*, Marshall won the war by losing the battle. Virginia had no court order to resist or disobey.

Federal power vis-à-vis that of the states

Two distinct lines of cases characterize this aspect of Marshall's legacy: a set of decisions that broadly construes the scope of federal power – particularly the necessary and proper clause and the interstate commerce clause, and a second set that concomitantly confines the scope of state power within a narrow compass. A pair of cases from each line illustrates the Marshall Court's policy position.

Unlike the establishment of national supremacy, but like the creation of judicial review, Marshall needed only one decision to settle the scope of federal power. The original charter of the Bank of the United States had expired the year before the War of 1812 began. The need for renewal had become painfully apparent during the course of the war as a result of the financial stringencies that afflicted the federal government. By the time Congress got around to rechartering the bank in 1816, the economy was too far gone for the bank to save it. Indeed, a number of the bank's branches made financial conditions worse by engaging in speculation, mismanagement of funds, and shady business practices.[13] In reaction, the states attempted to oust the bank from their territory by state constitutional prohibition or taxation. One such state was Maryland, whose legislature imposed a hefty tax that the state's courts upheld.

The case, *M'Culloch v. Maryland*, contained two questions requiring a judicial answer: Did Congress have the power to establish a national bank and, if so, could a state tax it? Although the Constitution nowhere makes reference to a bank, it does allow Congress to raise taxes, borrow money, regulate commerce, wage war, and raise and support armies and navies. From these expressly delegated powers, Marshall inferred the power to establish a national bank. ''[I]t may with great reason be contended'' that on the exercise of these powers ''the happiness and prosperity of the nation so vitally depends.'' If so, ''ample means for their execution'' must be available.[14] These means he found in the necessary and proper clause of Article I, Section 8, Clause 18:

---

[13]   The savings and loan banking scandals of the 1980s and 1990s are not without ancient, if less than honorable, lineage.

[14]   *M'Culloch v. Maryland*, 4 Wheaton 316 (1819), at 408.

Let the end be legitimate, let it be within the scope of the constitution, and all means which are appropriate, which are plainly adapted to that end, which are not prohibited, but consist with the letter and spirit of the constitution, are constitutional.[15]

Famous words these, as well-known and as oft-cited as those of any opinion. And though more than a century would elapse after Marshall's death in 1835 before this language overcame occasional nitpicking treatment,[16] no Court has ever formally qualified it.

Marshall answered *M'Culloch's* other question in the negative, basing his response on the supremacy clause. To allow the states to tax instrumentalities of the federal government "involves the power to destroy."[17] A half century later, the Court even-handedly concluded that the federal government could not tax the employees, property, or activities of the states.[18] The resulting scheme of intergovernmental tax immunity was not dismantled until the eve of World War II. Its major modern remnant exempts from federal taxation income derived from state and municipal bonds.

Marshall used the first interstate commerce clause case – *Gibbons v. Ogden* – as his vehicle to assert an expansive concept of federal power and, as in *Marbury v. Madison*, his opinion decided far more than what was needed to reach a decision. The controversy concerned a conflict over the licensing of steamboats between New York and Congress and was readily resolvable on the basis of the supremacy clause. But again Marshall seized his opportunity and eagerly leapt where others had not yet trod.

He began by defining commerce not only as "traffic, but it is something more; it is intercourse."[19] Noting that the key constitutional word is commerce "among" the several states, he defined it as "intermingled with. A thing which is among others, is intermingled with them." Therefore, "Commerce among the states cannot stop at the external boundary line of each state, but may be introduced into the interior."[20]

Did this mean that the states had no power at all over commerce, especially if Congress had acted?

It is not intended to say that these words comprehend that commerce which is completely internal, which is carried on between man and man in a state, and which does not extend to or affect other states. Such a power would be inconvenient, and is certainly unnecessary.[21]

Note that Marshall did not write that Congress has no power to regulate "completely internal" commerce, only that such power is "inconvenient"

---

[15]   Id. at 421.
[16]   For example, *Adair v. United States*, 208 U.S. 161 (1908); *Hammer v. Dagenhart*, 247 U.S. 251 (1918); and *Adkins v. Children's Hospital*, 261 U.S. 525 (1923).
[17]   4 Wheaton, at 431.
[18]   *Collector v. Day*, 11 Wallace 113 (1871).
[19]   *Gibbons v. Ogden*, 9 Wheaton 1 (1824), at 189.
[20]   Id. at 194.
[21]   Id.

and "unnecessary." But he does go on to say that "the completely internal commerce of a state, then, may be considered as reserved to the state itself."[22]

Particularly in light of hindsight, Marshall's position was clear. The commerce "among the several States" that Congress might regulate did not stop at a state line, and it certainly was not limited to business activities. And though Marshall's language did not foreclose all state regulation, any incompatibility would be resolved by the preference that the supremacy clause accords the federal government.

Independently of the expansive interpretation given federal powers, the Marshall Court narrowly construed those of the states. The primary basis was the language of Article I, Section 10, that forbids a state to "pass any . . . law impairing the obligation of contracts." It should occasion no surprise that the first case to construe the contract clause was the first decision to void a state law – *Fletcher v. Peck*.[23]

In 1795, enterprising schemers bribed the kakistocratic Georgia legislature into selling virtually all of Alabama and Mississippi for the munificent sum of $500,000. One year later, a new legislature revoked the grant. Meantime, the purchasers sold some of their ill-gotten gains to speculators and prospective settlers. Although the resulting litigation did not involve a bonafide "case or controversy" – which the Constitution limits federal courts to deciding – Marshall again disregarded jurisdictional limitations as he did in *Marbury v. Madison*.[24]

Emphasizing the harm that good-faith purchasers would suffer, Marshall equated a land grant with a contract by asserting that a grant "implies a contract" that estops the grantor from reneging.[25] As for the inclusion of public grants within the compass of the contract clause, Marshall simply asserted that "the words themselves contain no such distinction. They are general, and are applicable to contracts of every description."[26] Nine years later, Marshall extended the scope of the contract clause still further, ruling that corporate charters were also protected from abridgment.[27]

These decisions effectively positioned vested property rights alongside those that the Constitution explicitly protected from governmental abrogation, and presaged the use later Courts made of the Fourteenth Amendment to protect private property from hostile governmental regulation. If the individualistic tenor

---

[22]   Id. at 195.

[23]   6 Cranch 87 (1810).

[24]   The case was a friendly suit, a collusive action between parties whose real interests coincided. See C. Peter Magrath, *Yazoo: Law and Politics in the New Republic* (New York: Norton: 1966). Justice Johnson, in his concurring opinion in *Fletcher v. Peck*, also alluded to its feigned character. 6 Cranch, at 147–148.

[25]   Id. at 137.

[26]   Id.

[27]   *Dartmouth College v. Woodward*, 4 Wheaton 518 (1819).

of American life needed constitutional sanction, decisions such as *Fletcher v. Peck* and *Dartmouth College* convincingly provided it.

Although the division between North and South became increasingly institutionalized in the years following the death of Chief Justice Marshall in 1835, the Court did not directly address the slavery question until 1857. Before then, its major decisions, like those of the Marshall Court, concerned the supremacy, interstate commerce, and contracts clauses.

The Taney Court

No more than the Burger Court undid the decisions of the Warren Court did the Taney Court undo those of the Marshall Court. Expectations that the leveling influences of Jacksonian democracy would curtail vested property rights, commercial interests, and expand the sphere of states' rights went largely unrealized. President Jackson himself saw six of his nominees, including Chief Justice Taney, seated on the high court. Not since Washington had a single President been responsible for the appointment of a majority of the justices.

Two rulings typify the Taney Court's handling of the policy issues that characterized the Marshall Court. In *Charles River Bridge v. Warren Bridge*,[28] Taney ruled that states could reserve the right to alter, amend, or repeal corporate charters, and that no implied powers exist in the provisions of a public grant to a private organization. A corporation has only those specifically bestowed. Any ambiguity should be resolved in favor of the public. In drawing the foregoing line between private enterprise and government regulation, the Taney Court did not markedly deviate from Marshall's position. Marshall himself had observed that corporations are artificial entities created by law. As creatures of the law, they have only the powers their charters expressly confer.

In *Cooley v. Board of Port Wardens*,[29] the Taney Court spelled out the Marshall Court's ruling in *Gibbons v. Ogden*. Labeling their common position "selective exclusiveness," the majority held that Congress's power to regulate commerce was complete and to some extent exclusive. Only those subjects that "are in their nature national, or admit of only one uniform system, or plan of regulation, may justly be said to be of such a nature as to require exclusive regulation by Congress."[30] The states might regulate other matters if their regulations did not conflict with those of Congress.

Analysis of the Taney Court's nonunanimous decisions clearly shows that

[28]   11 Peters 420 (1837).
[29]   12 Howard 299 (1852).
[30]   Id. at 319.

cases concerning considerations of federalism dominated the docket. During the thirteen terms between January 1846 and December 1858,[31] 68 of the 181 non-unanimous decisions concerned federalism – 37.5 percent.[32] By contrast, only four cases concerned slavery, 2.2 percent.[33]

Various data reduction techniques reveal that the justices positioned themselves along an ideological continuum that undoubtedly also characterized the Marshall Court.[34] One end describes a Hamiltonian or Federalist orientation; the other, a Jeffersonian position. Most of the justices inclined toward Hamiltonianism, supportive of the United States in conflicts with the states, mercantile interests, vested property rights, the compensation claims of federal officials, hostility to jury determinations, and a broad interpretation of the Supreme Court's authority to resolve disputes.[35] Four justices appeared staunchly Hamiltonian: Wayne, McLean, Curtis, and Woodbury; three moderately so: McKinley, Clifford, and Grier. Nelson and Taney marginally adhered to Hamiltonianism, whereas Catron

[31] Although these terms are not coterminous with the Taney Court, 1836–1864, we chose them because the Court's membership was substantially stable during this period. A total of twelve justices sat, seven of whom were common to all thirteen years. As we point out in Chapter 6, validation of the attitudinal model becomes somewhat problematic – at least at the microanalytical level – if too many justices participate in too few cases. Furthermore, unless disagreement occurs, one cannot measure attitudinal differences among the justices. The ideal empirical condition, then, is one of much dissent among an unaltered set of justices. Between 1846 and 1858, almost 20 percent of the Court's decisions contained a dissent (181 of 918). These numbers are based on case citation as the unit of analysis.

[32] In addition to cases involving a conflict between federal and state authority, a set of seventeen land claims cases may also be considered pertinent to federalism, though not in a strictly legal sense. These cases concerned Spanish or Mexican land grants in California, Louisiana, and Texas. Private persons claimed title thereunder, with the United States maintaining in opposition that the lands were part of the public domain. In these cases, the individual justices voted as they did in the other issues that clearly concerned federalism. Adding them to the federalism proportion increases it to 47 percent.

[33] *Harris v. Runnels*, 12 Howard 79 (1851), involving a contract for the sale of slaves; *Moore v. Illinois*, 14 Howard 13 (1852), the constitutionality of Illinois' fugitive slave law; *Wanzer v. Truly*, 17 Howard 584 (1855), enjoining the sale of slaves to satisfy a garnishment; and *Scott v. Sandford*, 19 Howard 393 (1857).

[34] The non-unanimous decisions were formed into eleven cumulative scales compatibly with the procedures specified in Harold J. Spaeth, *Supreme Court Policy Making* (San Francisco: W. H. Freeman, 1979), pp. 120–125. The rank order of the justices on each scale was correlated with those of the other scales. These correlations were then factor analyzed and input into a non-metric multi-dimensional scaling program.

   The Marshall Court contained too many justices and not enough dissenting votes to allow for reliable empirical analysis. Our assertion about its ideological orientation is best described as a confident inference.

[35] Three issues do not correlate with those that comprise the Hamiltonian-Jeffersonian dimension: maritime conflicts between shippers and shipowners, rules of judicial procedure, and a small diversified set of cases pertaining to individual freedom. In addition to the slavery cases, this last set concerns such matters as the legal competence of women, governmental seizure of property, and the rights of criminal defendants.

and Campbell occupied a neutral position. The remaining justice, Daniel, was strongly Jeffersonian.

The case of Scott v. Sandford

The reputation of the Taney Court is thoroughly colored by its decision in *Scott v. Sandford*.[36] Its other contributions pale by comparison. Not only did the decision precipitate the Civil War, the self-inflicted wound that the ruling produced all but destroyed the public's perception of the Court as objective, dispassionate, and impartial.

Dred Scott, a slave, sought his freedom on his return to Missouri, a slave state, as a result of several years' residence in Wisconsin, a non-slave territory under the Missouri Compromise of 1820. After losing in the state supreme court, Scott brought suit in federal court alleging that because he and his owner were citizens of different states, the federal court had jurisdiction. When the case reached the Supreme Court, each justice wrote his own opinion. Taney's was dispositive. Because no black – slave or free – could be an American citizen, no black could sue in a federal court. The reason: At the time the Constitution was adopted, blacks were

considered as a subordinate and inferior class of beings, who had been subjugated by the dominant race, and whether emancipated or not, yet remained subject to their authority, and had no rights or privileges but such as those who held the power and the government might choose to grant them.[37]

Did no constitutional provision protect blacks? Again Taney said no: "For more than a century" blacks had

been regarded as beings of an inferior order; and altogether unfit to associate with the white race . . . and so far inferior, that they had no rights which the white man was bound to respect; and that the negro might justly and lawfully be reduced to slavery for his benefit. He was bought and sold, and treated as an ordinary article of merchandise and traffic, whenever a profit could be made by it. This opinion was at that time fixed and universal in the civilized portion of the white race.[38]

As a plain, unvarnished statement of unabashed racism, Taney's statement expressed a view shared by millions of Americans who did possess American citizenship. But might not language in the Declaration of Independence refute the "universal" perception of black inferiority? Specifically, the references to "all men" being "created equal," and the business about all men being "endowed by their Creator with certain inalienable rights?" Again Taney said no. "The language of the Declaration of Independence is equally conclusive."

[36] 19 Howard 393 (1857).
[37] Id. at 404–405.
[38] Id. at 407. If Taney's statement only applies to "the civilized portion of the white race," one may wonder what lesser status blacks might have been accorded by *uncivilized* whites.

... it is too clear for dispute, that the enslaved African race were not intended to be included, and formed no part of the people who framed and adopted this Declaration; for if the language, as understood in that day, would embrace them, the conduct of the distinguished men who framed the Declaration of Independence would have been utterly and flagrantly inconsistent with the principles they asserted; and instead of the sympathy of mankind, to which they so confidently appealed, they would have deserved and received universal rebuke and reprobation.[39]

If doubt had existed, by a vote of 7 to 2 the justices made it pellucid that the Constitution formed a government of, by, and for white males alone. The die was cast. Only civil war could alter the Court's decree. Four years later, hostilities began, and three years after they ended, the Fourteenth Amendment was ratified, permanently interring the most repellent decision in the Court's history.[40]

Given the ruling that Scott was not a citizen, the majority should simply have dismissed the case for want of jurisdiction. Instead, Taney took a page from Marshall's book on devious deviations from proper judicial procedure and declared the Missouri Compromise, which banned slavery in certain territories, unconstitutional. Note may also be made that the Constitution in Article IV, Section 3, explicitly authorizes Congress to "make all needful rules and regulations respecting the territory or other property belonging to the United States," not the Supreme Court or any other federal court.

RECONSTRUCTION

Following its decision in *Scott v. Sandford*, the power and influence of the Court hit bottom. The decision revolted large segments of the public, especially in the North. Congress displayed its contempt by altering the Court's size three times within a decade, all for purely political purposes. But with the end of the Civil War, the Court began to regain some of its lost luster. Lincoln placed five persons on the Court whom history regards highly: Swayne, Miller, Davis, Field, and the new Chief Justice, Salmon P. Chase. The American bar, newly organized and increasingly influential, regularly paid it homage. The justices themselves mostly kept to the middle of the ideological road, ratifying the policies of other officials rather than initiating their own.

Only once during this time did the Court inflict damage on itself – over the matter of legal tender. In an effort to finance the Civil War, Congress had enacted legislation that substituted paper money for gold as legal tender. In 1870, by a 4-to-3 vote, the Court held the legislation unconstitutional for the payment of

---

[39] Id. at 409, 410.

[40] One may quarrel about this being the most repulsive decision in the Court's history. Other racial alternatives are *Plessy v. Ferguson* and *Korematsu v. United States*, both of which are discussed later in this chapter. *Plessy*, of course, has also been interred – as a result of *Brown v. Board of Education*. Not so *Korematsu*, however.

debts that antedated the law's enactment in 1862.[41] One year later, the three dissenters, joined by two new appointees, reversed the earlier ruling and held that the Congress properly exercised the powers implied in the necessary and proper clause.[42] The Court managed to escape relatively unscathed, however, because criticism fell on President Grant for interfering with the independence of the judiciary by ''packing'' the Court.[43]

Military justice

Although the Court refused to decide the constitutionality of military tribunals during the Civil War on the basis that Congress had not given it jurisdiction to do so,[44] it effectively reversed itself once the War was over. In a two-part ruling, the Court unanimously held that the President lacks power to try civilians by military tribunals during wartime in places where the civil courts are open and functioning, and by a 5-to-4 vote that the combined war powers of President and Congress did not constitutionally authorize such tribunals where the regular courts were open.[45]

In a case that also arose from the actions of a military tribunal, but with ramifications that went beyond military justice, the Court meekly deferred to Congress and upheld a law that revoked its jurisdiction over a certain matter even though the case was already argued and awaiting decision.[46]

Civil rights

The Court first confronted the Fourteenth Amendment in the *Slaughterhouse Cases*[47] in 1873. Curiously, the case had nothing to do with blacks, but rather with a monopoly that Louisiana had granted to a slaughterhouse. Other butchers complained that the act put them out of business. Although the due process and equal protection clauses have been more litigated than any others in the Constitution, the provision of the Fourteenth Amendment on which the majority focused – the privileges and immunities clause – has been little used. The Amendment created no new rights, said the Court, but only allowed Congress, if it is so minded, to legislatively protect the handful of privileges and immunities that peculiarly derive from federal rather than state citizenship. The right to own and operate a butcher shop was not among them.

[41] *Hepburn v. Griswold*, 8 Wallace 603. Ironically, Chief Justice Chase, while Secretary of the Treasury in Lincoln's Administration, proposed and implemented the issuance of paper money as legal tender to finance the Civil War. As Chief Justice, he voted against its constitutionality.

[42] *Knox v. Lee*, 12 Wallace 457 (1870).

[43] Warren, op. cit. fn. 8 supra, III, 243–249.

[44] *Ex parte Vallandigham*, 1 Wallace 243 (1864).

[45] *Ex parte Milligan*, 4 Wallace 2 (1866).

[46] *Ex parte McCardle*, 7 Wallace 506 (1869). Congress feared that if the Court were to decide the case, it might declare Congress's efforts to reconstruct the South unconstitutional.

[47] 16 Wallace 36.

The first major Fourteenth Amendment decision that directly concerned blacks was the *Civil Rights Cases* of 1883.[48] The Court had previously gutted congressional legislation designed to protect blacks who exercised their right to vote under the Fifteenth Amendment.[49] The same fate befell congressional legislation designed to outlaw discrimination in places of public accommodation. The Amendment does not apply to private discrimination, said the justices, only that produced by affirmative state action. Discrimination by privately owned public utilities, though heavily regulated by government, does not constitute state action.

Over the solo dissent of a former Kentucky slave owner, John M. Harlan, the majority held that "individual invasion of individual rights is not the subject-matter of the Amendment." The power to enforce the Amendment "does not invest Congress with power to legislate upon subjects which are within the domain of state legislation," but only provides "relief against state legislation or state action."[50] Neither could the law be sustained under the Thirteenth Amendment:

It would be running the slavery argument into the ground, to make it apply to every act of discrimination which a person may see fit to make as to the guests he will entertain, or as to the people he will take into his coach or cab or car, or admit to his concert or theater, or deal with in other matters of intercourse or business.[51]

The decision in the *Civil Rights Cases* did not end the matter, of course. The racism that Chief Justice Taney had so ably rationalized in *Scott v. Sandford* was not to be eradicated simply because a bloody civil war had been fought and three constitutional amendments ratified. By legitimating white supremacy, the Court effectively declared these events null and void until the middle of the twentieth century, when a later Court, stricken with a guilty conscience, partially undid what its predecessors had wrought. In the meantime, the nation still needed a mechanism to implement white supremacy. Thirteen years later the Court provided it in *Plessy v. Ferguson*, when the justices – with Justice Harlan again dissenting – formulated the separate but equal doctrine. Thereafter, no sanction would befall even the most blatantly discriminatory state action so long as the governmental facilities or actions in question were separate, regardless of inequality.

FIGHTING THE WELFARE STATE

Following the Civil War the United States, previously an agrarian society, had become one of the world's industrial giants. As the Court reneged on the promises of the Fourteenth Amendment, it began to focus its attention on the economy.

---

[48]   109 U.S. 3.
[49]   In *United States v. Reese*, 92 U.S. 214 (1876), and *United States v. Cruikshank*, 92 U.S. 542 (1876).
[50]   109 U.S. at 11.
[51]   Id. at 24–25.

. . . as capitalism expanded, it impinged on the lives of individuals as never before; as it became the most important fact in American life, it became the most troublesome fact as well. Men began to say, first from scattered quarters, then in a steadily augmenting chorus, that the power of government should be used to control this giant, to mitigate the harm to individual and collective welfare that it might do if left unchecked. And conversely, others began to say, with a vengeance and volume far greater than in the past, that the giant would serve the community best if it were allowed to go its own way, that governmental tinkering with the economy was both futile and mischievous, that laissez faire should be the watchword of the day.[52]

More often than not the Supreme Court threw its lot with the plunderbunds who favored laissez-faire. We examine the three main areas where the Court applied the gospel of wealth: taxation, commerce, and substantive due process.

Taxation

The Articles of Confederation provided the Continental Congress with no direct authority to tax individuals. States could be solicited, but they could not be compelled to pay. This was one of the many deficiencies in the Articles that led to the calling of the Constitutional Convention in 1787.

The Framers of the Constitution granted Congress certain tax powers. Article 1, Section 8, Clause 1, declares that "Congress shall have the power to lay and collect taxes, duties, imposts and excises." The Framers restricted this broad tax power in three ways: duties, imposts and excises must be uniform (Article 1, Section 8); capitation and other "direct" taxes must be levied proportionate to population (Article 1, Section 2; Article 1, Section 9); and no tax or duty could be placed on goods exported from any state.

The first federal income tax was levied during the Civil War. The Supreme Court upheld it as an excise tax, not a direct tax, and thus one not subject to apportionment. Declared the Court: "Direct taxes, within the meaning of the Constitution, are only capitation taxes . . . and taxes on real estate."[53]

In 1894, Congress enacted the Wilson-Gorman Tariff Act, which placed a tax of 2 percent on the income of individuals and corporations from rents, interest, dividends, salaries, and profits over $4,000. Progressive and populist elements hailed the tax as a great victory. So much did the plunderbund fear the tax that they told the Court that the Act was part of a " 'Communist march' against the rights of property."[54] In April 1895, the Court declared in *Pollock v. Farmers' Loan and Trust*[55] that the tax on rents was in reality a tax on land and thus a direct tax that must be apportioned. Taxes on municipal bonds were invalidated

---

[52] Robert McCloskey, *The American Supreme Court* (Chicago: University of Chicago Press, 1960), pp. 102–103.

[53] *Springer v. United States*, 102 U.S. 586 (1880), at 602. The ruling sustained the 1796 precedent, *Hylton v. United States*, 3 Dallas 171.

[54] C. Herman Pritchett, *The American Constitution*, 3d ed. (New York: McGraw-Hill, 1977), p. 168.

[55] 157 U.S. 429.

on the grounds of intergovernmental immunity. With Justice Jackson ill, the Court split 4 to 4 on the constitutionality of the income tax. When Jackson recovered, the case was reargued. Jackson joined those who thought the income tax constitutional, but Justice Shiras switched, invalidating the tax.[56] According to Supreme Court historian Robert McCloskey, the direct tax clause "provided the judges with an objective formulation of their prejudice in favor of wealth."[57]

In a final blow to the Act, the Court also struck down the tax on business profits and employment income. It did not find such taxes unconstitutional; rather, it asserted that Congress would not have taxed these sources of income if it could not also tax dividends, interest, and rent. The *Pollock* decisions led to the ratification of the Sixteenth Amendment, one of four times an amendment undid a decision of the Court (see Chapter 2). The Amendment simply states that "the Congress shall have power to lay and collect taxes on incomes, from whatever source derived, without apportionment among the several States, and without regard to any census or enumeration." As noted in Chapter 1, the language did not prevent the Court from exempting themselves and their lower bench colleagues from its operation on the ground that the Constitution prohibits any lowering of judicial salaries. As we shall see next, the Amendment also did not prevent the Court from voiding taxes by labeling them constitutionally prohibited *non*taxes.

Interstate commerce and other national powers

The same year that the Supreme Court ruled the income tax unconstitutional, 1895, it rendered two additional decisions that supported the interests of laissez-faire economics. One week after the second *Pollock* ruling, the Court upheld an injunction prohibiting railroad workers led by Eugene Debs from obstructing the nation's railroads, and thus interstate commerce.[58] In effect, the Court declared the Pullman strike of 1894 illegal.

The Court's ruling in *Debs* was not the result of any principled belief in broad national powers over interstate commerce, such as Chief Justice Marshall had expressed in *Gibbons v. Ogden*. Typically, a cramped construction better enabled the Court to achieve a result consistent with its laissez-faire philosophy. The first relevant case, *United States v. E.C. Knight Co.*,[59] was decided a few months before the *Pollock* and *Debs* cases. It involved enforcement of the Sherman Antitrust Act, enacted by Congress in 1890, which made "every contract, combination . . . or conspiracy in restraint of trade or commerce among the several states, or with foreign nations . . . illegal."[60] The Department of Justice sought

---

[56]	*Pollock v. Farmers' Loan and Trust Co.*, 158 U.S. 601 (1895).
[57]	Op. cit. fn. 52 supra, p. 141.
[58]	*In re Debs*, 158 U.S. 564.
[59]	156 U.S. 1 (1895).
[60]	Id. at 6.

to break up the American Sugar Refining Company, which, through acquisitions, controlled over 98 percent of the nation's sugar refining.

The Court conceded that the sugar trust was an illegal monopoly. The relevant question, rather, was whether Congress had the authority to suppress monopolies. The Court said it did not. First, the Court asserted that the protection of life, health, and property is part of the police power, which belongs exclusively to the states. When monopolies burden the citizens of a state, the state's legislature must remedy the wrong. Second, although the Court recognized that Congress had plenary authority to regulate interstate commerce, it denied that the manufacture of 98 percent of the nation's sugar in several different states by one company constituted commerce. Drawing a distinction between manufacturing and commerce, the Court declared that "commerce succeeds to manufacture, and is not a part of it."[61] Monopolistic production only affects commerce indirectly, and thus is beyond the power of Congress to regulate.

The Court's commerce clause decisions did not invariably support business. In 1905, for example, it ruled that fixing prices through collusion at a stockyard violated the Sherman Act even though the activity took place within a single state. The Court held the activity to be part of "a current of commerce among the States"[62] that started with the raising of cattle and ended with the final retail sale. Other businesses did not deserve protection because of their incompatibility with the Puritan ethic that underlay laissez-faire economics. Thus, the Court held the commerce clause a perfectly appropriate vehicle for prohibiting the interstate sale of lottery tickets.[63] But such decisions were exceptions to the rule. More typical rulings invalidated the Child Labor Act of 1916, which prohibited the shipment of goods across state lines produced by children under the age of fourteen, or by those between fourteen and sixteen who worked more than forty-eight hours per week.[64] Concerned parent Roland Dagenhart, upset that his children would no longer be allowed to work in a North Carolina cotton mill, had sought to enjoin enforcement of the Act. According to the Court's 5-to-4 decision, Congress could not use the commerce power to regulate the conditions of production, because the Tenth Amendment reserved the matter to the states. The Court distinguished *Hammer* from the lottery case because the goods intended for interstate commerce were not in and of themselves harmful. Thus Congress could ban the sale of lottery tickets across state lines, but not goods made by child labor.

In reaction, Congress enacted a law that imposed a tax of 10 percent on the net profits of firms that hired children under the age of fourteen. With the passage of the Sixteenth Amendment, such taxing authority seemed clearly within Congress's power. Nevertheless, the Court struck the law on the ground that the

---

[61]   Id. at 12.
[62]   *Swift and Co. v. United States*, 196 U.S. 375, at 398–399.
[63]   *Champion v. Ames*, 188 U.S. 321 (1903).
[64]   *Hammer v. Dagenhart*, 247 U.S. 251 (1918).

imposition was not a tax, but a penalty.[65] This is similar to the Rehnquist Court's recent declaration that preventive detention – imprisonment for crimes the government believes one is likely to commit – is not punishment protected by the Fifth Amendment, but merely regulation.[66] Like Humpty Dumpty in *Through the Looking Glass*, words mean what the Court chooses them to mean – neither more nor less.[67]

With the onset of the Great Depression in 1929, the demand for federal regulation increased. When Franklin Roosevelt took office in 1933, he immediately proposed "New Deal" legislation to revive the national economy. Although the legislation sailed through Congress, it failed to receive Court approval.

First to fall was the National Industrial Recovery Act (NIRA), which required business and government to establish codes of fair competition that would result in higher prices and, so the government hoped, better wages and lower unemployment. In 1935 the Court struck down a provision that allowed (but did not require) the President to prohibit the transportation in interstate commerce of oil produced in excess of state and federal regulations.[68] With only Justice Cardozo dissenting, the Court ruled the provision to be a standardless delegation of legislative power that left the decision whether to ban such shipments entirely to the President's discretion.

The Court considered the remainder of the NIRA later in 1935. Although the Act would expire in three weeks, the Court nevertheless agreed to review it in *Schechter Poultry v. United States*.[69] The Schechter brothers owned slaughterhouses in New York that butchered out-of-state chickens. In violation of the authorized codes of fair competition, the brothers allegedly filed false sales and price reports and sold diseased chickens.

The Court voided the NIRA on two grounds. First, the establishment of codes of fair competition by businesses working with the executive branch unlawfully delegated legislative powers. The statute did not define "fair competition," thus leaving the codes to executive discretion. More troublesome to Roosevelt was the second part of the Court's opinion, which declared that the statute went beyond Congress's commerce power. Though out-of-state farmers supplied the chickens, their slaughter and sale occurred after "the flow of interstate commerce had ceased. The poultry had come to a permanent rest within the state."[70] Indeed they had. Once again, the Court ruled the effect on interstate commerce merely

---

[65] *Bailey v. Drexel Furniture*, 259 U.S. 20 (1922).

[66] *United States v. Salerno*, 481 U.S. 739 (1987).

[67] " 'The question is,' said Alice, 'whether you *can* make words mean so many different things.' " 'The question is, said Humpty Dumpty, 'which is to be master – that's all.' " The Supreme Court has obviously sided with Humpty. See Lewis Carroll, *Alice's Adventures in Wonderland and Through the Looking Glass* (New York: Oxford University Press, 1971), p. 190.

[68] *Panama Refining Co. v. Ryan*, 293 U.S. 388 (1935).

[69] 295 U.S. 495 (1935). Inasmuch as the Act was generally perceived to be an ineffective solution to the nation's economic woes, no substantial effort had been made to extend it.

[70] Id. at 543.

indirect and thus beyond the scope of the commerce clause. President Roosevelt criticized the Court for "relegat(ing) us to the horse-and-buggy definition of interstate commerce."[71]

In between the two NIRA cases, the Court invalidated by a 5-to-4 vote the Railroad Retirement Act of 1934, which had established a mandatory retirement plan for railroad employees covered by the Interstate Commerce Act. This was despite previous cases in which the Court had upheld extensive regulation of the railroads – the Interstate Commerce Commission's authority to set both interstate and intrastate railroad rates,[72] the Commission's authority to establish safety standards, including working hours,[73] and the regulation of labor relations, because of the effect strikes could have on interstate commerce.[74] The Court, in voiding the Railroad Retirement Act, argued that the previous cases dealt with railroad safety and efficiency, whereas the current case dealt only with "the social welfare of the worker, and therefore (was) remote from any regulation of commerce."[75]

The next act to be struck down was the Agricultural Adjustment Act of 1933.[76] The act attempted to increase depressed farm prices by subsidizing farmers who agreed to reduce crop production. Funds to pay the farmers came from a tax levied on the processors of the relevant commodities. Even though the Constitution gives Congress the power to tax for the general welfare, the Court ruled that the taxing and spending provisions of the Act, because they regulated agricultural production, violated the Tenth Amendment.

One of the biggest blows to the New Deal came in the 1936 case, *Carter v. Carter Coal Co.* The Court's decision invalidated the Bituminous Coal Conservation Act, which attempted to stabilize the coal industry by allowing a commission to set minimum and maximum prices. Maximum hour and minimum wage standards were also established. Coal producers were subject to a 15 percent sales tax from which they could be largely exempt if they abided by the commission's standards.

The Court's opinion focused on the scope of the commerce clause. Whereas in *Schechter* the attempted focus of regulation came *after* commerce allegedly ended, here the focus occurred *before* commerce began. According to the Court,

... the word "commerce" is the equivalent of the phrase "intercourse for the purposes of trade." Plainly, the incidents leading up to and culminating in the mining of coal do not constitute such intercourse. The employment of men, the fixing of their wages, hours of labor and working conditions, the bargaining in respect of these things – whether

[71] Gregory Caldeira, "Public Opinion and the Supreme Court: FDR's Court-Packing Plan," 81 *American Political Science Review* 1139 (1987), at 1141.
[72] *Houston, East & West Texas Railway Co. v. United States*, 234 U.S. 342 (1914).
[73] *Baltimore and Ohio Railway v. Interstate Commerce Commission*, 221 U.S. 612 (1911).
[74] *Texas & New Orleans Railroad Company v. Brotherhood of Railway and Steamship Clerks*, 281 U.S. 548 (1930).
[75] *Railroad Retirement Board v. Alton R. Co.*, 295 U.S. 330 (1935), at 368.
[76] *United States v. Butler*, 297 U.S. 1 (1936).

carried on separately or collectively – each and all constitute intercourse for the purposes of production, not of trade. The latter is a thing apart from the relation of employer and employee, which in all producing occupations is purely local in character. Extraction of coal from the mine is the aim and the completed result of local activities. Commerce in the coal mined is not brought into being by force of these activities, but by negotiations, agreements, and circumstances entirely apart from production. Mining brings the subject-matter of commerce into existence. Commerce disposes of it.[77]

By intruding into employer-employee relations the Act also interfered with the rights that the Tenth Amendment reserved to the states. Thus by a solipsistic reading of the commerce clause, the Court throttled much of the New Deal.

Freedom of contract

The preceding section shows that when the federal government attempted to regulate working conditions, the Court ruled that such legislative powers belonged to the states, not the federal government. What happened then when the states tried to regulate hours worked and wages paid? The short answer is that the Court generally ruled that such state legislation violated "freedom of contract," which the Court found implicit in the due process clause of the Fourteenth Amendment. Because these decisions are based on the subjects of state regulation, not the procedures states use, commentators classify these cases under the oxymoronic rubric, "substantive due process."

The idea behind substantive due process – that courts have the right to void government action even though it does not violate any explicit constitutional provision – can be traced back in American law at least as far as *Calder v. Bull*.[78] The Court in *Calder* upheld a Connecticut law setting aside a decree of a probate court against the claim that the statute constituted an ex post facto law. Speaking for himself, Justice Chase declared that he could not

subscribe to the omnipotence of a state legislature, or that it is absolute and without control; although its authority should not be expressly restrained by the constitution, or fundamental law of the state. . . . To maintain that our federal or state legislature possesses such powers, if they had not been expressly restrained, would, in my opinion, be a political heresy altogether inadmissable in our free republican governments.[79]

Justice Iredell replied that if

the legislature of the union, or the legislature of any member of the union, shall pass a law, within the general scope of their constitutional power, the court cannot pronounce it void, merely because it is, in their judgment, contrary to the principles of natural justice.[80]

[77]   298 U.S. 238, at 303–304.
[78]   3 Dallas 386 (1798).
[79]   Id. at 387–389.
[80]   Id. at 399.

The first known instance of a law being struck down on the grounds of substantive due process occurred in an 1856 case, *Wynehamer v. People.*[81] The New York Court of Appeals declared that a state law prohibiting the sale of liquor deprived saloon keepers of their property.

The judicial and economic impact of *Wynehamer* was felt quickly.

In less than twenty years from the time of its rendition the crucial ruling in *Wynehamer* was far on the way to being assimilated into the accepted constitutional law of the country. The "due process" clause, which had been intended originally to consecrate a mode of procedure, had become a constitutional test of the ever increasing reach of the substantive content of legislation. Thus was the doctrine of vested rights brought within the constitutional fold.[82]

Substantive due process first manifested itself in the jurisprudence of the Supreme Court in the dissenting opinion of Justice Bradley in the *Slaughterhouse Cases.* A "law which prohibits a large class of citizens from adopting a lawful employment, or from following a lawful employment previously adopted, does deprive them of liberty as well as property, without due process of law."[83] In *Munn v. Illinois,* the Court agreed that due process limited state interference with property rights, but ruled that such rights were limited by the state's power to regulate businesses "affected with a public interest."[84] In this case, the state's interest in regulating grain elevators overrode the owners' property interests.

The first case in which the Supreme Court struck down a state law on substantive due process grounds was the 1897 decision in *Allgeyer v. Louisiana.*[85] The Court invalidated a Louisiana statute that prohibited Louisiana companies from purchasing marine insurance from out-of-state businesses that did not comply with Louisiana regulations. The Court overturned Allgeyer's conviction for purchasing the insurance because

the statute is a violation of the fourteenth amendment of the federal constitution, in that it deprives the defendants of their liberty without due process of law. ... The "liberty" mentioned in that amendment means, not only the right of a citizen to be free from the mere physical restraint of his person, as by incarceration, but the term is deemed to

---

[81]   13 N.Y. 378.

[82]   Edward S. Corwin, *Liberty Against Government* (Baton Rouge, LA: Louisiana State University Press, 1948), pp. 114–15.

[83]   16 Wallace 36 (1873), at 122. Justice Bradley is the same person who, one day later, wrote: "Man is, or should be, woman's protector and defender. The natural and proper timidity and delicacy which belongs to the female sex evidently unfits it for many of the occupations of civil life. The constitution of the family organization, which is founded in the divine ordinance ... indicates the domestic sphere as that which belongs to ... womanhood. The harmony, not to say identity, of interests and views which belong ... to the family institution, is repugnant to the idea of a woman adopting a distinct and independent career from that of her husband. ...

   The paramount destiny and mission of woman are to fulfill the noble and benign offices of wife and mother. This is the law of the Creator." *Bradwell v. Illinois*, 16 Wallace 130 (1873), at 141.

[84]   94 U.S. 113 (1876), at 130.

[85]   165 U.S. 578.

embrace the right of the citizen to be free to . . . enter into all contracts which may be proper, necessary and essential to his carrying out a successful conclusion the purposes above mentioned.[86]

Whatever one might think of the political desirablity of laissez-faire capitalism, its constitutional basis is problematic. Reasonable people disagree whether the term "liberty" in the Fourteenth Amendment includes freedom of contract. But whatever the scope of this liberty, it is far from absolute. The plain words only prohibit deprivation without due process of law. The Court simply sought a result and reached it by the most convenient means possible.

A decision eleven years earlier magnified the consequences of *Allgeyer*, the ruling that corporations were "persons" within the meaning and protections of the Fourteenth Amendment.[87] Thus states could not limit the freedom of either individuals or corporations to contract.

However nugatory the substance of the *Allgeyer* decision might seem – allowing companies to let out-of-state contracts hardly seems momentous – the scope of the new right to contract became apparent in *Lochner v. New York*.[88] Under its police powers, the state had enacted a maximum-hour law limiting bakers to ten hours of work per day and sixty hours of work per week. In a 5-to-4 decision the Court ruled that the law necessarily interfered with freedom of contract. Rejecting evidence that long hours were injurious to bakers, the Court declared that the "real object and purpose were simply to regulate the hours of labor between the master and employer."[89] Never mind that when the federal government enacted such regulations the Court ruled that only the states could do so. Justice Holmes argued in dissent that this case

is decided upon an economic theory which a large part of the country does not entertain. . . . The Fourteenth Amendment does not enact Mr. Herbert Spencer's Social Statics. . . . A constitution is not intended to embody a particular economic theory, whether of paternalism and the organic relation of the citizen to the state or of *laissez faire*.[90]

On the authority of *Lochner* the Supreme Court invalidated the effort of both the federal and state governments to prohibit employers from forcing workers to agree not to join labor unions.[91] In the state case the Court acknowledged that it is "impossible to uphold freedom of contract and the right of private property without at the same time recognizing as legitimate those inequalities of fortune that are a necessary result of the exercise of those rights."[92]

The Court did not always uphold freedom of contract. In 1908 it sustained a law limiting women to ten hours of work per day in factories or laundries because

---

[86]   Id. at 589.
[87]   *Santa Clara County v. Southern Pacific R. Co.*, 118 U.S. 394 (1886).
[88]   198 U.S. 45 (1905).
[89]   Id. at 64.
[90]   Id. at 75.
[91]   *Adair v. United States*, 208 U.S. 161 (1908), and *Coppage v. Kansas*, 236 U.S. 1 (1915).
[92]   *Coppage v. Kansas*, 236 U.S. 1 (1915), at 17.

a "woman's physical structure, and the functions she performs in consequences thereof, justify special legislation."[93] In 1917 the Court upheld a maximum hour law for factory workers of both sexes without mentioning *Lochner*.[94] More often than not, though, state social legislation was invalidated. For example, in *Wolff Packing Co. v. Court of Industrial Relations*[95] the Court struck down a Kansas statute requiring binding arbitration of labor-management disputes when they threatened public well-being. In *Adkins v. Children's Hospital*[96] the Court voided a law setting minimum wages for women and children in the District of Columbia.

When the Great Depression began in 1929, the need for state regulation became acute. The validity of such legislation continued to depend on judicial approval. On the Supreme Court, a trifurcated alignment emerged: a four-person conservative coalition – McReynolds, Van Devanter, Sutherland, and Butler; a three-person liberal alliance of Holmes (replaced in 1932 by Cardozo), Brandeis, and Stone; and the two swing voters – Chief Justice Hughes and Justice Roberts. In 1934, Hughes and Roberts joined the liberals to uphold a New York law regulating the price of milk,[97] but in 1935 and 1936 they joined forces with the conservatives in a series of important cases. Shortly after concluding in *Carter* that the national government infringed on states' rights by regulating wages and prices, the Court ruled that New York's attempt to regulate minimum wages for women violated due process. By a 5-to-4 vote (Hughes split with Roberts and voted with the dissenters) the Court declared that "the State is without power by any form of legislation to prohibit, change or nullify contracts between employers and adult women workers as to the amount of wages to be paid."[98] As one commentator remarked:

The argument of the Chief Justice, who dissented, that the *Adkins* precedent need not be followed because of "material differences" in the two laws; the argument of Stone, Brandeis, and Cardozo, also dissenting, that precedent since *Adkins*, and "what is more important, reason" support state power to control wages, had no weight for five men now thoroughly deluded by the notion that the welfare state could be judicially throttled and the brave old world of their youth restored.[99]

The court-packing plan

By the middle of 1936 it was obvious that the Court would allow neither the federal nor the state governments to relieve the misery caused by the Depression. President Roosevelt made little issue of the Supreme Court in his 1936 reelection campaign, but following his landslide victory he made a bold move. On February

---

[93] *Muller v. Oregon*, 208 U.S. 412 (1908), at 420.
[94] *Bunting v. Oregon*, 243 U.S. 426 (1917).
[95] 262 U.S. 522 (1923).
[96] 261 U.S. 525 (1923).
[97] *Nebbia v. New York*, 291 U.S. 502.
[98] *Moorehead v. New York ex rel. Tipaldo*, 298 U.S. 587 (1936), at 611.
[99] McCloskey, op. cit. fn. 52 supra, pp. 166–67.

5, 1937, he proposed a court reform bill, ostensibly designed to improve judicial efficiency. The bill would allow the President to appoint one new justice for each gerontocratic member over seventy who chose not to resign. Given the ages of the justices, this would have amounted to six new appointments. Though many of the Court's decisions were unpopular, the notion of judicial indepenpence was not. The press vilified the plan and the public opposed it.[100] Progressive forces failed to rally behind the bill; Southern Democrats joined Republicans in opposition to it.[101]

The Court itself played no small role in defusing the plan. On March 29, 1937, by a 5-to-4 vote the justices overturned forty years of freedom-of-contract doctrine. Noting that the law in question allegedly violated the right to contract, the Court majority wondered:

What is this freedom? The Constitution does not speak of freedom of contract. It speaks of liberty and prohibits the deprivation of liberty without due process of law. In prohibiting that deprivation, the Constitution does not recognize an absolute and uncontrollable liberty. . . . Liberty under the Constitution is thus necessarily subject to the restraints of due process, and regulation which is reasonable in relation to its subject and is adopted in the interests of the community is due process.[102]

Then, on April 12, another 5-to-4 vote upheld the National Labor Relations Act, which guaranteed the right of labor to bargain collectively and authorized the National Labor Relations Board to prevent unfair labor practices. The case, *National Labor Relations Board v. Jones and Laughlin Steel Corp.*,[103] declared that a steel company, centered in Pittsburgh, with coal mines in Michigan, Minnesota, and Pennsylvania, warehouses in Chicago, Detroit, Cincinnati and Memphis, and factories in New York and New Orleans, conducted business in interstate commerce. Rejecting the dichotomy between manufacture and commerce, the Court instead asked whether steel production had a substantial effect on commerce. Clearly it did.

(Three subsequent decisions illustrate the scope of this ruling. In the first, *Wickard v. Filburn*,[104] The Court upheld a penalty on a farmer for harvesting twelve acres of unauthorized wheat that he grew for his own consumption. The Court pointed out that the excess wheat, when considered with all other wheat grown throughout the country for home consumption, could have a substantial effect on the price of wheat destined for interstate commerce. In the second case the Court upheld the constitutionality of the Civil Rights Act of 1964, which prohibits discrimination in places of public accommodation, because of the effect

---

[100]   Caldeira, op. cit. fn. 71 supra.
[101]   David Adamany, "Legitimacy, Realigning Elections, and the Supreme Court," 1973 *Wisconsin Law Review* 790 (1973).
[102]   *West Coast Hotel Co. v. Parrish*, 300 U.S. 379, at 391.
[103]   301 U.S. 1 (1937).
[104]   317 U.S. 111 (1942).

such discrimination had on interstate commerce.[105] The most recent case concerned a conspiracy among ophthalmologists at a local hospital to eliminate one competing practitioner. This, said the majority, restrains trade and commerce among the several states sufficient to violate the Sherman Antitrust Act.[106])

Finally, on May 24, 1937, a third 5-to-4 vote declared the Social Security Act to be within the tax powers of Congress.[107] This effectively overruled the limits on the taxing power decreed by the *Butler* case. In all three cases, Hughes and Roberts joined the three liberals to uphold the state or federal action in question. Because of the negative impact these decisions had on support for Roosevelt's plan, they have since become known as "the switch in time that saved nine."

Roosevelt's plan became fully superfluous when Justice Van Devanter resigned on May 18, 1937. Instead of a shaky 5-to-4 majority, the Court would soon have its first Roosevelt appointee and with it a 6-to-3 majority. Roosevelt lost the battle to enlarge the Court, but of course he had won the war.

THE CIVIL LIBERTIES AGENDA

At the same time that the Supreme Court began to remove itself from managing the nation's economic affairs, it began to pay closer attention to the non-economic rights and liberties of the Bill of Rights and the Civil War amendments. One of the first hints of the Court's switch from being a defender of economic freedoms to being a defender of other civil rights and liberties came in *United States v. Carolene Products Co.*[108]

The preferred freedoms doctrine

The *Carolene Products* case involved the constitutionality of the Filled Milk Act of 1923, which prohibited the interstate shipment of skimmed milk with oil-based fillers. Justice Stone, writing for the majority, made it clear that the Court would only minimally scrutinize such statutes:

Regulatory legislation affecting ordinary commercial transactions is not to be pronounced unconstitutional unless in light of the facts made known or generally assumed it is of such a character as to preclude the assumption that it rests upon some rational basis within the knowledge and experience of the legislators.[109]

At this point, Stone inserted a footnote that has shaped the Supreme Court's doctrinal developments to this day.

---

[105] *Heart of Atlanta Motel v. United States*, 379 U.S. 241 (1964), and *Katzenbach v. McClung*, 379 U.S. 294 (1964).
[106] *Summit Health Ltd. v. Pinhas*, 114 L Ed 2d 366 (1991).
[107] *Steward Machine Co. v. Davis*, 301 U.S. 548.
[108] 304 U.S. 144 (1938).
[109] Id. at 152.

There may be a narrower scope for operation of the presumption of constitutionality when legislation appears on its face to be within a specific prohibition of the Constitution, such as those of the first ten amendments, which are deemed equally specific when held to be embraced within the Fourteenth. . . .

It is unnecessary now to consider whether legislation which restricts those political processes which can ordinarily be expected to bring about repeal of undesirable legislation, is to be subjected to more exacting judicial scrutiny under the general prohibitions of the Fourteenth Amendment than are most other types of legislation. . . .

Nor need we inquire whether similar considerations enter into the review of statutes directed at particular religious . . . or national . . . or racial minorities . . . whether prejudices against discrete and insular minorities may be a special condition, which tends seriously to curtail the operation of those political processes ordinarily thought to be relied upon to protect minorities, and which may call for a correspondingly more searching judicial inquiry.[110]

Thus the formulation of what is known as the "preferred freedoms doctrine." Under this doctrine the Court assumes legislation constitutional unless it facially abridges a provision of the Bill of Rights, restricts access to normal political processes (e.g., the right to vote), or violates the equal protection rights of "insular minorities." If so, then the presumption of constitutionality does not obtain. The state can overcome the presumption of unconstitutionality if a law is "narrowly tailored" to sustain a "compelling" governmental interest.

As an example of this doctrine, consider the decision in *Regents of the University of California v. Bakke.*[111] The University of California Medical School at Davis had an affirmative action plan that reserved sixteen of its one-hundred seats for members of certain minority groups. The remaining eighty-four seats were open to people of all races. Bakke, a rejected white applicant, had higher admissions scores than many admitted under the affirmative action plan. The judgment of the Supreme Court, written by Justice Powell, subjected the school's admission policy to strict scrutiny (even though Bakke was not a member of a "discrete and insular minority") because it created a racial classification. Powell then considered whether California had a compelling interest in its special admission program. California argued that it had a compelling interest in (1) reducing the historic deficit of minority doctors, (2) countering the effects of societal discrimination, (3) increasing the number of doctors who would practice in poor communities, and (4) obtaining the benefits of a diverse student body.

Powell asserted that the first argument served no compelling governmental interest; this was discrimination for discrimination's sake. Powell suggested that redressing societal discrimination constituted such an interest, but as there was no evidence that Davis had previously discriminated against minorities in its admissions policies, the state's interest did not justify the violation of an innocent party's rights. Powell recognized a compelling interest in increasing health-care services to poor communities, but noted that the University did not narrowly draw its program to meet that goal: There was no evidence that those admitted

[110]   Id. at 152–153.
[111]   438 U.S. 265 (1978).

under the affirmative-action program had shown special interest in practicing in low-income communities. Powell, however, did find a compelling interest in Davis's desire for a diverse student body, but that the quota system again failed of narrow drafting. As an alternative, he suggested that a program that took race into account, but did not impose a quota, would be constitutionally permissible.

The preferred freedoms doctrine, which creates a double standard between economic and social rights on the one hand, and "political rights" such as First Amendment freedoms, equal protection, and the rights of persons accused of crime on the other, has by and large received majority support from the Supreme Court. The arguments in favor of the double standard are well presented by Henry Abraham.[112]

First, argues Abraham, is the crucial nature of political rights. We can be a free people and not have minimum wage laws, but we cannot be a free people without freedom of speech, press, and religion. Not all agree, though, that political rights outweigh economic rights. According to Justice Stewart in *Lynch v. Household Finance Corp.*,

> the dichotomy between personal liberty and property rights is a false one. Property does not have rights. People have rights. The right to enjoy property without unlawful deprivation, no less than the right to travel, is, in truth, a personal right. In fact, a fundamental interdependence exists between the right to liberty and the personal right to property. Neither can have meaning without the other.[113]

Abraham's second argument asserts that the Bill of Rights explicitly contains political rights, whereas many economic rights rest on creative interpretation of the due process clause. From an interpretivist standpoint, this justifies greater protection to freedom of commucation than to freedom of contract, but it does not fully resolve the matter. What of economic rights that the Constitution explicitly contains? For instance, Article 1, Section 10, of the Constitution prohibits states from impairing the obligation of contract. The Fifth Amendment prohibits the taking of property without just compensation. If support for the preferred freedoms doctrine rests on their explicit presence, shouldn't constitutionally explicit economic rights be similarly protected? And what of personal rights that lack plain constitutional language, such as the right to privacy, the right to travel, or the right to vote in presidential elections?[114] Should these rights receive less protection?

Abraham's third argument for the preferred freedoms doctrine rests on the appropriate responsibilities of judges. As James Madison declared when introducing the Bill of Rights in Congress:

---

[112] *Freedom and the Court*, 5th ed. (New York: Oxford University Press, 1988), pp. 28–34.
[113] 405 U.S. 538 (1972), at 552.
[114] Other than a prohibition against poll taxes, and discrimination in voting on account of sex, race, and age (for those over eighteen – plus the provision in Article I, Section 2, Clause 1 that authorizes persons whom the states have enfranchised to vote in federal elections – no constitutional language explicitly protects voting rights.

Independent tribunals of justice will consider themselves in a peculiar manner the guardians of those rights; they will be an impenetrable bulwark against every assumption of power in the legislative or executive; they will be naturally led to resist every encroachment upon rights expressly stipulated for in the Constitution by the declaration of rights.[115]

Or as Justice Fortas asserted: "The courts may be the principal guardians of the liberties of the people. They are not the chief administrators of its economic destiny."[116]

This defense of the preferred freedoms doctrine is also disputed. According to Judge Richard Posner of the Federal Court of Appeals, it is often claimed "that economic questions are more difficult for courts to decide sensibly than questions involving the rights of criminal defendants, political dissidents, or members of racial minorities; yet in fact less is known about those questions than about conventional economic problems."[117]

Incorporation of the Bill of Rights

A Court interested in following a civil liberties agenda must have jurisdiction over individual rights, most of which involve actions by state and local governments. Under the language of the original Constitution, the federal government was chiefly barred from abridging individual rights. States were prohibited only from passing bills of attainder, ex post facto laws, and impairing the obligation of contracts. The Bill of Rights, ratified in 1791, only limited the exercise of national power. So if Virginia wished to establish a state religion, or if New Jersey wished to punish persons who criticized governmental policies, nothing in the federal Constitution prevented their doing so.

The Supreme Court affirmed the inapplicability of the Bill of Rights to the states in the 1833 case of *Barron v. Baltimore*.[118] Marshall's unanimous decision categorically rejected Barron's claim that the Fifth Amendment, or indeed any of the Bill of Rights, applied to the states. Marshall noted that people of the United States established the Constitution for the governance of the United States, not for that of the respective states. If people wanted protection from their state governments, the state constitutions could so provide. Textually, the original Constitution speaks generally when it refers to the national government, and specifically mentions the states in those instances where limits on power are applicable to them. He therefore gave effect to the plain language of the Bill of Rights.

The potential application of the Bill of Rights to the states began with the passage of the Fourteenth Amendment, which says in part that "no State shall make or enforce any law which shall abridge the privileges or immunities of citizens of the United States; nor shall any State deprive any person of life,

---

[115] *Annals of Congress*, 1st Congress, 1st Session, June 8, 1789 (Washington D.C., 1834), I, 457.
[116] *Baltimore and Ohio Railroad Co. v. United States*, 386 U.S. 372 (1967), at 478.
[117] Richard Posner, *Economic Analysis of Law*, 2d ed. (Boston: Little, Brown, 1977), p. 498.
[118] 7 Peters 243.

liberty, or property, without due process of law.'' Despite the statements of some of the Framers that they meant the privileges and immunities clause to overturn *Barron* and apply the Bill of Rights to the states, the Supreme Court gave the clause a very limited construction, as we saw in the discussion of the *Slaughterhouse Cases*. To this day, the privileges and immunities clause does not significantly limit the behavior of state governments.

To the extent that the Bill of Rights binds the states today, it is through the due process clause. The first case to focus on whether this provision made any of the Bill of Rights binding on the states was *Hurtado v. California*.[119] California allowed indictment by information presented to a magistrate, rather than by a grand jury. Hurtado, who had been indicted and convicted of murder, argued that indictment by information violated the Fourteenth Amendment. The Supreme Court ruled in a 7-to-1 decision that (1) the due process clause in the Fourteenth Amendment means the same thing as the due process clause in the Fifth Amendment; (2) if due process in the Fifth Amendment included the requirement of indictment by grand jury, then the grand jury clause of the Fifth Amendment would be superfluous; and (3) nothing in the Constitution should be considered such. (This logic, though, did not prevent the Court from ruling that the Fourteenth Amendment's due process clause prohibited states from taking property without just compensation, even though the Fifth Amendment protects both due process and taking property without just compensation.[120]) Justice John Marshall Harlan dissented in *Hurtado*, arguing that the Fourteenth Amendment incorporated the Bill of Rights, and thus the right to indictment by grand jury. Following the *Hurtado* majority's logic, the Court ruled in 1900 that the due process clause did not prevent the states from employing an eight-person jury,[121] and in 1908 that nothing in the Fourteenth Amendment precluded compelled self-incrimination.[122] Harlan dissented alone in these cases also.

The Court reversed the logic of these decisions in its opinion in *Gitlow v. New York*.[123] Gitlow, a left-wing radical, was convicted under a New York statute that made it a crime to advocate the forceful overthrow of government. Though the Supreme Court upheld his conviction, it also ruled without dissent that ''freedom of speech and of the press – which are protected by the First Amendment from abridgment by Congress – are among the fundamental personal rights and 'liberties' protected by the due process clause of the 14th Amendment from impairment by the states.''[124] Soon thereafter the Court added freedom of religion and assembly.[125]

---

[119]   110 U.S. 516 (1884).
[120]   *Chicago, B. & Q. Railway Co. v. Chicago*, 166 U.S. 226 (1897).
[121]   *Maxwell v. Dow*, 176 U.S 581.
[122]   *Twining v. New Jersey*, 211 U.S. 78.
[123]   268 U.S 652 (1925).
[124]   Id. at 666.
[125]   *Hamilton v. Regents of the University of California*, 293 U.S. 245 (1934); *De Jonge v. Oregon*, 299 U.S. 353 (1937).

The landmark incorporation decision came in the 1937 case of *Palko v. Connecticut*,[126] for here the Court set the standard for incorporation that survives to this day. Justice Benjamin Cardozo, writing for the majority, declared that the due process clause incorporated those provisions of the Bill of Rights that are "implicit in the concept of ordered liberty" or "so rooted in the traditions and conscience of our people as to be ranked as fundamental."[127] Cardozo believed those fundamental rights to include First Amendment freedoms, but not indictment by grand jury, self-incrimination, or – in the case at hand – double jeopardy.

On-the-Court criticisms of the doctrine of selective incorporation elaborated in *Palko* have come from justices who believe the doctrine protects too much and justices who believe the doctrine protects too little. The former group includes Justices Felix Frankfurter, John Marshall Harlan II, who was the grandson of the first Justice John Marshall Harlan, Abe Fortas, and Lewis Powell. None of these justices believed that the due process clause "incorporated" amendments of the Bill of Rights as such. Finding no textual support in the due process clause for incorporation, Frankfurter would limit the clause to voiding state behavior that "shocks the conscience."[128] In the case at hand, that behavior included beating a suspect and forcing him to vomit so that morphine pills could be retrieved. Harlan, Fortas, and Powell were more expansive in their views. To them, the Bill of Rights gave evidence of those fundamental rights protected by due process, but in no way did the due process clause "incorporate" those provisions with all their bag and baggage or ancillary rules. Thus to Harlan, due process protected the fundamental right to trial by jury, but the Sixth Amendment's right to trial by jury, which Harlan believed meant twelve persons, did not bind the states.

Alternatively, several justices, most notably the first John Marshall Harlan and Hugo Black, believed in total incorporation of the Bill of Rights. Harlan and Black based their position on explicit statements made by the framers of the Fourteenth Amendment as to its intent. Two statements in particular back their claims. First, Senator Jacob Howard (R-MI), the Senate floor manager, stated that among the privileges and immunities protected by the Amendment were the unspecified privileges protected by Article IV, Section 2, of the Constitution, plus "the personal rights guaranteed and secured by the first eight Amendments to the Constitution. . . . The great object of the first section of this amendment is, therefore, to restrain the power of the States, and compel them at all times to respect these fundamental guarantees."[129] Second, Congressman John Bingham (R-OH), the principle author of Section 1 of the Amendment, stated three years after ratification that the first eight amendments "never were limi-

---

[126]   302 U.S. 319.

[127]   Ibid. at 325.

[128]   *Rochin v. California*, 342 U.S. 165, 172 (1952).

[129]   *Congressional Globe*, 39th Congress, 1st Session, p. 2765.

tations upon the power of the states, until made so by the fourteenth amendment.''[130]

Although total incorporation has never received the support of a majority of justices, the selective incorporation doctrine of *Palko* has been so extended that today most of the provisions of the Bill of Rights have been incorporated: the First, Fourth, and Sixth Amendments; the Fifth Amendment, except for the right to indictment by grand jury; and the Eighth Amendment protection against cruel and unusual punishments. Not binding are the Eighth Amendment protections against excessive bail and fines (but probably only because no appropriate case has reached the Court); Amendments Two (right to bear arms), Three (right not to have soldiers quartered in private homes in peacetime) and Seven (right to jury trials in civil suits where the amount in controversy exceeds $20).

The remaining question about incorporation concerns rights not explicitly listed in the Bill of Rights. In *Griswold v. Connecticut*[131] the Court ruled that Amendments One, Three, Four, and Nine, in conjunction with the Fourteenth Amendment, created a right to privacy that states could not abridge. The decisional coalitions in this case did not follow the usual ideological divisions on the Court: The majority included Justice Harlan, who did not believe in incorporation per se, and excluded Justice Black, who did. Harlan believed that the Connecticut statute, which prohibited married couples from using birth control, simply violated due process of law. Black argued that although due process includes all of the Bill of Rights, it does not include a single right beyond those mentioned there.

First Amendment freedoms

The Court's initial concern with the First Amendment occurred as the result of anti-subversive legislation enacted by Congress during World War I. To determine whether the statements of persons convicted under these laws were constitutionally protected, the Court, speaking through Justice Holmes, formulated the clear and present danger doctrine.[132] The doctrine, however, provided no protection for the challenged communications because these were wartime cases and ''when a nation is at war many things that might be said in time of peace are such a hindrance to its effort that their utterance will not be endured so long as men fight.''[133]

In 1951 the Supreme Court upheld Smith Act convictions of Eugene Dennis and associates for organizing the Communist Party of the United States and

---

[130]   *Congressional Globe*, March 31, 1871, p. 86.
[131]   381 U.S. 479 (1965).
[132]   In *Schenck v. United States*, 294 U.S. 47 (1919). Also see *Frohwerk v. United States*, 249 U.S. 204 (1919); *Debs v. United States*, 249 U.S. 211 (1919); and *Abrams v. United States*, 250 U.S. 616 (1919).
[133]   249 U.S. 47, at 52.

advocating the overthrow of the government,[134] despite the fact that no overt acts of violence or revolution were alleged. In 1956, however, a more liberal Court ruled in *Pennsylvania v. Nelson*[135] that the Smith Act preempted the states' authority to regulate subversive activity, despite the fact that the Smith Act specifically states that "nothing in this title shall be held to take away or impair the jurisdiction of the courts of the several States, under the laws thereof."[136] The following year the Court struck at the House Un-American Activities Committee (HUAC) by invalidating a contempt conviction of a labor leader for refusing to name associates who had worked for the Communist Party,[137] and severely limited Smith Act prosecution of those who organized the Communist Party.[138]

Congress reacted by attempting to limit the Court's authority. In July 1957, Senator William Jenner (R-IN) introduced a bill to limit the Supreme Court's appellate jurisdiction over a variety of anti-subversive laws. The compromise bill passed by committee kept the Court's appellate jurisdiction intact with a minor exception, but reversed the *Nelson* and *Yates* decisions. When the bill reached the Senate floor in August 1958, it was defeated by a 49-to-41 vote.

Two of the Court's decisions helped reduce any further congressional threat. In *Barenblatt v. United States* the Court distinguished the *Watkins* decision and upheld the authority of HUAC.[139] The same day the Court limited the *Nelson* case and upheld the authority of states to investigate subversive activities aimed at them.[140] Both cases were decided 5 to 4, and in both cases Justice Harlan switched from his earlier liberal position. This helped reduce the pressure on the Court, much as Owen Roberts' switch had in 1937.

Not until 1969 did the Court give clear and present danger its plain meaning: Government may not "forbid or proscribe advocacy of the use of force or of law violation except where such advocacy is directed to inciting or producing imminent lawless action and is likely to incite or produce such action."[141]

Not all communication receives constitutional protection, however. Obscenity,[142] fighting words,[143] and defamatory statements[144] do not because the Court considers them to lack "redeeming social value." At the other extreme, the

---

[134]   *Dennis v. United States*, 341 U.S. 494.
[135]   350 U.S. 497.
[136]   Title 18, U.S. Code, Section 3231.
[137]   *Watkins v. United States*, 354 U.S. 178 (1957).
[138]   *Yates v. United States*, 354 U.S. 298 (1957).
[139]   360 U.S. 109 (1959).
[140]   *Uphaus v. Wyman*, 360 U.S. 72 (1959).
[141]   *Brandenburg v. Ohio*, 395 U.S. 444 (1969), at 447.
[142]   *Roth v. United States*, 354 U.S. 476 (1957); *Miller v. California*, 413 U.S. 15 (1973); *Jenkins v. Georgia*, 418 U.S. 153 (1974).
[143]   *Terminiello v. Chicago*, 337 U.S. 1 (1949); *Cohen v. California*, 403 U.S. 15 (1971).
[144]   *New York Times v. Sullivan*, 376 U.S. 254; *Gertz v. Welch*, 418 U.S. 323 (1974); *Time v. Hill*, 385 U.S. 374 (1967; *Cox Broadcasting Corp. v. Cohn*, 420 U.S. 469 (1975); *Dun & Bradstreet, Inc. v. Greenmoss Builders Inc.*, 472 U.S. 749 (1985).

Court generally accords political communication more protection than that dealing with other subjects.[145] Decisions of the Warren, Burger, and Rehnquist Courts have extended First Amendment protection to symbolic speech (e.g., demonstrations, flag burning),[146] the right to silence,[147] and commercial communications (e.g., advertising).[148]

Among the First Amendment's freedoms, the least subject to governmental restriction has been the free exercise of religion. Individuals acting under religious auspices may constitutionally engage in certain otherwise illegal activities. Thus, ordinances prohibiting door-to-door solicitation in order to protect the right to privacy must exclude those distributing or selling religious materials, and communities may not require a license of those so engaged. A constitutional right to proselytize exists. Courts may not ascertain the truth or falsity of religious beliefs, and unconventional beliefs and denominations are as protected as traditional ones. The Amish may not be compelled to send their children to high school. No one may be compelled to salute the flag or display a state-mandated ideological message inimical to his or her religious beliefs. Individuals may not be denied unemployment compensation for refusing to work on their Sabbath day or to manufacture weapons. Congress may constitutionally authorize religious institutions to affirmatively discriminate against women and nonbelievers.[149] Of course, not all action is immunized. Bigamy is a crime whether or not one is a Mormon, and Indians are forbidden to use peyote.[150]

---

[145] For example, *Brown v. Hartlage*, 456 U.S. 45 (1982). "It is designed and intended to remove governmental restraints from the arena of public discussion, putting the decision as to what views shall be voiced largely into the hands of each of us, in the hope that use of such freedom will ultimately produce a more capable citizenry and more perfect polity and in the belief that no other approach would comport with the premise of individual dignity and choice upon which our political system rests." *Cohen v. California*, 403 U.S. 15 (1971), at 24. "There can be no doubt that the expenditures at issue in this case [an expenditure of more than $1000 by an independent political committee to further the election of a presidential candidate who has opted to receive public financing of his general election campaign] produce speech at the core of the First Amendment." *Federal Election Commission v. National Conservative Political Action Committee*, 470 U.S. 480 (1985), at 493.

[146] *Edwards v. South Carolina*, 372 U.S. 229 (1963); *Tinker v. Des Moines School District*, 393 U.S. 503 (1969); *Boos v. Barry*, 99 L Ed 2d 333 (1988); *United States v. Eichman*, 110 L Ed 2d 287 (1990).

[147] *NAACP v. Alabama*, 357 U.S. 449 (1958); *Shelton v. Tucker*, 364 U.S. 479 (1960).

[148] *Virginia State Board of Pharmacy v. Virginia Citizens Consumer Council*, 425 U.S. 748 (1976); *Bates v. State Bar of Arizona*, 433 U.S. 350 (1977); *First National Bank of Boston v. Bellotti*, 435 U.S. 765 (1978).

[149] *Cantwell v. Connecticut*, 310 U.S. 296 (1940); *Murdock v. Pennsylvania*, 319 U.S. 105 (1943); *United States v. Ballard*, 322 U.S. 78 (1944); *Saia v. New York*, 334 U.S. 558 (1948); *Kunz v. New York*, 340 U.S. 290 (1951); *Cruz v. Beto*, 45 U.S. 319 (1972); *Wisconsin v. Yoder*, 406 U.S. 205 (1972); *West Virginia State Board of Education v. Barnette*, 319 U.S. 624 (1943); *Wooley v. Maynard*, 430 U.S. 705 (1977); *Thomas v. Review Board of the Indiana Employment Security Division*, 450 U.S. 707 (1981); *Hobbie v. Unemployment Appeals Comn.*, 480 U.S. 136 (1987); *Corporation of the Church of Latter-Day Saints v. Amos*, 97 L Ed 2d 273 (1987). For decisions producing an opposite result when religion was not present, see *Kovacs v.*

In establishment clause cases the Supreme Court originally echoed Thomas Jefferson's sentiment for a "wall of separation" between church and state. Thus the Warren Court voided organized classroom prayer[151] and devotional bible readings.[152] Public outrage was tremendous. A New York Congressman called the prayer decision "the most tragic decision in the history of the United States."[153] A Georgia Congressman declared that first the Court "put the Negroes in the schools – now they put God out."[154] Yet the Court persisted in keeping explicitly sectarian influences out of public schools. More than forty years after the Scopes Monkey Trial the Court voided an Arkansas law that prohibited the teaching of evolution at public schools or universities,[155] and nineteen years later, over the dissents of Rehnquist and Scalia, struck down a follow-up law that required schools to teach "creation science" if they also chose to teach evolution.[156]

The Court has accomodated secular aid to parochial schools more than it has allowed religious influences in public schools. States may provide bus transportation[157] and loan secular books to parochial school students. Although the Court struck down plans to supplement the salaries of parochial school teachers,[158] it does allow states to provide tuition tax credits to parents who send their children to private schools.[159]

All told, the law of the First Amendment appears rather well settled, notwithstanding the Court's confrontation of a steady stream of such litigation. Though these cases frequently generate much political controversy, as in the flag-burning cases,[160] typically judicial resolution not only cools the fervor that formerly affected them, but it does so with little fluctuation in the Court's established policies.

Criminal procedure

The Bill of Rights provides extensive protection for the rights of persons accused of crime, including a prohibition on unreasonable searches and seizures and self-

Cooper, 336 U.S. 77 (1949); Feiner v. New York, 340 U.S. 315 (1951); Breard v. Alexander, 341 U.S. 622 (1951).

[150] Reynolds v. United States, 98 U.S. 145 (1879); Native American Church of Navajoland v. Arizona Corporation Comn., 405 U.S. 901 (1972); Employment Division, Oregon Dept. of Human Resources v. Smith, 108 L Ed 2d 876 (1990).

[151] Engel v. Vitale, 370 U.S. 421 (1962).

[152] Abington School District v. Schempp, 374 U.S. 203 (1963).

[153] Quoted in Fred Friendly and Martha Elliott, The Constitution: That Delicate Balance (New York: Random House, 1984), p. 109.

[154] Ibid.

[155] Epperson v. Arkansas, 393 U.S. 97 (1968).

[156] Edwards v. Aquillard, 482 U.S. 578 (1987).

[157] Everson v. Board of Education, 330 U.S. 1 (1947).

[158] Lemon v. Kurtzman, 403 U.S. 602 (1971).

[159] Mueller v. Allen, 463 U.S. 388 (1983).

[160] Texas v. Johnson, 105 L Ed 2d 342 (1989); United States v. Eichman, 110 L Ed 2d 287 (1990).

incrimination, and the right to counsel and a ban on cruel and unusual punishment. For all but the last of these, the leading decisions date from the Warren Court (1953–1969).

The fundamental Fourth Amendment question concerns the use of evidence obtained by an unreasonable search and seizure. In 1914 the Supreme Court ruled that such evidence could not be admitted in federal trials. It argued that without such a rule, Fourth Amendment protections would be "of no value, and, so far as those thus placed are concerned, might as well be stricken from the Constitution."[161]

Because most crimes are state matters, this federal exclusionary rule was of minor significance. In 1949, though, the Supreme Court made the Fourth Amendment binding on the states.[162] The Court specifically ruled that Colorado violated the Fourth Amendment rights of Dr. Julius Wolf by illegally seizing his appointment book, which was then used to convict him of conspiracy to commit an abortion. Nevertheless, the majority opinion rejected the extension of the exclusionary rule to the states, thus upholding Wolf's conviction and a one-to-five-year prison term.

The Court overruled its 1949 decision twelve years later in the first of the Warren Court's many landmark criminal rights decisions. The case in question, *Mapp v. Ohio*,[163] involved the warrantless search of the home of Dollree Mapp, who was believed to be harboring a man wanted for bombing the house of an alleged numbers racketeer, future boxing promoter Don King. The police found no fugitive but did seize some pornographic pictures. Mapp was arrested and convicted of violating Ohio's obscenity statute. Speaking for a five-person majority, Justice Clark declared that the Constitution requires states to abide by the *Weeks* exclusionary rule, which precludes admission of illegally seized evidence at trial.

This controversial decision came under attack in the 1970s and 1980s by the more conservative Burger Court, four of whose members were chosen by President Nixon precisely because they did not support expansion of the rights of persons accused of crime. The rallying cry against the exclusionary rule was a dissenting statement by Judge (later Justice) Benjamin Cardozo: "The criminal is to go free because the constable has blundered."[164] The Burger Court refused to extend the rule to grand jury hearings,[165] civil cases,[166] habeas corpus relief,[167] or deportation hearings.[168] In 1984 the Court created a good-faith exception to the exclusionary rule, whereby illegally obtained evidence would not be sup-

---

[161] *Weeks v. United States*, 232 U.S. 383 (1914), at 393.
[162] *Wolf v. Colorado*, 338 U.S. 25.
[163] 367 U.S. 643 (1961).
[164] *People v. Defore*, 242 N.Y. 13 (1926), at 21.
[165] *United States v. Calandra*, 414 U.S. 338 (1974).
[166] *United States v. Janis*, 428 U.S. 433 (1976).
[167] *Stone v. Powell*, 428 U.S. 465 (1976).
[168] *Immigration and Naturalization Service v. Lopez-Mendoza*, 468 U.S. 1032 (1984).

pressed if the police acted in objective good faith.[169] Given the increasing conservatism of the Rehnquist Court, the exclusionary rule rests on extremely shaky
ground.

The Fifth Amendment's protection against self-incrimination was an under-
standable reaction against British attempts to coerce confessions, as in Star
Chamber proceedings. Prior to the 1960s the Supreme Court decided on a case-
by-case basis whether the accused's will was overborne by physical or psychological duress.[170] Such determinations were not easily made, especially when
''facts'' about the interrogation itself were often in dispute. Despair over the
case-by-case approach led the Court to seek a prophylactic rule that it hoped
would not put an end to involuntary confessions. The vehicle for this new rule
was the 1966 case, *Miranda v. Arizona*,[171] which more than any other typifies
Warren Court activism in the realm of criminal procedure. Under *Miranda*,
police must inform suspects prior to any custodial interrogation that (1) they
have the right to remain silent, (2) if they choose to speak anything they say
may be used against them, (3) they have the right to an attorney, and (4) if they
cannot afford an attorney one will be provided them.

Not surprisingly this rule came under attack by the Burger Court. It ruled in
two cases that though incriminating statements made without *Miranda* warnings
could not be used in the prosecution's case-in-chief, they could be used to
impeach the credibility of witnesses if they took the stand and contradicted
anything they had said prior to receiving their *Miranda* warnings.[172] In 1984 the
Court created a public safety exception to *Miranda*, holding that the accused's
response to a question about the whereabouts of a gun hidden in a grocery store
could be used in evidence even though no warnings had been given.[173] Despite
these exceptions, the *Miranda* rule itself remains in place. In 1990, by a 6-to–
2 vote, the Rehnquist Court not only upheld *Miranda*, but also expanded it by
holding that once a suspect requests a lawyer, no future police-instigated interrogations may take place without the lawyer present, regardless of whether the
suspect subsequently waives the right or not.[174]

The right to counsel received strong support from the Court as early as 1932.
In *Powell v. Alabama*,[175] the Court required the states to provide indigent criminal
defendants with counsel under certain conditions. The case involved seven il-
literate black youths who, after a fight with several white youths on a train, were
falsely accused of raping two white girls. In a lynch-mob atmosphere, the youths
were convicted in a series of one-day trials. The presiding judge had appointed

[169]   *United States v. Leon*, 468 U.S. 897.
[170]   For example, *Brown v. Mississippi* 297 U.S. 278 (1936); *Ashcraft v. Tennessee* 322 U.S. 143
        (1944); *Fikes v. Alabama* 352 U.S. 191 (1957); *Jackson v. Denno* 378 U.S. 368 (1964).
[171]   384 U.S. 436.
[172]   *Harris v. New York*, 401 U.S. 222 (1971); *Oregon v. Hass*, 420 U.S. 714 (1975.).
[173]   *New York v. Quarles*, 467 U.S. 649.
[174]   *Minnick v. Mississippi*, 112 L Ed 2d 489 (1990).
[175]   287 U.S. 45 (1932).

all members of the local bar to defend them at their arraignment, but no one stepped forward to do so until the day of the trial. In reversing their convictions, the Supreme Court noted that

> during perhaps the most critical period of the proceedings against these defendants, that is to say, from the time of their arraignment until the beginning of their trial, when consultation, thorough-going investigation and preparation were vitally important, the defendants did not have the aid of counsel in any real sense, although they were as much entitled to such aid during that period as at the trial itself.[176]

The Court not only declared that the right to counsel begins at arraignment, but they also ruled that given the capital nature of the offense and the status of the defendants, a constitutional right to appointed counsel existed.[177] *Powell* further suggested that all indigent defendants should be afforded counsel; nevertheless, the ruling limited itself to capital cases where the defendants were unable to defend themselves because of illiteracy or other extenuating circumstances. In 1942 the Court ruled that the Constitution provided no unequivocal right to appointed counsel, only a right conditioned on the facts of each case existed.[178]

The Warren Court overruled the 1942 decision in 1963. The case, *Gideon v. Wainright*,[179] involved the trial and conviction of an individual for breaking and entering a pool hall with intent to commit a crime. Gideon had requested an attorney at his trial but was refused because Alabama only required appointed counsel in capital cases. The justices ruled unanimously that states must provide indigent defendants with appointed counsel in all felony cases.

The *Gideon* decision has fared reasonably well under the Burger and Rehnquist Courts. In 1972 the justices ruled that no indigent person could be jailed without court-appointed counsel or an intelligent waiver thereof.[180] On the other hand, whereas the Warren Court had pushed the entitlement to counsel back from the time of indictment to the time of arrest,[181] and extended the right to include the presence of an attorney at line-ups,[182] the Burger Court declined to combine the two rules and extend the right to counsel to pre-indictment lineups.[183] The 5-to-4 decision included all four Nixon appointees within the majority.

The most frequently litigated Eighth Amendment issue during the past twenty years has been the constitutionality of the death penalty. Unlike the *Mapp*,

---

[176] Id. at 57.
[177] Alabama subsequently retried four of the defendants, all of whom were again found guilty. Charlie Weems received a 75-year sentence in 1937 and was paroled in 1943; Andrew Wright received a 99-year sentence in 1937 and was paroled in 1944; Haywood Patterson received a 75-year sentence in 1936, escaped prison in 1948 and was later arrested and convicted for manslaughter; and Clarence Norris was convicted on retrial, sentenced to death, but had his sentence commuted to life. He was paroled in 1944.
[178] *Betts v. Brady*, 316 U.S. 455.
[179] 372 U.S. 335.
[180] *Argersinger v. Hamlin*, 407 U.S. 25.
[181] *Escobedo v. Illinois*, 378 U.S. 478 (1964).
[182] *United States v. Wade*, 388 U.S. 218 (1967).
[183] *Kirby v. Illinois*, 406 U.S. 682 (1972).

Miranda, or *Gideon* decisions, not until the Burger Court were latitudinal interpretations of the clause made.

The Court first upheld the death penalty in 1878,[184] and in 1890 it upheld electrocution on the mistaken assumption that the electric chair produced instantaneous and painless death.[185] Punishments are cruel and unusual, declared the Court, when they involve torture or a lingering death. In 1947 the Court even upheld the re-electrocution of a black youth who survived his first appointment with the chair.[186]

No successful challenge to the death penalty occurred before 1972. Then, in *Furman v. Georgia*,[187] a highly fractured Court declared unconstitutional capital punishment imposed at the untrammeled discretion of jurors. Justices Marshall and Brennan thought the death penalty always unconstitutional: Marshall because it is "morally unacceptable to the people of the United States at this time in their history",[188] and Brennan, not only because "its rejection by contemporary society is total," but because it is "severe," "degrading," and fails to respect murderers for "their intrinsic worth as human beings."[189] Douglas thought the death penalty as applied discriminated against minorities and the poor, a contention that the Court rejected in 1987. Stewart and White, without emphasizing race or class, also believed the death penalty to be cruel and unusual because it was arbitrarily and capriciously imposed on some and not on others. Along with Douglas, they reserved judgment on the constitutionality of mandatory death sentences. The four Nixon appointees dissented, claiming no constitutional violation in the death penalty in general or as imposed.

In response to *Furman*, thirty-five states and Congress reimposed the death penalty, some making it mandatory, others imposing guidelines for juries. In July 1976 the Court responded by declaring mandatory capital punishment to be just as arbitrary as the totally discretionary death penalties struck down in *Furman*,[190] but upholding the death penalty if juries were provided guidelines.[191] Brennan and Marshall dissented, again arguing that death is always cruel and unusual. Given overwhelming legislative support and massive public approval,[192] Marshall nevertheless argued that if only others knew as much about capital punishment as he did, they would find it "shocking, unjust, and unacceptable."[193]

The biggest blow to death penalty abolitionists since 1976 occurred when the

[184] *Wilkerson v. Utah*, 99 U.S. 130.
[185] *In re Kemmler*, 136 U.S. 436.
[186] *Louisiana ex rel. Francis v. Resweber*, 329 U.S. 459 (1947).
[187] 408 U.S. 238.
[188] Id. at 360.
[189] Id. at 305.
[190] *Woodson v. North Carolina*, 428 U.S. 280.
[191] *Gregg v. Georgia*, 428 U.S. 153.
[192] Thomas R. Marshall, *Public Opinion and the Supreme Court* (Boston: Unwin Hyman, 1989).
[193] *Gregg v. Georgia*, 428 U.S. 153 (1976), at 232.

Rehnquist Court rejected a claim that the death penalty was imposed in a racially discriminatory manner.[194] The abolitionists based their major claim not on the race of the convict, but on the race of the victim. A Georgia study of 2,000 murders found that killing a white person made one 4.3 times more likely to receive the death penalty than killing a black person, even after controlling statistically for dozens of other factors. The Court nevertheless ruled that even if the death penalty was discriminatorily imposed, petitioners would have to prove intentional bias.

The Rehnquist Court has continued to support the death penalty, upholding the states' right to apply it to a retarded adult with a mental age of six and a half years,[195] and to a youth of sixteen at the time of the murder.[196] The Court also upheld the death penalty in the context of the felony murder rule – for example, for two sons who helped their father escape from jail and kidnap a family, even though the father murdered the kidnap victims without the direct aid or prior knowledge of his sons.[197]

Equal protection

With its decision in *Plessy v. Ferguson*,[198] the equal protection clause became a dead letter insofar as black America was concerned. The separate but equal doctrine that *Plessy* formulated paid no heed to plain meaning; courts focused only on separation, not on whether the governmental facilities were "equal." Thus, the Court upheld the discontinuance of black high schools, but not white ones, on the basis that an injunction against funding the white schools would only make matters worse and, in any event, not help black students.[199] Similarly, the Court sustained segregation in all schools, public as well as private, for the nocuously paralogical reason that the private schools that the state chartered were creatures of the state to which the equal protection clause did not apply.[200]

Not until 1954 did the Court appreciably temper its racist hypocrisy by over-ruling separate but equal and replacing it one year later with a requirement that school desegregation proceed "with all deliberate speed."[201] Mindful that its decision almost caused the South to rise again, evidenced by a vogue in hooded sheets and burning crosses, the Court gave the federal district courts primary responsibility for applying its mandate. Fifteen years later, the Burger Court's

---

[194] *McCleskey v. Kemp*, 481 U.S. 279 (1987).
[195] *Penry v. Lynaugh*, 106 L Ed 2d 256 (1989). The Supreme Court reversed the death sentence because the trial court judge did not inform the jury that it could consider the defendant's retardation a mitigating factor.
[196] *Stanford v. Kentucky*, 106 L Ed 2d 306 (1989).
[197] *Tison v. Arizona*, 481 U.S. 137 (1987).
[198] 163 U.S. 537 (1986).
[199] *Cumming v. Richmond County Board of Education*, 175 U.S. 528 (1899).
[200] *Berea College v. Kentucky*, 211 U.S. 45 (1908).
[201] *Brown v. Board of Education*, 347 U.S. 484 (1954); 349 U.S. 294 (1955).

first formal decision capped this phase of desegregation by ordering immediate termination of dual school systems.[202] But desegregation in the South did not produce desegregation in the North. Violations of equal protection require purposeful governmental action. None occurs where discrimination is only the unintended effect of governmental action, or where no state action at all has occurred.[203] Moreover, if a Northern district does engage in intentional discrimination (e.g., Detroit), a judicially ordered remedy may not extend beyond the boundary of the district or districts that acted unconstitutionally.[204]

The Court has complemented the limited reach of equal protection with equally restrictive limitations on the action that the state and federal governments may *voluntarily* take under other constitutional provisions to alleviate the persistence of racism in American society. Although allegations of color-blindness are often asserted as a constitutional defense against preferential treatment of blacks and other racial minorities, only four justices in the Court's history have concurred – much less a majority in any given decision.[205] To pass constitutional muster, affirmative action programs may only set goals, not quotas. Race may only be one among a number of factors that determine eligibility. Moreover, the Court presumes the program unconstitutional unless the responsible governmental officials can show that it is narrowly tailored to remedy past evidence of discrimination.[206]

Needless to say, what is sauce for the black goose is not sauce for the white gander. Affirmative action programs – including those with quotas – that benefit whites do not violate the equal protection clause. Thus, public educational institutions typically give preferential treatment to children of alumni; seniority systems may constitutionally contain a last hired, first fired policy; and the states

---

[202] *Alexander v. Holmes County Board of Education*, 396 U.S. 19 (1969). The Burger Court's ruling was presaged by *Bradley v. Richmond School Board*, 382 U.S. 103 (1965), in which the Warren Court declared that "delays in desegregating school systems are no longer tolerable," at 105.

[203] As in a civil service examination where far more blacks than whites fail to pass. See *Washington v. Davis*, 426 U.S. 229 (1976), for an example. Housing segregation is commonly cited as an example of non-governmental or private discrimination, notwithstanding community zoning ordinances. On the other hand, the equal protection clause does reach some private acts of discrimination if they require judicial action for enforcement – for example, restrictive housing covenants (*Shelley v. Kraemer*, 334 U.S. 1 [1948]) or a white mother's loss of child custody because after her divorce she married a black (*Palmore v. Sidoti*, 466 U.S. 429 [1984]).

[204] *Milliken v. Bradley*, 418 U.S. 717 (1974).

[205] The original Justice Harlan in his dissent in *Plessy v. Ferguson*; Justice Stewart in a dissent in *Fullilove v. Klutznick*, 448 U.S. (1980), at 522, that then Justice Rehnquist joined; and Justice Scalia in his concurring opinion in *Richmond v. Croson Co.*, 102 L Ed 2d 854 (1989), at 899–900.

   President Bush's second nominee, Clarence Thomas, will likely join this group when an opportunity presents itself.

[206] *Regents of the University of California v. Bakke*, 438 U.S. 265 (1978); *Wygant v. Jackson Board of Education*, 476 U.S. 267 (1986); *Richmond v. Croson Co.*, 102 L Ed 2d 854 (1989).

may subsidize suburban school students much more generously than those who live in inner-city ghettos or rural slums.[207]

Apart from affirmative action, American racism is markedly less systematic than it was during the heyday of white supremacy and Jim Crow. Congress has enacted a number of major civil rights laws that have effectively outlawed discrimination in places of public accommodations[208] and in voting,[209] and to some limited extent in housing.[210] Although the Court delayed resolution of the most pathological of white America's racial fears – miscegenation – for thirteen years after it overruled the separate but equal doctrine, when it did void prohibitions on interracial marriage, it did so on a dual basis – due process as well as equal protection – in a most felicitously titled unanimous opinion: *Loving v. Virginia*.[211]

The Court has offset somewhat the niggardly treatment accorded blacks by extending the equal protection clause to other groups and classes. Notwithstanding what the framers of the Fourteenth Amendment may have intended, women, aliens, indigents, illegitimates, the mentally ill, the physically handicapped, and the elderly may not be subject to unreasonably discriminatory governmental action. And although the courts do not scrutinize laws and policies that classify people on these bases – with the exception of state laws that discriminate on the basis of alienage[212] – with the closeness imparted to racial classifications, all have received a measure of judicial inspection. With the exception of indigents, on whom the Warren Court looked favorably, beneficial treatment has primarily resulted from the policy making of the moderately conservative Burger Court. Women, for example, were "regarded as the center of home and family life" in the Warren Court's only sex discrimination case and as such properly subject to ostensibly protective disabling legislation – in this case automatic exemption from jury service, notwithstanding the constitutional right to an impartial jury.[213] Not until 1975 did the Court admit – over the dissent of Justice Rehnquist – that "no longer is the female destined solely for the home and the rearing of the family, and only the male for the marketplace and the world of ideas."[214]

---

[207] *Regents of the University of California v. Bakke*, 438 U.S. 265 (1978); *Firefighters Local Union v. Stotts*, 467 U.S. 561 (1984); *San Antonio Independent School District v. Rodriguez*, 411 U.S. 1 (1973).

[208] *Heart of Atlanta Motel v. United States*, 379 U.S. 241 (1964); *Katzenbach v. McClung*, 379 U.S. 294 (1964).

[209] *South Carolina v. Katzenbach*, 383 U.S. 301 (1966).

[210] *Jones v. Mayer Co.*, 392 U.S. 409 (1968).

[211] 388 U.S. 1 (1967). On the eve of the Court's decisions in *Brown v. Board of Education*, in the mid-1950s, approximately three dozen states had criminalized interracial marriage, thereby providing rather strong evidence – if any were needed – that legally sanctioned white supremacy flourished throughout the United States and not just in the South.

[212] *Bernal v. Fainter*, 467 U.S. 216 (1984).

[213] *Hoyt v. Florida*, 368 U.S. 57 (1961), at 62.

[214] *Stanton v. Stanton*, 421 U.S. 7, at 14–15.

Reapportionment

Despite the Warren Court's groundbreaking decisions in civil rights and criminal procedure, Chief Justice Warren believed that "reapportionment, not only of state legislatures, but of representative government in this country, is perhaps the most important issue we have had before the Supreme Court."[215]

Prior to the Warren Court's decisions on reapportionment, the Supreme Court had let stand arrangements whereby some congressional or state legislative districts might have ten or twenty times the population of other districts. For instance, in *Colegrove v. Green*[216] the Supreme Court dismissed an Illinois congressional reapportionment suit. The judgment of the Court, written by Felix Frankfurter, ruled reapportionment a nonjusticiable political question best solved by the democratic process. He admonished the courts "not to enter this political thicket."[217]

Reliance on democratic political processes is singularly poor advice when the problem at hand is minority control of that process through malapportionment. The 20 percent of the population that controls 55 percent of the legislative seats will not likely vote to undo their domination. With a liberal Warren Court majority firmly established, the Court ruled that federal courts can take jurisdiction over reapportionment suits.[218] Two years later the Court decided the merits of federal and state reapportionment cases. In *Wesberry v. Sanders*[219] the Court declared that the Constitution's command that representatives be chosen "by the People of the several States" means that each person's vote must be worth the same – in other words, one person, one vote. Thus, congressional districts within a given state must contain an equal number of people. Then, in *Reynolds v. Sims*,[220] the Court ruled that state legislative districts must be of approximately equal size. Despite the example of the U.S. Senate, even the upper house of state legislatures had to be apportioned on a one-person, one-vote basis.[221] The Court later extended its ruling to virtually all governmental units, such as school districts and sewer boards.[222]

The Court today allows different standards for national and state reapportionment. In *Karcher v. Daggett*[223] the Supreme Court overturned a congressional reapportionment where the difference between the largest district in New Jersey and the smallest was a mere seven-tenths of one percent. Yet the Court has

---

[215]   Quoted in David W. Rohde and Harold J. Spaeth, *Supreme Court Decision Making* (San Francisco: W.H. Freeman, 1976), p. 178.
[216]   328 U.S. 549 (1946).
[217]   Id. at 556.
[218]   *Baker v. Carr*, 369 U.S. 186 (1962).
[219]   376 U.S. 1 (1964).
[220]   377 U.S. 533 (1964).
[221]   *Lucas v. Forty-Fourth General Assembly*, 377 U.S. 713 (1964).
[222]   *Avery v. Midland County*, 390 U.S. 474 (1968); *Hadley v. Junior College District*, 397 U.S. 50 (1970).
[223]   462 U.S. 735 (1983).

consistently upheld state legislative districting with disparities approaching double figures.[224] The Court even upheld an 86 percent deviation in order to allow Wyoming's least populous county a single district.[225] Future battles will no doubt center on the Court's 1986 decision that gerrymandering – the drawing of legislative districts to favor one political party over another – is justiciable.[226] Whatever problems Frankfurter foresaw in requiring equal-population districts will be de minimis compared with a requirement that district lines not favor one or another political party.

The right to privacy

A number of constitutional provisions address the right to privacy, though not in so many words: the ban on unreasonable searches and seizures, the self-incrimination clause, the First and Ninth Amendments, and the due process clauses of the Fifth and Fourteenth Amendments. Among the most important privacy rights are those grounded in the freedom of association safeguarded by the First Amendment and the substantive due process liberties that pertain to marriage, family relationships, abortion, sexual activities, and the right to die.

The Court has positioned the right to associational privacy above human equality insofar as bona fide private organizations are concerned. "Members only" policies are constitutional as long as they are not hung on places of public accommodations or places that do not engage in intimate private relationships, such as large-membership all-male service clubs.[227] Consequently, B'nai B'rith need not accept non-Jews or the Knights of Columbus non-Catholics. The Society of Mayflower Descendants may deny membership to members of the Mafia, and the Daughters of the American Revolution may exclude the significant others of those who invaded Grenada and Panama in the 1980s. Social, sexual, racial, and religious exclusiveness – snobbery, if you will – is constitutionally protected for those engaged in truly private affairs, but government may mandate openness otherwise.

A landmark decision concerning marital privacy and family rights is *Griswold v. Connecticut*, in which the Court voided "an uncommonly silly law" that made it a crime for any person – including married couples – to use, assist, or counsel another to use "any drug, medicinal article or instrument for the purpose of preventing conception."[228] Relying somewhat on the Ninth Amendment, as

---

[224] *Mahan v. Howell*, 410 U.S. 315 (1973), upholding a 16.4 percent deviation; *Gaffney v. Cummings*, 412 U.S. 735 (1973), upholding a 7.8 percent deviation; and *White v. Regester*, 412 U.S. 755 (1973), upholding a 9.9 percent deviation.

[225] *Brown v. Thompson*, 462 U.S. 835 (1983).

[226] *Davis v. Bandemer*, 478 U.S. 109.

[227] Compare *Moose Lodge v. Irvis*, 407 U.S. 163 (1972), with the two Rehnquist Court sex discrimination cases, *Rotary International v. Rotary Club of Duarte*, 95 L Ed 2d 474 (1987); and *New York State Club Assn. v. New York City*, 101 L Ed 2d 1 (1988).

[228] 381 U.S. 479 (1965), at 480. The reference to the silliness of the law appears in Justice Stewart's dissent, at 527.

well as the due process clause of the Fourteenth Amendment, the majority stated that "specific guarantees in the Bill of Rights have penumbras, formed by emanations from those guarantees that help give them life and substance. . . . Various guarantees create zones of privacy," and concluded:

We deal with a right of privacy older than the Bill of Rights – older than our political parties, older than our school system. Marriage is a coming together for better or for worse, hopefully enduring, and intimate to the degree of being sacred. It is an association that promotes a way of life, not causes; a harmony in living, not political faiths; a bilateral loyalty, not commercial or social projects. Yet it is an association for as noble a purpose as any involved in our prior decisions.[229]

One might think that such stirring language – atypical of a majority opinion – would lay the issue to rest, but that was not the case. Seven years later the Court confronted a law enacted by Connecticut's neighbor, Massachusetts, that made the use of contraceptives by unmarried persons a felony. The State's Supreme Court explained that the law's "plain purpose is to protect purity, to preserve chastity, to encourage continence and self restraint, to defend the sanctity of the home, and thus to engender in the State and nation a virile and virtuous race of men and women."[230] Over the dissent of Chief Justice Burger, the majority held that "it would be plainly unreasonable to assume that Massachusetts has prescribed pregnancy and the birth of an unwanted child as punishment for fornication."[231]

On the other hand, the Court has clearly established that the fundamental rights encompassed by the right to privacy include childbirth, and that governments are free to promote policies toward that end notwithstanding the social and economic costs of a burgeoning population, unwanted and abused children, and homelessness. Accordingly, states may not refuse to issue a marriage license to persons who have failed to pay child support or whose children have become public charges, but states may promote and fully subsidize childbirth while refusing to pay for or provide public facilities for abortions.[232]

Notwithstanding the fundamental character of the rights surrounding child and family relationships, the Court has upheld the constitutionality of compulsory sterilization laws. "In order to prevent our being swamped with incompetence," said Justice Holmes, "It is better for all the world, if instead of waiting to execute degenerate offspring for crime, or to let them starve for their imbecility, society can prevent those who are manifestly unfit from continuing their kind. . . . Three

---

[229]   Id. at 484, 486.

[230]   *Eisenstadt v. Baird*, 405 U.S. 438 (1972), at 448. The opposition of the Roman Catholic Church prevented Massachusetts and Connecticut from repealing these legacies from their Puritanical past. William Cohen and John Kaplan, *Constitutional Law: Civil Liberty and Individual Rights*, 2d ed. (Mineola, NY: Foundation Press, 1982), p. 603.

[231]   405 U.S., at 448.

[232]   *Zablocki v. Redhail*, 434 U.S. 374 (1978); *Maher v. Roe*, 432 U.S. 464 (1977); *Poelker v. Doe*, 432 U.S. 519 (1977); *Webster v. Reproductive Health Services*, 106 L Ed 2d 410 (1989).

generations of imbeciles are enough."[233] At the time Holmes wrote, capital punishment was utilized with considerably greater frequency than it is today, and public welfare was not available as a way of life. Nonetheless, public squeamishness has largely made compulsory sterilization a dead letter, even though at least ten states authorize their judges to sterilize the mentally retarded.[234]

The right of a woman to secure an abortion without undue governmental interference has existed since the Burger Court's decision in *Roe v. Wade*.[235] The right, a classic example of substantive due process, rests among the liberties that government may not deprive persons of. The decision, an extreme example of an opinion that takes the form of judicial legislation, also exemplifies a rarity among court-made rules: one whose application is absolutely pellucid. Relying on the common law and the plain meaning of the operative word in the due process clause, the Court held that the constitutional right to life only protects persons, and personhood commences with birth.[236] When life begins – with the production of sperm, or an egg, at conception, at implantation, or at some later point – is constitutionally irrelevant. Though one may correctly argue that an all but delivered fetus is better endowed with potential life than a person born a vegetable, or a raving maniac, or a senescent victim of Alzheimer's disease, and that the Court's equation of personhood with birth is arbitrary, it is indisputable that the latter have been born, and a fetus by definition has not. Willynilly, the latter are persons protected by the Constitution.

Roe v. Wade was by no means the only instance in which the Burger Court deviated from the cautious conservatism that generally characterized its decisions. In *O'Connor v. Donaldson*,[237] the justices addressed the question of whether government may involuntarily confine without treatment persons who are mentally ill. The Court's unanimously negative answer rapidly depopulated the nation's mental hospitals and insane asylums into which American society had traditionally dumped the elderly, the poor, and the friendless. Institutionalizing those who are dangerous neither to themselves nor to others and who are capable of surviving in the outside world indisputably deprives them of liberty in violation of due process. The direct result of this decision has been the appearance of street people, particularly in larger cities. And though these £ersons offend the sensibilities of the tender-hearted,

---

[233] *Buck v. Bell*, 274 U.S. 200 (1927), at 207.
[234] Rorie Sherman, "Involuntary Sterilization Gains," *National Law Journal*, March 7, 1988, p. 3. Stephen Jay Gould argues that the Buck in the case of *Buck v. Bell* was not mentally defective, and that her case was rather "a matter of sexual morality and social deviance. . . . Who really cared whether . . . [she was] of normal intelligence; she was the illegitimate child of an illegitimate woman. Two generations of bastards are enough." "Carrie Buck's Daughter," 7 *Natural History* 14 (July 1984), at 17.
[235] 410 U.S. 113 (1973).
[236] Id. at 157–159.
[237] 422 U.S. 563 (1975). Also see *Addington v. Texas*, 441 U.S. 418 (1979); *Youngberg v. Romeo*, 457 U.S. 307 (1982).

the mere presence of mental illness does not disqualify a person from preferring his home [or the street] to the comforts of an institution. Moreover, while the State may arguably confine a person to save him from harm, incarceration is rarely if ever a necessary condition for raising the living standards of those capable of surviving safely in freedom . . .[238]

But not all activities that persons engage in under the rubric of privacy or personal autonomy are equally protected. The Burger Court, in one of its last decisions, sharply distinguished conventional sexual activities from those engaged in by consenting adult homosexuals. Only choices fundamental to heterosexual life – marriage, procreation, child rearing, and family relationships – are constitutionally protected. Although the law at issue flatly banned oral and anal sex regardless of marital status or sexual orientation, the majority rewrote the statute to apply only to homosexuals and, as so construed, justified its ruling because "proscriptions against that conduct have ancient roots" and at the time the Fourteenth Amendment was ratified "all but five of the 37 States in the Union had criminal sodomy laws."[239]

On the next privacy issue that the Court confronted, the right to die, the majority contradicted its sodomy case assertion that "the Court is most vulnerable and comes nearest to illegitimacy when it deals with judge-made constitutional law having little or no cognizable roots in the language or design of the constitution,"[240] by holding that persons who make their wishes clearly known have a constitutional right to terminate life-sustaining care: "The principle that a competent person has a constitutionally protected liberty interest in refusing unwanted medical treatment may be inferred from our prior decisions."[241]

THE SUPREME COURT AND THE DISTRIBUTION OF POWER, 1936–1991

The movement toward a civil liberties agenda that began with the *Carolene Products* case did not end the Supreme Court's role as arbiter of power among the three branches of government. Five cases dealing with executive, legislative, and judicial powers during this period deserve special attention because of their likely impact on future national controversies: *United States v. Curtiss-Wright Export Corporation*,[242] *Korematsu v. United States*,[243] *Youngstown Sheet and*

---

[238] *O'Connor v. Donaldson*, 422 U.S., at 575.
[239] *Bowers v. Hardwick*, 478 U.S. 186 (1986), at 200–201, 214–216, 190, 192, 193. In rebuttal, one of the dissenting opinions cogently observed that "neither history nor tradition could save a law prohibiting miscegenation from constitutional attack," even though the states treated it as a crime akin to sodomy. 478 U.S., at 216.
[240] Id. at 194. Three justices were common to both majorities: Rehnquist, O'Connor, and White.
[241] *Cruzan v. Director, Missouri Dept. of Health*, 111 L Ed 2d 224 (1990), at 241. Although the Court ruled that the petitioning party failed to provide clear and convincing evidence of her desire at trial, as Missouri law required, on remand the trial judge allowed the plaintiff's family to cease pumping chemical nutrition and water into her body. Six months after the Supreme Court's ruling, she died.
[242] 299 U.S. 304 (1936).
[243] 323 U.S. 214 (1944).

Tube Co. v. Sawyer,[244] *United States v. Nixon,*[245] and *Immigration and Naturalization Service v. Chadha.*[246]

The Curtiss-Wright Case

A joint resolution of Congress had authorized the President to prohibit arms sales to warring Paraguay and Bolivia. Following its indictment for violating the embargo, Curtiss-Wright sued to have the resolution invalidated as an unlawful delegation of power to the executive. The Court's decision not only upheld the resolution, but broadly defined the foreign affairs powers of the President. Distinguishing domestic powers, which are delegated to the national government by the Constitution, from foreign powers, which reside wholly in the national government, the justices held that within the national government the foreign powers vest almost exclusively in the presidency.

In this vast external realm with its important, complicated, delicate and manifold problems, the President alone has the power to speak or listen as representative of the nation. He *makes* treaties with the advice and consent of the Senate; but he alone negotiates. Into the field of negotiation the Senate cannot intrude; and Congress itself is powerless to invade it.[247]

Given the breadth of his foreign powers, the Court suggested that the President could have imposed the embargo even without Congressional authorization.

It is important to keep in mind that we are here dealing not alone with an authority vested in the President by an exertion of legislative power, but with such an authority plus the very delicate plenary and exclusive power of the President as sole organ of the federal government in the field of international relations – a power that does not require as a basis of its exercise an act of Congress . . .[248]

The broad dicta of *Curtiss-Wright* were progressively tested in both the Japanese internment and the Steel Seizure cases.

The Japanese internment cases

Two months after Japan attacked Pearl Harbor, President Roosevelt issued an executive order allowing the military to remove American citizens of Japanese descent from the West Coast and place them in "relocation centers." Congress ratified the President's order the following month.[249] No similar actions were

---

[244]   343 U.S. 579 (1952).
[245]   418 U.S. 683 (1974).
[246]   462 U.S. 919 (1983).
[247]   299 U.S. 304, at 319.
[248]   Id. at 319–320.
[249]   The Japanese in Hawaii were not interned, even though Hawaii had been attacked at Pearl Harbor. Unlike the Japanese on the West Coast, those in Hawaii provided the unskilled and "stoop" labor eseential to the operation of the Hawaiian economy that self-respecting whites would not perform. Bigotry thus took a back seat to economic well-being.

taken against German-Americans or Italian-Americans, even though the United States had also declared war against those nations. Indeed, no charges of disloyalty or subversion were ever filed against Japanese-Americans, many of whom fought bravely for their country in World War II. The pressure for the relocation came not from any realistic fear of an invasion, but from members of California farm associations envious of the fertile land owned and cultivated by Japanese-Americans, and from the state's then governor who, eleven years later, became Chief Justice of the United States – Earl Warren.

The Supreme Court upheld Roosevelt's orders in two decisions. In *Hirabayashi v. United States*[250] the justices sustained the dusk-to-dawn curfew imposed on Japanese-Americans by the military under the President's power as commander-in-chief. Far more damaging was the decision in *Korematsu v. United States*, which upheld their detention. Though noting a difference between the curfew in *Hirabayashi* and the relocation in *Korematsu*, the majority declared itself "unable to conclude that it was beyond the war power of Congress and the Executive to exclude those of Japanese ancestry from the West Coast war area at the time they did."[251] The decision, very much the law of the land today, means that a mere allegation of military necessity suffices to warrant the summary incarceration of any individual or group without any judicial determination of wrongdoing whatsoever.[252]

The steel seizure case

Whereas *Curtiss-Wright* involved presidential action subsequent to congressional authorization, and *Korematsu* involved presidential action followed by congressional ratification, the steel seizure case, *Youngstown Sheet and Tube Co. v. Sawyer*, involved unilateral presidential action that expressly contradicted congressional policy. Here, finally, the Court placed limits on presidential action related to foreign affairs.

The relevant facts are these: In December 1951, during the Korean War, the United Steelworkers Union announced plans to strike. Several attempts at federal

---

[250]   320 U.S. 81 (1943).
[251]   323 U.S. 214 (1944), at 217–218.
[252]   On the eve of the Persian Gulf War, reports such as the following appeared in the media: "Federal law enforcement agencies have . . . vastly stepped up intelligence-gathering activities directed at Iraqis and other allied Arab groups in this country, Administration officials said today. . . . Today, the Federal Bureau of Investigation ordered its agents throughout the country to interview business and community leaders of Arab descent, asking for information about possible terrorist activities by Iraqis . . . Some Arab representatives expressed the fear that a war could excite the same kind of hysteria that led Government officials to intern more than 110,000 Americans of Japanese ancentry during World War II, but officials insisted that no such plans had been considered or approved."

"Scrutiny of Iraqis Stepped Up in U.S.'', *New York Times*, January 8, 1991, p. A1. Note that the officials referred to in the last sentence of the quotation did not suggest that any such plan would be unconstitutional or illegal.

mediation failed. On April 4, 1952, the union announced an April 9 strike deadline. Because of the indispensability of steel production to the war effort, President Truman issued an executive order directing the Secretary of Commerce to take possession of the steel mills and keep them running. Under the United States flag, the workers returned to work.

Justice Black's majority opinion noted that the Constitution grants "all legislative powers" to Congress, not the President. As Congress had enacted no law authorizing such seizures, the President could not be acting under his constitutional authority to take "care that the laws be faithfully executed." Nor could the action be authorized under the President's authority as commander-in-chief, as the steel mills were not part of a theater of war. Had Truman's actions been upheld, it is not clear what limits, if any, would exist on unilateral presidential action in matters related to foreign affairs.

The Watergate tapes case

The President can conflict not only with Congress, as in the steel seizure case, but also with the judiciary. Unfortunately for the President, the judiciary itself decides the outcome of such conflicts.

On March 1, 1974, a grand jury indicted seven top aides to President Nixon for activities related to the Watergate burglary and coverup. Nixon himself was named as an unindicted co-conspirator. Following the indictments, Watergate Special Prosecutor Leon Jaworski sought and obtained a subpoena ordering Nixon to provide him with tape recordings and other evidence. Nixon refused to supply all the materials requested. The case quickly reached the Supreme Court, where Nixon's lawyer argued that executive privilege protected the requested conversations and asserted that the President might not comply with a decision of the Supreme Court that was not definitive.[253]

The threat of noncompliance was a tactical mistake. By questioning the Court's authority, Nixon all but guaranteed himself a definitive decision. Although other Presidents, such as Lincoln, successfully stood up to the Supreme Court, Richard Nixon in the summer of 1974 was in no position to do so. In a unanimous decision, the Court restated the position of Chief Justice Marshall in *Marbury v. Madison*: It is emphatically the province and the duty of the judiciary to say what the law is. After deciding that the courts alone had the authority to rule on the question of executive privilege, the Supreme Court found that such a right exists, but that it cannot outweigh the need to provide subpoenaed evidence in a criminal trial.

Following the decision, Nixon reluctantly agreed to turn over the tapes, which showed him to have directed the Watergate coverup from the beginning. Shortly

---

[253] Bob Woodward and Scott Armstrong, *The Brethren* (New York: Simon and Schuster, 1979), pp. 305–307.

thereafter, in the face of imminent impeachment by the House of Representatives, Nixon resigned.

The legislative veto case

As the role of the national government expanded during Franklin Roosevelt's New Deal, and again during Lyndon Johnson's Great Society, Congress found itself without the institutional capacity to make all the legislative decisions required of it. Thus, it doesn't have the inclination to set the rates truckers may charge, so it delegates the task to the Interstate Commerce Commission. It doesn't have the scientific wherewithal to set nuclear energy policy and delegates these decisions to the Nuclear Regulatory Commission. Such delegation is inevitable in any complex society.

When Congress delegates authority to the executive branch or independent agencies, a certain degree of responsiveness is lost. The federal bureaucrats whom Congress provides with quasi-lawmaking powers are obviously unelected. In an attempt to keep some control over the authority it delegates, Congress enacted almost 200 statutes since 1932 that provided for one-or two-house vetos of independent agency or executive branch decisions. The best known example is the War Powers Act, which limits the President's right to go to war without Congressional authorization to ninety days.

In *Immigration and Naturalization Service v. Chadha*,[254] the Court struck down the legislative veto on two grounds. A one-house veto violates the constitutional requirements that a law must be enacted by both houses of Congress and presented to the President for signature or veto. By contrast, the two-house veto only violates the Presentment clause. In its decision the Court voided 196 federal laws – more than it had in its previous history – and severely limited Congress's ability to oversee the bureaucracy to which it has delegated enormous power.

We may expect an increase in the frequency of conflicts among the legislative, executive, and judicial branches, especially with regard to the conduct of foreign policy and the exercise of the war powers that the Constitution divides between President and Congress. With the balkanization of the world resulting from the end of the cold war, long-dormant ethnic and religious animosities may be expected to flare anew. Some of these will undoubtedly threaten United States interests, response to which will become major matters of public concern. There is no reason to expect that these future controversies will be any less likely than those of the past to ultimately come to the Court for resolution.

---

[254]   462 U.S. 919 (1983). Also see Barbara Hinkson Craig, *Chadha* (Berkeley: University of California Press, 1990).

SUMMARY AND CONCLUSIONS

Our survey has outlined the ideological considerations that have motivated the thrust of the Court's decisions since its inception. Clearly, it has not marched to the beat of alien or enigmatic drums. The justices have responded rather to values central to the American heritage, to those that have shaped and guided the political behavior of Americans generally. Moreover, the leading decisions we have examined help demonstrate that plain meaning, intent, and precedent have not limited the Court's ability to achieve its political goals.

May we expect this political orientation to continue, or might we find the justices motivated by purely legalistic considerations? The behavior of the Burger and Rehnquist Courts suggests not. The values that motivated Warren Court policy making in the areas of civil liberties and civil rights – freedom and equality – continue to explain the voting of the incumbent justices. In matters economic, the justices whose service began on the Burger and Warren Courts appear to decide cases on considerations other than the New Deal economics that motivated their predecessors. A degree of libertarianism has emerged, coupled with attitudes toward the decision making of administrative agencies and the federal courts, and considerations pertaining to the authority of the federal government vis-à-vis the state.[255]

In other areas, the Court's recent policy making has provided it with a means to decide cases that heretofore had been the province of the state courts. Until 1983, the Court would not review cases containing intermixed questions of state and federal law unless the party invoking the Court's jurisdiction could show that the state court's decision rested on federal, rather than state, law. The Court reversed its policy, however, and decreed that it would now presume that state courts based their decisions on federal law in cases containing intermingled questions of federal and state law.[256] This had two effects. First, the Court has used *Long* to reach out and reverse state court decisions with which its conservative majority disapproves, particularly in the area of criminal procedure. Second, the threat of *Long* has forced liberally oriented state courts to rely on their own constitutional provisions instead of those in the federal Constitution in order to protect and safeguard individual rights and liberties.[257]

In order to avoid the first effect, we expect the state courts to use their own common, statutory, and constitutional law as the basis for an ever-increasing proportion of their decisions, not only in the area of civil liberties, but also rather broadly across the board. For example, in the aftermath of the Court's ruling that education is not a fundamental right protected by the Constitution,[258] states

---

[255] See Chapter 6.
[256] *Michigan v. Long*, 463 U.S. 1032 (1983).
[257] Harold J. Spaeth, "Justice Sandra Day O'Connor: An Assessment," in D. Grier Stephenson, Jr. (ed.), *An Essential Safeguard* (Westport, CT: Greenwood Press, 1991), pp. 92–95.
[258] *San Antonio Indpendent School District v. Rodriguez*, 411 U.S. 1 (1973).

began to look to their own constitutional and statutory provisions to equalize the financing of public education. Within a generation, virtually all of the states addressed this matter, and though their involvement produced mixed results, what is significant is that responsibility for the resolution of this major policy issue rests with the individual states rather than Washington.[259] Reliance on state law will not appreciably diminish the relevance of the Court's policy making, but will rather signal the emergence of the state courts from the shadow of the Supreme Court and a substantial increase in the importance of state constitutional law – the amount of which will depend on the ideological distance separating a given state's courts from the justices' Marble Palace. The Court, of course, is not solely dependent on *Long* in order to review state court decisions. Even if a state court exclusively relies on its own law, the Supreme Court may still rule the matter one that the states are preempted from regulating, either because Congress has already acted or because the matter is suited only for uniform national regulation. But because the Supreme Court will be dominated well into the twenty-first century by justices who couple their conservatism on substantive issues with deference to state action, we expect much more authoritative policy making on matters of major national moment by the state courts than has occurred at any previous time in the nation's history.[260]

[259]   For a summary of this development, see Rorie Sherman, "Tackling Education Financing," *National Law Journal*, July 22, 1991, pp. 1, 22–23.
[260]   In support of our judgment, see Ronald K.L. Collins, "Reliance on State Constitutions," 63 *Texas Law Review* 1095 (1985); Ronald K.L. Collins, "State Constitutional Law," *National Law Journal*, September 29, 1986, p. S-1; Barry Latzer, "The hidden conservatism of the state court 'revolution'," 74 *Judicature* 190 (1991).

4

Staffing the Court

On July 1, 1987, President Ronald Reagan nominated Robert Bork, U.S. Circuit Court Judge for the District of Columbia, to the Supreme Court. Bork, former professor at Yale Law School and erstwhile Solicitor General of the United States, had been confirmed to his post on what is reputedly the nation's second most prestigious court by a unanimous vote of the Senate. In November 1986, Senate Judiciary Committee Chairman Joseph Biden (D-DE) told the Philadelphia Inquirer that if a well-qualified conservative like Bork were nominated for the Supreme Court, "I'll have to vote for him, and if the groups tear me apart, that's the medicine I'll have to take."[1] Yet eleven months later after a change of wind, Biden's Judiciary Committee followed his lead and voted 9 to 5 against Bork. Less than three weeks after that the full Senate concurred, 58 to 42. History will undoubtedly regard the rejection of the radical-rightist Bork as the biggest legislative failure of the Reagan administration.

To the extent that the legal model of decision making is correct, it should not matter whom the President nominates or whether the Senate confirms, given a basic modicum of legal training and intelligence. If the text of the Constitution, legislative intent, and Supreme Court precedents decide cases, it simply should not matter much who holds life tenure on the Supreme Court. But if the Court largely bases its decisions on the attitudes and values of the justices, then clearly "the most important appointments a President makes are those to the Supreme Court of the United States."[2]

Following Nixon's contention, a case can be made that among the most important *decisions* a President makes are his nominations to the Supreme Court. What, for example, among Eisenhower's decisions compares to his appointments of Earl Warren and William Brennan? What among John Adams' compares to his nomination of John Marshall? The chief legacy of the Reagan Administration, when the twenty-first century rolls around, will likely be the Reaganizing of the judiciary.[3] In this chapter we examine the process by which Presidents nominate and senators confirm or reject appointees to the Supreme Court.

---

[1] *Philadelphia Inquirer*, November 16, 1986, p. A13.
[2] Richard Nixon, "Transcript of President's Announcements," *The New York Times*, October 22, 1971, p. 24.
[3] Sheldon Goldman, "Reaganizing the judiciary: the first term appointments," 68 *Judicature* 313 (1985); Sheldon Goldman, "Reagan's second-term judicial appointments: The battle at midway,"

PRESIDENTIAL SELECTION

Article 2, Section 2, Clause 2, of the United States Constitution gives the President the power "by and with the Advice and Consent of the Senate" to appoint "Judges of the Supreme Court." Despite the wording of this clause, the role of the Senate in Supreme Court nominations has been limited to consent; Presidents have only sought advice in the naming of lower court judges, especially those to the district courts, particularly when there is a senator of the President's party from the state in which the court is located. If the senator disapproves of the President's nominee, he or she can invoke "senatorial courtesy" and block the nomination. This process has not applied to the Supreme Court for nearly a century, nor was it ever intended to. According to Alexander Hamilton in Number 66 of *The Federalist Papers*,

> There will, of course, be no exertion of *choice* on the part of the Senate. They may defeat one choice of the Executive, and oblige him to make another; but they cannot themselves *choose* – they can only ratify or reject the choice of the President. They might even entertain a preference to some other person at the very moment they were assenting to the one proposed, because there might be no positive ground of opposition to him; and they could not be sure, if they withheld their assent, that the subsequent nomination would fall upon their own favorite.[4]

Modern Presidents usually delegate the initial phases of the selection process to the attorney general, chief of staff, or other top advisers. Recommendations from politicians, legal professionals, and interest groups are filtered through the Justice Department's Office of Legal Policy.[5] The President's advisers then pass the names of one or more top candidates to the FBI for exhaustive investigative checks.[6] The final choice is the President's, but the influence of others can be felt. Reagan Attorney General Edwin Meese lobbied hard, first for Robert Bork and next for Douglas Ginsburg, against a more moderate position urged by Chief of Staff Howard Baker. Nixon's choice of Harry Blackmun was obviously influenced by Blackmun's childhood friend, Chief Justice Warren Burger. Former President William Howard Taft lobbied successfully for his own appointment to the Chief Justiceship.[7]

---

70 *Judicature* 324 (1987); Sheldon Goldman, "Reagan's judicial legacy: Completing the puzzle and summing up," 72 *Judicature* 318 (1989).

[4] Alexander Hamilton, James Madison, and John Jay, *The Federalist* (New York: Mentor, 1961), p. 405.

[5] David O'Brien, *Storm Center* (New York: Norton, 1986), p. 53.

[6] Nescience rather than competence apparently characterizes many of these investigations. For example, the FBI's failure to uncover references in 1983 speeches of Bush's nominee, Clarence Thomas, that praised the anti-Jewish black leader, Louis H. Farrakhan, head of the Nation of Islam, while he – Thomas – was chair of the Equal Employment Opportunities Commission. See Pete Applebome, "Black Conservatives: Minority Within a Minority," *New York Times*, July 13, 1991, pp. 1, 7.

[7] On Taft, see Henry F. Pringle, *The Life and Times of William Howard Taft* (New York: Farrar and Rinehart, 1939), II, chap. 50.

Factors affecting nomination

Presidential selection undoubtedly involves complex choices. We doubt that any model will ever be able to explain the specific person chosen. But, as we shall see, we may be able to explain the type of person nominated. First, though, we examine some of the factors that influence presidential selection.

Partisanship and ideology. Given the Supreme Court's role as a national policy maker, it would boggle the mind if Presidents did not pay careful attention to the ideology and partisanship of potential nominees. This factor has been crucial from the Republic's beginning, with President Washington nominating eleven consecutive Federalists to the Court. Overall, 126 of 145 nominees (87 percent) have come from the President's party.[8] Simple partisanship paints an incomplete picture. In his discussions with Senator Henry Cabot Lodge about Democrat Horace Lurton, President Theodore Roosevelt observed that "the nominal politics of the man have nothing to do with his actions on the bench. His *real* politics are all important." Roosevelt had earlier sought assurances from Lodge that Oliver Wendell Holmes was "in entire sympathy with our views" before nominating him to the Supreme Court.[9]

In more recent times, Presidential candidate Richard Nixon campaigned in 1968 on the promise to appoint justices who would support the "peace forces" of society instead of those who favored the rights of accused criminals. As Chapter 6 demonstrates, his appointees have been consistently conservative on criminal procedure. Ronald Reagan's 1980 campaign platform included support for judicial nominees who were harsh on crime, opposed abortion, and favored school prayer. In 1986, Reagan argued that

the proliferation of drugs has been part of a crime epidemic that can be traced to, among other things, liberal judges who are unwilling to get tough with the criminal element in this society. . . . We don't need a bunch of sociology majors on the bench. What we need are strong judges who will aggressively use their authority to protect our families, communities and way of life; judges who understand that punishing wrongdoers is our way of protecting the innocent; judges who do not hesitate to put criminals where they belong, behind bars.[10]

Political environment. Although a rational President will wish to nominate someone with views as close to his as possible, political reality might make such a choice difficult. A President who chooses an unconfirmable nominee will lose more than he will gain.

---

[8] The data here and following were derived by the authors and include Bush's nomination of Clarence Thomas to replace Justice Marshall in the summer of 1991. We exclude from consideration two nominations: William Paterson, whose first nomination in 1793 was temporarily withdrawn so that he could officially resign from the Senate, and Homer Thornberry, whose nomination in 1968 was conditional on Fortas's promotion to Chief Justice.

[9] Henry Cabot Lodge, *Selections from the Correspondence of Theodore Roosevelt and Henry Cabot Lodge, 1894–1918* (New York: Scribner's, 1925) II, 228; I, 519.

[10] "Reagan Aims Fire at Liberal Judges," *New York Times*, October 9, 1986, p. A32.

A classic example of a President "trimming his sails" to avoid a battle with the Senate was Ford's nomination of John Paul Stevens. Ford, who became President following Nixon's resignation, entered office with the lowest initial approval ratings of any President since George Gallup began polling. That low level of popularity fell even further when Ford pardoned Nixon for any crimes he may have committed during his Administration. When Justice Douglas resigned, Ford faced a Senate that consisted of 62 Democrats and 38 Republicans. Further, Ford had to replace the Court's most liberal justice, one whom Ford himself had tried to impeach while House Minority Leader.[11] Under these circumstances, the conservative Ford pragmatically chose the moderate Stevens rather than conservatives such as Robert Bork or J. Clifford Wallace.[12]

Prior experience. All 145 individuals nominated to the high bench have been attorneys. Virtually all have had experience in public affairs of one sort or another, including several as senators or governors and one as a former President. Most commonly, they have previously served as jurists. Four of the five justices on the first Supreme Court had prior judicial experience. Overall, 91 of the 145 nominees (63 percent) have occupied judicial positions. This overall rate masks strong partisan differences: 73 percent of Republican nominees have had prior experience, versus only 48 percent of Democratic nominees. Looking only at the twentieth century doesn't change the picture much: The rates are 76 percent and 41 percent for Republicans and Democrats, respectively.

Region. The Judiciary Act of 1789 divided the nation into six circuits, then corresponding to the number of seats on the Supreme Court. As the number of circuits increased, so also did the number of justices. Until the end of the nineteenth century, each justice served in a dual capacity: as a circuit court judge and as a member of the Supreme Court. The assumption from the beginning was that the justice would reside within the circuit he served: The Judiciary Act of 1802 explicitly refers to "the justice of the supreme court residing within the said circuit."[13] Thus began the tradition of regional representation.

When circuit riding ended in 1891, the need for regional representation lessened. In fact, Lincoln ignored regional "rules" during the Civil War and, though such practices were revived after the War, "by the late 1880's presidents

---

[11] Ford's charges against Douglas concerned Douglas's publication of excerpts from his book, *Points of Rebellion*, in the *Evergreen Review*, a magazine that featured sexually explicit material. During the failed impeachment effort, Ford declared that "an impeachable offense is anything a majority of the House of Representatives considers [it] to be at a given moment of history." See Harold J. Spaeth, *Supreme Court Policy Making* (San Francisco: W.H. Freeman, 1979), p. 114.

[12] David O'Brien, "The Politics of Professionalism: President Gerald Ford's Appointment of Justice John Paul Stevens," 21 *Presidential Studies Quarterly* 103 (1991).

[13] Act of April 29, 1802, 2 Stat. 156–157.

disregarded it with increasing frequency."[14] In 1930, though, Hoover declined to nominate Judge Benjamin Cardozo on the ground that two New Yorkers were sitting on the Court, one of whom – like Cardozo – was Jewish. When another vacancy occurred, Justice Stone, one of the New Yorkers, offered to resign if that would secure Cardozo's nomination.[15] Hoover then selected Cardozo without calling Stone's bluff.

The most recent use of regionalism was Nixon's attempt to nominate a Southerner to replace Justice Black in 1971. Nixon hoped that doing so would win him electoral support from conservative Southerners who traditionally voted Democratic. The "Southern strategy" resulted in the failed nominations of Clement Haynsworth and G. Harrold Carswell, and the successful nomination of Lewis Powell.

Religion, race, and sex. Of the 145 people nominated to the Supreme Court, 143 have been white, 144 have been male, and 126 have been Protestant. The only African-Americans to date are Thurgood Marshall and Clarence Thomas; the sole female, Sandra Day O'Connor. Though it is often claimed that no Hispanics have served on the Court,[16] it is not clear why Benjamin Cardozo, a Sephardic Jew of Spanish heritage, should not count. Ethnically, virtually all of the white Protestant nominees have been Anglo-Saxon. Antonin Scalia was the first Italian-American. Of the nineteen non-Protestants named to date, seven were Jewish, twelve Roman Catholic.[17]

The first Catholic named to the Court was Roger Taney, who was nominated, defeated, renominated in 1835, and finally confirmed in 1836. A second Catholic, Edward White, was not named until 1894. Since then, for all but eight years, at least one Catholic has served on the Court. Three served simultaneously during the 1988 and 1989 terms: Brennan, Scalia, and Kennedy. A so-called Jewish seat existed from 1916, when Louis Brandeis was confirmed, until 1969, when Abe Fortas resigned. Douglas Ginsburg, who is Jewish, was nominated by

---

[14] Richard Friedman, "The Transformation in Senate Response to Supreme Court Nominations," 5 *Cardozo Law Review* 1 (1983), 50.

[15] Walter F. Murphy, *Elements of Judicial Strategy* (Chicago: University of Chicago Press, 1964), p. 76.

[16] For example, O'Brien, op. cit. fn. 5 supra, p. 66; Stephen Wasby, *The Supreme Court in the Federal Judicial System* (Chicago: Nelson-Hall, 1988), p. 117. John Schmidhauser, who is the "dean" of studies of judicial backgrounds, also states that no Hispanics have served on the Court; instead he labels Cardozo "Iberian." See his *Judges and Justices* (Boston: Little, Brown, 1979), p. 60. Our research indicates Schmidhauser's label to be accurate. Cardozo's family background is Spanish *and* Portuguese, and at the beginning of the twentieth century his family attended a Spanish-Portuguese synagogue. See George S. Hellman, *Benjamin N. Cardozo: American Judge* (New York: McGraw Hill, 1940), chap. 1.

[17] The numbers are based on nominations, not nominees. Thus Taney (Catholic) and Fortas (Jewish) are counted twice.

A focus on religious background is becoming increasingly fatuous. Justice Thomas, whom we count as a Protestant, was born of Protestant parents, raised a Roman Catholic, and at last word attends an Episcopalian church.

Reagan in 1987 but withdrew following allegations that he smoked marijuana. President Bush's choice of Clarence Thomas as Thurgood Marshall's successor did not surprise us. Indeed, we predicted as much six months before Marshall's retirement at the end of the 1990 term. It seems a virtual certainty that the Court will always count at least one woman among its number in the future.

Friendship and patronage. "Sometimes it isn't what you know, it's whom you know." About 60 percent of those named to the Supreme Court personally knew the President who nominated them.[18] Most of Washington's appointees, for instance, had personal ties to him.[19] Harry Truman nominated four close friends, Harold Burton, Fred Vinson, Tom Clark, and Sherman Minton. Lyndon Johnson named his longtime crony, Abe Fortas, as Associate Justice, and failed in his attempt to have him elevated to Chief Justice. Had Fortas been confirmed to the latter position, another friend of Johnson's, Homer Thornberry, would have been selected to fill Fortas's seat. Occasionally, though, the tie between President and potential nominee is not particularly close. Richard Nixon knew William Rehnquist from the latter's work at the Justice Department, but Nixon thought Rehnquist's name was "Renchler" and referred to him in a prenomination taped conversation as a "clown."[20]

A position on the Supreme Court may also be used to pay political debts. In 1952, Earl Warren, seeing his chances for obtaining the Republican presidential nomination falter, threw his support and that of the California delegation to General Eisenhower rather than Eisenhower's rival, Senator Robert Taft of Ohio. One year later, Eisenhower nominated Governor Warren to replace Fred Vinson. Similarly, Kennedy's friend, Byron White, best known as an all-American football player, received a seat on the Supreme Court in 1962, two years after organizing Citizens for Kennedy-Johnson.

Explaining presidential choice. As the nomination of Byron White exemplifies, reasons almost always exist that can explain, after the fact, why a President chose a particular person. Yet, of the dozens of people with appropriate experience, politics, and connections, there is no clear a priori explanation why Kennedy preferred White to other possible candidates. Indeed, social scientists can probably add little to the prenomination speculation over and above that provided by political pundits. Nevertheless, scholars have had some success in explaining the type (i.e., ideology) of person selected.

According to one analysis, Presidents interested in maintaining their popularity and prestige will attempt to avoid losing the confirmation battle, if at all pos-

---

[18]   Updated from Robert Scigliano, *The Supreme Court and the Presidency* (New York: Free Press, 1971), p. 95.
[19]   Henry Abraham, *Justices and Presidents*, 2d ed. (New York: Oxford, 1985), p. 72.
[20]   David Rosenbaum, "Tapes Say Nixon Saw Plot in Pentagon Papers' Release," *The New York Times*, June 6, 1991, p. B11.

sible.[21] Therefore, if one places the median senator, the President, and potential nominees on a liberal-conservative ideological spectrum, the President should always nominate someone in the space between himself and the Senate, rather than a nominee outside that range.

Presidents usually nominate individuals within this range, but occasionally they do not. One reason why they do not is if the President has very strong policy concerns about the Court. If the Court is very liberal and the President is conservative, the President might attempt to balance the liberalism of the Court with someone more conservative than himself, even if that person is outside the President-Senate interval. Similarly, if the Court is very conservative and the President is liberal, the President might attempt to balance the conservatism of the Court with a nominee more liberal than himself (and the Senate). Overall, a preliminary model, using the ideology of the President, median Senator, and Supreme Court, explains 80 percent of the variance in the ideology of presidential nominees.

SENATE CONFIRMATION

Following nomination by the President, the American Bar Association (ABA) conducts its own inquiry of the nominee, rating him or her on a qualified/not qualified scale. Although the ABA screens lower court appointees prior to nomination, it does not screen Supreme Court nominees until the President announces his choice.

The bar's involvement in Supreme Court nominations has been controversial. In 1969 it initially and unanimously ranked Haynsworth "highly qualified," then reconsidered and reaffirmed its judgment by a divided vote. In 1970 it labeled Carswell "qualified," though even his supporters thought him mediocre. For a short period of time following the Haynsworth debacle the Nixon Administration gave the ABA the right to pre-screen potential nominees. This practice ended when ABA votes against potential nominees Mildred Lillie and Herschel Friday were leaked to the press. When Nixon nominated Lewis Powell and William Rehnquist in 1972, he did not apprise the ABA until after he had sent their names to the Senate Judiciary Committee. In 1975, President Ford gave the ABA a list of names that included John Paul Stevens, who received the committee's top ranking. Reagan discontinued the pre-screening practice and gave the ABA no advance word on Sandra O'Connor. The committee found O'Connor "qualified," and Scalia and Rehnquist "highly qualified." Robert Bork received ten "highly qualified" votes, one vote "not opposed," and four votes "not qualified." Even before Anita Hill's sexual harassment charges Clarence Thomas received but a "qualified" rating from twelve of the Committee's

---

[21] Charles Cameron, Albert D. Cover, and Jeffrey A. Segal, "Supreme Court Nominations and the Rational Presidency." Paper presented at the 1990 annual meeting of the American Political Science Association, San Francisco.

fifteen members; two thought him unqualified, and one did not vote. Of twenty-three nominees, Thomas is the first who failed to receive at least a unanimous "qualified" rating or a majority superior rating.[22]

Following the submission of a nominee's name to the Senate, the Judiciary Committee holds hearings. The Committee will hear testimony from the legal community, interest groups, and the nominee. Nominees did not appear before the Committee prior to 1925, and the practice did not become established until the mid-1950s. Often nominees refuse to answer substantive legal questions because to do so would compromise their open-mindedness when such cases came before the Court. This avoids the appearance of partiality, not partiality itself, for it is not clear why the communication of a prior view biases one less than a flat refusal to communicate one's position. Such silence, though, does serve to keep nominees out of political trouble. For instance, had nominee Souter stated his views on abortion he would have instantly alienated half of the Senate. Nevertheless, the Judiciary Committee has generally recommended nominees who have refused to talk substance. Thus Clarence Thomas refused to admit that he had ever discussed the merits of *Roe v. Wade* with any one at any time.

The great exception is the Bork nomination. He had criticized certain Supreme Court decisions so outspokenly that he could not avoid telling senators under oath what he had repeatedly told the rest of the world in articles and speeches. Though Bork attempted to assume a moderate stance at the hearings, his previous writings and speeches, some of which he made only weeks before his nomination, led many to believe that his "moderation" was part of a confirmation conversion that would not last once he joined the Court.

If the Judiciary Committee does not table a nomination, it goes to the full Senate for consideration. The nomination will be debated on the floor, and unless filibustered, as was the second Fortas nomination, the full chamber will vote on it. Confirmation requires a simple majority.

Of the 145 nominees whom the Senate considered through 1991, 118 (81 percent) have been confirmed. Not all of the 118 have served; seven declined their seat. Robert Harrison, for instance, declined Washington's appointment in order to become Chancellor of Maryland, and John Jay declined reappointment due to the Court's low prestige.[23]

Of the twenty-seven rejections, the Senate formally repudiated twelve, failed to act on five, indefinitely postponed four, and forced the President to withdraw six.[24] The rejected nominees are listed in Table 4.1.

In order to gain insight into the factors that lead to rejection, we take three

[22] "Thomas: The Least Qualified Nominee So Far?" *National Law Journal*, September 16, 1991, p. 5. Also see Neil A. Lewis, "A.B.A. Is Split on Fitness of Thomas for High Court," *New York Times*, August 28, 1991, p. A1.

[23] Elder Witt, ed., *The Supreme Court and Its Work* (Washington: Congressional Quarterly, 1981), pp. 4, 74.

[24] The six withdrawn candidates includes Douglas Ginsburg, who withdrew as much because of misgivings within the Reagan administration as within the Senate.

Table 4.1. *Rejected Supreme Court nominees*

Name	President	Year[a]	Vote
John Rutledge	Washington	1795	10-14
Alexander Wolcott	Madison	1811	9-24
John Crittenden	J.Q. Adams	1828	Postponed
Roger Taney	Jackson	1835	Postponed
John Spencer	Tyler	1844	21-26
Reuben Walworth	Tyler	1844	Withdrawn
Edward King	Tyler	1844	Postponed
Edward King	Tyler	1844	Withdrawn
John Read	Tyler	1845	No Action
George Woodward	Polk	1845	20-29
Edward Bradford	Fillmore	1852	No Action
George Badger	Fillmore	1853	Postponed
William Micou	Fillmore	1853	No Action
Jeremiah Black	Buchanan	1861	25-26
Henry Stanbery	Johnson	1866	No Action
Ebenezer Hoar	Grant	1869	24-33
George Williams	Grant	1873	Withdrawn
Caleb Cushing	Grant	1874	Withdrawn
Stanley Matthews	Hayes	1881	No Action
William Hornblower	Cleveland	1893	24-30
Wheeler Peckham	Cleveland	1894	32-41
John Parker	Hoover	1930	39-41
Abe Fortas[b]	Johnson	1968	45-43[c]
Clement Haynsworth	Nixon	1969	45-55
G. Harrold Carswell	Nixon	1970	45-51
Robert Bork	Reagan	1987	42-58
Douglas Ginsburg	Reagan	1987	Withdrawn

Notes. [a]Year is year nominated. [b]Fortas's rejection led to the withdrawal of the nomination of Homer Thornberry, who was to take Fortas's place as associate justice. [c]Vote on cloture failed to reach two-thirds majority. Nomination subsequently withdrawn.

approaches. First, we examine the five nominations that failed between 1968 and 1988, along with the almost-failed nomination of Clarence Thomas in 1991. Then we conduct a systematic analysis of the factors affecting rejection since 1789. Finally, we examine the roll call votes of senators between the nomination of Earl Warren in 1953 and David Souter in 1990. Those results are then applied to the Thomas nomination.

The case studies

Between 1930 and 1967, Presidents nominated twenty-four consecutive persons to the Supreme Court without a single rejection. Thereafter, five of the next fifteen nominees were rejected. We examine them in sequence.

Abe Fortas. Following Lyndon Johnson's victory in the Democratic Senate nomination in the Texas primary in 1948,[25] he called on attorney Abe Fortas to prevent a legal maneuver by his opponent, former Governor Coke Stevenson, to keep him (Johnson) off the November ballot. Fortas's successful efforts resulted in a close personal and professional relationship that culminated in Johnson's naming him to the Supreme Court in 1965. Fortas remained a close adviser of Johnson while he was on the Court. According to one report, "few important Presidential problems are settled without an opinion from Mr. Justice Fortas."[26]

In June 1968, Chief Justice Warren announced his retirement from the Court, effective at Johnson's pleasure. Johnson declared that the retirement would not take effect until "such time as a successor is qualified."[27] This in essence told the Senate that if they didn't approve Warren's successor, Warren would simply stay on as Chief Justice, but it also allowed Senate opponents to claim that no actual vacancy existed. Fortas may in fact have suggested the contingent retirement scenario to Johnson.[28]

Johnson named Fortas to replace Warren, and another Johnson crony, Homer Thornberry, to occupy Fortas's place as associate justice.

The timing of the vacancy initially worked against Fortas. By the summer of 1968 a Presidential election was only months away. In and out of Washington, Johnson's popularity was plummeting. Republicans and Southern Democrats had every reason to believe that if they defeated the Fortas nomination, Richard Nixon would make the new appointment. Historically, Supreme Court nominees have fared poorly during the fourth year of a President's term in office. Johnson was particularly weak during his fourth year because he had already announced

[25]   Robert A. Caro, *The Years of Lyndon Johnson: Means of Ascent* (New York: Knopf, 1990), chs. 13–16.
[26]   *Newsweek*, July 8, 1968, p. 18.
[27]   "Warren-Johnson Letters," *New York Times*, June 27, 1968, p. A30.
[28]   John Massaro, *Supremely Political* (New York: State University of New York, 1990), p. 41.

his decision not to seek a second term. Presidential threats would not be effective; presidential promises could not be kept.

The second factor to work against the nomination was Fortas's and the Warren Court's liberal ideology. In his four terms, Fortas had supported the liberal position in civil liberties cases over 80 percent of the time, aligning himself with a bloc that included Warren, Douglas, Marshall, and Brennan.[29] Members of the Judiciary Committee grilled Fortas during the hearings about liberal decisions he had rendered,[30] and even for some that antedated his tenure.[31]

The third factor to work against the promotion of Fortas concerned a matter of ethics. The hearings disclosed that he had accepted a $15,000 fee for teaching a nine-week seminar at American University. The money was raised by Fortas's former law partner, Paul Porter, from wealthy businessmen involved in litigation that could come before the Supreme Court. Additionally, some senators questioned the propriety of Fortas's close relationship with Johnson. These considerations enabled conservative senators to oppose Fortas without appearing partisan.[32]

The motion to confirm Fortas never came up for a direct vote because of a filibuster on the Senate floor. The vote to invoke cloture shows the influence that ideology had on the nomination. The simple correlation between the support scores of senators compiled by Americans for Democratic Action (ADA), which measures how liberal senators vote, and their vote to invoke cloture is .79. Though there were 45 votes to invoke cloture and only 43 opposed, this was far less than the two-thirds needed to end Senate debate. With a direct vote on Fortas precluded, Johnson withdrew the nomination.

Clement Haynsworth. Following Richard Nixon's election, Warren announced his unconditional resignation at the end of the 1968 term. On May 21, 1969, Nixon named Warren Burger to replace him. Burger was confirmed on June 9 with little controversy. Meanwhile, a *Life* magazine story in May 1969 disclosed that in 1966 Fortas had accepted $20,000 as part of an annual "consulting" fee from Louis Wolfson, a millionaire businessman later convicted of stock manipulations. Though Fortas returned the money and accepted no future handouts from Wolfson, the ensuing controversy forced him to resign.

On August 18, 1969, Nixon chose Circuit Court of Appeals Judge Clement

---

[29] Jeffrey A. Segal and Harold J. Spaeth, "Decisional trends on the Warren and Burger Courts: results from the Supreme Court Data Base Project," 73 *Judicature* (1989) 103.

[30] For example, *Brown v. Louisiana*, 383 U.S. 131 (1966), which vacated the breach of peace conviction of blacks engaged in a stand-in at a segregated library.

[31] *Mallory v. United States*, 354 U.S. 449 (1957), which overturned the conviction and death sentence of an alleged rapist who confessed after a seven-hour unarraigned interrogation. Mallory was subsequently convicted of another rape in 1960, and died in a shootout with police following yet another rape in 1972.

[32] Donald Songer, "The Relevance of Policy Values for the Confirmation of Supreme Court Nominees," 13 *Law and Society Review* 927 (1979).

Haynsworth, a Democrat from South Carolina, to replace Fortas. The selection of Haynsworth was part of Nixon's "Southern strategy," by which he hoped to win the votes of conservative white Democratic Southerners in 1972.

Haynsworth at first appeared certain of confirmation. Though the Democrats controlled the Senate, a working majority of Republicans and conservative Southern Democrats existed. Confidence in Haynsworth began to erode when Judiciary Committee hearings began to focus on cases decided by Haynsworth in which he had a direct financial interest. One case concerned parties who had direct business dealings with a company in which he had a substantial stake. In another, Haynsworth bought stock in a company after deciding a case involving the company but before the decision was announced. Although Haynsworth gained but few dollars from these decisions, his behavior made him an easy target for one nominated to restore high ethical standards.

As in the Fortas case, Haynsworth's ideological opponents viewed the ethics charges as most serious. They alleged that Haynsworth had compiled an anti-union, anti-civil rights record as an appellate judge. On the union front, Haynsworth had ruled that businesses could shut down specific factories solely for the purpose of punishing union activity.[33] He also ruled that unions could not use authorization cards as a means to determine whether it had the support of a majority of a company's employees.[34] As for civil rights, Haynsworth had allowed private hospitals receiving federal funds to discriminate racially.[35] He also upheld "freedom of choice" school plans, where students were allowed to choose the schools they would attend, with the inevitable result that the schools remained segregated.[36]

Liberal opposition to Haynsworth produced vigorous lobbying. On November 21, 1969, the Senate rejected Haynsworth by a vote of 55 to 45. According to Nixon aide John Ehrlichman, Haynsworth "was not confirmed because of a highly expert, expensive and intensive lobbying campaign by organized labor and civil rights groups."[37] The correlation between ADA scores and the votes supporting Haynsworth was −.79.

G. Harrold Carswell. In angry reaction to Haynsworth's defeat, Nixon nominated G. Harrold Carswell, a little known federal judge from Florida who had graduated from a local Southern law school. So poorly qualified was he that the Dean of the Yale Law School was moved to declare that he "presents more slender credentials than any nominee put forth this century."[38] Carswell was reversed significantly more frequently – 40 percent – than the average district court judge

---

[33] *Darlington Manufacturing Company v. NLRB*, 325 F.2d 682 (1963).

[34] *NLRB v. S.S. Logan Packing Company*, 386 F.2d 562 (1967).

[35] *Simkins v. Moses H. Cone Memorial Hospital*, 323 F.2d 959 (1964).

[36] *Green v. County School Board*, 372 F.2d 338 (1967).

[37] Quoted in Massaro, op.cit. fn. 28 supra, p. 22.

[38] U.S. Senate, *Hearings on the Nomination of G. Harold Carswell, of Florida, to be Associate Justice of the Supreme Court of the United States*, 91st Congress, 2d Session, 1970, p. 242.

in the Fifth Circuit – the circuit in which he served.[39] So deficient were Carswell's qualifications that his Senate floor leader, Roman Hruska (R-NB), declared, "Even if he were mediocre, there are a lot of mediocre judges, and people and lawyers. They are entitled to a little representation, aren't they, and a little chance."[40] Even Nixon Administration insiders considered him a "boob" and a "dummy."[41]

Carswell's record as a federal judge and as a private citizen made him far more suspect on civil rights than Haynsworth. One of his decisions delaying implementation of desegregation was explicitly variant with higher court rulings; another made it virtually impossible to challenge segregation in public reform schools.[42] In 1956, Carswell, then a United States attorney, had helped transform a public golf club built with federal funds into a private club in order to avoid desegregation. While a U.S. attorney, he also helped charter a Florida State University booster club with membership limited to "any white person." But the most damaging blow to Carswell's candidacy occurred when a Florida television station found film of a 1948 speech in which he declared, "I yield to no man as a fellow candidate or as a fellow citizen in the firm vigorous belief in the principles of White Supremacy, and I shall always be so governed."[43] The defense of Carswell continued, though. Assistant Attorney General William Rehnquist later commented that Carswell's support for white supremacy amounted to no more than "some rather thin evidence of personal hostility toward blacks."[44]

Given the case against Carswell, the vote against him was surprisingly close, 51 to 45. More than two-thirds of the Republicans supported Carswell, as did fewer than a third of the Democrats. The correlation between ADA scores and pro-Carswell voting was − .84. If Nixon had had a Republican Senate majority, Carswell would have been confirmed.

Robert Bork. As noted at the beginning of the chapter, President Reagan nominated Bork to the seat vacated by the retirement of Justice Powell in 1987. Bork first came to public attention on October 20, 1973, when as Solicitor General he fired Watergate Special Prosecutor Archibald Cox at President Nixon's request after Attorney General Elliott Richardson and Deputy Attorney General William Ruckleshaus refused to do so. Richardson resigned in protest of Nixon's order; Rucklehaus was fired for refusing to obey. Bork executed Nixon's order, and thereafter remained in the Justice Department through Watergate, through Ford's pardon of Nixon, until the day Jimmy Carter became President.[45]

[39] Massaro, op. cit. fn. 28 supra, p. 6.
[40] Warren Weaver, Jr., "Carswell Nomination Attacked and Defended as Senate Opens Debate on Nomination," *The New York Times*, March 17, 1970, p. A21.
[41] Massaro, op. cit. fn. 28 supra, p. 116.
[42] Ibid., pp. 3–4.
[43] *New York Times*, "Excerpts from Carswell Talk," January 22, 1970, p. A22.
[44] Massaro, op. cit. fn. 28 supra, p. 109.
[45] Robert Bork, *The Tempting of America* (New York: Simon and Schuster, 1990), p. 272.

The turning point in Bork's confirmation came not in 1987 when he was nominated, but in 1986 when partisan control of the Senate switched from the Republicans to the Democrats. Reagan had worked feverishly to retain Republican control of the Senate. At campaign stops in Missouri and Alabama, he echoed concerns he first raised in North Carolina:

Today, Senator Strom Thurmond and Jim Broyhill are in a majority on the Senate Judiciary Committee, overseeing judicial appointments. Without Jim Broyhill and a Republican Senate majority, that job will be turned over to Teddy Kennedy and Joe Biden . . . You can strike a blow against drugs, thugs and hoodlums by casting your vote for Jim and keeping him as a force for law and order in the United States Senate. The future of our country, its safety and security, is in our hands.[46]

On November 4, 1986, the Democratic Party won 20 of 34 open Senate seats, taking a decisive 55-to-45 majority. Riding on a huge black vote, Democrats won Republican seats in Alabama, Florida, Georgia, and North Carolina.[47]

On the day of Bork's nomination, Ted Kennedy set the tone for the campaign to follow:

Robert Bork's America is a land in which women would be forced into back alley abortions, blacks would sit at segregated lunch counters, rogue police could break down citizen's doors in midnight raids, writers and artists could be censored at the whim of the government, and the doors of the federal courts would be shut on the fingers of millions of citizens[48]

Interest groups opposed to Bork joined the fray. People for the American Way, The Women's Legal Defense Fund, The Alliance for Justice, and the National Abortion Rights Action League immediately went on the attack. The AFL-CIO joined the anti-Bork forces in August 1987 along with the American Civil Liberties Union, which dropped its 51-year-old policy of non-involvement in Supreme Court nominations. Planned Parenthood ran advertisements that read, "State controlled pregnancy? It's not as far fetched as it sounds. Carrying Bork's position to its logical end, states could not ban or require any method of birth control, impose family quotas for population purposes, make abortion a crime, or sterilize anyone they choose."[49]

Opponent's allegations stemmed from Bork's published writings on and off the bench. In 1963, Bork declared that the proposed Civil Rights Act, which prohibited race discrimination in places of public accommodations, invoked a "principle of unsurpassed ugliness."[50] Most of the fodder, though, came from a 1971 article in which Bork criticized Supreme Court rulings that created a right to privacy, struck down prohibitions on the use of birth control by married

[46] "Reagan Aims Fire at Liberal Judges," *New York Times*, October 9, 1986, p. A32.
[47] Lena Williams, "Blacks Cast Pivotal Ballots in Four Key Senate Races, Data Show," *New York Times*, November 6, 1986, p. A33.
[48] James Reston, "Kennedy and Bork," *New York Times*, July 5, 1987, sec. IV, p. 15.
[49] "Robert Bork's Position on Reproductive Rights," *New York Times*, September 13, 1987, p. B9.
[50] Robert Bork, "Civil Rights–A Challenge," *The New Republic*, August 31, 1963, p. 22.

people, voided state court enforcement of racial covenants, and declared unconstitutional malapportioned state legislative districts.[51] He also argued that the equal protection clause of the Fourteenth Amendment should be limited to racial discrimination, to the exclusion, for instance, of sexual discrimination, and that the First Amendment is entirely inapplicable to scientific, literary, or artistic speech.[52]

During the Judiciary Committee hearings Bork repudiated many of his previous views: the Civil Rights Act of 1964 was fine, the Fourteenth Amendment protected women, and the First Amendment covered scientific, literary, and artistic communication. He did not, however, recant his views on the right to privacy. Moreover, his newly found moderation was seen as part of a "confirmation conversion," which impeached his credibility without softening his right-wing image.

Public pressure on the Senate to vote against Bork was enormous. Senator John Breaux (D-LA), who was first elected in 1986, told the *New York Times* that "many Southern Democrats were elected by black votes and that his black supporters were making the Bork vote a 'litmus test' issue. 'You can't vote maybe.' "[53] Constituent pressure was so great that even John Stennis, one-time leader of Southern segregationists, voted against Bork.

Bork was defeated by a 58-to-42 vote. Ideology played a huge role – the correlation between ADA scores and the confirmation vote was − .83, but so did partisanship. Because of constituent pressure, the anti-Bork coalition included moderate and conservative Southern Democrats who otherwise might have supported him. Ninety-six percent of the Democrats opposed Bork, while 87 percent of the Republicans supported him.

Douglas Ginsburg. During the floundering Bork campaign, President Reagan threatened to nominate someone liberals would abhor just as much as Bork, if Bork were rejected.[54] He attempted to accomplish that with the nomination of Douglas Ginsburg, a former Harvard Law Professor who had served for 14 months on the District of Columbia Circuit Court of Appeals. Unfortunately for Ginsburg's opponents, he had left no paper trail that tied him to unpopular views, à la Bork. A potential scandal inhered in a Ginsburg vote on a cable television contract decided while Ginsburg held $140,000 in another cable company directly benefited by the ruling. That story soon became secondary when Nina Totenberg of National Public Radio reported that Ginsburg smoked marijuana with some of his students while at Harvard. The anti-drug, anti-crime, "just say 'no' "

[51] Robert Bork, "Neutral Principles and Some First Amendment Problems," 47 *Indiana Law Journal* 1 (1971), at 8–11, 15–17, 18–19.
[52] Id. at 11–12, 20–35.
[53] Steven Roberts, "White House Says Bork Lacks Votes for Confirmation," *New York Times,* September 26, 1987, p. 1.
[54] *New York Times,* October 14, 1987, p. A1.

Administration quickly dropped its support of the nominee, who asked Reagan not to forward his nomination to the Senate.

Clarence Thomas. Though Clarence Thomas was narrowly confirmed by the Senate, his confirmation evidences the crucial variables associated with the five rejected nominees: ideologically motivated opposition spurred by serious questions as to the nominee's qualifications.

At the end of the 1990 Supreme Court term, Thurgood Marshall announced his intent to retire at such point that a successor was confirmed to take his place.[55] Marshall, a towering figure as a litigator for the NAACP Legal Defense Fund, Inc., probably influenced the Court more before he became a justice than after. He made history as a member of the Court more for what he was – the first African-American to sit on the tribunal – than for anything he did while there. Faced with replacing him, President Bush quickly nominated Clarence Thomas to the Court. In reply to charges that Bush nominated Thomas because he was black, Bush responded that Thomas was "the best man for the job on the merits. And the fact that he's a minority, so much the better."[56]

Clarence Thomas was an outspoken conservative who gained favor in the Reagan and Bush administrations by speaking forcefully against affirmative action and race-based preferences. Under Reagan he served as director of the Civil Rights office in the Department of Education and then as Chairman of the Equal Employment Opportunity Commission. President Bush nominated him to the United States Circuit Court for the District of Columbia, the same Court on which Warren Burger, Antonin Scalia, Robert Bork, and Douglas Ginsburg served prior to their Supreme Court nominations.

Liberal interest groups immediately expressed concern about the nominee. Civil rights groups were alarmed by his long opposition to affirmative action. Indeed, the NAACP executive board voted unanimously, with one abstention, to oppose the nominee. Women's groups were outraged by a speech in which Thomas seemingly endorsed using the Constitution to outlaw abortion. Senior citizens complained that Thomas let more than 1,000 age discrimination suits lapse during his tenure at EEOC.

Moreover, Thomas's qualifications came increasingly under question. Though Thomas had graduated from Yale Law School, University officials admitted that he was only admitted because of the school's affirmative action program,[57] the same sort of program Thomas now condemned. Thomas's career on the federal bench was short (one and a half years) and undistinguished. As noted earlier, the American Bar Association could do no better than give him a rating of "qualified."

---

[55] As the Thomas confirmation dragged on, Marshall chose to retire rather than serve into the 1991 term.

[56] John E. Yang and Sharon LaFraniere, "Bush Picks Thomas for Supreme Court," *Washington Post*, July 2, 1991, p. A1, at A6.

[57] "Judge Thomas Takes the Stand," *New York Times*, September 8, 1991, Section 4, p. 18.

At the first round of confirmation hearings, Thomas attempted a middle ground between the stonewalling of Souter and the conversion of Bork. Thomas refused to state where he stood on abortion, and even tried to suggest that he had never really thought about the issue. At the same time he tried to disown his previous statements on fetal rights. He also, for the first time in his career, managed to praise affirmative action programs. This, of course, led to Democratic charges of a Bork-like confirmation conversion.[58]

Neither the conservative ideology, nor the interest group opposition, nor the questions of qualifications were enough to bring Thomas down. Four days before the scheduled October 8 vote only about 40 senators opposed the nominee. Then, on October 6, an article by Timothy Phelps in *Newsday*[59] and a report by Nina Totenberg on National Public Radio broke the story that a law school professor in Oklahoma, Anita Hill, had told Senate Judiciary Committee staffers that Thomas had sexually harassed her in the early 1980s while she worked for him at the Department of Education and later at the EEOC. Hill, who had spoken to the Committee on conditions of confidentiality, was drawn out by the media after someone on or working for the Committee leaked the story to Phelps and Totenberg.

The Senate delayed the vote for a week in order to give the Judiciary Committee time to consider the charges. It would take a book-length manuscript to recount the charges and countercharges leveled during the hearings. Most persuasive from Hill's side was the fact that she told several people of the alleged harassment

---

[58] The Democrats appear to have been right. Four months after being seated on the Supreme Court, Thomas returned to the Court of Appeals to issue the decision in a major affirmative action case that had been gathering dust for over a year, *Lamprecht v. Federal Communications Commission*. Such cases are normally resolved within two to three months. In his opinion, Thomas ruled that Congress's effort to diversify white male ownership in broadcasting by authorizing the FCC to advantage women in the competition for new licenses was unconstitutional. Although the Supreme Court had upheld a more advantageous parallel program for blacks in *Metro Broadcasting, Inc. v. FCC*, 111 L Ed 2d 245 (1990), Thomas distinguished it by holding that the black program did produce programming diversity, whereas the female program did not.

In an unusually critical editorial, the *New York Times* ("Justice Thomas's Late Hit," February 25, 1992, p. A12) said: " . . . manipulation, even if it occurred, was not the worst feature of the decision. . . . The major vice is something Presidents Reagan and Bush pledged that their high court nominees would not engage in: legislating from the bench, making law rather than interpreting it, substituting personal policy preferences for those of duly elected legislatures."

"Chief Judge Abner Mikva, in strong dissent, showed how – until recently – the Supreme Court had deferred to Congress over just such judgments about how much linkage between diverse ownership and diverse programming was significant. Thus at the very moment Judge Thomas testified he would be content to apply the high court's precepts, he was busy misapplying them."

"This kind of flyspecking jurisprudence, demanding unreasonably precise proof when the judiciary disagrees with Congress, is not new to the courts [see Chapter 8 for evidence]. But it's a salient feature of the new legal culture ushered in by Presidents Reagan and Bush, who swore to combat it."

[59] "The Thomas charge: Law prof told FBI that he sexually harrassed her at EEOC," October 6, 1991, p. 7.

at the time it occurred. Most persuasive from Thomas's side was the fact that Hill never filed a complaint against Thomas at the time, and actually followed him from the Department of Education to the EEOC.

Democrats and Republicans treated the hearings quite differently from one another. "The Democrats made a pass at figuring out what had happened in the case. The Republicans tried to win. While the Democrats were pronouncing themselves flummoxed by two diametrically opposing stories, the Republicans had already launched a scorched-earth strategy against Professor Hill."[60] Bush himself endorsed the policy to attack Hill.[61] Thus, Arlen Specter (R-PA) charged Hill of commiting perjury, Orrin Hatch (R-UT) accused her of concocting her story in coordination with liberal interest groups, and Alan Simpson (R-WY) even questioned her sexual proclivities.[62] The Democrats, either not understanding that the Republicans were playing hardball, or unable to compete in the game, never asked Thomas about his alleged penchant for watching pornographic movies, which would have corroborated part of Hill's testimony; didn't call witnesses who claimed that Thomas had harassed them; and didn't introduce into evidence the positive results of Hill's lie detector test.[63]

The final vote for Thomas was 52 to 48. Again, charges against the qualifications of the nominee were acted upon only by those ideologically opposed to the nominee: The correlation between ADA scores and the vote on the Thomas nomination was $-.81$. Partisanship was similarly in evidence: 41 of 43 Republicans supported Thomas; 46 of 57 Democrats opposed him.

These five rejections, plus Thomas, lead to the following tentative conclusions. First, the probability of rejection is greatest when the President is in a weak position. Every rejection occurred when either the nominating President was in the fourth year of his term of office or when his party did not control the Senate. Second, qualifications play a crucial role in confirmation politics. Every rejected nominee confronted a serious question of ethics or competence. Third, the role of qualifications is largely interactive. Lack of qualifications only leads ideologically opposed Senators to vote against the nominee. Fourth, electoral politics influence confirmation voting. Interest groups and constituents have an impact.

These conclusions are tentative as they are based only on case studies of rejected nominees. To assess the impact of these and other variables on confirmation voting, we turn to more systematic analyses. We start with an aggregate analysis that examines confirmation decisions since 1789. Because we lack reliable information about relevant variables for many eighteenth and nineteenth

---

[60] Maureen Dowd, "Going Nasty Early Helps G.O.P. Gain Edge on Thomas," *The New York Times*, October 15, 1991, p. A1.

[61] Andrew Rosenthal, "White House Role in Thomas Defense," *The New York Times*, October 14, 1991, p. A1.

[62] Anthony Lewis, "Time of the Assassins," *New York Times*, October 14, 1991, p. A19; William Safire, "The Plot to Savage Thomas," *New York Times*, October 14, 1991, p. A19.

[63] That lie detectors are not allowed as courtroom evidence is largely irrelevant. Hearsay is generally not allowed either; yet no objections to hearsay were raised during the Committee hearings.

century nominees, we supplement the aggregate analysis with an individual-level focus on the votes of senators, starting with the nomination of Earl Warren.

An aggregate analysis

From 1789 through 1990, 145 people have been nominated to the Supreme Court,[64] of whom the Senate has confirmed 118 (81 percent). Recent research has suggested that the Senate's decision to confirm particular nominees can be explained by partisan and institutional politics between the Senate on the one hand and the President or the Court on the other.[65] Senators may cast votes that either increase the power or prestige of the Senate or decrease that of the President or Court.

From this framework we test several hypotheses about the confirmation process. First, a pro-Senate bias that manifests itself rather simply – namely, that the Senate should be more likely to confirm those nominees who are U.S. senators than those who are not.

Second, an anti-President bias should most likely surface when the President's party does not control the Senate (e.g., Reagan and Bork, Nixon and Haynsworth/Carswell), and during the fourth year of the President's term of office (e.g., Johnson and Fortas), except for the period between reelection and the start of a new term. Such Presidents are likely to have minimal influence over senators of either party.

A President's strength may also depend on his electoral base. For instance, one presidential scholar has found moderate relationships between a President's electoral strength in a Representative's home district and that Representative's support for the President's policies.[66] If this relationship also holds for the Senate, then the larger the President's previous electoral victory, the more likely his nominees are to be confirmed. Although the President and Vice-President are elected as a team, the electoral coalition may not remain loyal if the Vice-President succeeds to office through the death or resignation of the President. Thus, elected Presidents should more readily secure confirmation of their nominees than succession Presidents. John Tyler, for instance, the successor to William Henry Harrison, failed in four consecutive attempts to secure confirmation of his nominees.

---

[64] This list excludes William Paterson, whose nomination was withdrawn by President Washington so that Paterson could officially resign from the Senate; Homer Thornberry, whose nomination for associate justice became moot when the Senate refused to promote Abe Fortas to chief justice; and Douglas Ginsburg, whose name was never officially forwarded to the Senate. Ginsburg asked President Reagan not to forward his name after revelations that Ginsburg had smoked marijuana while a professor at Harvard Law School. It also excludes Clarence Thomas, whose nomination had not been acted on at the time this analysis was undertaken.

[65] Jeffrey A. Segal, ''Senate Confirmation of Supreme Court Justices: Partisan and Institutional Politics,'' 49 *Journal of Politics* 998 (1987).

[66] George C. Edwards, *Presidential Influence in Congress* (San Francisco: W.H. Freeman, 1980).

Although the Senate might add to its prestige by confirming one of its own, it may particularly damage the President by rejecting those closest to him, such as members of his cabinet. Similarly, an anti-Court motivation can manifest itself by a refusal to promote an associate justice to chief justice (e.g., Fortas).

We begin with a bivariate analysis of our hypotheses. First, we find little independent support for a pro-Senate bias in confirmation voting. The Senate has confirmed eight of its own (89 percent), but this proportion is virtually indistinguishable from the 81 percent of non-Senators whom the Senate has confirmed.

Substantial support is found for anti-Presidential motivations, however. Only 56 percent of nominees (14 of 25) have been confirmed in the fourth year of a President's term, versus 87 percent in the first three years (104 of 120). Similarly, the Senate has confirmed only 59 percent of nominees when the President's party was a minority (23 of 39), compared with 90 percent when the President's party controlled the Senate (95 of 106). Additionally, elected Presidents appear to fare substantially better (86 percent) than succession Presidents (53 percent). Nevertheless, such success does not depend on the size of the President's electoral coalition. The correlation between the percent of the President's electoral college vote and Senate approval or disapproval is slightly negative, $-.15$. Nominees politically close to the President fare especially poorly: 29 percent of current cabinet members have been rejected versus only 17 percent of non-cabinet nominees.

Finally, the simple relationship between promotion from associate justice to chief justice lacks strength. Eighty-two percent of non-justices have been confirmed compared with only 71 percent of promoted associate justices.

To determine the independent impact of each variable while controlling for all other variables, we conduct a logit analysis of the 145 aggregate-level Senate confirmation votes.[67] The dependent variable is the decision to confirm a particular nominee; the independent variables are the factors specified earlier. Table 4.2 presents the results.

The results include the "impact" or substantive significance of each variable. This is calculated by measuring the difference in the probability of confirmation when that variable is present as opposed to its absence.[68] For instance, the President's control of the Senate increases the probability of a nominee's confirmation by .35. This is clearly a substantial effect.

The results indicate a fair degree of support for the aggregate confirmation model. Four out of the seven variables in the model reach statistical significance. Overall, the model predicts 87 percent of the confirmation votes correctly, for a 32 percent reduction of error.[69] Senate control substantially increases the like-

---

[67] A description of logit may be found in the appendix at the back of the book.

[68] The impact is measured from a baseline of a .50 prior probability of confirmation.

[69] The percent reduction in error statistic compares the error rate from the model with the error rate by predicting the modal value every time.

Table 4.2. *Logit estimates of aggregate confirmation votes*

Variable	MLE[a]	SE[b]	Sig[c]	Impact
U.S. Sen.	.08	1.37	n.s.[d]	---
4th Year	-1.55	.58	.01	-.32
Control Sen	1.89	.61	.01	.35
Elected	.55	.69	n.s.	---
Elec Coll	-.01	.01	n.s.	---
Cabinet	-1.53	.66	.01	-.32
AJ to CJ	-1.78	.99	.05	-.35
Constant	1.56	.92	.09	.83[e]
Percent reduction in error		32		

Notes. [a]Maximum Likelihood Estimate. [b]SE=Standard Error. [c]Sig=significance level. [d]n.s. = not significant. [e]Probability of confirmation when all independent variables equal zero.

lihood of success, except for fourth-year nominations, which are substantially more likely to be defeated.

The model, of course, distorts reality to some extent. We treat Senate confirmation votes as single units when in fact they consist of as many as 100 individual voters, each of whom faces a unique decision calculus. Additionally, crucial factors that might influence confirmation votes, such as the ideology or qualifications of the nominee, are excluded. Because of data limitations, we cannot measure such factors for all confirmation votes. Nevertheless, we can measure most of the factors that influence confirmation from the nomination of Earl Warren in 1953 to that of David Souter in 1990.[70] We then apply the results to the 1991 nomination of Clarence Thomas.

An individual-level analysis

Any examination of the individual votes of senators must begin with an explanation of their motivations. First, senators should be concerned with reelection.

[70] The following section is based on work conducted with Charles Cameron and Albert Cover.

Though it may be too much to claim that senators are "single-minded seekers of reelection," to use David Mayhew's description,[71] one cannot long enjoy the perquisites of Senate life if one's roll-call behavior systematically antagonizes one's constituents.

Scientific analyses of confirmation voting usually suggest that public concern over nominees turns on the nominees' perceived judicial ideology and perceived qualifications. Ideologically proximate nominees should be perceived as attractive, poorly qualified nominees unattractive, and ideologically distant and poorly qualified nominees very unattractive.

Senators may pay careful attention to their constituents, but six-year terms give senators the potential to "shirk" and vote in accordance with their own preferences at the expense of their constituents. For example, Jacob Javits (R-NY) and George McGovern (D-SD) often voted their personal preferences in disregard of their constituents.[72] Though they ultimately suffered electoral defeat, a complete model of confirmation voting should attempt to account for senators' personal preferences.

Beyond these factors, the President may take an active role in the confirmation process, particularly if the confirmation becomes controversial. The President will generally have more political resources to deploy and can use them more effectively when his party controls the Senate and when he is not in the final year of his term. In addition, Presidential resources are likely to have an effect on members of his own party more than those of the other party. We also include the President's popularity, which has been extensively linked to executive success in the legislative arena.[73]

Finally, we account for organized interest groups, representing as they do more active citizens and potential campaign contributions. Historical evidence clearly indicates that lobbying has influenced the confirmation process. For example, Peter Fish argues that the rejection of Judge Parker in 1930 was due in large part to the activity of organized labor and the NAACP.[74] The nomination of Haynsworth brought forth a torrent of interest group activity, which in turn was exceeded by the almost frenetic mobilization of groups during the Bork nomination.

Data and variables. The dependent variable consists of the 2,153 confirmation votes cast by individual senators from the nomination of Earl Warren through the nomination of David Souter.

---

[71] *Congress: The Electoral Connection* (New Haven: Yale University Press, 1974), p. 17.

[72] See Alan Abramowitz and Jeffrey Segal, *Senate Elections* (Ann Arbor: University of Michigan Press, 1992), chaps. 3, 6.

[73] George C. Edwards, *At the Margins: Presidential Leadership of Congress* (New Haven: Yale University Press, 1989).

[74] "Spite Nominations to the United States Supreme Court: Herbert Hoover, Owen J. Roberts, and the Politics of Presidential Vengeance in Retrospect," 77 *Kentucky Law Journal* 545 (1989).

Nominee ideology and qualifications. To determine perceptions of nominees' qualifications and judicial philosophy, we use a content analysis from statements in newspaper editorials from the time of the nomination until the Senate voted.[75] The analysis used four of the nation's leading papers – two with a liberal stance, *The New York Times* and *The Washington Post*, and two with a more conservative outlook, *The Chicago Tribune* and *The Los Angeles Times*. Table 4.3 reports the results. Qualifications range from 0 (most unqualified) to 1 (most qualified). Ideology ranges from 0 (extremely conservative) to 1 (extremely liberal).

As indicated elsewhere, the data are reliable and appear to be valid.[76] The ideology scores meet the strictest test for validity – predictive validity. The ideology scores correlate at .80 with the overall ideological direction of the votes the approved nominees later cast on the court.[77]

Constituent ideology. We measure constituent ideology from statewide voting in selected presidential election voting and partisanship. Details are provided in Appendix 4.1.

Constituent distance. Constituent distance is the squared distance between nominee ideology and constituent ideology. The scaling procedure employed is discussed in Appendix I.

Personal Ideology. We measure each senator's personal "ideology" as the difference between his or her actual and predicted ADA scores, based on constituent ideology.[78] Those more liberal than their constituents should be more likely to vote for liberal nominees (Case 1) and less likely to vote for conservative nominees (Case 2) than "faithful" representatives would be, whereas those more conservative than their districts should be more likely to vote for conservative nominees (Case 3) and less likely to vote for liberal nominees (Case 4) than "faithful" representatives would be. We expect Cases 1 and 3 (Shirk +) to be positive and Cases 2 and 4 (Shirk −) to be negative.

Presidential strength and same-party status. We measure presidential strength as a dummy variable that takes the value "1" when the President's party controls the Senate and the President is not in the fourth year of his term, and zero otherwise. We measure same party as a dummy variable that takes the value "1" when a senator is of the same party as the President and zero otherwise.

---

[75] Charles M. Cameron, Albert D. Cover, and Jeffrey A. Segal, "Senate Voting on Supreme Court Nominees: A Neoinstitutional Model," 84 *American Political Science Review* 525 (1990).

[76] *Ibid.*

[77] Jeffrey A. Segal and Albert D. Cover, "Ideological Values and the Votes of U.S. Supreme Court Justices," 83 *American Political Science Review* 557 (1989).

[78] These scores do not represent the senators' ideology per se, but rather the direction of their ideology compared with that of their constituents.

Table 4.3. *Nominee margin, vote status, ideology, and qualifications*

Nominee	Year	President's Status[a]	Margin	Qual[b]	Ideol[c]
Warren	1954	Strong	96-0d	.74	.75
Harlan	1955	Weak	71-11	.86	.88
Brennan	1957	Weak	95-0d	1.00	1.00
Whittaker	1957	Weak	96-0	1.00	.50
Stewart	1959	Weak	70-17	1.00	.75
White	1962	Strong	100-0d	.50	.50
Goldberg	1962	Strong	100-0d	.92	.75
Fortas 1	1965	Strong	100-0d	1.00	1.00
Marshall	1967	Strong	69-11	.84	1.00
Fortas 2	1968	Weak	45-43e	.64	.85
Burger	1969	Weak	74-3	.96	.12
Haynsworth	1969	Weak	45-55	.34	.16
Carswell	1970	Weak	45-51	.11	.04
Blackmun	1970	Weak	94-0	.97	.12
Powell	1971	Weak	89-1	1.00	.17
Rehnquist 1	1971	Weak	68-26	.89	.05
Stevens	1975	Weak	98-0	.96	.25

O'Connor	1981	Strong	99-0	1.00	.48
Rehnquist 2	1986	Strong	65-33	.40	.05
Scalia	1986	Strong	98-0	1.00	.00
Bork	1987	Weak	42-58	.79	.10
Kennedy	1988	Weak	97-0	.89	.37
Souter	1990	Weak	90-9	.77	.33
Thomas	1991	Weak	52-48	.41	.16

Source.   Updated from Cameron, Cover, and Segal: "Senate Voting on Supreme Court Nominees: A Neoinstitutional Model," 84 American Political Science Review 526 (1990).

Notes.   [a]The President is labelled "Strong" in a non-election year in which the President's party controls the Senate, and "Weak" otherwise.   [b]Qualifications [Qual] are measured from 0.00 (least qualified) to 1.00 (most qualified).   [c]Ideology [Ideol] is measured from 0.00 (most conservative) to 1.00 (most liberal).   [d]Voice vote.   [e]Vote on cloture--failed to receive necessary two-thirds majority.

Presidential popularity. We measure the President's popularity as the percentage of people who approve of the job the incumbent is doing as measured by the Gallup survey prior to the Senate vote.

Interest-group activity. In the best of all possible situations we would have senator-level data on the amount of lobbying by organized interests dating back to 1954. Obviously, such data are unavailable. Thus, while recognizing that some senators will be lobbied more than others, we choose a variable that measures lobbying activity with respect to each nominee, the number of organized interests presenting testimony for (Interest Group Pro) and against the nominee (Interest Group Con) at the Senate Judiciary Committee hearings. Though this process treats all groups as fungible, we know that some groups are more powerful than others. Unfortunately for the purposes of political research, the Constitution protects the membership lists of organized interests. Despite this problem, we presume that the more opposition a nominee has, the less support he or she will have, and alternatively, the more organized support for a nominee, the more support he or she will have.

Results. Again, we first present the bivariate results and then proceed to the multivariate analysis. The substantive results, though, are largely the same. We present both because those without extensive statistical backgrounds may find the logit analysis daunting, whereas those with such a background may be skeptical of bivariate results. Those preferring bivariate analyses can skip the multivariate section; those preferring more multivariate analyses can skip the bivariate section.

We begin our examination with the influence of qualifications. Although we expect that ideology should strongly affect votes, other nominee characteristics also influence senators. If they did not, it would be impossible to explain how certain strong liberals (e.g., Brennan) and conservatives (e.g., Burger) breezed through the Senate. Senators may find it difficult, for instance, to justify opposition to highly qualified nominees. As our qualifications variable is skewed toward the high end, we classify nominees as highly qualified if their qualifications score from the content analysis is greater than .90, moderately qualified if their score is greater than or equal to .50 and less than .90, and unqualified if their score is less than .50. We see in Table 4.4 a strong positive relationship between qualifications and votes. Senators voted for highly qualified nominees 98 percent of the time, for moderately qualified nominees 80 percent of the time, and for lesser qualified nominees but 53 percent of the time. In other words, if 100 votes are cast, a poorly qualified nominee will receive 45 fewer votes on average than a highly qualified nominee. We can measure the strength of the bivariate relationship by gamma, a measure of association that runs from -1.0 (perfect negative relationship) through 0.0 (no relationship) to 1.0 (perfect positive relationship). The gamma of .81 indicates that senators are much more likely to vote for nominees who are perceived as well qualified.

Table 4.4. *Confirmation voting by nominee qualifications*

	Qualifications		
Vote	Low	Moderate	High
No	139	158	21
	47.4%	19.0%	2.0%
Yes	154	672	1,009
	52.6%	81.0%	98.0%
γ=.81			

Table 4.5. *Confirmation voting by constituent ideological distance*

	Distance		
Vote	Close	Moderate	Far
No	9	174	135
	1.2%	17.7%	33.1%
Yes	754	808	273
	98.8%	82.3%	66.9%
γ=-.71			

We next examine ideology, or more explicitly, the ideological distance between a senator's constituents and the nominee. To examine this relationship
we categorize constituencies and nominees as liberal, moderate, and conservative
using the data described earlier. Senators should be most likely to vote for
nominees who are ideologically close to their constituents (e.g., liberal constituents and liberal nominees) and least likely to vote for nominees who are ideologically distant from their constituents (e.g., liberal constituents and
conservative nominees). This is exactly what we find. We see in Table 4.5 the
percentage of senators voting for ideologically proximate, ideologically moderate, and ideologically distant nominees. Overall, senators voted almost 99
percent of the time for nominees who were close to the average views of their
constituents, 83 percent of the time for nominees who were a moderate distance
from their constituents, and but 67 percent of the time for nominees who were
distant from their constituents. The gamma of − .71 indicates that senators are
much less likely to vote for nominees who are distant from their constituents.
What is perhaps most interesting about ideology is the manner in which it
interacts with qualifications. Table 4.6 examines the percentage of "yes" votes
senators cast by both constituent ideological distance and qualifications. The

Table 4.6. *Confirmation voting by qualifications and distance:*
percentage pro

Qualifications	Constituent Ideological Distance		
	Close	Moderate	Far
High	99.9	96.0	98.9
Medium	99.3	78.4	55.2
Low	90.6	53.8	8.3

results couldn't be clearer. Senators are willing to vote for highly qualified candidates regardless of ideological distance. They are also willing to vote for ideologically close nominees regardless of qualifications. Charges against Fortas no more influenced liberals than charges against Thomas did conservatives. But when nominees are both distant and poorly qualified, opposition is virtually certain.

Although senators will be concerned with the ideology of their constituents, they should also pay some attention to their own policy preferences. Here we classify senators as "liberal" if their ADA scores fall one standard deviation above where they should be given the ideological preferences of their constituents, and "conservative" if their ADA scores fall more than one standard deviation below where they should be given the ideological preferences of their constituents. All others are considered moderates. Again we note that these scores do not represent the actual personal ideology of senators, but rather the extent and direction of their "shirking" in a liberal or conservative direction.

Similar to this presentation, liberal-liberal, moderate-moderate, and conservative-conservative matches between senators and nominees are considered proximate, liberal-moderate and conservative-moderate matches are considered moderate, and liberal-conservative matches are considered distant. Senators voted 92 percent of the time for nominees close to themselves, 87 percent of the time for nominees a moderate distance from themselves, and 64 percent of the time for nominees distant from themselves (see Table 4.7). The gamma, $-.51$, though not as strong as the relationship between constituent ideology and vote, suggests that a substantial amount of shirking does take place in confirmation votes.

Confirmation votes occur in the political world, not in a vacuum. The most important player in this political world is the President, who is expected to use his influence to secure a successful nomination. The President's resources will be lower, and thus he will have less influence, when he is in the final year of his term and when his party does not control the Senate. In fact, Presidents have secured 94 percent of the votes on the average when they are in a strong position

Table 4.7. *Confirmation voting by senator ideological distance*

Vote	Close	Moderate	Far
No	13	233	72
	7.6%	13.1%	35.6%
Yes	157	1,548	130
	92.4%	86.9%	64.4%
$\gamma = -.51$			

Table 4.8. *Confirmation voting by Presidential status*

Vote	Weak	Strong
No	274	44
	19.7%	5.8%
Yes	1,115	720
	80.3%	94.2%
$\gamma = .60$		

vis-à-vis the Senate and 80 percent of the votes when in a weak position (gamma = .60) (see Table 4.8). Thus, a weakly positioned President can cost his nominee an average of fourteen votes. Additionally, the President's influence is likely to be lower on members of the opposition party. Senators of the President's party support his nominees with 93 percent of their votes, whereas senators of the opposition party do so only 78 percent of the time (gamma = .59) (see Table 4.9). Additionally, popular Presidents – those with approval ratings greater than 70 – average 98 percent of the votes, whereas unpopular Presidents – those with approval ratings less than 50 – average only 79 percent (gamma = .44). This indicates that an unpopular President costs a nominee an average of almost 20 votes (see Table 4.10).

Finally, we expect interest groups to influence the votes of senators. When nominees face fierce opposition by organized interests at confirmation hearings – for example, Haynsworth, Bork, and Kennedy – they receive on average 71 percent of the votes, but when they have no opposition, they average 97 percent of the votes (gamma = − .60) (see Table 4.11). Because supportive interest-group mobilization arises largely in reaction to interest-group mobilization against

Table 4.9. *Confirmation voting by Presidential partisanship*

No	244	74
	22.5%	6.9%
Yes	840	995
	77.5%	93.1%
γ=.59		

Table 4.10. *Confirmation voting by Presidential popularity*

No	139	168	11
	21.5%	16.1%	2.4%
Yes	507	876	452
	78.5%	83.9%	97.6%
γ=.44			

Table 4.11. *Confirmation voting by interest-group opposition*

No	20	117	181
	2.7%	16.1%	29.3%
Yes	722	608	505
	97.3%	83.9%	70.7%
γ=-.60			

nominees, there is little likelihood of a bivariate relationship between votes and positive group support. In fact, none is found: gamma = −.03. However, if we control for other factors, interest-group support should help a nominee.

Because our bivariate tables do not allow us to control for the influence of

Table 4.12. *Dependent and independent variables*

Variable	Mean	Minimum	Maximum	Std. Dev.
Vote	.85	0.00	1.00	.35
Distance	.14	.00	.65	.13
Qualifications (lack of)	.20	.00	.89	.25
Qualifications x Distance	.03	.00	.47	.05
Shirk +	.08	.00	.69	.12
Shirk -	.03	.00	.68	.09
Strong President	.35	.00	1.00	.48
Presidential Popularity	59.56	40.00	79.00	10.89
Same Party	.50	.00	1.00	.50
Interest Group +	4.86	.00	21.00	6.09
Interest Group -	5.27	.00	17.00	6.17

other factors, and because they do not allow us to predict individual results based on the complete set of specified factors, we move to a multivariate analysis of our confirmation model.

We estimated the model using logit analysis.[79] The independent variables are the original interval-level measures discussed in the "Data and Variables" section. Table 4.12 presents the means, ranges, and standard deviations of the dependent and independent variables. Table 4.13 provides the results of the logit equation. As the data are largely interval level, we use the column labeled "Impact" to measure the change in the probability of a "yes" vote given a one standard deviation change in each independent variable for an undecided senator. So, for example, a one standard deviation or "typical" increase in ideological distance between a senator's constituents and a nominee decreases the probability of a "yes" vote by .27.

As shown, the results for the model are quite impressive. All of the estimated logit coefficients are of the predicted sign, are of reasonable magnitudes, and are highly significant. The model predicts 95 percent of the votes correctly, for a 67 percent reduction in error.

As the results indicate, the ideological distance between senators' constituents and nominees decisively affects confirmation voting. A one standard deviation increase in that distance decreases the likelihood of a "yes" vote by .27. Qualifications by themselves have a less direct effect on voting. A one standard deviation change in qualifications, which accounts for a full quarter of the scale, affects the probability of a "yes" vote by .16. We do not say that qualifications matter only slightly, for that is not correct. Qualifications have a substantial effect on voting when they interact with ideological distance. Here, a one standard

---

[79] Logit is explained in the appendix at the back of the book.

Table 4.13. Logit estimates of individual-level confirmation model

Variable	MLE[a]	SE[b]	Impact[c]
Constant	1.62	.58	- - - -
Distance	-9.31	1.34	-.27
Qualifications (lack of)	-2.75	.74	-.16
Distance x Qualifications	-21.30	4.22	-.24
Shirk +	14.71	2.84	.14
Shirk -	-8.67	3.03	-.19
Strong President	2.90	.34	.30
Same Party	.68	.21	.09
Presidential Popularity	.06	.01	.16
Interest Group +	.05	.02	.07
Interest Group -	-.21	.03	-.27
x2/df	753/2142		
percent predicted correctly	95		
percent reduction error	67		

Notes. [a]Maximum Likelihood Estimate. [b] Standard Error. All coefficients
significant at p<.001 except Interest Group + (p=.005). [c]"Impact" measures
the change in probability of a yes vote given a one standard deviation change
in the independent variable for an undecided (p=.5) senator.

deviation change lowers the probability of a "yes" vote by .24. Thus, senators overwhelmingly vote for close nominees who are well qualified, and for the most part they also vote for close nominees who are not so well qualified. Senators are moderately likely to vote against highly qualified distant nominees; they almost never vote for poorly qualified distant nominees.

Because we have no direct measures of the personal ideology of senators, we can say nothing about the effect of ideological distance between the personal ideology of senators and that of nominees. Nevertheless, the results do suggest that even when measured indirectly, the personal ideology of senators does have a significant impact on confirmation voting. When both the senator and the nominee are either to the right or the left of the senator's constituents, the senator is more likely to vote for the nominee. Alternatively, when the senator is on the opposite side of his or her constituents from the nominee, the senator is less likely to vote for the nominee.

We next examine presidential influence on the votes of senators. First, Presidents clearly are more successful when they are in a strong legislative position – that is, when their party controls the Senate and it is not an election year. A strong legislative position especially sways senators who remain undecided after examining the characteristics of the nominee. According to the model, a switch from a weak to a strong President raises to .80 the probability of a "yes" vote from a previously undecided senator. Membership in the President's party produces a lesser effect, increasing the probability of a "yes" vote from .5 to .59.

The final presidential variable we examine is the President's approval rating. Unquestionably, no one-to-one relationship between presidential popularity and confirmation approvals exists. President Nixon, for instance, was at the height of his popularity when Haynsworth and Carswell were rejected (65 and 63 percent approval, respectively). President Johnson's approval rating was only at 39 percent when Thurgood Marshall was confirmed. Yet it is also true that Johnson's approval ratings were almost as low when Fortas was rejected as Chief Justice (42 percent), and President Reagan was near his second-term low when Bork was defeated (50 percent). On average, the difference between an unpopular President (e.g., 40 percent approval) and a popular one (e.g., 60 percent approval) increases the likelihood that an undecided senator will vote "yes" from .50 to .77.

Finally, strong interest-group mobilization against a nominee can hurt a candidate, whereas interest-group mobilization for a nominee only has substantively slight, but still statistically significant, positive effects. The Bork nomination provides an interesting example. Seventeen organized groups testified against Bork at the Judiciary Committee hearings; 20 supported him, but negative pressure has more influence. In probabilistic terms, a moderate-to-conservative Southern senator who would have voted for Bork with a probability of .95 without any interest-group pressure would have voted for him at a probability of only .61 after the intensive interest-group mobilization.

Interest groups appear to have had an even more devastating effect on the

Table 4.14. *Actual versus predicted "no" votes*

Nominee	Actual	Predicted
Warren	0	0
Harlan	11	2
Brennan	0	0
Whittaker	0	0
Stewart	17	0
White	0	0
Goldberg	0	0
Fortas 1	0	0
Marshall	11	2
Fortas 2	43	44
Burger	3	0
Haynsworth	55	48
Carswell	51	53
Blackmun	0	0
Powell	1	0
Rehnquist 1	26	29
Stevens	0	0
O'Connor	0	0
Rehnquist 2	33	31
Scalia	0	0
Bork	58	46
Kennedy	0	0
Souter	9	6

Mean Absolute Error all votes	3.00
r actual vs. predicted	.97

Haynsworth nomination. Sixteen groups spoke against Haynsworth; only three testified favorably. Senators with a .95 probability of voting for him in the absence of interest-group involvement had only a .45 probability of support following the extensive lobbying campaign. Though many conservatives blamed the Reagan White House for failing to mobilize behind Bork, the Nixon White House was far more culpable in its failure to support Haynsworth.

Beyond the parameter estimates, the model does an excellent job in predicting confirmation outcomes. Table 4.14 presents the actual and predicted "no" votes for every confirmation from Earl Warren (1954) through David Souter (1990).

Overall, the model's mean absolute error is but 3.00 votes per confirmation. The correlation between actual and predicted "no" votes is .97. On a nomination-level basis, the model underpredicts the low levels of opposition to the Harlan,

Stewart, Marshall and Bork nominations. In the first three cases, conservative Southern senators voted against nominees who strongly supported desegregation. Though most of the opposition to Bork is predicted, he did considerably worse than expected given his high qualifications. On the other hand, the model predicts 44 votes against Fortas's elevation to Chief Justice, almost exactly the 43 votes he actually received. The same is true for Carswell (actual, 51; predicted, 53) and Rehnquist (1986) (actual, 33; predicted, 31).

Gauging the success of the model in terms of confirmation outcomes is not a straightforward task. The vote on the Fortas nomination as Chief Justice was 45 Yea and 43 Nay, a majority insufficient to invoke cloture. Under current rules, 41 "no" votes precludes invocation of cloture. If we use these as our decision rule for passage, then we correctly predict the outcome of every nomination.

We further tested our model for the possibility of violated assumptions. The final result is that our substantive conclusions do not change. Details are reported in Appendix 4.2.

Finally, we apply the model to the 1991 vote for Clarence Thomas. Though there were unique aspects to this nomination – most notably, the charges of sexual harassment by Anita Hill – the model well accompanies the charges through the effect this has on the nominee's perceived qualifications. Thomas's score of .41 places him above Carswell, but in a low-level echelon with Haynsworth and Rehnquist (1986). Our resulting prediction is 57 votes against the nominee, 9 votes different from the actual total of 48.

SUMMARY AND CONCLUSIONS

Presidents nominate individuals to the Court in order to satisfy certain goals. For some Presidents, policy concerns are paramount, whereas others are more concerned with patronage. Although we cannot predict nominees with any overall accuracy, we can predict the ideology of the President's choice. In short, that ideology will be a function of the President's ideology, the ideological composition of the Senate, and the ideological makeup of the Supreme Court.

Although the Senate routinely confirms most nominations, it rejects a substantial number. Five nominees failed to be confirmed between 1968 and 1987. We find that the senators' votes greatly depend on the ideological distance between their constituents and the nominee, the perceived qualifications of the nominee, and the interaction between the two. The personal ideology of senators also appears to matter. In short, a nominee's reception hinges on the characteristics of the nominee and the composition of the Senate.

Finally, the context of a nomination strongly influences the outcome. The strength and popularity of the President emerge as important determinants of individual votes. In addition, the relative mobilization of interest groups around a nominee also has pronounced effects.

APPENDIX 4.1: MEASURING CONSTITUENT
IDEOLOGY, PERSONAL IDEOLOGY, AND IDEOLOGICAL
DISTANCE

We develop here a measure of state-level ideology so that ADA scores can be partitioned into constituent preferences and those based on the personal preferences of senators. The measure we develop must be usable as far back as the 1953 Warren nomination.

Because state-level survey data do not allow us to measure ideology in the 1950s or 1960s, we examine presidential voting as an indicator of state-level ideology. We know that certain elections tap the traditional liberal-conservative dimension. In these elections, the difference between a state's Democratic vote and the national Democratic vote might be a good indicator of state-level liberalism. For instance, in 1972, Massachusetts was 16.7 percentage points more Democratic than the nation, followed by Rhode Island (9.3) and Minnesota (8.6). At the other extreme, Mississippi was 17.9 points less Democratic than the national average, followed by Oklahoma, Georgia, Alabama, and Utah. Two criteria determine our use of an election: It had to evidence strong ideological content, and no significant third party could participate. Because of third parties, we excluded 1948, 1968, and 1980. Of the remaining elections, we eliminated 1952 and 1956 as non-ideological. Although the 1976 election did have a marginal ideological component, a strong regional reaction to Carter's candidacy makes it inappropriate for inclusion. The elections that fit the criteria are 1964, 1972, and 1984. These comport with MacDonald's and Rabinowitz's choices, who find these to be three of the four most ideological presidential elections since 1920.[80]

The average ideological proclivity of a state's voters does not necessarily provide us with the average ideological proclivity of a senator's constituents. As Fiorina, Fenno, and others have demonstrated, Democrats and Republicans in Congress represent different constituencies.[81] One study, for instance, demonstrates that as elections approach, senators often move closer to the median voter within their party, not the median voter within their state.[82] Thus the predicted ADA scores that we seek, those expunged of personal influence, will have to represent partisan differences as well. The residuals from the model become our measure of shirking.

To this end we regressed each senator's actual ADA score in the year of a

---

[80] Stuart Elaine MacDonald and George Rabinowitz, ''The Dynamics of Structural Realignment,'' 81 *American Political Science Review* 775 (1987).

[81] Morris Fiorina, *Representatives, Roll Calls, and Contituencies* (Lexington, MA: D.C. Heath, 1974); Richard Fenno, *Home Style: House Members in Their Districts* (Boston: Little Brown, 1978).

[82] Catherine R. Shapiro, David Brady, Richard Brody, and John Ferejohn, ''Linking Constituency Opinion and Senate Voting Scores: A Hybrid Explanation,'' 15 *Legislative Studies Quarterly* 599 (1990).

confirmation vote on state-level presidential election results from our key ideological elections (1964, 1972, and 1984) along with two dummy variables for the partisanship of the senator, "Democrat" and "Southern Democrat."[83] For nominations through 1968, we used the 1964 election; for nominations from 1969 through 1975, the 1972 election; and for nominations from 1981 through 1988, the 1984 election. Constituent preferences are simply the predictions from the equation. The effects of personal ideology and partisanship do not contaminate them.[84]

To measure constituent ideological distance we could simply take predicted ADA scores, divide them by 100 (to place them with our nominee ideology scores on a 0–1 scale), and then use the squared distance between nominee ideology and predicted ADA scores. This process assumes that a 0 in ADA scores is equivalent to a 0 in nominee ideology, and that a 100 in ADA scores is equivalent to a 1 in nominee ideology. In other words, if a = ADA/100, NI = nominee ideology, and a = α + β_1NI, then α = 0 and β = 1. There is no explicit reason to believe this is so. As the scaling question is largely an empirical one, we conducted a search for the α and β that minimized the -2^* log likelihood ratio in the logit equation, a procedure analogous to the Hildreth-Lu procedure for autocorrelation. We end with an α of .2 and a β of .5, but note that the results are robust: An α of 0 and a β of 1.0 fit the data almost as well.

APPENDIX 4.2: CORRELATED ERROR STRUCTURES

Because of the pooled cross-sectional time series design of the study, errors can correlate with one another in three distinct ways: over time, over space, and

---

[83] We controlled for home state advantage in presidential election voting using the formula derived by Michael Lewis-Beck and Thomas Rice, "Localism in Presidential Elections: The Home state Advantage," 27 *American Journal of Political Science* 548 (1983).

[84] The results of the regressions through 1968, from 1969 through 1975, and from 1981 forward are respectively,

> ADA = 27.3 + .95 × DVote + 42.3 × Dem − 25.7 × SDem, adj R^2 = .49.
> ADA = 35.3 + 2.4 × DVote + 37.5 × Dem − 21.0 × SDem, adj R^2 = .58.
> ADA = 29.5 + 2.1 × DVote + 49.5 × Dem − 21.4 × SDem, adj R^2 = .69.

All variables are significant at p<.05. One potential problem with this methodology is that to the extent that pure representational behavior is not entirely explained by our predictor variables, the residuals will pick up some of that representational behavior and treat it as shirking. For instance, the ideological distance between Democratic and Republican constituents may not be the same within every Southern state. Similar studies, however, show that these residuals do behave as if they measure shirking; for instance, they wax and wane over the electoral cycle and correlate with previous electoral margins. Joseph P. Kalt and Mark A. Zupan, "Capture and Ideology in the Economic Theory of Politics," 74 *American Economic Review* 279 (1984). With these caveats in mind, we treat the residuals as largely representing non-constituent interests.

over both time and space.[85] Correlations over time would most likely exist if the error of a particular senator at time t correlated with the error of that senator at any time beyond t. Correlations over space would most likely occur if the errors of one or more senators on a particular vote correlate with the errors of other senators on that same vote. For instance, our residual analysis suggests that we consistently overpredicted the number of pro-Potter Stewart votes (see Table 4.13). Correlations over time and space would occur if the true slope coefficients vary from one nomination to another.

To control for the possibility of correlated errors in time and space we employed a logit variant of the Least Squares Dummy Variable technique. First, to control for correlations across time, we added a dummy variable for the hundreds of senators who voted in more than one confirmation. The results suggest that auto-correlated errors are not a problem.[86]

The more likely problem, as noted, is correlation across space, or heteroskedasticity. We therefore attempted to include a dummy variable for all but one of the nominees, but extremely high multicollinearity between subsets of the nominee dummies and some of the nominee-level variables prevented the equation from being estimated. Because we could not enter the complete set of nominee dummies, we chose to enter those in which the model mispredicted the total number of ''no'' votes by more than three, for it is most likely that we will have correlated errors across senators here. The results are presented in Table 4.15.

As seen, the new model does significantly improve the overall fit. The χ^2 drops from 753 to 631 with only four additional degrees of freedom. The mean absolute error of predicted ''no'' votes drops to 1.5 per confirmation. The percent predicted correctly barely improves though, increasing from 94.6 to 95.1. Most importantly, virtually no change in the substantive interpretations of the coefficients occurs. Significance levels remain extremely high, and the impact of the variables, though changed somewhat, are relatively the same. For instance, distance and qualifications have an increased impact in the new model, but the interaction between distance and qualifications has a lesser impact. One significant difference is the greater effect of positive interest-group mobilization, but that still pales by comparison with negative interest group mobilization.[87]

If the slope coefficients for the independent variables vary for each nomination,

[85] See Lois Sayrs, *Pooled Time Series Analysis* (Beverly Hills: Sage, 1989); and James Stimson, ''Regression in Space and Time: A Statistical Essay,'' 29 *American Journal of Political Science* 914 (1985).

[86] See Jeffrey A. Segal, Charles M. Cameron, and Albert D. Cover, ''A Spatial Model of Roll Call Voting: Senators, Constituents, Presidents, and Interest Groups in Supreme Court Confirmations,'' 36 *American Journal of Political Science* 96 (1992).

[87] If we add dummy variables for all nominees whose ''no'' votes are mispredicted by two votes or more, multi-collinearity starts to become an extreme problem. For instance, the correlation between Strong President and the remaining variables in the model increases to .9 and its standard error jumps from .6 to 2.5. Nevertheless, the parameter estimates remain basically the same.

Table 4.15. Logit estimates of dummy variable confirmation model

Variable	MLE[a]	SE[b]	Impact[c]
Constant	3.88	1.00	- - - -
Distance	-11.30	2.04	-.31
Qualifications (lack of)	-4.61	1.24	-.26
Distance x Qual	-20.38	6.30	-.25
Shirk +	15.95	2.93	.37
Shirk -	-9.16	3.16	-.20
Strong President	2.41	.64	.26
Same Party	.90	.24	.11
Presidential Popularity	.08	.03	.20
Interest Group +	.15	.05	.21
Interest Group -	-.26	.05	-.33
Harlan	-.60	.72	- - - -
Stewart	-4.55	.66	- - - -
Marshall	.53	.91	- - - -
Haynsworth	-.39	.76	- - - -
Bork	-3.01	.78	- - - -
χ^2/df	631/2137		
percent predicted correctly	95		
percent reduction in error	67		

Notes. [a]Maximum Likelihood Estimates. [b]Standard Error. All substantive coefficients significant at $p<.005$. Stewart and Bork significant at $p<.005$; Harlan, Marshall and Haynsworth not significant. [c]"Impact" measures the change in probability of a "yes" vote given a one standard deviation change in the independent variable for an undecided ($p=.5$) senator.

then the model will produce correlated errors in time and space. The usual method of estimating the extent of such problems is to run separate logit analyses for each nomination and use a χ^2 test to determine whether restricting the coefficients to the same value across nominations (i.e., pooling) results in a significant reduction in overall fit.

Unfortunately, the nature of our data makes such a test impossible. First, several of the nominations were unanimous, and thus there is no variance to explain within those cross-sections. We could exclude these cross-sections from our pool, but to do so leaves unexplained why those nominees received such high levels of support relative to other nominees (presumably because they are ideologically moderate or highly qualified) and simultaneously creates a serious selection bias problem. Second, our model necessarily makes use of nominee-level independent variables such as the qualifications of the nominee. These variables could not be used to predict votes in individual nominations as the scores only vary across nominations.

Because of these problems, we attempted a simpler test to determine whether the slope for ideological distance varies across nominations by including interaction terms between each of the N-1 nominees and ideological distance. Unfortunately, the logit results did not converge. We were able to test whether the slope for ideological distance differed from the first eleven nominations to the next eleven by adding a dummy variable for the first set and an interaction between the dummy variable and ideological distance. Neither estimate came close to being significant. The results, though, are only a necessary condition for assuming constant slopes, not a sufficient condition.

We are left without an explicit test of whether the nominations should be pooled or not. We note, however, that the case for pooling is reasonable given the overall fit of the model. We could not predict 96 percent of the votes correctly and obtain a mean absolute error of 1.5 votes per nomination if the slope coefficients across nominations were randomly distributed.[88]

---

[88]   T. D. Wallace, "Weaker Criteria and Tests for Linear Restrictions in Regression," 40 *Econometrica* 689 (1972) shows that even in circumstances where coefficients do differ between different cross sections, pooling can lead to more precise estimates than the individual estimator variances.

5

Getting into court

Assertions by persons about to initiate a lawsuit, as well as by those who have already lost, that they will take their cases all the way to the United States Supreme Court undoubtedly bespeak their deeply felt intentions, but in most cases their avowals lack credibility. Individuals who wish to file a lawsuit must be proper parties – that is, they must have standing to sue. If they have such credentials, they must also bring their cases to the proper forum: The court in question must have jurisdiction – the capability to resolve their dispute. Assuming that the plaintiff is a proper party and is in the proper forum, a third hurdle to Supreme Court resolution still remains: The justices themselves must deem the matter worthy of their consideration. The last is by far the most difficult to surmount.

Decisions about access, whether they concern proper parties or proper forum, have important policy effects. Although such questions do not resolve the merits of the cases before the Court, they serve as a "gate" that litigants must pass through in order to obtain a meritorious resolution of their disputes.[1] The policies that govern access, like decisions on the merits, impact and bind the operation of the judicial system generally. Analyses show that the Warren Court provided relatively open access, a policy that the Burger Court continued during its very early years.[2] But by the mid-1970s, the Burger Court had established policies that narrowed access to the federal courts.[3] The cited analyses both show that the individual justices' votes opening or closing access covary with their overall rankings on a general liberal-conservative dimension.[4] Liberals vote to open access; conservatives to close it.

---

[1] The original "gate" through which litigants must pass is the justices' decision whether or not to decide the case at all – that is, whether to grant the petition for certiorari or, in the case of an appeal, to note probable jurisdiction. Absent reconsideration, which almost never occurs, denial ends further Supreme Court consideration of the case. We discuss this "gate" in the section on case selection in this chapter.

[2] Gregory J. Rathjen and Harold J. Spaeth, "Access to the Federal Courts: An Analysis of Burger Court Policy Making," 23 *American Journal of Political Science* 360 (1979), at 361–364.

[3] Gregory J. Rathjen and Harold J. Spaeth, "Denial of Access and Ideological Preferences: An Analysis of the Voting Behavior of the Burger Court Justices, 1989–1976," 36 *Western Political Quarterly* 71 (1983). Also see Table 5.1.

[4] The overall ranking of the justices on a liberal-conservative continuum is taken from David W.

In this chapter we begin by detailing the legal requirements for getting into federal court by specifying the jurisdiction of the federal courts in general and that of the Supreme Court in particular, and the elements that determine whether a litigant has standing to sue. We will also present the procedure whereby cases reach the Supreme Court and the factors that affect the justices' decision to accept a case for consideration. We conclude with a discussion of the Court's caseload.

LEGAL REQUIREMENTS

There are two legal considerations for gaining access to a court: Does the petitioned court have jurisdiction and does the petitioning party have standing to sue. These considerations apply to all courts, state and federal. They vary inasmuch as courts differ from one another in the jurisdiction they have; furthermore, the state courts generally insist much less that plaintiffs meet all the technical requirements of standing to sue.

Jurisdiction

In its broadest sense, jurisdiction means the authority by which a court accepts and decides matters brought to its attention. Jurisdiction takes three forms: geographical, hierarchical, and subject matter. The federal courts organize themselves along state lines, whereas the state courts basically rely on their counties and the subdivisions thereof – cities, towns, and townships – to separate the geographical jurisdiction of one court from another. Hierarchically, the federal courts have a three-tiered system: trial or courts of first instance, inferior or intermediate courts of appeals, and a supreme court. Most states adhere to the same arrangement, although some of the less populous states do without an intermediate court of appeals.

The federal district courts try the vast majority of cases heard in the federal system. Each state has at least one district Court. If a state has more than one, the additional district courts carry a geographical designation – northern, southern, eastern, western, central, or middle.[5] Except for the District Court for the

Rohde and Harold J. Spaeth, *Supreme Court Decision Making* (San Francisco; W.H. Freeman, 1976), pp. 142–144.

[5] Twenty-six states and the District of Columbia have a single district court: the six New England states (Maine, New Hampshire, Vermont, Massachusetts, Rhode Island, Connecticut), New Jersey, Delaware, Maryland, South Carolina plus sixteen states west of the Mississippi River (Minnesota, North and South Dakota, Nebraska, Kansas, Montana, Wyoming, Colorado, New Mexico, Arizona, Utah, Idaho, Nevada, Oregon, Alaska, Hawaii. Twelve states have two, all but one of which (Washington) are in the Midwest or South (Ohio, Indiana, Michigan, Wisconsin, Iowa, Missouri, Kentucky, Arkansas, Mississippi, Virginia, and West Virginia). Seven of the nine states with three are in the South: Alabama, Florida, Georgia, Louisiana, North Carolina, Oklahoma, Tennessee. The other two are Illinois and Pennsylvania. Three states have four: New York, Texas, and California. Four territories of the United States also have a district court: Puerto Rico, the Virgin Islands, Guam, and the Northern Mariana Islands.

District of Columbia, those in the states and other territories of the United States are gathered together into eleven numbered courts of appeals, which are identified as United States Courts of Appeals for the [N]th Circuit. A given circuit court will hear appeals from all of the district courts in the adjacent states that comprise its geographical jurisdiction.[6] The sole exception is the court of appeals for the District of Columbia, which hears appeals only from the District's district court. Panels of three judges decide the vast majority of the cases in the courts of appeals. Depending on the rules of the specific circuit, some cases may be heard by the full bench (en banc).

The foregoing courts, plus the Supreme Court, resolve most every matter that the Constitution authorizes the federal courts to resolve. Although their subject matter is thereby limited, within its confines the district courts, courts of appeal, and the Supreme Court may be described as courts of general jurisdiction.[7]

The source of the federal courts' and the Supreme Court's subject-matter jurisdiction is Article III of the Constitution and acts of Congress based thereon. The heart of this jurisdiction consists of federal questions – "all cases, in law and equity, arising under this Constitution, the laws of the United States, and treaties." The federal courts make policy because they authoritatively resolve these questions. Ancillary to federal questions are those arising under diversity of citizenship, and supplementary jurisdiction. We discuss each in turn.

Federal questions. To invoke federal question jurisdiction, parties seeking access to a federal court must demonstrate to the court's satisfaction that their cases in chief substantially concern some provision of the Constitution, an act of Congress, or a treaty of the United States. The action of federal administrative agencies and officials or an action to which the United States is party are, for all practical purposes, also federal questions. Article III also makes reference to suits between states, admiralty and maritime jurisdiction, and cases to which foreign diplomatic personnel accredited to the United States are party. Though such controversies technically constitute federal questions, they arise infre-

---

[6] The states and territories that each Circuit encompasses are as follows: First: Maine, New Hampshire, Massachusetts, Rhode Island, Puerto Rico. Second: Vermont, New York, Connecticut. Third: Pennsylvania, New Jersey, Delaware, Virgin Islands. Fourth: Maryland, West Virginia, Virginia, North and South Carolina. Fifth: Mississippi, Louisiana, Texas. Sixth: Michigan, Ohio, Kentucky, Tennessee. Seventh: Wisconsin, Illinois, Indiana. Eighth: Minnesota, Iowa, Missouri, Arkansas, North and South Dakota, Nebraska. Ninth: Montana, Idaho, Washington, Oregon, California, Nevada, Arizona, Alaska, Hawaii, Guam, Northern Marianas. Tenth: Kansas, Oklahoma, Wyoming, Colorado, New Mexico, Utah. Eleventh: Alabama, Georgia, Florida.

[7] There are also five "specialized" federal courts with their own judges. Three trial courts: the Tax Court, the Court of Claims, and the Court of International Trade; and two appellate courts: the Court of Appeals for the Federal Circuit and the Court of Military Appeals. The Tax Court hears federal tax cases, the Court of Claims entertains suits for damages against the federal government, and the Court of International Trade decides tariff and related sorts of disputes. The Federal Circuit hears appeals from the specialized trial courts other than the Tax Court and appeals in intellectual property cases. The Court of Military Appeals reviews decisions of courts martial.

quently. And when they do, their litigation comports more with private disputes than it does with the resolution of matters of public policy that characterizes cases arising under the Constitution, acts of Congress, or treaties.[8]

Because the federal courts, as noted, are courts of limited jurisdiction, plaintiffs must show that a right or immunity arising under federal law is an integral element of their causes of action and not merely a collateral issue, or introduced as a defense, or in response to respondents' counterclaims. Two additional conditions must also be met. If the facts alleging federal jurisdiction are challenged, the burden of proof falls on the party seeking access to the federal courts. Second, all federal courts have a continuing obligation to notice a lack of jurisdiction and to dismiss cases on their own motion if either of the parties fails to so move.

Diversity of citizenship. Apparently because of concern that state courts would be biased in favor of their own residents in cases involving an out-of-state litigant, the Framers authorized the federal courts to decide cases "between citizens of different states" or between citizens of one state and aliens. These cases rarely contain an issue of policy consequence. Instead, they tend to be the kinds of everyday tort, contract, and property cases that predominately find their way into state courts.

In order to avoid inundating the federal courts with diversity cases, the Supreme Court as well as Congress have imposed conditions on those who would bring them. In an early decision, the Supreme Court ruled that diversity must be complete – that is, every litigant on one side of the controversy must be domiciled in a different state from those on the other side.[9] Domicile rather than residence controls. An individual may have several residences, but only one domicile – the place where he or she currently resides, so long as he or she intends to remain there for some indefinite period of time.[10] Resident aliens are not citizens of a state because they have not been naturalized. Neither are unincorporated associations, such as a labor union. The domicile of their members controls, which in the case of a union with members throughout the United States effectively means that the organization can neither sue nor be sued in diversity. Congress, however, has exempted corporations from this rule by providing them with citizenship in the state of their incorporation as well as in their primary

---

[8]   One may argue that suits between states have a public-policy dimension because of the character of the parties to such litigation. Though that is true, these disputes typically involve title to land bordering the states in question or the allocation of water or other resources. As such, they rarely involve more than a dispute over a few acres of real property – for example, *Georgia v. South Carolina*, 111 L Ed 2d 309 (1990), or a matter of contract – for example, *Texas v. New Mexico*, 96 L Ed 2d 105 (1987), 108 L Ed 2d 98 (1990). But cf. *Wyoming v. Oklahoma*, 117 L Ed 2d 1 (1992), which declared unconstitutional an Oklahoma statute that discriminated against an out-of-state product.

[9]   *Strawbridge v. Curtis*, 3 Cranch 267 (1806).

[10] *Gilbert v. David*, 235 U.S. 561 (1915); *Mississippi Band of Choctaw Indians v. Holyfield*, 104 L Ed 2d 29 (1989).

place of business.[11] Thus, in order for General Motors to be involved in a diversity action, no adverse party may be a citizen of Michigan – its principal business place, or Delaware – its state of incorporation.[12]

Congress has also specified a jurisdictional dollar amount that must be met so that the federal courts may avoid petty lawsuits. It was set at more than $50,000 in 1989. The amount claimed controls.[13] Once a jurisdictionally sufficient amount is established, subsequent events cannot destroy it.[14] Aggregation of claims is permissible as long as one jurisdictionally sufficient claim exists. But a defendant's counterclaim may not be aggregated with the plaintiff's claim in order to meet the jurisdictional amount of $50,000. In multiple-party litigation, aggregation may occur if the relevant party has a joint and common interest in the disputed property (e.g., a $75,000 painting jointly owned by a husband and wife) rather than a several interest (e.g., two passengers in a car each of whom suffers a $40,000 injury).

Congress has excepted class actions and interpleaders from the foregoing requirements. Although every class member must meet the jurisdictional amount,[15] only the named or representative party – not every individual class member – need be diverse from the party or parties on the other side of the controversy. With regard to interpleader – an action whereby a stakeholder who does not claim title to property, such as a bank or an insurance company, deposits the proceeds with a court when ownership or title is in question, thereby forcing the claimants to resolve the matter without subjecting the stakeholder to multiple liability – diversity is satisfied as long as at least two claimants have citizenship in different states and the amount in controversy exceeds a mere $500.[16]

---

[11]   28 *United States Code* 1332 (c). Federal courts differ about the location of a corporation's "principal place of business." Some hold it to be its home office; others where the bulk of its activity occurs. See *Kelly v. United States Steel*, 284 F.2d 850 (1960); *Egan v. American Airlines*, 324 F.2d 565 (1963).

[12]   Note the fictional character of corporate citizenship. The Supreme Court had originally ruled that for diversity purposes the citizenship of the individual stockholders controlled. *Bank of the United States v. Deveaux*, 5 Cranch 84 (1810). Subsequently, the increasing geographical spread of corporate stockholders began to preclude corporations from suing in federal court because of a want of complete diversity. The Court rectified the matter in 1845 by qualifying *Deveaux* and limiting corporate citizenship to its place of incorporation. *L.C.& C. RR. Co. v. Letson*, 2 Howard 497. As a result, "every one of the shareholders of the General Motors Corporation is a citizen of Delaware despite the fact that there are more stockholders than there are Delawareans." John P. Frank, *Justice Daniel Dissenting* (Cambridge: Harvard University Press, 1964), pp. 51–52.

[13]   If the plaintiff's cause of action does not allege a dollar amount – as in an injunction, nuisance abatement, or specific performance of a contract – the court will determine the jurisdictional amount either by the value of the relief to the plaintiff or by the cost that the respondent would incur if the relief is granted.

[14]   28 *United States Code*, 1331(a), 1332(a). *St. Paul Mercury Indemnity Co. v. Red Cab*, 303 U.S. 283 (1938).

[15]   *Zahn v. International Paper Co.*, 414 U.S. 291 (1973).

[16]   Strictly speaking, only statutory interpleader, 28 *United States Code* 1335, 1397, 2361, is exempt

Supplementary jurisdiction. This pertains to pendent and ancillary jurisdiction, which largely result from decisional rather than statutory law. Both arise in the context of multiple-claim litigation and permit a federal court to hear an entire case and not just the federal portion of it. Invocation requires the presence of at least one claim sufficient to establish either federal question or diversity jurisdiction. If all the claims in the case "derive from a common nucleus of operative fact," the entire dispute may be heard.[17] Pendent jurisdiction allows a question of state law over which the federal court has no jurisdiction to be adjudicated along with the federal question that occasioned the parties' dispute, whereas ancillary jurisdiction allows parties other than the original plaintiff to join their jurisdictionally insufficient claims with that which is sufficient so that a single proceeding may resolve them all.

The purpose of supplementary jurisdiction – to promote judicial economy and preclude piecemeal litigation – was undermined in *Finley v. United States*[18] when the Court appeared to rule that the federal courts lack pendent jurisdiction absent explicit congressional legislation that says they do. Congress responded by codifying supplemental jurisdiction, thereby overriding *Finley* and preventing erosion of the federal courts' authority to resolve an entire case or controversy.[19]

Summary and conclusion. In exercising their jurisdiction, the federal courts – including the Supreme Court – not only depend on Article III of the Constitution, but also on acts of Congress. Indeed, the lower federal courts owe their very existence to Congress, to say nothing of their subject-matter jurisdiction. And although the Constitution established the Supreme Court, it only specifies its original jurisdiction. It receives all of its appellate jurisdiction – the heart of its policy-making capacity – from Congress, and what Congress grants, Congress may revoke. In our discussion of national supremacy in Chapter 1, such congressional legislation – particularly Section 25 of the Judiciary Act of 1789 – played a key role in checking the centrifugal force of states' rights. In the twentieth century, Congress relieved the federal courts of the power to issue labor injunctions, thereby presaging the ultimate victory of organized labor, a few years later, to bargain collectively. More recently, Congress has expressed, but not acted on, opposition to cross-district busing as a remedy for unconstitutionally segregated public schools.

In order to function as effective policy makers, courts depend on their subject-

from the ordinary jurisdictional requirements. Not so interpleader arising under Rule 22 of the Federal Rules of Civil Procedure.

[17] *United Mine Workers v. Gibbs*, 383 U.S. 715 (1966), at 725.

[18] 104 L Ed 2d 593 (1989).

[19] In the Federal Courts Study Committee Implementation Act of 1990, 28 *United States Code* 1367. Also see, T.M. Mengler, S.B. Burbank, and T.D. Rowe, Jr., "Recent Federal Court Legislation Made Some Noteworthy Changes," *National Law Journal*, December 31, 1990 – January 7, 1991, pp. 20–21.

matter jurisdiction. The federal courts, however, are not free agents in this regard. Congress determines which courts – if any – shall exercise which segments of the constitutionally provided subject-matter jurisdiction. As a result, Congress has the power to check judicial decision making on and about matters of which it disapproves.

Standing to sue

The mere appearance of a plaintiff before the proper federal court does not guarantee access. Litigants must be proper parties – that is, they must have standing to sue. Unlike the state courts, the federal courts are quite finicky in this regard. Whether a plaintiff is a proper party turns on a number of constitutional and prudential considerations. We discuss each element separately, paying special attention to the one that has dominated access policy making since the beginning of the Burger Court: the presence of personal injury.

Case or controversy. The words of Article III limit the federal courts to deciding "cases" or "controversies." The difference between them is purely technical. Compatibly with legal definitions generally, the requirement does not have precise definition: a legal dispute between two or more persons whose interests conflict. As such, the federal courts may not decide hypothetical questions, render advisory opinions, or resolve collusive cases.

Hypothetical questions typically result when a live dispute becomes moot because of changes affecting a litigant's contentions. Thus, an out-of-court settlement moots further proceedings; the repeal of a law precludes a challenge to its constitutionality. If, however, the controversy is sufficiently short-lived through no fault of the plaintiff, it may be "capable of repetition, yet evading review."[20] This is especially likely because "the usual rule in federal cases is that an actual controversy must exist at stages of appellate or certiorari review, and not simply at the date the action is initiated."[21] If such be the situation, as when individuals challenge a denial of their right to vote, or a woman challenges an anti-choice abortion statute, the matter does not become moot because the election is over or the woman is no longer pregnant. Even in matters where mootness can be avoided, the Court can find a way around the doctrine if it so desires. One recent example is the 1986 homosexual sodomy case in which Michael Hardwick brought his challenge to the Georgia statute to the Supreme Court even though the state refused to prosecute Hardwick after his arrest.[22] The Court accepted his rather unlikely claim that he was in imminent danger of arrest.

[20] *Southern Pacific Terminal Co. v. Interstate Commerce Commission*, 219 U.S. 498 (1911), at 515.
[21] *Roe v. Wade*, 410 U.S. 113 (1973), at 125.
[22] *Bowers v. Hardwick*, 478 U.S. 186.

An advisory opinion typically results when a governmental official requests a court's opinion about a hypothetical matter – for example, the constitutionality of a bill introduced but not yet enacted by the legislature, or the legality of certain proposed administrative action. Not only do advisory opinions lack liveliness, they also force the courts to trench on separation of powers. Nonetheless, a number of states do permit their supreme court to respond to them if the governor or attorney general so requests.

Collusive, or feigned, disputes most often occur in the guise of a stockholder's suit. When, for example, shareholders seek to enjoin their corporation from complying with a tax, the interests of the parties do not conflict; they coincide. Collusion is not always apparent, however. The decisions that voided the federal income tax and applied the contract clause to actions of a state legislature were brought by non-adversarial parties.[23] On the other hand, the parties need not necessarily disagree formally. Courts may accept guilty pleas and enter default judgments.

Legal injury. Access requires more than a mere conflict of interest. The conflict must also pertain to a right that is statutorily or constitutionally protected, or to some personal or property interest that the law recognizes. A business, for example, has no right to avoid ordinary commercial competition. Traditionally, only injuries susceptible to liquidation were actionable. Today, the courts also recognize aesthetic, conservational, recreational, cultural, and religious interests. In large part because of the immunity that surrounds government officials, a clearcut injury may not be redressible – for example, persons found innocent after serving their sentence, or a property whose value declines because of a change in a zoning ordinance that does not rise to the level of a taking. The gravity of injury does not necessarily determine whether it is legally protected. Under the common law, such trifles as a single footstep on another's land, unwanted touching, or the pointing of a gun constitute trespass, battery, and assault, respectively, even though no discernible damage may have resulted.

Personal injury. Closely related, but nonetheless separate and independent from legal injury, is the requirement that plaintiffs show they have suffered or are threatened with personal injury. Individuals may not sue solely on behalf of third persons who themselves are competent to bring their own lawsuits. Non-individuals, however, may sometimes bring action on behalf of others. Thus, a group may represent its members and a state may occasionally sue in a *parens patriae* capacity for persons fully competent to bring their own lawsuits.[24] The

---

[23] *Pollock v. Farmers' Loan & Trust Co.*, 157 U.S. 429, 158 U.S. 601 (1895); *Fletcher v. Peck*, 6 Cranch 87 (1810).

[24] *United Automobile Workers v. Brock*, 477 U.S. 274 (1986), which permitted the union to sue for benefits for members laid off because of import competition; and *Snapp & Son, Inc. v. Puerto Rico*, 458 U.S. 592 (1982), which allowed the Commonwealth to seek an injunction against apple growers who were discriminating against migrant Puerto Rican farm workers.

Table 5.1. *Disposition of standing to sue cases*

Court	Warren			Burger			Rehnquist		
Access	pro	anti	% pro	pro	anti	% pro	pro	anti	% pro
Personal Injury	8	3	72.7	18	34	34.6	7	10	41.2
Other Aspects	23	11	67.6	14	9	60.9	6	2	75.0
Total	31	14	68.9	32	43	42.7	13	12	52.0

rule does not prohibit class actions, of course, where an individual sues to vindicate his or her own rights, plus those of similarly situated persons. The prohibition of taxpayer's suits best illustrates the rigor with which the federal courts – though not the state courts – adhere to this prudential aspect of standing. On the rationale that a person subject to a federal tax does not suffer an injury more severely or more peculiarly than taxpayers generally, but only suffers in an indefinite way along with millions of others, individuals may not initiate a judicial challenge to the constitutionality of a federal tax.[25] The Court subsequently limited the scope of this precedent when it excepted from the ban on taxpayer's suits those that allege the challenged tax exceeds some specific limitation on the power of Congress to tax or to spend money.[26] Recent examples in which the plaintiffs were denied standing include an organization of taxpayers dedicated to the separation of church and state who sought to contest the no-cost transfer of government property to religious educational institutions, and the parents of black school children who wished to challenge the action of the Internal Revenue Service granting tax exemptions to racially discriminatory schools.[27]

Table 5.1 shows that the anti-access decision making of the Burger and Rehnquist Courts results from their treatment of cases raising claims of personal injury, an element of standing with which the Warren Court was little concerned.[28] Thirty-four of the Burger Court's 43 anti-standing decisions pertained to personal injury (79 percent), as did 10 of the Rehnquist Court's 12 (83 percent). Moreover, only 11 of the Warren Court's 45 standing cases

[25] *Frothingham v. Mellon*, 262 U.S. 447 (1923). Of course, taxpayers may refuse to pay a tax and, having been indicted, defend their non-payment on the ground that the tax violates the Constitution. If they lose, they will likely incur a markedly more severe sanction than if they merely lost a taxpayer's suit brought while the tax was held in abeyance.

[26] *Flast v. Cohen*, 392 U.S. 83 (1968). The challenged expenditure provided aid to parochial schools.

[27] *Valley Forge Christian College v. Americans United for Separation of Church and State*, 454 U.S. 464 (1982); *Allen v. Wright*, 468 U.S. 737 (1984).

[28] These data span the Warren and Burger Courts, plus the 1986–1990 terms of the Rehnquist Court. The unit of analysis is docket number and excludes memorandum decisions.

pertained to personal injury claims (24 percent), compared with 52 of the Burger Court's total of 75 (69 percent) and 17 of the Rehnquist Court's 25 (68 percent).[29]

Within the personal injury facet of standing, the Burger Court, and to a lesser extent the Rehnquist Court, have together disproportionately addressed private or implied causes of action. The Warren Court, by contrast, decided nary a one. These cases present the question whether an identifiable group of litigants have standing under various federal statutes. For example, does the Parental Kidnapping Prevention Act allow parents to determine in federal court the validity of state child custody orders? Does the Civil Service Reform Act of 1978 authorize federal employees to sue their unions for breach of the duty of fair representation?[30]

The Court has formulated four criteria for determining the existence of an implied cause of action:

> First, is the plaintiff "one of the class for whose *especial* benefit the statute was enacted" . . . that is, does the statute create a federal right in favor of the plaintiff? Second, is there any indication of legislative intent, explicit or implicit, either to create such a remedy or to deny one? . . . Third, is it consistent with the underlying purposes of the legislative scheme to imply such a remedy for the plaintiff? . . . And finally, is the cause of action one traditionally relegated to state law, in an area basically the concern of the States, so that it would be inappropriate to infer a cause of action based solely on federal law?[31]

Justice Scalia argues somewhat persuasively that the second of these factors alone has controlled the Court's implied cause of action decisions. Compatibly with his hostility to interpretivism, which we documented in our discussion of legislative and framers' intent in Chapter 2, Scalia has taken the position that federal private rights of action simply ought not to be implied, period.[32]

Although Scalia's colleagues do not agree with him on the reasons for non-implication of private rights of action, the Court has been markedly unsympathetic toward such claims. The Burger Court denied access in 17 of 23 such cases (74 percent), the Rehnquist Court in 3 of 4 (75 percent).

Political questions. If the Supreme Court believes it inappropriate for the federal courts to resolve the merits of a controversy, it labels the matter a "political question," thereby sending a message to the other branches of government that they should resolve it rather than the judiciary. History records few such decisions. Among them are the ratification of a constitutional amendment, the legitimacy of two competing state governments, the boundary between the United

---

[29] Both the Burger and Rehnquist Courts uncharacteristically began with a string of decisions supporting access – seven and five, respectively. If these be excluded from the totals in Table 5.1, their pro-access proportions decline to 36.8 and 40.0 percent, respectively.

[30] The Court unanimously answered "no" to both questions. *Thompson v. Thompson*, 98 L Ed 2d 512 (1988); *Karahalios v. National Federation of Federal Employees*, 103 L Ed 2d 539 (1989).

[31] *Cort v. Ash*, 422 U.S. 66 (1975), at 78.

[32] *Thompson v. Thompson*, 98 L Ed 2d 512 (1988), at 525–528.

States and Spain, and the adequacy of national guard training.[33] One matter that
the Court initially refused to adjudicate, but now finds justiciable, is legislative
apportionment and districting.[34] In so ruling, the Court devised a set of criteria
for determining if a question were political that raised the nebulosity level of
the standard legal definition to new heights:

Prominent on the surface . . . is found a textually demonstrable constitutional commitment
of the issue to a coordinate political department; or a lack of judicially discoverable and
manageable standards for resolving it; or the impossibility of deciding without an initial
policy determination of a kind clearly for nonjudicial discretion; or the impossibility of
a court's undertaking independent resolution without expressing lack of the respect due
coordinate branches of government; or an unusual need for unquestioning adherence to
a political decision already made; or the potentiality of embarrassment from multifarious
pronouncements by various departments on one question.[35]

Notwithstanding the inherent subjectivity of the foregoing criteria, one should
not overlook the utility of the label, "political question." It bespeaks a decision
qualitatively different from those that courts render, and reminds all concerned
that courts carefully avoid intruding themselves into the unprincipled domain of
bureaucrats and politicians. As such, the political question doctrine helps preserve
the mythology of judging discussed in Chapter 1.

Finality of decision. In order to avoid any diminution of the authoritativeness
of their decisions, courts scrupulously avoid controversies where their decisions
may be overruled by non-judicial decision makers. As we pointed out in our
discussion of jurisdiction earlier, Congress must provide the federal courts with
the authority to decide the cases they hear. Only the Supreme Court's original
jurisdiction is activated by the Constitution directly. Congress, however, has not
seen fit to bestow on the various federal courts all of the subject-matter jurisdiction
that the Constitution contains. Instead, it vests some of it in various nonjudicial
agencies and officials. The classic example dates from the Court's fifth reported
case and governs eligibility for veterans' pension and disability benefits, where
the final and binding decision was originally made by the War Department and
today is made by the Veterans' Administration.[36]

The ability of a court to make the final and binding decision is not precluded
because a higher court may overturn it. Neither does the possibility that Congress
at some time in the future may amend a statute adverse to the construction that

[33] *Coleman v. Miller*, 307 U.S. 433 (1939); *Luther v. Borden*, 7 Howard 1 (1849); *Foster v.
Neilson*, 2 Peters 253 (1829); *Gilligan v. Morgan*, 413 U.S. 1 (1973).

[34] *Colegrove v. Green*, 328 U.S. 549 (1946); *Baker v. Carr*, 369 U.S. 186 (1962).

[35] 369 U.S. at 217.

[36] *Hayburn's Case*, 2 Dallas 409 (1792). Questions about the constitutionality of a veterans' benefits
statute or the meaning of the words therein are, of course, matters for judicial determination.
For example, *Traynor v. Turnage*, 99 L Ed 2d 618 (1988), which presented the question of
whether Congress statutorily authorized a Veterans' Administration regulation disqualifying
alcoholic veterans from education benefits under the G-I Bill.

a court had put on it. The same applies to proposed constitutional amendments. The rule only requires that at the time of decision the court's judgment bind the parties and not be susceptible to alteration administratively or legislatively.

Estoppel. Courts, state as well as federal, rather rigorously limit litigants to a single bite of the apple – to but one figurative day in court. Because estoppel is so thoroughly entrenched throughout the judicial system, few cases involving it reach the Supreme Court. It takes two general forms. *Res judicata*, or claim estoppel, precludes a party from relitigating the same cause of action against the same party if it was resolved by a final judgment that addressed the merits of the controversy. Although the common law defined causes of action narrowly, most court rules, including the Federal Rules, require the merger and joinder of claims. This "transactional" definition of cause of action is designed to avoid piecemeal litigation and to promote judicial economy. The same party re-quirement governs those in privity with the relevant party, as well as employment and agency relationships, and successors in interest. *Res judicata* does not bar relitigation if the cause of action lacks meritorious resolution. Thus, dismissal for want of subject-matter jurisdiction does not bar relitigation in the proper forum.

The other component – collateral estoppel or issue preclusion – may be invoked only on a showing that an earlier proceeding actually decided the identical issue, and that it had to be decided in order to resolve the original case. Although the doctrine of mutuality prevented the assertion of collateral estopped against non-parties to the original proceeding, most jurisdictions have discarded the doctrine. Consequently, a party may be collaterally estopped from raising an issue if the original proceeding fully and fairly litigated it. The concept of full and fair litigation is increasingly limited to issues whose relitigation was reasonably foreseeable at the time of the original action. Thus, the second of two passengers in an automobile may not relitigate the driver's negligence if the other passenger had previously lost his suit for damages for injuries suffered in a resulting accident. If, however, the first passenger had won, the driver may not relitigate his negligence in the case of the second passenger.

Estoppel's preclusion of multiple lawsuits serves several purposes. In addition to enhancing the efficient use of judicial time and energy, it enables litigants to rely on a court's final judgment, and thereby plan for the future. It also prevents the judicial system from being used as a tool of harassment.

Exhaustion of administrative remedies. To avoid trenching on other methods of dispute resolution, the Court requires potential litigants to exhaust any admin-istrative remedies that may exist before gaining access to the federal courts. Exhaustion occupies a position with regard to agency action similar to the re-lationship of the abstention doctrine to state court action – a matter discussed in the last major section of Chapter 1. They differ in that abstention only applies if state court proceedings have commenced, whereas exhaustion applies regardless of the onset of agency action.[37] If a state has not initiated proceedings, persons may take their grievances – assuming the existence of federal jurisdiction – directly to the proper federal court. That is not true of agency action. Because exhaustion applies whether or not the agency has launched proceedings, exceptions exist. These include inadequate agency remedies, an unduly dilatory agency, irreparable injury, or an agency acting *ultra vires*.

The utilities of standing. The elements of standing determine whether litigants are proper parties, thereby enabling the federal courts to avoid hypothetical, officious, and redundant decisions, and unnecessary conflicts with other decision makers. The rules governing standing enable judges to avoid issues they prefer not to resolve and to cite good legal form to justify their doing so.

The policies that govern access to the federal courts necessarily have substantive as well as procedural effects. Denial of access may equally readily produce conservative or liberal effects depending on the orientation of the non-judicial decision makers who serve as the justices' surrogates. Conversely, opening access may again produce liberal or conservative effects depending on the justices' policy preferences about the substantive matters that cases gaining access contain.

Jurisdiction over the parties

A final legal requirement that governs getting one's case into court concerns the question of whether the court has jurisdiction over the respondent. By initiating lawsuits, plaintiffs voluntarily subject themselves to the court's jurisdiction. Not so the party who is sued. Due process of law requires that the court have the power to act on defendants or their property.[38] Courts have such power if defendants have ''minimum contacts'' with the state in which the court is located, ''such that the maintenance of the suit does not offend 'traditional notions of fair play and substantial justice.' ''[39]

Minimum contacts obviously exists if the respondent resides in or is domiciled in the forum state. It similarly exists in actions about property located in the state (e.g., quiet title to real estate) or a status granted individuals by the state

---

[37] Exhaustion should be distinguished from the doctrine of primary jurisdiction. Although both seek to thwart the courts from impinging on agency resolution of disputes, exhaustion only applies where an agency has exclusive primary jurisdiction over a matter. Primary jurisdiction, by contrast, is a form of abstention that a court may exercise even though it and the agency have concurrent jurisdiction.

[38] Due process, of course, also requires that the respondent receive notice of the pendency of legal action, and a hearing.

[39] *International Shoe Co. v. Washington*, 326 U.S. 310 (1945), at 316.

 With some relatively minor exceptions, the federal courts are treated as though they are courts of the state in which they sit for purposes of determining the territorial reach of their jurisdiction. This is especially true of cases that raise a federal question.

in question (e.g., dissolution of a marriage).[40] Nor is there any question of minimum contacts if the respondent voluntarily agrees to suit in a given state's courts. The test's application becomes crucial only over an unwilling out-of-state respondent. For such persons, the effect may be enormous. If, at one extreme, the Court construes minimum contacts to require that the defendant be resident or domiciled in the forum state, individuals could avoid legal responsibility by merely crossing the state line.[41] At the other extreme, a loose definition of minimum contacts could paralyze commercial activity if a retailer or other small business could be required to defend itself in a distant state's courts solely on the basis of an injury involving its product that occurred within that state. Such a policy would deter sellers from doing business with nonresidents because exposure to suit would travel with every item sold.

Collectively, the Court's decisions have staked out a position more or less midway between these extremes. In its most instructive decision, the Court rejected foreseeability of an injury as a permissible criterion for suit, and focused instead on the defendant's conduct and connections with the forum state. Did it solicit business there, close sales, perform service, or avail itself of the benefits of the forum state's laws to the extent that it "should reasonably anticipate being haled into court there"?[42] More recent decisions require a "substantial connection" between the defendant and the forum state, which, according to at least four of the justices, "must come about by *an action of the defendant purposefully directed toward the forum State*."[43]

Justice Brennan had been least supportive of the Court's position. Although he accepted minimum contacts as the appropriate standard, he regularly dissented when a majority ruled that the contacts were insufficient to establish jurisdiction. In only four of nineteen Burger and Rehnquist Court cases decided before his retirement in 1990 did he vote against a state's exercise of extraterritorial jurisdiction. All the other justices supported the state at least twice as frequently. For Brennan, the purposeful interjection of goods into the stream of commerce

---

[40] In addition to jurisdiction over persons (*in personam*) and jurisdiction over things (*in rem*), the Court has also subjected *quasi in rem* jurisdiction to the minimum contacts test. See *Shaffer v. Heitner*, 433 U.S. 186 (1977). *Quasi in rem* actions attempt to seize the defendant's tangible or intangible property in order to satisfy a judgment. They are brought in a state where the defendant has property, but the plaintiff lacks sufficient contacts to establish *in personam* jurisdiction over the defendant.

[41] This was effectively the Court's original policy. *Pennoyer v. Neff*, 5 Otto 714 (1877). "Process from the tribunals of one State cannot run into another State, and summon parties there domiciled to leave its territory and respond to proceedings against them." 5 Otto, at 727. Also see *Harris v. Balk*, 198 U.S. 215 (1905). *Shaffer v. Heitner*, 433 U.S. 186 (1977), overruled them both. 433 U.S., at 212, note 39.

[42] *World-Wide Volkswagen Corp. v. Woodson*, 444 U.S. 286 (1980), at 297.

[43] *Burger King Corp. v. Rudzewicz*, 471 U.S. 462 (1985), at 475; *Asahi Metal Industry Co. v. Superior Court*, 480 U.S. 102 (1987), at 112.

sufficed to establish minimum contacts, as did situations where the burden on the out-of-state defendant was slight.[44]

CASE SELECTION

The procedure that the Court employs to select the cases that it wishes to decide is formally uncomplicated. But because the justices provide very little information about this stage of their decision making, we do not know if its formal simplicity also characterizes its operation. We can at least infer that the procedure the Court uses to choose its cases does work efficiently. The justices manage to stay abreast of their docket, unlike the vast majority of courts, state and federal. Little time elapses between receipt of a case and its disposition: A decision not to hear a case may be made within a week or two, but not for several months if the case reaches the Court during the summer when it is not in session. Cases that the Court agrees to review are usually heard and decided within a year. Finally, lay and professional criticism is notable by its absence, which assuredly would not be true if an affected public considered the Court dilatory or ducking important issues.

The Court has authority to adopt rules governing its own operations, and a goodly number of these rules lay out (1) the processes whereby losing litigants bring cases to the Court's attention, and (2) the criteria that govern the justices' decision to review the lower court's judgment.[45]

For all practical purposes, the justices are free to accept or reject cases brought to their attention as they see fit. That is to say, the Court has full control over its docket.[46] But that is not to say that the Court has no obligation to decide certain sorts of cases. The justices would not likely refuse to review a decision by a lower federal court that voided a major act of Congress, nor would it decline to consider a state court's decision that substantially redefined the scope of the First Amendment, absent extenuating circumstances.

Procedure[47]

Because the Court had far less control over its docket in the nineteenth and early twentieth centuries than it does now, a remnant of this situation still persists in

---

[44] *World-Wide Volkswagen Corp. v. Woodson*, 444 U.S. 286 (1980), at 299, and *Rush v. Savchuk*, 444 U.S. 320 (1980). In *Woodson*, Brennan labelled his opinion in *Shaffer v. Heitner*, 433 U.S. 186 (1976), at 219, a dissent. 444 U.S., at 301.

[45] *The Rules of the Supreme Court of the United States* are published at periodic intervals in the *United States Reports*. The most recent compilation appears at 445 U.S. 983 (1980). The Court frequently changes the number that identifies a given rule. Our numbers refer to those in volume 445 of the *United States Reports*.

[46] Especially since 1988 when Congress eliminated virtually all of what remained of the Court's mandatory jurisdiction. See Lynn Weisberg, "New law eliminates Supreme Court's mandatory jurisdiction," 72 *Judicature* 138 (1988).

[47] The most authoritative treatise on the procedures that govern the practice of law before the

the technical distinction between the two major methods for accessing the Court: the writ of certiorari and the writ of appeal.[48] Within one to three months from the date the highest state or federal court with authority to hear the matter has entered its judgment, the losing litigant may petition the Supreme Court for a writ of certiorari if the case is one that Congress has not required the Court to review. If Congress has mandated review, the losing litigant files a writ of appeal. Although the effect of a denial differs, the Court uses the same procedure to grant either writ, the Rule of Four: the vote of four of the nine justices, three if only six or seven participate.[49]

Statutes and court rules specify the time within which losing litigants must petition the Court to review their cases. In all but the most exceptional circumstances, petitioning parties must have exhausted the remedies provided by the lower courts. Most often, this is either a final judgment of a state supreme court or a federal court of appeals. Many states, however, permit their supreme courts to deny a litigant leave to appeal, in which case the loser may petition the Supreme Court on the issuance of a judgment or decree by the inferior court of appeals or the trial court, as the case may be. The Supreme Court's Rules specify the format that petitions for writs of certiorari and appeal must take, the information they shall include, and the number of copies to be filed. Other parties to the litigation are notified and provided an opportunity to submit briefs in opposition to Supreme Court review.

Additionally, interested third parties or interest groups have the opportunity to file amicus curiae (friend of the court) briefs supporting or opposing a petition for certiorari.[50] Nongovernmental entities may do so with the consent of both

---

Supreme Court is Robert L. Stern, Eugene Gressman, and Stephen Shapiro, *Supreme Court Practice*, 6th ed. (Washington: Bureau of National Affairs, 1986). The most detailed analysis of the Court's internal procedures is H.W. Perry, Jr., *Deciding to Decide: Angela Setting in the United States Supreme Court* (Cambridge; Harvard University Press, 1991). On the workload of the Supreme Court, see Gerhard Casper and Richard A. Posner, *The Workload of the Supreme Court* (Chicago: American Bar Foundation, 1976).

[48]   Litigants may petition the Court through other writs, such as certification, mandamus, injunction, stay of execution, rehearing, etc. The Court also accepts cases under its original jurisdiction and has authority to entertain various motions and to issue such orders on its own motion as it deems appropriate. These alternative routes are rarely used and, except for the exercise of original jurisdiction, are almost always handled summarily.

   The Court does not consider itself obliged to hear all cases arising under its original jurisdiction. *Illinois v. City of Milwaukee*, 406 U.S. 91 (1972); *Arizona v. New Mexico*, 425 U.S. 794 (1976). If it grants leave to file a complaint thereunder, it almost always appoints a special master to hear the issues of fact and file a written report for the justices' consideration.

[49]   According to the opinion of Justice Douglas in *Pryor v. United States*, 404 U.S. 1242 (1971), at 1243.

[50]   See, for example, Lucius Barker, "Third Parties in Litigation: A Systemic View of the Judicial Function," 29 *Journal of Politics* 41 (1967); Lee Epstein, *Conservatives in Court* (Knoxville: University of Tennessee Press (1985); and Karen O'Connor, *Women's Organizations Use of the Courts* (Lexington, MA: Lexington Books, 1980).

parties, or, failing that, with the consent of the Court. National, state, and local governmental units are automatically granted the right to file briefs. The Court will occasionally request third parties, usually the United States or a state, to file amicus briefs.

Until recently, following receipt of a petition and the winning party's brief in opposition, plus an optional reply by the petitioner, the Clerk of the Supreme Court compiled and reviewed the documents, along with the lower court's record of the case. If the Clerk deemed the petition ''frivolous'' – undeserving of review – he so informed the chief justice who, in turn, had his clerks prepare a digest of the case. If the chief justice and his clerks agreed that the case did not merit review, it was ''deadlisted.'' The material and recommendations pertaining to the case were sent to the other justices who, assisted by their clerks, reviewed the file. If all the justices agreed with deadlisting, the case would not be discussed in conference and would automatically be denied review. This fate apparently befell well over half the petitions. But if the chief justice or any of the associate justices objected to deadlisting, the case would be discussed in conference.

Today the procedure is just the reverse: A discuss list has replaced the deadlist. The Chief Justice compiles a list of cases that he or any other justice considers sufficiently worthy of formal decision. ''Certworthiness'' is determined in each justices's chambers, where memos are prepared by the clerks. To cut down on the work of the clerks, several justices have instructed their clerks to form a cert pool, where the participating clerks divide the petitions among themselves. Other justices have their clerks write memos on each case, or those considered important.[51] In conference, the justices discuss the cases on the discuss list and vote on the basis of seniority. If, following discussion, at least four justices support review (three if seven or fewer participate) the petition is granted and the case is scheduled for oral argument. Out of the more than 5,000 petitions the Court receives per term, approximately 150 are granted and become candidates for formal decision.[52] The petitions for review are divided fairly evenly between cases in which the Court's filing fee is paid and the requisite number of copies are filed, and *in forma pauperis* petitions in which the filing fee and the requirement of multiple copies are waived. The vast majority of these are filed by incarcerated indigents. The justices accept and decide only a handful of these cases per term, well under 1 percent of the total submitted.[53]

[51] Jan Palmer, *The Vinson Court Era* (New York: AMS, 1990), pp. 24–30. Perry, op. cit. fn 47 supra, pp. 41–91, provides a detailed discussion of the current procedure. His perceptive analysis shows that very little bargaining occurs among the justices whether to accept a case for review. Ibid., pp. 140–197.

[52] Granting a petition does not necessarily preclude a summary decision on the merits without the benefit of oral argument or a formal opinion of the Court. Rules 16.7 and 23.1 specifically so provide.

[53] Linda Greenhouse, '' 'Pauper' Cases Reshape High Court's Caseload,'' *New York Times*, Jan. 28, 1991, p. A13.

Criteria for selection[54]

In adumbrating the criteria for granting a writ of certiorari, the justices give heaviest emphasis to decisions "in conflict" with another court of appeals, a state court of last resort, or "applicable decisions" of this Court.[55] The other two stipulated criteria are decisions that have "departed from the accepted and usual course of judicial proceedings, or so far sanctioned such a departure," and those that have "decided an important question of federal law which has not been, but should be, settled by this Court." Although conflict may be amenable to objective determination, the Court does not limit itself only to the enumerated considerations which, according to Rule 17, are "neither controlling nor fully measuring the Court's discretion."[56]

Although no comparable rule addresses the granting of writs of appeal, the rules provide indirect guidance by instructing appellants and appellees about the kind of arguments and considerations their briefs should contain. The fact that the Court uses the same procedure – the Rule of Four, described earlier – to dispose of petitions for certiorari as well as writs of appeal suggests that their criteria for selection may be fungible.[57]

That four or more justices agree to review a case does not necessarily insure a decision on the merits of the controversy. After oral argument, a majority may rule that the writ was improvidently granted, or dismiss an appeal for lack of jurisdiction or for want of a substantial federal question, or for one of the other reasons specified in Table 5.2. From the beginning of the Warren Court through the end of the 1990 term, the justices addressed the advisability of a non-meritorious decision after oral argument in 3.26 cases per term. In over 90 percent of these cases, the justices did deny the plaintiffs access notwithstanding their initial decision to the contrary (112 of 124). In only twelve cases did the justices reconfirm the grant of access. Ten denied the states' contentions that their state court decisions rested on adequate non-federal grounds (out of a total of twenty cases, as Table 5.2 indicates).[58] The other two reconsidered cases that

---

[54]   Most of the data in this section and the remaining sections of this chapter date from the beginning of the Warren Court in 1953 because highly reliable data are available for this period. We certainly do not intimate that nothing of importance in this – or any other – regard occurred between the time of Chief Justices Marshall and Warren. See Perry, op. cit. fn 47 supra, pp. 113–139, for a cogent critique of earlier studies of criteria that putatively govern the decision whether or not to decide a case, and an assessment of the considerations pertinent to such decisions during the five terms of the Burger Court that he analyzed.

[55]   Rule 17.1, 445 U.S., at 1003.

[56]   Id. Also see Perry, op. cit. fn. 47 supra, pp. 32–40.

[57]   Robert L. Stern and Eugene Gressman, *Supreme Court Practice*, 5th ed. (Washington: Bureau of National Affairs, 1978), pp. 374–377. Perry, op. cit. fn. 47 supra, pp. 25–26.

[58]   The seven of the fourteen Warren Court cases in which the Court held that the state court's decision did not rest on an adequate nonfederal ground are *Staub v. Baxley*, 355 U.S. 313 (1958), in which the Court proceeded to void a municipal solicitation ordinance; the four cases decided under *Ivanhoe Irrigation District v. McCracken*, 357 U.S. 275 (1958), which concerned

Table 5.2. *Non-meritorious resolution of orally argued cases*

Non-meritorious action	Court			
	Warren	Burger	Rehnquist	Total
writ improvidently granted	34	32	10	76
want of adequate federal question	7	2	2	11
want of jurisdiction	1	2	1	4
adequate non-federal grounds	14	6	0	20
to determine basis of state decision	3	2	3	8
miscellaneous	2	2	1	5
total	61	46	17	124

reconfirmed the grant of access were *Aldrich v. Aldrich* and *Virginia v. American Booksellers Assn.*, both of which requested the state supreme court to answer certain questions of law.[59]

Reconsideration following a grant of access does not necessarily undermine the integrity of the Rule of Four. But as Justice Douglas pointed out: "If four can grant and the opposing five dismiss, then the four cannot get a decision of the case on the merits. The integrity of the four-man vote rule ... would then be impaired."[60] This occurs when five justices vote to dismiss a writ as improvidently granted, or to deny access for lack of jurisdiction or for want of a substantial federal question over the dissent of the other four. The justice who most assiduously subverted the rule was Frankfurter. In workers' compensation cases, he regularly refused to address the merits after he had voted to deny cert. He rationalized his position as follows:

The right of a Justice to dissent from an action of the Court is historic. . . . Not four, not eight, Justices can require another to decide a case that he regards as not properly before the Court. The failure of a Justice to persuade his colleagues does not require him to yield to their views, if he has a deep conviction that the issue is sufficiently important. . . . Even though a minority may bring a case here for oral argument, that does not mean that the majority has given up its right to vote on the ultimate disposition of the case as conscience directs. This is not a novel doctrine. As a matter of practice, members of the

land and water reclamation contracts that were part of California's Central Valley Project; *NAACP v. Alabama*, 355 U.S. 449 (1958), which pertained to the compelled disclosure of membership lists; and *Wright v. Georgia*, 373 U.S. 284 (1963), which involved an effort to desegregate a city park.

The three of the six counterpart Burger Court decisions that confirmed the grant of access are *Oregon v. Kennedy*, 456 U.S. 667 (1982), a double jeopardy case; *Ake v. Oklahoma*, 470 U.S. 68 (1985), which involved the assistance of a psychiatrist when the sanity of a defendant charged with a capital offense is questioned; and *Longshoremen v. Davis*, 476 U.S. 380 (1986), preempting state court jurisdiction of a labor dispute.

[59] 375 U.S. 249 (1963), and 98 L Ed 2d 782 (1988).
[60] *United States v. Shannon*, 342 U.S. 288 (1952), at 298.

Court have at various times exercised the right of refusing to pass on the merits of cases that in their view should not have been granted review.[61]

If, however, one or more of those voting to dismiss originally voted to grant, no impairment of the Rule of Four results.

Five dissenters from cert appeared to have voted to dismiss in five cases between the beginning of the Warren Court in 1953 and the end of the fourth term of the Rehnquist Court in 1990.[62] Although these instances may be too few to jeopardize the Rule, the episodes are worth noting. In the first case, the Yonkers, New York, Board of Education denied a left-wing group use of school facilities after hours while allowing other organizations to do so. Although the case had been argued twice, five justices dismissed the writ as improvidently granted. The four dissenters, however, merely wrote a twenty-word opinion that simply stated their belief that the case warranted meritorious decision.[63] A year later, the same four dissenters – Warren, Black, Douglas, and Clark – objected at length to the majority's refusal to address the merits of a state prisoner's contentions. But they said nothing about the Rule of Four.[64] Neither did the dissenting opinion in the next case.[65] In the two remaining cases, however, the issue of the integrity of the Rule of Four was raised and joined. Speaking for himself, Black, Brennan, and Marshall in an early Burger Court case, Douglas noted that "the four who now dissent were the only ones to vote to grant the petition. The rule should not be changed to a 'rule of five' by actions of the five justices who originally opposed certiorari. . . . it is the duty of the five opposing certiorari to persuade others at Conference, but, failing that, to vote on the merits of the case."[66]

The final and most recent case raised the question of whether the constitutional right to privacy extended to homosexual solicitation.[67] In a per curiam opinion, five justices dismissed the writ as improvidently granted because the lower court did not make clear the constitutional basis of its ruling. The four dissenters, in a thirty-nine-word opinion, said the case was properly before the Court and that dismissal "is not the proper course."[68] Justice Stevens, one of the majority, attempted to rationalize the result. After pointing out that the dissenters themselves did not address the merits nor "attempt to refute the sound reasons offered

[61] *Rogers v. Missouri Pacific R. Co.*, 352 U.S. 500 (1957), and *Ferguson v. Moore-McCormick Lines*, 352 U.S. 521 (1957), at 528. Also see Glendon Schubert, *Quantitative Analysis of Judicial Behavior* (Glencoe, IL: Free Press, 1959), pp. 210–267, and Glendon Schubert, "Policy Without Law: An Extension of the Certiorari Game," 14 *Stanford Law Review* 284 (1962).

[62] The articulation of the problem dates to at least the Vinson Court. See the opinions of Douglas and Frankfurter in the *Shannon* case, op. cit. fn. 60 supra.

[63] *Ellis v. Dixon*, 349 U.S. 458 (1955).

[64] *Durley v. Mayo*, 351 U.S. 277 (1956).

[65] *Wolfe v. North Carolina*, 364 U.S. 177 (1960). Brennan joined Warren, Black, and Douglas.

[66] *Triangle Improvement Council v. Ritchie*, 402 U.S. 497 (1971), at 508.

[67] The Court ruled it did not in a case decided two years later, *Bowers v. Hardwick*, 479 U.S. 186 (1986).

[68] *New York v. Uplinger*, 467 U.S. 246 (1984), at 252.

by the majority for dismissing the writ," he observed that "the Members of the Court have always considered a case more carefully after full briefing and argument on the merits than they could at the time of the certiorari conference, when almost 100 petitions must be considered each week." Therefore,

If a majority is convinced after studying the case that its posture, record, or presentation of issues makes it an unwise vehicle for exercising the "gravest and most delicate" function that the Court is called upon to perform, the Rule of Four should not reach so far as to compel the majority to decide the case.[69]

Effects of denial or dismissal

The Court's refusal to decide a case arising on certiorari whether or not the petition had been granted has no precedential effect. With regard to appeals, unqualified assertions that "dismissal and affirmance are treated legally as decisions on the merits of cases, and they have some weight as precedents for future cases" are not quite correct.[70] Affirmation, with or without opinion, whether on certiorari or appeal, clearly has precedential value. So also when an appeal is dismissed for want of a substantial federal question as distinct from lack of jurisdiction. When the Court rules a question insubstantial, it says something about the merits of the case. But when it dismisses for want of jurisdiction, it has "no occasion to address the merits of the constitutional questions presented in the jurisdictional statements."[71]

THE SUPREME COURT'S CASELOAD

Tremendous growth has occurred in the Supreme Court's caseload over time. As shown in Table 5.3, little change occurred in the number of cases filed between 1880 and 1920. Steady growth ensued in the number filed in the 1930s and 1940s, with explosive growth since 1950.

Table 5.4 contains a more detailed analysis of the filings since the first term of the Warren Court. As can be seen, the total number of filings almost quadrupled between the 1953 and 1989 terms. Between 1789 and 1950 the number of cases filed climbed from under 10 per term to slightly over 1,000. By 1961 the Court faced 2,000 filings. It took only five years after that to reach 3,000, and but another seven to reach 4,000. Though 5,000 filings have not been reached as of the 1989 term, it fell only 105 filings short.

Filings come under either the paid or miscellaneous (unpaid) dockets. Through 1958 the paid cases annually exceeded the unpaid cases. During the Warren Court, the number of unpaid cases grew substantially and exceeded the paid

---

[69]   Id. at 250, 251.

[70]   Perry, op. cit. fn. 47 supra, pp. 31–32, 37–40; Lawrence Baum, *The Supreme Court*, 2d ed. (Washington: Congressional Quarterly, 1985), p. 89.

[71]   *Hopfmann v. Connolly*, 471 U.S. 459 (1985), at 460–461.

Table 5.3. *Cases filed, 1880–1980*

Term	Cases Filed
1880	417
1890	636
1900	406
1910	516
1920	565
1930	845
1940	977
1950	1,181
1960	1,940
1970	3,419
1980	4,175
1985	4,421
1989	4,895

Source. **Updated** from Casper and Posner: The Workload of the Supreme Court, Chicago: American Bar Foundation, 1976.

cases every year from 1959 until 1979. Miscellaneous cases held steady through the early 1980s but began to grow dramatically at the end of the decade, jumping from 2,254 in 1987 to 2,878 in 1989.

The Supreme Court can of course only review a small percentage of the cases filed. Indeed, the Court reviews only about 10 percent of the paid cases and 1 percent of the miscellaneous cases. Moreover, only about half of these cases receive full treatment by the Court – oral argument and written opinions. The remainder result in summary dispositions. Since 1953, the Supreme Court has decided approximately 129 cases per term through oral argument and written opinion, counting by case citation, not docket number. The early Warren Court decided less than 100 cases per year, but the early Burger Court heard as many as 153 cases in the 1972 term. That appears to be close to the Court's institutional limit, for since then the Court has never decided more than 155 cases in a single term. The 1989 term of the Court, which made headlines for the rate at which it rejected petitions for review,[72] decided but 130 cases, the lowest total since 1980. The 1990 term promptly bettered it, however, dropping to a low of 116, and the 1991 term bodes to drop still lower.[73]

[72] Linda Greenhouse, "As Its Workload Decreases, High Court Shuns New Cases," New York Times, November 28, 1989, p. A1.

[73] Linda Greenhouse, "Lightening Scales of Justice: High Court Trims Its Docket," *New York Times*, March 7, 1992, p. 1.

The types of cases heard by the Warren, Burger, and Rehnquist Courts through the 1990 term are presented in Table 5.5. Again we count by citation, not docket. As can be seen, continuity characterizes the types of cases heard. Criminal procedure was most frequently litigated in the Burger and Rehnquist Courts, and was second only to economic cases in the Warren Court. Economic activity, civil rights, judicial power, and the First Amendment have received substantial attention from all three Courts. Yet, although economic activity is second overall in type of case heard, it occupies a decreasing share of the Court's agenda. A full quarter of the Warren Court's cases dealt with economic activity, compared with barely one-sixth of the Rehnquist total. Also showing a substantial decrease are cases dealing with unions and federal taxation. Alternatively, issues of federalism are more frequently litigated before the Rehnquist Court than its two predecessor Courts. A likely explanation for these trends may be the justices' perception that business, labor, and tax matters have relatively little salience, and a resurgent focus on the state and local governments as a result of deregulation. Finally, although the types of cases heard might give some guide to the type of questions the Court deems important, it is not foolproof. Criminal procedure covers a wide array of constitutional issues including Fourth, Fifth, Sixth, and Eighth Amendment rights. Privacy, on the other hand, has largely dealt with contraception and abortion. This does not necessarily make privacy a less important issue to the Court.

WHICH CASES FOR DECISION

The decision whether to grant review has received much scholarly attention. The substantive importance of agenda setting has no doubt attracted scholars, as has the game-theoretic context in which certiorari voting arguably takes place, and the unusual richness of the data now available.[74] We examine first the factors linked with decisions to grant certiorari and then examine the aggregate decisions of the Court itself.

Unfortunately, analyses of whether to grant review, with but a couple of exceptions, are limited to cases arising on writ of certiorari and exclude writs

---

[74] We say "arguably" because there are cases that for various non-strategic reasons do not warrant review. Many are clearly frivolous. Others may not be a "good vehicle," in the sense that the issue on which review would turn is presented neither clearly nor straightforwardly. Relatedly, the justices may believe that a better case will shortly appear. Or they may consider the issue to be one that has not had sufficient lower court or scholarly attention, and consequently view the matter as one where avoidance outweighs the benefits of decision. On the other hand, except for frivolous cases, one should not consider avoiding decision for these reasons as necessarily non-strategic. Perry, op. cit. fn. 47 supra, discusses these considerations at pp. 222–245. But in presenting a model of such decision making, at 271–284, Perry deemphasizes strategic considerations in favor of legalistic ones. As for the richness of the data concerning the decision to decide, see Palmer, op. cit. fn. 51 supra.

Table 5.4. *Supreme Court case load, 1953–1989*

Term	Total		Paid			Miscellaneous			
	Filed	Disposed	Disp	Grant	%Grant	Disp	Grant	%Grant	Oral
1953	1302	1293	694	78	11.2	599	10	1.7	84
1954	1397	1352	721	108	15.0	631	12	1.9	93
1955	1644	1630	865	123	14.2	761	18	2.4	98
1956	1802	1670	900	139	14.4	767	38	5.0	121
1957	1639	1765	967	109	11.3	797	34	4.3	127
1958	1819	1763	886	116	13.1	874	24	2.7	118
1959	1862	1787	860	122	14.2	927	55	5.9	115
1960	1940	1911	887	89	10.0	1023	22	2.2	128
1961	2185	2142	860	103	12.0	1282	39	3.0	101
1962	2369	2324	972	115	11.8	1349	95	7.0	125
1963	2295	2401	1036	118	11.4	1363	59	4.3	130
1964	2792	2180	1027	116	11.3	1151	22	1.9	106
1965	2752	2683	1172	134	11.4	1502	44	2.9	102
1966	3106	2890	1232	121	9.8	1653	58	3.5	112
1967	3271	2946	1338	166	12.4	1606	89	5.5	122
1968	3383	3117	1228	101	8.2	1829	64	3.5	111
1969	3419	3357	1433	95	6.6	1922	38	2.0	107
1970	3419	3318	1540	101	6.6	1771	83	4.7	125

1971	3639	3645	1628	131	8.0	2009	30	1.5	147
1972	3752	3748	1771	133	7.5	1969	21	1.1	153
1973	4187	3876	1868	166	8.9	2004	17	0.8	148
1974	3465	3847	1877	155	8.3	1966	19	1.0	139
1975	3940	3806	1810	154	8.5	1989	18	0.9	151
1976	3775	4006	1929	147	7.6	2075	22	1.1	143
1977	3971	3845	1901	146	7.7	1950	14	0.7	135
1978	3881	3943	1955	210	10.7	1988	27	1.4	134
1979	3993	3812	1983	199	10.0	1828	32	1.8	141
1980	4175	4280	2256	235	10.4	2017	27	1.3	128
1981	4447	4456	2417	299	12.4	2033	13	0.6	148
1982	4224	4188	2174	292	13.4	2011	12	0.6	155
1983	4264	4162	2168	247	11.4	1987	14	0.7	155
1984	4013	4269	2179	241	11.1	2082	23	1.1	142
1985	4421	4289	2107	244	11.6	2180	29	1.3	153
1986	4254	4339	2099	242	11.5	2239	26	1.2	153
1987	4484	4401	2142	239	11.2	2254	32	1.4	144
1988	4790	4806	2178	223	10.2	2626	29	1.1	140
1989	4895	4908	2028	171	8.4	2878	32	1.1	131

Sources. Harvard Law Review; U.S. Supreme Court Judicial Database.

Table 5.5. *Case selection by issue area controlled for court*

Issue Area	Warren Court	Burger Court	Rehnquist Court	row total
Criminal procedure	352 (19.6%)	517 (21.5%)	167 (24.5%)	1036 (21.2%)
Economic activity	448 (25.0%)	427 (17.8%)	112 (16.4%)	937 (19.2%)
Civil rights	224 (12.5%)	496 (20.6%)	97 (14.2%)	817 (16.7%)
Judicial power	228 (12.7%)	269 (11.2%)	85 (12.5%)	582 (11.9%)
First amendment	155 (8.6%)	208 (8.7%)	58 (8.5%)	421 (8.6%)
Unions	127 (7.1%)	108 (4.5%)	29 (4.3%)	264 (5.4%)
Federalism	81 (4.5%)	87 (3.6%)	42 (6.2%)	210 (4.3%)
Federal taxation	115 (6.4%)	68 (2.8%)	21 (2.9%)	203 (4.2%)
Due process	37 (2.1%)	128 (5.3%)	34 (5.0%)	199 (4.1%)
Attorneys	10 (0.6%)	32 (1.3%)	17 (2.5%)	59 (1.2%)
Privacy	2 (0.1%)	40 (1.7%)	10 (1.5%)	52 (1.1%)
Interstate relations	9 (0.5%)	17 (0.7%)	4 (0.6%)	30 (0.6%)
Miscellaneous	5 (0.3%)	7 (0.3%)	7 (1.0%)	19 (0.4%)
Column total	1793	2404	682	4879

of appeal. The cert studies consequently omit a quarter of the Court's cases.[75] Although the Court gives no stated reason for review of non-cert cases, other factors that account for much of the Court's behavior are knowable – for example, the "cues" that the cases contain, the direction, whether liberal or conservative, of the lower court's decision, whether any judges on this court dissented, and whether the Supreme Court affirmed or reversed the decision of the lower court. Only the analyses reported later that use the Supreme Court Judicial Database and Jan Palmer's masterful work on the Vinson Court[76] include appeals. Though Palmer finds similarity in how the justices voted between granting cert and noting jurisdiction on appeals, the model he formulates to explain cert voting does not adequately explain appeals voting.[77]

Individual-level models

The major premise behind most prior work on certiorari is the assumption that the justices prefer to hear cases they wish to reverse. Given a finite number of cases that can be reviewed in a given term, the Court must decide how to utilize its time, the Court's most scarce resource. Certainly, overturning unfavorable lower court decisions has more of an impact – if only to the parties to the litigation – than affirming favorable ones. Thus, the justices should hear more cases with which they disagree, other things being equal.

The first person to actually test this simple reversal strategy in cert voting was S. Sidney Ulmer.[78] He proposed that justices who voted for cert would support the applicant on the merits, whereas justices who voted against cert would not. Ulmer found a significant relationship between the cert vote and the vote on the merits for eight of eleven justices, but the correlations were quite low, ranging from .00 to .157.

Ulmer used his evidence of a reversal strategy to suggest an attitudinal approach to certiorari voting, but the low correlations could just as easily support the conclusion that justices do not pursue policy goals in their certiorari voting. Doris Marie Provine, for example, so argues.[79] She reaches this conclusion by operating under the assumption that if the attitudinal model were correct, justices would virtually always vote to hear cases whose result they disapproved of and deny review to decisions they approve of. Provine therefore expects the attitudinal

---

[75] According to the Supreme Court Judicial Database, the Supreme Court formally decided 5,597 cases from the beginning of the Warren Court in 1953 through the end of the fourth term of the Rehnquist Court in 1990, excluding cases on the original docket and using docket number as the unit of analysis. For the Warren Court, 25.2 percent did not arise on cert, along with 26.5 percent of those on the Burger Court, and 18.1 percent of those on the Rehnquist Court.

[76] Op. cit. fn. 51 supra, ch. 6.

[77] *Ibid.*, p. 95.

[78] S. Sidney Ulmer, "The Decision to Grant Certiorari as an Indicator to Decision 'On the Merits,' " *Polity* 429 (1972).

[79] "Deciding What to Decide: How the Supreme Court Sets its Agenda," 64 *Judicature* 320 (1981).

model to produce very few unanimous certiorari decisions, that justices will almost always vote to reverse decisions when they vote to grant cert, and that justices who vote to deny will almost always vote to affirm on the merits. She finds little support for these hypotheses, however.

Although reversal is the major premise of deciding which cases to review, one ought not consider it the only factor guiding the certiorari votes of policy-minded justices. First, with more than 4,000 cases confronting the Court annually, justices who voted to review every case with which they disagreed would generate institutional paralysis. Salience will obviously matter. Moreover, even if the Court could hear all cases with which a justice disagreed, it is not necessarily in that justice's best policy interest to have all such cases reviewed. If the justice will likely lose on the merits, it is preferable that the case not be heard at all. A series of obscenity cases during the 1970s exemplifies this. By a 5-to–4 vote in *Miller v. California*,[80] the majority decided that states and local governments could ban sexually explicit patently offensive work that lacked serious literary, artistic, political or social value, and that violated contemporary community standards. The four dissenters preferred constitutional standards more protective of freedom of communication. When lower courts upheld convictions based on *Miller*, three of the dissenters – Brennan, Stewart, and Marshall – voted to grant certiorari. Justice Stevens, who replaced Justice Douglas, also opposed *Miller*, but nevertheless voted to deny cert:

> Nothing in Mr. Justice Brennan's opinion dissenting from the denial of certiorari in this case persuades me that any purpose would be served by such argument. For there is no reason to believe that the majority of the Court which decided *Miller v. California* . . . is any less adamant than the minority. Accordingly, regardless of how I might vote on the merits after full argument, it would be pointless to grant certiorari in case after case of this character only to have *Miller* reaffirmed time after time.[81]

Alternatively, justices who favored a particular lower court decision might vote to grant cert if they were confident of affirmation. Finally, unanimity in cert decisions does not indicate that they are non-ideological. The overwhelming majority of unanimous cert denials occur in *in forma pauperis* petitions submitted by convicted criminals. As they incur virtually no cost in filing such petitions, largely frivolous appeals result.[82] If the majority of trials do comport with due process, from an attitudinal perspective we would expect unanimous denials. Presumably even liberal justices don't want to free criminals just because they disapprove of incarceration.

To adequately determine whether an attitudinal focus can explain certiorari voting requires more sophisticated strategies than simple reversal.

Glendon Schubert's "Certiorari Game,"[83] represents the first systematic at-

---

[80]   413 U.S. 15 (1973).

[81]   *Liles v. Oregon*, 425 U.S 963 (1976), at 963–964.

[82]   The Court is cognizant of this problem and has taken steps to alleviate it. See *In re Demos*, 114 L Ed 2d 20 (1991).

[83]   *Quantitative Analysis of Judicial Behavior*, pp. 210–254.

tempt to explain the justices' behavior in game-theoretic terms. Schubert examined the strategies of the four-member liberal bloc of the 1942 term: Rutledge, Murphy, Black, and Douglas. According to Schubert's analysis, the bloc voted to grant cert in thirteen of the fourteen cases in which an appellate court overturned a lower court decision favorable to the employee. The bloc apparently eschewed a simple reversal strategy of voting to hear every anti-worker appellate court decision by focusing instead only on those where the appellate court reversed a trial court decision favorable to the worker. Unfortunately, Schubert's analysis was limited by the fact that he could only infer the justices' conference votes from the actual granting of cert; he had no data on how they actually voted. Indeed Provine has since contested his specific conclusions.[84]

Strong support for strategic certiorari voting can be found in the work of Saul Brenner.[85] He assumed that justices will behave most strategically when only four vote to grant cert, because then each vote is essential. He therefore argues that a justice who wants to affirm will not provide the fourth vote unless he or she is quite certain that the Court will in fact affirm. As he predicts, when a four-person certiorari bloc includes justices who want the court to affirm, the affirmance-preferring justices in that bloc will be more likely to prevail than the reversal-preferring justices. He also finds the justices to be less strategic when more than four vote for cert, because in these cases each justice's vote does not affect the decision to hear the case. Voting for cert in such cases neither aids nor hinders the justice's policy designs, making predicted outcomes irrelevant to the decisional outcome. In a later study, Brenner and John Krol found that, consistent with the attitudinal model, justices were more likely to vote for cert if they wanted to reverse, if their side would win on the merits, and if they were liberals on a liberal Court or conservatives on a conservative Court.[86] These results coincide with the findings of Jan Palmer, who found that the justices' votes on cert correlate with their vote on the merits and whether their side wins on the merits.[87] More recent work by Palmer extends these findings to the appeals docket and finds overwhelming evidence for reversal strategies, but little evidence that those who vote for cert are overall more likely to win on the merits.[88]

[84] Doris Marie Provine, *Case Selection in the United States Supreme Court* (Chicago: University of Chicago Press, 1980), ch. 5. Brennan did not follow Schubert's strategy. The other liberal justices adhered to it between 62 and 100 percent of the time. One can dispute the criteria of success, but we consider Schubert's model reasonably accurate empirically.

[85] Saul Brenner, "The New Certioraric Game," 41 *Journal of Politics* 649 (1979).

[86] Saul Brenner and John F. Krol, "Strategies in Certiorari Voting on the United States Supreme Court," 51 *Journal of Politics* 828 (1989); reprinted in Harold J. Spaeth and Saul Brenner, eds., *Studies in U.S. Supreme Court Behavior* (New York: Garland, 1990), pp. 7–23. Also see John F. Krol and Saul Brenner, "Strategies in Certiorari Voting on the United States Supreme Court: A Reevaluation," 43 *Western Political Quarterly* 335 (1990).

[87] Jan Palmer, "An Econometric Analysis of the U.S. Supreme Court's Certiorari Decisions," 39 *Public Choice* 387 (1982).

[88] Op. cit. fn. 51 supra, chap. 6.

Table 5.6. *Affirmation and reversal by court*

Decision	Warren Court	Burger Court	Rehnquist Court	row total
Affirm	775 (35.9%)	995 (35.7%)	352 (45.3%)	2122 (37.1%)
Reverse	1382 (64.1%)	1795 (64.3%)	425 (54.7%)	3602 (62.9%)
Column total	2157	2790	777	5724

According to Brenner, though, a "prediction" strategy is only likely to be followed under the circumstances just described.[89]

Aggregate-level models

If the justices tend to vote to review decisions with which they disagree, as suggested by the attitudinal model, and if at least four justices must so vote, then the Court should tend to reverse those cases that it does review. We examine the extent to which the Supreme Court reverses lower court decisions for the Warren, Burger, and Rehnquist Courts in Table 5.6. Our data consist of all orally argued cases decided from the 1953 through the 1990 terms except those that arose on original jurisdiction. This period includes the Warren and Burger Courts and the first five terms of the Rehnquist Court. We use docket number as our unit of analysis because the Court does not necessarily dispose of all cases decided by a single opinion in the same fashion. We also count as separate cases the handful that contain split votes, in the sense that one or more of the justices voted with the majority on one aspect or issue of the case and dissented on another. We include these to avoid making an arbitrary judgment about whether the Court affirmed or reversed the lower court's decision.

Because the Court's formal disposition of the cases it decides does not unerringly indicate affirmation or reversal, we focus instead on whether the petitioning party prevailed or not. If the petitioning party prevailed, we count the case as a reversal of the lower court. If the petitioning party did not prevail, we count the case as affirmed.

As can be seen, the Warren, Burger, and Rehnquist Courts all reversed more cases than they affirmed, though the difference is markedly smaller for the Rehnquist Court. When we break the data into different terms (see Table 5.7),

---

[89]   Op. cit. fn. 85 supra.

Table 5.7. *Reversal rate by term*

Term	Rate	Term	Rate	Term	Rate	Term	Rate
53	48.2	62	74.7	71	61.2	81	65.0
54	66.7	63	76.2	72	68.2	82	62.6
55	53.3	64	72.5	73	67.5	83	72.1
56	66.0	65	71.1	74	68.1	84	63.6
57	56.6	66	69.9	75	65.5	85	58.3
58	57.1	67	68.0	76	64.6	86	61.7
59	60.3	68	72.1	77	68.7	87	49.7
60	53.1	69	64.5	78	66.9	88	50.0
61	68.9	70	60.1	79	61.5	89	57.0
				80	66.7	90	60.8

we find that except for the first term of the Warren Court and the 1987 and 1988 terms of the Rehnquist Court, reversals invariably outnumber affirmances. (We discuss the peculiar findings for the Rehnquist Court later.) Reversals peaked in the 1962 and 1963 terms at 74.7 and 76.2 percent, respectively.

Conflict. A focus on reversal rates allows us to make inferences about the cases the Court chooses to hear, but it does not allow for inferences about cases the Court chooses not to hear. If the attitudinal model, as applied to conference voting, is correct, the cases the justices decline to review are more likely to be cases with which the Court agrees. Sidney Ulmer provides strong support for this conclusion by showing that conflict between lower court decisions and his predicted Supreme Court preferences to be the most important factor affecting the grant of certiorari. Among the cert petitions he sampled, review was granted in only 12 percent. Breaking the percentage into conflict and no-conflict categories reveals grants of cert in 44 percent of the conflict cases, but only 7 percent of those without. Thus, if we accept Ulmer's subjective operationalization of conflict with contemporary Supreme Court preferences, such conflict appears almost a necessary condition for review.[90]

In a similar vein to Ulmer's, Donald Songer found that presumed conflict with lower court decisions in economic cases was a crucial factor in cert decisions during the four years he analyzed: 1935, 1941, 1967, and 1972.[91]

As a sizeable number of cases that don't conflict do in fact get heard, we examine other factors affecting cert. The major theoretical focus of studies examining aggregate cert decisions is cue theory, first applied to judicial behavior

---

[90] S. Sidney Ulmer, "The Supreme Court's Certiorari Decisions: Conflict as a Predictive Variable," 78 *American Political Science Review* 901 (1984).
[91] "Concern for Policy Outputs as a Cue for Supreme Court Decisions on Certiorari." 41 *Journal of Politics* 1185 (1979).

by Joseph Tanenhaus and associates.[92] Arguing that the justices can give petitions no more than cursory consideration, they hypothesize that certain cues will merit further consideration, whereas those without any cues will be dropped. The cues they examined were the parties involved, the subject area of the case, and conflict in the court below.

Parties and groups as cues for review. Various parties might have an effect on the grant of review. One party that might particularly be advantaged is the United States, whose cases are usually briefed and argued by the office of the Solicitor General. The Solicitor General appears before the Court more than any other attorney, and appears to benefit from this repeat experience.[93] According to one justice, "the ablest advocates in the U.S. are the advocates in the Solicitor General's Office."[94] The office has been considerate of the Court's caseload, appealing only about one-tenth of the cases that the government loses.[95] These are presumably the most meritorious ones.

Tanenhaus et al. find that between 1947 and 1958, when the United States sought review, cert was granted 47 percent of the time, but when the United States did not seek review and no other cues were present, cert was granted only 6 percent of the time. After controlling for the presence of other cues, they estimate that if the United States favored review, the probability of cert being granted increased by about .38. Provine's data, which cover the same period as Tanenhaus's, show the United States granted review 66 percent of the time.[96] This discrepancy probably results because Provine includes cases containing multiple cues. Ulmer and associates found that if the United States requested review, the probability of cert being granted in the 1955 term increased from 32 percent to 66 percent after deadlisted cases were dropped.[97]

Analyses of more recent terms confirm these findings. Studies by Teger and Kosinski, and Armstrong and Johnson, show that the United States as a party, alone or together with other cues, greatly increased the probability of review in

---

[92]   Joseph Tanenhaus, Marvin Schick, Matthew Muraskin, and Daniel Rosen, "The Supreme Court's Certiorari Jurisdiction: Cue Theory," in Glendon Schubert, ed., *Judicial Decision-Making* (New York: Free Press, 1963), pp. 111–132.

[93]   See generally, Marc Galanter, "Why the 'Haves' Come Out Ahead: Speculations on the Limits of Legal Change," 9 *Law and Society Review* 95 (1974), and specifically Provine, op. cit. fn. 84 supra, pp. 86–92.

[94]   Karen O'Connor and Lee Epstein, "States Rights or Criminal Rights: An Analysis of State Performance in U.S. Supreme Court Litigation." Paper presented at the annual meetings of the Northeastern Political Science Association, Philadelphia, 1983. Quoted in Jeffrey A. Segal and Cheryl Reedy, "The Supreme Court and Sex Discrimination: The Role of the Solicitor General," 41 *Western Political Quarterly* 553 (1988), 556.

[95]   Robert Scigliano, *The Supreme Court and the Presidency* (New York: Free Press, 1971), p. 169.

[96]   Provine, op. cit. fn. 84 supra, p. 87.

[97]   S. Sidney Ulmer, William Hintze, and Louise Kirklosky, "The Decision to Grant or Deny Certiorari: Further Consideration of Cue Theory," 6 *Law and Society Review* 637 (1972).

the 1967–1968 and 1975–1977 terms.[98] Results reported by Caldeira and Wright for the 1982 term demonstrate that when the Solicitor General requests review, the probability of cert being granted increased, depending on the other variables present, between .36 and .64.[99] In sum, the evidence is overwhelming: Solicitor General requests for review enormously increase the probability of acceptance.

Influences on cert decisions are not limited to the parties. As noted, interest groups and various organizations can file amicus curiae briefs. These briefs, in addition to providing legal arguments that the parties themselves might not make, may enable the Court to judge the importance of the litigation. Indeed, in one recent case, Justice Stevens in dissent buttressed his view that the case was an unimportant one that never should have been reviewed, noting that ''not a single brief amicus curiae was filed.''[100] If briefs amicus curiae signal a case's importance, then briefs both in favor and in opposition should further enhance review. This is exactly what Caldeira and Wright found.[101] Cert was granted in 36 percent of the cases they examined that had at least one brief, but in only 5 percent of those without any. Whereas briefs favoring review produced stronger effects, briefs opposed also increased the probability of review.

Lower court conflict. When circuits conflict with one another, or when state supreme courts conflict with one another on national questions, ''federal law is being administered in different ways in different parts of the country; citizens in some circuits are subject to liabilities or entitlements that citizens in other circuits are not burdened with or otherwise entitled to.''[102] Thus the Court should grant review to such cases even though they otherwise would not merit review. Indeed, Rule 17 of the Supreme Court specifically lists conflicts between or among lower courts as a reason for granting cert.

Not all justices agree that sufficient credence is paid to lower court conflicts. In a dissent to a denial of review on the final day of the 1989 term, Justice White pointed out that he had dissented from denial of certiorari 67 times during the term:

My notes on these dissents indicate that on 48 occasions I dissented because in my view there were conflicts among courts of appeals sufficiently crystallized to warrant certiorari if the federal law is to be maintained in any satisfactory uniform condition. In 7 other cases, there were differences on the same federal issue between courts of appeals and state courts; in another case state courts of last resort differed with each other. Finally,

---

[98] Stuart H. Teger and Douglas Kosinski, ''The Cue Theory of Supreme Court Certiorari Jurisdiction: A Reconsideration,'' 42 *Journal of Politics* 834 (1980); Virginia Armstrong and Charles A. Johnson, ''Certiorari Decisions by the Warren and Burger Courts: Is Cue Theory Time Bound?'' 15 *Polity* 143 (1982).

[99] Gregory A. Caldeira and John Wright, ''Organized Interests and Agenda Setting in the U.S. Supreme Court,'' 82 *American Political Science Review* 1109 (1988).

[100] *United States v. Dalm*, 108 L Ed 2d 548 (1990), at 564.

[101] Op. cit. fin. 99 supra.

[102] *Beaulieu v. United States*, 111 L Ed 2d 811, (1990), at 812.

there were 11 cases that did not involve a conflict but in my view presented important issues that had not been settled but should be settled by this Court.[103]

White admitted that though some of these conflicts may not have been "real" or "square," in most cases the court of appeals "expressly differs" with another court.

... yet certiorari is denied because the conflict is "tolerable" or "narrow," or because other courts of appeals should have the opportunity to weigh in on one side or another of the unsettled issue, or for some other unstated reason.[104]

At the other extreme, the Court sometimes manufactures a conflict in order to justify review. Thus, in a suit for equitable recoupment of a time-barred tax refund, the majority asserted that the "approach taken" by two courts of appeals conflicted with that "adopted" by another.[105] The dissenters, however, persuasively documented the absence of conflict.[106] Significantly, the majority made no effort to refute the dissenters' assertions.

Systematic analyses find Justice White's concerns somewhat overstated. Though Ulmer et al. found little evidence that conflict affected the grant of cert in the 1955 term,[107] his more extensive treatment of the issue indicates the cruciality of intercircuit conflict to cert decisions of the Vinson and Warren Courts, but less to Burger Court decisions, after controlling for other factors.[108] Caldeira and Wright also show conflict to have significant effects, but unfortunately they do not distinguish between conflict among lower courts and conflict with the prevailing direction of the Supreme Court's decisions on the issue that the case concerns.[109]

Tanenhaus et al. studied a variant of the conflict hypothesis: whether disagreement within the court below or disagreement between different courts in the same case affected the likelihood of review. They found that the Court granted review 13 percent of the time when there is dissension between or within lower courts and no other cues present, versus 6 percent of the time when these cues are absent.[110] They estimate that conflict between or within lower courts in the same case increases the probability of review by .11 after controlling for other cues.

Subject matter. Although much evidence shows that conflict with Supreme Court preferences, conflict between and among lower courts, the presence of the United States as a party, and activity by interest groups as amici curiae affect cert, less evidence indicates that the type of case does so. Scholars have inquired whether civil liberties or economic claims are more likely to be reviewed than other types

---

[103]   Id. at 811–812.
[104]   Id. at 812.
[105]   *United States v. Dalm*, 108 L Ed 2d 548 (1990), at 556.
[106]   Id. at 565, note 2, 569, 571.
[107]   Op. cit. fn. 97 supra.
[108]   Op. cit. fn. 90 supra.
[109]   Op. cit. fn. 99 supra.
[110]   Op. cit. fn. 92 supra.

of cases. The evidence that they are is underwhelming. Tanenhaus et al. found that the Vinson and Warren Courts were more likely to hear non-criminal civil liberties cases than other types of cases, but were only marginally more likely to hear economic cases.[111] Ulmer found no effect for either civil liberties or economic cases after controlling for other factors,[112] whereas Caldeira and Wright similarly found that a civil liberties cue did not significantly increase the probability of review after other factors were considered.[113] Issue as a cue was found to be significant in the Teger-Kosinski and Armstrong-Johnson studies, but these do not fully control for other factors.[114]

Petition type. We note again that the Court is more likely to grant review to paid petitions than to unpaid ones. Approximately 10 percent of the former gain review in a given year, as opposed to only 1 percent of the latter. Although this might suggest a bias against indigent petitioners, the lack of filing fees no doubt produces a large number of completely frivolous claims.[115]

Entirely apart from the factors we have addressed are questions of standing and jurisdiction. Also relevant are such considerations as "good" facts on which an authoritative opinion may be based; whether the issue the case poses is sufficiently "ripe" for review or whether it should be allowed to "percolate" further in the lower courts and among scholars; and whether or not a more appropriate case may already be on its way to the Court. Though all but unexamined by political scientists, they obviously affect the Court's decisions concerning review.

Rehnquist Court affirmations Finally, we examine the Rehnquist Court's recent penchant for affirming lower court decisions. It is an important matter because it not only indicates a basic change in most, if not all, of the justices' strategies to grant and deny review, but it also suggests that marked changes are occurring in the Court's management and control of its docket.

What accounts for this difference? One may plausibly assume that the frequency of reversal will be less in cases that are reviewed because of conflict between or among courts below than in cases where these courts do not conflict. The Court's usual proclivity to reverse should be mitigated when the Court reviews because of conflict below. Consider the following scenarios. In situation one, a lower court rules one way on an issue unresolved by the Supreme Court. Like the overwhelming majority of cases, it is either not appealed or denied review. The following year, a different court hears a similar case and, not bound by horizontal *stare decisis*, rules in the opposite direction. Now conflict exists and the Court is much more likely to grant review. But because the order

[111]   Ibid.
[112]   Op. cit. fn. 90 supra.
[113]   Op. cit. fn. 99 supra.
[114]   Op. cit. fn. 98 supra.
[115]   For example, *In re Demos*, 114 L Ed 2d 20 (1991).

in which the lower courts decided the case is unrelated to the preferences of the justices, the Court should be no more likely to reverse the recent case than affirm it.

In situation two, both lower courts again decide the question differently, but this time do so at the same time. Although the Court could take only the case with which it disagrees, it is more likely to decide both cases together.[116] Presumably, one case will be affirmed and the other reversed, thus precluding the possibility of a reversal strategy. Thus, the Rehnquist Court's affirmation policy may stem from reviewing a higher proportion of cases with conflict.

Four caveats should be noted when analysis considers conflict in the lower courts. First, the Court gives no reason for reviewing cases except on writ of certiorari. Of the 5,597 orally argued cases other than those arising under the Court's original docket that were decided between the beginning of the Warren Court in 1953 and the end of the 1989 term, only 4196 arose on cert. Second, the Court does not provide a reason for review in every cert case. In 1,744 such cases, the Court gave no reason. Mitigating this concern is the fact that the Rehnquist Court was less derelict in providing reasons for review than its predecessor Courts. It gave reasons 64 percent of the time, whereas the Warren and Burger Courts each did so in about 58 percent of their cert cases. Moreover, slightly more of the Rehnquist Court's cases rose on certiorari (81.9 percent) than did those of the Warren and Burger Courts (74.8 and 73.5 percent, respectively). Third, not all authors of opinions and judgments of the Court give reasons at an equal frequency. Douglas did so in barely a third of his Warren Court assignments, whereas Frankfurter gave a reason in over 92 percent of his. The variation among the Rehnquist Court justices is much less marked, however. Except for White, who gave a reason in only 41.2 percent of his assignments, and Brennan, 60 per cent, the others range between Kennedy's 68.0 and Powell's 87.5.[117] Fourth, a statement in the majority opinion that conflict exists may be false. One occasionally will find dissents from such statements.[118] With these caveats in mind, the data indicate that more than two-thirds of the cases in which the Court either gives no reason for review or provides a reason other than conflict were reversed (67.0 percent), as opposed to 53.1 percent that specify conflict as the reason for review. The differences in these proportions are highly significant.

Table 5.8 shows that during its first five terms, the Rehnquist Court did in fact take a much higher percentage of cases with conflict than did either the Warren or Burger Courts. Almost 40 percent of the Rehnquist Court's cert decisions involved conflict (248 of 658), as opposed to only 21.9 percent for

---

[116]   For example, *Traynor v. Turnage*, 99 L Ed 2d 618 (1988).

[117]   The others' percentages are: Stevens 68.2, O'Connor 68.3, Marshall 70.6, Rehnquist 74.4, Scalia 77.3, and Blackmun 85.0.

[118]   For example, ''The majority states that certiorari was granted in this case to resolve a conflict among the Courts of Appeals. . . . but in fact no such conflict exists.'' *United States v. Dalm*, 108 L Ed 2d 548 (1990), at 565.

Table 5.8. *Conflict as a reason for granting cert by court*

	Warren Court	Burger Court	Rehnquist Court	row total
No Conflict	1370 (84.8%)	1617 (78.1%)	410 (62.3%)	3397 (78.2%)
Conflict	245 (15.2%)	454 (21.9%)	248 (37.7%)	947 (21.8%)

Table 5.9. *Affirmation and reversal by court controlled for conflict*

	Warren Court	Burger Court	Rehnquist Court	row total
Conflict below				
affirmed	114 (46.5%)	198 (43.6%)	124 (50.0%)	436 (46.0%)
reversed	131 (53.5%)	256 (56.4%)	124 (50.0%)	511 (54.0%)
column total	245	454	248	947
No Conflict below				
affirmed	460 (33.6%)	534 (33.0%)	166 (41.5%)	1160 (34.1%)
reversed	910 (66.4%)	1083 (67.0%)	244 (59.5%)	2237 (65.9%)
column total	1370	1617	410	3397

the Burger Court (454 of 2071) and a mere 15.3 percent for the Warren Court (245 of 1,615). This, though, does not fully explain the Rehnquist Court's low reversal rates. Although all three Courts affirm more cases involving conflict than they do those without, the Rehnquist Court affirms more frequently than the Warren and Burger Courts even after controlling for conflict (see Table 5.9). Specifically, the Rehnquist Court reverses only half the time in cases involving

Table 5.10. *Affirmation rates by lower court direction and court*

Lower Court Direction	Warren Court	Burger Court	Rehnquist Court
Liberal	51.5%	32.3%	41.0%
Conservative	28.8%	39.3%	48.7%

conflict, compared with 53.5 percent and 56.4 percent for the Warren and Burger Courts respectively; the Rehnquist Court reverses 59.5 percent of the time in cases not involving conflict, compared with 66.4 percent and 67.0 percent for the Warren and Burger Courts respectively.

These data lead to the following conclusions: If the Rehnquist Court decreased its granting of cert to cases in which conflict was present from 38 percent to 20 percent, and if its percentage of reversals within the conflict and no conflict cases remained the same, its overall reversal rate in certiorari cases would increase from 54.7 percent to 57.6 percent. Thus the Rehnquist Court's affirmation posture is partially, but not entirely, explained by its acceptance of a higher percentage of cases with conflict below.

In an effort to explain the Rehnquist Court's higher rate of affirmations regardless of conflict, we examine the ideological "direction" (liberal or conservative) in which the Courts resolved their cases. What we want to know is the extent to which the conservative Rehnquist Court affirms liberal and conservative lower court decisions. Phrased differently, are the conservative members of the Rehnquist Court so well entrenched that the additional benefit of strengthening a conservative lower court decision might, under some circumstances, be worth the risk of reversal?

This, too, provides a partial explanation. The Rehnquist Court affirms almost half the conservative lower court decisions it hears, compared with only 39.3 percent for the Burger Court (see Table 5.10). This explanation is only partial because the Rehnquist Court's 48.7 percent affirmation rate is virtually identical to the rate at which the Warren Court affirmed liberal decisions. Most surprising is the Rehnquist Court's affirmation of a remarkably high 41.0 percent of its liberal lower court decisions, versus 32.3 percent for the Burger Court. Alternatively, the Warren Court only affirmed 28.8 percent of the conservative lower court decisions it heard.

Thus, the Rehnquist Court, during its first five terms, has not adhered as strictly to a simple "error correction" strategy as did the Warren and Burger Courts because it accepts for review a significantly higher proportion of cases in which the lower courts conflict. What we do not know, and will not know until docket books for the recent terms become available, are the particular strategies, if any, employed by the justices during these most recent terms.

PROPOSALS FOR REFORM

Proposals to reform the Court's workload have been notably unsuccessful. The system that the First Congress created in 1789 exists today with only a few significant structural changes. The most important occurred in 1891 when Congress created nine circuit courts of appeals, and in 1925 when the Judges' Bill of that year drastically reduced the Court's obligation to decide certain cases.

The most recent major proposals date from the early 1970s and, like most of their predecessors, fell on deaf ears. In 1971, Chief Justice Burger appointed a seven-member group of distinguished jurists and scholars to recommend measures to enable the Court to keep up with and perform its work adequately. Since then the Court has kept abreast of its workload notwithstanding a small but steady increase in the filings per term – an increase, however, markedly less than the rate that prevailed during the 1960s.[119] Because the Court has not fallen behind in disposing of cases, Burger's committee – the Federal Judicial Study Group on the Case Load of the Supreme Court – focused on the adequacy of the Court's performance. It dusted off and resubmitted a proposal that initially surfaced in the 1880s, the establishment of a national court of appeals.[120] In the Study Group's version, this court would screen all petitions for review filed with the Supreme Court and deny about 80 percent as unworthy of the justices' consideration. No appeal could be taken from its denial of review. Important cases involving real intercircuit conflicts would be sent to the Supreme Court for decision, whereas the national court of appeals would decide conflicts of lesser importance.

At about the same time – 1983 – Congress also got into the act with its formation of a Commission on Revision of the Federal Court Appellate System. This body also recommended the establishment of a national court of appeals, although one substantially different from that of the Study Group. It would not screen cases; rather the Supreme Court would refer cases to it for decision, as would the various circuit courts of appeals. This scheme assumed that the Court was failing to decide a number of important cases, particularly those involving statutory construction.[121] The Supreme Court would have discretion to review decisions of the new court.

Response to the proposals of the two commissions and variations subsequently

---

[119] Arthur D. Hellman, "Caseload, conflicts, and decisional capacity: does the Supreme Court need help?" 67 *Judicature* 28 (1983), at 31. As we noted in connection with our discussion of the Court's workload, at the beginning of the 1990s the Court began to accept fewer cases for review, notwithstanding small increases in the total number of filings. Also see Linda Greenhouse, "As Its Workload Decreases, High Court Shuns New Cases," *New York Times*, Nov. 28, 1989, p. 1; Ruth Marcus, "High Court's Caseload Is Unprecedentedly Light," *Washington Post*, Feb. 5, 1990, p. A4.

[120] Statement of Linda Greenhouse in the panel discussion "Rx for an overburdened Supreme Court: Is relief in sight?" 66 *Judicature* 394 (1983).

[121] Stern and Gressman, op. cit., fn. 57 supra, pp. 44–45.

proposed was sufficiently mixed to nix them. The justices themselves disagreed about their desirability,[122] as did lower court judges and commentators.[123] In addition to disagreement within the judicial and legal communities, many reasons seem to mitigate reformist inclinations.

First, the justices do not sit from late June or early July until the first Monday in October.[124] Because they may visit their offices, hire staff, and evaluate petitions for certiorari and writs of appeal during this time, they are not totally free of duties.[125] But though it may not be accurate to view the inter-term recess as a three-month vacation, it is markedly lengthier than that of the average fulltime worker. Second, the burdens of office do not preclude the justices from speaking at bar and other associational meetings, granting interviews, and writing books and articles. The same year he became Chief Justice, Rehnquist published a book on the Court,[126] and throughout his tenure, Chief Justice Burger heavily involved himself in matters of judicial administration. Third, notwithstanding generous retirement benefits, recent Courts have been among the most aged in history. The presence of sitting justices who are in their eighties belies an overburdened bench.

Fourth, the most time-consuming portion of the justices' work consists of writing opinions. The justices equally divide the task of writing the opinion of the Court among themselves, which requires each to write an average of fifteen or sixteen per term.[127] At their own volition, the Warren Court justices also wrote an average of 1.24 special opinions (concurrences and dissents) per orally argued case, the Burger Court justices an average of 1.59.[128] Table 5.11 displays the frequency with which the Rehnquist Court justices have written opinions during the 1986–1990 terms. The difference between 11.1 percent – the share

[122] Miriam Krasno, "What the justices have said about the Court's workload," 66 *Judicature* 404 (1983).
[123] See notes 119–121 supra, and the references cited therein. Also see Donald P. Lay, "Query: Will the proposed national court of appeals create more problems than it solves?" 66 *Judicature* 447 (1983); Samuel Estreicher and John Sexton, "Improving the process: Case selection by the Supreme Court," 70 *Judicature* 41 (1986); and Robert L. Stern, "Remedies for appellate overloads: The ultimate solution," 72 *Judicature* 103 (1988).
[124] Special sessions in 1958 and 1972 cut into this hiatus. The justices issued half a dozen orders between August 28 and September 17, 1958, in addition to hearing arguments and deciding the school desegregation ruckus in Little Rock, AR: *Cooper v. Aaron*, 358 U.S. 1. In 1972, they reconvened on July 7, a week after adjournment, to stay three judgments of the D.C. Circuit concerning the seating of delegates to the Democratic National Convention. *O'Brien v. Brown*, 409 U.S. 1.
[125] Their clerks are certainly busy. See Stuart Taylor, Jr., "When High Court's Away, Clerks' Work Begins," *New York Times*, Sept. 23, 1988, p. A12.
[126] William H. Rehnquist, *The Supreme Court: How It Was, How It Is* (New York: Morrow, 1987).
[127] Harold J. Spaeth, "Distributive justice: Majority opinion assignments in the Burger Court," 67 *Judicature* 299 (1984); reprinted in Spaeth and Brenner, op. cit. fn. 86 *supra*, pp. 80–92.
[128] Harold J. Spaeth and Michael F. Altfeld, "Influence Relationships within the Supreme Court: A Comparison of the Warren and Burger Courts," 38 *Western Political Quarterly* 70 (1985); reprinted in Spaeth and Brenner, op. cit. fn. 86 *supra*, p. 263.

Table 5.11. *Frequency of opinion writing by justice by term*

Justice	1986	1987	1988	1989	1990	total
			Term			
Blackmun	41	29	48	32	24	174
	25.6	19.6	32.2	23.2	18.9	24.1
Brennan	48	40	45	46		179
	30.0	27.0	30.2	33.3		30.1
Kennedy		14	29	32	30	91[a]
		9.5	19.5	23.2	23.6	22.0
Marshall	37	29	32	32	32	162
	23.1	19.6	21.5	23.2	25.2	22.4
O'Connor	43	36	34	28	26	167
	26.9	24.3	22.8	20.3	20.5	23.1
Powell	39					39
	24.4					24.4
Rehnquist	26	24	23	22	21	116
	16.2	16.2	15.4	15.9	16.5	16.1
Scalia	42	43	44	41	43	213
	26.2	29.1	29.5	29.7	33.9	29.5
Souter					12	12
					9.4	9.4
Stevens	62	44	53	57	44	260
	38.7	29.7	35.6	41.3	34.6	36.0
White	40	44	33	29	30	176
	25.0	29.7	22.1	21.0	23.6	24.4

Note. [a]Full terms only (1988-1990).

of the opinions of the Court that each justice is expected to bear – and the figures that appear in Table 5.11 indicates the extent to which each of them engages in special opinion writing.[129] Except for the Chief Justice and the freshman Souter, they all write approximately twice the minimum required, with Stevens more than three times the minimum, and Brennan slightly less. Overworked justices would hardly display such behavior.

[129] The N for each term in Table 5.11 is the number of citations to orally argued and *per curiam* cases, excepting decrees and those decided by a tied vote. The N per term is: 1986, 160; 1987, 148; 1988, 149; 1989, 138; 1990, 127. We did not exclude from our calculations the handful of cases in which a given justice did not participate.

Fifth, the proposed reforms would further bureaucratize the judiciary by adding another layer of appellate review and decision. Given the cost and delay already inherent in litigation, additional expense precludes support. Finally, Congress effectively eliminated the last vestiges of the Court's obligatory jurisdiction in 1988. No longer must the Court hear appeals in which a state court voided an act of Congress or upheld a state law against a challenge to its constitutionality. Although these cases comprised less than 5 percent of the Court's docket, the justices had complained that they usurped too much of their time and resources.[130]

SUMMARY AND CONCLUSIONS

The link that connects the various factors that determine who gets into the Supreme Court are the individual justices' personal policy preferences. Given the freedom to select for review such cases as the justices wish, the factors that govern selection and the strategies that the various justices employ in voting to review a case are matters of individual determination.

Although analyses of case selection have primarily focused on petitions for certiorari rather than writs of appeal – with the exception of Palmer's work on the Vinson Court and our own analyses – a fairly detailed picture of the con-siderations that enter into the justices' choice has emerged.

We have demonstrated that even the two legal requirements for getting into Court – jurisdiction and standing to sue – are subject to the justices' control, although Congress, compatibly with the provisions of Article III of the Constitution, determines the Court's jurisdiction. As with other congressional legislation, the Court interprets the language and intentions of Congress. So also here. And though some of the elements of standing to sue are constitutionally grounded, whereas decisional law has produced others, the precedents governing both kinds are no less subject to judicial manipulation than are those governing other areas of the law, as we documented in Chapter 1. Needless to say, such jurisprudential considerations as the importance of the case, whether it contains good facts, whether it clearly presents an issue, whether a better case is in the pipeline, and such other factors as constitute "certworthiness," also lie wholly within the individual justice's discretion.

As for the non-legal factors that govern case selection, although a fully ex-plainable model remains to be constructed, we do know that the following factors incline the Court toward review: 1) desire to reverse the decision of the lower court; 2) conflict between or among lower courts, especially the cirucit courts of appeal; and 3) the United States as a party to the lawsuit. A special relationship exists between the Solicitor General and the justices. The Solicitor General's

---

[130] Weisberg, op. cit. fn. 46 supra, p. 138. The number of clerks to which each justice is entitled has increased with the growth in the Court's caseload, from one to two following World War II, to three in the 1960s, and to four in the 1970s. "Rx for an overburdened Supreme Court," op. cit. fn. 120 supra, p. 397.

petitions are generally granted on the understanding that the office exercise restraint in choosing the cases for the Court's consideration. Other cues that enhance review include the presence of amicus curiae and issues that the justices consider salient.

Proposals to reform the process for getting cases into the Supreme Court dating from the 1970's have largely fallen on deaf ears. Unlike the vast majority of American courts, state and federal, the justices remain abreast of their docket. Notwithstanding a substantial increase in the number of cases the Court is petitioned to review over the past half century, the justices make their decisions to grant or deny review within a few weeks of their receipt. If accepted during the first four months of the Court's term, the case will likely be decided before adjournment, otherwise the following term. Because of the currency of its docket, the luxury of a three-month summer vacation, and the justices' failure to speak with a single unequivocal voice, all proposals for reform have fallen on deaf ears to date.

6

The decision on the merits

This chapter begins where Chapter 5 left off – with the considerations that apply once the Court has agreed to hear a litigant's case. Accordingly, we start with a discussion of the stages that follow the decision to decide a case and the considerations that govern the disposition of these cases. We will especially emphasize the factors that affect the justices' decisions and the policies that characterize their decisions.

PROCESS

Cases that receive full treatment from the Court – those that are argued orally and decided with a full opinion (referred to as formally decided cases)[1] – are subject to three votes. We considered the first of these – the decision to decide – in Chapter 5. If the Court votes to grant cert or to note probable jurisdiction, the other two votes occur following oral argument. These are the original vote on the merits and the final vote on the merits. Palmer refers to them more accurately and descriptively as "conference votes on the merits" and "report votes on the merits."[2] We know relatively little about the former vote, a great deal about the latter. First we present a discussion of oral argument.

Oral argument

Oral argument is the only publicly visible stage of the Court's decision-making process. The extent to which it affects the justices' votes is problematic. The justices aver that it is a valuable source of information about the cases they have agreed to decide,[3] but that does not mean that oral argument regularly, or even

---

[1] But a formally decided case need not be decided on the merits of the controversy, as we pointed out in Chapter 5.

[2] Jan Palmer, *The Vinson Court Era: The Supreme Court's Conference Votes* (New York: AMS Press, 1990), p. 97.

[3] Robert L. Stern and Eugene Gressman, *Supreme Court Practice*, 5th ed. (Washington: Bureau of National Affairs, 1978), pp. 730–735; William H. Rehnquist, *The Supreme Court: How It Was, How It Is* (New York: Morrow, 1987), pp. 271–285. Political scientists are just beginning to analyze the influence of oral argument systematically. See Steven A. Peterson, James N.

infrequently, determines who wins and who loses. The conference vote on the merits occurs within seventy-two hours of oral argument; hence, it is likely to be fresh in the justices' minds. On the other hand, the Court rigorously limits the time for argument to 30 minutes for each side, with a few exceptions when an hour is allotted.[4]

The Court devotes fourteen weeks per term to oral argument, two weeks each during the months of October through April. During this time, it sits in public session on Mondays, Tuesdays, and Wednesdays, from 10 a.m. to noon, and from 1 to 3 p.m. This schedule provides an upper limit for the number of orally argued cases that the Court will consider during a term: four per day for three days over each of fourteen weeks, for a normal maximum of 168 cases. The Clerk of the Court schedules oral argument; it typically occurs between four and six months after the justices have agreed to review the case. Several weeks before the date of argument, the justices receive the briefs filed by the parties to the litigation, along with those that interested non-parties may have submitted (*amici curiae*). Such non-parties receive permission from the parties themselves or the Court gives them leave to submit their views on the proper resolution of the controversy. The parties' consent need not be had for the Solicitor General to file a brief on behalf of the United States, or for the authorized official of a federal agency, state, territory, or political subdivision of a state or territory to file on its behalf.[5] Nongovernmental interests generally have little trouble gaining permission from the Court to file briefs. Between 1969 and 1981, only 11 percent of motions for leave to file amicus briefs were denied.[6] Most frequently participating as amici are states, followed by corporations and business groups, and citizen organizations. Individuals rarely participate.[7]

Lawyers filing amicus briefs on behalf of organized interests are not allowed to present oral argument except "in the most extraordinary circumstances."[8] Nevertheless, interest groups are often parties, in which case their lawyers may engage in the oral argument. For instance, the NAACP Legal Defense Fund

Schubert, Glendon Schubert, and Stephen L. Wasby, "Patterns in Supreme Court Oral Argument," paper presented at the 1991 meetings of the Law and Society Assn., Amsterdam, The Netherlands; and Stephen L. Wasby, Steven A. Peterson, James N. Schubert, and Glendon Schubert, "The Supreme Court's Use of Per Curiam Dispositions: The Connection to Oral Argument," paper presented at the 1991 meetings of the Midwest Political Science Assn., Chicago.

[4] Rules limiting the time of oral argument are a modern phenomenon. They did not exist early in the Court's history. Before the current time limits, the Court allowed each side an hour in important cases, thirty minutes in the remainder. Rehnquist, op. cit. fn. 3 supra, pp. 274–275.

[5] Rule 36 of the *Rules of the Supreme Court of the United States*, 445 U.S. at 1031–1032.

[6] Karen O'Connor and Lee Epstein, "Court Rules and Workload: A Case Study of Rules Governing Amicus Curiae Participation," 8 *Justice System Journal* 35 (1983).

[7] Gregory Caldeira and John Wright, "Amici Curiae Participation Before the Supreme Court: Who Participates, When, and How Much," 52 *Journal of Politics* 782 (1990).

[8] Supreme Court Rule 38.7.

(LDF) sponsored the historic case of *Brown v. Board of Education*,[9] with the plaintiffs' represented by the LDF's chief counsel, Thurgood Marshall. For public interest lawyers representing groups like the NAACP or the ACLU, the Supreme Court serves as a forum not just for winning clients' cases, but for promoting the cause that the group espouses.[10]

The conference

No one is permitted to attend the justices' conferences except the justices themselves. At these meetings, the justices decide whether or not to hear the cases they have been asked to review; they discuss and vote on whether to affirm or reverse the cases before them; and justices are assigned cases in which they are to write the opinion of the Court. What transpires in the conference is often described as Washington's best kept secret. What little we know we learn long after the fact, apart from an occasional statement in an opinion, from the justices' private papers and their off-the-bench communications.

According to Chief Justice Rehnquist, conferences convene on Wednesday afternoons following oral argument and on Friday mornings. The Wednesday conference votes on the cases at which oral argument was heard the preceding Monday, whereas the Friday conference disposes of the orally argued cases from Tuesday and Wednesday. The second part of the conferences that dispose of orally argued cases is devoted to the consideration of cases the Court has been asked to review.[11]

Evidencing the lack of knowledge about conference procedures is the misinformation that commentators have provided about the order in which the justices speak and vote. At one time, the process apparently involved two stages, with the Chief Justice speaking first, followed by the others in descending order of seniority. The second stage, in which the justices voted to affirm or reverse, proceeded in the opposite order: the most junior voted first, the Chief Justice last. Sometime between the Vinson Court (1946–1952) and the Warren Court (1953–1968), the process became a single stage, with the justices speaking and voting in order of seniority.[12] In his book, Rehnquist states:

For many years there has circulated a tale that although the discussion in conference proceeds in order from the Chief Justice to the junior justice, the voting actually begins with the junior justice and proceeds back to the Chief Justice in order of seniority. I can testify that, at least during my fifteen years on the Court [dating from 1971], this tale is very much of a myth . . .[13]

[9] 347 U.S. 483 (1954).
[10] Jonathan Casper, *Lawyers Before the Warren Court* (Urbana: University of Illinois Press, 1972).
[11] Rehnquist, op. cit. fn 3 supra, pp. 287–288, 289.
[12] Saul Brenner and Jan Palmer, "Voting Order in Conference on the Vinson Court," unpublished manuscript, 1991.
[13] Op. cit. fn. 3 supra, pp. 289–290.

The Court follows basically the same procedure with regard to the decision to decide a case, except that discussion "is much less elaborate."[14] If the Chief Justice has placed the case among those to be discussed, he explains why he has done so. If one of the associate justices has put a case on the discuss list, that justice begins the discussion. The justices vote in order of seniority and are free to preface their vote to grant or deny review with a statement of their reasons why.

In response to correspondence with Professor Robert Bradley, Rehnquist elaborated on conference procedures as follows:

I am quite surprised that this very obvious "question of fact" still remains in dispute, and yet your reference to academic texts . . . shows that it plainly does.
Because the references . . . piqued my curiosity, I talked this over with Justice Brennan, who has the longest service of any present member of the Court. He confirms that since he came to the Court in the fall of 1956, the procedure has been as I describe it to you.[15]

As far as conference discussions are concerned, Rehnquist reports that "with occasional exceptions, each justice begins and ends his part of the discussion without interruption from his colleagues." He further states:

When I first went on the Court, I was both surprised and disappointed at how little interplay there was between the various justices during the process of conferring on a case. Each would state his views, and a junior justice could express agreement or disagreement with views expressed by a justice senior to him earlier in the discussion, but the converse did not apply; a junior justice's views were seldom commented upon, because votes had been already cast up the line. Like most junior justices before me must have felt, I thought I had some very significant contributions to make, and was disappointed that they hardly ever seemed to influence anyone because people did not change their votes in response to my contrary views. I thought it would be desirable to have more of a round-table discussion of the matter after each of us had expressed our views. Having now sat in conferences for fifteen years [as of 1987], and risen from ninth to seventh to first in seniority, I now realize – with newfound clarity – that while my idea is fine in the abstract it probably would not contribute much in practice, and at any rate is doomed by the seniority system to which the senior justices naturally adhere.[16]

Justice Scalia has echoed Rehnquist's sentiments, but without endorsing Rehnquist's approval of the lack of interchange among the justices. In response to questions following a speech at the George Washington University Law School, Scalia said that "not very much conferencing goes on" in conference. He used "conferencing" in the sense of efforts to persuade others to change their minds by debating matters of disagreement. "In fact," he said, "to call our discussion of a case a conference is really something of a misnomer.

---

[14] Ibid. p. 289. For a description of the Court's decision to decide practices during the Vinson Court, see Palmer, op. cit. fn. 2 supra, pp. 26–30.

[15] Reprinted in 7 *Law, Courts, and Judicial Process Section Newsletter* 8 (Fall, 1989). Also see H.W. Perry, Jr., *Deciding to Decide: Agenda Setting in the United States Supreme Court* (Cambridge: Howard University Press, 1991), pp. 85–91.

[16] Op. cit. fn. 3 supra, pp. 290–291.

It's much more a statement of the views of each of the nine Justices, after which the totals are added and the case is assigned.'' He went on to say that he doesn't like this: ''Maybe it's just because I'm new. Maybe it's because I'm an ex-academic. Maybe it's because I'm right.'' He concurred with Rehnquist's observation that his own remarks ''hardly ever seemed to influence anyone because people did not change their votes in response to my contrary views.''[17]

Although the other branches of government have opened their proceedings to a degree of public scrutiny, the Supreme Court has adamantly refused to follow this trend. On the other hand, unlike Congress and the executive branch, the Court has provided the public with all relevant materials pertaining to its decisions: briefs, transcripts of oral argument, the record of lower court proceedings, as well as the opinions of the justices themselves. The Court justifies its refusal to open its conferences to public examination on the ground that it would jeopardize its effectiveness as an authoritative policy-making body. While still an associate justice, Rehnquist provided what appears to have been the first full-blown defense of the practice. He gave four reasons for the secrecy:

First, ''A remarkably candid exchange of views'' occurs. ''No one feels at all inhibited'' about being quoted out of context or that ''half-formed or ill conceived ideas'' might subsequently be ''held up to public ridicule.'' Second, each justice is required to do his or her own work. Unlike members of the president's cabinet, who are ''generally flanked by aides,'' the justices are forced to prepare themselves personally for the conference. Third, public scrutiny or press coverage could subject the Court to ''lobbying pressures'' intended to affect the outcome of decisions. Fourth, ''occasionally short-tempered remarks or bits of rancorous rhetoric'' are uttered which might transcend the cordiality that exists among the justices if they became part of a public record.[18]

THE CONFERENCE VOTE ON THE MERITS

We know precious little about conference voting, and much of what we do know may be incorrect. For instance, Professor J. Woodford Howard contended that changes in the justices' voting between the original and final votes on the merits are ''so extensive in empirical reality as to pose very serious problems of clas-

[17] ''Ruing Fixed Opinions,' *New York Times*, Feb. 22, 1988, p. 20; reprinted in Harold J. Spaeth and Saul Brenner, eds., *Studies in U.S. Supreme Court Behavior* (New York: Garland, 1990), pp. 256–257. Also see Paul M. Barrett, ''Despite Expectations, Scalia Fails to Unify Conservatives on Court,'' *Wall Street Journal*, April 28, 1992, pp. A1, A6.

[18] Mort Mintz, ''Rehnquist Strongly Defends Secrecy in Supreme Court,'' *Washington Post*, January 28, 1977, p. A2; Harold J. Spaeth, *Supreme Court Policy Making* (San Francisco: W.H. Freeman, 1979), p. 24.

sification and inference.''[19] Yet support for his assertion that voting fluidity belies the validity of the attitudinal model as the explanation for the justice's behavior rests exclusively on anecdotal evidence. We refute Howard's assertion here.

The justices' docket books contain the records of their conference voting.[20] The justices are provided these books at the beginning of each term so that they may individually keep a record of the votes cast in conference; the dates of votes; and to whom the opinion of the Court was assigned, by whom, and when. Although these books become the private property of the justice to whom it is issued, several have made them available to posterity along with their other private papers. Seven of the eleven justices who served on the Vinson Court have opened their docket books to the public, as well as several who served on the Warren Court.[21]

Fluidity and the attitudinal model

Not until 1980 did the first scientific analysis of the original vote on the merits appear[22] – Professor Saul Brenner's reexamination of Howard's assertions about voting fluidity.[23] Brenner found that the Vinson Court justices voted the same way at the original and final votes on the merits 86 percent of the time overall, and 91 percent of the time in major cases. In 8.6 percent of the cases, a voting change transformed a minority or a tie into a majority. Similar findings resulted from his study of the latter portion of the Warren Court.[24]

Apart from the incidence of fluidity, current work has directly assessed the

[19] "On the Fluidity of Judicial Choice," 52 *American Political Science Review* 43 (1968), at 44.

[20] Jan Palmer and Saul Brenner, "Working with Supreme Court Docket Books," 81 *Law Library Journal* 41 (1989); Palmer, op. cit. fn. 2 supra, pp. 34–49.

[21] Palmer, op. cit. fn. 2 supra, contains a meticulous compilation of conference voting on the Vinson Court, with a complete case-by-case record of the justices' voting and opinion assignments, along with an assortment of other pertinent identifying information. As a result of Palmer's work, scholars now have a highly accurate record of at least three voting data points for each of the Court's formally decided cases: the vote whether or not to accept the case for review, conference voting, and the report vote. Palmer's Vinson Court data includes every available vote, not just those cast in the formally decided cases.

[22] Earlier and contemporaneous studies using docket book data did appear, but they focused on the cert vote, not the conference vote – for example, S. Sidney Ulmer, "The Decision to Grant Certiorari as an Indicator to Decision 'On the Merits,' " 4 *Polity* 429 (1972); Saul Brenner, "The New Certiorari Game," 41 *Journal of Politics* 649 (1979); Doris Marie Provine, *Case Selection in the United States Supreme Court* (Chicago: University of Chicago Press, 1980); Jan Palmer, "An Econometric Analysis of the U.S. Supreme Court's Certiorari Decisions," 39 *Public Choice* 387 (1982).

[23] "Fluidity on the United States Supreme Court: A Re-examination," 24 *American Journal of Political Science* 526 (1980); reprinted in Spaeth and Brenner, op. cit. fn. 17 supra, pp. 53–60.

[24] Saul Brenner, "Fluidity on the Supreme Court, 1956–1967," 26 *American Journal of Political Science* 388 (1982); reprinted in op. cit. fn. 17 supra., pp. 61–65.

compatibility of the attitudinal model with changes between the original and final votes on the merits. Not only do these studies find no incompatibility, they also show that the attitudinal model explains those that do occur, while the role and small-group explanations favored by other scholars do not. Thus, ideological voting on the Vinson Court did not decrease between the original and final votes on the merits, which would clearly be the case if non-attitudinal variables intervened.[25] When minimum winning coalitions on the Warren Court broke up, they most often did so when the marginal justice in the majority was ideologically closer to a dissenting justice than he was to any member of the majority.[26] Attitudinal factors also accounted for majority-minority voting shifts by members of the Warren Court when the original vote coalition did not break up. Conversely, a set of non-attitudinal factors did not explain these voting shifts: the length of service of the shifting justice[27]; the importance of the case; whether the Court affirmed or reversed the decision of the lower court; whether dissent occurred on the lower court; whether the original vote coalition was large or small; whether the Court declared action unconstitutional or overruled one of its precedents.[28]

THE REPORT (OR FINAL) VOTE ON THE MERITS

At any point between the conference vote on the merits and the day a decision is announced, justices are free to change their votes. Their position when the decision is announced constitutes the final vote on the merits. In examining and analyzing the report vote, we pay particular attention to the influence of the

[25]   Saul Brenner, "Ideological Voting on the Vinson Court: A Comparison of the Original Vote on the Merits with the Final Vote," 21 *Polity* 102 (1989).

[26]   Saul Brenner and Harold J. Spaeth, "Majority Opinion Assignments and the Maintenance of the Original Coalition on the Warren Court," 32 *American Journal of Political Science* 72 (1988); Saul Brenner, Timothy M. Hagle, and Harold J. Spaeth, "The Defection of the Marginal Justice on the Warren Court," 42 *Western Political Quarterly* 409 (1989).

[27]   Howard posits the existence of a so-called "freshman effect" as the first of his nonideological intervening variables. He defines it as "unstable attitudes that seem to have resulted from the process of assimilation to the Court. It is not uncommon for a new Justice to undergo a period of adjustment, often about three years in duration, before his voting behavior stabilizes into observable, not to mention predictable, patterns." Op. cit. fn. 19 supra, p. 45. Recent studies all discount the existence of a freshman effect. See Edward V. Heck and Melinda Gann Hall, "Bloc Voting and the Freshman Justice Revisited," 43 *Journal of Politics* 852 (1981); John M. Scheb II and Lee W. Ailshie, "Justice Sandra Day O'Connor and the 'freshman effect,' " 69 *Judicature* 9 (1985); Thea F. Rubin and Albert P. Melone, Justice Antonin Scalia: A first year freshman effect?" 72 *Judicature* 98 (1988); Albert P. Melone, "Revisiting the freshman effect hypothesis: The first two terms of Justice Anthony Kennedy," 74 *Judicature* 6 (1990). Cf. Timothy M. Hagle and Carolyn I. Speer, "A New Test for the Freshman Effect: Justices Scalia and Kennedy," paper presented at the 1991 meetings of the American Political Science Assn., Washington, D.C; Timothy M. Hagle, "Freshman and Court Effects for Supreme Court Justices," paper presented at the 1992 meetings of the Midwest Political Science Assn., Chicago.

[28]   Timothy M. Hagle and Harold J. Spaeth, "Voting Fluidity and the Attitudinal Model of Supreme Court Decision Making," 44 *Western Political Quarterly* 119 (1991).

factors that are crucial to the operation of the attitudinal model: facts (or case stimuli), which are central to both attitudinal and legal models, and attitudes, which are central only to the former. We then examine a series of nonattitudinal factors to determine what effect, if any, they have.

Facts

Case stimuli or facts are central to the decision making of all judges. Trial judges and juries must determine, for example, whether criminal suspects committed the deeds alleged by the prosecution. Appellate courts often must decide, based on the facts of the case as determined by the trial court judge and jury, whether the defendant's conviction was obtained in violation of the Constitution. Determinations of whether a given conviction or a given law violates constitutional rights necessarily depend on the facts of the case. Speaking out against the President is not the same as exposing nuclear secrets. Nor is libeling the President the same as libeling a private individual. Prohibiting abortion after conception is not the same as prohibiting abortion after viability.

To phrase the matter from the standpoint of attitude theory, behavior may be said to be a function of the interaction between an actor's attitude toward an "object" (i.e., persons, places, institutions, and things) and that actor's attitude toward the situation in which the object is encountered.[29] Insofar as judicial decision making is concerned, attitude objects are the litigants who appear before a court, whereas attitude situations consist of the "facts" – that is, what the attitude object is doing, and the legal and constitutional context in which the attitude object is acting. The examples in the preceding paragraph illustrate the situational context. "Objects," on the other hand, include indigents, businesses, persons accused of a crime, women, minorities, labor unions, juveniles, and so on. As far as the Supreme Court is concerned, research has shown that situations predict behavior much better than objects.[30] Indeed, matters could hardly be otherwise. Responses to a survey of people's attitude toward the President of the United States or toward students lack meaning unless the inquiry is placed in a specific context: students doing what? Rioting in the streets or studying in the library?

To a greater extent than attitude objects, situations are subjectively perceived. Justices not uncommonly dispute the facts of a case. Sometimes the justices

---

[29] Milton Rokeach, *Beliefs, Attitudes, and Values* (San Francisco: Jossey-Bass, 1968), pp. 112–122.

[30] Harold J. Spaeth and Douglas R. Parker, "Effects of Attitude Toward Situation Upon Attitude Toward Object," 73 *Journal of Psychology* (1969), 173–182; Milton Rokeach and Peter Kliejunas, "Behavior as a Function of Attitude-Toward-Object and Attitude-Toward-Situation," 22 *Journal of Personality and Social Psychology* (1972), 194–201; Harold J. Spaeth, David B. Meltz, Gregory J. Rathjen, and Michael V. Haselswerdt, "Is Justice Blind: An Empirical Investigation of a Normative Ideal," 7 *Law and Society Review* (1972), 119–137.

accept as true what is empirically false. Consider the Court's acceptance of the lower court's finding in *Buck v. Bell*[31] that the Buck family had produced three generations of imbeciles. Contrary to the "facts" of the case, Carrie Buck was a woman of normal intelligence whose daughter made the first-grade honor roll.[32] Conversely, what is empirically true the justices may assert to be false. Consider, for example, its unanimous decision that Long Island is not an island but an extension of the mainland.[33]

With these caveats in mind, we examine the role of facts in the decisions of the Supreme Court. We choose search and seizure as our substantive area of investigation, and we do so for two reasons. First, the situational context – the facts – in which law enforcement authorities conduct searches and seizures are readily identifiable and limited in number. Second, search and seizure is one of the many areas about which justices and scholars bewail the Court's alleged inconsistencies.[34] The question of whether a given search or seizure violates the Fourth Amendment is also of great substantive importance, for as this book goes to press, evidence seized in violation of the Constitution may not be used in criminal trials.[35] Thus, in the immortal words of Benjamin Cardozo, "the criminal is to go free because the constable has blundered."[36]

Specification. In determining what variables to include for analysis, we consider those facts that relate to the prior justification for the search (warrant and probable cause), the place of the intrusion (e.g., home, car, etc.), the extent of the intrusion (full searches versus lesser intrusions, such as frisks), and various exceptions to the warrant requirement, including searches incident to arrest.[37]

The most basic requirements for the reasonableness of a search are a warrant and probable cause. Probable cause is generally required whether there is[38] or is not a warrant,[39] though evidence from warrants issued without probable cause can be used in court if the police officers acted in good faith.[40]

For a search to be unreasonable it generally must occur at a place where the accused has an expectation of privacy.[41] The greatest expectation of privacy is in one's home. "At the very core [of the Fourth Amendment] stands the right

---

[31]   274 U.S. 200 (1927).
[32]   Stephen Jay Gould, "Carrie Buck's Daughter," *Natural History*, July 1984, p. 14.
[33]   *United States v. Maine*, 469 U.S. 504 (1985).
[34]   See Jeffrey A. Segal, "Predicting Supreme Court Cases Probabilistically: The Search and Seizure Cases, 1962–1981," 78 *American Political Science Review* 891 (1984), at 891, 893.
[35]   *Mapp v. Ohio*, 367 U.S. 643 (1961). But see *United States v. Leon*, 468 U.S. 897 (1984), creating a "good-faith" exception to the exclusionary rule.
[36]   *People v. Defore*, 242 N.Y. 13 (1926), at 21.
[37]   See Segal, op. cit. fn. 34 supra.
[38]   *United States v. Harris*, 403 U.S. 573 (1971).
[39]   *Chambers v. Maroney*, 399 U.S. 42 (1970).
[40]   *United States v. Leon*, 468 U.S. 897 (1984).
[41]   *Katz v. United States*, 389 U.S. 347 (1967).

of a man to retreat into his own home and there be free from unreasonable governmental intrusion."[42] Commercial premises are likewise given great protection. "The businessman, like the occupant of a residence, has a constitutional right to go about his business free from unreasonable official entries."[43] Yet, "commercial premises are not as private as residential premises."[44] Still receiving protection, but to a lesser degree, are one's person[45] and one's car (or other motorized vehicle),[46] but the protection afforded them is nevertheless great compared with places where one has no property interest,[47] such as the home of a third party.

The type of search can be as determinative of reasonableness as the place of the search. Limited intrusions such as stop-and-frisks or detentive questioning require less prior justification than do full searches.[48]

Finally, there are well-established exceptions to the warrant requirements. The most important of these is the right to search incident to a lawful arrest.[49] This right generally extends to immediate searches of the arrestee and the area under his control. Lesser authority exists for arrests that follow upon but are not incident to lawful arrests.[50] Other exceptions include searches of evidence in plain view,[51] searches with the permission of those having a property interest in the area being searched,[52] searches after hot pursuit,[53] searches at fixed or functional borders,[54] searches explicitly authorized by Congress,[55] and searches for evidence to be used at non-criminal trials or hearings.[56]

Methods and results. We examine all Supreme Court decisions dealing with the reasonableness of a search or seizure from the beginning of the 1962 term through the end of the 1989 term (N = 196). The independent variables are the facts of the case discussed earlier. We note here that it may be improper to rely on the Supreme Court's written opinion to ascertain the facts of the case. Thus, the Court may assert that certain variables are or are not present, such as probable cause, in order to justify its decision, even though reality is to the contrary. Occasionally, opinions even differ about "objective" determinations, such as

[42] *Silverman v. United States*, 365 U.S. 505 (1961), at 511.
[43] *See v. Seattle*, 387 U.S. 541 (1967), at 543.
[44] Wayne LaFave, *Search and Seizure* (St. Paul: West, 1978), I, 338.
[45] *Davis v. Mississippi*, 394 U.S. 721 (1969).
[46] *Carroll v. United States*, 267 U.S. 132 (1925).
[47] *United States v. Calandra*, 414 U.S. 338 (1974).
[48] *Terry v. Ohio*, 392 U.S. 1 (1968).
[49] *Chimel v. California*, 395 U.S. 752 (1969).
[50] *Chambers v. Maroney*, 399 U.S. 752 (1970).
[51] *Coolidge v. New Hampshire*, 403 U.S. 443 (1971).
[52] *Schneckloth v. Bustamonte*, 412 U.S. 218 (1973).
[53] *Warden v. Hayden*, 387 U.S. 294 (1967).
[54] *United States v. Ramsey*, 431 U.S. 606 (1977).
[55] *Colonade Catering v. United States*, 397 U.S. 72 (1970).
[56] *United States v. Calandra*, 414 U.S. 338 (1974).

where the search took place. For instance, in *California v. Carney* the California Supreme Court considered the warrantless search of respondent's motor home to be akin to a search of a home,[57] whereas the U.S. Supreme Court considered it closer to a search of a car, and thus found the search reasonable.[58] To guard against the possibility that the Supreme Court's statement of facts is influenced by the decision it desires to reach, we use the lower court record to determine the facts of each case.[59]

Our dependent variable is the decision of the Supreme Court whether or not to exclude evidence or find a search unreasonable. A liberal decision is one that prohibits the use of questionably obtained evidence; a conservative decision is one that admits such evidence. Overall, the Court ruled in a liberal direction in 37 percent of the cases.

We begin by examining the percentage of liberal or conservative decisions based on the presence or absence of the fact in question. We initially consider the nature of the search, which involves the locus of the search and the extent of the intrusion. As expected, the Court gave greatest protection to one's home, upholding only 51 percent of the searches conducted there. Less protection is given to places of business, where 58 percent of searches have been upheld. One's person receives still less protection (66 percent upheld), whereas searches of one's car or other motor vehicle are very likely to be upheld (72 percent). The least protection is given to places where the suspect does not have a property interest (85 percent upheld).

The extent of the intrusion involves the difference between full searches and lesser intrusions, such as detentive questioning or a stop-and-frisk. Overall, 59 percent of full searches have been upheld compared with 84 percent of limited intrusions.

Against the nature of the search the Court must consider the prior justification for the search – a warrant and probable cause. Even though cases with warrants typically involve questions as to the validity of that warrant, the Court still upholds more cases with warrants (72 percent) than without (61 percent). Alternatively, the lower court's decision as to whether probable cause exists negatively correlates with the Supreme Court's decisions. Fifty-nine percent of cases with probable cause are upheld compared with 65 without. This suggests

[57]   668 P.2d 807 (1983).
[58]   471 U.S. 386 (1985).
[59]   Certain facts cannot be ascertained independently of the Court's decision, such as whether the case concerns statutory construction or constitutional interpretation. Similarly, unobserved preferences that underlie the justices' decisions, such as whether the decision supports or opposes considerations of federalism (i.e., state action) or upholds or overturns administrative agency action. Although such factors have an ideological component that exists independent of and prior to any given decision, they can only be measured concomitantly with that decision. See Timothy M. Hagle and Harold J. Spaeth, "The Emergence of a New Ideology: The Business Decisions of the Burger Court," 54 *Journal of Politics* 120 (1992).

that the Supreme Court views lower court probable-cause decisions rather subjectively.

Next we consider the exceptions to the warrant requirement, the most important of which is a search incident to a lawful arrest. The Supreme Court upheld 90 percent of the searches that the lower court ruled took place incident to a lawful arrest. Surprisingly, the Court did not uphold more searches after, but not incident to, a lawful arrest (61 percent) than it did searches after arrests that the lower court considered unlawful (64 percent).

Other exceptions to the warrant requirement rarely occurred, so we simply note that the Court upheld all of the nine searches when two or three exceptions were present, 73 percent of those containing one exception, and only 56 percent of those without any exceptions.

More interesting than the bivariate effect of facts of the Court's decision is the independent influence of each fact when the influence of every other fact has been controlled. To examine this we conducted a logit analysis of the 196 Supreme Court search and seizure decisions. (See the Appendix at the end of the book for a description of logit.) We used the decision of the Court in each case as our dependent variable and the facts of the case identified earlier as our independent variables. Because of the Court's tendency to reverse the decisions it reviews, we include the direction of the lower court decision as a control variable that should negatively associate with the Supreme Court's decision. The results are presented in Table 6.1.

The coefficients show the change in the log of the odds ratio for a conservative decision given the presence of each fact. As this is not readily interpretable to most readers, we provide under the column ''Impact'' the estimated increase or decrease in the probability of a conservative decision when the variable in question is present. The impact estimate assumes that the search otherwise has a 50-50 chance of being upheld. Note that the places where seaches occurred are all compared with a search where one does not have a property interest, and that the arrest estimates are all compared with a search that was not preceded by an arrest.

We see from the maximum likelihood estimates (MLEs) that every variable has a significant impact on the likelihood of a search being upheld except probable cause and unlawful arrest. All four places we examine (home, business, person, and car) decrease the probability of a search being upheld when compared with a search where one does not have a property interest.[60]

The only substantive difference between the bivariate and multivariate results is that the latter show a clear ordering in terms of searches following arrests: searches incident to arrest receive the most leeway, searches after lawful arrests

---

[60] Though logit's S-shaped specification suggests that the impact of home is not much different than the impact of the other ''place'' variables, measuring the impact at prior levels higher than 50–50 would show a much stronger effect.

Table 6.1. *Logit analysis of search and seizure cases*

Variable	MLE[a]	SE[b]	Impact[c]
House	-3.63[f]	.96	-.47
Business	-2.94[e]	.98	-.45
Person	-2.24[e]	.89	-.40
Car	-2.65[e]	.99	-.44
Search	-1.60[e]	.60	-.33
Warrant	1.83[f]	.57	.36
Probable Cause	-.02	.44	.00
Incident Arrest	3.32[e]	1.24	.47
After Arrest	.93[d]	.59	.22
After Unlawful	.49	.59	.12
Exceptions	1.48[f]	.39	.82
Lower Court Dec	-1.47[f]	.38	.31
Constant	4.25[f]	1.04	--

percent predicted correctly   76

Notes. [a]Maximum Likelihood Estimate. [b]Standard error. [c]Impact equals change in probability of a liberal decision when the fact is present for a search with a 50% chance of being upheld. [d]Significant at p<.10. [e]Significant at p<.01. [f]Significant at p<.001.

receive less leeway, and searches after unlawful arrests receive virtually no additional leeway.

The model predicts 76 percent of the Court's cases correctly for a 30 percent reduction in error over the null model. Though the facts presented do strongly influence the Court's decisions, obviously other considerations also enter the equation. One problem with fact models is that they are static. That is, they do not consider how changing membership on the Court influences decisions. For instance, if we add a variable that counted each time a Warren Court appointee was replaced by a Nixon, Ford, or Reagan appointee, we get a highly significant variable (MLE = .24; p < .005) that indicates that the current Court evaluates search and seizure cases much more leniently than did the Warren Court. This suggests that the exclusionary rule may soon be overturned directly, or simply made irrelevant because so few searches are ruled unreasonable. This also betokens a need to explicitly consider the attitudes and values of the justices as a factor affecting their decisions.

Facts obviously affect the decisions of the Supreme Court, but on that point the attitudinal model does not differ from the legal model. The models differ in that proponents of the legal model conjoin facts with such legalistic considerations as the intent of the Framers, the plain meaning of the law, and prior decisions of the Court, whereas proponents of the attitudinal model describe the justices' votes as an expression of fact situations applied to their personal policy preferences. Unfortunately, the legal model has heretofore failed the most basic test of a scientific model: It has not been tested and perhaps cannot be tested. This is because intent, plain meaning, and precedent are so nebulous that they can be used to support both sides of any case that comes to Court, as we pointed out in Chapter 2.

Focusing on facts to evidence the operation of the attitudinal model has its own set of problems, however. First, we do not know for a fact that "facts" explain the justices' behavior except in those areas where they have been identified. Outside of search and seizure, only a handful of other subjects have successfully been put to such a test.[61] Whether facts cause the justices to vote as they do in areas such as antitrust litigation, involuntary confession, state taxation, national supremacy, First Amendment, and so on has not been determined. Furthermore, certain justices in certain areas may deem facts irrelevant. Justice Harlan, for example, never once supported a judicially imposed legislative apportionment plan, asserting that it was a matter that the Supreme Court had no authority to resolve.

Attitudes

As we noted in Chapter 2, an attitude is a relatively enduring set of interrelated beliefs. Thus, if attitudes are the proximate cause of the votes of Supreme Court justices, their votes must be relatively stable and consistent. Beginning in the late 1950s, scholars, under the leadership of Glendon Schubert, began to use cumulative (or Guttman) scaling and factor analysis to demonstrate the existence of and to measure the extremeness of the justices' attitudes.[62] This

---

[61] Timothy M. Hagle, "But Do They Have to See It to Know It? The Supreme Court's Obscenity and Pornography Decisions," 45 *Western Polical Quarterly* 1039 (1992); Tracey George and Lee Epstein, "On the Nature of Supreme Court Decision Making," 86 *American Political Science Review* 323(1992) (death penalty cases); Robin Wolpert, "Explaining and Predicting Supreme Court Decision-Making: The Gender Discrimination Cases, 1971–1987," paper delivered at the 1991 annual meeting of the Midwest Political Science Association, Chicago; Joseph A. Ignagni, *Explaining and predicting Supreme Court decision-making: The Establishment Clause cases, 1970–1986* (unpublished Ph.D. dissertation, Michigan State University, 1990); Kevin McGuire, "Obscenity, Libertarian Values, and Decision Making in the Supreme Court," 18 *American Politics Quarterly* 47 (1990); Jeffrey Segal and Cheryl Reedy, "The Supreme Court and Sex Discrimination: The Role of the Solicitor General," 41 *Western Political Quarterly* 553 (1988).

[62] Samuel Stouffer, Louis Guttman, Edward Suchman, Paul Lazersfeld, Shirley Star, and John Clausen, *Measurement and Prediction* (New York: Wiley, 1950). Judicial applications include: Glendon A. Schubert, *Quantitative Analysis of Judicial Decisions* (Glencoe, IL: The Free Press, 1959), ch. 5; S. Sidney Ulmer, "Supreme Court Behavior and Civil Rights," 13 *Western Political Quarterly* 288 (1960); Harold J. Spaeth, "Warren Court Attitudes Toward Business: The "B" Scale," in Glendon Schubert, ed., *Judicial Decision Making* (New York: Free Press, (1963),

work focused on the justices' votes, which was an eminently proper thing to do. Unfortunately, because no earlier studies existed, these analysts used their scales and their factor analyses[63] to explain the justices' votes, with the scales themselves being used as evidence of the attitudinal model. Circular reasoning necessarily resulted. The validity of such reasoning could have been determined if in using votes to construct scales, the scales (or more precisely the rank ordering of the justices) were used to *predict* votes in subsequently decided cases instead of using the votes in previously decided cases to infer the existence of specified attitudes that motivated the justices' votes in these same cases. One study arguably did use past votes to infer future behavior, but the evidence is less than clear.[64]

In short, the early attitudinal modelers should have formally reversed matters by using the patterns of past voting to predict how the justices would vote in future cases. Their failure to do so presumably resulted from insufficiently longitudinal data. Assume, for example, that we wish to apply the attitudinal model to the voting behavior of the justices in the death penalty cases decided by the Rehnquist Court. On the generally accepted assumption that the attitudes of adults who occupy a relatively fixed position in society are relatively stable,[65] we order the Burger Court's death penalty decisions along a liberal-conservative continuum from 9 to 0 – against the death penalty at one end to the unanimous decisions upholding the death penalty at the other. We find the holdover justices – those who served on both Courts – array themselves as follows: Marshall and Brennan are most liberal, voting the same in all the cases in which they both participated, Stevens is third, followed by Blackmun. Powell is fifth, with O'Connor, White, and Rehnquist anchoring the conservative end of the continuum.

On the basis of this ordering we expect that the justices' past votes will predict those they cast in the future. As we have no Burger Court track record for Scalia and Kennedy, we look to other indicators to determine their death penalty attitudes. Newspaper editorials between nomination and confirmation indicated that both were conservative overall, Scalia more so than Kennedy. Assessment of their record as lower federal court judges and their off-the-bench speeches and writings suggests that Scalia is likely to match Rehnquist's support for capital punishment, with Kennedy a notch less supportive, but more so than White, who was closest to Rehnquist among the

pp. 79–108; Glendon Schubert, *The Judicial Mind* (Evanston: Northwestern University Press, 1965).

[63] Harry H. Harman, *Modern Factor Analysis*, 2d ed. rev. (Chicago: University of Chicago Press, 1967).

[64] Harold J. Spaeth, *Supreme Court Policy Making: Explanation and Prediction* (San Francisco: W.H. Freeman, 1979), pp. 122–123; 154–164.

[65] Milton Rokeach, op. cit. fn. 29 supra, pp. 112–122.

Burger Court holdover justices.[66] We arrive, then, at the following ordinal ranking from liberal to conservative:

Mar	Stev	Blkm	Pow	Souter	O'Con	White	Ken	Scal
x . . .	x . . .	x . . .	x . . .	x	x	x	x . . .	x . . . x
Brn								Rehn

Accordingly, we predict that if the Court affirms the death penalty by a 7-to-2 vote, the dissenters will be Marshall and Brennan[67]; if they do so by 6 to 3, Stevens will join them; and if the vote is 5 to 4, Blackmun will be the fourth dissenter. In liberal decisions, Rehnquist and Scalia are the most likely dissenters, followed by Kennedy, and then White.

Application of this model to the twenty-one formally decided death penalty cases and the two per curiam decisions[68] decided from the beginning of the Rehnquist Court in October 1986 through the end of the 1990 term correctly identified which participating justices voted with the majority and which in dissent in nineteen of these twenty-three cases.[69]

Note that at this level of generality, the attitudinal model does not necessarily predict the direction of a given decision (i.e., liberal or conservative); neither does it enable us to necessarily predict how many – if any – justices will dissent. We use the modifier, "necessarily," to qualify the statements because not only do we know the track record of each participating justice, but we also know the outcome of previous death penalty cases. Thus, because the Burger Court split its decisions almost exactly between pro-death and anti-death, with the proportion of pro-death increasing as the Burger Court aged, we could have simply predicted that each Rehnquist Court case was more likely to be decided conservatively than liberally.[70] Such a prediction would have been correct almost two-thirds of the time (fifteen of twenty-three). At the level of the individual justices, we could have predicted with considerable confidence that no death penalty case in

---

[66] Our placement of Souter is a bit tentative because of his limited service on the Court. During his initial term on the Court – 1990 – which was the last we were able to consider prior to publication, he voted conservatively except in *Parker v. Dugger*, 112 L Ed 2d 812 (1991), a 5-to-4 decision. His conservative vote in *Lankford v. Idaho*, 114 L Ed 2d 173 (1991), suggests more support for capital punishment than O'Connor provides. We accordingly judge him to be conservative, but less so than Rehnquist, Scalia, Kennedy, and White.

[67] In the interim between the retirement of Brennan in 1990, and that of Marshall one year later, any case in which only one vote opposed the death penalty would have been cast by Marshall.

[68] *Hildwin v. Florida*, 104 L Ed 2d 728 (1988), and *Delo v. Stokes*, 109 L Ed 2d 325 (1990).

[69] The four errors occurred in cases in which we incorrectly predicted Kennedy as a dissenter in *McKoy v. North Carolina*, 108 L Ed 2d 369 (1990), and *Lankford v. Idaho*, 114 L Ed 2d 173 (1991), and two cases in which O'Connor rather than White was the fourth dissenter (*Mills v. Maryland*, 100 L Ed 2d 384 [1988], and *South Carolina v. Gathers*, 104 L Ed 2d 876 [1989]).

[70] Of course, as the Court decides predicted cases, these may be added to the set of past decisions, thereby allowing analysts to refine their predictions by detecting any shifts in the justices' voting.

either direction would ever be decided unanimously because of the behavior of Douglas, Brennan, and Marshall at the liberal extreme, and Rehnquist at the Conservative extreme.[71] But such precise predictions better depend on knowledge of specific facts that explain why a justice votes as he or she does in one case compared with another. We exemplified such specific application of the attitudinal model with regard to search and seizure in the preceding section of this chapter. But at the macro-level at which we apply the attitudinal model here, we can only identify how each justice voted inasmuch as we are given no information other than the direction of the Court's decision and the number of justices who dissented.[72] And though these limitations produce predictions less than full and complete – that is, that case X will concern the death penalty and will be decided liberally (conservatively) by a vote of Y to Z – the accuracy of the limited prediction validates the explanatory power of the independent variable: the operational effect of the individual justices' attitudes toward the death penalty.

Though our ability to predict how each justice voted provides a test of the validity and reliability of the attitudinal model, just how powerful a test it is depends on the likelihood that results such as those in the death penalty cases occur. The probability that a certain voting pattern results is rather problematic.[73] We could assume randomness and simply assert that because each justice is a free agent, together they may form a 7-to-2 decision in 36 different ways, with the probability of predicting the actual one being .0278. And because there are 126 ways in which nine individuals may produce a 5-to-4 vote, the probability of choosing the correct one is .0079. If we are correct in both picks, arguably the probability of doing so becomes .0278 $\times$ .0079, which equals .00022, or 1 in 4536.

For two reasons, the astronomical probabilities that an assumption of random combinations of dissenters produces overstates reality. First, if Justice A is correctly selected as the sole liberal dissenter in an 8-to-1 decision, the attitudinal model postulates that Justice A must also be among the liberal dissenters in all other conservative decisions. Consequently, A must be among the dissenters in cases with two, three, and four liberal dissents. Similarly Justice B, who is predicted to be a dissenter in the 7-to-2 case. He should again be a given in the cases that have three or four liberal dissents. Second, certain patterns or combinations are extremely improbable. Although each justice may theoretically be the solo liberal dissenter in a conservative decision,

---

[71] The Burger and Rehnquist Courts have never been unanimously pro-death, and have been unanimously anti-death only five times: *Skipper v. South Carolina*, 376 U.S. 1 (1986); *Hitchcock v. Dugger*, 481 U.S. 393 (1987); *Maynard v. Cartwright*, 100 L Ed 2d 372 (1988); *Johnson v. Mississippi*, 100 L Ed 2d 575 (1988); and *Shell v. Mississippi*, 112 L Ed 2d 1 (1990).

[72] To be completely accurate, we should also be provided with the name(s) of any non-participating justice(s).

[73] We wish to thank Professor Timothy Hagle for helping us conceptualize and formulate the theoretical and empirical measure of probability that we use here.

the likelihood that it will be a Rehnquist or a Scalia borders on absolute zero. Conversely, the likelihood is the same that Marshall or Brennan would be the solo dissenter in a liberally decided case. Thus, for example, not only were Brennan and Marshall not among the solo dissenters in any of the eight liberally decided civil rights or liberties cases decided during the first four terms of the Rehnquist Court, neither did they cast any of the 24 conservative votes in liberal decisions containing two dissents, nor any of the 114 dissents in liberal decisions containing three dissents. However, each did cast a single conservative dissent in a 5-to-4 decision. By contrast, Rehnquist cast 5 of the 8 solo dissents in liberally decided civil rights and liberties cases. He also dissented in 8 of the 12 two-dissent cases, 31 of the 38 three-dissent cases, and 36 of the 37 four-dissent cases.

Accordingly, we take a conservative approach to estimating the probability of a correct prediction. We arbitrarily assume that no more than three justices are likely to be the marginal dissenter. Thus, in the solo dissent situation, the probables are I, H, and G. If two justices dissent, I is a given, with H, G, and F the possibly marginal member. Similarly, for the cases with three and four dissenters. The probability of correctly predicting how all the justices voted in any given case then become .33. Hence, the probability of correctly predicting nineteen of the twenty-two death penalty cases, as we did, is $(.33)^{19}$ $\times$ $(.67)$ $\times$ 8,855. We multiply the initial part of the equation by 8,855 because there are 8,855 ways to get any nineteen of twenty-three predictions correct (i.e., 23!(19! $\times$ 4!). The answer, therefore, is .000004. By contrast, if we use the same formulation in a hypothetical set of 10 cases, only half of which we correctly predict, an insignificant probability of .13 results: $(.33^5$ $\times$ $(.67)^5$ $\times$ 252. (10!/(5! $\times$ 5!) = 252 different ways in which to get 5 of 10 cases correct.)

As the Appendix to this chapter shows, the use of past voting behavior to predict what occurs subsequently exceeds conventional levels of significance for 18 of the 21 issues into which criminal procedure has been divided, 10 of the 21 categories of civil rights, and 8 of the 14 First Amendment areas in which the Burger and Rehnquist Courts have rendered decisions. Although the ranking of the justices in their support/opposition for the civil liberty/civil rights claimant in these cases correlates from one issue to the next with a few exceptions,[74] enough variation exists to indicate that the attitudinal model augments its explanatory power as content refinement increases. That is, the justices' undifferentiated attitudes toward civil liberty do not predict their votes, but rather their less global attitudes toward the specific civil liberty issue – for example, attitudes toward the death penalty, affirmative action, race discrimination, double jeopardy, commercial speech, and so on.

Less success obtains in predicting the justices' votes in various economic,

[74] Harold J. Spaeth, "The Dimensions of Civil Liberties Decision Making on the Burger Court," in Spaeth and Brenner, *op. cit.* fn. 17 *supra*, pp. 184–194.

judicial power, and federalism areas, as the Appendix shows. This appears not to result from failure to refine the content of these categories, but either because some of the justices view these issues as tapping attitudes different from those that motivate their colleagues,[75] or because behavior results from interrelationships among a set of facts whose existence scholars have not yet identified.

Content analysis

In addition to the past voting of the justices to predict their future votes, a second independent measure of the justices' attitudes has been formulated for the purpose of testing the attitudinal model. This second measure, which is wholly unrelated to either facts or votes, is newspaper editorials that characterize nominees prior to confirmation as liberal or conservative on civil rights and civil liberties.[76] Although this measure is gross and imprecise by comparison with facts and votes, it nonetheless avoids the circularity problem, and is reliable and replicable. As a result, it provides additional evidence – if such be needed – to confirm the behavioral existence of the attitudinal model.

Segal and Cover created this measure by content analyzing editorials about nominees from selected newspapers that appeared between the time of their nomination by the President until their confirmation by the Senate.[77] The scores of the confirmed justices are given in Table 6.2.

We believe that the scores accurately measure the perceptions of the justices' values at the time of their nomination. Given the lack of past votes from which to predict future votes, editorial judgments do provide a starting point for prediction. Although not everyone would agree that every score precisely measures the perceived ideology of each nominee, Fortas, Marshall, and Brennan, are expectedly the most liberal, and Scalia and Rehnquist are the most conservative.[78] Harlan and Stewart come out liberal because the debate about them centered around their support for the overriding issue of the day – segregation. Goldberg is not perceived to be as liberal as Fortas or Marshall because of an even-handedness at the Department of Labor that even the *Chicago Tribune* could support. O'Connor comes out as a moderate, given her previous support for

[75]   See Hagle and Spaeth, op. cit. fn. 59 supra.

[76]   David Danelski suggested coding the qualitative content of speeches made by Justices Brandeis and Butler prior to their appointment to the Court as a measure of their attitudes. He found that support for or opposition to laissez-faire correlated with the direction of these two justices' dissents in economic cases. "Values as Variables in Judicial Decision-Making: Notes Toward a Theory," 19 *Vanderbilt Law Review* 721 (1966).

[77]   Jeffrey A. Segal and Alber D. Cover, "Ideological Values and the Votes of U.S. Supreme Court Justices," 83 *American Political Science Review* 557 (1989). See Chapter 4 for details.

[78]   Rehnquist is included twice, once as associate justice and once as Chief Justice. Although his ideological scores are the same both times, the scores are separate measures, taken from 1972 and 1986, respectively. That they are identical to the second decimal place is partially a coincidence, but mostly a result of the fact that he was viewed as staunchly conservative both times.

Table 6.2. *Justices' values and votes*

Justice	Values[a]	Votes[b]
Warren	.50	78.1
Harlan	.75	41.4
Brennan	1.00	78.4
Whittaker	.00	42.6
Stewart	.50	51.1
White	.00	41.2
Goldberg	.50	89.0
Fortas	1.00	79.6
Marshall	1.00	80.4
Burger	-.77	28.9
Blackmun	-.77	48.1
Powell	-.67	36.9
Rehnquist[c]	-.91	18.8
Stevens	-.50	57.9
O'Connor	-.17	29.4
Rehnquist[d]	-.91	18.4
Scalia	-1.00	29.5
Kennedy	-.27	26.1

Notes. [a]From Segal and Cover, op. cit. fn. 77 supra. The range is -1.00 (extremely conservative) to 1.00 (extremely liberal). [b]Percentage liberal in civil liberties cases, 1953-1990. [c]Values and votes as Nixon appointee. [d]Values and votes as Reagan appointee.

women's rights and abortion. Indeed, the only hint of opposition to her nomination came from right-wing interest groups and the arch-conservative Senator, Jesse Helms (R-NC).

Measures of perceived attitudes are obviously imperfect measures of those the justices actually possess. Given the impossibility of surveying the justices themselves (even if one rashly assumed that such surveys would be scientifically valid and reliable), content analysis has its place. To the extent that measurement error exists in the data, we will undoubtedly find weaker correlations than would otherwise be the case.[79] Therefore, the correlation be-

[79] William D. Berry and Stanley Feldman, *Multiple Regression in Practice* (Beverly Hills: Sage, 1985) pp. 30–31.

tween ideological values and votes that we present is lower than the true correlation.

Because statements in newspaper editorials deal almost exclusively with support by the justices for civil liberties and civil rights, we use as our dependent variable the votes of all justices appointed since the beginning of the Warren Court in all formally decided civil liberties cases from the beginning of the 1953 term through the end of the 1989 term, as derived from the Supreme Court database.[80] Civil liberties issues are those involving criminal procedure, civil rights, the First Amendment, due process, and privacy. Liberal decisions are (1) pro-person accused or convicted of crime, (2) pro-civil liberties or civil rights claimant, (3) pro-indigent, (4) pro-Indian, and (5) anti-government in due process and privacy. The data are presented in Table 6.2.

The results are straightforward: The correlation between the ideological values of the justices and their votes is .79 (r^2 = .62, adjusted r^2 = .60). Regressing votes on our measure of values yields a constant of 49.7 and a slope of 25.2 (t = 4.86). The largest residuals belong to Goldberg, who is 27 percentage points more liberal than expected, and Harlan, who is 27 points more conservative than expected. Ten of the seventeen justices are within 10 points of their expected scores. Given the fact that our correlation is attenuated by the measurement error that no doubt exists in the independent variable, the results supply exceptional support for the attitudinal model as applied to civil liberties cases.

Critics of the attitudinal model might present the following alternative scenario: If judges and justices base decisions on legal values (e.g., precedent, the intent of the Framers, and so on) and not political values, editorials on nominees with lower court experience would be based on those legal values. Our measures will correlate with their votes on the Supreme Court because as justices they are again basing their votes on their legal values. But if this were the case, lower court experience would provide crucial information that does not exist for those without such experience – the legal (as opposed to political) values of the nominees. If the editorials provided information on legal values, and if such values were relevant to the justices' decisions, the correlation for those with such information should be higher than the correlation for those without such information. This is clearly not the case. Though the N's are small, the correlation between values and votes for those with lower court experience is .69 (adjusted r^2 = .41) whereas the correlation for those without lower court experience is .94 (adjusted r^2 = .85). If anything, the voting record of lower court judges, who *are* bound by Supreme Court precedents, might constitute *disinformation*

---

[80]   The paucity of editorials prior to Warren prevents us from beginning with earlier justices. Because the Supreme Court database begins with the appointment of Warren, we have the complete voting record on all included justices.

about their true values and thus their likely voting behavior once on the Supreme Court.

Combining "facts" and attitudes. Consistent with the attitudinal model, we have seen that both facts and attitudes affect the decisions of the Supreme Court. The attitudinal model, though, does not hold that these are separate influences on the Court's decisions. Rather, it holds that facts or case stimuli are juxtaposed against the attitudes of the justices in determining how any particular justice reaches a decision in any particular case.

Facts explain why a particular justice votes one way in certain cases, and differently in others. They cannot explain differences in decisions among justices; attitudes, as manifest in previous voting, can. By focusing on facts, we explain why a justice votes liberally in one case and conservatively in other. By focusing on attitudes, we explain why one justice is conservative over a series of cases whereas another is not. Facts and attitudes do not contradict one another; they are complementary parts of a common model. They differ only in their respective units of analysis.

We now come to our most specific test of the attitudinal model by using as our dependent variable the decision of each justice in each search and seizure case from 1962 through 1989 (N = 1, 550).[81] The independent variables are the facts of each case plus each justice's attitudes. Because our content analysis was not designed with criminal justice cases specifically in mind, we develop a more robust measure from a factor analysis of three different surrogates for criminal justice attitudes: the content analysis used earlier, the judicial ideology of the appointing President, as defined by Tate and Handberg,[82] and the party identification of the justice. The scores ranged from 4.18 for Marshall and Fortas to −2.71 for Scalia.

We first entered only attitudes into the equation and achieved a 68 percent prediction rate, for a 27 percent reduction in error over the justices' mean of 56 percent. We then entered just the twelve fact-based variables described and achieved a 62 percent prediction rate, for a relatively low 14 percent reduction in error. This suggests that in predicting votes, one is clearly better off knowing the attitudes of the justices than the facts of the case. Finally, we combined the attitude measure with the fact variables into a single model. The results are presented in Table 6.3. Seventy-four percent of the individual justices' decisions were predicted correctly for a 41 percent reduction in error. Nine of the twelve variables were significant at p < .001.

Results from the model can be presented in pictorial form as in Figure 6.1,

---

[81] Because of data limitations, we include only those justices appointed since the beginning of the Warren Court.

[82] C. Neal Tate and Roger Handberg, "Time Binding and Theory Building in Personal Attribute Models of Supreme Court Voting Behavior, 1916–88," 35 *American Journal of Political Science* 460 (1991).

Table 6.3. *Search and seizure analysis with attitudes*

Variable	MLE[a]	SE[b]
House	-1.90[e]	.29
Business	-1.76[e]	.31
Person	-1.50[e]	.28
Car	-1.53[e]	.30
Search	-1.10[e]	.19
Warrant	.84[e]	.19
Probable Cause	.20[c]	.15
Incident Arrest	1.24[e]	.31
After Arrest	.17[d]	.20
After Unlawful	.14[d]	.20
Exceptions	.93[e]	.12
Attitudes	-.46[e]	.03
Constant	2.22[e]	.31

percent predicted correctly   74

Notes. [a]Maximum Likelihood Estimate.   [b]Standard error. [c]Significant at p<.10. [d]Significant at p<.01. [e]Significant at p<.001.

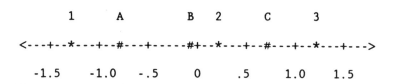

Legend: *— Justices: 1—Brennan; 2— Stevens; 3— Rehnquist.

#— Cases: A—Terry v. Ohio; B— U.S. v. Leon; C— Mapp v. Ohio.

Figure 6.1   Justices and cases in attitudinal space

which places the case stimuli and justices' values in attitudinal space. Any justice will vote to uphold any search to the left of his or her indifference point and will vote strike any search to the right of his or her indifference point. For instance, the search for evidence in *Mapp v. Ohio*, at .78 would be allowed in court by Rehnquist (1.20) but not by Stevens (.32) or Brennan (–1.28).[83] As this is an empirical model, prediction errors will occur. Justice Stevens, for instance, dissented in *United States v. Leon*, and is generally more liberal in search and seizure than predicted. Nevertheless, with 74 percent of the individual-level votes predicted correctly, the model demonstrates the overall validity of the attitudinal model.[84]

The source of attitudes

As demonstrated, political attitudes are crucial to understanding the decisions made by Supreme Court justices. If that is the case, it may be worth considering where attitudes originate. The leading explanation in the political science literature – though one that is highly contested – is that attitudes can be explained through the social background characteristics of the justices.

Social background theory has two main virtues according to its proponents, elegance and plausibility. In its most basic form it holds the following: 1) ascriptive and acquired social attributes affect one's political attitudes and values; 2) attitudes and values affect behavior; 3) these processes apply to Supreme Court justices. Proponents of such models claim impression success.[85]

Critics, including at least one of the original pioneers of this approach, claim that "the sociological (background) model of decision making does not make sense. It is inaccurate to assert that someone behaves in a certain way *because* that person is black, female, Catholic, Democratic, old, Harvard educated, in solo law practice, and so forth."[86]

---

[83] Scale points for the justices are created by multiplying their factor scores by the slope coefficient for Attitude in Table 6.3. Scale points for case stimuli are − 1 times the predicted log of the odds ratio of upholding the search given the facts of the case and an Attitude score of 0.

[84] There are several causes of error in the model, including measurement error on the attitudinal variable, incomplete specification of relevant case stimuli, and measurement error of case stimuli (caused by measuring case stimuli by the lower court record). Others sources of error might include excluding non-attitudinal factors, such as the presence of the United States as a party to the suit or excluded role values. To the extent the first set of problems exists, the attitudinal model is stronger than our empirical model demonstrates.

[85] C. Neal Tate, "Personal Attribute Models of Voting Behavior of U.S. Supreme Court Justices: Liberalism in Civil Liberties and Economics Decisions, 1946–1978. 75 *American Political Science Review* 355 (1981).

[86] Sheldon Goldman and Austin Sarat, eds., *American Court Systems*, 2d ed., (New York: Longman, 1985), p. 382. The same language also appears in the first edition (San Francisco: W.H. Freeman, 1978), p. 374. See, however, Sheldon Goldman, "Voting behavior in the United States Courts of Appeals, 1961–1964," 60 *American Political Science Review* 374 (1966); and Sheldon Goldman "Voting Behavior on the United States Courts of Appeals Revisited," 69 *American Political Science Review* 491 (1975).

In a communication to Harold Spaeth dated September 27, 1989, Linda Greenhouse, the award-winning Supreme Court reporter for the *New York Times*, rhetorically inquired: "Do people seriously put forward the theory that it is a justice's social background rather than views that determines whether he is a frequent dissenter?"

The empirical evidence indicates that the critics have the upper hand. With one exception,[87] virtually every study of background and behavior has either failed to explain a large percentage of the variance in decisions[88] or explained a large percentage of variance by employing as many or more variables than cases,[89] which makes it mathematically impossible not to explain a large percentage of the variance.[90]

No doubt the best effort in this vein is the recent work by Tate and Handberg cited earlier. Using a relatively small number of variables they explain up to 47 percent of the variance in the decisions of Supreme Court justices since the turn of the century. Does this demonstrate that social background characteristics have a significant *effect* on the voting behavior of the justices? Only partially. Although some of the most significant variables are independent of the latent attitudes they attempt to explain (e.g., agricultural and southern origins), two of the most important variables – partisanship and appointing president – are probably best considered surrogates for judicial attitudes, not causes of them – and, as such, are at least potentially independent of social background. Thus they are useful for predicting attitudes, but are of less help in explaining them. For instance, President Reagan nominated Antonin Scalia because Scalia is a staunch conservative; Scalia is not a staunch conservative because he was nominated by Reagan. Similarly, among political elites, ideology might influence party identification at least as much as party identification influences ideology.[91] Presumably, former Justice Douglas did not become a liberal because he was a Democrat; rather, he chose the Democratic Party because he was a liberal. True background characteristics – those that influence attitudes without reciprocal linkage – have still not been able to explain significant proportions of judges' attitudes or votes. Thus, although the ability to *predict* behavior from social attributes may be possible, we are still largely unable to *explain* behavior from social background characteristics.

[87] Tate and Handberg, op. cit. fn. 82 supra.
[88] Goldman, op. cit. fn. 86 supra (1966); Goldman, op. cit. fn. 86 supra (1975); S. Sidney Ulmer, "Dissent Behavior and the Social Background of Supreme Court Justices," 32 *Journal of Politics* 580 (1970); S. Sidney Ulmer, "Are Social Background Models Time-Bound?" 80 *American Political Science Review* 957 (1986).
[89] Richard Johnston, "Supreme Court Voting Behavior: A Comparison of the Warren and Burger Courts," in Robert L. Peabody, ed., *Cases in American Politics* (New York: Praeger, 1976); Tate, op. cit. fn. 85 supra; S. Sidney Ulmer, "Social Background as an Indicator to the Votes of Supreme Court Justices in Criminal Cases: 1947–1956," 17 *American Journal of Political Science* 622 (1973).
[90] James Payne and James Dyer, "Betting After the Race is Over," 19 *American Journal of Political Science* 559 (1975). Payne and Dyer achieved results better than Ulmer's (ibid.) using a random number generator to create independent variables.
[91] See, for example, Charles Franklin and John Jackson, "The Dynamics of Party Identification," 77 *American Political Science Review* 957 (1983); Robert Erikson, "The 'Uncorrelated Errors' Approach to the Problem of Causal Feedback," 44 *Journal of Politics* 863 (1982). Cf. Donald Green and Bradley Palmquist, "Of Artifacts and Partisan Instability," 34 *American Journal of Political Science* 872 (1990).

The reasons for this deficiency are several. First, because independent measures of the attitudes and values of justices (i.e., those not taken from their voting behavior) have only recently been created, the models have not tested what the theory expects – the effect of attributes on attitudes. What is tested is only the indirect link – attributes on behavior. Testing the direct link between backgrounds and attitudes might prove more fruitful.

Second, the social background model as applied to Supreme Court justices necessarily relies on the assumption that social backgrounds affect attitudes in the population at large, or at least in the highly educated segment thereof. Evidence from political socialization indicates this is simply false.[92]

The most direct evidence of the limited relationship between social attributes and political attitudes comes from the biannual National Election Studies conducted by the University of Michigan Survey Research Center. Using its 1984 data we attempt to predict the ideology of respondents with various social and demographic variables. Predictors include age, sex, race, religion, social class, party identification, region, and an interactive variable for Southern Democrats. The analysis is limited to those with a college education or better, for these are the people for whom ideology and ideological constraint should be most meaningful.[93] The results, presented in Table 6.4, demonstrate that much of the variance between individuals' ideology cannot be explained by social attributes: The adjusted R^2 is but .31; only two variables are significant, party and age, and, as noted, the former is partially a surrogate for ideology, not just a cause of it. Clearly, the within-group variance overwhelms the between group variance: There is much more variance among Southerners, for example, than there is between the average Southerner and the average Northerner. The only realistic conclusion to draw from these results is that social backgrounds do affect political ideology on the individual level, but only moderately. We would not expect models that predict behavior from social backgrounds, which is one step removed from attitudes, to perform particularly well.

When we examine social attributable models of judicial behavior, our expectations should be even lower. These models take an extremely small (N = 25 or so) non-random sample and expect good results when only moderate relationships exist in the (highly educated) population from which judges come. The fact that Jews or Catholics may be more liberal on average than the general population should not lead to great expectations that a particular Jew or a particular Catholic non-randomly chosen will be more liberal than a particular Protestant non-randomly chosen, – for example, an Antonin Scalia versus a William Douglas.

[92] Donald Searing, Joel Schwartz, and Alden Lind, "The structuring Principle," 67 *American Political Science Review* 415 (1973); David O. Sears, "Political Socialization," in Fred Greenstein and Nelson Polsby, eds., *Handbook of Political Science, Vol. 2* (Reading, MA: Addison-Wesley, 1975).
[93] Philip E. Converse, "The Nature of Belief Systems in Mass Publics," in David Apter, ed., *Ideology and Discontent* (New York: Free Press, 1966).

Table 6.4. *Ideology by social attributes*

Regressor	Standardized β
Age	.15[a]
Sex	.03
Class	-.03
Religion	.07
Race	-.02
Party	-.57[a]
Region	.10
Southern Democrats	.08
R^2	.33
F-Ratio	16.29[a]
N	269

Source. Survey Research Center.
Notes. [a]$p<.05$.

Finally, heredity may limit social background explanations of political behavior insofar as personality and ideology are concerned. Although genetic explanations of behavior may not be "politically correct" in a culture that uses
environmental deprivation of one sort or another to excuse everything from
temper tantrums to serial murder, the evidence from the famous Minnesota studies
of identical twins reared apart is compelling: About half of the variance in
personality traits, including several that tie closely to political attitudes, can be
attributed to genetic diversity.[94] The total effect of all environmentally based
variance is between 20 and 35 percent.[95] Thus, although we know how crucial
attitudes are to decisions, sociological efforts to examine the origin of attitudes
are likely to produce limited results.

NON-ATTITUDINAL FACTORS
AND SUPREME COURT DECISIONS

In this section we assess the extent to which various factors outside of facts and
attitudes affect the justices' decisions. With one notable exception, the influence

[94] The intra-group correlations among monozygotic twins reared apart is as high as the correlation
for monozygotic twins reared together and across the board is higher than that for dizygotic
twins reared together. See Auke Tellegen, David Lukken, Thomas Bouchard, Jr., Kimerly
Wilcox, Nancy Segal, and Steven Rich, "Personality Similarity in Twins Reared Apart and
Together," 54 *Journal of Personality and Social Psychology* 1031 (1988).
[95] The rest of the observed variance is attributable to measurement error.

of the Solicitor General, there appears to be little systematic evidence that these factors have any appreciable effect.

Roles

We start with role orientations, which are "norms of behavior which constrain the activities of the role occupant."[96] The role that has received most attention from twentieth-century commentators is judicial restraint, along with its converse, judicial activism.[97] Although evidence exists that both trial court judges and federal appellate judges may be influenced by role perceptions,[98] virtually no such evidence exists for those who sit at the top of the judicial hierarchy.[99] Some evidence of roles is easily dismissed. For instance, Justice Blackmun, dissenting from a Court opinion striking down the death penalty, declared:

I yield to no one in the depth of my distaste, antipathy, and indeed abhorrence, for the death penalty, with all its aspects of physical distress and fear and of moral judgment exercised by finite minds. That distaste is buttressed by a belief that capital punishment serves no useful purpose that can be demonstrated. For me, it violates childhood's trainings and life's experiences, and is not compatible with the philosophical convictions I have been able to develop. It is antagonistic to any sense of "reverence for life." Were I a legislator, I would vote against the death penalty.[100]

This, of course, sounds like judicial restraint. A justice hates the death penalty but votes for it because he finds no basis for declaring it unconstitutional (notwithstanding the fact that it is the Supreme Court that must give meaning to the Constitution's prohibition on cruel and unusual punishment).

This would be a bit more plausible were it not for the fact that Justice Blackmun wrote the majority opinion in *Roe v. Wade*,[101] which supporters and detractors alike consider a classic example of judicial legislation, and as such one of the most activist decisions in the Court's history. The point is not that *Roe* was rightly or wrongly decided. The point is simply that a justice capable of finding a right to first and second trimester abortions in the words "due process of law"

[96] James Gibson, "Judges' Role Orientations, Attitudes and Decisions," 72 *American Political Science Review* 911 (1978), at 917.
[97] We provide a full discussion of the behavioral effects of judicial activism and restraint in Chapter 8.
[98] J. Woodford Howard, *Courts of Appeals in the Federal Judicial System* (Princeton: Princeton University Press, 1981); Gibson, op. cit. fn. 96, supra.
[99] Joel Grossman argues that some of Justice Frankfurter's conservative positions can be explained by a role-based belief in "denial of judicial responsibility (DJR)." But because Grossman operationalizes DJR as those cases in which any justice (often Frankfurter himself) raises the DJR issue, the results are tautological. They are also perfectly consistent with a strategy of using DJR as a convenient justification for desired results. Moreover, even when the DJR factor is not present, Frankfurter votes conservatively. See "Role Playing and the Analysis of Judicial Behavior," 11 *Journal of Public Law* 285 (1963). We further discuss the judicial restraint of Justice Frankfurter later.
[100] *Furman v. Georgia*, 408 U.S. 238 (1972), at 405–406.
[101] 410 U.S. 113 (1973).

engages in pure hypocrisy when he complains that the words "cruel and unusual punishment" don't allow him to void death penalties. A claim of judicial restraint from Justice Blackmun is simply bunkum.

Three reasons support judicial restraint: 1) justices, along with lower federal court judges, should defer to publicly accountable decision makers because as lifetime appointees they are remote from public needs and sentiments; 2) because the constitutional system is federal, deference also ought to be paid state decision makers; and 3) because not all wisdom emanates from courtrooms, judges should accede to the expertise and technical competence of administrative officials. Because friend and foe alike agree on the synonymity of Justice Frankfurter and judicial restraint, we will use him to illustrate the vagaries of this role.[102]

If a justice adheres to restraint, it ought to be manifest, among other litigation, in cases involving state and administrative agency regulation. During Frankfurter's tenure on the Warren Court, when his reputation peaked, he did indeed defer to the states when they regulated labor unions. But he did not do so when the states regulated business, when the NLRB regulated labor, or when other federal agencies regulated business. Instead, like all of his colleagues, he used judicial restraint solely to rationalize his substantive policy preferences,[103] which, in his case, were those of a staunch economic conservative: pro-business and anti-union.[104] He supported state regulation of labor because the states' regulations opposed labor. He refused to support their business regulations, as well as federal agency regulation, because these decisions were predominately economically liberal. Surprisingly perhaps, Frankfurter did not hesitate to accompany his activist votes with opinions. When he wrote in opposition to state anti-business regulation, his lack of restraint appeared starkly naked. But when he wrote in opposition to liberal agency regulation, he was able to partially conceal his activism because he could rationalize his anti-agency votes on the basis of support for decisions of the courts of appeals and congressional legislation.[105] It boggles the mind that even the most Pollyannaish belief in the reality of Frankfurter's restraint could survive his dissenting opinion in *F.H.A. v. The Darlington*, in which he unequivocally asserted that an act of Congress was

---

[102] E.g., Charles M. Lamb, "Judicial Restraint on the Supreme Court," in Stephen C. Halpern and Charles M. Lamb, eds., *Supreme Court Activism and Restraint* (Lexington, MA: D.C. Heath, 1982); Martin Shapiro, *Law and Politics in the Supreme Court* (New York: Free Press, 1964); Rogers Smith, *Liberalism and American Constitutional Law* (Cambridge: Harvard University Press, 1985).

We discuss judicial restraint and its converse, judicial activism, systematically in Chapter 8.

[103] See Harold J. Spaeth and Stuart H. Teger, "Activism and Restraint: A Cloak for the Justices' Policy Preferences," in Halpern and Lamb, op. cit. fn. 102 supra, pp. 277–301.

[104] Harold J. Spaeth, "The Judicial Restraint of Mr. Justice Frankfurter – Myth or Reality," 8 *American Journal of Political Science* 22 (1964); Harold J. Spaeth and Michael F. Altfeld, "Felix Frankfurter, Judicial Activism, and Voting Conflict on the Warren Court," in Sheldon Goldman and Charles M. Lamb, eds., *Judicial Conflict and Consensus* (Lexington, KY: University of Kentucky Press, 1986), pp. 87–114.

[105] Spaeth and Altfeld, *ibid.*, pp. 102, 106, 109–110.

unconstitutional because it "did substantially impair the 'vested rights' " of a housing developer.[106] This was, remember, a generation after the Court terminated laissez-faire economics as a limitation on the economic powers of government.[107] The majority's opinion caustically concluded: "Invocation of the Due Process Clause to protect the rights asserted here would make the ghost of *Lochner v. New York* . . . walk again."[108]

External influences

The behavior of Blackmun and Frankfurter seems to suggest that judicial restraint cloaks, rather than motivates, judicial behavior. But from an environmental standpoint, certain external factors might produce a bit of deference. To determine if this be so, we examine sequentially the influences of the Solicitor General, Congress, public opinion, and interest groups.

Before we begin this investigation, a brief methodological note is in order. One cannot demonstrate that the Supreme Court is influenced by the Solicitor General, Congress, public opinion, interest groups, or any other external factor by the simple expedient of correlating the Court's decisions with the preferences of any of these actors. For instance, it may be possible to show that the Warren Court supported the position taken by the NAACP Legal Defense Fund, Inc. (LDF) in every desegregation case before it. But this does not necessarily mean that the Court was *influenced* by the LDF. The liberal Warren Court most likely would have supported desegregation with or without the support of the LDF.[109] Before influence can be inferred, we must show that an actor in the Court's environment had an independent impact after controlling for other factors.

The Solicitor General. As discussed in Chapter 5, the Solicitor General represents the executive branch of the United States before the Supreme Court, and is quite successful in getting cases heard by the Court. The favorable treatment accorded the United States at access continues when the case is decided on the merits. Scigliano sampled cases at 10-year intervals and showed that the United States won 62 percent of its cases in the nineteenth century and 64 percent in the twentieth.[110] The search and seizure data set provides evidence that the United States as a party significantly affects the Court's decisions even when the facts of the case are controlled. Adding the United States to the model presented in Table 6.1 increases the reasonableness of a search by .20. The coefficient is statistically significant at p < .05.

Many times the United States is not a direct party, but nevertheless has a

---

[106] 358 U.S. 84 (1958), at 93.
[107] See the section entitled "The Court-packing plan" in Chapter 3, supra.
[108] 358 U.S. 84, at 91–92.
[109] This is not to say that the LDF did not have an influence on agenda setting. See Chapter 5 for a discussion of the role of groups in getting cases into the Court.
[110] *The Supreme Court and the Presidency.* (New York: The Free Press, 1971).

substantial interest in the outcome of the case. For instance, in *Brown v. Board of Education*,[111] the famous racial desegregation suit, the Solicitor General only filed an amicus brief. It was in the government's brief in the second *Brown* case that the Court found the "all deliberate speed" proposal.[112]

Looking at the amicus cases more generally, it becomes clear that despite the government's success as a litigant, it "has an even better record as amicus curiae."[113] For the years 1943, 1944, 1963, and 1965, Scigliano reports that the party supported by the Solicitor General won 87 percent of the time. Such results are consistent with more recent findings.[114]

Again, preliminary evidence suggests that these results hold after controlling for the facts of the case. One tested area is the sex discrimination cases heard by the Supreme Court between 1971 and 1984.[115] The Court supported the Solicitor General 64 percent of the time when it favored a conservative (anti-equality) decision and 90 percent of the time when it favored a liberal (pro-equality) decision. After controlling for several case facts, changes in the Court's membership, and the Court's tendency to reverse, the position taken by the Solicitor General still had a large influence, affecting the probability of a liberal or conservative decision by as much as .28. So too has evidence of solicitor general influence been found in death penalty cases.[116] Obviously, though, to make a case for broadly based Solictor General influence, such findings need replication in a broad array of subject areas.

Congress. Unlike the President, who has no control over sitting members of the Supreme Court, Congress possesses explicit constitutional power to check and balance judicial and Supreme Court decision making: It can impeach and remove judges, it can increase or decrease the size of any federal court, and it can limit – or even terminate – the Court's appellate jurisdiction, along with all the jurisdiction of the lower federal courts. Congress has the power, for example, to eliminate the Court's ability to hear abortion or flag burning or reapportionment cases. Thus, more so than the executive branch, one might expect Congress to impact the Court's decisions.

Perhaps because of public belief in the mythology of judging (see Chapter 1), Congress has rarely exercised its constitutional powers to sanction the Supreme

[111] 347 U.S. 483 (1954).
[112] Lincoln Caplan, *The Tenth Justice* (New York: Knopf, 1987), p. 31.
[113] Scigliano, op. cit. fn. 110 supra, p. 179.
[114] Karen O'Connor, "The Amicus Curiae Role of the U.S. Solicitor General in Supreme Court Litigation," 66 *Judicature* 256 (1983); Steven Puro, "The Role of the Amicus Curiae in the United States Supreme Court," unpublished Ph.D. dissertation, State University of New York at Buffalo, 1971; Steven Puro, "The United States as Amicus Curiae," in S. Sidney Ulmer, ed., *Courts, Law and Judicial Processes* (New York: Free Press, 1983); and Jeffrey A. Segal, "Amicus Curiae Briefs by the Solicitor General During the Warren and Burger Courts," 41 *Western Political Quarterly* 135 (1988).
[115] Segal and Reedy, op. cit. fn. 61 supra.
[116] George and Epstein, op. cit. fn. 61 supra.

Court. Only one justice, Samuel Chase, was impeached, and that was a blatant partisan attempt of the Jeffersonians to gouge the Federalists. The Senate's attempt to remove Chase fell short of the requisite two-thirds majority. Congress has been circumspect in limiting the Court's appellate jurisdiction. It has on occasion played with the number of justices – during Reconstruction, for example, it shrank the size of the Court – but that was due to Congress's battles with President Andrew Johnson rather than efforts to curb the Court. When Ulysses Grant was elected President, Congress quickly restored the seats. Recall our discussion in Chapter 3 of Franklin Roosevelt's inability to secure passage of his Court-packing plan, notwithstanding his landslide reelection in 1936 and the overwhelming Democratic control of Congress.

Although anecdotes can be told of occasional justices who switched votes in response to political pressure from Congress and elsewhere – for example, Hughes and Roberts in 1937, and Harlan in 1959 – no systematic evidence of Congressional influence on the justices' decisions exists. The closest is a study that argues that periods of attempted Court curbing follow periods of low Court support for the United States, which in turn are followed by higher periods of support for the United States.[117] Unfortunately, the article does not indicate whether increased support results from the justices' reaction to the Court curbing effort, the appointment of new justices with different views, or simply regression-to-the-mean effects.[118] Thus, we cannot point to any systematic demonstration of congressional influence on the Court's decisions.

Public opinion. Supreme Court decisions by and large correspond with public opinion.[119] This should not be surprising, as Supreme Court justices are chosen by the President, who in turn is selected by vote of the people. Again, the question of concern is whether public opinion – however defined – *influences* the Court.

Theoretically, there is little reason to think so. Institutionally, the justices are immune from majoritarian pressures. The public neither elects nor removes them from office. Moreover, from a normative perspective, the justices are not supposed to represent majoritarian concerns. As Justice Jackson so eloquently stated in *West Virginia Board of Education v. Barnette*:

The very purpose of a Bill of Rights was to withdraw certain subjects from the vicissitudes of political controversy, to place them beyond the reach of majorities and officials and

[117] Roger Handberg and Harold F. Hill, Jr., "Court Curbing, Court Reversals, and Judicial Review: The Supreme Court versus Congress," 14 *Law and Society Review* 309 (1980).
[118] Regression to the mean is a well known statistical result that indicates that when scores on any measure, such as support for the United States by the Supreme Court, are unusually high or low, they can be expected to be closer to the mean the following time. Among other things, it explains why children of tall parents tend not to be quite as tall and why people who make the cover of *Sports Illustrated* seem to be jinxed in their performance in subsequent weeks.
[119] David Barnum, "The Supreme Court and Public Opinion: Judicial Decision Making in the Post-New Deal Period," 47 *Journal of Politics* 652 (1985); and Thomas Marshall, *Public Opinion and the Supreme Court* (New York: Longman, 1989).

to establish them as legal principles to be applied by the courts. One's right to life, liberty, and property, to free speech, a free press, freedom of worship and assembly, and other fundamental rights may not be submitted to vote; they depend on the outcome of no elections.[120]

In interpreting certain clauses, "cruel and unusual punishments" being a notable example, the Court claims to look to public opinion for guidance. But if, as we have shown in Chapter 2, the watchword of the plain meaning rule is that words mean what the Court wants them to mean, the watchword of the Court's use of public opinion data is that there are three types of lies: lies, damn lies, and statistics. In determining whether the Constitution prohibited the death penalty for retarded individuals, the Court noted that in Texas, Florida, and Georgia, three states with overwhelming support for the death penalty, opinion opposed execution of the retarded by 73 percent, 71 percent, and 66 percent, respectively. Yet the Court declared that "there is insufficient evidence of a national consensus against executing retarded people."[121] Recall as well that Justice Marshall, defeated in his quest for a nation opposed to the death penalty, justified his continued antagonism on the belief that an "informed public" would agree with him if they knew all the facts.[122]

We know of no empirical study that systematically demonstrates that public opinion has any influence on the decisions of the justices. Indeed, although public opinion might influence state court judges,[123] evidence on unelected, life-tenured federal counterparts shows no such influence.[124]

Interest groups. Interest groups are among the prime shapers of public policy in the United States. They contribute vast amounts of money and personnel to political campaigns. Additionally, they can organize and support grass roots lobbying of representatives, as the frenetic campaign for and against Judge Bork exemplified. Interest groups also lobby the judiciary through direct sponsorship of cases and through the filing of briefs amicus curiae. They certainly play a

[120]   319 U.S. 624, at 638.
[121]   *Penry v. Lynaugh*, 106 L Ed 2d 256 (1989), at 289.
[122]   *Gregg v. Georgia*, 428 U.S. 153 (1976), at 232.
[123]   See, for example, Paul Brace and Melinda Gann Hall, "Neo-Institutionalism and Dissent in State Supreme Courts," 52 *Journal of Politics* 54 (1990); James Gibson, "Environmental Constraints on the Behavior of Judges," 14 *Law and Society Review* 343 (1980); and James Kuklinski and John Stanga, "Political Participation and Governmental Responsiveness," 73 *American Political Science Review* 1090 (1979).
[124]   Micheal Giles and Thomas G. Walker, "Judicial Policy-Making and Southern School Segregation," 37 *Journal of Politics* 917 (1975). Beverly B. Cook shows that as public opinion turned against the Vietnam War, sentencing by federal judges in draft-dodger cases became more lenient, but this probably occurred because federal judges, like most other groups, were themselves turning against the war. No independent effect of public opinion is demonstrated. "Public Opinion and Federal Judicial Policy," 21 *American Journal of Political Science* 567 (1977). See Herbert M. Kritzer, "Federal Judges and Their Political Environment: The Influence of Public Opinion," 23 *American Journal of Political Science* 194 (1979).

crucial part in getting cases and issues on the Court's agenda.[125] The question this section considers, though, is once a case is on the docket, do interest groups have an ability to influence the Court's decisions?

Like public opinion, it is not clear why they should. Unlike legislators and elected judges, interest groups have little tangible to offer the justices, apart from some information – occasionally not otherwise available – that may marginally ease their reaching a decision. Nor do normative reasons support interest group influence on the judiciary. Although pluralist theory suggests that some public good might emerge from a battle of competing interest groups in the legislative arena, no definition of the public good, not even Richard Posner's, includes buying and selling judicial decisions.

Nevertheless, journals of political science are awash with "evidence" that interest groups are invincible litigators,[126] most of which consists of case studies of particular groups, such as the NAACP Legal Defense Fund, who are examined precisely because of their success. Few people want to spend a year or two studying losing litigators. Systematic analysis, however, shows them to have relatively little impact. The best such study, using precision matching to compare interest group-sponsored cases with similar non-group-sponsored cases found no evidence of interest group efficacy in the federal district courts.[127] Simply put, we have virtually no evidence to date that interest groups have an independent impact on Supreme Court decisions on the merits.

The final decision on the merits: Conclusions

According to Oliver Wendell Holmes, law is nothing more than "the prophesies of what the courts will do in fact."[128] By this he meant that statutes and constitutional commands do not give citizens a fair understanding of what the law permits and what the law prohibits. It is a judge's decision that tells us what we may and may not do. Because decisions about the legality of today's activity will be made by judges tomorrow, law becomes the prophesies of what judges will do. "The object of our study, then, is prediction."[129]

---

[125] See, for example, Lucius Barker, "Third Parties in Litigation: A Systemic View of the Judicial Function," 29 *Journal of Politics* 41 (1967); Gregory Caldeira and John Wright, "Interest Groups and Agenda-Setting in the Supreme Court of the United States," 82 *American Political Science Review* 1109 (1988); Lee Epstein, *Conservatives in Court* (Knoxville: University of Tennessee Press, 1985); Karen O'Connor, *Women's Organizations Use of the Courts* (Lexington, MA: Lexington Books, 1980); Frank Sorauf, *The Wall of Separation: Constitutional Politics of Church and State* (Princeton: Princeton University Press, 1976); and most notably, Clement Vose, *Caucasians Only* (Berkeley: University of California Press, 1959).

[126] For refutation, see Lee Epstein and C.K. Rowland, "Debunking the Myth of Interest Group Invincibility in the Courts," 85 *American Political Science Review* 205 (1991).

[127] Ibid.

[128] Oliver Wendell Holmes, "The Path of the Law," 10 *Harvard Law Review* 457 (1897), 460–461.

[129] Ibid. at 457.

What do we need to predict decisions from the types of cases that come to the Supreme Court? Let us take as an example a statute regulating abortion in the second and third trimesters. The facts that gave rise to the controversy are indisputable. Beyond them, proponents of the legal model would presumably want to know the text of the Constitution, what the framers of the Ninth and Fourteenth Amendments said, and the content of the majority opinion in *Roe v. Wade*.[130] Others might want to know public opinion on the issue, or the role of interest groups in the case. Proponents of the attitudinal model would want nothing more than the attitudes – the personal policy preferences – of the justices toward second and third trimester abortions. Predictions with that information, we believe, will outperform predictions with all other information combined.

JUDICIAL BEHAVIOR

In Chapter 3 we presented an overview of the Court as an authoritative policy maker. Our historical summary there focused on landmark decisions that typified the Court's ideological orientation at various points in time and the political effects of the justices' decisions. In this section we present a more systematic picture of the policy making of the Warren, Burger, and Rehnquist Courts. We limit our focus to these three Courts because we have highly reliable data pertaining to them.

We describe our approach here as more systematic than that presented in the historical overview of Chapter 3 because we focus on all of the Court's formally decided cases.[131] These we group into ten discrete policy or issue areas. By grouping the cases into these rather grossly defined issues, however, we lose much of the detail and the consequent richness that a microanalytical fix provides. And though such a focus accords with the attitudinal model, our analysis nonetheless mixes rather indiscriminately, if not arbitrarily, the objects of the justices' attitudes – the litigants and the interests they vicariously represent – and the situations in which the objects are encountered. Thus, for example, although litigation involving blacks, women, aliens, juveniles, and indigents properly concerns civil rights, the justices do not consistently vote as though the cases concerning each of these groups are fungible with those of the others. Similarly with regard to labor unions. A conflict between a union and a Fortune 500 company, on the one hand, and a controversy between a union and one of its members, on the other, both involve unions, but the situational context could hardly differ more. Nonetheless, we believe our approach strikes something of a middle ground between the poles of micro- and macroanalysis.

By dividing the Court's decisions and the justices' voting into a number of

---

[130]   410 U.S. 113 (1973).

[131]   That is, all orally argued cases except those decided by a tied vote, whose issue usually cannot be determined, and decrees, which may or may not show a date of oral argument and which typically resolve state boundary disputes.

policy or issue areas, we are able to characterize the decisions and votes from an attitudinal or ideological perspective. That is, we may properly speak of a case outcome, as well as a justice's vote, as "liberal" or "conservative." These labels, of course, do not necessarily denote any semantically fixed outcomes. It is therefore incumbent on us to define what we mean when we use these terms, in addition to specifying the scope of each of our ten policy areas. For the most part, our specification of the "liberal" and "conservative" positions accords with common usage, as does our division of the Court's decisions into policy areas.

We have divided the Court's decisions compatibly with the policy areas that the Supreme Court database identifies: criminal procedure, civil rights, First Amendment, privacy, due process, unions, economic activity, judicial power, federalism, and federal taxation.[132] The database defines a "liberal" outcome or vote in each of these policy areas as follows (a "conservative" vote or outcome is the opposite): support of persons accused or convicted of crime, or those denied a jury trial, support of those alleging violation of their civil rights, or support of those alleging deprivation of First Amendment freedoms. With regard to privacy, a liberal vote supports females in matters of abortion, and disclosure in actions concerning freedom of information except for student and employment records. With regard to due process, a liberal position opposes government action where deprivation of due process is alleged except in takings clause cases where conservatives oppose the governmental action. A liberal vote supports labor unions except where the union is alleged to violate the antitrust laws; in these cases, a liberal vote supports competition. In economic activity, the liberal position opposes business, the employer, and arbitration, while supporting competition, liability, indigents, small businesses vis-à-vis big ones, debtors, bankrupts, consumers, the environment, and accountability. In judicial power, a "liberal" – more accurately, a judicial activist as opposed to judicial restraintist – supports the exercise of judicial power, including review of administrative agency action. In federalism, a liberal vote supports national supremacy – that is, is pro-national and anti-state. In federal taxation, the liberal position supports the United States and opposes the taxpayer.

We use all signed opinion and per curiam cases that were orally argued in the analyses that follow. As we mentioned, we exclude cases decided by a tied vote and decrees. Our unit of analysis is docket number rather than case citation. Analysis begins with the Warren Court in 1953 and terminates with the end of the fifth term (that began in October 1990) of the Rehnquist Court. We consider the three most recent Courts first, then the justices who sat on each of them.

---

[132] The database also contains small attorneys, interstate relations, and miscellaneous sets, which we do not analyze because of the difficulty in assigning direction to the outcome and votes in these cases. Attorneys concerns bar membership, fees, and advertisements. Interstate relations concerns boundary and other disputes between states.

Table 6.5. *Liberal policy output by area and court*

	Court					
	Warren		Burger		Rehnquist	
Policy Area	%	N	%	N	%	N
criminal procedure	58.5	(386)	34.4	(550)	32.6	(175)
civil rights	77.1	(262)	51.7	(576)	54.4	(114)
First Amendment	71.7	(180)	49.2	(236)	42.5	(73)
due process	55.8	(43)	35.6	(146)	34.3	(35)
privacy	50.0	(2)	28.6	(49)	23.1	(13)
unions	65.8	(152)	55.7	(131)	40.0	(30)
economic activity	70.9	(592)	50.7	(533)	51.5	(132)
judicial power	39.9	(273)	29.1	(323)	42.1	(95)
federalism	64.4	(90)	60.4	(101)	60.5	(43)
federal taxation	79.2	(130)	70.7	(75)	73.9	(23)

Courts

As Table 6.5 shows, the three Courts display a remarkable similarity about which issues they most frequently decide, even though the proportion liberally decided varies across the Courts. Criminal procedure was the second most litigated policy on the agenda of the Warren and Burger Courts (18.1 and 19.8 percent, respectively), rising to first on the Rehnquist Court with a 22.9 percent share.[133] Civil rights was of primary concern on the Burger Court, fourth on the Warren Court, and third on the Rehnquist Court. First Amendment occupied fifth place on all three Courts. These three areas, collectively denominated as civil liberties, garnered 38.8 percent of the Warren Court's agenda, and reached almost half of that of the Burger and Rehnquist Courts (49.0 and 47.4 percent, respectively). These findings clearly document the continued dominance of the civil liberties agenda that initially manifested itself following the switch in time of the late 1930s, as we pointed out in Chapter 3.

As for the other two major issues, economic activity appears to be slowly declining in overall frequency, though not in rank: from more than 25 percent of the Warren Court's cases, to 19.2 percent on the Burger Court, and 17.3 percent on the Rehnquist Court. The supervisory and housekeeping responsi-

---

[133] These and the other proportions reported for Table 6.5 include the small attorneys, interstate relations, and miscellaneous areas.

bilities of the Supreme Court – judicial power – have remained basically constant over the past four decades, constituting respectively one-eighth, one-ninth, and one-eighth of the last three Courts' formal output.

Table 6.5 also shows the extent to which the Burger and Rehnquist Courts have abandoned the liberalism of the Warren Court. These data, however, are less informative than a term-by-term analysis would show. On economic and labor policy, the Warren Court was extremely liberal almost from its beginning. On civil liberties, however, it did not become liberal until the 1961 term, as other analysis has shown, and remained well above 70 percent in six of its remaining seven terms.[134] Interestingly, the Rehnquist Court remains slightly more liberal in civil rights than the Burger Court (54.4 percent versus 51.7 percent). Other research also suggests that the precipitous drop in liberal economic decisions is more a function of a new ideological orientation that began to manifest itself by the mid-1970s than it is an infusion of conservative pro-business sentiments.[135]

On other issues, privacy continues to comprise less than 2 percent of the Court's output. The presence of abortion decisions here may give the impression of judicial preoccupation that the frequency of decisions clearly does not support. Though the last two Courts decided far fewer tax cases than the Warren Court did, all three overwhelmingly support the Internal Revenue Service and other federal tax collection efforts. Comparing the Burger and Rehnquist Courts, restraint better characterized the former than the latter, even though in criminal procedure, First Amendment, due process, and privacy the Rehnquist Court issues more conservative decisions. Indeed, the conservative Rehnquist Court is *less* restraintist – that is to say, more activist – than was the liberal Warren Court. On the other hand, though the Rehnquist Court is not especially willing to defer to the lower federal courts and administrative agencies, it defers to state action with a frequency approximately equivalent to that of its predecessors.

Justices

Tables 6.6–6.8 display by Court each justice's percentage of support for each of the policy areas that we identified, along with the justice's rank order toward that policy relative to the other justices. Because each area is a heterogeneous composite of a number of more specifically defined issues in which the behavior of given justices may vary widely (e.g., Black who supported persons accused or convicted of crime except those who pled the

---

[134] Jeffrey A. Segal and Harold J. Spaeth, "Decisional trends on the Warren and Burger Courts: Results from the Supreme Court Data Base Project," 73 *Judicature* 103 (1989), at 104; reprinted in Elliot E. Slotnick, ed., *Judicial Politics* (Chicago: American Judicature Society, 1992), pp. 475–481.

[135] Hagle and Spaeth, op. cit. fn. 59 supra.

Table 6.6. *Liberal policy output of Warren Court justices by percentage and rank*

Justice	crim pro[a]	civil rts[b]	1A[c]	dp[d]	Policy Areas union[e]	bus activ[f]	jud power[g]	fed[h]	tax[i]
Black	71.2 / 7	75.8 / 7	90.4 / 3	62.8 / 7	77.9 / 2	82.5 / 2	50.6 / 4	68.2 / 5	84.3 / 3
Brennan	73.1 / 6	82.5 / 6	85.6 / 5	57.1 / 9	62.1 / 9	75.9 / 4	40.5 / 8	62.2 / 6	75.5 / 9
Burton	31.8 / 16	47.8 / 15	44.7 / 13	15.0 / 15	54.5 / 12	50.3 / 11	39.0 / 11	44.0 / 16	76.2 / 8
Clark	35.6 / 13	58.4 / 11	36.2 / 15	48.7 / 11	64.2 / 7	74.9 / 5	39.7 / 10	53.9 / 13	81.1 / 6
Douglas	89.0 / 1	92.7 / 2	98.9 / 1	65.1 / 6	69.5 / 5	85.7 / 1	58.0 / 2	70.0 / 3	39.8 / 16
Fortas	78.6 / 3	82.7 / 4	79.2 / 7	80.0 / 1T	57.7 / 11	61.8 / 8	40.0 / 9	52.9 / 15	52.9 / 15
Frank-furter	45.5 / 10	59.6 / 10	51.2 / 11	34.6 / 13	45.9 / 16	36.8 / 15	28.9 / 16	61.9 / 7	77.8 / 7
Goldberg	80.0 / 2	98.4 / 1	90.9 / 2	80.0 / 1T	61.9 / 10	66.0 / 7	41.1 / 7	60.0 / 9	75.0 / 10

	Criminal procedure[a]	Civil rights[b]	First Amendment[c]	Due process[d]	Unions[e]	Economic activity[f]	Judicial power[g]	Federalism[h]	Federal taxation[i]
Harlan	38.3 12	42.5 17	46.2 12	43.6 12	53.7 13	38.2 14	32.9 15	53.2 14	71.2 12
Jackson	35.0 15	72.7 8	60.0 10	0.0 17	50.0 15	30.0 17	14.3 17	80.0 1	25.0 17
Marshall	75.0 4	86.0 3	85.7 4	66.7 4	85.7 1	50.0 12	37.5 14	20.0 17	100 1
Minton	35.3 14	50.0 13	18.8 17	14.3 16	52.0 14	60.2 9	51.2 3	71.4 2	87.5 2
Reed	27.3 17	47.5 16	23.5 16	33.3 14	70.4 3	50.4 10	58.3 1	58.8 10	74.1 11
Stewart	46.0 9	57.8 12	65.0 8	60.9 8	62.5 8	47.5 13	43.1 6	58.7 11	69.0 13
Warren	74.4 5	82.6 5	82.9 6	65.8 5	69.8 4	79.7 3	45.1 5	69.1 4	82.8 5
White	48.0 8	66.2 9	60.5 9	75.0 3	68.6 6	69.6 6	38.8 12	61.4 8	83.3 4
Whittaker	41.9 11	48.3 14	39.0 14	50.0 10	37.8 17	34.7 16	38.0 13	56.5 12	62.0 14

Notes. [a]Criminal procedure. [b]Civil rights. [c]First Amendment. [d]Due process.
[e]Unions. [f]Economic activity. [g]Judicial power. [h]Federalism. [i]Federal taxation.

Table 6.7. *Liberal policy output of Burger Court justices by percentage and rank*

Justice	crim pro[a]	civil rts[b]	1A[c]	dp[d]	priv[e]	union[f]	bus activ[g]	jud power[h]	fed[i]	tax[i]
					Policy Areas					
Black	45.3	50.8	73.0	60.0	0.0	56.3	68.8	18.9	50.0	100
	6	7	4	4	12T	6	2	12	10T	1
Blackmun	32.2	54.7	50.5	32.4	51.1	62.1	51.4	29.6	69.1	71.2
	8	6	7	10	4	5	7	8	3	5
Brennan	75.0	82.6	82.5	57.5	62.5	67.9	65.9	42.3	66.0	69.3
	3	3	3	5	2	2	3	3	5	7
Burger	19.6	37.0	30.8	31.5	14.3	40.0	42.8	23.1	69.3	70.7
	11	12	12	11	8	12	10	10	2	6
Douglas	87.7	92.6	91.4	94.6	88.9	51.0	82.2	63.6	72.2	38.5
	1	1	1	1	1	8	1	1	1	13
Harlan	38.9	47.5	40.5	80.0	0.0	37.5	45.5	13.5	50.0	81.8
	7	8	9	2	12T	13	8	13	10T	3

	Criminal procedure[a]	Civil rights[b]	First Amendment[c]	Due process[d]	Privacy[e]	Unions[f]	Economic activity[g]	Judicial power[h]	Federalism[i]	Federal taxation[j]
Marshall	77.9 2	83.2 2	82.9 2	64.5 3	60.9 3	69.5 1	62.9 4	41.0 4	68.5 4	77.3 4
O'Connor	17.2 12	46.5 9	37.3 10	23.1 12	6.3 11	50.0 9	42.4 12	33.0 5	45.5 12	65.2 8
Powell	28.7 10	39.8 11	48.6 8	39.7 8	31.1 7	48.1 10	42.5 11	26.1 9	61.7 7	55.0 11
Rehnquist	14.0 13	24.4 13	18.3 13	19.5 13	6.5 10	43.1 11	41.5 13	22.4 11	32.3 13	61.9 10
Stevens	56.3 4	57.7 4	63.6 6	45.9 7	48.7 5	64.2 4	53.8 5	44.0 2	51.3 9	52.2 12
Stewart	45.7 5	45.7 10	66.7 5	51.6 6	42.4 6	51.6 7	45.3 9	30.6 7	55.1 8	63.3 9
White	31.4 9	55.0 5	33.1 11	36.8 9	8.2 9	66.2 3	52.9 6	30.9 6	64.4 6	85.3 2

Notes. [a]Criminal procedure. [b]Civil rights. [c]First Amendment. [d]Due process.
[e]Privacy. [f]Unions. [g]Economic activity. [h]Judicial power. [i]Federalism. [j]Federal taxation.

Table 6.8. *Liberal policy output of Rehnquist Court justices by percentage and rank*

Policy Areas

Justice	crim pro[a]	civil rts[b]	1A[c]	dp[d]	priv[e]	union[f]	bus activ[g]	jud power[h]	fed[l]	tax[l]
Blackmun	60.3 / 4	86.6 / 3	69.9 / 3	48.1 / 4	53.8 / 5	56.7 / 4	55.4 / 4	48.4 / 3	61.9 / 5	73.9 / 4
Brennan	87.4 / 2	91.6 / 2	86.6 / 2	59.4 / 2	60.0 / 4	63.6 / 2	68.2 / 2	50.0 / 2	63.2 / 4	68.4 / 6
Kennedy	21.6 / 9	38.0 / 7	35.3 / 6	22.2 / 10	9.1 / 10	25.0 / 10	52.9 / 6	44.3 / 5	50.0 / 10	66.7 / 7
Marshall	88.5 / 1	93.9 / 1	87.7 / 1	57.1 / 3	69.2 / 2	70.0 / 1	70.5 / 1	52.6 / 1	65.9 / 3	65.2 / 8
O'Connor	23.6 / 8	35.7 / 8	33.3 / 7	37.1 / 6T	38.5 / 6	30.0 / 9	41.1 / 10	39.4 / 7	52.5 / 9	52.2 / 9T

	Criminal procedure[a]	Civil rights[b]	First Amendment[c]	Due process[d]	Privacy[e]	Unions[f]	Economic activity[g]	Judicial power[h]	Federalism[i]	Federal taxation[j]
Powell	29.5 5	42.3 5	46.2 5	61.5 1	100 1	60.0 3	53.6 5	11.8 10	66.7 2	83.3 2
Rehnquist	16.6 10	22.8 10	14.1 10	25.7 9	15.4 8T	33.3 8	45.0 9	29.5 9	53.5 8	78.3 3
Scalia	27.6 6	33.0 9	27.8 8	31.4 8	30.0 7	36.7 6T	47.3 8	32.6 8	60.5 6	69.6 5
Stevens	69.9 3	67.3 4	61.6 4	42.9 5	61.5 3	50.0 5	64.1 3	45.3 4	54.8 7	52.2 9T
White	24.7 7	41.2 6	26.0 9	37.1 6T	15.4 8T	36.7 6T	51.5 7	42.1 6	67.4 1	91.3 1

Notes. [a]Criminal procedure. [b]Civil rights. [c]First Amendment. [d]Due process. [e]Privacy. [f]Unions. [g]Economic activity. [h]Judicial power. [i]Federalism. [j]Federal taxation.

251

Fourth Amendment,[136] and Warren, a strong supporter of civil rights, except for indigents[137], the entries in these tables are relatively gross and imprecise indicators of support and rank. Privacy does not appear on Table 6.6 because the Warren Court decided only two such cases.[138] Among the Warren Court justices, Jackson's rankings are especially suspect because he participated in so few cases during his single term on it, as are those of Souter's single Rehnquist Court term.[139]

The Warren Court justices greatly vary their support for the policy areas that comprise civil liberties: criminal procedure, civil rights, First Amendment, and due process. Justices shown to be liberals in other research[140] generally exceed an 80 percent level of support: Douglas, Goldberg, Fortas, Warren, Marshall, and Brennan, along with Black insofar as First Amendment freedoms are concerned. A marked difference separates the liberally inclined from the other justices: twenty-three points between Black, seventh ranked on criminal procedure, and the eighth-ranked White. At the other extreme, Truman's remaining justices, Minton and Burton, along with Roosevelt's second nominee, Reed, least support civil liberties generally. Matching their conservative orientation are Harlan and Whittaker toward civil rights, Clark and Whittaker toward the First Amendment, and Frankfurter toward due process.

---

[136]   See Harold J. Spaeth and David J. Peterson, "The Analysis and Interpretation of Dimensionality: The Case of Civil Liberties Decision Making," 15 *American Journal of Political Science* 415 (1971); reprinted in Spaeth and Brenner, op. cit. fn. 17 supra, pp. 161–183.

[137]   For example, *Shapiro v. Thompson*, 394 U.S. 618 (1969); *Moya v. DeBaca*, 369 U.S. 825 (1969).

[138]   *Société Internationale v. Rogers*, 357 U.S. 197 (1958); *Griswold v. Connecticut*, 381 U.S. 479 (1965).

[139]   It is not our purpose in this section to document further the operation of the attitudinal model of the justices' decision making, but rather to describe the policy output resulting from their votes. We do, however, note that a focus on dissenting votes graphically displays the attitudinal model at work. The attitudinal model simply holds that justices will dissent when the majority's position is further from their "ideal," or indifference, points than a dissenting vote would be. If the attitudinal model is operative, individual justices should differentially vary their dissent rates between liberal and conservative decisions. Liberal justices should dissent from conservative outcomes, and vice-versa. This indeed is what occurs. The twenty-three justices who sat on the Warren and Burger Courts varied their rate of dissent between liberally and conservatively decided civil liberties cases by an average of 31.2 points, and in business and union cases by an average of 20.9 points. Douglas, for example, dissented from only 1.3 percent of the liberally decided civil liberties cases, but from 77.7 percent of the conservative ones. Rehnquist, on the other hand, dissented from 54.8 percent of the liberal decisions, but from only 0.9 percent of the conservative ones. Goldberg never dissented from a liberal civil liberties decision and Clark never dissented from a conservative one. The same pattern obtains in the economic cases. Warren dissented from 29.0 percent of the conservative decisions, but only 0.4 percent of the liberal ones. Frankfurter and Harlan, on the other hand, dissented from 43.3 and 42.3 percent of the liberal decisions, respectively, but from only 4.1 and 1.7 percent of those that were conservatively decided. See Segal and Spaeth, op. cit. fn. 134 supra, pp. 106–107.

[140]   Spaeth, op. cit. fn. 64 supra, pp. 128–137; Segal and Spaeth, op. cit. fn. 134 supra, pp. 105–106.

Except for federal taxation, which the Warren Court supported more than any other policy area,[141] the justices display markedly less extreme behavior toward the other issues in Table 6.6. Whereas twenty-one of the justices' civil liberties cells reach 75 percent or higher, only seven justices' cells reach this level in the other four areas. Low levels of support are also absent. Again excluding Jackson, relatively few justices support a policy area at rates below 40 percent. More typical is a proximate clustering of the justices in their support or opposition to a given policy area. For example, excluding the three most extreme justices, the others support federalism between the narrow range of 71.4 and 52.9 percent. Whereas support for judicial power, except for Jackson, Frankfurter, and Harlan, extends from Reed's 58.3 percent to Marshall's 37.5. Although the remaining policy, federal taxation, is supported by all the justices save Jackson and Douglas, that support also operates within relatively narrow limits. Excluding Marshall's five supportive votes, the others range from 87.5 to 52.9 percent.

The Burger Court justices, like their predecessors, also display a pattern of great variation in their individual levels of support for the various components of civil liberties. They differ from their Warren Court brethren in that they fluctuate very little in rank order from one component of civil liberties to another. Thus, Douglas is most supportive of all five policies. Marshall and Brennan consistently follow him, except for Brennan in due process. On the conservative side, Burger, O'Connor, and Rehnquist rank no higher than ninth among the thirteen justices on any aspect of civil liberties, except Burger on privacy, with Rehnquist anchoring the scale on all but privacy. Excluding the infrequently participating Black and Harlan, the other justices, except White and Stewart, also display a consistency in rank across the five issues. White, fifth most supportive of civil rights, a notch below Stevens and ahead of Blackmun, ranks no higher than ninth on the other components, whereas Stewart, fifth or sixth otherwise, ranks tenth on civil rights.

Even more so than the Warren Court justices, those on the Burger Court divided their pro and anti votes almost equally in the five other issues. In only four instances did support exceed 80 percent: economic activity by Douglas (82.2), and federal taxation by Black (100.0), White (85.3), and Harlan (81.8). Except for judicial power, in which only Douglas was an activist, non-support rarely fell below 40 percent: Harlan (37.5) toward unions, the states' rights oriented Rehnquist toward federalism (32.3), and Douglas on federal taxation (38.5).

Because the heterogeneity of the non-civil liberties issue areas appears indistinguishable from that of civil liberties, the small variance among the justices' levels of support in the former compared with the latter areas probably results from the relatively low salience of these issues and the apparent emergence, at

---

[141] This is also true of the Burger and Rehnquist Courts, the difference being that these two Courts produced markedly less output supportive of the other policies than did the Warren Court.

least among the justices new to the Rehnquist Court, of a new ideological orientation in cases concerning business and economic activities generally, an orientation, moreover, that seems to include aspects of judicial power and federalism.[142]

As for the Rehnquist Court justices,[143] the variance between supporters and opponents of the civil liberties policy areas is substantial. Marshall and Brennan remain staunchly liberal, followed for the most part by either Stevens or Blackmun. The conservatively voting justices greatly distance themselves from their colleagues. In criminal procedure, for example, the fourth ranked justice, Blackmun, supports the accused 60 percent of the time, whereas the fifth ranked Powell votes supportively only half as often. Stevens, fourth in support of civil rights with a score of 67.3 percent, is followed by Powell at 42.3 percent. Stevens, fourth most supportive of First Amendment at 61.6 percent, is followed by Powell at 46.2. Blackmun, fifth in support of privacy, is followed by O'Connor who is fifteen points distant (53.8 to 38.5). Powell's high levels of support for due process and privacy are misleading. He cast only one privacy vote, whereas on due process his support occurred in takings clause cases, an aspect of due process distinct from the questions of notice and hearing that otherwise characterize this policy area.

On the conservative side, the Reagan nominees – O'Connor, Rehnquist, Scalia, and Kennedy – plus White, form a cohesive group. Across all five civil liberties categories, their support rarely exceeds the mid–30s, and falls below 20 percent for at least one of their number in criminal procedure, First Amendment, and privacy. Rehnquist surrenders his anchoring position to Kennedy in due process and privacy, which hardly evidences a moderation of his views.[144]

The Rehnquist Court justices' behavior in the five non-civil liberties areas parallels that of the justices on the earlier Courts. Although a rather wide distance separates Marshall, who is most pro-union, from Kennedy, who is least (70.0 versus 25.0), the five most anti-union justices vary by less than twelve points (36.7 to 25.0). In economic activities, less than thirty points separates the most and least anti-business justices, Marshall and O'Connor. In judicial power, except for Powell, the poles of activism and restraint span scarely 23 points, whereas only 17 points distinguishes the nationalist White from the states' righter Kennedy. If we exclude the two justices who supported federal taxation with more than 80 percent of their votes (White and Powell),

---

[142]   Hagle and Spaeth, op. cit. fn. 59 supra.

[143]   We exclude Souter from consideration because of the skewed effect his few votes in his first term on the Court have on the other justices' rankings. He cast a grand total of six votes, all conservative in due process, privacy, and federal taxation. In the other issue areas, his liberal vote percentage was: criminal procedure 15.4, civil rights 72.2, First Amendment 33.3, unions 37.5, economic activity 40.9, judicial power 50.0, and federalism 66.7.

[144]   See David W. Rohde and Harold J. Spaeth, "Ideology, strategy and Supreme Court decisions: William Rehnquist as chief justice," 72 *Judicature* 247 (1989).

the other eight vary by only 26 points (Rehnquist at 78.3 to O'Connor and Stevens at 52.2).

SUMMARY

This chapter examines the Court's decisions on the merits. Following oral argument, the justices vote in conference on each case heard in the preceding two or three days. Between the conference vote and the final vote there exists a certain degree of fluidity, but such switches are generally toward greater rather than lesser attitudinal consistency. The two aspects of the attitudinal model, facts and attitudes, are crucial to explaining the votes of the Supreme Court, both separately and in conjunction with one another. Conversely, virtually no support is found for non-attitudinal factors, such as judicial restraint, public opinion, and interest group activity. An examination of the votes actually cast by the justices of the Warren, Burger, and Rehnquist Courts shows that the issues they most frequently addressed remained remarkably constant over the last half of the twentieth century, even though the proportion decided liberally and conservatively varied across the three Courts. As for the individual justices, they vary greatly in their support and/or opposition to the policy areas that encompass civil rights and liberties (criminal procedure, civil rights, First Amendment, due process, and privacy). In the other issue areas, the voting of the justices on all three Courts varies but little by comparison.

APPENDIX 6.1: PREDICTING THE JUSTICES' VOTES

This appendix specifies the probability that the justices' past voting will predict their future votes. We have categorized the decisions of the Warren, Burger, and Rehnquist Courts compatibly with the issues listed in the United States Supreme Court Judicial Database that have been the subject of previous research (N = 116). The direction (e.g., liberal or conservative) of these issues is also as specified in this database. Where the definition of an issue remained constant between the Warren and Burger Courts, we use the votes in the former set to predict those in the latter. Where a new issue emerged during the Burger Court, or an old issue subdivided (e.g., the separation of the due process-hearing and due process-government employees cases from due process, and the division of the liability set between governmental and non-governmental tortfeasors), we used the votes of the Burger Court justices to predict the voting in the Rehnquist Court cases. For example, the Warren Court decided only a single sex discrimination case, and none that concerned affirmative action or abortion. Hence, we use the behavior of the Burger Court justices to predict that of the Rehnquist Court justices in these and other newly emerging issues.

This procedure entails a cost – the relative paucity of Rehnquist Court decisions. Whereas the Burger Court spanned seventeen terms, only the decisions of the first four and a half terms of the Rehnquist Court are available – that is, those decided between the beginning of the 1986 term and the end of Volume 113 of the *Lawyers' Edition* of the *United States Reports*, the last decision date of which is April 23, 1991.

We compute the probability (P) for each issue according to the procedure specified in the text:

$$p = \frac{N!}{C! \times W!}$$

where N = the number of non-unanimous decisions in the issue area, C = the number of non-unanimous decisions correctly predicted, and W = the number incorrectly predicted. A probability $\tau.05$ ($.5^{-1}$) is listed as not significant (ns). If we have attempted to predict the voting of the Rehnquist Court, an R appears in the final column of the relevant row.

Criminal procedure

Votes arrayed in support/opposition to the rights of persons accused or convicted of crime, or the right to a fair jury trial.

	N	C	W	p	
involuntary confession	10	8	2	$.28^{-2}$	
contempt of court	7	5	2	$.37^{-1}$	
habeas corpus	10	7	3	$.14^{-1}$	R
plea bargaining	17	11	6	$.5^{-2}$	
retroactivity	28	20	8	$.3^{-4}$	
search and seizure	73	53	20	$.4^{-11}$	
search and seizure, vehicles	3	3	0	$.36^{-1}$	R
search and seizure, Crime Control Act	1	1	0	ns	R
self-incrimination	29	26	3	$.3^{-9}$	
Miranda warnings	8	4	4	ns	
self-incrimination, immunity	0				R
right to counsel	32	19	13	$.1^{-2}$	
line-up identification	5	4	1	$.4^{-1}$	
cruel and unusual punishment, death penalty	40	25	15	$.9^{-4}$	
cruel and unusual punishment, non-death	0				R
discovery and inspection	7	3	4	ns	
double jeoparady	40	23	17	$.75^{-3}$	
extra-legal jury influences	30	25	5	$.1^{-6}$	
confrontation	15	11	4	$.14^{-2}$	
subconstitutional fair procedure	24	16	8	$.6^{-3}$	
Federal Rules of Criminal Procedure	11	9	2	$.75^{-3}$	
statutory construction	36	18	18	$.1^{-1}$	
jury trial	13	10	3	$.55^{-3}$	
speedy trial	1	1	0	ns	

Civil rights

Votes arrayed in support/opposition to the civil rights claimant.

	N	C	W	p	
voting	17	9	8	$.5^{-1}$	
Voting Rights Act of 1965	1	1	0	ns	R
ballot access	3	1	2	ns	R
desegregation	17	14	3	$.4^{-4}$	
desegregation, schools	2	2	0	ns	R
employment discrimination	8	7	1	$.2^{-2}$	R
affirmative action	8	6	2	$.2^{-1}$	R
reapportionment	26	15	11	$.5^{-2}$	
debtors' rights	0				R
sex discrimination	0				R
sex discrimination, employment	4	2	2	ns	R
deportation	5	1	4	ns	
aliens, employability	0				R
Indians	1	1	0	ns	R
Indians, state jurisdiction	5	4	1	$.5^{-1}$	R
juveniles	1	1	0	ns	R
poverty law, constitutional	4	4	0	$.1^{-1}$	R
poverty law, statutory	7	2	5	ns	R
handicapped	2	1	1	ns	R
illegitimates	0				R
residency requirements	4	2	2	ns	R
military	8	8	0	$.14^{-3}$	
immigration and naturalization	8	4	4	ns	
indigents	24	15	9	$.2^{-2}$	
civil rights acts, liability	15	8	7	$.5^{-1}$	R

First Amendment

Votes arrayed in support/opposition to freedom of communication.

	N	C	W	p	
First Amendment	64	36	28	$.7^{-4}$	
commercial speech	3	1	2	ns	R
libel, defamation	20	13	7	$.26^{-2}$	
libel, privacy	4	3	1	ns	
federal internal security legislation	5	4	1	$.3^{-1}$	
legislative investigations	1	1	0	ns	
security risks	9	8	1	$.75^{-3}$	
conscientious objectors	0				R
campaign spending	2	0	2	ns	R
protest demonstrations	31	25	6	$.6^{-7}$	
religious freedom	9	2	7	ns	
establishment of religion	7	5	2	$.4^{-1}$	
parochial school aid	1	1	0	ns	R
obscenity, state	24	21	3	$.5^{-7}$	
obscenity, federal	7	6	1	$.1^{-1}$	

Due process

Votes arrayed in support/opposition to government.

	N	C	W	p	
due process	34	22	12	$.1^{-3}$	
due process, hearing	2	1	1	ns	R
due process, government employees	1	0	1	ns	R
prisoners' rights	4	4	0	$.1^{-1}$	R
impartial decision maker	1	0	1	ns	R
takings clause	4	3	1	ns	R
due process, jurisdiction	3	2	1	ns	R

Privacy

Votes arrayed in support/opposition to abortion and disclosure.

	N	C	W	p	
abortion	4	4	0	$.1^{-1}$	R
freedom of information acts	2	0	2	ns	R

Attorneys

Votes arrayed in support/opposition to attorneys.

	N	C	W	p	
attorneys' fees	9	5	4	ns	R
commercial speech, attorneys	2	2	0	ns	R

Unions

Votes arrayed in support/opposition to unions, trial in arbitration, and competition in union antitrust.

	N	C	W	p	
arbitration	12	8	4	$.1^{-1}$	
union antitrust	9	3	6	ns	
union/union member conflict	15	4	11	ns	
union and closed shop	1	0	1	ns	
Fair Labor Standards Act	7	6	1	$.1^{-1}$	
OSHA	0				R
rights of unions vis-à-vis business	28	15	13	$.1^{-1}$	
rights of business vis-à-vis unions	20	9	11	ns	

Economic activity

Votes arrayed in support/opposition to business, employers, competition, liability, injured persons, indigents, debtors, bankrupts, consumer, environment, accountability

	N	C	W	p	
antitrust	35	16	19	$.4^{-1}$	
mergers	14	9	5	$.1^{-1}$	
bankruptcy	6	2	4	ns	
sufficienty of evidence	17	11	6	$.1^{-1}$	
election of remedies	19	11	8	$.2^{-1}$	
liability, governmental	10	6	4	$.5^{-1}$	R
liability, non-governmental	5	1	4	ns	R
ERISA	3	1	2	ns	R
state tax	20	5	15	ns	
state regulation	15	5	10	ns	
natural resources	23	12	11	$.3^{-1}$	
securities regulation	22	8	14	ns	
governmental corruption	8	0	8	ns	
zoning	0				R
consumer protection	0				R
patents and copyrights	13	4	9	ns	
transportation regulation	11	1	10	ns	
public utility regulation	17	6	11	ns	

Judicial power

Votes arrayed on pro/anti-judicial activism.

	N	C	W	p	
comity, criminal and First Amendment	0				R
comity, civil procedure	1	1	0	ns	R
Federal Rules of Civil Procedure	18	9	9	ns	
judicial review of agency action	40	13	27	ns	
mootness	29	17	12	$.3^{-2}$	
venue	5	0	5	ns	
standing to sue	8	7	1	$.2^{-2}$	R
judicial administration	43	21	22	$.1^{-1}$	

Federalism

Votes arrayed on pro-U.S. anti-state basis.

	N	C	W	p	
preemption state court jurisdiction	1	0	1	ns	R
preemption state regulation	9	1	8	ns	R
national supremacy	24	15	9	$.2^{-2}$	
Submerged Lands Act	3	0	3	ns	

Federal taxation

Votes arrayed on pro-U.S./anti-taxpayer basis.

	N	C	W	p
federal tax	36	18	18	$.1^{-1}$
gifts, professional, and personal expenses	9	0	9	ns
priority of federal fiscal claims	5	0	5	ns

7

Opinion assignment and
opinion coalitions

The decision on the merits merely indicates whether the ruling of the court whose decision the Supreme Court reviewed is affirmed or reversed and, consequently, which party has won and which has lost. The opinion of the Court, by comparison, constitutes the core of the Court's policy-making process. It specifies the constitutional and legal principles on which the majority rests its decision, it guides the lower courts in deciding future cases, and it establishes precedents for the Court's own subsequent rulings – even if such decisions and their supporting opinions can be overturned by future Supreme Courts.

Although the opinion of the Court is controlling and authoritative, the non-majority opinions that the justices write – concurrences and dissents – are by no means exercises in futility. Concurring opinions punctuate overstated or understated aspects of the Court's opinion, indicate its scope insofar as the concurring justice is concerned, address related matters, and exhibit the extent to which the members of the majority coalition are in agreement. Dissenting opinions obviously express disagreement with the majority's holding. They may also provide the rationale whereby the majority's opinion may be undermined and/or eventually qualified or overruled. Thus, the first Justice Harlan's dissent in *Plessy v. Ferguson* formed the basis for the majority's overruling in *Brown v. Board of Education*,[1] and opinions dissenting from the Court's refusal to apply portions of the Bill of Rights to state criminal procedure during the 1940s and 1950s laid the groundwork for the liberal Warren Court majority of the 1960s to do so.[2] Charles Evans Hughes – later Chief Justice – probably stated best the function of the dissenting opinion:

... an appeal to the brooding spirit of the law, to the intelligence of a future day, when a later decision may possibly correct the error into which the dissenting judge believes the court to have been betrayed.[3]

Although the justices are free to write concurring and dissenting opinions as they individually see fit, that is not true of opinions of the Court. If the Chief

---

[1]   163 U.S. 537 (1896), at 552; 347 U.S. 483 (1954).
[2]   See the discussion of these matters in Chapter 3.
[3]   Charles Evans Hughes, *The Supreme Court of the United States* (New York: Columbia University Press, 1928), p. 68.

Justice is among the majority in the original (conference) vote on the merits, he determines who will write the Court's opinion. If he is not a member of this group, the senior justice who is makes the assignment. In this chapter we initially identify the patterns of opinion assignment and the reasons for their existence. We then investigate opinion coalitions – who joins with whom, and why.

OPINION ASSIGNMENT

As we noted, the Chief Justice assigns the Court's opinion when he is among the majority at the conference vote on the merits. If he is not, the senior associate justice makes the assignment. The operation of this rule in practice has meant that Chief Justices from Vinson through Rehnquist have assigned approximately 80–85 percent of the Court's opinions, with the remaining percentage divided among the two or three senior associate justices.[4] Except for Professor Palmer's study of the Vinson Court, other analyses of opinion assignment have been based on membership in the final vote coalition – the one listed in the Reports – rather than membership in the final conference vote on the merits. Because the justices are free to change their votes between the conference vote and the report vote, we do not know for a fact that the ostensible assigner was a member of the final conference coalition at which the opinion of the Court was assigned. Although the justices' private papers make occasional reference to their changing sides,[5] Saul Brenner's systematic comparison of the justices' conference votes with their final votes shows switching to be fairly unusual, and that when it does occur it tends to increase the size of the final coalition rather than to transform the conference majority into either a minority or a smaller majority.[6] If, however, the original majority opinion coalition does break up and the author of a dissenting or a concurring opinion gains a majority, he or she is by that fact automatically reassigned the opinion of the Court without another conference vote.[7] Moreover, if the Chief Justice switches to the majority prior to the report vote, he also may

[4]   Jan Palmer, *The Vinson Court Era* (New York: AMS Press, 1990), p. 125; S. Sidney Ulmer, "The Use of Power on the Supreme Court: The Opinion Assignments of Earl Warren, 1953–1960," 30 *Journal of Public Law* 49 (1970), at 53; Harold J. Spaeth, "Distributive justice: Majority opinion assignments in the Burger Court," 67 *Judicature* 299 (1984), at 301. Sue Davis, "Power on the Court: Chief Justice Rehnquist's opinion assignments," 74 *Judicature* 66 (1990).

[5]   Walter F. Murphy, *Elements of Judicial Strategy* (Chicago: University of Chicago Press, 1964), pp. 68–73; J. Woodford Howard, "On the Fluidity of Judicial Choice," 62 *American Political Science Review* 43 (1968), at 44–49; S. Sidney Ulmer, "Earl Warren and the Brown Decision," 33 *Journal of Politics* 689 (1971).

[6]   Saul Brenner, "Fluidity on the United States Supreme Court: A Reexamination," 24 *American Journal of Political Science* 526 (1980); Saul Brenner, "Fluidity on the Supreme Court, 1956–1967," 26 *American Journal of Political Science* 388 (1982); both reprinted in Harold J. Spaeth and Saul Brenner, eds., *Studies in U.S. Supreme Court Behavior* (New York: Garland, 1990). Saul Brenner, Strategic Choice and Opinion Assignment on the U.S. Supreme Court: A Reexamination," 35 *Western Political Quarterly* 204 (1982).

[7]   Palmer, op. cit. fn. 4 supra, p. 127.

reassign the Court's opinion without taking another conference vote. Chief Justice Warren exemplified this practice in a memo to the Court:

> You will recall that when we discussed No. 24 – *Halliburton Oil Well Cementing Co. v. Reily* – I did not vote because I was uncertain as to what my decision would be, and Justice Black assigned the case further. I have decided to vote to reverse. I am, therefore, reassigning the case to myself.[8]

Consequently, in the findings we report next, we assume that both the opinion assigner and his assignee were members of the original majority (conference) vote coalition.

Assignment patterns

We start our analysis with a complete listing of all opinion assignments made during the Warren, Burger, and the first five terms of the Rehnquist Court. Tables 7.1–7.3 contain the results.

The most obvious feature of the tables is that the Chief Justice makes most of the assignments. Warren made 1,319 out of 1,538 (86 percent), Burger made 1,835 out of 2,157 (86 percent), and Rehnquist has made 543 out of 659 (82 percent) through the end of the 1990 term. During the Warren Court, Hugo Black was the senior associate justice, but as he overwhelmingly sided with Warren on the merits, he assigned only seventy-one cases in sixteen years. Felix Frankfurter, who was fourth in seniority (including the Chief Justice) through 1957 and third until his retirement in 1962, assigned ninety-one opinions during his nine Warren Court terms, the most of any associate justice. Following Frankfurter's retirement, the conservative bloc almost never won a majority unless joined by Warren, so Clark and Harlan assigned precious few cases.

Eight of the twelve justices on the Burger Court made opinion assignments, including one unlikely assignment by Blackmun, who at the time was fifth in seniority.[9] Douglas assigned more than any other associate until his resignation in 1975; Brennan thereafter made virtually every associate assignment. In less than 1 percent of all cases did Douglas or Brennan dissent along with Burger.

Brennan was the only associate justice to have assigned opinions through the 1989 term of the Rehnquist Court. In the term following his resignation, the bulk of Brennan's assignments were picked up by White and Marshall.[10] Through the 1989 term these two had served a total of fifty-two years while making but six assignments, but in 1990 they almost tripled the number, to a total of sixteen.

The Chief Justices we consider have not attempted to assign themselves a

---

[8]   Quoted in David M. O'Brien, *Storm Center*, 2d ed. (New York: Norton, 1990), p. 287.

[9]   In *Williams v. United States*, 458 U.S. 279 (1982).

[10] But Marshall's opportunity aborted with his retirement at the end of the 1990 term, after only one year as senior associate.

Table 7.1. *Opinion assignment in the Warren Court*

Majority Opinion Writer	Majority Opinion Assigner							
	Warren	Black	Reed	Frank-furter	Doug-las	Clark	Harlan	Total
Warren	170							170
Black	162	14						176
Reed	14	3	10					27
Frankfurter	50	2	4	28				84
Douglas	176	6			2			184
Jackson	4	1	2					7
Burton	29	1	3	3				36
Minton	18	4						22
Clark	140	4	5	20		3		172
Harlan	106	14	3	20	3	4	2	152
Brennan	137	7		6	4	1	2	157
Whittaker	37	2		5				42
Stewart	105	7		11	2	2	1	128
White	75	5			1	1		82
Goldberg	35	1						36
Fortas	40							40
Marshall	21						2	23
Total	1319	71	27	91	12	11	7	1538

large number of cases overall.[11] Warren self-assigned in 12 percent of his opportunities, whereas Burger and Rehnquist each did so about 14 percent of the time. Associate justices did not manifest the same restraint, however. They very much prefer to write themselves. During the Warren Court, Black self-assigned 20 percent of the time, whereas Frankfurter did so at a frequency of 31 percent and Reed at 37 percent. On the Burger Court, Douglas assigned to ally Brennan (26 percent) more often than he assigned to himself (14 percent), whereas Brennan overwhelmingly wrote himself (38 percent) in preference to his ally Marshall (7 percent). Stewart gave himself four of his nine assignments, White retained three of his five, and Marshall and Blackmun self-assigned at their only opportunity. On the Rehnquist Court, Brennan self-assigned 34 percent of the time.

---

[11]   They did, however, assign themselves a disproportionate number of important cases, as we point out later.

Table 7.2. *Opinion assignment in the Burger Court*

Majority Opinion Writer	Burger	Black	Doug-las	Bren-nan	Stew-art	White	Mar-shall	Black-mun	Total
Burger	258								258
Black	17	7							24
Douglas	61	4	11						76
Harlan	12	3	4						19
Brennan	135	3	21	76					235
Stewart	143	2	18	19	4				186
White	238	5	10	23		3			279
Marshall	202	2	7	15	1		1		228
Blackmun	189		3	28				1	221
Powell	209		5	19	1				234
Rehnquist	235		1	3	2	1			242
Stevens	136			18	1				155
Total	1835	26	80	201	9	4	1	1	2157

Equality

An unwritten rule of the Court decrees that each justice should receive an equal share (one-ninth) of the Court's opinions, deviation from which apparently produces disharmony.[12] As Chief Justice Warren phrased it:

I do believe that if [assigning opinions] wasn't done . . . with fairness, it could well lead to gross disruption in the Court. . . . During all the years I was there . . . I did try very hard to see that we had an equal work load.[13]

The equality to which the norm refers is absolute equality, not that which is conditioned on the frequency with which any given justice is a member of the conference vote coalition. Thus, if A is available for assignment in fifty cases and B in twenty-five, and A receives the assignment in ten and B in five, equality would not result even though the frequency with which they were assigned opinions when members of the conference vote coalition was identical: 1 in 5.

[12] Alpheus T. Mason, *Harlan Fiske Stone: Pillar of the Law* (New York: Viking, 1956), pp. 602–603, 793; Nina Totenberg, "Behind the Marble, Beneath the Robes," *New York Times Magazine,* March 16, 1975, pp. 64–65.

[13] Anthony Lewis, "A Talk with Warren on Crime, the Court, the Country," *New York Times Magazine,* October 19, 1969, p. 130.

Table 7.3. *Opinion assignment in the Rehnquist Court, 1986–1990 terms*

Majority Opinion Writer	Majority Opinion Assigner					
	Rehn-quist	Bren-nan	White	Mar-shall	Black-mun	Total
Rehnquist	77					77
Brennan	27	34				61
White	75	6	4			85
Marshall	58	12		1		71
Blackmun	51	14		1		66
Powell	18	2				20
Stevens	59	14	3	1	1	78
O'Connor	73	6		1		80
Scalia	60	5				65
Kennedy	38	6	3	1		48
Souter	7		1			8
Total	543	99	11	5	1	659

We present the extent of overall equality of opinion assignments in Table 7.4, which contains the number of majority opinions – plus plurality judgments[14] – written by the justice holding each seat on the Court for the 1953–1990 terms. The assignments include those by the Chief Justice plus whatever assignments are made by associate justices. The holders of each seat are detailed at the bottom of the table. Thus, in the 1953 term, Douglas, Minton, and Burton wrote six Court opinions, Reed, Jackson, and Clark wrote seven, Frankfurter wrote eight, and Warren and Black wrote nine apiece.

We measure the equality of each term's opinion assignments in two ways: by standard deviation (s.d.) and the coefficient of relative deviation (CRV), both of which increase as equality decreases. The standard deviation measures the typical deviation of a justice from the Court mean. Thus, in the 1953 term, the justices averaged 7.22 assignments and the typical justice located within 1.1 assignments of that average. The CRV divides the standard deviation by the mean in order to control for the total number of opinions in a term. For example,

---

[14] That is, those opinions with which less than a majority concur.

Table 7.4. *Majority opinion writing, 1953–1990 terms*

Term	1[a]	2[b]	3[c]	4[d]	5[e]	6[f]	7[g]	8[h]	9[i]	St.d.[j]	CRV[k]
1953	9	9	8	6	6	7	6	7	7	1.1	.16
1954	12	9	11	11	7	6	6	2	14	2.8	.29
1955	8	9	9	10	9	9	8	9	11	.9	.10
1956	12	11	11	13	11	8	9	11	14	1.7	.16
1957	11	12	10	13	13	8	7	15	15	2.7	.23
1958	10	10	11	12	13	10	10	12	11	1.1	.10
1959	11	11	8	11	12	7	11	10	16	2.4	.22
1960	11	14	12	13	12	12	12	11	13	.84	.07
1961	10	12	4	11	10	5	12	10	11	.83	.08
1962	12	11	12	13	13	13	12	12	12	.63	.05
1963	11	12	14	12	14	11	14	10	13	1.4	.11
1964	10	10	10	10	10	10	9	10	12	.7	.07
1965	9	11	10	12	13	11	12	8	11	1.5	.14
1966	11	11	11	12	11	12	11	9	12	.9	.08
1967	11	13	11	13	13	12	14	13	10	1.2	.10
1968	12	11	8	12	12	10	11	10	13	1.4	.13
1969	11	10	0	13	10	13	12	9	10	1.4	.13
1970	13	14	10	14	11	13	16	10	9	2.2	.18
1971	12	12	12	13	18	18	18	11	15	2.8	.19
1972	19	17	14	16	13	17	16	16	12	2.1	.13
1973	14	16	15	14	15	19	17	17	13	1.8	.11
1974	14	17	13	6	15	16	16	15	11	1.8	.12
1975	17	16	16	9	16	15	16	16	17	.6	.04
1976	15	15	14	13	13	15	14	15	12	1.1	.08
1977	16	15	12	14	14	14	15	14	15	1.1	.07
1978	17	12	13	15	13	16	15	16	13	1.6	.11
1979	15	16	14	14	14	15	15	15	14	.7	.05
1980	13	15	12	11	13	15	16	15	13	1.6	.11
1981	16	16	15	15	15	19	13	17	15	1.8	.10
1982	17	18	15	15	15	19	16	20	16	1.8	.10
1983	18	18	16	16	14	18	17	19	15	1.6	.09
1984	17	13	16	16	13	18	16	17	13	1.8	.12
1985	14	18	14	17	13	19	17	19	15	2.2	.13
1986	17	20	13	16	16	17	18	12	16	2.3	.14
1987	15	7	15	19	16	20	16	16	15	1.8	.11

Table 7.4. (*cont.*)

Term	Seat 1[a]	2[b]	3[c]	4[d]	5[e]	6[f]	7[g]	8[h]	9[i]	St.d.[j]	CR[k]
1988	15	15	14	16	16	17	13	12	14	1.5	.10
1989	15	13	13	13	13	17	17	14	14	1.6	.11
1990	15	13	11	14	8	14	16	11	12	1.5	.12

Notes. [a]Warren (1953-1968), Burger (1969-1985), Rehnquist (1986-   ). [b]Black (1953-1970), Powell (1971-1985), Kennedy (1986-   ). [c]Frankfurter (1953-1961), Goldberg (1962-1964), Fortas (1965-1968), Blackmun (1970-   ). [d]Douglas (1953-1974), Stevens (1975-   ). [e]Minto (1953-1955), Brennan (1956-1989), Souter (1990-   ). [f]Reed (1953-1956), Whittaker (1956-1961), White (1961-   ). Reed wrote 5 opinions in the 1956 term, Whittaker wrote 3. Whittaker wrote 2 opinions in the 1961 term, White wrote 3. [g]Burton (1953-1957), Stewart (1958-1980), O'Connor (1981-   ). [h]Jackson (1953), Harlan (1954-1970), Rehnquist (1971-1985), Scalia (1986-   ). [i]Clark (1953-1966), Marshall (1967-1990). [j]Standard deviation. [k]Coefficient of relative variation. The standard deviation and coefficient of relative variation exclude the following due to incomplete service during a term: Harlan, 1954; Frankfurter, 1961; Whittaker and White, 1961; Seat 3, 1969; Douglas, 1974; Stevens, 1975; an Kennedy, 1987.

the standard deviations of the 1953 and 1977 terms were both 1.1. But the mean in the latter was 14.33, nearly twice the mean in 1953. Thus the typical deviation relative to the mean was much lower in 1977 – that is, a standard deviation of 1 from a mean of 14 is more equal than a standard deviation of 1 from a mean of 7.

CRVs during the 1953-1990 terms range from a high of .29 during the 1954 Warren Court (Harlan's assignments excluded) to a low of .04 during the 1975 term of the Burger Court (Stevens' assignments excluded). Overall, opinion assignments have been slightly more equitably apportioned during the Burger (average CRV = .11) and Rehnquist Courts (CRV = .116) than during the Warren Court (CRV = .13). Nevertheless, substantial equality has prevailed on all three Courts.

Ideology

Despite the overall equality of opinion assignments, the data in Table 7.4 mask the fact that the various Chief Justices dramatically over-assign to those ideologically closest to them and under-assign to those furthest from them. Counterbalancing this behavior is that of senior associates at the other end of the Court's ideological spectrum. To an appreciable extent, equality occurs in spite of the Chief's assignment patterns, not because of them. Examples abound. Perhaps the most egregious violation of the equality norm happened during the 1959 term when Warren assigned twelve opinions to Brennan and Clark, eleven to himself, ten to Black and Douglas, and but one to Frankfurter. During Frankfurter's eight full terms on the Warren Court he averaged less than six assignments from Warren per term, whereas Black and Clark averaged about ten and Douglas almost eleven during that same period. Burger displayed comparable behavior during the 1981 term, when he assigned to himself, White, and Rehnquist sixteen times, while assigning only three to Brennan. Rehnquist also under-assigned to Brennan, who received only four assignments from him in the 1986 term.

The chief justices' CRVs appear in Table 7.5. Burger is the most egalitarian (.21), followed closely by Warren (.22) and then Rehnquist (.23). Although each Chief practices substantial inequality in his own assignments, the average CRVs are more equal than those that Elliot Slotnick compiled for the Taft (.32), Hughes (.35), Stone (.39) and Vinson (.35) Courts.[15]

Absent equal distribution, the assigning justice would be expected to assign opinions disproportionately to himself or to the justice whose policy preferences most closely approximated his own, thereby insuring congruence between the assigner's preferences and the contents of the majority opinion. Indeed, Burger so behaved, preferring the two justices to whom he was ideologically closest during the 1981 through 1985 terms – Rehnquist and White. They ranked either first, second, or tied for second. At the other extreme, the two justices from whom he most distanced himself – Brennan and Marshall – received the fewest assignments except for O'Connor in 1981, her first term, and Blackmun and Burger himself in 1985. Thus, attitudinally based choices clearly limit the operation of equal assignment.

Two additional factors besides the ideological proclivities of the Chief Justice constrain the equality norm: the assignment practices of the senior associate justices, and the (in)frequency with which each junior associate votes with the senior associate when he is in the majority at the conference vote on the merits. Thus, for example, Brennan, who became the Burger Court's senior associate when Douglas retired in 1975, never once assigned himself the opinion in his eight opportunities prior to becoming senior associate. He did, however, self-assign in three of his thirteen opportunities during the 1975 term. Thereafter, through the end of the Burger Court in the summer of 1986, he self assigned in 71 of 180 cases (39.4 percent). The data do not disclose whether he self-assigned because Burger disfavored him or whether Burger disfavored him because he self-assigned so much, or whether they were simultaneously influenced by each others assignments.

As for availability, Douglas was a member of Burger's majority vote coalition less than 50 percent of the time (in 303 of 613 cases), whereas White was available for a Burger assignment in almost 90 percent of the cases during the first twelve terms of the Burger Court (1,126 of 1,279 occasions).[16] Thus, although ideological distance makes assignment a bit more difficult, it does not preclude achievement of absolute equality, if a Chief Justice is so inclined.

A final factor that may occasionally limit equal assignments is the tendency

---

[15] "Who Speaks for the Court? Majority Opinion Assigments from Taft to Burger," 23 *American Journal of Political Science* 60 (1979). Also see Elliot Slotnick, "The Chief Justices and Self-Assignment of Majority Opinions," 31 *Western Political Quarterly* 219 (1978).

[16] Spaeth, op. cit. fn. 4 supra, p. 301.

Table 7.5. *Chief Justice opinion equalization by term*

Warren		Burger		Rehnquist	
Term	CRV	Term	CRV	Term	CRV
1953	.30	1969	.29	1986	.38
1954	.37	1970	.20	1987	.18
1955	.22	1971	.10	1988	.19
1956	.26	1972	.19	1989	.24
1957	.33	1973	.11	1990	.14
1958	.29	1974	.17		
1959	.41	1975	.10		
1960	.23	1976	.22		
1961	.15	1977	.24		
1962	.12	1978	.27		
1963	.10	1979	.15		
1964	.17	1980	.24		
1965	.14	1981	.35		
1966	.23	1982	.22		
1967	.13	1983	.18		
1968	.14	1984	.23		
		1985	.26		
Average	.22		.21		.23

to give fewer assignments to newcomers. From 1953 through 1990, six of the seven freshman associate justices (Goldberg excluded) who began service from the first day of the October term received fewer assignments than the Court average during their first full term on the Court: Fortas (1965), Marshall (1967), Blackmun (1970), O'Connor (1981), Scalia (1986), and Souter (1990).[17] Fortas

[17] Excluding Chief Justices, six of the nine new appointees during the quarter century between

received the third fewest assignments in the 1965 term and Blackmun the second fewest in the 1970 term, whereas Marshall, O'Connor, Scalia, and Souter all obtained the fewest in their first terms. The six justices averaged more than 2.5 fewer opinions in their first full term than their more senior colleagues.

These behaviors complicate attainment of equality in assignment, and may engender pointed media criticism. Burger, for example, was said to have "generated hostility among the other justices because of the ways he has chosen to assign opinions." He was charged with assigning "a majority opinion when he was in the minority," and that "some justices even believe that . . . [he] has on occasion cast 'phony votes' in conference — voting with the majority so that he can assign the opinion and then dissenting from it when it is finally written."[18] Belieing the accuracy of these statements is Burger's record during his term of office, a record unmatched for equal distribution by any of his five immediate predecessors.[19]

Important cases

Within the goal of equality of assignment, assigners are free – and the Chief Justice is expected – to retain important cases for themselves.[20] This guarantees that the opinion will conform as closely as possible to the Chief's personal policy preferences. Arguably all the Court's cases are important because at least four of the justices have agreed to review and decide the matter. Nonetheless, external indicators may be employed to enable analysts to establish degrees of importance. Citation in constitutional law casebooks is perhaps the most popular. In order to overcome the bias against statutory construction that these materials contain and to provide a more legalistic focus than that of most public law scholars, we employ an alternative measure: a headline on the cover of the issue of the privately printed *Lawyers' Edition* of the *U.S. Reports* in which the text of the case appears.[21]

1965 and 1990 wrote least during their first full term. The three exceptions are Powell, Stevens, and Kennedy, all of whom – not incidentally – were the only ones to take their seats midway through the preceding term.

[18] Totenberg, op. cit. fn. 12 supra, pp. 64–65. Similar assertions may be found in Glen Elsasser and Jack Fuller, "The Hidden Face of the Supreme Court," *Chicago Tribune Magazine*, April 22, 1978, p. 50; and in Bob Woodward and Scott Armstrong, *The Brethren* (New York: Simon and Schuster, 1979), pp. 64–65, 170–171, 178–180, 262–263, 359, 416–423, 435–436.

[19] Spaeth, op. cit. fn. 4 supra, p. 304.

[20] Slotnick, "The Chief Justices and Self-Assignment," op. cit. fn. 15 supra, p. 225. David W. Rohde, "Policy Goals, Strategic Choice and Majority Opinion Assignments in the U.S. Supreme Court," 16 *American Journal of Political Science* 652 (1972), at 656–657.

[21] This decision rule is by no means perfect, but at the least it seems to overcome any bias against statutory construction and provide an appropriately legalistic focus. The editors do not headline cases in every issue of the *Lawyers' Edition*, although as many as eight have appeared in at least one issue. Hence, we assume that headlining is a function of editorial judgment of importance rather than available space.

To determine the operational relevance of self-assignment, we consider the first twelve terms of the Burger Court. Slightly more than 14 percent of the cases were identified as important, of which approximately 64 percent involved constitutional interpretation, whereas the remainder did not. Burger assigned 79.5 percent of these cases, compared with his overall percentage of 84.8. Brennan assigned 18.3 percent, two and a half times his general frequency, whereas Douglas assigned 2.9 percent, half his overall proportion. Burger assigned himself almost a quarter of his important cases (59 of 252), Brennan did so in almost 40 percent of his (22 of 58), whereas Douglas did not self-assign in any of his six important cases.[22] Burger's ratio is only 1.4 percent different from the average amassed by the chief justices from Taft through the first five terms of the Burger Court.[23]

In the most recent study, Davis, using the same definition of importance as ours, found that Rehnquist, during his first three terms as Chief Justice, assigned himself the same percentage of these cases as Burger did.[24] But unlike Burger, who assigned important cases to his colleagues with frequencies ranging from 16.7 percent to 0 percent (with an overall average of 10.9),[25] Rehnquist assigned to his ideological colleague White one of every three such cases, while retaining only one in four for himself. He averaged one in eight for the associate justices overall.[26]

Issue specialization. Another consideration that affects opinion assignments is the disproportionate assignment of certain types of cases to specific justices. Unlike self-assignment in important cases, issue specialization does not characterize the assignment patterns of all Chief Justices. Palmer reports that Hughes, Stone, and Vinson did not allow it.[27] But it apparently did occur on the Warren and Burger Courts.

Issue specialization seems to serve three important purposes. First, given the Court's work load, the division of labor that specialization allows may increase the Court's productivity. Some areas of the law are complex – for example, tax, energy, transportation – and efficiency may warrant assignment of the Court's opinions to specialists. Second, certain justices may prefer to write on certain subjects. Third, specialization may facilitate the development of judicial expertise, which enhances the credibility and legitimacy of the Court's decisions.[28]

Despite claims that Warren expressly disapproved of issue specialization,[29]

---

[22] Spaeth, op. cit. fn. 4 supra, pp. 303–304
[23] Slotnick, "Who Speaks for the Court," op. cit. fn. 15 supra, p. 69.
[24] Davis, op. cit. fn. 4 supra.
[25] During his first twelve terms (1969–1980).
[26] Davis, op. cit. fn. 4 supra, p. 70.
[27] Op. cit. fn. 4 supra p. 125.
[28] Burton Atkins, "Opinion Assignment on the United States Courts of Appeal: The Question of Issue Specialization," 27 *Western Political Quarterly* 409 (1974).
[29] David M. O'Brien, *Storm Center* (New York: Norton, 1986), p. 246.

analysis of the Warren Court's civil liberties decisions shows that in approximately two-thirds of the narrowly defined issues into which civil liberties were divided, a particular justice wrote the Court's opinion significantly more frequently than any of his colleagues. The specialists, moreover, were justices who attitudinally positioned themselves close to Warren, who made most of the assignments.[30] For example, Brennan specialized in the First Amendment, right to counsel, and discovery and inspection; Douglas in courts martial and indigents. A more inclusive study of the 1969–1983 terms of the Burger Court produced similar results. In 63 percent of the civil liberties issues and in 62 percent of those that did not concern civil liberties, at least one justice wrote sufficiently frequently to qualify as a specialist. As on the Warren Court, the Burger Court's civil liberties specialists are the ideological allies of the chief justice – for example, Rehnquist in double jeopardy and confrontation, Powell in commercial speech and attorneys' fees, White in jury trial and reapportionment. In areas of arguably less substantive importance, justices attitudinally distant from Burger – Douglas (judicial review of agency action), Brennan (arbitration and priority of federal fiscal claims), and Marshall (state jurisdiction over Indians and non-governmental tort liability) – emerged as specialists.[31]

This research seems to indicate that the achievement of equal distribution does not preclude opinion assigners from realizing their personal policy preferences. The Chief Justice can over-assign to ideological clones, knowing that his opponents will get more than their share of cases assigned by associate justices. Further, by disproportionately retaining the important cases, opinion assigners insure maximum congruence between enunciated policy and their personal preferences. The creation of issue specialists in the highly salient area of civil liberties who are attitudinally aligned with the Chief Justice further enables him to correlate equal distribution and the realization of his own policy preferences. On the other hand, the appearance of specialists in only two-thirds of the issues into which the Court's decisions are apportioned suggests that division of labor, the desire of a justice to write on certain subjects, and the development of expertise sufficient to enhance the credibility and legitimacy of the Court's decisions are secondary objectives, at best.[32]

---

[30]   Saul Brenner, "Issue Specialization as a Variable in Opinion Assignment on the U.S. Supreme Court," 46 *Journal of Politics* 1217 (1984).

[31]   Saul Brenner and Harold J. Spaeth, "Issue Specialization in Majority Opinion Assignment on the Burger Court," 39 *Western Political Quarterly* 520 (1986); reprinted in Spaeth and Brenner, op. cit. fn. 6 supra.

[32]   Two other factors appear to have had some limited impact on opinion assignment: perceived competence and the time justices take to write majority opinions. A study of competence found that of the thirty-two justices who served between 1921 and 1967, those whom law professors considered less competent received fewer assignments. Saul Brenner, "Is Competence Related to Majority Opinion Assignment on the United States Supreme Court?" 15 *Capital University Law Review* 35 (1985). With regard to time, an analysis of the Vinson Court's opinion assigners showed them to be partial to those who wrote most quickly. Saul Brenner and Jan Palmer, "The

OPINION ASSIGNMENTS AND OPINION COALITIONS

The Court delivers an opinion only if a majority agrees on an explanation for its decision. If less than a majority do so, then the plurality view becomes a "judgment" of the Court, not an "opinion," and lacks precedential value. For example, in *Houchins v. KQED*,[33] four of the seven participating justices voted to reverse an appellate court ruling granting the press expansive rights to investigate prison conditions. The three-member plurality declared that the press has no special access to prisons. The three dissenters argued that the media have such entrance under the First Amendment. Justice Stewart's special concurrence regarded the lower court's ruling to be too broad, but nevertheless upheld limited access. Hence, the plurality's view of no special access lacked a majority and has no authoritative bearing on future decisions. Because a majority opinion usually depends on the approval of the marginal (usually fifth) justice, he or she receives a greater share of assignments.[34]

Thus, David Danelski, in an often reprinted but never published paper, asserts that "the selection of the Court's spokesman may be instrumental in . . . holding the . . . majority together in a close case," and that the assignment of the opinion to the justice "whose views are closest to the dissenters" might increase the size of the majority."[35] Unfortunately, both assertions are false.

Concerning the former assertion, inspection of the minimum winning coalitions on the Warren Court shows that though the marginal justice – the one attitudinally closest to the dissenters on the narrowly based cumulative scale to which the case pertains – was hugely advantaged in the number of assignments received (more than twice the random expectation), his selection did not increase the probability that the coalition would survive.[36] Neither self-assignment nor assignment to the justice in the middle of the conference coalition enhanced its preservation. As the authors concluded, "Apparently, whenever a justice decided to leave the original coalition, he did so, and the fact that he had been assigned to author the majority opinion did not forestall his defection."[37]

---

time taken to write majority opinions as a determinant of opinion assignments," 72 *Judicature* 179 (1988). Also see Palmer, *op. cit.* fn. 4 *supra*, pp. 132–149.

[33]   438 U.S. 1 (1978).

[34]   David W. Rohde and Harold J. Spaeth, *Supreme Court Decision Making* (San Francisco: W.H. Freeman, 1976), ch. 8.

[35]   "The Influence of the Chief Justice in the Decisional Process," in Sheldon Goldman and Austin Sarat, eds., *American Court Systems* (San Francisco: W.H. Freeman, 1978), p. 514; in Walter F. Murphy and C. Herman Pritchett, eds., *Courts, Judges, & Politics*, 4th ed. (New York: Random House, 1986), p. 574. Murphy and Howard, op. cit. fn. 5 supra, essentially make the same allegations.

[36]   Saul Brenner and Harold J. Spaeth, "Majority Opinion Assignments and the Maintenance of the Original Coalition on the Warren Court," 32 *American Journal of Political Science* 72 (1988); reprinted in Spaeth and Brenner, op. cit. fn. 6 supra. This study used conference vote data from the justices' docket books to determine the membership of the original (conference) vote coalition.

[37]   Ibid. p. 80.

Concerning the latter of Danelski's assertions, – assignment so as to increase the size of either the final vote or the final opinion coalition – analysis of the Warren Court shows that the marginal justice's authorship of the Court's opinion does not increase the size of either coalition.[38]

If the justice attitudinally closest to the dissenters cannot increase the size of minimum winning decisional coalitions when assigned to write the opinion of the Court, why then is this justice so disproportionately favored with assignments?

First, the probability that the majority opinion will have to be reassigned to another justice because the conference vote coalition breaks up is lessened. Breakups occur when the vote coalition shifts from affirm to reverse, or the converse. The reassignment of the opinion obviously takes time and slows the Court's productive process.[39] Research, however, has shown that once assigned the Court's opinion, the marginal member of the vote coalition retains it, regardless of whether or not the coalition breaks up. But when non-marginal members receive the assignment, they are much less likely to retain it when the coalition breaks up.[40]

Other considerations that may cause assigners to favor the marginal justice include an opinion of moderate content that should help retain support for the Court's position in future cases. Tension may also be reduced between the majority and minority.[41] And because the marginal justice is attitudinally closer to the minority than any other member of the majority, assigning the opinion to this justice may keep the original coalition intact.

One may ask why assignment to the marginal justice does not attract those who dissented at the conference vote. The answer seems to be that the main task of assignees, whether they are marginal or not, is to write an opinion that garners the votes of the other members of the original vote coalition. This job is especially important in the minimum winning situation. It does not make sense to attempt to satisfy justices who voted the other way at the final conference vote when such attempts might cause one or more of the original majority to refuse to join the Court's opinion.[42]

OPINION COALITIONS

In arriving at their decisions, the individual justices are free actors in two separate senses. First, they may vote as they see fit: either as a member of the majority

---

[38] Saul Brenner, Timothy M. Hagle, and Harold J. Spaeth, "Increasing the Size of Minimum Winning Coalitions on the Warren Court," 23 *Polity* 309 (1990). This study also utilized the justices' docket books to ascertain membership in the final conference vote coalition.

[39] Saul Brenner, "Reassigning the Majority Opinion on the United States Supreme Court," 11 *Justice System Journal* 186 (1986).

[40] Brenner and Spaeth, op. cit. fn. 36 supra, p. 78.

[41] William P. McLauchlan, "Ideology and Conflict in Supreme Court Opinion Assignment, 1946–1962," 25 *Western Political Quarterly* 16 (1972), at 26.

[42] Brenner, Hagle, and Spaeth, op. cit. fn. 38 *supra*, p. 318.

vote coalition or in dissent. Second, except for the opinion of the Court, the justices may write such opinions as they desire to explain their individual votes. As a consequence, a justice may be a member of a particular voting coalition, but not a member of the opinion coalition that supports that vote. For example, a justice may specially concur by agreeing with the disposition the Court makes of the case, while disagreeing with the reasons the majority gives for its disposition. We preface our discussion of opinion coalitions with a systematic listing of the nine voting and opinion options available to the justices.

Voting and opinion options

1. A justice may be assigned to write the opinion of the Court. As noted in our discussion of opinion assignment, a justice does not freely decide to write the opinion of the Court, with the possible exception of the assigning justice.

2. A justice who is assigned to write the opinion of the Court fails to get a majority of the participating justices to agree with the contents of the opinion. In this case, the justice's opinion becomes a "judgment of the Court." Because only a plurality instead of a majority of the participating justices join it, the opinion – unlike an opinion of the Court – lacks precedential value.

3. A justice may be a voiceless member of the majority (or plurality) vote and opinion coalitions – that is, the justice writes no opinion, but simply agrees with the opinion or judgment of the Court.

4. A justice may write an opinion notwithstanding membership in the majority or plurality opinion coalition. Such an opinion is a regular concurrence. It manifests itself only by the writing of an opinion or the joining of one written by another justice. Absent the writing or joining of such an opinion, the justice has exercised option 3, willy-nilly.

5. A justice may agree with the disposition made by the majority or plurality, but disagree with the reasons contained in its opinion. Unlike a regular concurrence, this option may occur with or without opinion. At least one justice must cast such a special concurrence to produce a judgment of the Court.

6. A justice may dissent. Like a special concurrence, a dissent may be coupled with an opinion. A dissent indicates that the justice in question disagrees with the disposition that the majority has made of the case.

7. A justice may dissent from a denial or a dismissal of certiorari, or from the summary affirmation of an appeal. Such votes, plus any accompanying opinion that a justice may see fit to write, only pertain to cases that the Court refuses to hear and decide.

8. A justice may render a jurisdictional dissent, which, like the preceding action, may or may not be accompanied with an opinion. This type of dissent disagrees with the Court's asertion of jurisdiction or with the Court's failure to afford the parties time for oral argument.

9. A justice may refuse to participate in a case. The justices most commonly recuse themselves because of illness. Other reasons, which the justices exercise at their own discretion, include previous involvement in a case or with a party to it. Thus, justices promoted from a lower court will not participate in cases in which they previously voted. Justices will typically recuse themselves if they hold stock in a company before the Court. Because he served as Solicitor General before he was appointed to the Court, Justice Thurgood Marshall recused himself from all of the cases in which his office had represented the United States. For this and perhaps other reasons, he failed to participate in 98 of the 171 docketed cases that were formally decided during the 1967 term (57.3 percent).

The frequency with which the justices engaged in these behaviors during the first five terms of the Rehnquist Court (1986–1990) is shown in Table 7.6. The unit of analysis in this table is case citation, and cited cases are defined as those on the Court's appellate docket that were formally decided – that is, following oral argument (N = 695).[43]

The table shows that silent membership in the majority vote coalition is by far the most common action of each of the justices. Brennan, Marshall, and Stevens so behaved slightly less than half the time, in contrast to Souter, Powell, Rehnquist, and White, whose averages exceed two out of three votes. Marshall and Brennan, the Court's liberals, lead in proportion of dissents, with 33.2 and 31.6, followed by Stevens (27.2) and Blackmun (23.1). At the other extreme, Souter, Kennedy, Powell, and White do so with frequencies of 1 vote in 13, 10, 10, and 8, respectively.

Although commentators now accept the propriety of judicial dissent,[44] many disapprove of concurrences as unnecessary nitpicking.[45] Most culpable from this point of view is Scalia, 11.4 percent of whose votes are special concurrences. Blackmun and Stevens follow with 8.2 and 7.3 percent, respectively. Powell, Scalia, and O'Connor lead in proportion of regular concurrences, with 5.8, 4.9, and 4.9 percent, respectively. The Chief Justice set the best example, casting only 1.4 and 2.0 percent of his votes as regular and special concurrences.

The slight deviations from the flat distribution of opinions of the Court results

---

[43] We exclude cases decided by a tied vote, and decrees of the Court, even though they were orally argued. Tied votes almost never contain any kind of opinion, and decrees typically ratify, automatically and without any justice authoring a special opinion, the report of the special master whom the justices chose to hear the dispute. Because dissents from denials of certiorari or the summary affirmation of an appeal can only occur in cases the Court refuses to hear, none appears in Table 7.6 because it contains only those options the justices exercise in formally decided cases – those that are orally argued.

[44] Thomas G. Walker, Lee Epstein, and William Dixon, "On the Mysterious Demise of Consensual Norms in the United States Supreme Court," 50 *Journal of Politics* 361 (1988).

[45] For example, Robert W. Bennett, "A dissent on dissent," 74 *Judicature* (1991), 255–260.

Table 7.6. *Behavioral options of Rehnquist Court justices,
1986–1990 terms*

Justice	Behavior							
	1[a]	2[b]	3[c]	4[d]	5[e]	6[f]	7[g]	8[h]
Blackmun	10.1	0	54.4	3.0	8.2	23.1	.4	0.6
Brennan	10.1	.5	47.1	3.3	6.4	31.6	.2	0.7
Kennedy	9.7	.2	60.7	4.3	3.3	10.1	0	11.8
Marshall	10.1	.4	47.9	1.9	5.9	33.2	.3	0.3
O'Connor	10.8	.7	60.6	4.9	5.8	16.0	0	1.3
Powell	12.2	.6	68.9	5.8	1.9	10.3	0	0.6
Rehnquist	10.9	.3	68.1	1.4	2.0	16.8	0	0.4
Scalia	8.9	.4	57.6	4.9	11.4	15.4	.1	1.3
Souter	6.0	.9	72.4	1.7	2.6	7.8	0	8.6
Stevens	10.6	.6	49.5	3.7	7.3	27.2	.5	0.6
White	11.7	.6	66.9	3.3	4.5	12.8	.0	0.3

Notes. [a]Opinion of the Court. [b]Judgment of the Court. [c]Member, majority
or plurality coalition. [d]Regular concurrence. [e]Special concurrence.
[f]Dissent. [g]Jurisdictional dissent. [h]Nonparticipation.

from the variant frequency with which the individual justices engaged in other
kinds of behavior. Judgments of the Court and jurisdictional dissents rarely
occurred, as was also true of recusals, except for Kennedy. His high percentage
(11.8) results because he joined the Court midway through the 1987 term, which
precluded his participation in cases argued prior to his seating. All of the other
justices, save the next junior (Souter, Scalia, and O'Connor), recused themselves
less than 1 percent of the time. Given the ages of the justices, this is a rather
remarkable participation rate overall.

Patterns of interagreement

Although the frequency with which the justices locate in the majority vote
coalition, and the proportion of votes cast in dissent, provide possible bases for
identifying who agrees and disagrees with whom, the extent to which individual
justices join one another in their special opinions (regular and special concurrences, and jurisdictional and regular dissents) comprises a much richer source
of information about judicial relationships. We limit our focus to these opinions
because, as noted, the justices are completely free actors insofar as concurrences
and dissents are concerned. That is, no justice can be forced to or prevented
from concurring or dissenting; nor can any justice be required to or prevented
from joining a special opinion of another justice. This, of course, is not true of

opinions and judgments of the Court. To the extent that the justices value the opportunity to write the Court's opinion, the opinion assigner possesses something akin to a coercive instrument as do other members of the opinion coalition, especially when the coalition is minimum winning in size: One or more may withdraw from the coalition, thus precluding formation of a majority opinion.[46]

Thus, the writing and joining of special opinions bespeak an ability to persuade or convince another of the correctness of one's position in that case. Such an effect occurs without the use of coercion, authority, or political control. As such, it constitutes what Webster defines as "influence,"[47] and as such is distinct from the related construct of power, which does involve the use of coercion, authority, or control.[48] Note also that the writing and joining of special opinions occur in a context in which side payments are not made. That is, justices do not do something to induce others to do something they would not otherwise do. The fact that a justice may be motivated to write a special opinion for reasons other than to exert influence – to curry favor with a segment of the public, to enhance his reputation, or to express disapproval of certain conduct – does not gainsay the absence of side payments. We view influence as an effect, not as a motivation. As a result, concurrences and dissents reflect the strongly held policy views of their authors. And because those who join such opinions may be said to be "persuaded" of the correctness of the positions they espouse, one may – given our operationalization – easily infer who is "influencing" whom.

In what follows, we focus on the patterns of interagreement that occur in the justices' special opinions as a form of "influence." Such a focus warrants comparing each justice with his colleagues. We begin by paralleling the frequency with which each justice joins another's special opinion and the frequency with which other justices join the authoring justice's opinions.

Table 7.7 presents these data for the first four terms of the Rehnquist Court. The rows represent the frequency with which the named justice functioned as a joinee – a joiner of the opinions of another justice. The columns represent the

[46] We could have divided each justice's special opinions between concurrences and dissents and analyzed them separately. We chose not to do so because no theoretical reasons support one rather than the other as a vehicle for the expression of personal policy preferences. Suffice it to say that most of the justices write dissents more often than they do concurrences. The justices' proportion of dissents to concurrences during the first four terms of the Rehnquist Court is as follows: Marshall 89.7, Rehnquist 80.6, Brennan 62.8, Stevens 59.7, Blackmun 59.6, White 54.7, Powell 50.0, O'Connor 48.1, Kennedy 41.0, and Scalia 34.5. Given the disfavor with which many judges and commentators view concurrences, and for whatever it may be worth, the three individuals whom Reagan chose as associate justices may be characterized as the Court's nitpickers.

[47] *Webster's Seventh New Collegiate Dictionary* (Spring field, MA: G. & C. Merriam, 1972), p. 433.

[48] See Michael F. Altfeld and Harold J. Spaeth, "Measuring Influence on the U.S. Supreme Court," 24 *Jurimetrics Journal* (1984), 236–247; and Bernard Schwartz, *Super Chief: Earl Warren and His Supreme Court* (New York: New York University Press, 1983), pp. 302–303, 352–353, 381, 437, 719–720.

Table 7.7. *Interagreement in special opinions, 1986–1989 terms*

Justice	Mar-shall	Bren-nan	Ste-vens	Black-mun	O'Con-nor	White	Pow-ell	Ken-nedy	Rehn-quist	Scalia
Marshall	**58**	92	38	39	5	5	2	1	0	7
Brennan	46	**113**	33	40	6	6	3	1	0	6
Stevens	16	27	**149**	12	8	4	1	0	3	5
Blackmun	18	43	27	**94**	7	5	1	2	3	5
O'Connor	1	2	9	7	**77**	16	9	11	12	21
White	0	2	9	0	2	**75**	1	4	9	11
Powell	0	0	0	2	5	3	**18**	-	1	1
Kennedy	0	1	2	0	7	3	-	**39**	2	11
Rehnquist	0	0	8	1	19	22	5	10	**31**	24
Scalia	0	0	7	1	18	9	2	16	10	**116**
joiners/ opinion	1.40	1.48	.89	1.09	1.0	.97	1.33	1.15	1.29	.78

frequency with which the various justices joined the opinions of the named justice. Thus, Marshall joined Brennan's special opinions 92 times, Blackmun's 39 times, and Rehnquist not at all. Conversely, Brennan joined Marshall only half as frequently (46 times) as Marshall joined him. Blackmun joined Marshall only 18 times, whereas Rehnquist reciprocated Marshall's failure to join him. The bold-faced entry along the principal diagonal specifies the number of special opinions each justice wrote during the first four terms of the Rehnquist Court. The figure at the foot of each column indicates the number of joiners each justice got per authored special opinion. This number can theoretically range from 0.0 to 4.0. The former indicates a situation where no one ever joined the authoring justice, whereas a range exceeding 4.0 is not possible because beyond that point a special opinion becomes an opinion of the Court.

Table 7.7 presents several interesting results. First, not much interagreement occurs, and that which does tends to be among like-minded individuals. For example, the liberal Marshall joined his fellow liberal, Brennan, almost as frequently as he did the rest of the justices combined. Neither of them either joined or was joined by Rehnquist. They agreed with Kennedy once, and he reciprocated only by joining an opinion of Brennan's. Thus, it superficially appears as though the justices exert little influence on one another, except for those with whom they most commonly vote. And bloc voting arguably results from likemindedness, not influence.

The ratio of joiners per opinion appears independent of the frequency with which a justice writes. Thus, though the two most prolific justices, Stevens (149)

and Scalia (116) obtained the lowest proportion of joiners per opinion – .
.78, respectively, – the third most prolific, Brennan, garnered the high
portion, 1.48. Brennan was followed by Marshall, who wrote less fre
than any member of the Court except the two part time members, Powell and
Kennedy, and the Chief Justice. But Brennan and Marshall join one another in
a much greater proportion of their opinions than is true of any of the other pairs:
Marshall, 92 of Brennan's 113 (81.4 percent), and Brennan, 46 of Marshall's
58 (79.3 percent). By contrast, five justices never concurred in a single one of
Marshall's special opinions. Thus, whatever "influence" either of these justices
exerted did not extend to the Court's conservative majority. Overall, the justices
appear to join the opinions of those who join them, and this appears to mean
the two liberals, plus the moderate Stevens and Blackmun, versus the conservative majority. This further substantiates the fact that the attitudinal attribute,
likemindedness, explains interagreement, not the social characteristic, influence.

Among the pairs who interacted a dozen or more times, only White-O'Connor
and Kennedy-Rehnquist display a one-sided relationship by markedly exceeding
a 2:1 ratio. O'Connor joined eight times as many opinions of White (16) as he
did of hers (2), whereas Rehnquist joined five times as many of Kennedy's
opinions (10), as he did of Rehnquist's (2).

The relative infrequency of special opinion coalitions, as revealed by the first
four terms of the Rehnquist Court, suggests that evidence of "influence" will
only be manifest – if at all – over an extended period of time. Hence, we
separately consider the full span of the Warren and Burger Courts, sixteen terms
and seventeen terms, respectively.[49] We define a special opinion as we did in
Table 7.7: an author's specification of the reason for his or her vote. A mere
citation of a precedent or a simple statement that the author supports the rationale of the court below suffices. Joint authorship counts as an opinion for each
author. (No jointly written opinions occurred in any formally decided Rehnquist
Court case during its first four terms.) Where a justice states that the opinion
governs an additional case or cases, it is multiply counted.[50] The unit of analysis
is the same as before: orally argued cases by citation, excluding tied votes and
decrees.[51]

The foregoing rules produce 1,821 Warren Court cases that contain 2,251
special opinions (1,475 dissents and 776 concurrences), an average of 1.24
special opinions per case. For the Burger Court, there are 2,440 cases that contain
3,698 special opinions (2,191 dissents, 1,507 concurrences), an average of 1.52

---

[49] Much of the data that follow initially appeared in Harold J. Spaeth and Michael F. Altfeld,
"Influence Relationships within the Supreme Court: A Comparison of the Warren and Burger
Courts," 38 *Western Political Quarterly* (1985) 70.

[50] For example, Brennan's and Marshall's opinions in *Mobile v. Bolden*, 446 U.S. 55 (1980), also
apply to *Williams v. Brown*, 446 U.S. 236 (1980).

[51] A small handful of Warren and Burger Court cases in which one or more of the justices concurred
in some of the majority's holdings and dissented in others were counted compatibly with the
smallest whole number necessary to account for the variant behavior of the justices involved.

per case. For the first four terms of the Rehnquist Court, there are 568 cases with 770 special opinions (434 dissents, 336 concurrences), an average of 1.36 per case. Although the frequency of special opinions has remained relatively stable across the three Courts, it is interesting to note that there is a steady increase from one Court to the next in the proportion of concurring special opinions at the expense of dissents – from 34.5 to 40.8 to 43.6. Is there something about judicial conservatives that causes them to haggle about the details of opinions that support conservatively decided outcomes?

Who "influences" whom?

Previous efforts to measure influence have indicated that the construct is best captured by focusing on the behavior of particularized individuals.[52] Because influence may be one-sided or mutual, a measure that centers on pairs of justices needs to be formulated. Accordingly, we consider the number of times each justice joins a given author's special opinions as a percentage of the number of opportunities that the justice has to join. Thus, if A joins B in 10 of 20 opportunities, while C joins B in 15 of 45, A's ratio is .5 and C's is .33. The use of opportunities automatically corrects for justices who were not on the Court for the full period under analysis and also for recusals by sitting justices. In order to assess the mutuality of the pairwise relationship, we calculate the number of times B joined each colleague's special opinions as a percentage of B's opportunities to do so. Assume B joined A 45 percent of the time and joined C 10 percent of the time. We would characterize the A-B relationship as mutual and that of B-C as one-sided, with C influencing B but not vice-versa.

Tables 7.8 and 7.9 present these data. The columns represent the influencer, the rows the influencee. The empty cells indicate pairs of justices who never served together. The entry at the bottom of each justice's column specifies the average pairwise relationship for each justice: the proportion of the time the other justices who served with the columnar justice joined the author's special opinions.

Several interrelated results emerge from these tables. First, the mean percentage with which any justice joined another barely exceeded 10 percent on the Warren Court, and fell slightly below it on the Burger Court. Second, approximately 40 percent of the pairwise relationships on the two Courts fell below 5 percent. Third, although 17 percent of the Warren Court pairs joined in less than 1 percent of their opportunities to do so (34 of 197), compared with 5 percent of the Burger Court's (7 of 134), the Warren Court had a markedly higher percentage of pairs who joined together at least a quarter of the time: 17.8 percent versus 7 percent.

Observe the Chief Justice's behavior. Warren did not join a single one of

[52]   Michael F. Altfeld and Harold J. Spaeth, "Measuring Influence on the U.S. Supreme Court," 24 *Jurimetrics Journal* (1984), 236–247.

Frankfurter's special opinions in cases in which he participated; neither did he join any of Burton's 44 or Reed's 13. These justices reciprocated: None joined Warren. Further, Harlan also failed to join any of Warren's 75, whereas Warren joined 2 of Harlan's 452. Similarly, neither Stewart nor White ever joined Warren, whereas Warren joined 1 of Stewart's 157 and 2 of White's 110. As for Burger, he joined 2 of Marshall's 373 and 6 of Harlan's 76, but neither ever joined him. Burger joined only 7 of Brennan's 521; Brennan reciprocated, joining only 2 of Burger's 243. Douglas similarly: Burger joined 6 of 303, Douglas 2 of 88.

The failure of these justices to join the Chief supports the absence of side payments, to which we alluded. One such payment would involve joining the Chief's special opinions in return for future majority opinion assignments. But eight of Warren's colleagues never joined even one such opinion, and eight of Burger's joined less than 5 percent of his.

The gist of these results is that few pairwise relationships involve a substantial degree of influence, especially on the Burger Court. Indeed, most special opinions appear to be exertions without effects. However, some relationships occur frequently enough to warrant the label, "influential." Unfortunately, no theory exists by which we can derive a threshold level of joining that establishes this condition. Nonetheless, in order to distinguish the few that appear to be such, we employ a modest criterion of one standard deviation above the respective mean of each Court.[53] These pairs are boxed in Tables 7.8 and 7.9.

The dyadic relationships that meet our definition of influential are portrayed in Figures 7.1 and 7.2. The head of the arrows indicates the direction of influence. Combining these figures with Tables 7.8 and 7.9 shows that two justices on the Warren Court and one on the Burger Court neither influence nor are influenced by any other justice: White and Fortas on the Warren Court and Harlan on the Burger Court. Burger influenced no one, but was influenced by Powell, O'Connor, and Rehnquist. Two Warren Court justices – Brennan and Clark — and five Burger Court justices – Stewart, White, Powell, Blackmun, and Stevens – influenced at least one other justice, but are not influenced by any. By comparison, no influenced justice fails to influence at least one other.

Where exertions produced effects that meet our definition of influential, they are largely limited to justices who share the influencer's ideology. The only exceptions are Marshall's influence on Harlan and Stewart during his service on the final two years of the Warren Court, and Stewart's influence on Douglas, Marshall, Brennan, and Rehnquist – plus White's on Brennan and Rehnquist – on the Burger Court. The interagreement of joiners with authors whose policy preferences they generally share evidences the dominance of such preferences in the Court's opinion coalitions, and extends the utility of the attitudinal model

---

[53] Two Warren Court and three Burger Court pairs sufficiently closely approximate this criterion to warrant inclusion: Harlan joining Clark and Frankfurter joining Burton on the Warren Court, and Marshall, Brennan, and Rehnquist joining Stewart on the Burger Court.

Table 7.8. *Dyadic influence matrix, Warren Court*

	Blk	Brn	Bur	Clk	Dou	For	Frk	Gol	Har	Jac	Mar	Min	Ree	Stw	War	Whi	Wht
Black	---	18.2	4.9	11.3	**38.8**	3.3	1.6	9.4	3.5	0	0	5.0	0	11.2	**43.2**	9.1	5.8
Brennan	6.1	---	0	2.4	11.6	3.3	7.9	13.2	1.1		12.5		0	6.2	21.1	5.4	1.4
Burton	1.6	13.3	---	**32.4**	2.1		15.9		**29.0**	**33.3**		**30.0**	**37.5**	0	0		**27.8**
Clark	4.8	0	20.9	---	3.0	13.8	10.1	0	13.4	12.5		10.0	12.9	10.3	7.2	16.9	8.3
Douglas	**44.0**	**33.6**	0	6.3	---	18.6	4.7	20.8	1.5	11.1	**37.5**	15.0	3.2	6.2	**47.0**	4.5	6.9
Fortas	2.3	10.5		7.1	16.1	---			2.1		16.7			1.6	16.7	1.5	
Frankfrtr	3.8	10.3	**24.4**	19.1	3.0		---		**35.2**	22.2		5.0	6.3	11.8	0		18.2
Goldberg	6.9	**29.4**		0	12.5			---	1.7					16.3	**25.0**	0	
Harlan	4.0	8.4	**45.7**	24.6	2.0	6.8	**35.9**	13.7	---		28.6	0	0	**27.0**	0	22.9	20.8
Jackson	7.7	**33.3**		0	0	20.0	20.0			---		20.0	0		[a]		

Justice	Values (reading across the row)
Marshall	3.7 **25.0** 4.5 4.3 1.3 --- 0 0 7.5
Minton	11.1 18.8 **30.8** 4,2 9.8 6.7 **33.3** --- **26.7** --- 0 0
Reed	2.4 0 **36.8** **42.9** 6.0 7.6 6.9 22.2 **36.8** --- --- 0 0
Stewart	5.1 3.2 15.5 3.1 11.7 16.0 23.1 **26.5** **37.5** --- 0 22.7 19.6
Warren	20.5 **38.5** 0 9.3 20.5 23.3 0 **26.4** 0.4 0 **37.5** 10.0 0.6 1.8 2.8
White	4.3 8.3 10.5 0 3.5 3,8 7.7 0 7.7 10.2 0 ---
Whittaker	3.6 0 **38.5** **31.9** 3.5 19.3 **36.3** **36.3** 15.2 7.5 ---
average	8.2 14.2 20.3 16.3 8.2 9.8 12.4 13.8 11.6 16.8 21.3 14.6 8.7 9.7 11.2 9.2 12.4

average = 12.49
std. dev. = 12.27

Notes: columns = influencer
       rows = influencee

a = Warren wrote no opinions in cases in which Jackson participated

Table 7.9. *Dyadic influence matrix, Burger Court*

	Blk	Blm	Brn	Brg	Dou	Har	Mar	Pow	Reh	Stv	Stw	Whi
Black	---	10.5	3.6	13.6	**25.4**	1.3	4.2				2.4	2.9
Blackmun	4.2	---	5.1	10.4	1.1	2.9	5.9	9.9	7.9	2.9	7.2	14.2
Brennan	4.3	12.7	---	1.1	**18.7**	1.3	**47.8**	7.1	1.4	**19.0**	**18.4**	**20.7**
Burger	10.3	16.9	1.4	---	2.0	7.9	0.4	**25.2**	**31.5**	5.1	11.7	15.6
Douglas	**21.9**	2.5	**36.7**	2.3	---	1.4	**25.4**	5.1	3.1		**19.5**	11.1
Harlan	2.9	15.8	0	0	2.8	---	0				17.5	2.9
Marshall	1.6	12.6	**57.8**	0	14.7	5.6	---	5.7	0.9	16.4	**18.3**	14.2
Powell		4.5	3.2	8.2	2.0		1.3	---	9.5	3.9	11.1	4.6
Rehnquist		12.4	0.3	**20.9**	2.5		1.7	**23.1**	---	9.6	**18.0**	**19.1**
Stevens		2.5	11.2	3.5			5.7	3.8	4.3	---	11.4	8.5
Stewart	2,9	2.7	11.1	3.3	5.3	4.0	8.2	12.7	13.2	10.0	---	5.8
White	1.4	5.8	11.6	3.8	1.9	1.3	3.7	4.3	9.2	2.8	3.2	---
average	6.2	9.0	12.9	6.1	7.6	3.2	9.5	10.8	9.0	8.7	12.6	10.9

```
Notes: columns = influencer      average   = 9.07
         rows   = influencee      std. dev. = 9.35
```

to this type of behavior as well. Accordingly, our Rehnquist Court conclusion applies to the Warren and Burger Courts as well: The attitudinal attribute of likemindedness explains interagreement, not influence.

As the figures indicate, both Courts are essentially bifurcated between a liberal and a non-liberal cluster. On the Warren Court, Marshall and the five justices to his left form the liberal grouping, with those to his right comprising the non-liberals. On the Burger Court, Black, Douglas, Brennan, and Marshall appear as liberals, with Powell, Rehnquist, O'Connor, and Burger forming a conservative wing.

Marshall on the Warren Court and Stewart on the Burger Court occupied extremely pivotal positions. Marshall, of course, sat during only two Warren Court terms, and recused himself from a very substantial number of cases, especially during his first term. The fact that his pivotal place did not survive the Warren Court diminishes its importance. If we discount his position, the Warren Court appears to have been completely bifurcated, with no justice exerting influence on both wings. Stewart, though a "moderate" on the Burger Court,[54] influenced three liberal justices (Douglas, Marshall, and Brennan), while simultaneously

[54] Harold J. Spaeth, *Supreme Court Policy Making* (San Francisco: W.H. Freeman, 1979), p. 135.

influencing the conservative Rehnquist. Justice White, a moderate then, if not on the Rehnquist Court, occupied a secondarily pivotal spot, influencing one liberal (Brennan) and one conservative (Rehnquist). Indeed, if we only consider White's behavior after Stewart retired at the end of the 1980 term, we find that he continued to influence Rehnquist, but his link with Brennan fell four points below our threshold. During the Burger Court's last five terms, then, complete bifurcation obtained.

The apparently disproportionate size of the non-liberal cluster on the Warren Court is an artifact of Figure 7.1. No more than six of these nine justices served together – Jackson, Minton, Reed, Burton, Frankfurter, and Clark (1953 term), with Harlan thereafter replacing Jackson. At the end of the 1955 term, this grouping shrunk to five when Brennan replaced Minton. Although Whittaker's replacement of Reed early in the 1956 term and Stewart's succession of Burton at the beginning of the 1958 term maintained its size at five, Whittaker's and Frankfurter's departures early in 1962 reduced the cluster to three. Clark's departure at the end of the 1966 term shrank the number to two: Harlan and Stewart. By contrast, three of the liberals served throughout the Warren Court: Douglas, Black, and the Chief.

Notwithstanding the limited number of influential relationships, only twenty-six of sixty (43 percent) involve mutuality. This finding suggests that to some extent the justices do differ in their ability to persuade others of the correctness of their views, and that joining special opinions is not solely a matter of offering quid pro quos. Also note that on both Courts, mutual relationships predominate among the minority cluster. Thus, fourteen of the twenty-three non-liberal relationships (61 percent) on the Warren Court are mutual, compared with but four of twelve among the liberals. Conversely, on the Burger Court, the liberals are mutual influencers to a greater extent than the other justices. These findings suggest that mutuality may be a function of a group's loss of power (as distinct from influence). As personnel changes shrink a group's domination of the Court's decisions, ideological reinforcement (via agreement in special opinions) occurs.

Within the bifurcated ideological structure of each Court, Warren and Brennan were most influential on the Warren Court. Brennan retained this position in the shrunken Burger Court cluster, along with Douglas. On the non-liberal side of the Warren Court, Clark appeared most influential,[55] with Burton and Harlan pivotal therein. Interestingly, the two justices most influential within their respective clusters were uninfluenced by anyone else: Brennan and Clark. On the Burger Court, Powell was the most influential conservative. He also was uninfluenced by any justice. Brennan, however, was.

---

[55] Notwithstanding the judgment of the President who nominated him, Truman, that he was "such a dumb son of a bitch." Merle Miller, *Plain Speaking* (New York: Berkley, 1973), p. 226.

By contrast, Frankfurter, deemed by many to be highly influential – for example, Wallace Mendelson, *Justices Black and Frankfurter: Conflict on the Court* (Chicago: University of Chicago Press, 1961); G. Edward White, *The American Judicial Tradition* (New York: Oxford University Press, 1976), p. 325 – actually influenced only Harlan.

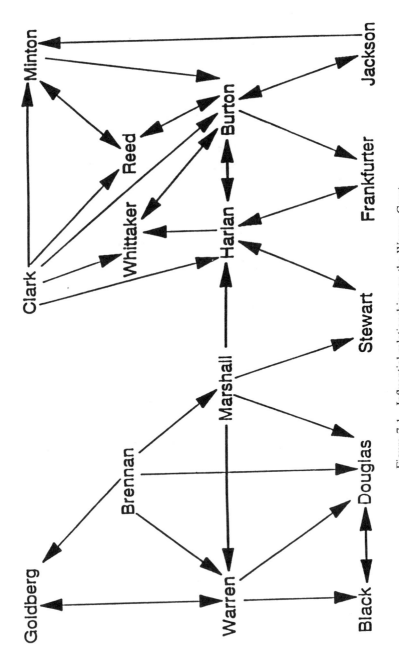

Figure 7.1   Influential relationships on the Warren Court

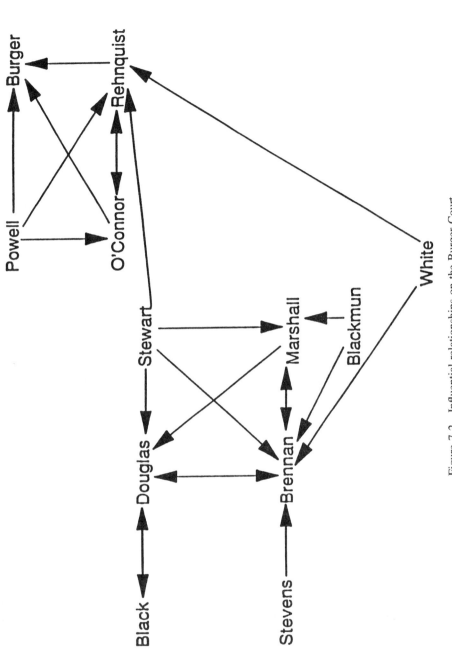

Figure 7.2   Influential relationships on the Burger Court

Finally, seniority (or the lack thereof) appears to have little, if any, effect on influence. This further supports the exclusion of side payments from the operational definition of influence, and further substantiates the dominance of likemindedness. Burton, Clark, and Harlan, highly influential members of the Warren Court, were relatively junior. Burton began the Warren Court sixth in seniority, and ended as fourth. Clark rose from seventh to third, Harlan from junior to fourth. On the liberal side, Marshall was junior and Brennan rose no higher than fifth. Other junior members, by contrast, exerted relatively little influence: Goldberg, Fortas, Stewart, and White – none of whom exceeded the sixth position. As for the most senior members – Black, Reed, Frankfurter, and Douglas – only Reed influenced as many as two of his colleagues. Similar patterns – or lack thereof – characterize the Burger Court.

Of the 37 influential relationships displayed in Figure 7.1, 21 included a senior influencing a colleague junior to himself, 16 the reverse. In Figure 7.2, the 23 relationships divide in the opposite manner: 8 between senior-junior and 15 junior-senior.

THE FAILURE OF COALITION FORMATION

To a markedly greater extent than in earlier Courts, the Burger and Rehnquist justices have failed to produce opinions of the Court to explain their decisions and guide affected publics and lower courts in the resolution of all similar cases. Instead, judgments of the Court have resulted, precluding an authoritative resolution of the controversy at issue. Although the number of judgments is not large – 4.4 percent of the Burger Court's signed opinions and 3.8 percent of those of the Rehnquist Court during its first five terms (1986-1990) – it compares unfavorably with the Warren Court's 2.3 percent.[56]

---

[56]   For analytical purposes. we consider all orally argued signed opinion cases using case citation, rather than docket number, as the unit of analysis. Where one or more of the justices in the decisional coalition only partially supported the Court's decision while dissenting on another part, we count the case compatibly with the smallest whole number necessary to account for the variant behavior. For example, *Regents of the University of California v. Bakke*, 438 U.S. 265 (1978).

We scrupulously define a judgment according to the Court's own language. Though only a small part of the prevailing opinion may comprise the "opinion of the Court," we exclude the case from consideration. Thus, the convoluted statement in *Arizona v. Fulminante*, 113 L Ed 2d 302 (1991), as reported in the *New York Times*, March 27, 1991, p. C21, constitutes an opinion, not a judgment: "JUDGES: WHITE, J., delivered an opinion, Parts I, II, and IV of which are for the Court, and filed a dissenting opinion in Part III. MARSHALL, BLACKMUN AND STEVENS, JJ. joined Parts I, II, III and IV of that opinion; SCALIA, J., joined Parts I and II; and KENNEDY, J., joined parts I and IV. REHNQUIST, C.J., delivered an opinion, Part II of which is for the Court, and filed a dissenting opinion in Parts I and III. O'CONNOR, J., joined Parts I, II and III of that opinion; KENNEDY and SOUTER, JJ., joined Parts I and II; and SCALIA, J., joined Parts II and III. KENNEDY, J., filed an opinion concurring in the judgment." We know of no other case that required so cumbrous a statement to specify an opinion – or even a judgment – of the Court.

The vast majority of these cases concern civil rights and liberties — 85 percent of the Burger Court's and 76 percent of the Rehnquist Court's. These proportions suggest that judgments of the Court occur in cases the justices deem highly salient. Supporting the salience of these cases is the inordinate number of opinions they contain – an average of 4.47 in the Burger Court and 3.72 in the Rehnquist Court.

The evidence shows that the individual justices vote their attitudes – their personal policy preferences – in cases decided by a judgment with at least as much regularity as they do overall. The problem seems to be the unusual amount of conflict that these cases engender – an inability to compromise and resolve differences among the justices' ideal points. An appropriate focus, therefore, from which to analyze these cases is conflict-of-interest theory.[57] Although we do not formally apply the theory here, our focus on the three key actors who, given the Court's rule structures, bear most responsibility for judgments, implicitly rests on it.

These three actors are those who specially concur, the justice assigned to write the opinion of the Court, and the justice who made the assignment. Failure to form a majority opinion coalition may result because the policy preferences of one or more of the members of the majority vote coalition are insufficiently satisfied. Conversely, the fault may lie with the opinion assignee who fails to bargain effectively because he gives primacy to his own policy preferences, or the opinion assigner may have selected an assignee unable to effect the necessary compromises.

Special concurrences

Although the frequency with which the justices specially concurred varies little relative to the number of times each held membership in majority vote coalitions, these data tell us nothing about the cruciality of a justice's special concurrences insofar as the preclusion of a majority opinion coalition is concerned. Clearly, a justice who specially concurs when the Court is split between a four-member plurality and an equal number of dissenters is more crucial to the formation of the majority opinion coalition than a justice who is one of several special concurrers, only one of whom is needed to form a majority opinion coalition.

What we need, therefore, is a measure that will specify how crucial each special concurrence is to the preclusion of a majority opinion. Such a measure may readily be formulated. Simply divide the number of special concurrences into the number of votes needed to form a majority opinion coalition in a given case. Thus, if the plurality opinion coalition contains four votes, and four justices

---

[57]   See Robert Axelrod, *Conflict of Interest* (Chicago: Markham, 1970). David W. Rohde applied conflict-of-interest theory to the formation of majority opinion coalitions in the civil liberties decisions of the Warren Court. See op. cit. fn 20 supra, and "Policy Goals and Opinion Coalitions in the Supreme Court," 16 *American Journal of Political Science* (208) (1972).

Table 7.10. *Culpability index*

Justice	Number of Special Concurrences	Weight
Kennedy	2	1.000
Douglas	6	.845
O'Connor	10	.817
Scalia	8	.770
Black	6	.750
Powell	24	.736
Harlan	8	.729
Stevens	13	.727
Rehnquist	17	.699
White	31	.698
Stewart	16	.649
Burger	22	.647
Blackmun	36	.640
Marshall	26	.587
Brennan	31	.581

dissent, the specially concurring justice receives a score of 1. Similarly, if the plurality has three members, while three others specially concur, only two of their votes are needed. Cruciality thus becomes .67. This measure may range from 1.00 to .20. The latter obtains in a case where a four-member plurality confronts five special concurrers.[58]

Table 7.10 displays the application of this measure to the special concurrences

[58] For example, *Texas v. Brown*, 460 U.S. 730 (1983). Other unanimous decisions, though containing concurrences with slightly greater weight are *United States v. Mandujano*, 425 U.S. 564 (1976), and *McDaniel v. Paty*, 435 U.S. 618 (1978), both decided 8 to 0, with four special concurrences; *Ballew v. Georgia*, 435 U.S. 223 (1978), in which a two-member plurality was arrayed against seven special concurrences written by three different justices; and *Burnham v. California Superior Court*, 109 L Ed 2d 631 (1990), in which a three-member plurality confronted six special concurrences written again by three different justices.

cast in the 121 cases decided by a judgment of the Court during the 1969–1989 terms. Viewed solely from the standpoint of each justice's special concurrences on the preclusion of a majority opinion coalition, the measure may be labeled the culpability index. Except for Kennedy, who cast only two special concurrences, we deem the measure indicative of the extent to which each justice allows his policy preferences to ride roughshod over judicial norms supporting cohesion and the enunciation of binding policy. It is interesting to observe that three of the four most culpable justices are members of the conservative wing of the Rehnquist Court. At the other extreme, the concurrences of the liberal Brennan and Marshall least adversely affected the formation of majority opinion coalitions. As a result, they may be considered the Court's institutional loyalists. Closest to them is the moderate Blackmun.

These findings may be explained in light of the conservative orientation of the Burger and Rehnquist Courts. At least since the seating of O'Connor at the beginning of the 1981 term, conservative justices have constituted a majority. As such, they have less to lose than their opponents when they fail to avail themselves of their built-in majority to articulate binding policy. The liberals, along with a moderate such as Blackmun, find themselves in the majority far less frequently. When they do, they may be more reluctant to eviscerate their victory by unyielding adherence to their individual policy preferences.

Opinion assignees

Although the foregoing results seem to clearly establish responsibility for the Court's failure to produce opinions of the Court, we should also assess the behavior of the other actors in the process – the assignees and their assigners. Assignees may bear responsibility because they may bargain ineffectively or because they may disregard the preferences of one or more of the members of the majority vote coalition. On the other hand, as Table 7.10 shows, the justices vary in the extent to which they are willing to subordinate their views in the interests of institutional loyalty. Hence, the task of a given assignee may correspondingly vary depending on the members in the majority vote coalition. Table 7.11 contains an index that specifies the degree of difficulty assignees faced in their unsuccesful efforts to write an opinion of the Court.

The N in Table 7.11 is slightly reduced from that of Table 7.10 to avoid multiply counting the split vote cases. Each citation comprises only a single assignment. Three of the justices received none: Douglas, Scalia, and Kennedy. In calculating the index we used the culpability scores of Table 7.10. If only a single justice precluded formation of a majority opinion, that justice's culpability score indicates the difficulty the assignee had in arriving at an opinion of the Court. Where several justices specially concurred, we total their scores and divide by their number. The scores of each assignee's cases are totaled and divided by the number of assignments made to that justice.

By this measure, O'Connor faced the greatest difficulty in forming a majority,

Table 7.11. *Assignee difficulty in judgments cases as measured by culpability scores of special concurrers*

Justice	Number of Assignments	Difficulty
O'Connor	5	769.5
Marshall	3	724.0
Blackmun	8	714.4
Brennan	17	705.0
Rehnquist	13	699.6
White	17	696.9
Powell	12	681.3
Stewart	10	679.0
Black	4	676.0
Harlan	1	666.0
Stevens	13	655.9
Burger	11	654.4

followed at some distance by Marshall, Blackmun, and Brennan. At the other extreme, Stevens and Burger had the easiest task. Their failure to do better appears to be less a result of stubborn special concurrers than of their abilities as assignees. And because Burger can only be an assignee when he assigns himself the case, his shortcomings may result from self-selection. Be this as it may, three of the four justices who faced greatest difficulty in authoring an opinion of the Court are the three who were least culpable as special concurrers — Brennan, Marshall, and Blackmun. This suggests that their failure to produce opinions of the Court stems not from a lack of accommodation, but from the intransigence of the special concurrers with whom they had to deal. O'Connor, however, was among the worst offenders in precluding formation of majority opinion coalitions.[59] Her unwillingness to yield when others were assigned to

---

[59] For example, *Wygant v. Jackson Board of Education*, 476 U.S. 267 (1986), an affirmative action case; *Pennsylvania v. Delaware Valley Citizens' Council*, 483 U.S. 711 (1987), the fee-shifting provisions of the Clean Air Act; (*Thompson v. Oklahoma*, 101 L Ed 2d 702 (1988), death penalty for minors; *Florida v. Riley*, 102 L Ed 2d 835 (1989), warrantless helicopter searches; and *Price Waterhouse v. Hopkins*, 104 L Ed 2d 268 (1989), the burden of proof in sexually based employment discrimination.

Table 7.12. *Proportion of majority opinion coalitions achieved by assigners*

Justice	Number of Assignments	Percent of Majority Opinions
White	5	100.0
Marshall	1	100.0
Blackmun	1	100.0
Rehnquist	447	99.5
Douglas	81	97.5
Burger	1910	96.4
Brennan	300	90.7
Stewart	8	87.5
Black	26	76.9

write the opinion of the Court may have exacerbated the intransigence of those who specially concurred when she was assigned the opinion of the Court.

Opinion assigners

To complete the picture, we investigate the performance of opinion assigners. As we observed, the Reports do not tell the reader who made the assignment. Absent access to the justices' docket books, the contents of which have been made available only for the Vinson Court,[60] we have relied on the Court's rules to obtain this information.[61] As Table 7.12 shows, the two Chief justices, followed by Brennan, who was the senior associate for the fifteen terms following Douglas' retirement in 1975, made the vast majority of the assignments. These three justices also assigned all but nine of the cases that resulted in judgments.

Justices Black and Brennan have a success rate far lower than they should have had, given their proportion of assignments. As with the assignees, the reasons for these disproportionalities may have been the relative level of difficulty they faced in the cases with which they had to deal. Analysis, however, shows

---

[60] Palmer, op. cit. fn. 4 supra.
[61] If the Chief Justice is in the majority vote coalition, he assigns the opinion. If not, the senior associate justice who voted with the majority does so.

that none of the assigners' performance correlates with the difficulty he faced due to the size of the decision coalitions with which he had to work. Two other factors, however, appear to explain their lack of success.

First, among the five leading assigners, both Black and Brennan self-assigned a greater proportion of the cases that resulted in judgments: 66.7 and 38.5 percent, respectively. By comparison, Douglas never self-assigned, whereas Burger and Rehnquist did so with frequencies of only 14.7 and 8.3 percent. Thus, Black and Brennan's poor performance as assigners may result from their proclivity for self-assignment.

Second, one may expect an assigner to join the opinion of his assignee. Both Black and Brennan egregiously failed to do so. In the two cases that Black assigned that resulted in judgments that he did not assign to himself, he specially concurred, whereas Brennan did so in 12 of the 16 judgments in which he served as assigner that he did not self-assign. Rehnquist, by contrast, specially concurred in only 1 of the 11 he did not self-assign, whereas Burger did so in 20 of 75.

Although the Court's rule structures badly skew assigner data, they nonetheless clearly show that performance is lessened when assigners either disproportionately self-assign or remove themselves from the plurality opinion coalition by specially concurring.

Accommodation versus jurisprudential purity

The justices appear to divide themselves into three groups in the cases resolved by a judgment of the Court. At one extreme are those who reach their goals only by treading a straight and narrow path. They are unskilled or uninterested in bargaining, stubborn individuals unwilling to compromise. One may consider them self-righteous rectitudinarians, willing to sacrifice the common or institutional good for their individual goals. Included in this group are almost half the justices who served between the 1969 and 1989 terms: O'Connor, Scalia, Black, Powell, Harlan, Stevens, and perhaps Kennedy. Opposite them are the accommodationists – the institutional loyalists – who do not obstruct the formation of an opinion of the Court, even at the cost of their individual policy preferences. Located here are Marshall and Blackmun. Douglas and Brennan display schizoid behavior characteristic of both extremes. Douglas functions very effectively as assignee and assigner, but is among the most dogmatic as a special concurrer. Perhaps his institutional loyalty only extends to cases in which he is charged with an institutional output – as assignee or assigner. When he had no such responsibility, he felt free to act independently, even though it precluded formation of a majority opinion. Brennan, by contrast, displays the least culpability as a special concurrer, but when he had responsibility for an institutional output he seemed to have allowed his personal preferences to dominate the group product. Assertions of his skill as a bargainer[62] are not manifest in these cir-

---

[62]   For example, Woodward and Armstrong, op. cit. fn. 18 supra, pp. 46–47, 77, 215.

cumstances. With the possible exceptions of the Chief Justices, the others –
Stewart and White – fall between the poles of accommodation and jurisprudential
purity. Rehnquist and Burger manifest skill as opinion assigners/assignees, although neither tended to suppress a special concurrence to save an opinion of
the Court.

SUMMARY AND CONCLUSIONS

As far as opinion assignment is concerned, The Warren, Burger, and Rehnquist
Courts have achieved aggregate equality, in spite of the ideologically based
opinion assignments by the Chief Justices and, even more notably, the senior
associates. Bias from the left counterbalances bias from the right, and vice versa.
The various chiefs have further enhanced their ideological goals through retention
of a disproportionate segment of the important cases for themselves.

A modicum of specialization manifests itself, with certain justices – usually
those closest to the opinion assigner – called upon to write the Court's opinions
in certain issue areas. Thus although the Court does achieve substantially equal
workloads, and does allow specialization in aid of efficiency, neither of these
goals impede ideologically based opinion assignments by individual assigners.

Indeed, when we consider the formation of opinion coalitions, our analyses
of the Warren, Burger, and Rehnquist Courts demonstrate that such activity is
substantially absent, notwithstanding the emphasis that the conventional wisdom
gives to judicial bargaining and negotiation. The frequency with which the
justices write special opinions, which barely average a single joiner, bespeaks
a lack of effective interaction, to say nothing of exerting "influence." Interaction
and evidence of influence seems to be a function of like-mindedness – for
example, the Brennans and Marshalls, the Frankfurters and Harlans, and the
O'Connors and Rehnquists.

Given that the Court's ability to arrive at decisions efficiently – the vast
majority of which are supported by an opinion in which a majority of the justices
concur – evidences strong institutional characteristics, nevertheless, as Justice
Powell pointed out, the Court

is perhaps one of the last citadels of jealously preserved individualism. To be sure, we
sit together for the arguments and during the long Friday conferences when votes are
taken. But for the most part, perhaps as much as 90 percent of our total time, we function
as nine small, independent law firms.[63]

More recently, Chief Justice Rehnquist[64] and Justice Scalia have echoed Powell's remarks:

---

[63] Lewis F. Powell, Jr., Report to the Labor Law Section of the American Bar Assn., Atlanta, GA, August 11, 1976.
[64] *The Supreme Court: How It Was, How It Is* (New York: Morrow, 1987), pp. 289–295.

Justice Scalia says one thing has disappointed him . . . the absence of give and take among the Court's members . . . efforts to persuade others to change their views by debating points of disagreement.

. . . he said his own remarks "hardly ever seemed to influence anyone because people did not change their votes in response to my contrary views."

But he added that he now realized that his initial hope for "more of a round-table discussion" would probably not contribute much in practice and "is doomed by the seniority system."[65]

---

[65] "Ruing Fixed Opinions," *New York Times*, February 22, 1988, p. 20; reprinted in Spaeth and Brenner, op. cit. fn. 6 supra, pp. 256–257.

8

The Supreme Court and constitutional democracy

As we pointed out in Chapter 1, the Supreme Court is a major policy-making body. This fact, for the reasons specified, precludes it from being responsive to the vagaries of public opinion. At the other extreme, no one credibly alleges that the Court should lightly upset the actions of the other branches of the federal government or those of the state and local governments. Rather, the Court should lard its policy making with restraint.

The wisdom of such a course rests on several postulates. Judges, especially those holding lifetime appointments, are insulated and remote from the public's wishes and sentiments. Hence, they should defer to publicly accountable decision makers. Deference should also be accorded to state and local governmental officials because of the federal character of the constitutional system. Not all political wisdom emanates from Washington, and the bit that does may occasionally originate elsewhere than from the justices' marble palace. Furthermore, many issues, especially those of an economic, environmental, and technological nature, are increasingly complex. Such matters require expertise for optimal resolution. Judges, consequently, should defer to the experts and not impose their amateurish judgments on the professionally competent. In sum, the Court should not declare unconstitutional congressional or executive action, except in the most blatant and wanton circumstances; the Court should uphold the decisions of state and local officials; and the rules and regulations of the federal bureaucracy – especially those of the federal regulatory commissions – should receive the Court's support.

The normative appeal of judicial restraint does not guarantee its empirical operation, however. Furthermore, there is the opposite persuasion: that the Court has the authority to make policy precisely to curb and check the actions of those government officials who possess the coercive capability of purse and sword. Thus, a posture of judicial activism is preferable to that of restraint. But this persuasion is rarely articulated.[1] It is obviously much more politic for judges to

---

[1] But see Arthur S. Miller, "In Defense of Judicial Activism," in Stephen C. Halpern and Charles M. Lamb, eds., *Supreme Court Activism and Restraint* (Lexington MA: Lexington Books, 1982), pp. 167–199; Christopher Wolfe, *Judicial Activism: Bulwark of Freedom or Precarious Security?* (Pacific Grove, CA: Brooks/Cole, 1990).

affect a posture of restraint rather than activism, just as it is for politicians who oppose the Court's ideological orientation to mouth demands for the seating of "strict constructionists," or whatever the code words for judicial restraint happen to be at a given point in time. But the mere fact that justices may wrap themselves in the mantle of restraint does not mean that they actually practice what they preach.

Indeed, even the most nodding acquaintance with the real world ought to make such a posture suspect. A decision maker may indeed defer to the judgment or action of another. But rational people do not do so blindly. They, along with judges, only defer to the course of action or to the policies of which they approve. Nonetheless, though scientific scholarship to date holds no brief for judicial restraint, in the sense that it actually motivates the justices' votes, not all are convinced. Consider, for example, the pair of following quotations:

An "important constraint on judges' decisions is that they exercise judicial restraint. This expectation . . . asks judges to do what is legally proper rather than what they prefer on ideological grounds. This means that judges must on occasion vote against their political values. Judges' ideological preferences are tempered by what they think they ought to do."[2]

Some have made uncertainty the servant of selected business interests. Others have been guided by more generous considerations. In Mr. Justice Frankfurter's view this "sovereign prerogative of choice" is not for judges. He would resolve all reasonable doubt in favor of the integrity of sister organs of government and the people to whom they must answer. . . . He is wary of judicial attempts to impose Justice on the community; to deprive it of the wisdom that comes from self-inflicted wounds . . . In his view, humanitarian ends are served best in that allocation of function through which the people by a balance of power seek their own destiny.[3]

Readers also ought to be disabused of the notion that restraint correlates with conservatism, and activism with liberalism, notwithstanding their equation by persons who should know better.[4] One highly salient example should suffice: the affirmative action case, *Metro Broadcasting, Inc.* v. *Federal Communications Commission*, in which the Court upheld FCC policies that give preference to

---

[2]   James A. Gibson, "Decision Making in Appellate Courts," in John B. Gates and Charles A. Johnson, eds., *The American Courts* (Washington: Congressional Quarterly, 1990), p. 262.

[3]   Wallace Mendelson, *Justices Black and Frankfurter: Conflict on the Court* (Chicago: University of Chicago Press, 1961), pp. 130–131. Sad to say, but otherwise reputable scholars have accepted as gospel the pseudologue of Frankfurter's restraint. For example, "Frankfurter . . . who would become one of the most ardent and consistent advocates of judicial restraint . . . " Henry J. Abraham, "Line-Drawing between Judicial Activism and Restraint: A Centrist Approach and Analysis," in Halpern and Lamb, op. cit. fn. 1 supra, p. 203. We document the falsity of such assertions later.

[4]   As Gibson notes, "The major difference between activists and restraintists is in their respective processes of decision making, not their liberalism-conservatism per se." Gibson, op. cit. fn. 2 supra, p. 265.

minorities in the licensing of broadcasters.[5] The liberals adopted a restraintist rationale to uphold the affirmative action:

... we are "bound to approach our task with appropriate deference to the Congress, a co-equal branch charged by the Constitution with the power to 'provide for the ... general Welfare" ... and 'to enforce ... the equal protection guarantees of the Fourteenth Amendment." ... We explained that deference was appropriate in light of Congress' institutional competence as the national legislature ...[6]

Further, not only should deference be paid Congress, but also the FCC: "we must pay close attention to the expertise of the Commission and the factfinding of Congress when analyzing the nexus between minority ownership and programming diversity."[7] Why? Because "both Congress and the Commission have concluded that the minority ownership programs are critical means of promoting broadcast diversity. We must give great weight to their joint determination."[8]

The conservative dissenters – O'Connor, Rehnquist, Scalia, and Kennedy – wrapped themselves in the mantle of constitutional activism: "The Court's application of a lessened equal protection standard to congressional actions finds no support in our cases or in the Constitution."[9] They concluded: "The Court has determined ... that Congress and all federal agencies are exempted, to some ill-defined but significant degree, from the Constitution's equal protection requirements. This break with our precedents greatly undermines equal protection guarantees, and permits distinctions among citizens based on race and ethnicity which the Constitution clearly forbids."[10] Justice Kennedy separately observed: "In upholding this preference, the majority exhumes Plessy's deferential approach to racial classifications."[11]

In what follows, we first examine the literature on Supreme Court activism through history, focusing on the influential work of Robert Dahl. We then assess the extent to which the various justices on the Warren, Burger, and Rehnquist Courts exercised judicial restraint in three broad areas where it ought to be most manifest: cases that challenge the decisions of federal regulatory commissions, cases concerning federalism, and those governing access to the federal courts. We pay particular attention to Frankfurter because of his reputation as the judicial restraintist par excellence. We then consider how well the Solicitor General fares, and conclude by assessing the record of the Warren, Burger, and Rehnquist Courts insofar as declarations of unconstitutionality and the overruling of precedent are concerned – actions quintessentially incompatible with the exercise of judicial restraint.

---

[5]   111 L Ed 2d 445 (1990).
[6]   Id. at 462 (citations omitted).
[7]   Id. at 466.
[8]   Id. at 472.
[9]   Id. at 487.
[10]   Id. at 505.
[11]   Id. at 506. The reference is to the separate but equal doctrine formulated in *Plessy v. Ferguson*, 163 U.S. 537 (1896).

DAHL AND HIS CRITICS

Although many have written on the propriety of judicial review, we examine the influence of judicial review instead. To what extent has the Court used its power to check the powers of the legislative branch? The empirical debate over judicial review began with the work of Robert Dahl in 1957.[12] His argument can be divided into several parts. First, he argues that the Court has rarely attempted to overturn the wishes of contemporary lawmaking majorities. In the 167 years between the adoption of the Constitution and Dahl's study, the Court had voided only eighty-six different provisions of federal law. Of those eighty-six, thirty-eight were declared unconstitutional within four years of enactment and thus opposed *contemporary* lawmaking majorities. Twelve of the thirty-eight occurred during the New Deal. Of these twelve, two were "trivial," two were "minor," and one was about to expire anyway. The remaining seven were "unceremoniously swept under the rug"[13] following the Court's historic switches on substantive due process and the interstate commerce clause. Of the twenty-six cases during periods other than the New Deal, Dahl labeled eleven "minor" and fifteen "major." Thus, other than New Deal decisions that were quickly reversed, the Court voided only fifteen major legislative provisions representing contemporary and national lawmaking majorities.

Second, Dahl claims that the Court has been unsuccessful in almost every case when it has tried to thwart contemporary lawmaking majorities. He ascribes this to the fact that on average the President appoints a new justice every twenty-two months. Democratically elected Presidents, representing the national political majority, will no doubt use that power to appoint justices whose views coincide with that majority. Thus, an intransigent Court will soon be replaced through turnover by one more accepting of congressional authority on the issues at hand. Dahl finds that of the fifteen major provisions declared unconstitutional within four years of enactment (excluding the New Deal), ten were reenacted in similar form by later Congresses. Dahl declares, "although the Court seems never to have succeeded in holding out indefinitely, in a very small number of important cases it has delayed the application of policy up to as much as twenty-five years."[14]

Finally, Dahl argues that the few cases in which the Court successfully blocked policy for an extended period were not those in which the Court protected powerless minorities against the tyranny of the majority. The six cases (five that later Congresses did not reenact, plus one New Deal case) questioned whether Congress could limit child labor, require workmen's compensation, or tax certain forms of income. In each case the Court supported vested interests against such

---

[12] Robert Dahl, "Decision-Making in a Democracy: The Supreme Court as National Policy-Maker," 6 *Journal of Public Law* 179 (1957).

[13] Ibid.

[14] Ibid., p. 291.

congressional power. If this is all the Supreme Court can or will do, why then do we allow such an undemocratic institution? Dahl concludes that the role of the Court in our society can be justified by its ability to "confer legitimacy on the fundamental policies of the successful (lawmaking) coalition."[15]

Evaluation of the Court's policy making that merely scrutinizes declarations of unconstitutionality, while totally ignoring the many other policy-making devices that the Court has at its disposal, is obviously simplistic. We do so nonetheless because of the credence such work has received. Fortunately, the attention that Dahl's article has received results more from the debate it has engendered than belief in the accuracy of his findings.

The first significant criticism demonstrated that Dahl's findings did not apply to the period 1958 to 1974.[16] The Warren Court declared unconstitutional much more national legislation than its predecessors. During the period Casper studied, the Court voided thirty-two provisions of federal law in twenty-eight cases. Six occurred within four years of their enactment and thus fell within Dahl's definition of a contemporary lawmaking majority. Only one of the original thirty-two provisions – lowering the voting age to eighteen in state and local elections – was reenacted. With the exception of the eighteen-year-old vote, every one of these provisions was struck because of incompatibility with the Bill of Rights or the Fourteenth Amendment. The Warren Court clearly protected powerless minorities.

Casper also found Dahl's research design defective. Most troublesome was Dahl's exclusion of cases that voided national legislation more than four years after enactment. Dahl simply presumed the lawmaking majority to be out of office. Thus, notwithstanding his ineffably myopic focus, Dahl further excluded more than half the potentially relevant cases from his substantive analysis. Finally, Casper noted the narrowness of Dahl's study, which measured activism only in terms of judicial review of federal legislation. Dahl did not consider cases in which the Court emasculated federal legislation under the guise of statutory interpretation, nor did he consider cases in which the Court struck state or local legislation, no matter how pervasive such legislation may have been: *Roe v. Wade*,[17] for example, which struck down or amended abortion laws in forty-nine of fifty states.

Dahl asserts without evidence that the Court's importance is to legitimize congressional policy. David Adamany critiqued this view, noting that the Court historically had failed to grant legitimacy to administrations when they needed it most: in the period following critical or realigning elections.[18] This point, though, is actually consistent with Dahl's major thesis, for it is the appointment

[15] Ibid., p. 294.
[16] Jonathan Casper, "The Supreme Court and National Policy Making," 70 *American Political Science Review* 50 (1976).
[17] 410 U.S. 113 (1973).
[18] David Adamany, "Legitimacy, Realigning Elections and the Supreme Court," 1973 *Wisconsin Law Review* 790 (1973).

process that supposedly keeps the Court representative. A President elected by a realigning vote should not expect support from the Court until he has replaced several justices.

Richard Funston sought to verify this proposition.[19] Funston deduces from Dahl's work that the Court should not deviate long from the dominant political coalition, except during realigning phases. Overall, he finds the Court only slightly more likely to strike down federal legislation during critical periods, the eight years following the onset of realignment. Yet he finds the Court to be three times more likely to void federal legislation within four years of enactment during critical periods than during non-critical periods. Canon and Ulmer, though, point out that Funston's conclusions result entirely from the Court's clash with the New Deal.[20] Elimination of the New Deal cases shows the Court significantly more likely to strike down legislation in non-critical periods than in any of the other critical periods.

Although the Court's responsiveness to national policy making has been extensively studied, less attention has been paid to the Court's responsiveness to state legislatures. One recent study, though, found that since Reconstruction, state laws struck down by the Supreme Court pertained to the most salient of the issues that had produced contemporary electoral realignments. Moreover, laws that the Court voided tended to be those enacted by state legislatures under partisan control different from the Court.[21] Indeed, one may readily note that the resolution of such convulsing controversies as employment discrimination, affirmative action, and the rights of persons accused and convicted of crime do not depend on the action of either Congress or the state legislatures. As these matters became burning issues in the early 1970s, legislators, as is their wont, avoided them like a social disease. Instead, prevailing polices have been forged by judges and bureaucrats, under the direction of the justices of the U.S. Supreme Court.[22]

Fitting this work into the attitudinal model leads to the following hypotheses: 1) The Supreme Court will generally support policies passed by the dominant lawmaking coalition. 2) Deference or restraint toward the lawmaking coalition will not produce such support, but rather the shared values that the appointment process produces. 3) When the values of the justices conflict with the values

---

[19] Richard Funston, "The Supreme Court and Critical Elections," 69 *American Political Science Review* 795 (1975).

[20] Bradley Canon and S. Sidney Ulmer, "The Supreme Court and Critical Elections: A Dissent," 70 *American Political Science Review* 1215 (1976).

[21] John B. Gates, "Partisan Realignment, Unconstitutional State Policies, and the U.S. Supreme Court, 1837–1964" 31 *American Journal of Political Science* 259 (1987).

[22] See our discussion of these matters in Chapter 3 and in Isabelle Katz Pinzler, "A Major Change in Bias Law for the Workplace," *National Law Journal*, August 21, 1989, pp. S5, S12; Paul Gewirtz, "Discrimination Endgame," *The New Republic*, August 12, 1991, pp. 18–20, 22–23. Also compare *Griggs v. Duke Power Co.*, 401 U.S. 424 (1971), with *Wards Cove Packing Co. v. Atonio*, 104 L Ed 2d 733 (1989).

of the relevant lawmaking coalition, no restraint will be apparent. We examine these hypotheses next.

JUDICIAL ACTIVISM/RESTRAINT: MYTH AND REALITY

By the mid-1960s, empirical analyses had begun to appear that systematically showed that the justices used judicial activism and restraint as a means to cloak their personal policy preferences – that is, that justices who disapproved the action under review justified their opposition in terms of judicial activism, whereas those who supported the action adopted a restraintist posture.[23] These analyses make two assumptions: that justices wedded to either restraint or activism should display such adherence by their votes as well as their opinions, and that their use of activism or restraint will be even-handed, that it will apply across the policy-making board.[24]

The independent regulato₁ ᵧ commissions

Because of their expertise and the highly technical and complex matters that they regulate, judges putatively ought to defer to the decision making of these agencies. One of them, the National Labor Relations Board, regulates labor-management relationships; the others various sorts of business activities – for example, power, transportation, securities. Analysis of the first seven terms of the Warren Court (1953–1959) reveals that a majority of the justices deferred either to the pro- or anti-union decisions of the NLRB, but not to both. Furthermore, those who deferred to pro-union NLRB decisions opposed the pro-business decisions of the other agencies, whereas those who supported anti-union NLRB decisions only supported pro-business agency decisions. What explains these results? The substantive policy preferences of the justices: liberals support anti-buisness and pro-labor decisions; conservative the opposite, as Table 8.1 indicates. The patterns displayed in this table do not occur by chance. The consistently selective pattern of support and non-support clearly indicates that neither judicial restraint nor judicial activism motivates these justices' votes.[25]

Analyses of the Burger and Rehnquist Courts produce similar findings.[26] During the first nine terms of the former (1969–1977), only White and Blackmun

[23]   For example, Harold J. Spaeth, "The Judicial Restraint of Mr. Justice Frankfurter – Myth or Reality," 8 *American Journal of Political Science* (1964) 22.

[24]   We exclude unanimously decided cases from the analyses that follow because they evidence no disagreement among the justices with regard to restraint or activism.

[25]   Of the thirteen justices who sat between the 1953 and 1960 terms, only Burton, Reed, Minton, and Jackson evidenced restraint toward the NLRB by casting more than half their votes in support of the agency's pro- and anti-union decisions. Only Minton and Burton supported pro- and anti-business agency decisions with more than half their votes. See Spaeth, op. cit. fn. 23 supra, pp. 34–36.

[26]   Harold J. Spaeth and Stuart H. Teger, "Activism and Restraint: A Cloak for the Justices' Policy Preferences," in Halpern and Lamb, op. cit. fn. 1 supra, pp. 278–282.

Table 8.1. *Voting behavior of selected justices toward agency action,*
1953–1959 terms

Justice	NLRB Pro-Union			NLRB Anti-Union		
	Pro	Con	% Pro	Pro	Con	% Pro
Frankfurter	2	5	29	7	1	88
Harlan	0	5	0	4	2	67
Whittaker	0	5	0	5	1	83
Black	6	1	86	0	8	0
Douglas	6	1	86	0	8	0
Warren	7	0	100	3	5	38

Justice	Agency Pro-Business			Agency Anti-Business		
	Pro	Con	% Pro	Pro	Con	% Pro
Frankfurter	12	2	86	8	15	35
Harlan	10	2	83	7	11	39
Whittaker	5	2	71	1	10	9
Black	3	11	21	20	1	95
Douglas	2	12	14	16	7	70
Warren	3	11	21	20	3	87

among the twelve justices who served during this time supported agency action regardless of whether it was pro- or anti-business or labor. Unlike behavior on the Warren Court, two justices failed to support the agencies with at least half their votes regardless of the agencies' economic posture: Stewart and Stevens.[27]

[27] When the agency was pro-business, Stewart supported it 64 percent of the time, but only 17 percent of the time when it was anti-business. He voted to uphold pro-union decisions at a frequency of 53 percent, compared with 25 percent of the anti-labor decisions. Combined, he supported economically conservative outcomes 47 percent of the time; economically liberal ones 43 percent of the time. Stevens, who participated in only six agency business decisions and five involving labor, supported a conservative outcome at a frequency of 43 percent, and a liberal outcome at a frequency of only 25 percent.

Table 8.2. *Voting behavior toward agency action, 1981–1989 terms*

Justice	1 Pro Business	2 Anti Business	3 Pro Union	4 Anti Union	% Conser- vative (1+4)	% Lib- eral (2+3)
Marshall	0-11	8-3	8-1	1-4	6	80
Brennan	1-10	8-3	8-1	1-4	13	80
White	6-5	11-0	8-1	1-4	44	95
Burger	8-0	2-5	3-4	2-2	83	36
Blackmun	7-4	7-4	7-2	1-4	50	70
Powell	4-0	1-6	2-6	3-2	78	20
Rehnquist	7-4	3-8	3-6	4-1	69	30
Stevens	5-6	6-5	7-2	3-2	50	65
O'Connor	6-1	3-8	1-8	3-2	75	20
Scalia	2-1	2-2	1-1	0-1	50	50
Kennedy	2-1	2-2	0-1	0-0	67	40

The behavior of the justices who sat during some portion of the last five terms of the Burger Court and the first four of the Rehnquist Court (1981–1989) is displayed in Table 8.2. Again, the justices as a group support economically conservative agency decisions or economically liberal agency decisions, but not both. Blackmun again does so, as he did during the early years of the Burger Court (but barely insofar as conservative decisions are concerned), but not White, who opposes more conservative decisions than he supports. Stevens's apparent activism now appears to have been a function of his limited participation in agency action cases during the early Burger Court. He reveals himself as a compatriot of Blackmun, supporting both conservative (though barely) and liberal agency action. Scalia's ten participations and Kennedy's eight are too few to enable us to characterize either as an activist or as a restraintist. Their behavior during this limited period, however, marks neither as a principled supporter of judicial restraint.

Viewed from the perspective of the justices' differential support for liberal/conservative outcomes, the twelve justices on the early Warren Court showed an average difference of 45.5 points as between liberal and conservative outcomes,[28] and the dozen who sat during the first seven terms of the Burger Court

[28] The data exclude Jackson, who participated in only one agency action case.

had an average differential of 38.3 points, an average that drops to 31.9 if the infrequently participating Black and Harlan – six votes each – are excluded. For the 1981 through 1989 terms, the average difference is 41.1 points. Clearly, something other than judicial restraint (or judicial activism) motivates behavior toward agency action regulatory of business and labor.

Considerations of economic federalism

The same results obtain when we analyze the same three periods – the 1953–1959 terms, the 1969–1977 terms, and the 1981–1989 terms – to ascertain the extent to which the justices defer to state action when such action concerns regulation of business or labor.

Keying on the same six justices listed in Table 8.1 shows Frankfurter, Harlan, and Whittaker supporting state regulation of labor at percentages of 91, 86, and 100 percent, respectively. But when the state's regulation pertained to business, these justices' percentages fell to only 31, 53, and 14 percent. Conversely, Black, Douglas, and Warren supported state regulation of labor at a low 10, 8, and 9 percent, respectively, but upheld business at proportions of 73, 69, and 72.

What accounts for these discrepant results? The same explanation as accounts for their behavior toward agency action: the justices substantive economic attitudes. State labor regulation in all twelve of the cases decided nonunanimously during the 1953–1959 terms was anti-union. Hence, the economically conservative Frankfurter, Harlan, and Whittaker supported it, whereas the economically liberal Black, Douglas, and Warren did not. State regulation of business, however, produced the reverse effect: A pro-state vote in twenty of these twenty-six cases was simultaneously anti-business. Hence, a pattern of support opposite to that for the labor cases obtains. Of the twelve justices other than Jackson (who participated in only a single case) who sat during these terms, only Clark and Brennan supported the states with more than half their votes in both the labor and business cases.[29]

On the early Burger Court (1969–1977), only Rehnquist appears to exercise restraint toward state economic regulation.[30] He invariably supported state labor regulation whether it was pro- or anti-union. Similarly, he always supported the states when their regulations simultaneously supported business, while doing so at an 80 percent rate when they opposed business. At the other extreme, Douglas upheld the states with barely a third of the fifteen votes he cast during this time. Joining him as an unabashed activist was Justice Powell, whom many view as a restraintist "in the mold of Frankfurter and Harlan."[31] Indeed, Powell sup-

---

[29]   Brennan, 71 percent toward both labor and business; Clark, 75 percent in the labor cases and 67 percent in the business cases.

[30]   Spaeth and Teger, op. cit. fn. 26 supra, pp. 282–287. See also Sue Davis, *Justice Rehnquist and the Constitution* (Princeton: Princeton University Press, 1989).

[31]   Jacob W. Landynski, "Justice Lewis F. Powell, Jr.: Balance Wheel of the Court," in Charles M. Lamb and Stephen C. Halpern, eds., *The Burger Court* (Urbana: University of Illinois Press,

Table 8.3. *Voting behavior toward state economic regulation,*
1981–1989 terms

Justice	state anti-union pro-con	state pro-business pro-con	% pro	state anti-business pro-con	% pro
Brennan	0-3	4-22	15	17-7	71
Marshall	0-3	4-22	15	15-10	60
White	1-4	1-26	4	10-15	40
Burger	3-1	0-20	0	5-9	36
Blackmun	3-2	3-24	11	8-17	32
Powell	1-3	4-17	19	6-8	43
Rehnquist	5-0	24-3	89	22-3	88
Stevens	1-4	12-14	46	15-9	63
O'Connor	4-1	11-13	46	17-4	81
Scalia	1-0	5-2	71	5-6	45
Kennedy	1-0	1-1	50	1-2	33

ported state business regulation even less than Douglas: one-third of the time when the regulation supported business and barely a fourth of the time when it was anti-business. On the other hand, Powell did cast supportive state votes in four of the five cases in which the state was anti-union, whereas Douglas did so in only two of his six votes. The other nine justices either supported liberal or conservative state decisions, but none supported or opposed both.

Table 8.3 displays the behavior of the justices who sat during some portion of the the 1981–1989 terms. As the first column indicates, the states decided the handful of labor cases reviewed by the Court in an anti-labor fashion, with Rehnquist, O'Connor, Burger, and Blackmun supporting the states with more than half their votes among those who participated in more than one of these cases. Concerning cases involving business, only Rehnquist supported the states

1991), p. 308. Cf. Vincent Blasi, "The Rootless Activism of the Burger Court," In Vincent Blasi, ed., *The Burger Court: The Counter-Revolution That Wasn't* (New Haven: Yale University Press, 1983), pp. 210–211. The quoted statement is literally correct, though ironically so. As our tables and discussion reveal, neither Frankfurter nor Harlan practiced the restraint for which they were reputed. Even less so, Justice Powell, notwithstanding assertions to the contrary. For example, Henry J. Abraham, *Justices & Presidents*, 2d ed. (New York: Oxford University Press, 1985), p. 318.

with more than half his votes regardless of whether state action supported or opposed business, and he did so overwhelmingly: in 89 percent of the pro-business cases, and in 88 percent of those decided antithetically to business. Significantly, four justices opposed the states regardless of the effects on business: White, Burger, Blackmun, and Powell. Of these, the only constant from the early Burger Court was Justice Powell.

So much for judicial restraint insofar as considerations of federalism are concerned. On the basis of our analyses, the justices deferred to state action even less than they did to the federal regulatory commissions.

Civil liberties

The operation of judicial restraint insofar as considerations of federalism are concerned may be assessed from one additional perspective: cases concerning civil liberties. To the extent that the provisions of the Bill of Rights and the various provisions of the federal civil rights acts apply to the state and local governments, they do so in precisely the same fashion as they bind the federal government, with the exception of the size of juries in criminal cases and the need for unanimity insofar as guilty verdicts are concerned.[32] Accordingly, because of the generally accepted view that the states serve as laboratories for political experimentation and innovation, coupled with the principle of state sovereignty and the fact that nothing in the Constitution explicitly makes the Bill of Rights binding on the states, one may expect a restraint oriented justice to give the state and local governments a bit more leeway than the federal government in their activities affecting civil liberties.

Spaeth and Teger[33] selected four sets of Burger Court civil liberties cases decided between the beginning of the 1969 term and March 1979, in which the federal government and the states had separately participated frequently enough to allow for the formation of cumulative scales in which the justices array themselves in a highly consistent fashion on the basis of their hypothesized attitude toward the civil liberty issue each set of cases contains: First Amendment freedoms,[34] double jeopardy, search and seizure, and poverty law. Only the formally decided and per curiam decisions in which the position of the federal or state governmental unit was antithetical to the contentions of the civil liberty claimant were included. Table 8.4 specifies the frequency with which the Court supported governmental restrictions on the exercise of civil liberty in each of the four areas.

---

[32] See *Williams v. Florida*, 399 U.S. 78 (1970); *Apodaca v. Oregon*, 406 U.S. 404 (1972); *Ballew v. Georgia*, 435 U.S. 223 (1978); *Burch v. Louisiana*, 441 U.S. 130 (1979). The states, however, need not adhere to the Second, Third, or Seventh Amendments, nor to the requirement that persons be indicted by a grand jury.

[33] Op. cit. fn. 26 supra, pp. 287–294.

[34] The First Amendment scale excludes the religion clauses, commercial speech, obscenity, and libel actions for defamation and invasion of privacy. These issues scale separately.

Table 8.4. *Comparison of the proportion of decisions that upheld governmental action in four areas of civil liberties, 1969–1979*

Issue	Decisions pro-anti state	% pro	Decisions pro-anti U.S.	% pro
First Amendment	11-14	44	13-3	81
Double Jeopardy	8-11	42	13-7	65
Search & Seizure	15-9	63	28-13	68
Poverty Law	17-28	38	17-3	85

As the table shows, the Court exercised markedly more restraint in the federal cases than it did toward the states. Only in search-and-seizure did the Court support the states with more than half its decisions, but even here its restraint was slightly less than that accorded the federal government. In the other three areas, the Court displayed marked activism, upholding state action less than two and a half times as frequently as that of the federal government: 30 percent versus 77 percent.

The voting of the individual justices parallels the Court's behavior. With but five incidental exceptions, not a single justice exercised greater restraint toward the states than he did the federal government. Because of his single participation in a federal double jeopardy case, Black appears more supportive of the states than the federal government. Similarly Douglas, Brennan, and Marshall in search-and-seizure, but the differences are minuscule: 13, 10, and 13 percent, respectively, versus 7, 8, and 7 percent in the federal cases. Douglas also supported the states slightly more in poverty law: two of thirty-two state cases (6 percent) compared with none of eight federal cases.

As still further evidence of the subordination of the canons of restraint to the justices' individual policy preferences, we may note the similarity of each justice's rank order between the two scales that comprise each of the four civil liberties issues we have considered. These coefficients[35] range from + .81 in double jeopardy to + .95 in First Amendment and search-and-seizure. The probability of the rank orders being this similar is substantially less than one in a thousand.

At the risk of repetition, we undertake further consideration of civil liberties on the off chance that we may uncover some evidence of judicial restraint. Instead of a narrow focus on selected civil liberty issues, we proceed in a

[35]   Kendall's tau-b rank order correlation coefficient which is corrected for tied rankings. See Sidney Siegel, *Nonparametric Statistics for the Behavioral Sciences* (New York: McGraw-Hill, 1956), pp. 213–219.

Table 8.5. *Support of state and federal action affecting civil liberty,*
1981–1989 terms

Justice	1981-1985 Terms			1986-1989 Terms		
	State	Federal	Fed-St	State	Federal	Fed-St
Marshall	15.0	27.3	+12.3	8.8	17.1	+8.3
Brennan	20.5	30.6	+10.1	10.6	17.2	+6.6
White	65.0	69.2	+4.2	66.4	74.2	+7.8
Burger	73.8	77.3	+3.5			
Blackmun	46.2	51.2	+5.0	34.4	34.5	+0.1
Powell	62.0	72.0	+10.0	57.4	65.5	+8.1
Rehnquist	85.0	80.0	-5.0	81.3	80.2	-1.1
Stevens	35.9	51.9	+16.0	32.9	37.3	+4.4
O'Connor	72.2	70.6	-1.6	70.9	71.9	+1.0
Scalia				68.2	71.4	+3.2
Kennedy				64.5	76.1	+11.6

thoroughly global fashion and simultaneously examine the justices' behavior across the sum total of individual freedom.[36] As previously, we use docket number as our unit of analysis, rather than case citation, and we again include all orally argued and per curiam cases. Instead of requiring conflict between exercise of civil liberty and governmental action, we also include the collusive cases, those where government supports the civil liberty claimant – for example, some civil rights actions. We separately consider the last five terms of the Burger Court and the first four of the Rehnquist Court.

Table 8.5 shows the results of this analysis. To a lesser extent, but virtually without exception, the justices support the state and local governments appreciably less than they do the federal government. Judicial restraint, in the form of considerations of federalism, remains notable by its absence. Only Rehnquist and O'Connor on the Burger Court, and Rehnquist alone on his Court, support state action affecting civil liberty to a greater extent than they do that of the federal government.

---

[36] Criminal procedure, civil rights, First Amendment freedoms (including the religion clauses, obscenity, commercial speech, and libel), due process, privacy, and attorneys.

Support for the Solicitor General

As noted in Chapters 5 and 6, the Solicitor General is the President's representative before the Supreme Court. As the President (along with the Vice-President) is the only official elected by the entire country, justices might show restraint by supporting the policies supported by his representative in Court. Previous research has in fact shown that virtually every justice serving between 1953 and 1982 supported the party favored by the Solicitor General in amicus curiae briefs over half the time.[37] Nevertheless, such support was largely conditioned on the ideological position of the party being supported. Fifteen of the twenty justices examined demonstrated significantly different levels of support when the Solicitor General favored the liberal side than when he favored the conservative side. Rehnquist, who has appeared to be restraintist elsewhere, supported the Solicitor General 77 percent of the time in conservative briefs but only 39 percent of the time in liberal ones, the largest difference among the Court's conservatives.

We supplement these results with findings from the 1983-1988 terms of the Court. Overall, the party supported by the Solicitor General won 65.7 percent of the time. The percentage of votes cast by the justices in support of the Solicitor General's position, presented in Table 8.6, ranged from 83.9 percent for Kennedy to 44.4 percent for Marshall. The average level of support for the eleven justices who served during this period is 61.6 percent. This level of support is not surprising, as it largely represents support by conservative justices for conservative positions taken by the Solicitor General.[38] The question of interest is whether there is any evidence of deference or restraint.

Here again the answer is "no." Of the eleven justices considered, only three – Burger, Powell, and O'Connor – supported both the liberal and conservative briefs of the Solicitor General more than half the time.[39] The typical response: Liberals support liberal briefs and conservatives support conservative briefs. Clearly, judicial restraint remains a sometime thing.

Access to the federal courts

We have focused thus far on judicial restraint as deference, either to the federal regulatory commissions, to the states, or to the Solicitor General. But it is also possible for restraint to manifest itself at the point of access rather than after the Court has bid the plaintiff to enter. That is, restraint operates before the case reaches the decision stage, not afterward.[40]

[37] Jeffrey A. Segal, "Amicus Curiae Briefs by the Solicitor General During the Warren and Burger Courts," 41 *Western Political Quarterly* 135 (1988).
[38] The Solicitor General supported the conservative position in 66 percent of the ideological briefs filed during this period.
[39] Kennedy's 50 percent support for liberal briefs is based on only four votes.
[40] See Alexander Bickel, *The Least Dangerous Branch* (New York: Bobbs-Merrill, 1962), ch. 4.

Table 8.6. *Voting behavior toward the Solicitor General, 1983–1988 terms*

Justice	Votes	Total % pro	SG liberal % pro	SG conservative % pro
Brennan	175[a]	45.7	75.0	25.8
Marshall	171	44.4	83.0	19.8
White	172	67.4	47.9	76.7
Burger	92	68.5	55.2	75.0
Blackmun	172	54.7	74.5	42.9
Powell	118	63.6	58.8	72.3
Rehnquist	174	64.9	39.6	82.6
Stevens	172	50.6	66.7	41.3
O'Connor	171	64.3	53.2	72.8
Scalia	81	69.1	47.4	77.3
Kennedy	31	83.9	50.0	91.7

Note. [a]Only 142 out of 175 briefs involved issues categorized as liberal or conservative.

With reference to the Supreme Court, the word, "access," has two meanings: to describe the narrow gatekeeping function that the justices perform at the "decision to decide" stage of its process,[41] which is largely governed by the Rule of Four.[42] The other meaning concerns the formal technical requirements, such as standing to sue, mootness, exhaustion of remedies, and so on, that determine who has access to the judicial forum at all levels of the federal court system. We discuss both meanings in Chapter 5. We limit our investigation here to the second meaning.

The ideal method would determine whether the justices vote their preferences toward access per se in such cases or their preferences toward the substantive issues the case contains – the merits of the controversy. That is, do liberal justices grant access to liberal litigants and deny it to conservatives, and vice-versa? Such an approach is not feasible here because access decisions have both a tactical and strategic component. Justices, for example, may vote against access

---

[41]   For example, Lawrence Baum, "Policy Goals in Judicial Gatekeeping," 21 *American Journal of Political Science* (1977), 13–35; Stuart H. Teger and Douglas Kosinski, "The Cue Theory of Supreme Court Certiorari Jurisdiction: A Reconsideration," 42 *Journal of Politics* (1980), 834–846.

[42]   See Jan Palmer's elegant and meticulous analysis, *The Vinson Court Era* (New York: AMS Press, 1990).

simply because they consider it an appropriate means to allocate a scarce resource, a means to facilitate the handling of a pressing case load. Or they may vote to deny access because they believe themselves to be a minority on the Court and view the decision making of various administrative agencies, the states, and the lower federal courts as more congruent with their substantive policy preferences than those of a majority of their colleagues.

An analysis of all formally decided access cases disposed of during the first seven terms of the Burger Court indicated that the justices responded to a mixture of motivations: For some, the dominant consideration was administrative/legal concerns – that is, judicial restraint. Others focused on the substantive policy outcome, whereas the largest group was motivated by both considerations. Significantly, the justices' access choices covaried with their rank ordering on a general liberal-conservative dimension. Liberal justices, headed by Douglas, vote to open access and the moderates occupy a middle position, whereas the conservatives vote to close access, with Rehnquist anchoring the scale regarding closure and conservatism.[43] Further analysis focusing only on cases in which access was denied found that denial produced conservative results, which correlated extremely closely with the individual justice's ideological preferences.[44]

We emphasize that no necessary association exists between access and ideological orientation. Closing access can produce a liberal result, whereas a vote for opening the judicial door may as easily have a conservative effect. As we pointed out in Chapter 3, at an earlier time, when legislative bodies were more progressive in their policy making than the courts, a vote for access closure usually coincided with a liberal posture, whereas the openness of judicial activism supported the maintenance of dual federalism and economic laissez-faire. If preferred policy outcomes depend on implementation elsewhere in the political system, we can rest assured that those who prefer those outcomes will support access closure, but not because they are true believers in judicial restraint, any more than those who prefer Court-made policy are true believers in judicial activism.

We should also note that one ought neither be surprised nor saddened to find that judicial restraint has so little operational force among Supreme Court justices. As Spaeth and Teger pointed out:

If not to decide is to decide (and it surely is), then even the restrained jurist is promulgating policy decisions when he defers. Can anyone of reason and conviction really believe that someone who has attained the office of Supreme Court justice is able to submerge his politics entirely in deference to vague notions of judicial restraint? One may defer, but

[43] Gregory J. Rathjen and Harold J. Spaeth, "Access to the Federal Courts: An Analysis of Burger Court Policy Making," 23 *American Journal of Political Science* (1979) 360.

[44] Gregory J. Rathjen and Harold J. Spaeth, "Denial of Access and Ideological Preferences: An Analysis of the Voting Behavior of the Burger Court Justices, 1969–1976," 36 *Western Political Quarterly* (1983) 71.

blindly. Justices, like most mere mortals, defer to the ideas and institutions of
.. they approve. We would not want them on the Supreme Court otherwise.[45]

The accommodation of a restraintist reputation
in the face of activist behavior

Given the largely mythical character of judicial restraint, how is it possible for
an activist justice to maintain a reputation for restraint? The short answer, of
course, is that large numbers of otherwise rational people acerebrally refuse to
be confused by facts. Self-deception, the ostrich posture, is an endemic human
trait. Even scholars, whose function it is to create and disseminate truth, are by
no means immune.[46] Because no other justice has a reputation for judicial restraint
that matches that of Frankfurter, we focus our attention on him.[47]

We may assume that justices with a reputation for restraint will take pains to
explain their position when they vote incompatibly with their reputation because
such votes deviate from their presumed philosophical position. Alternatively, to
the extent that such justices value their reputation, yet are restraintist only insofar
as restraint accords with their substantive policy preferences, they will take pains
not to explain the conflict between restraint and their activist votes, but rather
to explain these votes *away*.

To determine which option Frankfurter chose, we rely on an analysis of
Frankfurter's opinion behavior in the business and labor cases involving state
and regulatory commission action decided during his tenure on the Warren Court
(1953–1961).[48] In the labor cases, Frankfurter had no opportunity to show his
true colors. In each of these cases, a pro-state vote was concomitantly anti-
union. Hence, he easily cloaked his anti-union attitude by writing pro-state
opinions. But a different picture emerges from the more structurally complex
state business regulation cases. In these thirty-three cases, only Douglas wrote
as frequently as he. Moreover, he had no reticence in writing anti-state opinions
– a total of nine. Three anti-state opinions occurred in cases that received front-
page coverage. One concerned an effort by a state to tax federal property leased
to private persons. Frankfurter wrapped himself in the nationalistic mantle of
Chief Justice Marshall in *M'Culloch v. Maryland* to justify his opposition to the
state tax.[49] In the second case, Frankfurter vigorously argued that an apportioned
income tax on an out-of-state company's instate activities violated the commerce

---

[45] Op. cit. fn. 26 supra, p. 297

[46] For a dated list of such, see Spaeth, op. cit. fn. 23 supra, notes 4, 10, and 11.

[47] Professor Abraham seems to demur as far as Rehnquist is concerned. Op. cit. fn. 31 supra,
p. 318.

[48] Harold J. Spaeth and Michael F. Altfeld, "Felix Frankfurter, Judicial Activism, and Voting
Conflict on the Warren Court," in Sheldon Goldman and Charles M. Lamb, eds., *Judicial
Conflict and Consensus* (Lexington, KY: University of Kentucky Press, 1986), pp. 87–114.

[49] *Detroit v. Murray Corp.*, 355 U.S. 489 (1958), at 608.

clause.[50] In the final case he sounded an unabashedly nationalistic refrain in asserting that another state tax violated the import-export clause:

... guided by the experience of the evils generated by the *parochialism* of the new States, the wise men at the Philadelphia Convention took measures to make of the expansive United States a free trade area and to withdraw from the States the *selfish* exercise of power over foreign trade, both import and export.[51]

Significantly, eight of Frankfurter's nine anti-state opinions took a pro-business stance. Moreover, seven of the eight appear as dissents. Indeed, he did not fail to couple each of these pro-business dissents with an opinion. Perhaps Frankfurter's apologists ignore his dissenting opinions. Others have not.[52] Although Frankfurter displayed deference in the state labor cases, his votes were simultaneously anti-union. In the state business cases, his deference disappeared, but his economic conservatism remained.

Similar to his behavior in the state business cases, Frankfurter did not hesitate to author anti-NLRB opinions. In fact, he accompanied each of his eight anti-NLRB votes with an opinion, six of which were dissents. It is also noteworthy that his five opinions supporting the NLRB all appeared in cases in which the NLRB was anti-union. Unlike the state business cases where his activism appeared starkly naked, here Frankfurter behaved somewhat deviously by using deference to Congress and to the courts of appeals to mask his lack of deference to the NLRB.[53] Naked activism still emerged, but less frequently.[54]

In the agency cases regulating business, Frankfurter continued to have no qualms about writing when he disapproved of the agency's action. He wrote in half the twenty cases in which he voted anti-agency. Conversely, he wrote in support of only seven of twenty-seven pro-agency votes. Eight of his ten anti-agency opinions supported a pro-business result, as did all of his opinions upholding agency action.

Although Frankfurter wrote almost as often when he exercised restraint as when he did not (twenty-four versus twenty-six opinions), the twenty-four restraintist opinions applied to only 40 percent of his sixty restraintist votes. His twenty-six activist opinions, by comparison, applied to 52 percent of his fifty activist votes. Moreover, twenty of the activist votes appeared as dissents (77 percent). Only ten

---

[50] *Northwestern States Portland Cement Co. v. Minnesota*, 358 U.S. 450 (1959), at 470.

[51] *Youngstown Sheet & Tube v. Bowers*, 358 U.S. 534 (1959), at 551 (italics added).

[52] An analysis of *Northwestern States* and *Youngstown* labels Frankfurter's dissents as "fervent," and contrasts them with Professor Paul Freund's characterization of the majority opinions as having "shown a marked degree of self-restraint." Anthony Lewis, "A Gain for States' Rights," *New York Times*, March 1, 1959, p. 56.

[53] For example, *Mastro Plastics v. NLRB*, 350 U.S. 270 (1956), where he argued that the NLRB's construction of a provision of the Taft-Hartley Act conflicted with its plain meaning. Deference to the courts of appeals rather than the NLRB characterized his opinions in *NLRB v. Electrical Workers*, 346 U.S. 464 (1953); *NLRB v. Lion Oil Co.*, 352 U.S. 282 (1957); and *NLRB v. Walton Manufacturing Co.*, 369 U.S. 404 (1962).

[54] For example, *NLRB v. Truitt Manufacturing Co.*, 351 U.S. 149 (1956).

of his pro-state and pro-agency opinions were such (42 percent). As noted, such behavior is exactly what one would expect from a spokesperson for restraint who believes it necessary to explain deviations from such a course. It is also exactly what one would expect from a justice who practices restraint only when state and agency action is congruent with the justice's substantive policy preferences. Clearly, the latter conclusion is more correct.[55]

Why, then, the persistence of Frankfurter's restraintist reputation? Several hypotheses may be proposed. 1) Frankfurter's attachment to restraint antedates his appointment to the Court. This suggests that he changed his tune notwithstanding his verbalization of restraint during the 1920s and 1930s. 2) Frankfurter became more conservative and more activist with age. This runs counter to empirical findings, most notably those of Glendon Schubert, who finds him to be conservative from the beginning of the Vinson Court in 1946 until his retirement sixteen years later.[56] 3) The cases considered do not run the gauntlet of those amenable to the exercise of restraint. Technically, this is true. Previous research has identifed a very small set of cases in which Frankfurter, along with all the other justices, did decide on the basis of their attitudes toward activism/restraint. Frankfurter clearly did exercise restraint here, but these cases bear little resemblance to any underlying hypothesized variable other than the propriety of the Supreme Court's resolution of the controversy they presented.[57] That Frankfurter behaved as a restraintist in this small universe does not gainsay his activism in the cases we have considered. 4) Frankfurter's reputation rests exclusively on his opinions of the Court. On the Warren Court, ten of his thirteen majority opinions supported the states and federal agencies. Yet if an exclusive focus on majority opinions explains Frankfurter's reputation, what does this say about the scholarship of those who have so sharply limited their focus? 5) Assertions of consistent restraint came not from Frankfurter, but rather from scholars and commentators. That some analysts dress Frankfurter in such a mantle is their problem, not his.

Whatever the explanation, the research reported here reveals Frankfurter to have been nothing more than a stalwart economic conservative who, along with his other economically oriented colleagues, used judicial restraint and judicial activism with equal facility to achieve his substantive policy objectives.

DECLARATIONS OF UNCONSTITUTIONALITY

Certainly the most dramatic instances of a lack of judicial restraint – or conversely, the manifestation of judicial activism – are decisions that declare acts

---

[55]　Inasmuch as the majority of Frankfurter's activist opinions were dissents, in each of these cases a majority of his colleagues were the ones who displayed restraint, whether verbalized or not, which Frankfurter, the putative restraintist, refused to do.

[56]　*The Judicial Mind* (Evanston: Northwestern University Press, 1965), pp. 127–141.

[57]　Harold J. Spaeth, "Judicial Power as a Variable Motivating Supreme Court Behavior," 6 *American Journal of Political Science* (1962), 54. Most of these cases concern the Federal Rules of Civil Procedure, comity, diversity of citizenship, and venue.

of Congress and, to a lesser extent, those of state and local governments unconstitutional. Here, the conflict between an unelected, lifetime judiciary and the public's representatives is most acute. Absent a constitutional amendment, the Court's decision is final. Only four times in history has Congress successfully proposed an amendment that undid a decision: the Eleventh Amendment that undid *Chisholm v. Georgia*; the Fourteenth Amendment that overturned *Scott v. Sandford*; the Sixteenth Amendment that authorized an income tax; and the Twenty-Sixth Amendment that allowed 18-year-olds to vote in state and local elections.[58]

The Supreme Court first declared an act of Congress, or portion thereof, unconstitutional in the 1803 case *Marbury v. Madison*.[59] Over fifty years passed before the Court again did so.[60] Following the Civil War, though, the Court began using its power of judicial review on a more regular basis. Peaks of activism occured "during the late 1860s; during the administration of Theodore Roosevelt; after World War I; during the 1920s and 1930s; and during the 1960s, a cycle that has not yet begun to decline."[61]

Ideally, from the standpoint of activism/restraint, one should analyze declarations of unconstitutionality by contrasting them with cases in which the Court upholds the challenged law's constitutionality. We do not follow this course, however, for several reasons. First, a declaration of unconstitutionality is not simply the activist side of a restraintist coin. The numismatic analogy is inapposite because it compares qualitatively different outcomes. A fetus, labeled an "unborn person" by those of an anti-choice persuasion, is not the opposite of an undead individual. Nor is attempted homicide the antithesis of murder. Second, many declarations of unconstitutionality do not pertain to legislation. They commonly concern such matters as the *ultra vires* activity of unduly zealous police officers, the unauthorized action of an administrative agency, or the ruling of a lawless jury. Although such activities are usually not legislatively authorized, in many cases it is far from clear whether the Court has voided a statute or ordinance. Lastly, it is even less clear whether the Court's ruling has sustained the constitutionality of a statute. The inherent subjectivity in such judgments gives us pause. Consequently, we consider only those cases in which the Court rather clearly says it has voided a legislative enactment or the provision of a state constitution or municipal charter.

From the beginning of the Warren Court through the first four terms of the Rehnquist Court, the justices have declared fifty-five acts of Congress unconstitutional, only one of which has been reversed by congressional action: the 18-year-old vote. Compared with all considerations of constitutionality, this number

---

[58] 2 Dallas 419 (1793); 19 Howard 393 (1857); *Pollock v. Farmers' Loan and Trust Co.*, 157 U.S. 429, 158 U.S. 601 (1895); and *Oregon v. Mitchell*, 400 U.S. 112 (1970).

[59] 1 Cranch 137.

[60] *Scott v. Sanford*, 19 Howard 393 (1857).

[61] Gregory A. Caldeira and Donald J. McCrone, "Of Time and Judicial Activism: A Study of the U.S. Supreme Court, 1800–1973," in Halpern and Lamb, op. cit. fn. 1 supra, p. 113.

– less than an average of 1.5 per term – represents a small fraction. Because the Court upholds the overwhelming majority of challenged federal laws, these Courts, as well as all their predecessors, may accurately be characterized as restraintist.[62] Nonetheless, marginal differences in deference may be specified. Thus, the Burger Court, notwithstanding its reputation for restraint, declared proportionately more laws unconstitutional than the reputably activist Warren Court or the Rehnquist Court to date: twenty-eight, an average of 1.65 per term. The comparable figures for the Warren Court are 22 and 1.38, and 5 and 1.25 for the Rehnquist Court.

These Courts display much more activism when confronted with the actions of state and local governments. Again, by our subjective count, of 75 state and local ordinances and constitutional provisions challenged as unconstitutional during the first four terms of the Rehnquist Court, the justices voided 35 – 46.7 percent. This contrasts with the 16.1 percent reported earlier for federal enactments.

As it did toward federal legislation, the Burger Court declared that of the state and local governments unconstitutional at a higher frequency than the other two: 13.24 per term (225 total). The Rehnquist Court averaged 9.3 (37), and the Warren Court only 8.69 per term (139). Note also that the Warren Court's liberally activist reputation was primarily based on its opposition to state action with regard to persons accused of crime, First Amendment freedoms, and race discrimination.

Table 8.7 displays the votes of the twenty-five justices who participated in the 456 cases in which the Court declared legislation unconstitutional during the 1953–1989 terms. We again caution the reader that these data display only the overruling aspect of constitutionality. They tell us nothing about voting behavior in cases where the majority upheld a statute or constitutional provision. They only indicate the relative extent the individual justices conformed to their colleagues' judgment of unconstitutionality.

Given these caveats, only one justice, Rehnquist, exercised restraint by voting against unconstitutionality less than half the time. His support, 38.9 percent, places him far distant from the next least activist justice, Burton, who is at 61.5 percent. At the other extreme, seven justices supported unconstitutionality with more than 90 percent of their votes, all of whom, with the exception of the infrequently participating Jackson, were liberals: Brennan (96.6 percent), Douglas (95.1), Fortas (93.9), Goldberg (94.8), Marshall (94.4), and Warren (92.5). Indeed, Brennan never voted to sustain the law in any of the 146 Warren Court's declarations of unconstitutionality in which he participated. Liberal justices obviously supported declarations of unconstitutionality not because they are activ-

---

[62] During the first four terms of the Rehnquist Court, for example, we count thirty-one federal laws the constitutionality of which litigants disputed. The Court declared five of them unconstitutional, 16.1 percent.

Table 8.7. *Votes in support and opposition to decisions declaring legislation unconstitutional, 1953–1989 terms*

Justice	total	%	Congress only	%
Black	152-39	79.6	24-6	80.0
Blackmun	234-45	83.9	21-8	72.4
Brennan	421-15	96.6	51-3	94.4
Burger	174-80	69.0	20-8	71.4
Burton	16-10	61.5	0-3	0.0
Clark	94-31	75.2	6-8	42.9
Douglas	255-13	95.1	30-3	90.9
Fortas	46-3	93.9	11-0	100.0
Frankfurter	35-11	76.1	3-3	50.0
Goldberg	55-3	94.8	6-0	100.0
Harlan	114-70	62.0	16-14	53.3
Jackson	8-0	100.0	0-0	--
Kennedy	25-3	89.3	2-0	100.0
Marshall	304-18	94.4	35-4	89.7
Minton	11-2	84.6	0-0	--
O'Connor	71-34	67.6	13-1	92.9
Powell	191-23	89.3	20-3	87.0
Reed	13-2	86.7	0-0	--
Rehnquist	96-151	38.9	13-13	50.0
Scalia	30-12	71.4	5-0	100.0
Stevens	149-28	84.2	14-6	70.0
Stewart	264-55	82.8	29-10	74.4
Warren	147-12	92.5	18-6	75.0
White	319-89	78.2	30-20	60.0
Whittaker	22-5	81.5	2-2	50.0
totals	3247-754	81.2	369-121	75.3

ists, but rather because the bulk of the legislation at issue restricted individual liberty.

Conservatives likewise do not hesitate to declare unconstitutional laws of which they disapprove. Powell and Kennedy, for example, almost reach the 90 percent level (89.3), and are appreciably more inclined to void statutes in cases where a majority of the Court does so than such moderate justices as Stevens (84.2 percent), Blackmun (83.9), and Stewart (82.8). Inasmuch as we are concentrating only on declarations of unconstitutionality, the justices as a group must display an activist posture. But they do so with something of a vengeance, voting to void at better than an 80 percent rate, instead of the 55 to 67 percent range that would obtain if on average only five or six of the participating justices so voted. Frankfurter, for example, though he is more restrained than the justices collectively, nonetheless voted to void in more than three of four opportunities (76.1 percent) when a majority of the Court also did so.

Not surprisingly, the justices showed more reluctance to declare congressional legislation unconstitutional than that of the state and local governments. But the difference is slight: 75.3 percent of their votes compared with 81.2 percent. Of course, this merely indicates that the majority coalition in federal cases was slightly smaller on average than those voiding state and local enactments. Burton and Clark exercised most restraint: the former supporting Congress with all three of his votes, Clark with eight of his fourteen. Three other justices split their votes equally: Frankfurter, Rehnquist, and Whittaker. Unlike the overall pattern displayed in Table 8.7 where the liberal justices were most activist, we find two conservatives among those most willing to void acts of Congress: Scalia and Kennedy, both of whom voted to void at every opportunity. Note also that Scalia, along with O'Connor, are much more willing to upset federal legislation than they are that of the states: 71.4 versus 100 percent, and 67.6 versus 92.9 percent, respectively.

This survey of voting in cases where the Court declares legislation unconstitutional further documents the sometime character of judicial restraint. We consider one final aspect of the Court's decision making in our effort – unsuccessful thus far – to discover evidence of judicial restraint: decisions in which the Court overturned or otherwise formally altered the Court's precedents.

Alterations of precedent

The caveats we supplied to our analysis of declarations of unconstitutionality also apply to alterations of precedent. As before, we consider only those cases in which a majority of the justices said in so many words that they were formally altering one of the Court's own precedents. With one empirically unexamined difference, we exclude decisions that upheld challenged precedents for the same reasons as before. The difference is that the Court rarely says that it accepts a case to consider the continued vitality of one of its precedents, and when it does say so it is the prelude to formal alteration.[63] Accordingly, if we compared formal alterations with formal non-alterations, very few cases would populate the latter side.

To a greater extent than with respect to legislation, courts are expected to defer – to adhere to – what they have previously decided. Courts are not responsible for legislative action, but they are responsible for the decisions they themselves have made. When a legislative body behaves in an outrageously unconstitutional manner, we expect Courts to void such action. But courts are supposed to remain true – that is, consistent – unto themselves, to respect the decisions made by their predecessors.[64] Hence, a court should overrule itself far less frequently than it overrules other decision-making bodies, notwithstanding that in the case of the Supreme Court no one else can correct its constitutional errors, short of a constitutional amendment. This is why the Court has formulated a rule that leaves all constitutional questions open for reconsideration.[65] Some, however, more so than others, according to a recent opinion of Chief Justice Rehnquist, which overruled two precedents[66] that held that victim impact evidence could not be constitutionally used to impose the death penalty on a defendant. In rationalizing the overrulings, Rehnquist, speaking for himself and five colleagues – White, O'Connor, Scalia, Kennedy, and Souter – formulated what may be called the "preferred precedents doctrine": that *stare decisis* should apply to economic decisions with especial force because people need stability to conduct their business affairs.[67] But in cases involving "procedural and evidentiary rules" – the essence of due process, equal protection, and the Fourth through the Eighth Amendments – "the opposite is true."[68]

With regard to the Supreme Court, we find precedent formally altered markedly less often than laws declared unconstitutional. It voided 456 legislative actions

---

[63] For example, *California v. Acevedo*, 114 L Ed 2d 619 (1991), "We granted certiorari . . . to reexamine the law applicable to a closed container in an automobile . . . " at 626–627. *Payne v. Tennessee*, 115 L Ed 2d 720 (1991), "We granted certiorari . . . to reconsider our holdings in Booth and Gathers that the Eighth Amendment prohibits a capital sentencing jury from considering 'victim impact' evidence relating to the personal characteristics of the victim and the emotional impact of the crimes on the victim's family." at 730.

[64] As an extreme example, consider that the supreme English court – the House of Lords – did not assert the authority to overturn its own decisions until 1966. See Ruggero J. Aldisert, "The English appellate process: A distant second to our own?" 75 *Judicature* 48 (1991), at 49.

[65] *The Passenger Cases*, 7 Howard 283 (1849), at 470; *Mitchell v. W.T. Grant Co.*, 416 U.S. 600 (1974), at 527–628. Also see *Glidden Co. v. Zdanok*, 370 U.S. 530 (1962), at 543; *Patterson v. McLean Credit Union*, 491 U.S. 164 (1989), at 172–173.

[66] *Booth v. Maryland*, 96 L Ed 2d 440 (1987), and *South Carolina v. Gathers*, 104 L Ed 2d 876 (1989). The overruling occurred in *Payne v. Tennessee*, 115 L Ed 2d 720 (1991).

[67] "Considerations in favor of stare decisis are at their acme in cases involving property and contract rights, where reliance interests are involved . . . " 115 L Ed 2d 720, at 737.

[68] Id. Also see Linda Greenhouse, "A Longtime Precedent for Disregarding Precedent, " *New York Times*, July 21, 1991, Sec. 4, p. 4.

during the 1953–1989 terms, while formally overruling itself only 104 times, barely one-fifth as frequently.[69]

But when the justices split in cases overruling precedent, canons of restraint are abandoned. A classic example concerned the constitutionality of the minimum wage and overtime requirements of the Fair Labor Standards Act as applied to employees of state and local governments.[70] By a 5-to-4 vote, the Court sustained the Act and in the process overruled a contrary nine-year-old precedent.[71] The disenters – Burger, Rehnquist, Powell, and O'Connor – could not have matters both ways. They could not advocate restraint toward Congress as well as the states. Activism had to be unsheathed in defense of deference. Given that the state regulation here supported their conservative policy preferences, they championed judicial activism in support of considerations of federalism in a series of rousing opinions. The one to which they all subscribed went so far as to echo Chief Justice Marshall's reasoning in *Marbury v. Madison*: "The fact that Congress generally does not transgress constitutional limits on its power to reach State activities does not make judicial review any less necessary to rectify the cases in which it does do so."[72] The states' possession of equal Senate representation makes no difference:

This Court has never before abdicated responsibility for assessing the constitutionality of challenged action on the ground that affected parties theoretically are able to look out for their own interests through the electoral process.[73]

This from justices, three of whom had apotheosized "normal democratic processes" as the justification for the states – as well as Congress – to deny pregnant indigents abortions for which they could not pay.[74] All but Burger concurred in O'Connor's statement that in the aftermath of the majority's decision in *Garcia,* the only protection for "the remaining essentials of state sovereignty" is Congress' "underdeveloped capacity for self-restraint."[75]

The voting data that bear on the overrulings that occurred during the 1953–1989 terms are presented in Table 8.8. We employ a somewhat different format in this table than we did in Table 8.7, which contains the justices' voting in the

---

[69] By formal overruling, we mean a statement in the prevailing opinion that the decision "overruled" one or more of the Court's precedents, or a statement that the decision formally altered the applicability of a precedent short of an overruling: for example, limited a precedent in principle. A formal overruling or alteration excludes cases in which a precedent is "distinguished" or is otherwise held to be inapplicable to the case at hand.

[70] *Garcia v. San Antonio Metropolitan Transit Authority*, 469 U.S. 528 (1985).

[71] *National League of Cites v. Usery*, 426 U.S. 833 (1976).

[72] 469 U.S., at 566–567.

[73] Id. at 567, n. 12.

[74] *Maher v. Roe*, 432 U.S. 464 (1977), at 480; *Poelker v. Doe*, 432 U.S. 519 (1977), at 521. Also see *Beal v. Doe*, 432 U.S. 438 (1977). The three justices were Burger, Rehnquist, and Powell. Clearly, "normal democratic processes" are fine when they support one's preferences; not so fine when they do not.

[75] 469 U.S., at 588.

Table 8.8. *Votes in support and opposition to decisions formally altering precedents*

Justice	Court Warren	Court Burger	Court Rehnquist	total	%
Black	33-7	3-1		36-8	81.8
Blackmun		42-4	10-5	52-9	85.2
Brennan	38-0	31-16	9-6	78-22	78.0
Burger		41-8		41-8	83.7
Burton	2-1			2-1	66.7
Clark	13-15			13-15	46.4
Douglas	37-3	9-3		46-6	88.5
Fortas	15-1			15-1	93.8
Frankfurter	3-5			3-5	37.5
Goldberg	12-0			12-0	100.0
Harlan	16-23	3-1		19-24	44.2
Jackson	1-0			1-0	100.0
Kennedy			7-0	7-0	100.0
Marshall	9-0	33-15	8-7	50-22	69.4
Minton	1-0			1-0	100.0
O'Connor		11-2	11-4	22-6	78.6
Powell		39-4	4-1	43-5	89.6
Reed	1-0			1-0	100.0
Rehnquist		32-11	11-4	43-15	74.1
Scalia			13-2	13-2	86.7
Stevens		24-9	9-6	33-15	68.8
Stewart	24-13	33-3		57-16	78.1
Warren	37-2			37-2	94.9
White	21-11	39-8	14-1	74-20	78.7
Whittaker	3-2			3-2	60.0
totals	266-83	340-85	96-36	702-204	77.5

cases in which the Court declared legislative actions unconstitutional. Though the number of cases is much fewer than the number that pertains to unconstitutionality, we nonetheless divide the individual justices' votes among the three Courts whose behavior we assess. We do this because we have found that votes toward formal alterations of precedent more prominently display liberal/conservative patterns than they do in declarations of unconstitutionality.

In this regard, compare, for example, the decreasing proportions of Brennan's and Marshall's votes across the three Courts with those of White. As the Court has grown more conservative, their responses to alteration of precedent have also changed. Although the overall proportion of altering votes (77.5 percent) compares to those supporting unconstitutionality (81.2 percent total, 75.3 percent toward congressional action), the justices most supportive of formally altering precedents do not exhibit a common ideological stripe. The liberal Fortas, Goldberg, and Warren supported overruling with 93.8, 100, and 94.9 percent of their votes, respectively, when a majority of the Court did so. So also the conservatives Kennedy (100 percent) and Powell (89.6 percent). The explanation, of course, is that conservative Courts alter liberal precedents, whereas liberal courts do the opposite.

Although it appears superficially that three conservative justices defer most to precedent – Frankfurter 37.5 percent, Harlan 44.2 percent, and Clark 46.4 percent – deference did not motivate their behavior. Clark, for example, voted to overrule with eight of his first twelve Warren Court votes, all of which were cast prior to the Court's shift to a liberal orientation in the early 1960s.[76] Conversely, eight of Clark's last eleven votes affirmed the overruled precedent. So also, Frankfurter. Three of his first four votes supported alteration; all of his last four opposed it. A similar pattern obtains on the liberal side: All seven of Marshall's initial Burger Court votes supported alteration, as did all of Brennan's initial eight. Of Marshall's final sixteen, only seven were such, as were six of Brennan's last fifteen.

THE SUBORDINATE STATUS OF JUDICIAL RESTRAINT

Our efforts to uncover evidence of judicial restraint of a principled sort in the behavior of the twenty-five justices who have sat on the Court during the 1953-1989 terms have been fruitless. With the single exception of Rehnquist, all of the justices clearly appear to use restraint – along with judicial activism – as a means to rationalize, support, and justify their substantive policy concerns. If they support a policy – whether it concerns economics, civil liberties, access to the federal courts, unconstitutionality, or precedent – restraint serves as a useful

---

[76]   Jeffrey A. Segal and Harold J. Spaeth, "Decisional trends on the Warren and Burger Courts: Results from the Supreme Court Data Base Project," 73 *Judicature* 103 (19-89), at 104; reprinted in Elliot E. Stotrick, ed., *Judicial Politics*, Chicago: American Judicature Society, 1992), pp. 475–481.

cloak to conceal the nakedness of a barefaced statement of substantive preferences. On the other hand, activism works equally well to justify a high-handed
course toward action of which they disapprove.

Only Rehnquist appears to deviate from the foregoing course, and he does so
only insofar as consideration of federalism is concerned. He does defer to the
states regardless of whether the state's action was liberal or conservative, or
whether it concerned economics or civil liberties. He also appears reluctant to
declare actions unconstitutional, a reluctance, however, that does not extend to
constitutional issues on which the government generally takes a liberal position,
such as affirmative action under the Fourteenth Amendment and the taking of
property under the Fifth Amendment. Here, Rehnquist displays an activism that
in other areas would do Justice Douglas proud. Nor does Rehnquist's restraint
apply to formal alternations of precedent or to access to the federal courts. Toward
these matters he gives preference to his substantively conservative attitudes.
White and Blackmun also appeared to exercise restraint toward federal agencies
during the Burger Court, but not toward state economic regulation. White,
however, exercises no such restraint on the Rehnquist Court, and Blackmun did
so but barely. Stevens arguably also displays restraint toward the federal agencies,
but only on the Rehnquist Court, whereas O'Connor displays more deference to
state action impinging on civil rights and liberties on the Burger Court than to
that of the federal government.

REACTIONS TO THE COURT'S DECISIONS

Rarely does a Court decision provoke retaliatory action from other political
actors. Not uncommonly, however, members of Congress, the President or one
of his minions, local officials, and elements of affected publics may complain
that the Court has upstaged other actors by encroaching on their decision-making
turf. As we document in Chapter 9, the Court's status and authority are such
that its decisions are generally complied with, no matter how distasteful certain
elements find them. This being so, the likelihood that the basis for a decision,
as distinct from the decision itself, will give rise to anything more substantial
than rhetoric is highly unlikely.

Heightening the likelihood of futility is the double-edged quality of the canons
of judicial activism and restraint. A given vote or decision may simultaneously
manifest activism toward one decision-making body and restraint toward another,
as our discussion of *Garcia v. San Antonio Metropolitan Transit Authority* with
regard to the alteration of precedent illustrates.[77] To take a legislative example,
consider the matter of legislative reapportionment and districting. After overruling *Colegrove v. Green*[78] – its precedent that held that the matter was a political

---

[77] Also note the observation about Frankfurter's behavior in fn. 53 supra.
[78] 328 U.S. 549 (1946).

question, the Court in *Baker v. Carr*[79] held that the constitutional standard governing apportionment is one person, one vote – that legislative districts must be approximately equal in population.[80] From the legislative perspective, the one-person, one-vote requirement was fairly characterized by one authority as ''the most remarkable and far-reaching exercise of judicial power'' in American history.[81] But from the voters' standpoint, the decisions may properly be viewed as supportive of the ''normal democratic processes'' to which the Court paid obeisance in the Medicaid-abortion decisions of 1977.[82] By activistically destroying the system of ''rotten boroughs'' that allowed rural districts to dominate and control the state legislatures and Congress, the Court enabled urban – and especially suburban – communities to exercise power congruent with their proportion of the total population.

Congress

Congress typically fails to react to the Court's decisions that construe its legislation.[83] Individual members, of course, may mount a soap box, but such sound and fury – like most congressional utterances – is merely so much kakistocratic posturing that signifies nothing. Not uncommonly, the Court's prevailing opinion will invite Congress to change the law if it disagrees with the interpretation that the justices have given it. And equally commonly, if Congress does choose to overturn one of the Court's decisions, it will do so with little or no fanfare.

A recent case in point concerned the Federal Tort Claims Act, which governs the liability of federal employees who cause an injury within the scope of their employment. In *Westfall v. Erwin*,[84] the Court unanimously ruled that the judicially created doctrine of official immunity did not absolutely immunize federal employees who exercised decision-making discretion for torts committed within the scope of their employment. In other words, they could be personally sued for common law torts committed on the job. The Court, however, invited Congress to change the law if it so desired: ''We are also of the view . . . that Congress is in the best position to provide guidance for the complex and often highly empirical inquiry into whether absolute immunity is warranted in a particular context.''[85] Congress quickly and quietly accepted the invitation by amending the Federal Tort Claims Act to make an FTCA action against the United States the exclusive remedy for torts committed by federal employees.

---

[79]   369 U.S. 186 (1962).
[80]   *Gray v. Sanders*, 372 U.S. 368 (1963); *Wesberry v. Sanders*, 376 U.S. 1 (1964); *Reynolds v. Sims*, 377 U.S. 533 (1964); *Avery v. Midland County*, 390 U.S. 474 (1968); *Hadley v. Junior College District*, 397 U.S. 50 (1970).
[81]   Richard C. Cortner, *The Apportionment Cases* (New York: Norton, 1970), p. 253.
[82]   Op. cit. fn. 74 supra.
[83]   See Beth Henschen, ''Statutory Interpretations of the Supreme Court,'' 11 *American Politics Quarterly* 441 (1983).
[84]   98 L Ed 2d 619 (1988).
[85]   98 L Ed 2d, at 628.

Such invitions are by no means atypical of Court decisions construing legis-lative language. Neither is it unusual for Congress to react as it did. Furthermore, when Congress does respond to the Court's invitation, the Court takes pains to give primacy to that pronouncement. Thus, in its first construction of the FTCA amendment, the justices broadly read the language about the exclusivity of the FTCA as the sole remedy for persons seeking money damages for injuries caused by federal employees, even though this meant that persons injured by certain employee actions were barred from suing under other legal provisions.[86] Justice Stevens, in dissent, argued that the majority's holding will "deprive an important class of potential plaintiffs of their pre-existing judicial remedy" and will once again invite "congress to step in and 'provide guidance.' "[87]

President

Such interstitial, back-and-forth accommodation to somebody else's decision making primarily manifests itself only when the constitutionality of congressional action is not at issue. The Court does not invite Congress to void its interpretations of the Constitution. Such determinations are exclusively the province of judi-cial review. The fact that the President may support congressional legislation is constitutionally irrelevant, as the flag-burning controversy of 1989 and 1990 make clear.

In reaction to the 5-to-4 decision upholding a ruling of the Texas Supreme Court that flag burning violated the First Amendment,[88] the effect of which voided the laws of the forty-eight states that had prohibited such action, both Congress and the President vehemently expressed their displeasure. When Con-gress and President together unite in opposition to a Court's decision, the Court's position becomes rather precarious. At such times a threat to the Court's power and/or authority may realistically exist.

Illustrating such threats were the school desegregation cases, in which resistance emanated from the Southern states rather than from Congress or the President, and the controversy over divulging the contents of President Nixon's Watergate tapes. In such situations, when the Court persists in adhering to the opposed policy, the justices tend to arrive at a decision greater than minimum winning in size.[89] Ideally, they should unite and speak with a single voice, as they did in both *Brown v. Board of Education* and *United States v. Nixon*.[90] But neither the ideal nor the modal result occurred in the flag burning controversy.

The President initially pressed for a constitutional amendment that would

---

[86] *United States v. Smith*, 113 L Ed 2d 134 (1991).

[87] 113 L Ed 2d, at 156, 157. The important class of potential plaintiffs are persons injured by medical malpractice in military hospitals overseas.

[88] *Texas v. Johnson*, 105 L Ed 2d 342 (1989).

[89] David W. Rohde and Harold J. Spaeth, *Supreme Court Decision Making* (San Francisco: W.H. Freeman, 1976) pp. 193–205.

[90] 347 U.S. 483 (1954); 418 U.S. 683 (1974).

exclude flag burning as a mode of expressive conduct protected by the First Amendment. But instead of an amendment, Congress enacted the so-called Flag Protection Act, which imposed criminal penalties on those who knowingly mutilated, defaced, physically defiled, burned, or trampled on a flag of the United States, unless such conduct disposed of worn or soiled flags. The Court, however, by the same vote and with the same alignment of the justices, voided the federal law for the same reasons and in much the same language as it did the Texas law a year earlier.[91]

Instructively, the majority rejected the Bush Administration's invitation to reconsider its original decision "in light of Congress' recent recognition of a purported 'national consensus' favoring a prohibition on flag-burning," by asserting that even if such a consensus existed, "any suggestion that the Government's interest in suppressing speech becomes more weighty as popular opposition to that speech grows is foreign to the First Amendment."[92] Efforts to propose a constitutional amendment following the Court's decision came to naught when both the House and Senate failed to muster the necessary two-thirds vote.[93]

Direct confrontations between the Court and the President are few and far between. Much more frequent are cases in which the Court is called upon to construe the rules, regulations, and activities of various officials within the executive branch, such as the Internal Revenue Service, the Immigration and Naturalization Service, and the various cabinet-level departments. Litigation here, however, tends to manifest the interstitial back-and-forth decision making displayed when the Court construes the meaning of congressional statutory language, notwithstanding that a goodly portion of such controversies concerns the constitutionality of agency and department action. Although affected publics subject to administrative regulation may fulsomely praise certain decisions and as readily damn others, rarely does the Court or the agency itself speak harshly of the other. The advice given to junior members of Congress – to get along, go along – fairly describes relationships between the Court and the bureaucracy.

The public

Although pollsters commonly quiz the public about its attitudes toward various Court decisions, their polls indicate that the public is largely ignorant and ill-informed about the Court's rulings. Given that the questions asked do not necessarily have a common meaning to all respondents and that public opinion may vacillate like a weather vane, negative judgments about the public's knowledge

---

[91]   *United States v. Eichman*, 110 L Ed 2d 287 (1990).

[92]   110 L Ed 2d, at 296.

[93]   Richard L. Berke, "Fruitless Debate on Flag in Senate," *New York Times*, June 26, 1990, p. A12; "Senate Rejects New Move to Outlaw Flag Burning," *New York Times*, June 27, 1990, p. A11.

and understanding may result more from polling deficiencies than from any significant shortcoming on the part of the public itself.

With these caveats in mind, we note the Court's position that the public's opinion about any given decision is irrelevant. The justices pay obeisance to the Constitution and to the actions of the people's representatives, not to the public itself. The Court made this clear in the the the language quoted earlier about the supposed national consensus concerning flag burning. Probably the best examples of public reaction to the Court's decisions are found in the actions of state and local elected officials, along with those matters that require a vote of the electorate itself.

Great attention attended the Court's right-to-die decision in which the majority held that though individuals have the right to refuse or to have withdrawn life-sustaining treatment, the due process clause did not prohibit a state from requiring clear and convincing evidence of an incompetent's wish to terminate such treatment.[94] At the other extreme, the due process clause also did not preclude a state from using a standard that made euthanasia available on demand if it wished.

The Missouri requirement (in the Cruzan Case), which the Court upheld, was one of the most stringent. The state's supreme court, in construing the relevant statutes, ruled that Missouri had an "unqualified interest in life." As a result, no patient had a legal interest that could outweigh the state's interest as long as the treatment that the patient was receiving was not "oppressively burdensome," regardless of the lack of quality of the patient's life.[95] In Cruzan, this was a surgically implanted feeding tube for a woman brain-dead since 1983.

Following the Supreme Court's decision, the state dropped its opposition to removing Cruzan's tube, thereby permitting a local judge to authorize its removal. In 1991, Missouri's legislators changed its law by overwhelming margins, so that a patient need only express in writing the wish to be allowed to die when hope for recovery no longer exists.[96] Note that Congress also responded to the Court's decision by enacting the Patient Self-Determination Act in the fall of 1990. This legislation requires all health care centers receiving federal aid to inform patients of their rights to accept or refuse medical treatment and to use living wills and durable powers of attorney to realize their wishes.[97]

A final, unrelated example of a public reaction to a Supreme Court decision concerns the most pathological aspect of America's racial fears: miscegenation. Thirteen years after the Court declared the separate but equal doctrine of *Plessy*

[94]   *Cruzan v. Director, Missouri Department of Health*, 111 L Ed 2d 224 (1990).
[95]   Linda Greenhouse, "Does Right to Privacy Include Right to Die? Court to Decide," *New York Times*, July 25, 1989, pp. 1, 8.
[96]   Lisa Belkin, "State Asks to Quit Right-to-Die Case," *New York Times*, October 12, 1990, p. A9; Andrew H. Malcolm, "Right-to-Die Case Nearing a Finale," *New York Times*, December 7, 1990, p. A12; "A Stronger Right-to-Die Law Is Likely in Missouri," *New York Times*, May 17, 1991, p. A11.
[97]   Andrew H. Malcolm, "Judge Allows Removal of Woman's Feeding Tube," *New York Times*, December 10, 1990, pp. 1, 9.

v. Ferguson unconstitutional, the justices finally got around to deciding the constitutionality of laws prohibiting interracial marriage. By a unanimous vote, in what may well be the most felicitously titled case in the Court's annals, they voided such statutes as violations of both due process and equal protection.[98] Twenty years later, the voters of the state generally reputed to be the most rabidly racist of all – Mississippi – approved an amendment that formally removed the offending language from their state's constitution.

CONCLUSION

In this chapter we have assessed the relationship between the Supreme Court and representative democracy, especially with regard to congressional and presidential action, that of administrative agencies, and the action of state and local governments. We have shown that assertions that the Court merely ratifies congressional policy not only to be false, but remarkably simple-minded as well. We have found some evidence of judicial support for the decision making of the other branches and levels of government. But, overwhelmingly, such support results because these nonjudicial actions comport with the policy preferences of the justices themselves. Assertions to the contrary – as typified by the rubric of judicial restraint – is gerontocratic balderdash, unworthy of credence by any but the most gullible.

Indeed, not only judicial restraint, but also judicial activism, serve only to cloak the individual justices' policy preferences.

Although the infrequency with which the justices declare legislative actions unconstitutional indicates a measure of deference to the public and its representatives, appearance again belies reality. The displacement of the liberal Warren Court with increasingly conservative Burger and Rehnquist Courts did not result because of congruence with public sentiment. It resulted because Nixon, Reagan, and Bush populated the judiciary with persons in their own ideological image.

Still less does the record of the Warren, Burger, and Rehnquist Courts' adherence to precedent evidence conformity to public or publicly accountable sentiments. The infrequency with which they have formally altered their own precedents superficially evidences restraint. But the reality of adherence speaks instead to a policy-making capacity that enables the Court to appear as relatively fixed and stable while it pursues its preferred policy-making course.

---

[98] *Loving v. Virginia*, 388 U.S. 1 (1967).

The impact of judicial decisions

In Chapter 1 we described the Court's authoritative policy-making capacity. Alexis deTocqueville, more than a century before the activism of the Warren Court, stated that "there is hardly a political question in the United States which does not sooner or later turn into a judicial one."[1] Thus, "the judge is one of the most important political powers in the United States."[2] In this final chapter we go beyond the decisions of the Supreme Court to examine what happens after the Court announces its policies.

Broadly speaking, this chapter concerns the impact of the Court's decisions, a somewhat nebulous concept. Consider the Supreme Court's 1973 decision striking down state anti-abortion laws.[3] On the most concrete level, the ruling impacted the parties to the suit. The pseudonymous "Jane Roe" won an injunction barring Henry Wade, the District Attorney of Dallas County, Texas, from enforcing the state's anti-abortion statute. Roe, though, was unable to obtain the abortion she desired as it took nearly four years from filing the original suit until the Supreme Court disposed of the case. Because the Constitution and the Court's interpretation of it are the supreme law of the land,[4] Roe impacted the abortion laws in the forty-nine states that were not in complete compliance with its holding.[5] Thus, under the broad wording of Justice Blackmun's majority opinion, state and local governments could neither ban abortions during the first six months of pregnancy nor regulate them in the first trimester. Prosecutors and law enforcement officials could not enforce unconstitutional laws.

Which laws are unconstitutional is debatable because no single decision ever provides a completely definitive answer to all questions about a subject area; so lower court judges would need to determine whether local regulations complied with Roe. Impact would also extend to the millions of women who obtained

---

[1] *Democracy in America* (Garden City, NY: Anchor, 1969, p. 270.
[2] Ibid.
[3] *Roe v. Wade*, 410 U.S. 113 (1973).
[4] *Cooper v. Aaron*, 358 U.S. 1 (1958).
[5] Although four states allowed abortion on demand in 1973, only New York allowed it through the end of the second trimester with no hospitalization during the first trimester.

legal abortions since 1973, to medical professionals, hospital administrators, potential fathers, and of course, the unwanted fetuses.

Roe also impacted the political arena. Public attitudes toward abortion polarized. Partisans on both sides claimed that the public supported them. Thus, a survey paid for by Planned Parenthood indicated that the public opposed a decision banning abortion counseling in federally subsidized family planning clinics,[6] 65 percent to 33 percent. Not to be outdone, the National Right to Life Committee conducted its own poll two weeks later and reported supportive results of 69 percent to 27 percent.[7] So much for the objectivity of public opinion polls. As in other respects, the piper's payer calls the tune.

The legalization of abortion occasioned the creation of the pro-life movement, contributed to the rise of the "New Right," and substantially demobilized pro-choice forces. As a prime example of the law of unintended consequences, one may plausibly claim that *Roe* helped nominate and elect Ronald Reagan in 1980. Similarly, the remobilization of pro-choice forces following a 1989 decision that appeared to restrict abortion rights is credited with the election of Douglas Wilder as governor of Virginia.[8] And if *Roe* is overruled in the future, the prime beneficiary may be the Democratic Party.

A FRAMEWORK FOR UNDERSTANDING IMPACT

As the previous discussion makes obvious, "impact" is a multifaceted concept, subject to examination at three different levels at least: the result of the decision on the parties; compliance with the decision by judges, public officials, and citizens; and the impact of the decision on society at large.[9]

Result on the parties

A decision most narrowly influences the parties to the suit. In *Roe*, the result on the parties was fairly small. The plaintiff already had had her unwanted child;

---

[6] *Rust v. Sullivan*, 114 L Ed 2d 233 (1991).

[7] The Planned Parenthood question, in a Louis Harris poll, asked: "A few weeks ago, the U.S. Supreme Court, by a 5-4 vote, upheld the Government's rule prohibiting any discussion about abortion in family-planning clinics that receive federal funds. The only exception would be if a pregnant woman's life was in danger. Do you favor or oppose that Supreme Court decision preventing clinic doctors and medical personnel from discussing abortion in family planning clinics that receive federal funds?" The Right to Life question as posed by the Withlin Group asked: "If you knew that any government funds not used for family-planning programs that provide abortion will be given to other family-planning programs that provide contraception and other preventive methods of family planning, would you then favor or oppose the Supreme Court's ruling?" See Adam Clymer, "Abortion Foes Say Poll Backs Curbs on Counseling at Clinics," *New York Times*, June 25, 1991, p. A7.

[8] *Webster v. Reproductive Health Services*, 106 L Ed 2d 410 (1989).

[9] See Stephen Wasby, *The Impact of the United States Supreme Court* (Homewood, IL: Dorsey, 1970), chap. 2, for a similar typology.

so the result of the decision affected her no more than it did any other woman of child-bearing age. We don't know if she has availed herself of her newly won rights since then. The result of the case probably had even less effect on Henry Wade. He would no longer be prosecuting women who sought, or doctors who performed, abortions, but no evidence indicates that he spent much time before *Roe* doing that anyway.

By contrast, decisions on other issues may be far more consequential to the parties. In capital punishment cases, for example, the result is literally life or death. In other lawsuits, victory may be entirely Pyrrhic. Some of the winning litigants in *Brown v. Board of Education*,[10] for example, never attended a desegregated public school.

Compliance

Beyond the effect of a decision on the parties, we can examine compliance by those charged with interpreting and implementing it.[11] As we stated, few Supreme Court decisions definitively answer all questions about an issue. *Roe*, for instance, said nothing about spousal consent, parental consent, or Medicaid funding. Until such time as the Supreme Court authoritatively speaks to such issues, the lower courts are responsible for interpreting *Roe* and filling in the gaps. In the second *Brown* desegregation decision,[12] the Supreme Court expressly mandated Southern federal district court judges to determine the pace at which desegregation was to proceed within their states.

When the Supreme Court or lower courts declare that abortion rights must be protected, or that schools must be desegregated, it is usually up to public, and sometimes up to private, officials to implement those decisions. In *Roe*, prosecutorial implementation was quite simple: No longer could women who obtained or doctors who performed first and second trimester abortions be prosecuted. For public and private health care administrators, implementation was a bit more complex, for they had to decide whether to use their facilities for abortions. In *Brown*, the implementing population consisted largely of local school boards, who in conjunction with federal district courts had to develop plans that would produce desegregation "with all deliberate speed," a standard that gave them wide-ranging discretion.

Thus, compliance with a decision by the interpreting and implementing populations can be problematic. At one end of the spectrum, automatic compliance results. That fairly well described the situation in *Roe*. At the other end of the compliance spectrum is obstruction, which consists of attempts to prevent enforcement of Supreme Court decisions. Obstruction by the interpreting population

[10]   347 U.S. 483 (1954).
[11]   Charles A. Johnson and Bradley C. Canon, *Judicial Policies: Implementation and Impact* (Washington, DC: Congressional Quarterly, 1984).
[12]   349 U.S. 294 (1955).

rarely occurs; lower courts seldom defy a higher court's decisions. Obstruction occasionally manifests itself in the implementing population, however. A classic example occurred when Governor Faubus of Arkansas mobilized the national guard to prevent court-ordered desegregation in Little Rock in 1957. Less dramatic but more pervasive is the action of Bible Belt public school teachers who continue to lead their students in prayer in violation of *Engel v. Vitale* and *School District of Abington Township v. Schempp*.[13] "Secondary populations"[14] – those not directly affected by a Court decision, – can engage in obstruction as well. These include racists who stand in schoolhouse doors and Operation Rescue workers who mob abortion clinics.

A large gray area called "evasion" occupies the space between compliance and obstruction.[15] Evasion can be said to exist when interpreting and implementing populations comport with the letter but not the spirit of a ruling. For instance, the Court's reliance on the special character of education in *Brown* led some lower courts to exclude other public facilities from its compass, such as public transportation, swimming pools, and so on.[16] Yet such decisions conflicted with the basic notion of *Brown*: the inherent inequality of racially separate institutions. As we noted in Chapter 4, many of the complaints against Judge Carswell's nomination to the Supreme Court centered around his niggardly application of *Brown* to related litigation.

On the other hand, strictly speaking, a court's decision binds only the parties thereto. Its extension either to other litigants or to those situated similarly to the original parties may not be warranted. The Court itself commonly limits the scope and applicability of its precedents. For example, the justices ruled unanimously that prosecutors have only qualified immunity for the legal advice they give to police in the course of criminal investigations. The Court so held notwithstanding its precedent that prosecutors were absolutely immune from a civil suit for damages even though the prosecutor used perjured testimony, deliberately withheld exculpatory evidence, or failed to make full disclosure of facts harmful to the state's case.[17] Over the objections of thirty-seven states and the Department of Justice,[18] the Court asserted that "absolute immunity is designed to free the *judicial process* from the harassment and intimidation associated with litigation."[19] The justices' emphasis on the judicial process as the justification for absolute immunity significantly narrows its scope.

---

[13] 370 U.S. 421 (1962), and 374 U.S. 203 (1963).
[14] Johnson and Canon, op. cit. fn. 11 supra, ch. 5.
[15] Wasby, op. cit. fn. 9 supra, pp. 30–32.
[16] See Walter F. Murphy, "Lower Court Checks on Supreme Court Power," 53 *American Political Science Review* 1017 (1959).
[17] *Imbler v. Pachtman*, 424 U.S. 409 (1976).
[18] Marcia Coyle and Fred Strasser, "Justices Define Prosecutorial-Advice Immunity," *National Law Journal*, June 10, 1991, pp. 5, 12.
[19] *Burns v. Reed*, 114 L Ed 2d 547 (1991), at 563.

Impact

Although compliance and impact greatly overlap, impact is generally considered to be broader in scope than compliance because it includes consequences directly attributable to a given decision. On the other hand, impact is narrower than what has been called "aftermath," which includes everything that happened after a decision, whether directly caused by it or not. The trick of course is to determine which consequences are directly attributable to a decision and which are not. For instance, *Brown* presumably caused the end of Southern school segregation, but districts did not actually desegregate until Congress enacted the 1964 Civil Rights Act, denying funds to segregated schools. And although *Roe* undoubtedly increased abortions, the number of legal abortions was in fact climbing prior to *Roe* and may have continued upward without it.[20]

A final aspect of impact that is frequently overlooked or disregarded merits attention. Private persons and public officials, not party to litigation, are substantially free to adapt their conduct to accord with court decisions as they individually see fit. For example, in reaction to the possibility that the justices might overrule *Roe v. Wade*, the Connecticut legislature approved legislation that makes abortion a statutory right under state law.[21] Because the Constitution provides a floor for individual rights, not a ceiling, any state is free to provide individuals with more liberty than the Constitution mandates. The revocation of a woman's federal constitutional right to an abortion without undue governmental interference does not prevent a state from reading such a right into its own constitution or enacting legislation to that end.[22]

With this framework in mind we undertake a more systematic examination of compliance and impact.

COMPLIANCE

Normative models of judicial decision making – those that attempt to explain how courts should act – hold that lower courts ought to adhere to the decisions of their judicial superiors. Nevertheless, lower court judges, like Supreme Court justices, have their own policy preferences about the issues in a particular case, which they might seek to follow to the extent possible. Because of the finality of the overwhelming majority of trial court cases, and because the Court grants review to markedly less than 5 percent of petitioned cases, the potential exists for less than full compliance by lower courts – that is, the interpreting population.

---

[20] See the text following.

[21] Kirk Johnson, "Connecticut Acts to Make Abortion a Statutory Right," *New York Times*, April 28, 1990, pp. 1, 7.

[22] The irony of Connecticut's action should not be overlooked. Recall that a short twenty-five years earlier, Connecticut had a law that criminalized the sale, use, or distribution of any contraceptive drug or device, even between married couples. *Griswold v. Connecticut*, 381 U.S. 479 (1965). Clearly, what goes around, comes around.

Interpreting population[23]

Many early studies of lower courts found striking examples of lower courts' ignoring or misinterpreting Supreme Court decisions. J. W. Peltason, for instance, noted that the first six years of litigation following *Brown*

> produced negligible results. There were exceptions, but by and large federal judges applied the law adversely to the claims of Negroes. Some judges were so opposed to integration that they believed the safety of the nation depended on their minimizing the scope of the Supreme Court's decisions.[24]

Other scholars found dramatic examples of noncompliance over juvenile justice,[25] search and seizure,[26] and a variety of other areas.[27] Larry Baum concluded that these studies evidenced a view of lower court decision making that was one "of a judicial system in which judges reach decisions with little regard for the rulings of the highest court – in effect a system in near anarchy."[28]

Nevertheless, this work arguably focused on an unrepresentative sample of trees in the forest of compliance by investigating only state court implementation of controversial Warren Court civil liberties decisions. Their authors were no doubt motivated to examine compliance where the probability of finding it was relatively low. Recent systematic analysis has found that the federal courts overwhelmingly comply with express commands of the Supreme Court.[29] In the field of libel, only a handful of district court decisions failed to comply during a ten-year period.[30] Undoubtedly, lower courts are more likely to avoid or mitigate Supreme Court rulings than to defy them outright.[31] Songer concludes

---

[23] This section is based in part on Jeffrey A. Segal, Donald Songer, and Charles M. Cameron, "The Hierarchy of Justice: A Principle-Agent Perspective on Supreme Court-Circuit Court Interactions," proposal submitted to the National Science Foundation, 1991.

[24] *Fifty-eight Lonely Men: Southern Federal Judges and School Desegregation* (New York: Harcourt, Brace & World, 1961) p. 93.

[25] Bradley Canon and K. Kolson, "Compliance with *Gault* in Rural America: the Case of Kentucky," 10 *Journal of Family Law* 300 (1971).

[26] D. R. Manwaring, "The Impact of *Mapp v. Ohio*," in D.H. Everson, ed., *The Supreme Court as Policy-Maker: Three Studies on the Impact of Judicial Decisions* (Carbondale, IL: Southern Illinois University Press, 1968).

[27] Jerry K. Beatty, "State Court Evasion of United States Supreme Court Mandates During the Last Decade of the Warren Court," 6 *Valparaiso Law Review* 260 (1972).

[28] "Lower Court Response to Supreme Court Decisions: Reconsidering a Negative Picture," 3 *Justice Systems Journal* 208 (1978), at 208.

[29] Donald Songer, "The Impact of the Supreme Court on Trends in Economic Policy Making in the United States Courts of Appeals," 49 *Journal of Politics* 830 (1987); Donald Songer and Reginald Sheehan, "Supreme Court Impact on Compliance and Outcomes: *Miranda* and *New York Times* in the United States Courts of Appeals," 43 *Western Political Quarterly* 297 (1990).

[30] John Gruhl, "The Supreme Court's Impact on the Law of Libel: Compliance by Lower Federal Courts," 33 *Western Political Quarterly* 502 (1980).

[31] Beatty, op. cit. fn. 27 supra.

accordingly that "the overall extent and frequency of such noncompliance and evasion is unclear."[32]

Implementing population

The implementing population consists of those public and (occasionally) private officials charged with carrying out the Court's commands. To an appreciable extent, the implementing population's compliance with Supreme Court decisions is also unclear. A major deficiency of compliance studies is their inability to measure compliance validly and reliably. Typical methods include asking whether respondents have complied with particular Supreme Court decisions, or following them around to see if they do so. Needless to say, such studies substantially overestimate compliance. People generally do not admit to breaking the law, and are less likely in fact to do so when they are being monitored. As one critic noted,

Asking movie censors . . . or district attorneys . . . whether they conform to Supreme Court guidelines on obscenity and inquiring of school teachers whether they lead prayers in school is not much more revealing than it would be to ask taxpayers whether they declare all their income or fabricate any deductions. It is naive to expect people to incriminate themselves, and it can be assumed that those implicated in unlawful actions will generally take steps to conceal or whitewash them.[33]

Alternatively, compliance will be dramatically underestimated if, for example, one asks criminal defendants whether the police read them their rights.[34]

Findings of noncompliance are particularly dramatic, then, when substantial numbers of people admit they disobey the law. Robert Birkby, for instance, wrote to Tennessee school superintendents inquiring whether they were adhering to the decision in *Abington School District v. Schempp*,[35] which prohibited devotional bible readings. Despite the fact that such inquiries should overestimate compliance, only 1 out of 121 reporting districts admitted to the elimination of all bible reading and devotional exercises. Fifty-one districts altered their policies somewhat, whereas 70 made no changes whatsoever.[36] And despite the fact that surveilled police are more likely to abide by the *Miranda* requirements, only 25 of 118 suspects in a New Haven study received the full warnings required by

---

[32] Donald Songer, "An Overview of Judicial Policymaking in the United States Courts of Appeals," in John B. Gates and Charles A. Johnson, eds., *The American Courts: A Critical Assessment* (Washington, DC: Congressional Quarterly, 1990), p. 43.

[33] James Levine, "Methodological Concerns in Studying Supreme Court Efficacy," 4 *Law and Society Review* 583 (1970).

[34] Richard Medalie, Leonard Zeitz, and Paul Alexander, "Custodial Police Interrogation in Our Nation's Capital: The Attempt to Implement *Miranda*," 66 *Michigan Law Review* 1347 (1968).

[35] 374 U.S. 203 (1963).

[36] Robert Birkby, "The Supreme Court in the Bible Belt: Tennessee Reaction to the *Schempp* Decision," 10 *American Journal of Political Science* 304 (1966).

the Supreme Court ruling in a study conducted shortly after the ruling was made.[37] Noncompliance also occurs in other settings as well. The University of California, under state legislative prodding, set racial quotas on admissions that severely limit the number of Asian students despite the express prohibition on quotas in *Regents v. Bakke.*[38]

Nevertheless, as is true of the interpreting population, noncompliance may be easily overestimated among the implementing population. Prosecutions against women who obtained, or doctors who performed, first and second trimester abortions stopped immediately when *Roe* was decided. Readings of the *Miranda* requirements did increase after the police began to understand the rule better.[39] No executions took place in the United States between the striking down of the death penalty in *Furman v. Georgia*[40] and its reimposition in *Gregg v. Georgia.*[41]

Congressional compliance. Examples of congressional and presidential compliance also have their drama. In 1962 the Supreme Court decided the first in a short series of cases that in the words of one observer, "involved the most remarkable and far-reaching exercise of judicial power in our history."[42] The issue was the reapportionment of Congress and the legislatures of each and every one of the fifty states.

The Court initially asserted that legislative apportionment was properly a matter for judicial resolution,[43] thereby overruling a precedent in which Justice Frankfurter had held such controversies to be political questions inappropriate for judicial resolution.[44] In his dissent in *Baker v. Carr*, Frankfurter had asserted that the fact that courts "could effectively fashion" a remedy for "the abstract constitutional right" of electoral districting was mere "judicial rhetoric . . . not only a euphoric hope. It implies a sorry confession of judicial impotence in place of a frank acknowledgment that there is not under our Constitution a judicial remedy for every political mischief, for every undesirable exercise of legislative power." Appeal for relief, he said, "does not belong here," but belongs rather "to an informed, civically militant electorate." He then predicted: "There is nothing judicially more unseemly nor more self-defeating than for this Court to make *in terrorem* pronouncements, to indulge in merely empty rhetoric, sounding a word or promise to the ear, sure to be disappointing to the hope."[45]

The majority paid him no heed and in the process proved him to be a false

---

[37]   Michael Wald, Richard Ayres, David W. Hess, Mark Schantz, and Charles H. Whitebread II, "Interrogations in New Haven: The Impact of Miranda," 76 *Yale Law Journal* 1519 (1967).

[38]   438 U.S. 265 (1978). See Dinesh D'Souza, *Illiberal Education: The Politics of Race and Sex on Campus* (New York: Free Press, 1991), ch. 2.

[39]   Wald, et al., op. cit. fn. 37 supra.

[40]   408 U.S. 238 (1972).

[41]   428 U.S. 153 (1976).

[42]   Richard C. Cortner, *The Apportionment Cases* (New York: Norton, 1970), p. 253.

[43]   *Baker v. Carr*, 369 U.S. 186 (1962).

[44]   *Colegrove v. Green*, 328 U.S. 549 (1946).

[45]   369 U.S. 186 at 269–70.

prophet. In its next decision, the Court stipulated that within a single legislative constituency the operative districting principle must be one person, one vote.[46] This was followed by a ruling that in congressional elections, one person's vote "as nearly as practicable . . . is to be worth as much as another's."[47] The Court topped off its policy making four months later when it made its one-person, one-vote standard binding on *both* houses of the state legislatures.[48] Lest it appear that the Court only rode herd on Congress and the state legislatures, note also that the justices subsequently penned all popularly elected local government officials in the same barnyard as the legislators.[49]

Thus in the 27-month period from March 1962 to June 1964, the Court utterly abolished the stranglehold that farm and rural interests had had on the nation's legislatures since the time of Thomas Jefferson. This was no mean accomplishment for the governmental branch that has neither the purse nor the sword – especially because it concerned a matter that is not exactly of minor moment to legislators. The name of the legislative game is reelection, and reelection depends on the boundaries and characteristics of constituencies. Nonetheless, within one year of the decision in *Reynolds v. Sims*, forty-five of the fifty states took action to comply with the one person, one vote principle. It ought to be kept in mind that this occurred at a time when substantial segments of the population were more than a little riled at the Court's policies: God-fearing citizens outraged about the ban on organized prayer and bible reading in the public schools; police, prosecutors, and law-and-order elements muttering about the crippling of law enforcement[50]; and prudes and blue-noses dismayed and distraught over the demise of Victorian morality.[51]

Presidential compliance. The court has also successfully imposed its will on the executive branch, and again a theoretically co-equal branch has acceded to judicial supremacy at its own peril. The prime example is the Watergate Tapes case.[52] The circumstances that gave rise to the litigation were unprecedented: President Nixon threw down the gauntlet and dared the Court to force him to turn over his confidential papers.

Federal District Court Judge John Sirica had ordered Nixon to hand over sixty-four specified tapes and documents that related to private conversations between him and his closest and most trusted advisers, so that they could be used as evidence in a pending criminal trial involving seven of those advisers, all of

---

[46] *Gray v. Sanders* 372 U.S. 368 (1963).
[47] *Wesberry v. Sanders*, 376 U.S. 1 (1964), at 7–8 (footnote omitted).
[48] *Reynolds v. Sims*, 377 U.S. 533 (1964).
[49] *Avery v. Midland County*, 390 U.S. 474 (1968); and *Hadley v. Junior College District*, 397 U.S. 50 (1970).
[50] For example, *Mapp v. Ohio*, 367 U.S. 643 (1961); *Escobedo v. Illinois*, 378 U.S. 478 (1964).
[51] For example, *Manual Enterprises v. Day*, 370 U.S. 478 (1962); *Jacobellis v. Ohio*, 378 U.S. 184 (1964); and *A Quantity of Books v. Kansas*, 378 U.S. 205 (1964).
[52] *United States v. Nixon*, 418 U.S. 683 (1974).

whom a federal grand jury had previously indicted for various offenses including conspiracy to defraud the United States and obstruction of justice. On several occasions, including oral argument before the Supreme Court, Nixon and his henchmen hinted that they might not comply with a decision ordering the surrender of the tapes.

The justices, however, were not intimidated. They accepted Nixon's challenge to their authority. With a lapse of only sixteen days between oral argument and the announcement of their decision, the justices delivered a unanimous opinion (written, ironically, by the man whom Nixon himself had nominated as Chief Justice) that unequivocally subjected the President to the rule of law. The opinion stated that the aphorism "the King can do no wrong" has no place in the American constitutional system; that when a President claims the privilege of confidentiality in his communications, that claim "cannot prevail over the fundamental demands of due process of law in the fair administration of criminal justice. The generalized assertion of privilege must yield to the demonstrated specific need for evidence in a pending criminal trial."[53]

Nixon promptly released the tapes, which included specific conversations ordering aides to cover up the Watergate break in. Six weeks later, Nixon resigned under threat of impeachment and removal from office.

Potential reasons for noncompliance

Several explanations exist for the potential lack of compliance. More often than not these reasons, though limiting the Court in theory, do not limit it in practice.

The lack of coercive capacity. The justices possess neither the power of the purse nor of the sword.[54] Hence they must rely on the executive branch to give force and effect to their decisions when resistance occurs. In 1958, for example, an order by a reluctant President Eisenhower to nationalize the Arkansas Guard was required to enforce desegregation in Little Rock. The sole weapon the Court has at its disposal is its moral authority, and though moral authority may appear to be a fragile weapon compared with dollars, nightsticks, nuclear weapons, and other elements of *Realpolitik*, the Court's policy-making capacity – based on the respect and reverence accorded justices, the perceived legitimacy of the Court's decisions even when they are disapproved of by substantial segments of society, and the factors described in Chapter 1[55] – compares favorably with these tangible forms of persuasion, whether they are gently or roughly applied.

---

[53]   Id. at 713.
[54]   See *Missouri v. Jenkins*, 109 L Ed 2d 31 (1990), however, in which the Court upheld the authority of lower courts to order elected officials to raise taxes.
[55]   See Walter F. Murphy and Joseph Tanenhaus, *The Study of Public Law* (New York: Random House, 1972), pp. 40–44.

Decisions bind only the parties to litigation. The decision of a court, at all levels of the judicial system, technically binds only the parties to the litigation. Other persons, though similarly situated, have no legal duty to comply. Even so, the Supreme Court virtually never finds it necessary to spend time applying a decision to other persons simply because they were not formally parties to the litigation. School desegregation and obscenity do constitute important exceptions, however. Other exceptions are cases on their way to the Court at the time the Court announces its decision. These merely receive summary treatment – that is, the Court simply cites its controlling decision as authority for the action to be taken. Thus, four days after its July 1976 death penalty decisions, in which the majority declared that a mandatory death sentence for premeditated murder constituted cruel and unusual punishment,[56] the Court took summary action in the cases of sixty-three other persons who were under sentence of death: thirty-eight from North Carolina, nine from Georgia, seven from Oklahoma, six from Florida, and three from Louisiana. In each instance the summary action rested on the formal decisions announced four days earlier.

The Court's 1976 decisions were not its first encounter with the death penalty. Four years earlier, in *Furman v. Georgia*,[57] the justices, with one fell swoop, had voided the capital punishment laws of thirty-nine states, plus the District of Columbia. Thereupon, thirty-five states and Congress enacted new legislation to comply with what they perceived to be the Court's mandate, even though the laws of only two states – Georgia and Texas – were at issue in *Furman*. But over half of the reenacting states found that their new laws still failed to pass muster when the Court handed down its 1976 decision, which held the death penalty constitutionally permissible, at least for murder, only if the judge and jury have been given adequate information and guidance to enable them to take account of aggravating and mitigating circumstances and the character of the defendant before passing sentence.

As evidence of compliance, the states' response to the Court's decisions regarding capital punishment is instructive. From the time the Court first grappled with the constitutionality of the death penalty in a 1968 decision[58] until Utah's execution of Gary Gilmore in January 1977, not a single one of the several hundred occupants of death row was executed – notwithstanding American society's overwhelming endorsement of capital punishment and the rapidity with which all but fifteen of the fifty states successfully managed to crank up their creaky legislative machinery in order to comply with the Court's 1972 decision declaring existing capital punishment constitutionally defective.

The Court's opinion lacks clarity. We observed in Chapter 7 that a majority of the justices must agree on an opinion for it to become the opinion of the Court. When the Court is closely divided, bargaining, negotiation, and compromise among the majority coalition are especially costly and difficult to come by.

---

[56] *Gregg v. Georgia*, 428 U.S. 153; and *Woodson v. North Carolina*, 428 U.S. 280.
[57] 408 U.S. 238.
[58] *Witherspoon v. Illinois*, 391 U.S. 510.

Sometimes the majority justices cannot accommodate their differences, and in such cases only a "judgment of the Court" results. These judgments provide little guidance to the lower courts or to those affected by the Court's decision. Even those who desire to comply with the Court's mandate find determination of the Court's position difficult. Nonetheless, compliance typically occurs. Consider again the Court's 1972 death penalty decision. Although the opinion of the Court was announced *per curiam* rather than as a judgment of the Court, it approximated the latter more than the former. In pertinent part it read as follows:

> The Court holds that the imposition and carrying out of the death penalty in these cases constitute cruel and unusual punishment in violation of the Eighth and Fourteenth Amendments. The judgment in each case is therefore reversed insofar as it leaves undisturbed the death sentence imposed, and the cases are remanded for further proceedings.[59]

Each of the five justices who constituted the majority wrote his own separate opinion. Nonetheless, as previously mentioned, fully 70 percent of the states and the Congress promptly rewrote their capital punishment laws, hoping they had accurately fathomed the Court's inscrutable position. More then half of these states found they had guessed wrong when the Court handed down its five 1976 death penalty decisions, every one of which was announced via a judgment of the Court to which only Justices Stewart, Powell, and Stevens subscribed. Again, compliance was complete. Moreover, a systematic analysis of lower court decision making by Charles A. Johnson found that neither the size of the voting majority, the size of the opinion majority, the number of dissenting justices, the number of dissenting opinions, or the author of the majority opinion affected compliance.[60]

But even when every single justice joins the opinion of the Court, its position may still be no more clear than mud. The decisions in *Brown v. Board of Education*[61] again provide an apt illustration. The Court first said that "separate educational facilities are inherently unequal,"[62] and that the segregation the plaintiffs complained of deprived them of the equal protection of the laws guaranteed by the Fourteenth Amendment. This was a perfectly clear and comprehensible statement. The Court then addressed the matter of implementation, and one year later ruled that public schools must desegregate "with all deliberate speed," and that the task of eradicating this racist legacy belonged to the federal district courts "because of their proximity to local conditions."[63] Needless to say, the formula "with all deliberate speed" hardly lent itself to consensual application. No wonder that a decade elapsed before any appreciable changes occurred in the Deep South – especially because the Court itself chose to say

[59]   *Furman v. Georgia*, 408 U.S. 238, at 239–40.
[60]   "Lower Court Reactions to Supreme Court Decisions: A Quantitative Examination," 23 *American Journal of Political Science* 792 (1979).
[61]   347 U.S. 484 (1954), and 349 U.S. 294 (1955).
[62]   347 U.S., at 495.
[63]   349 U.S. 294, at 301, 299.

virtually nothing more on the subject until 1965, when it tersely asserted that "delays in desegregation of school systems are no longer tolerable."[64] Not until the Burger Court was the matter of implementation clarified. And then clarity resulted only because the Court discarded the "all deliberate speed" formula:

... continued operation of segregated schools under a standard of "all deliberate speed" for desegregation is no longer constitutionally permissible. . . . the obligation of every school district is to terminate dual school systems at once and to operate now and hereafter only unitary schools.[65]

Thus did desegregation finally come to the South, the border states, and parts of the North, aided and abetted by provisions in the Civil Rights Act of 1964 that permitted a cutoff of federal funds from school districts that failed to desegregate. If the fifteen-year interval between 1954 and 1969 constitutes noncompliance with the Court's mandate in *Brown v. Board of Education*, the blame should at least partially fall on the occupants of the Marble Palace.

IMPACT

The impact of a Supreme Court decision includes those societal consequences that directly or indirectly result from its decision. As we noted, the basic difficulty in determining impact is separating all that comes after a decision from all that is *caused* by the decision – that is, the impact.

Methodological problems

One of the least effective methods of determining impact is what is called a postest design or "one-shot case study."[66] Here the researcher waits for the Court's decision, and at some later point measures one or more types of responses to that decision. For instance, after the decision in *In re Gault*[67] we might measure the number of juveniles granted procedural rights.[68] Without knowing the extent of pre-*Gault* rights, we cannot even begin to assess the impact of the decision. According to research design gurus Donald Campbell and Julian Stanley, "such studies have such a total absence of control as to be of almost no value."[69]

Another typical but flawed method of assessing impact measures a certain activity at one time-point before and one time-point after the decision in question.

---

[64] *Bradley v. Richmond School Board*, 382 U.S. 103, at 105; and *Rogers v. Paul*, 382 U.S. 198, at 199.

[65] *Alexander v. Holmes County Board of Education*, 396 U.S. 19 (1969), at 20.

[66] Donald Campbell and Julian Stanley, *Experimental and Quasi-Experimental Designs for Research* (Chicago: Rand McNally, 1963), p. 7.

[67] 387 U.S. 1 (1967). The *Gault* decision extended due process protections to juvenile court proceedings.

[68] For example, Norman Lefstein, Vaughn Stapleton, and Lee Tietelbaum, "In Search of Juvenile Justice: *Gault* and its Implementation," 3 *Law and Society Review* 491 (1969).

[69] Op.cit. fn. 66 supra, p. 6.

This is called a "one-group pretest-postest design." Thus, to measure the impact of *Roe* we could count the number of legal abortions in 1972 and the number of legal abortions in 1973. Indeed, if we did so we would find a 27 percent increase, from about 587,000 to approximately 745,000.[70] Based on these numbers, we might then assume that *Roe* had a substantial impact on abortion rates. Yet such a jump could be consistent with any of the trends depicted in Figure 9.1 except D, where O_4 represents the number of 1972 abortions and O_5 represents the number of 1973 abortions. Yet only A provides justification for inferring impact, whereas almost nothing justifies inferring impact in E, F, G, or H. According to Campbell and Stanley, the one-group pretest-postest design is simply a "bad example" of how to do research.[71]

The difficulty of assessing impact increases when the Court focuses on fundamental principles rather than on the specific controversy before it – that is, on the larger question or issue, of which the case before it represents only a part. The opinion of the Court is, after all, the core of the justices' policy-making power. The opinion lays down the broad constitutional and legal principles that bind the lower courts, other governmental instrumentalities, and affected private persons; establishes precedents for the Court's future decisions; and, least importantly, resolves the litigation at hand.

Thus, in *M'Culloch v. Maryland*,[72] Chief Justice Marshall upheld the power of Congress to establish a national bank and concomitantly prohibited the states from taxing or regulating it. If the outcome of the controversy were analyzed twenty years after the decision was announced, the conclusion would be inescapable: The "case was more interesting as a monument to judicial impotence than as an example of judicial power."[73] In 1832, President Jackson vetoed a bill to extend the charter of the Bank of the United States. One year later, he withdrew federal funds from the Bank's vaults, and in 1837 its charter expired. The Bank, a shell of its former self, lingered for a few more years until bankruptcy put it out of business in 1841.

But the significance of *M'Culloch* is not that it affected the eventual fate of the Bank, but rather that in that decision Marshall formulated the doctrine of implied powers. His assertion of this principle provided the basis for the expansion of federal power and the rise of the welfare state that began during the depression of the 1930s. Though these developments did not occur until more than a century after *M'Culloch*, the decision in that case doomed the strict constructionists of federal power to defeat; thereafter, assertions that that government is best that governs least would have an unmistakably hollow ring.

---

[70] Gerald Rosenberg, *The Hollow Hope: Can Courts Bring About Social Change* (Chicago: University of Chicago Press, 1991), p. 180.
[71] Op. cit. fn. 66 supra, p. 7.
[72] 4 Wheaton 316 (1819).
[73] Murphy and Tanenhaus, op. cit. fn. 55 supra, p. 56.

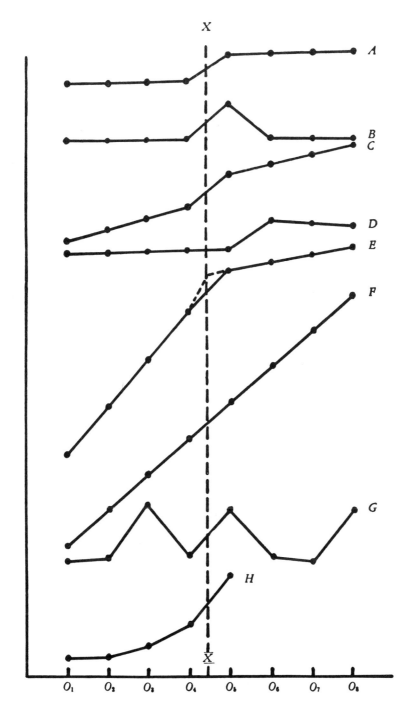

Figure 9.1 Problems with the pretest-postest design. Source: Campbell and Stanley, op. cit. fn. 66 supra.

Case studies of impact

Despite the problems of discerning the impact of the Court's decisions, examples of well-crafted, informative research do abound. We will examine studies in four such areas: the Fourth Amendment's exclusionary rule, reapportionment, desegregation, and abortion.

The exclusionary rule. The Fourth Amendment's exclusionary rule – as this book goes to press – holds that evidence obtained in violation thereof typically cannot be used in criminal trials. The Supreme Court imposed the rule on the federal government in 1914[74] and on the states in 1961.[75] Critics of the exclusionary rule, such as Chief Justice Burger, have claimed that the rule does not deter the police.[76] The truth is quite the contrary, for as Bradley Canon demonstrates, police compliance with the warrant requirement of the Fourth Amendment surged from the pre-*Mapp* to post-*Mapp* periods.[77] For example, only three search warrants were obtained by the Cincinnati police in 1958, and not one was issued in 1959. In the five months prior to the 1962 decision, three warrants were issued.[78] Yet, by 1963, 100 warrants were issued to the Cincinnati Police. A less dramatic but similar situation existed in Boston.[79] The deterrent effect of the exclusionary rule is the only plausible explanation for these data.

Alternatively, supporters of the exlusionary rule claim that the rule does not hamper the police. According to Tom Wicker, "the myth has spread that streams of criminals are going free because the exclusionary rule prevents the evidence from being used in court."[80] He cites statistics that only a miniscule number of cases – less than 1 percent – are dropped because of flaws in obtaining evidence. But by failing to consider cases where the police make no arrest because the rule deters them from making a questionable search in the first place, Wicker's findings lack validity. Both Burger and Wicker take internally inconsistent views: Burger, that the rule hampers police but does not deter; Wicker, that the rule deters but does not hamper. Clearly, the rule deters. Clearly, arrests are not made but for the presence of the rule. The latter, though, is true of any rule, exclusionary or not, that enforces the Fourth Amendment. But such a tradeoff was made when the Fourth Amendment was adopted.

[74]   *Weeks v. United States*, 232 U.S. 383.

[75]   *Mapp v. Ohio*, 367 U.S. 643.

[76]   *Bivens v. Six Unknown Federal Agents*, 403 U.S. 388 (1971), at 416.

[77]   "Is the Exclusionary Rule in Failing Health? Some New Data and a Plea Against a Precipitous Conclusion," 62 *Kentucky Law Journal* 681 (1974). Of course, the absence of a warrant is not per se unreasonable, so there is no absolute proof that the police were acting in outright disregard of the Fourth Amendment prior to *Mapp*.

[78]   Ibid. No data are availailable on the number of warrants requested but they could hardly be substantially more than the number obtained.

[79]   Ibid.

[80]   "Exploding a Myth," *New York Times*, May 10, 1983, p. A25.

Reapportionment. As discussed earlier in this chapter, Supreme Court rulings in the early 1960s required the apportionment of the House of Representatives and both houses of state legislatures on a one person, one vote basis. The rulings, though hostile to the well being of incumbents, received almost immediate compliance.

The question here, though, is not compliance, but impact. Chief Justice Warren, for one, thought the impact of these decisions enormous. Reflecting on his tenure, he viewed the reapportionment decisions as the most important,[81] for it freed the cities from the stranglehold of rural rule.

The reapportionment decisions clearly affected the number of urban and rural representatives, increasing the former at the expense of the latter. But if the reapportionment decisions were more than just a jobs program for big-city politicians, the influx of urban legislators should have had an impact on the budget priorities set by states following reapportionment. This is the question that was examined in a 1973 article by Roger Hanson and Robert Crew.[82] Using a pooled cross-sectional time-series design, they compare reapportioned states with non-reapportioned states, and states prior to reapportionment to states after reapportionment. State aid to cities, they found, increased significantly in 31 percent of the reapportioned states but in only 23 percent of the nonreapportioned states. Superficially surprising was their finding that reapportionment benefited suburbia more than central cities.[83] But because central cities antedated suburban sprawl, states commonly malapportioned the former to a lesser extent than the latter.

School desegregation. A more pessimistic view about the Court's impact on American life is presented in a book by Gerald Rosenberg, which contains a series of case studies that challenge the conventional wisdom about the efficacy of Supreme Court decisions.[84] Two of the more interesting accounts concern school desegregation and abortion.

It has been said of *Brown v. Board of Education*[85] that

probably no case ever to come before the nation's highest tribunal affected more directly the minds, hearts, and daily lives of so many Americans. Already, just two decades later, scholars have assigned the case a high place in the literature of liberty. The decision marked the turning point in America's willingness to face the consequences of centuries of racial discrimination.[86]

---

[81] David W. Rohde and Harold J. Spaeth, *Supreme Court Decision Making* (San Francisco: Freeman, 1976), p. 178.
[82] "The Effects of Reapportionment on State Public Policy Out-Puts," in Theodore Becker and Malcolm Feeley, eds., *The Impact of Supreme Court Decisions* (New York: Oxford University Press, 1973), pp. 155–174.
[83] Ibid., p. 172.
[84] Op. cit. fn. 70 supra.
[85] 347 U.S. 483 (1954).
[86] Richard Kluger, *Simple Justice* (New York: Vintage, 1977), p. x.

Nevertheless, in 1955, the year after the *Brown* decision, only twenty-three black school children in the entire South attended desegregrated schools.[87] And in 1956, the year after the *Brown* implementation decision,[88] only .11 percent of black school children did so. In 1959, a year after *Cooper v. Aaron*[89] held that threats of violence could not delay desegregation, the proportion had increased to only .16 percent. By the end of the 1963–64 school year, ten years after *Brown I*, only 1.2 percent of black children were enrolled in desegregated schools.

A phenomenal increase occurred thereafter. The rate was 2.3 percent in 1964, 6.1 percent in 1965, 16.9 percent in 1966, 32.0 percent in 1968, 85.9 percent in 1970, and 91.3 percent in 1972. A crucial intervening factor – in Rosenberg's analysis *the* crucial intervening factor – was the passage of the Civil Rights Act of 1964. Title VI of the act declared that ''no person in the United States shall, on the ground of race, color, or national origin, be excluded from participation in, be denied the benefits of, or be subjected to discrimination under any program or activity receiving Federal financial assistance.'' This became significant when, in 1965, Congress began pouring billions of dollars into education as part of President Lyndon Johnson's Great Society. Following the 1964 Act, the Department of Health Education and Welfare (HEW) set increasingly rigid standards for compliance with Title VI, culminating in 1968 regulations that required complete desegregation by the fall of 1969.

The Supreme Court, though, had not completely abandoned the field of school desegregation. A 1965 decision declared that ''delays in desegregation of school systems are no longer tolerable.''[90] And in 1969 the Supreme Court ended the era of ''all deliberate speed,'' declaring that ''the obligation of every school district is to terminate dual school systems at once.''[91]

Apportioning credit for desegregation is no simple task. Rosenberg relies on a survey conducted by the U.S. Commission on Civil Rights. The Commission found that between 1954 and 1975, federal district courts desegregated 207 Southern districts, whereas 152 were desegregated under HEW.[92] We need not accept Rosenberg's conclusion that ''*Brown* and its progeny stand for the proposition that courts are impotent to produce significant social change,''[93] to realize that the courts acting alone on desegregation did not get very far. On the other hand, nothing prevented Congress and its administrative agent from desegregating schools before 1954, or even in the immediate aftermath of *Brown*.

---

[87]   All figures are from Rosenberg, op. cit. fn. 70 supra, p. 50.
[88]   349 U.S. 294.
[89]   358 U.S. 1 (1958).
[90]   *Bradley v. Richmond School Board*, 382 U.S. 103, at 105.
[91]   *Alexander v. Holmes County Board of Education*, 396 U.S. 19, at 20.
[92]   Rosenberg, op cit. fn. 70 supra, p. 53. The survey probably underestimated HEW's effectiveness by giving only the courts credit for responses that listed both the courts and HEW as the primary sources of desegregation pressure.
[93]   Ibid., at 71.

Congress did not do so. Suffice it to say that the Court's leadership was a necessary but insufficient cause of Southern school desegregation.

Yet the impact of *Brown* cannot be measured simply in terms of desegregated schools. We turn again to Richard Kluger:

> The mass movement sparked by *Brown* was unmistakenly thriving as soon as six months after the Court handed down its implementation decree. It began in the Deep South, in Montgomery, Alabama, when a forty-three-year-old seamstress and active NAACP member named Rosa Parks refused to move to the back of a city bus to make room for a white passenger. Within days, and thanks to the leadership of Mrs. Parks's pastor, the Reverend Martin Luther King, Jr., all blacks were staying off the buses of Montgomery in a massive show of resentment over the continuing humiliation of Jim Crow. . . . Lunch counter sit-ins started in North Carolina in 1960, and soon in hundreds of communities blacks were making personal statements of protest – and risking their necks – to demonstrate the depth of their demand for equal treatment as human beings.[94]

Abortion. Many believe that absent the decision in *Roe v. Wade*,[95] legal abortions would be oxymoronic. Senator Edward Kennedy expressed the fears of millions of pro-choice women when he declared in 1987 that Robert Bork's America, one in which *Roe* was overturned, would be one in which "women would be forced into back alley abortions."[96]

Roe undoubtedly had a substantial impact on the number of abortions in the United States. As one text declares, the response to *Roe* was "immediate from women who sought abortions. In the first three months of 1973, 181,140 abortions were performed in the United States; and during the first year following the Supreme Court's decision a total of 742,460 abortions were performed nationwide."[97] The upward trend continued, exceeding 1 million in 1975.[98] The number plateaued in 1979 at approximately 1.5 million.

The conventional wisdom, which gives the Supreme Court full and total credit (or blame) for abortion rights in the United States, is not completely correct. Although the number of legal abortions climbed strikingly following *Roe*, the number of legal abortions actually escalated dramatically prior to *Roe*, as shown in Figure 9.2. In 1969, 22,000 legal abortions were performed in the United States; in 1970, three years prior to *Roe*, 194,000, a 752 percent increase. The following year saw the number jump to 486,000, a 151 percent increase. The largest increase since *Roe*, 27 percent, occurred in the year of the decision. From a purely statistical viewpoint, the year of *Roe* did not produce a substantial change in the incidence of abortion.

What impact, then, did the Court have? Clearly, it did not instigate abortions. That responsibility locates elsewhere. First, from the mid–1960s through the early 1970s, public opinion increasingly liberalized. One study found approval

---

[94] Op. cit. fn. 86 supra, pp. 749–750.

[95] 410 U.S. 113 (1973).

[96] James Reston, "Kennedy and Bork," *New York Times*, July 5, 1987, Sec 4, p. 15.

[97] Johnson and Canon, op. cit. fn. 11 supra, p. 6.

[98] All figures are from Rosenberg, op. cit. fn. 70 supra, p. 180.

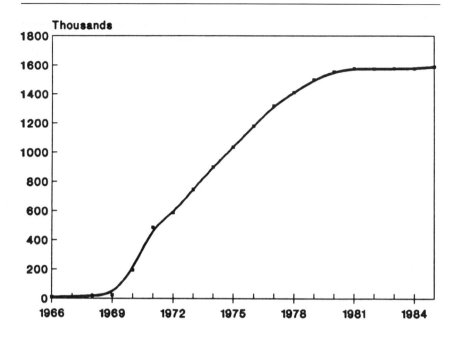

Figure 9.2   Legal abortions in the United States. Source: Rosenberg, op. cit. fn. 70
supra.

at 41 percent in 1965, reaching 63 percent in 1972. According to the National
Opinion Research Center, by 1972, 40 percent endorsed the broadest abortion
alternative, abortion on demand.[99] These increases can be traced to several
factors, including the burgeoning women's movement, dramatic changes in attitudes toward sexual relations, and fetal deformities caused by the drug tha-
lidomide and the rubella virus.

Second, state legislatures began to react to these changes in public opinion.
In 1967, with 73 percent of Californians supporting abortion reform,[100] Governor
Ronald Reagan signed a liberalization bill into law. The first state to virtually
legalize abortion on demand was Hawaii, which acted in 1970. Three more states
did so that year: New York, which acted despite a large Catholic population;
Alaska, whose legislature overturned a gubernatorial veto; and Washington,
whose liberalization provisions were duly enacted following a referendum that
passed by a margin of 12 percent.

Following the pro-choice victories of 1970, the legislative movement stalled
somewhat. Though substantial liberalization of abortion laws took place, no state
completely legalized abortion in 1971 or 1972. After the January 1973 *Roe*
decision, repeal became superfluous. Though it cannot be proven, it seems likely

[99]   Ibid., pp. 260–61.
[100]   Ibid., p. 261.

that several other states would have repealed their laws in part or in whole during the remainder of the 1970s had *Roe* not been decided. But it is just as probable that many states would never have eliminated their anti-abortion laws without *Roe*, whereas others would have adopted a position between no choice and *Roe*. Thus the Supreme Court dramatically boosted abortion rights, but like school desegregation, the Court did not act alone. Public opinion (and legislative) changes preceded the Court's action.

THE SUPREME COURT AND PUBLIC OPINION

Robert Dahl's seminal article on the Supreme Court, discussed in Chapter 8, declares that its significance as a national policy maker limits it to legitimizing congressional and presidential policies.[101] Whatever theoretical merit might exist in Dahl's notion, empirical reality demonstrates its falsity. The ignorance of the public about the workings and decisions of the Court precludes it from making much of an impact, much less a legitimizing one.

Public ignorance about the Court is substantial, though perhaps no more so than other areas of politics. A 1964-1966 national study, during the height of Warren Court activism, found that less than half of all respondents could name a single thing the Court had done recently that they liked or disliked.[102] Moreover, having an opinion does not guarantee its rationality. The minority of people who mentioned a specific like or dislike included one person who opposed the Court for "getting us mixed up in this war," and another who supported the Court because "they gave us Medicare."[103] Perhaps the best example of the public's ignorance of the Court was a 1989 *Washington Post* survey.[104] Nine percent correctly named William Rehnquist as Chief Justice of the United States. Among associate justices, recall ranged from 23 percent for Sandra Day O'Connor, to .6 percent for John Paul Stevens. All this pales by comparison with the 54 percent who correctly named Joseph Wapner as the judge on the TV show "The People's Court."

It should occasion no surprise then that public support for various issues is totally unaffected by the Court's decisions. Examination of national surveys taken on eighteen issues before and after Supreme Court decisions between 1937 and 1983 support this judgment.[105] The issues, typically controversial, received significant media play. They included the death penalty, abortion, miscegenation, and affirmative action. "Overall, the average poll shift was virtually zero – a

---

[101] Robert Dahl, "Decision-Making in a Democracy: The Supreme Court as National Policy-Maker," 6 *Journal of Public Law* 179 (1957).

[102] Murphy and Tanenhaus, op. cit. fn. 55 supra, p. 41.

[103] Ibid., p. 42.

[104] Richard Morin, "What Americans Think: The Case for TV in the Highest Court," *Washington Post National Weekly Edition*, June 26-July 2, 1989, p. 37.

[105] Thomas R. Marshall, *Public Opinion and the Supreme Court* (Boston: Unwin Hyman, 1989), chap. 6.

bare + .06, or six one-hundredths of one percent. These results provide little evidence that Court rulings influence mass public opinion. The polls shifted away from the Court's position more often than toward it.''[106]

One partial explanation for these nonfindings, particularly among highly salient issues, is provided by Charles Franklin and Liane Kosaki.[107] Rather than an increase or decrease in support, they found that *Roe* polarized public opinion. White Protestants, for instance, showed increased support for abortion rights while white Catholics decreased theirs. The applicability of their results to other areas, though, has not been demonstrated. But their findings comport with the judgment that the Court's decisions have little or no aggregate impact on public opinion.

SUMMARY AND CONCLUSION

In Chapter 1 we noted the Court's role as the predominant shaper of American public policy. Abortion, busing, affirmative action, and flag burning are but a few of the highly salient issues that the Court has addressed. In the first eight chapters, and particularly in Chapter 6, we demonstrate how the justices base their decisions on their ideological attitudes and values. In this chapter we have altered our focus to consider what happens to issues after the Court articulates its policy. In doing so we distinguish between compliance and impact. Compliance refers to the extent that those charged with interpreting and implementing Supreme Court rulings obey them, whereas impact refers to the effect of such rulings on society.

Despite a few contrary instances, compliance with Supreme Court decisions occurs. Lower court judges don't like to be overruled, and thus outright defiance rarely happens. Nevertheless, lower court judges, no less than Supreme Court justices, have tools that enable them to mitigate the full import of High Court rulings. Precedents can be found on both sides of cases, unfavorable precedents can be distinguished, facts can be obfuscated. Given the small percentage of appealed cases, and the even smaller percentage of cases that the Court reviews, lower court judges have substantial leeway to act independently.

Compliance with Supreme Court rulings by those in the implementing population may also be problematic. If a teacher in a small, homogenous, Bible Belt community leads class in prayer and no one complains, there is little the Supreme Court or the American Civil Liberties Union can do about it. So too is there little that the Court can do to sanction police officers who inaccurately claim to have read defendants their rights or who routinely assert that incriminating evidence came into their possession not because of an unreasonable search or seizure, but because the defendant suffered from "dropsy." In sum, full

---

[106]   Ibid., at 146.
[107]   "Republican Schoolmaster: The U.S. Supreme Court, Public Opinion, and Abortion," 83 *American Political Science Review* 751 (1989).

compliance with the Court's decisions is no more likely than full compliance by motorists with speed limits. Even so, compliance is the rule rather than the exception, even among those who disagree with the law.[108]

Decisional impact is much more difficult to assess than compliance. *Post hoc, propter hoc* has no more validity impact-wise than otherwise. Apportionment of credit and blame bedevils all analysts. The Civil War is blamed on the Court's most despicable decision[109]; the end of Southern apartheid is a claimed result of what may be its most respected decision[110]; and tens of millions of abortions are both claimed and blamed on what may be its most controversial decision.[111] Yet in none of these decisions did the Court solely shape public policy. With or without *Scott v. Sandford*, a nation divided between slavery and freedom could not endure. Though Congress may never have acted without the Court's lead in civil rights, acting alone the Court accomplished precious little in the fight against school segregation. The increased incidence in abortion was initially spurred by public opinion and state legislatures, which is where the fight will return if *Roe* is overturned. The Supreme Court is but one actor, albeit a leading one, impacting public policy.

[108] Tom R. Tyler, *Why People Follow the Law: Procedural Justice, Legitimacy, and Compliance* (New Haven: Yale University Press, 1990).
[109] *Scott v. Sandford*, 19 Howard 393 (1857).
[110] *Brown v. Board of Education*, 347 U.S. 483 (1954).
[111] *Roe v. Wade*, 410 U.S. 113 (1973).

Conclusion: Response to criticisms of the Attitudinal Model

We end this book with our response to the charges that critics of the attitudinal model typically make. Although we have addressed most of them in the course of formulating and applying the attitudinal model, we did not consider them as so many direct challenges to the propriety of our workways. This we do here.

We note first that we exclude from criticisms of the attitudinal model allegations that courts and judges do not make policy. Such criticism flourished at an earlier time, when jurisprudes as well as the lay public uncritically accepted as gospel the assertion that judges merely found or discovered the law – in the same sense that gardners discover weeds in their shrubbery, or diners find flies in their soup. What little credibility this argument had it lost when judges themselves began to formally admit that they made policy.[1] And though some members of the Supreme Court, as well as lower courts, remain equivocal, that no more warrants rebuttal than the argument that people kill, not guns.

Because attitudinal research within the judiciary has focused on the U.S. Supreme Court largely to the exclusion of other courts – and done so, moreover, by an analysis of the Court's twentieth century decisions – critics have suggested that the model is both institutional and time bound. We address each criticism in turn.

THE TIME-BOUND CRITICISM

Political scientists have disproportionately analyzed the Warren, Burger, and Rehnquist Courts. They have done so in part because much more data exist about these Courts, including a widely ranging database of known reliabliity that is designed for multi-investigator use.[2] Apart from the ready availablility of data, political scientists tend to concentrate on matters of current import. We are not historians. Though these two factors militate against the past, such analyses do exist. The initial formulation of the attitudinal model, by Glendon

---

[1] See the section of Chapter 1, ''Judges as policy makers,'' which contains examples of such recognition.

[2] Harold J. Spaeth, *United States Supreme Court Judicial Database, 1953- Terms* (Ann Arbor, MI: Interuniversity Consortium for Political and Social Research, 1990, 1991, 1992).

Schubert, was partially tested against decisions of the Vinson Court (1946–1952), which at that time was the Court of most recent vintage.[3] Three unpublished dissertations addressed the first half of the twentieth century,[4] and in our presentation of the Court's political history in Chapter 3 we did subject the decisions of the Taney Court to attitudinal analysis, discovering that the justices located themselves along an ideological axis of Hamiltonianism-Jeffersonianism.[5]

Two other factors also work to lessen consideration of earlier Courts: the absence of dissent relative to more recent Courts, and the existence of obligatory jurisdiction. In all probability, these two factors are closely interrelated: The relative absence of dissent presumably resulted because of the Court's mandatory jurisdiction, which in turn produced vast numbers of decisions on well settled questions.

Although infrequency of dissent does not preclude application of the attitudinal model, as we point out in Chapter 6, it obviously makes it much more difficult to reach confidence levels beyond the conventional range of improbability. And, needless to say, an explanation of judicial decision making as antithetical to the conventional wisdom as the attitudinal model needs an abundance of highly persuasive data to achieve even a modicum of acceptance. Admittedly, we cannot unequivocally substantiate that the absence of dissent results from the mandatory jurisdiction that preceded enactment of the Judges' Bill of 1925. It may have resulted from intra-group norms that disapproved of dissent. Or the costs of writing dissents may have been higher before clerks were readily available to draft opinions. These, of course, stem from non-attitudinal considerations. Nonetheless, the fact that the attitudinal model explains the justices' behavior in those issue areas and across the periods examined warrants that the burden of proving an alternative explanation fall on our critics.

THE INSTITUTIONAL CRITICISM

As for the institutional criticism – that the attitudinal model governs only the Supreme Court – one cannot gainsay the peculiar position the justices occupy. The Court completely controls its docket, and thus eliminates meritless claims at the certiorari stage. It is the court of last resort; no judicial decision makers can alter its decisions. Furthermore, the justices clearly lack ambition for higher office. Asked what her next career step would be following service on the

---

[3] *Quantitative Analysis of Judicial Behavior* (Glencoe, IL: Free Press, 1979); *The Judicial Mind* (Evanston, IL: Nortwestern University Press, 1965).

[4] Donald C. Leavitt, *Attitudes and Ideology on the White Supreme Court, 1910–1920* (East Lansing, MI: Michigan State University, 1970); Mary R. Mattingly, *The Hughes Court, 1931–1936: Psychological Dimensions of Decision Making* (East Lansing, MI: Michigan State University, 1969); Peter G. Renstrom, *The Dimensionality of Decision Making of the 1941–1945 Stone Court* (East Lansing, MI: Michigan State University, 1972).

[5] See pp. 210–213 supra.

Supreme Court, Justice O'Connor said: "I have no next career step. This is it."[6]
Her response has typified the behavior of her colleagues and predecessors, except
for those who antedated the nineteenth century. These institutional factors – if
not lifetime incumbency without electoral accountability – distinguish the justices
from those who sit on other benches. Too little research has been conducted on
lower courts to establish the necessity of a position at the apex of the judicial
hierarchy and lack of ambition as prerequisites for the operation of the attitudinal
model in any across-the-board fashion. The research that does exist suggests
that non-attitudinal factors supplement, but do not displace, the attitudinal
model.[7] The anecdotal and impressionistic use of common ideological descriptors
for the behavior of judges – state and federal, trial and appellate – indicates that
lay and journalistic court watchers detect the operation of personal policy preferences.

Be this as it may, we should not be faulted for the failure – such as it may
be – of the attitudinal model to manifest itself at lower court levels. Our book
concerns the U.S. Supreme Court. And although we do not think the Supreme
Court is necessarily unique in being driven attitudinally, we suspect that intervening variables of a non-attitudinal sort appreciably affect lower-court decision
making – that of the states more than that of the federal government – if only
because of the lifetime appointments and the consequent lack of electoral accountability that federal judges enjoy. If neo-institutionalism has taught political
science anything over the past decade, it is that institutional structures shape
incentives. Theories of presidential power don't necessarily apply to county
executives; theories of Supreme Court decision making don't necessarily apply
to traffic courts.

Behavioral research has concentrated on civil rights and liberties; relatively
little emphasis has been given behavior involving economic and fiscal activities,
the exercise of judicial power, or considerations of federalism. This should
occasion no surprise. Salience affects scholars – at least those who pride themselves on timeliness – as much as it does the mass media and the public at large;
hence, the attention accorded individual rights and liberties. The lesser heed paid
other issue areas does not infer the presence of non-attitudinal variables. The
limited work in these areas does not so suggest.[8]

---

[6] Lawrence Bodine, "Sandra Day O'Connor," 69 *American Bar Association Journal* 1394 (1983),
at 1398.

[7] See Henry R. Glick, "Policy Making and State Supreme Courts," and Lynn Mather, "Policy
Making in State Trial Courts," both in John B. Gates and Charles A. Johnson, eds., *The American
Courts: A Critical Assessment* (Washington, D.C: Congressional Quarterly, 1991).

[8] See, for example, Glendaon A. Schubert, *Quantitative Analysis of Judicial Behavior*, op. cit.
fn. supra, pp. 290–299; Harold J. Spaeth, "Judicial Power As a Variable Motivating Supreme
Court Behavior," 6 *American Journal of Political Science* 54 (1962); Harold J. Spaeth and Stuart
H. Teger, "Activism and Restraint: A Cloak for the Justices' Policy Preferences," in S.C.
Halpern and C.M. Lamb, eds., *Supreme Court Activism and Restraint* (Lexington, MA: Lexington
Books, 1982); Robert L. Dudley and Craig R. Ducat, "The Burger Court and Economic Lib-
eralism," 39 *Western Political Quarterly* 236 (1986); Craig R. Ducat and Robert L. Dudley,

THE ABSENCE OF NON-ATTITUDINAL FACTORS

This does not mean that attitudinal variables explain behavior across the board. As far as the modern Court is concerned – that is, since Warren became Chief Justice in 1953 – we have not discovered any narrowly defined issues in which variables of a non-attitudinal sort operate. If non-attitudinal factors have not been found at the microanalytic level, it follows, a fortiori, that no such discovery has occurred at the macroanalytic level. That is not to say that the opposite holds: that the attitudinal model explains the totality of the justices' decision making. As the appendix to Chapter 6 clearly shows, we do not achieve acceptable levels of predictive validity in many issue areas – especially those pertaining to unions, economic activity, judicial power, federalism, and federal taxation. It may well be that intervening variables of a non-attitudinal sort preclude predictive validity. If so, no one has discovered them in these or any other policy-making area. The lack of any testable alternative explanation, coupled with the relatively little attention analysts have paid these issue areas, suggests that inaccurate specification of the relevant attitudinal variables may well account for the lack of predictive validity.

Note also our use of predictive validity as the criterion for operational evidence of the attitudinal model here. Less rigorous analyses, such as those employed in the references cited in footnote 9, find that attitudinal variables explain the great majority of the behavior there examined. In short, perhaps we have set our sights too high: that our expectations surpass either our analytic or our measurement skills, or both. If so, the appropriate response to an allegation that the justices may have no preferences in at least some policy areas is to shift the evidentiary burden to those who so allege.

THE SUPREME COURT IS STILL A COURT

This criticism acknowledges that although the justices exercise choice, they do so as judges rather than as legislators or administrators. We obviously do not dispute this assertion; what we do dispute is the spin these critics give the assertion. It usually quotes the following language:

... political scientists who have done so much to put the "political" in "political jurisprudence" need to emphasize that it is still "jurisprudence." It is judging in a political context, but it is still judging; and judging is something different from legislating or administering. Judges make choices, but they are not the "free" choices of congressmen. ... There is room for much interpretation in the texts of constitutions, statutes, and ordinances, but the judicial function is still interpretation and not independent policy making. It is just as false to argue that judges freely exercise their discretion as to contend they have no policy functions at all. Any accurate analysis of judicial behavior must have

"Dimensions Underlying Economic Policy Making in the Early and Later Burger Courts," 49 *Journal of Politics* 521 (1987); Timothy M. Hagle and Harold J. Spaeth, "The Business Decisions of the Burger Court: The Emergence of a New Ideology," 54 *Journal of Politics* 120 (1992).

as a major purpose a full clarification of the unique limiting conditions under which judicial policy making proceeds.[9]

Pious stuff this, fully compatible with modern manifestations of the mythology of judging that we described in Chapter 1. Unlike the classic formulations of Chief Justice Marshall[10] or Justice Roberts,[11] it does admit – albeit grudgingly – that judges do make policy.

Spin results from 1) characterizing congressional options as "free," and conversely by 2) positing "limiting conditions" that presumably confine judicial discretion within narrow bounds. According to these critics, legislators presumably behave as so many loose cannons unconstrained by constituent or reelection concerns, and operate in an environment where laws are made as easily as checks are bounced or budgets deficited. As for the "limiting conditions" under which justices presumably operate, we have tried our utmost to identify and empirically validate them – unsuccessfully – in our discussion of the legal model in Chapter 2, non-attitudinal factors in Chapter 6, and the existence of judicial restraint in Chapter 8.

On the other hand, we have regularly noted that the justices are not completely free agents. Their jurisdiction is limited; they cannot avoid deciding some cases, while rejecting others; a plurality may not render an opinion of the Court; four justices may not overrule five; authoritative decisions should be accompanied by an opinion that is larded with citation to previously decided cases. They should justify their decisions by formalistically relying on plain meaning and/or legislative (or Framers') intent, by writing their opinions in legal language, and by employing legal (i.e., syllogistic) reasoning.

But these limitations overwhelmingly pertain to the rules of the judicial game, not to its outcome. And although rules of procedure are often outcome-determinative, those to which the Supreme Court is subject are minimally so relative to other decision-making bodies – judicial and nonjudicial – as we pointed out in Chapters 1 and 5. To the extent that the Court's "limiting conditions" are "unique," it is because they are so overwhelmingly insubstantial, not because they pertain to the substantive controversies their cases contain.

Courts, of course, do not decide all disputes; and when they do do so, they adhere to certain procedures. But as we have documented, at the level of the U.S. Supreme Court, how the justices decide their cases depends upon the free play of their individual personal policy preferences. This does not mean that any conceivable outcome is as likely as any other – theoretically, perhaps, but not in any real world sense. Thus, one need not worry that the justices will overrule the doctrine of judicial review, even though they might cut it back here and there as they have done with regard to state criminals who seek federal court

---

9   C. Herman Pritchett, "The Development of Judicial Research," in Joel B. Grossman and Joseph Tanenhaus, eds., *Frontiers of Judicial Research* (New York: Wiley, 1969), p. 42.

10   *Osborn v. Bank of the United States*, 9 Wheaton 738 (1824), at 866.

11   *United States v. Butler*, 297 U.S. 1 (1936), at 62.

review of their convictions. Nor is it likely that the justices will limit the scope of the equal protection clause to its original beneficiaries – blacks – or disregard the language of the Fifth Amendment and allow government to take property without compensating its owners; or declare women's suffrage to be the product of an unconstitutionally ratified constitutional amendment.

On the other hand, to assert that the Court's discretion is severely constrained substitutes myth for reality. A Court capable of defining due *process* to include matters as *substantive* as minimum wage and maximum hour legislation, freedom of communication, and a woman's right to an abortion hardly wants for discretion. Or one capable of asserting that governmental racial segregation in the District of Columbia violates due process rather than equal protection. Or one that reads into the Ninth Amendment a right to buy, sell, and use contraceptive devices. Or includes corporations among citizens. Or justifies the exclusion of professional baseball, alone among sports, as exempt from the antitrust laws because of Congress's "positive inaction."[12] Or defines Long Island as part of the mainland,[13] and tomatoes – though botanically a fruit – as vegetables.[14]

It is precisely because the justices exercise virtually untrammelled discretion – and do so, moreover, authoritatively – that enables them to blink at reality and incorporate illogic and falsehood into the law of the land.

CIRCULAR REASONING

The most damning criticism of the attitudinal model in earlier days was that it employed circular reasoning inasmuch as the attitudes used to explain the justices' votes are based on these self same votes. As we point out in Chapter 6, early attitudinal theorists used the results of their cumulative scales and factor analyses to explain the justices' votes, with the scales and factors used to evidence the explanatory power of the attitudinal model. Although the robustness of many of these scales and the excellent structure of recovered factors supports a "confident inference" that attitudes affect behavior,[15] confident inferences are no substitute for unimpeachable scientific evidence.

To this end, we have formulated and applied three separate and independent ways in which to eliminate the circularity problem: the use of facts derived from the lower court records of cases decided by the Supreme Court; content analysis of editorials appearing in advance of nominee confirmation; and the use of the justices' past voting behavior to predict their votes in subsequent cases. Although

---

[12] *Flood v. Kuhn*, 407 U.S. 258 (1972), at 283–284.

[13] *United States v. Maine*, 469 U.S. 504 (1985).

[14] *Nix v. Hedden*, 149 U.S. 304 (1894).

[15] Joseph F. Kobylka, "Leadership on the Supreme Court of the United States: Chief Justice Burger and the Establishment Clause," 42 *Western Political Quarterly* 545 (1989), at 550. Also see Lee Epstein, Thomas G. Walker, and William J. Dixon, "The Supreme Court and Criminal Justice Disputes: A Neo-Institutional Perspective," 33 *American Journal of Political Science* 825 (1989).

each has its shortcomings,[16] these imperfections in no way pertain to circularity. This failing is totally alien to all three of these techniques.

ANECDOTAL EVIDENCE

Whereas we have systematically presented the attitudinal model, our criticisms of the legal model largely rest on anecdotal evidence. To this charge we plead guilty, but not culpable. As we have indicated, the legal model's concepts – plain meaning, intent (original or otherwise), interpretivism, precedent, and balancing – to say nothing of activism, restraint, strict construction, or interpretivism, have not been and perhaps cannot be operationalized. Their vagueness is so chameleon-like that they fit either side of any but the most open and shut case, as we demonstrate in Chapter 2. The elasticity of these concepts precludes systematic testing, and because they cannot be tested, the legal model fails the most basic criterion of a scientific model. This being the case, criticism of the legal model must be rendered anecdotally.

One can, however, test the operation of two of the legal model's subordinate concepts: judicial activism and restraint. On the assumption that justices who display activism or restraint in their voting behavior will do so in an even-handed fashion, we examined those policy areas in which activism/restraint normatively ought to operate. Here we did proceed systematically, as the relevant sections of Chapter 8 indicate. But here also, the result is the same: This aspect of the legal model is no more operative than those we examined anecdotally.

The inoperative character of the legal model does not mean that, for example, every established precedent forms no guide for decision. We do not so allege. Beyond peradventure, some precedents will remain forever impervious to change. Others have been permanently interred, never to rise again. One might have thought that the separate but equal doctrine was among them. Apparently not, as the argument of blacks seeking greater funding for Mississippi's historically black public colleges seems to indicate.[17] What we do allege is that justices pick and choose among applicable contradictory precedents, some of which are indeed set in concrete. But the fact that a precedent is firmly grounded is entirely independent of the question of whether it *actually* guides decision in any given case. Most assuredly, precedents rationalize decisions; as we have shown, they do not function as independent variables.

THE FAILURE OF THE LEGAL MODEL

Critics also maintain that one should not expect the legal model to explain and predict judicial decisions. To impose such expectations transforms the legal

---

[16]   In particular, fact models are consistent with both legal and attitudinal models, predictive validity is a necessary but not sufficient condition for acceptance of the attitudinal model, and editorials measure perceived as opposed to actual attitudes.

[17]   Linda Greenhouse, "Justices Weigh Bias Legacy at Colleges," *New York Times*, November 14, 1991, p. A8; "Post-*Brown*," *National Law Journal*, November 25, 1991, p. 9.

model into a straw man. Instead, these critics assert, the model should be viewed as exclusively normative – that society expects the good judge to try to follow precedent, adhere to plain meaning and lawmakers' intentions, and balance conflicting interests in arriving at a decision.[18] We do not dispute the normative correctness of the legal model. That indeed is how judges should decide their cases – if only they could. But we emphatically and unequivocally demur from the charge that expecting the legal model to explain and predict decisions sets up a straw man. Legalists do claim that their model not only should explain decisions, but also that it actually does do so.

The inability of the legal model to explain and predict decisions reduces its utility to normative rationalization – normative rationalization, moreover, that occurs after the fact of decision. It cloaks, it masks the reality of choice based on the individual justices' personal policy preferences as triggered by their individual attitudes and values. There *is* conflict between the legal and the attitudinal models as *explanations* of judicial behavior. On the other hand, we do not dispute that normative rationalization of attitudinally based decisions does take place, that judicial opinions do normatively rationalize the attitudinally based decisions they govern.

A final criticism to which we may be subject more than other attitudinal modelers is our failure to recognize any operative effects on decisions other than those of the attitudinal model. We believe we have sensitively analyzed the relevant internal and external non-attitudinal factors. Their impact on decisions appears to be minimal. The eminently testable role of judicial activism and restraint effectively masks behavior; it doesn't explain it, as we show in different contexts in Chapters 6 and 8. Such highly plausible external influences – such as the Solicitor General, Congress, public opinion, and interest groups – come up empty for the most part. With the possible exception of the Solicitor General, we are simply unable to demonstrate that these forces cause the justices to behave in any *systematic* way. This is not to say that these or other factors have never had any influence whatsoever in any case. There will always be fleeting and idiosyncratic factors that influence Supreme Court decisions from time to time. But we must never forget it is a *model* we are expoundng – one intended to endure for years to come.

---

[18]   But apparently not Justice Scalia, at least as far as the First Amendment is concerned. See his opinions expressly rejecting balancing in *Employment Division, Oregon Human Resources Dept. v. Smith*, 108 L Ed 2d 876 (1990), at 888–893, and *Barnes v. Glen Theatre, Inc.*, 115 L Ed 2d 504 (1991), at 515–521. The former concerns religious use of peyote, the latter expressive nude dancing. Also see Paul M. Barrett, ''Despite Expectations, Scalia Fails to Unify Conservatives on Court,'' *Wall Street Journal*, April 28, 1992, pp. A1, A6.

Appendix: Logit analysis

In Chapters 4 and 6 we rely on a statistical tool called "logit" to estimate the influence of a variety of independent variables on three different dependent variables: the aggregate decision to confirm or not confirm a Supreme Court nominee; the individual-level decision of a senator to vote for or against a nominee; and the decision of the Court to hold a search reasonable or unreasonable. In this appendix we attempt to explain logit analysis in as straightforward a manner as possible. We hope, though, that even without this appendix readers will be able to grasp the substantive significance of the results from the explanations in the text.

In logit analysis we start with a dependent variable, such as a senator's decision to vote for or against a nominee, that we believe can be explained by one or more independent variables, such as the number of interest groups opposed to the nominee or the institutional strength of the President. Our goals include: 1) determining weights for each independent variable, so that we know how much each independent variable contributes to or detracts from the probability that a senator votes for a nominee; 2) determining whether those weights statistically differ from zero; and 3) using the weights to determine the probability that any given senator will vote "yes" or "no."

THE LINEAR REGRESSION PROBABILITY MODEL

Before discussing logit analysis itself, it is appropriate to explain a precursor of logit, the linear regression probability model. With one independent variable, the linear regression probability model initially takes the form

$$Y_i = \alpha + \beta X_i + \epsilon_i \tag{1}$$

where Y_i is the dependent variable. In our examples the variable is dichototomous – that is it takes on two values – 1 if the senator voted for the nominee and 0 if the senator voted against the nominee; X_i is the value of the independent variable – for example, the number of interest groups opposing the nominee; β is the slope, or the increase (or decrease) in the probability of a "yes" vote given a one-unit increase in the number of opposing interest groups; α is the constant, representing here the probability of confirmation when the independent variable equals 0, in this case, when no groups oppose the nominee; and ϵ_i is an error term, representing the effects of unmeasured variables and random errors.

As we stated, Y_i can take on only two values, 0 or 1.[1] Let us say, though, that for a given level of interest group opposition, eight senators vote "yes," while two vote "no." The *expected value* of Y_i is neither 0 nor 1, but .8. Thus the probability of a "yes" vote is .8. If we think of Equation 1 in terms of expected value, then,

$$P_i = \alpha + \beta X_i + \epsilon_i \qquad (2)$$

where P_i is the *probability* of a senator voting for a nominee.

Assume that we determine (or more accurately, a computer program determines), based on a random sample of votes, that the values of α and β that best predict the probability of a "yes" vote are 1.0 and $-.05$, respectively. Then our estimated model becomes

$$P_i = 1.0 - .05X_i + \epsilon_i$$

We interpret α as follows: The predicted probability of a "yes" vote when no interest groups oppose the nominees is 1.0. We interpret β as follows: For each additional interest group opposing the nominee, the probability of confirmation decreases by .05. Thus, if five groups oppose the nominee, the probability of a "yes" vote is .75; if ten groups oppose the nominee, the probability of a "yes" vote is .50; and if fifteen groups oppose the nominee, the probability of a "yes" vote is .25.

Statistical significance

These hypothetical results, as we stated, come from a particular sample of data. Had our sample been different, our results would almost inevitably be different. With different samples we might have obtained an α of .90 and a β of $-.10$, or an α of .75 and a β of .02. The statistics (for example, α's and β's) that we get from any particular sample are thus *estimates* of the true population *parameters*, which are unknown.

If we get an estimate of β from our sample of $-.10$, it can be shown that that value is more likely to have come from a population whose true β is $-.10$ than it is likely to have come from a sample whose true β is any other value – for example $-.9$, 1.2, or 0. It is possible, however, to calculate the probability that the estimate did come from a population whose true value is one of the above, or any other number. By analogy, if we found that 80 percent of people in a sample survey ($n = 100$) approved of the job the President is doing, it is more likely that this

---

[1] Otherwise we would be dealing simply with the linear regression model, sans "probability."

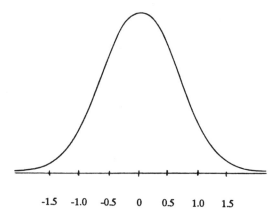

-1.5   -1.0   -0.5   0   0.5   1.0   1.5

Figure A.1   Frequency distributions of estimated β's

percentage came from a population where 80 percent of the people supported the President than it is to have come from any other population. Nevertheless, it is virtually as likely that this percentage came from a population where 77 percent of the people support the President, plausible that this percentage came from a population where 70 percent of the people support the President, and possible but unlikely that this sample came from a population where only 50 percent of the people support the President. Thus, both our estimated β of −.10 and our estimated presidential support percent of 80 can be considered *maximum likelihood estimates*. What we are most often interested in is the likelihood that our sample estimate, −.10, came from a population where the true value of β equals 0. If it is plausible that the estimate came from a population where the true value of β equals zero, then we cannot reject the hypothesis that β = 0. In other words, we cannot reject the hypothesis that interest-group opposition has no influence on the probability that a senator will vote to confirm.

We proceed as follows. First, we can demonstrate that *if the true value of β equals 0*, then by taking a large number of samples and estimating β from each of them, we would get a *sampling distribution* of estimated β's centering around 0, as in Figure A.1. The various estimated β's from the sampling distribution have a standard deviation, which is known as the *standard error* of the estimate. In this case, the standard error is .5, which means that the typical deviation of any estimated β from the true value of 0 is .5. Note that most of the estimated β's are close to zero, with fewer present as we move away from 0 in either direction. Sixty-eight percent of all observed β's will be within one standard error of 0(between −.05 and .05), 95 percent will be within two standard errors of 0 (between −1.0 and 1.0), and 99 percent within three standard errors of 0 (between −1.5 and 1.5) *if the true value of β is 0*. Judging from Figure A.1, we see in our example that if we observe from a sample estimate of β of .03, it is highly conceivable that the estimate emanates from a population where the true population is 0. On the other hand, if we observe a sample estimate of -1.5, it is very unlikely that the estimate came from a population where the true value is 0, as less than 1 percent of the time could we get an estimate as far from zero as -1.5 if the true value of β were 0. Thus, we can say that an estimate of -1.5 is significantly different from 0 at the .01 level. So too, in our example, less than 5 percent of the time would we get an estimate as far from 0 as -1.0 if the true value of β were 0. Thus, in this example, an estimate of -1.0 would be significant at the .05 level. Generally, significance levels at the either the .01 or .05 level are considered strong enough to conclude that the true value of β is not 0. The lower the significance level, the more certain one is that this is true.

The multivariate model

Many times we will be interested in the effect of a number of variables simultaneously. For instance, the probability of a senator voting for confirmation might depend on the number of interest groups in opposition, in addition to the institutional strength of the President, where the President's strength is measured as 1 if his party controls the Senate and 0 if it does not. This type of independent variable, which takes only two values – usually 1 if the variable is present and 0 if the variable is absent – is called a categorical or dummy variable, and is used extensively in Chapters 4 and 6. With two variables, the linear regression probability model takes the form,

$$P_i = \alpha + \beta_1 X_1 + \beta_2 X_2 + \epsilon_i$$

where P_i is the probability of a senator voting to confirm; X_1 is the value of the first independent variable, the number of opposition interest groups; X_2 is the value of the second independent variable, the institutional strength of the President, and takes on either the value 0 or the value 1; α is the constant (the value of P_i when all independent variables are equal to 0); β_1 is the slope of X_1 (the change in the probability of a yes vote given a one-unit change in the number of opposition groups, *controlling for the strength of the President*); β_2 is the slope of X_2 (the change in the probability of a "yes" vote given a shift in institutional strength of the President from 0 [does not control the Senate] to 1 [does control the Senate], *controlling for the number of opposition interest groups*); and ϵ_i, as before, is the error term.

Accordingly, each slope estimate represents the independent effect of that variable, controlled for whatever other variables are included in the model. Thus we might obtain the following results from a sample of cases:

$$P_i = .80 - .08X_1 + .25X_2 + \epsilon_i$$

which would be interpreted as follows. The probability of a "yes" vote when no interest groups oppose the nominee ($X_1 = 0$) and the President does not control the Senate ($X_2 = 0$) is .80. Each unit increase in the number of opposition interest groups lowers the probability of a "yes" vote by .08, controlling for the institutional strength of the President. A change from no partisan control of the Senate ($X_2 = 0$) to partisan control of the Senate ($X_2 = 1$) increases the probability of a "yes" vote by .25.

Note that the absolute size of β_1 ($-.08$) and β_2 (.25) cannot be compared directly. Both are slope coefficients, but their units of measurement differ. A one-unit change in the number of opposition groups – for example, from 8 to 9 – is a small shift relative to the range of the variable, but a one-unit change in control of the Senate (from 0 to 1) takes us across the entire range of the variable. Finally, both X_1 and X_2 have standard errors that will help us determine whether their estimated β's are statistically significant from 0.

Mathematical problems[2]

Due to the relative ease in interpreting the linear regression probability model, it is often used as a method for analyzing dichotomous choice data. Unfortunately, several mathematical problems afflict the model that outweighs its interpretability.

First, probabilities are bounded by 0 and 1, but that need not necessarily be the case. In the example, if no interest groups opposed the nominee and the President's party controlled the Senate, the probability of a "yes" vote would be 1.05, an impossible situation. So, too, if the President's party did not control the Senate and twelve groups opposed the nominee, the probability of a "yes" vote would be $-.16$, an equally impossible situation.

Second, the linear regression probability model is, as its name indicates, a linear model. Each unit increase in an independent variable has the same effect on the probability of a "yes" vote as each other increase. A change from 9 to 10 has the same influence as an increase from 25 to 26. It may be the case, though, that once a certain level of opposition is reached, a senator will be likely to vote "no," with little marginal effect from additional groups. Similarly, a senator might totally discount a unit decrease at very low levels of opposition.

An alternative example of the problem of assuming linearity in a probabilistic relationship is the likelihood of home ownership, which no doubt will be a function of the purchaser's income. The greater the income, the more likely an individual will buy. Yet, clearly, the relationship between income and purchase is not linear. Consider a person with no annual income. Such a person is not

---

[2]   This section can be skipped by those willing to take our word for it that the linear probability model contains statistical and theoretical problems that require the use of alternative techniques.

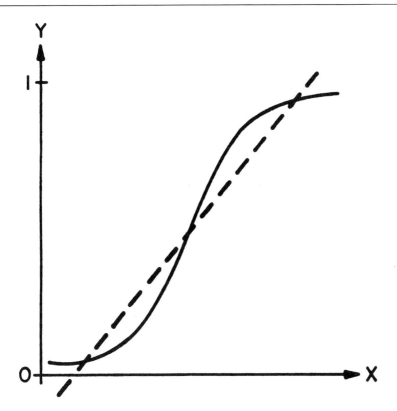

Figure A.2 Linear and S-shaped (logit) probability functions

likely to buy a house. If such a person's income increased to $10,000, a purchase would still be extremely unlikely. Next, consider a person with $40,000 annual income. That person might be inclined to buy. If he received a $10,000 increase in income, his probability of purchasing a house would likely increase substantially. Finally, let's consider a millionaire. Such a person might be highly likely to purchase a home, but an extra $10,000 in income would have virtually no effect on that decision. Thus, the influence of added income on purchasing a home is small at low levels, strong at moderate levels, and low again at high levels. This suggests that the model should have an S-shaped slope, as in Figure A.2, rather than the straight slope of the linear regression probability model.

Finally, for the linear regression probability model to be appropriate, certain assumptions about the error term must be met. One of them, constant variance, is clearly violated in the example. The variance is higher for expected probabilities closer to .5 and lower for expected probabilities closer to 0 or 1. Although this problem can be solved through techniques such as weighted least squares, the linear specification problem discussed remains.

THE LOGIT MODEL

Because of the methodological problems discussed, linear regression probability model estimates can be poor indicators of the true population values. If the functional form is incorrectly specified, the β estimates will be biased, and if the variance is not constant, tests of significance will be incorrect. Faced with these problems, alternative methods, such as probit and logit, are commonly used. From a statistical viewpoint, either markedly improves on the linear regression probability model, though it must be noted that the statistical gain comes at the cost of comprehensible results.

In logit analysis, the model is transformed to the form

$$\log (P_i/(1 - P_i)) = \alpha + \beta X_i + \epsilon_i \tag{3}$$

That is, the dependent variable is no longer the probability of an event happening, but the *log of the odds ratio* of that event happening. The "odds ratio" is a fairly simple concept. If the probability of an event happening (P_i) is .80, then the odds ratio is .80/.20, or 4. If the probability of an event happening is .10, then the odds ratio is .10/.90 = .11. If the probability of an event happening is .50, the odds ratio is .50/.50 = 1.

The dependent variable is not the odds ratio itself, but the natural log of the odds ratio. The natural log of a number is the exponent that e is raised to in order to equal that number, where e equals 2.718. Thus, when we say that the (natural) log of 20 equals 3, that means that $e^3 = 20$. Taking the log of the odds ratio flattens the slope at odds ratios much greater than 1 (at probabilities much greater than .50) and at odds ratios much less than 1 (at probabilities much less than .50). Thus, independent variables will have the greatest effect when the probability of an event happening is close to .50 and the least effect when the probability of an event happening is close to 0 or 1.

Consider the following example:

$$\log (P_i/(1 - P_i)) = 2.20 + -.20X_1 + .60X_2 + \epsilon_i$$

where all variables are as defined before. The estimated α of 2.20 means that the log of the odds ratio of a "yes" vote is equal to 2.20 when no interest groups oppose the candidate and the President's party does not control the Senate. We can turn the "log of the odds ratio," which has virtually no intuitive meaning, into a simple probability with two steps. First, we can turn the log of the odds ratio into the simple odds ratio by taking the anti-log of 2.20, a task that many hand calculators can accomplish. We determine that the anti-log of 2.20 equals 9.03. Thus the odds ratio of a "yes" vote with no interest group opposition and a President whose party does not control the Senate is 9.03. The second step turns the odds ratio into a probability. We do this with the formula P = OR/(1 + OR), where P is the probability and OR is the odds ratio. Thus, with an odds ratio of 9.03, the probability of the event happening is 9.03/10.03 = .90. Thus, the probability of a senator voting to confirm a nominee when there are no interest groups in opposition and the President's party controls the Senate is .90.

Next, consider the estimate − .20 for β_1. This means that the log of the odds ratio decreases by − .20 for each interest group that opposes the nominee. This estimate is not so easy to turn into a probability because the change in the probability of "yes" vote for a one-unit change in interest group opposition depends on the values of the other variables. When the probability approaches .50, the influence will be greatest; when the probability is close to 0 or 1, the effect will be minimal. Thus, to turn the estimate into a probability, we must make a prior assumption what the probability of a "yes" vote would be absent the influence of the variable in question.

One common method is to examine the impact of a given independent variable when the other independent variables are at levels that leave the probability of the event happening at .50 − a toss up. Among other advantages, changes in probability are symmetrical around .50; they are not symmetrical around any other point. Thus, at any other prior probability level, the influence of the variable in question will arbitrarily depend on whether the variable is being increased or decreased.

If the prior probability of a senator voting "yes" is .50, then the odds ratio of a "yes" vote is 1.0. The log of the odds ratio becomes 0.0, as the log of 1 is 0. If an additional interest group opposed the nominee, the log of the odds ratio drops by − .20 from its prior value (in this case, 0). Thus, the log of the odds ratio with an additional group in opposition is − .20. As we did with α, we can turn the log of the odds ratio (OR) into a probability by taking the anti-log of the log of the OR (the anti-log of − .20 is .82), and then dividing the resulting OR (.82) by 1 + OR. The result is .45. This means that the addition of one extra interest group lowers the probability of a "yes" vote from .50 (the prior value we chose to start with) to .45. Thus, the addition of one additional interest group lowered the probability of a "yes" vote by .05, *given a prior probability of .50*. Had we started at a different prior, the influence would be less.

Finally, we determine the influence of the estimate .60 for β_2. Technically, this says that when the President's party controls the Senate, the log of the odds ratio of a positive vote increases by .60. Again, if we start with a prior probability of a "yes" vote of .50, then the beginning log of the odds ratio is zero. If the President's party shifts from no control to control, then the new log of the odds ratio is .60. The anti-log of .60 is 1.82, which is the new odds ratio of a "yes" vote. We turn the new odds ratio into a new probability value by dividing 1.82 by 2.82. The new probability is .65. Thus, in this example the President's control of the Senate increases the probability of a "yes" vote by .15 from a prior probability of .50.

To determine the influence of a one (or more) unit change in any independent variable from any prior probability level, we take the following steps:

1. Choose a prior probability level.

2. Determine the odds ratio OR $= (P_i/(1 - P_i))$ for that prior probability level.

3. Take the log of the OR of the prior probability level.

4. For a one-unit change in the independent variable, determine the new log of the odds ratio by adding or subtracting the estimated β for the coefficient of interest. This is the new log of the odds ratio after the influence of the variable in question. If we are interested in the change of a two-unit increase in the variable of interest, add or subtract $2 \times \beta$, if a three-unit increase, add or subtract $3 \times \beta$, and so on.

5. Take the anti-log of the new OR. This is the new odds ratio.

6. Divide the OR by $1 +$ OR. This is the new probability of the event happening.

7. Compare the new probability with the prior probability of the event happening.

If we choose a prior probability of .50, the task is simplified mathematically as we finish step 3 with an original log of the odds ratio of 0.

The logit model solves all of the mathematical problems of the linear probability model. Predicted probabilities can never fall outside the [0,1] range, because they only approach 0 and 1 as the log of the odds ratio approaches negative and positive infinity, respectively. The model has the desired S-shaped curve. As probabilities approach 0 or 1, the slope levels out, as Figure A.2 shows. Here, the S-shaped curve is the actual logit curve. Finally, no automatic violations occur in any of the error-term assumptions.

Subject/name index

Case index

Milligan, Ex parte, 85
Milliken v. Bradley, 112
Mills v. Maryland, 223
Minnick v. Mississippi, 108
Miranda v. Arizona, 108, 110, 339, 340
Mississippi Band of Choctaw Indians v. Holyfield, 168
Missouri v. Jenkins, 342
Mitchell v. W.T.Grant Co., 45, 323
Mobile v. Bolden, 281
Moore v. Illinois, 82
Moorehead v. New York ex rel. Tipaldo, 95
Moose Lodge v. Irvis, 115
Mortensen v. United States, 35
Moya v. DeBaca, 252
Mueller v. Allen, 106
Muller v. Oregon, 95
Muniz v. Hoffman, 42
Munn v. Illinois, 93
Murdock v. Pennsylvania, 105
Myers v. United States, 49

NAACP v. Alabama, 52, 105, 183
National Labor Relations Board v. Electrical Workers, 317
National Labor Relations Board v. Jones and Laughlin Steel Corp., 96
National Relations Board v. Lion Oil Co., 317
National Labor Relations Board v. S.S. Logan Packing Co., 136
National Labor Relations Board v. Truitt Manufacturing Co., 317
National Labor Relations Board v. Walton Manufacturing Co., 317
National League of Cities v. Usery, 324
Native American Church of Navajoland v. Arizona Corporation Comn., 106
Nebbia v. New York, 95
Nevada v. Hall, 25
New Jersey Welfare Rights Organization v. Cahill, 48
New York v. Quarles, 108
New York v. Uplinger, 184, 185
New York State Club Assn. v. New York City, 115
New York Times v. Sullivan, 104
Nix v. Hedden, 361
Northwestern States Portland Cement Co. v. Minnesota, 317
Norton v. Mathews, 48

O'Brien v. Brown, 204
O'Connor v. Donaldson, 117, 118
O'Malley v. Woodrough, 3
Ohio v. Akron Reproductive Health Center, 43
Ohio v. Betts, 2
Ollman v. Evans, 57
Olmstead v. United States, 60–61

Oregon v. Hass, 108
Oregon v. Kennedy, 183
Oregon v. Mitchell, 3, 72, 75, 319
Oregon ex rel. State Land Board v. Corvallis Sand & Gravel Co., 51
Osborn v. Bank of the United States, 5, 360

Palko v. Connecticut, 102, 103
Palmore v. Sidoti, 112
Panama Refining Co. v. Ryan, 90
Parker v. Dugger, 223
Passenger Cases, 45, 323
Patterson v. McLean Credit Union, 323
Payne v. Tennessee, 48, 323
Pennoyer v. Neff, 178
Pennsylvania v. Delaware Valley Citizens' Council, 294
Pennsylvania v. Nelson, 104
Penry v. Lynaugh, 111, 240
People v. Defore, 107, 216
Planned Parenthood v. Ashcroft, 43
Plessy v. Ferguson, 84, 86, 111, 112, 261, 301, 331–332
Poelker v. Doe, 116, 324
Pollock v. Farmers' Loan and Trust Co., 3, 72, 75, 87–88, 172, 319
Powell v. Alabama, 108–109
Price Waterhouse v. Hopkins, 294
Pryor v. United States, 180

Quantity of Books, A v. Kansas, 341

Railroad Commission of Texas v. Pullman Co., 23
Railroad Retirement Board v. Alton R. Co., 91
Reed v. Reed, 3
Regents of the University of California v. Bakke, 41, 42, 98, 112, 113, 290, 340
Reynolds v. Sims, 114, 328, 341
Reynolds v. United States, 106
Richmond v. Croson Co., 112
Rochin v. California, 102
Roe v. Wade, 50, 54–55, 117, 132, 171, 235, 242, 333–334, 334–335, 337, 346, 351, 352–353, 354, 355
Rogers v. Lodge, 41
Rogers v. Missouri Pacific R. Co., 184
Rogers v. Paul, 345
Rogers v. Richmond, 51
Rotary International v. Rotary Club of Duarte, 115
Roth v. United States, 104
Rush v. Savchuk, 179
Rust v. Sullivan, 334

Saia v. New York, 105
San Antonio Independent School District v. Rodriguez, 113, 123